a stitch in time

a stitch in time

Knitting and Crochet Patterns of the 1920s 1930s & 1940s

Introduced & edited by JANE WALLER

Duckworth

First published in 1972 by
Gerald Duckworth & Co. Ltd.
The Old Piano Factory,
43 Gloucester Crescent, London N.W.1.

Designed by Tony Birks in association
with Mike Ricketts and Jim Bulman

Cloth ISBN 0 7156 0653 0

Paper ISBN 0 7156 0693 X

Printed by C. Tinling & Co. Ltd,
London and Prescot

*To give complete accuracy, the patterns in this book have
been photographed straight from the original magazines.
The publishers hope that the authenticity of the lay-out
and designs will compensate for any imperfections in
the reproduction.*

Preface

The knitting and crochet patterns in this book, selected from the pages of English fashion magazines of the 20s, 30s and 40s, are perfectly in tune with today's fashions, and also provide exciting ideas for the future. Sixteen of the patterns have been specially knitted up and photographed for this book, to show how well they look today. The patterns themselves are presented complete with their original illustrations.

In my introduction, I have described the changes of style in knitting and crochet patterns and other clothes, showing how social changes and the fashionable crazes of the times influenced their design. A word of warning is needed here about terminology, which can be confusing. For instance, what Americans call a "sweater" is in England more commonly called a "jumper"—which in America means something quite different. In such cases, I have used American terms when these differ from the English. The patterns themselves, however, which are photographed from English originals, have English terms. For convenience, an Anglo-American glossary is provided at the end of the book.

The garments in the old patterns are always beautifully designed. The areas of pattern are carefully placed; the shape is well thought out and the final appearance is considered down to the last detail. The patterns can be knitted up in modern yarns, and can be changed to suit your taste. At the end of the book, in addition to the glossary, is a section of information and suggestions for knitting and crocheting from the patterns. This includes some good advice on the essentials of knitting by "Finella", written in 1936, and some modern hints; equivalent knitting needle and crochet hook sizes; and, most important, an index giving a modern yarn for each pattern. This index ensures that the tension given in the pattern is maintained when modern yarns are used—very important for a good result. Advice on how to check your tension is included in the knitting hints. Modern yarns generally have less yardage weight for weight than the old yarns, and no longer always come in ounce balls; so it is impossible to give an accurate estimate of the amount of yarn needed for each garment. Any difficulties should be taken to your local knitting shop or department store. Finally, if you cannot already knit, it is easy to begin, or mothers and grandmothers can be enrolled to knit for you!

Thanks are due to the editors both past and present of the following magazines: *Everywoman* (IPC), *Good Housekeeping* (The National Magazine Co.), *Good Needlework and Knitting* (IPC), *Miss Modern* (IPC), *Modern Home* (IPC), *Modern Woman* (IPC), *My Home* (IPC), *Stitchcraft* (Patons and Baldwins), *Wife and Home* (IPC), *Woman and Home* (IPC), *Woman's Illustrated* (IPC), *Woman's Magazine* (United Society for Christian Literature), *Woman's Pictorial* (IPC) and *Woman's Weekly* (IPC). Out of the fourteen magazines, only four are still going strong: *Good Housekeeping*, *Stitchcraft*, *Woman and Home* and *Woman's Weekly*. The editors cannot be held responsible for any errors in the original patterns and cannot enter into any correspondence.

Thanks are also due to Tony Birks who organised and designed the book; to IPC library for permission to use five of their patterns; to Beatrice Bellini of Women's Home Industries, 11 West Halkin Street, London W.1., for knitting the garments for the modern photographs; to Scaioni's Studio for the photography (hair by Vidal Sassoon); and to Norah Marshall, Mrs Lowe, Mik Dunn, my mother and many friends for all their knitting and help.

This book is dedicated to Daisy Groombridge-Harvey, who luckily never threw her magazines away.

Contents

Early 20's sweater

Introduction

20s

The Twenties girl tried to create a chaste, virginal impression. Her simplicity, youthfulness and even boyishness were intended to "attract the demobilised soldier, disillusioned by the woman of experience".* Her head had to be small, with a boyish shingle or bob and later the very short Eton crop. Often this was hidden beneath a close-fitting cloche hat pulled well down over the eyebrows. Her expression was dictated by the newly popular movies; her make-up had to follow as closely as possible that of the film star she "most nearly" resembled. With her unnaturally colored mouth a pout full of innocence—hopefully like Lillian Gish—and eyes staring under her plucked eyebrows, her own expression was carefully concealed.

The Twenties sweater was also designed to conceal. It abolished the bosom and ignored the hips, by hanging like a sack from the neck to just below the hips. All the natural lines of the figure were mysteriously hidden, and the colors of the sweaters—mostly pale pastel, beige or white—added to the "chaste" look. In the early Twenties, the tubular sweater was baggy, loose-fitting and generally rather large in appearance. The main part had to be in an "easy to knit" stitch and made in one long strip, and was often given shape and lightness by the addition of a lacy crocheted border in a more complex stitch. Low round necks or v-necks were edged with a firm line of crochet. Knitted suits consisted of a long tunic top falling over a baggy skirt which often had a border of fur. By 1927, the sweater was not quite so ample, and clung to the hips. The sleeves were long and fitted at the cuffs, and the neck was v-shaped as on a boy's pullover, while on the cardigan the v-shape was fastened very low with three or four buttons. The sweater could be turned into a knitted suit by the addition of a tubular skirt, the silhouette always being a straight line. Below her skirt, the Twenties girl wore flesh-colored stockings. "Woman was a curious pink-legged creature with a scarlet mouth, no waist and almost no hair."

Underwear was minimal. If the figure was too curvy and feminine, an elastic belt was worn over the hips or breasts to give an impression of flatness. The camibocker, a bodice and pants all in one, was popular, since it flattened the breasts above by being drawn tight over the chest, and the loose-fitting knickers gave considerable flexibility—a revolt from the bodices which on the curvy Edwardian figure had constricted the waist and pushed the breasts upwards almost to exposure. Woman had at last reached the age when she was no longer hampered by her clothes. Though her sexuality was minimized, she had escaped from convention and asserted her independence. The craze for movies, automobiles, jazz and tennis expressed itself strongly in the style of the sweater. The Twenties girl could now take pleasure in being fit and young. The freedom of a sweater was especially useful to her on the tennis court, where it allowed her ease of movement and miraculous speed. For "reckless" car-driving it gave her an outdoor look, the v-neck a sporting appearance; and when dancing the Charleston, she could fling her arms wildly around without any danger of not being always perfectly covered.

But by the late Twenties and early Thirties, her new looks had begun to worry her. "In destroying the mystery of our complexion we have killed man's curiosity about it. I sometimes wonder if in gaining freedom we have not lost something more precious." Women became more "subtle" and acquired a maturer and more feminine appearance. Skirts were lengthened and began to flare at the bottom, and the rather stereotyped straight-line sweater was relieved of its monotony by the addition of horizontal lines on the cuffs and bottom edge in darker and brighter tones; by 1931 diagonal lines set into the front and cuffs gave greater variety. Now that there was a little more style, it

* Acknowledgments for this and most other quotations that follow from old magazines are due to C. Willett Cunnington, *English Women's Clothing in the Present Century*.

7

30s

could be stated with conviction that "a woman who is subtle is a most attractive creature—a bit dangerous, but well worth knowing". A border appeared around the pocket and hem, which was often decorated with embroidery and floral motifs. Prettiness had arrived, and with it a mood of amusement and superficiality. The cloche hat could now be "tilted ever so little to the back and just a thought sideways".

By 1932, the fashionable woman was tall, slender and elegant. She had acquired two new images. She was a feminine and pretty woman reacting against the immaturity of the Twenties. But she was also, from necessity, a working woman, smart and intelligent, rising above the economic stresses of the Great Depression and filling a position of responsibility. By knitting her own sweaters, she found that she could add a little character and individuality to the increasing number of mass-produced clothes. In fact, instead of producing a dearth of knitting and crochet, the Depression, with all its hardships, turned out to be the greatest and most exciting age of these crafts, and an enormous number of original and varied styles were created.

There were sweaters "to dash about town in", or to look demure in; sweaters for golfing, sailing and tennis; sweaters for a party; even sweaters to wear to the movies which continued to be as popular as ever. It was the great age of Hollywood. Stars like Mae West, Greta Garbo and Marlene Dietrich became the "ideal woman". They were the new "fulfilled" women, fascinating and pretty, with warm romantic personalities and softly curving, distinctly feminine figures. The overgrown schoolgirl of the Twenties with her mask-like face had matured. Now her complexion was natural. Make-up, if used at all, "should increase the expression of the face, but it should not look odd". She grew her hair longer, and like Garbo, she wore it swept back behind the ears to fall on the neck in soft curls that had a "combed up look about them". Her carriage was elegant and graceful, her figure pencil-thin. Her skirt was long, and was fitted around the hips and down to the knee, where it then flared out with perhaps a lift in front or a train behind. Her suits were knitted to look like gowns, falling in one long line from neck to hem and always showing the natural curves: "We must have curves where nature intended curves to be." Her sweater was soft and warmly colored in peach, oyster, pale green, mauve and innumerable other pastel shades. Often it was

Tubular sweater with stripes

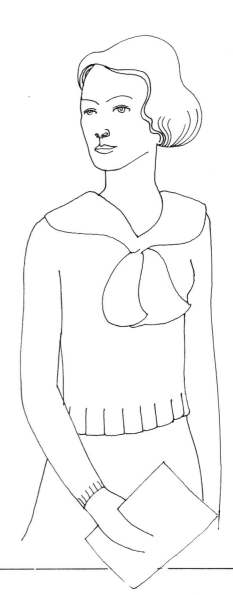

◁ *Early 30's 'feminine' sweater*
Working woman's sweater ▽

slightly bloused, with a cowl neckline and a draped look about the breasts, which were now natural-looking: "Bare your bosom as low as your figure will allow and conscience will permit." The sleeves were short and floppy, with perhaps a scallopped or lacy edge, or long and loose-fitting to the cuff. The cardigan opened into a deep v-neck and was fastened with one button just above the waistline, giving an air of charm and simplicity. For a party, the sweater would be light and lacy and enhanced with frills, ruffs, bows and tucks, or decorated with crocheted or embroidered flowers.

Although she wanted to appear feminine again, the Thirties girl was not going to lose her new-found freedom. She could be charming and sweet without becoming weak. Like Mae West, she presented a more overtly sexual image, acquiring style, flare and a calculated feminity. But—since most women had to work during the Depression—she also had to look strong and capable of holding down a job. She had to have a cool, collected personality and an air of competence and intelligence. The working woman's sweater was therefore a smart affair. It was usually high-necked, fastening at the back with perhaps a neat row of buttons, or it was plain and practical, long-sleeved, with an insert in the elbow knitted in a different

A slip 'that fits like wallpaper'

The Thirties woman wanted above all to be slim and fit. "Slenderness is the one attribute of the chic." This was achieved either by slimming and dieting, or by taking part in some outdoor activity. There was sailing, swimming, walking or hiking; and golf was overtaking tennis in popularity. If you were fat, you could look thin by means of clever optical illusions incorporated into the sweater. Diagonals were slimming and were often used in a neat pattern or in a cross-over neck or lapels. The waistline was higher than the natural waist, to give an appearance of height and longer legs. The tall girl was much admired, and all fashion drawings were slightly elongated to make the figure look slender. Skirts and dresses were cut on the bias to make them cling to body. Underneath, it was important to have a slip "that fits like wallpaper to the wall" or a knitted "deliciously enchanting camiknicker" in oyster pink. (see p. 132.) For the woman who had difficulty with her figure—"one must not be fat"—a rubber roll-on garment was worn to give a molded look, but usually corsets were felt to be unnatural.

The most obvious characteristic of the Thirties sweater was the emphasis on the shoulder. This was perhaps the cleverest way of making one look slimmer, since the puffed sleeves or cape not only made the head look small but also flatteringly diminished the hips. The cape was for the feminine girl, broadening her shoulders and making her look neat, pretty and "demure". The puffed sleeve was as varied as it was exciting. There were leg-of-mutton sleeves, Bishop sleeves, small, huge or bell-shaped puffed sleeves, and Schiaparelli square padded sleeves. There might also be a giant butterfly as the collar (see p. 69) or fins like a prehistoric animal's (see p. 91). The sense of humour apparent in the knitwear and crochet of the Thirties remains unrivalled. One could be "amusing to look at, rather than beautiful". Little designs were often embroidered on the sweater from the transfers that were given away in almost every magazine. Sometimes one's initial was embroidered on the collar or pocket. Folk art

color and pattern. A scarf-collar with the end of the scarf knitted into the sweater could look "chic" and provide "variety without losing the slender line". But the most popular working clothes were brightly colored two-tone or striped sweaters and outfits. The useful outfit was sometimes very dashing and courageous. The "Magpie" set (see p. 67) had exciting diagonal stripes in contrasting colors. The "lightning" sweater (see p. 125) was in vivid diagonal patterns that looked as if they were moving. Every kind of accessory would be knitted or crocheted to make a girl look stylish and original. There were matching hats, belts, scarves and gloves. There were also handbags and other items such as gauntlets worn over the sleeves. Not only was the ambitious working girl progressive and hardworking: she looked exciting and colorful. "Depressions sociological or meteorological cannot depress the woman who has just discovered an extremely daring combination of colors".

Puffed sleeves

able, the sweater being longer and worn over the skirt, often with a belt to give sharp emphasis to the waist. The pencil-slim skirt now flared below the hips and was often pleated or gored.

was fashionable, with gigantic peasant puffed or long full-bloused sleeves. It was an age of originality and vitality.

The aim was to have a physically perfect body. Once it became generally accepted that the sun was not only not harmful but actually good for you, there was a craze for sun-bathing. "We have become sportswomen and sun-worshippers." At last it was no longer necessary to have a pale bleached complexion, and it was actually fashionable to be healthy. But it soon became obvious that for sun-bathing to be worthwhile one would have to expose more of the body, and so for the first time women wore a really sensible bathing-suit instead of remaining fully dressed on the beach. Even "nudity" was encouraged, and there arrived the first daring one-piece backless bathing-suit. This was a smart knitted garment with thin shoulder straps and décolletage effects (see p. 182). For the feminine girl the bathing-suits were in soft pastel shades and for the bolder girl in colorful stripes. Play-clothes for the beach, slacks and shorts, and trousers worn with halter-neck tops were all the rage. Men too wore multi-striped bathing-suits (see p. 96).

The period from 1935 to 1938 "was a tense, nervous age" threatened by the approach of war and women reacted by becoming more alert and energetic. Some adopted an escapist attitude, with clothes that were cheerful and exuberant, while others began to look more stylish and adult. Hair was cut shorter and curled higher on the head. Shoulders were often squarer, and "uplift" was the new style for the bust. Hemlines rose and waists were lowered to their natural position. The neckline was raised on the sweater and could be polo, square, round, cowl or rolled. The fitted, tailored look became fashion-

Puffed sleeves

Fitted, tailored sweater

Knitting and crochet blossomed. Pattern became important, either with a challenging "Fair Isle" or by variation of the stitch itself. The working girl knitted smart cables and ribbing, often in difficult and intricate designs. The cables were bold and thick, and with the advent of the popular "quick-knit" or double knit wools she could make a really chunky-looking sweater in no time at all. Her sweater was usually one striking all-over color, such as emerald green, cherry red, or bright navy. "Color is a mania today."

The feminine girl knitted complex lacy patterns in chevron, diamond or butterfly stitch, with unusual "petal" collars and "sunray" ribbing in colors such as cornflower blue, jade green or daffodil yellow. Magyar-sleeved sweaters with roll necks were popular. Pompoms, frilly bows and feathery collars and cuffs decorated the intricate design. Crazy ruffs and crocheted frills were added to the front of the sweater: for the Coronation of George VI in 1937 one could knit a sweater with cascades of gathered ruffs in red, white and blue (see p. 163).

The sportswoman aimed at the opposite effect. Her sweater would be plain, with a small neat area of pattern and smart pockets, a knitted belt or a necktie. She dressed with style and distinction; a tailored look was essential. Buttons, clips and buckles were still attractive and ex-

citing, and a hat, scarf and gloves would match her sweater in deep browns, greys and greens. For casual sports she had to look carefree, and wore either a short-sleeved, patterned sweater or a long-sleeved pullover with a cowl or polo neck. Small flecks, moss stitch or knots looked "fun", and the sweater set, or twin-set, with the outer cardigan buttoned up to the neck, was found to be practical and flattering.

By 1938, when the threat of war in Europe had grown more real, women wanted to be feminine in a calmer way and to be prepared for whatever might happen. "We must cultivate an erect carriage and perfect balance." A more dignified and elegant "suity" look arrived. Suits, sweater sets and jackets were popular, with most of the figure being modestly covered up. A complete dress with a full skirt could be knitted, or a two-piece suit with lapels on the fitted jacket. Tunic tops began to have bunched cartridge pleats at the back. These pleats, together with the neat little belt, emphasised the waist, which had to be no more than 24″–25″ round. The skirt, though still fitted round the hips, was now often flared immediately below. These suits of the late Thirties were always beautifully styled and cheerfully colored or patterned (see p. 200), and "the force of their chic would knock you down a mile away". The "Tyrolean" look became popular, and an interest developed in folk-art fashions. Among the soft puffed sleeves there started to appear heavier-looking square-puffed shoulders and leg-of-mutton sleeves. Stripes and two-tone sweaters were popular again; but now they were more reserved and formal, the mood generally becoming discreet, "with a calculated modesty and even an exotic prudery at times".

With the outbreak of World War II in September 1939, the great age of knitting and crochet was at an end, and over the following years most knitting energy, at any rate in England, was diverted into making squares for blankets, or socks, gloves and cold weather hoods (balaclavas) for the Forces.

40s

In Europe, the wartime woman had lost the softness of the Thirties and had grown by necessity into a harder, more severe-looking adult. Her carriage was erect and dignified. Her emotions were controlled. Her outlook was responsible.

Fashion as such came to a standstill. In America, the restrictions which governed fashion designers and the making of new clothes, passed in 1942 under Public Law 85, were not lifted until 1947. In France, women brightened up the Occupation as best they could with the available material, ribbons and bows. Most of the Paris fashion houses were allowed to stay open under careful controls. Schiaparelli, for example, fled to America, but her staff managed to keep her House going. In England, evening gowns, party frocks and formal dinner dresses were put away, and utilitarian "siren suits" (jump suits), warm comfortable slacks and sweaters, and practical regulation working clothes took their place. With nothing new available, it became unimportant what one wore. It was often a relief not to have to keep up appearances and to be able to wear shabby dull clothing without feeling inferior. Indeed, it was almost fashionable to be unfashionable, and the only noticeable tendency was for women's clothes to become masculine. Women had become part of the war effort, either joining the women's forces or working at home. This meant filling a man's job, and one wanted to look capable and strong. "Women fought side by side with their men—in the Services as well as on the home front. Competition no longer existed, since each had an equally important part to play." Women's clothes began to have a military look. Army caps and brogues were worn, and sweaters and jackets were padded at the shoulders like epaulettes to make them look square and wide. Skirts were shortened to just below the knee, but slacks or trousers often replaced the skirt, being more practical for work.

The only areas of the body that could remain feminine all the time were the face, hair and hands. The Forties woman concentrated on these, and was often extravagant

Knitted suit

Square shoulders

over make-up or a permanent wave. The permanent wave kept the hair manageable, either in tidy flat curls or rolled back from the side of the face. Otherwise the hair was swept severely upward from the neck and rolled inwards on the crown of the head, or it was worked into a neat chignon which was tidy and practical to wear under a uniform cap. A crocheted snood or turban kept hair out of the way at work, or a knitted hood worn in the cold. But more often, a silk print scarf or peasant square was knotted on the front of the head, replacing the many knitted hats and berets of the Thirties. The face was no longer soft and natural-looking. Now a bright smooth complexion was needed, with "cake" face powder hiding every wrinkle. Eyebrows were carefully plucked and a hard black line was pencilled in, arching over the eyes. Lips were firmly outlined in an alluring red "Badge of Courage" lipstick. Fingernails matched in a hard shining polish, and were expertly manicured.

Apart from face, head and hands, individuality was disapproved of. There was very little freedom of choice in clothing, and it was easier to work if one looked the same as everyone else. Thus a pair of slacks worn with a comfortable sweater became almost a uniform. The sweater was plain and unglamorous and had to be simple and cheap to make. Wool was scarce and expensive. Old sweaters were unravelled and re-knitted, or old scraps were used up, and there was generally a "make-do" attitude towards knitting. Style in knitwear remained static, and there was one "prototype" sweater which became fashionable in 1938 and was hardly changed till after the war. This was essentially a square-looking sweater in a dark green, brown, or red, or any color available. It ended just on the hips and was worn outside the skirt or slacks. There was usually a yoke and a high round or square neckline. A collar, if there was one, was a small buttoned opening with little lapels. The sleeves were plain and either long and close-fitting, or short, ending just above the elbow. The soft puffed sleeve of the Thirties had turned into a heavy, hard, square puff which was flattened out on top in a continuation of the shoulder.

All the exciting frills, ruffs, puffed sleeves, belts and bows of the Thirties were regarded as unnecessary detail. Lacy stitches and fancy cables were thought frivolous. The points to emphasize now were practicality, warmth and economy. The number of buttons was restricted by regulation, and they were not used as decoration. A pattern, if any, was a simple but effective raised lattice work covering all or part of the sweater in large diamonds. A plain ribbed yoke could occasionally be relieved by a little embroidery. Woman longed to be sweet and sentimental again, and to acquire a romantic, "chocolate box" kind of femininity—to wear frilly underwear and pretty clothes. Silk stockings were yearned after, and many women made do with a black pencilled line on the bare leg to imitate a stocking seam.

When victory came at last in 1945, there was peace and high spirits, but not plenty. In Europe, taxes and clothes-rationing meant few new clothes for most women, and the implications of post-war austerity were felt also in American fashion. But interest in clothes returned, and it was announced joyfully: "Fashion is going Feminine." The

14

Lattice pattern sweater

knitted sweater still had a cosy, homely look and a square yoke, but there had begun to be additions like the occasional bow. The hard, square puffed sleeve softened a little, and the shoulders lost most of their padding. By 1946 colors were cheerful and bright in reds, greens and blues, and an interest in stitches returned. Most popular were the Fair Isle patterns. A natural-colored wool sweater would have an intricate multi-colored Fair Isle pattern across the yoke or pocket, or as a border round the neck. Fair Isle sweater sets were the smartest thing to wear, and buttons returned on cardigans and a v-neck on pullovers. Lacy stitches like feather-stitch returned, and the end of the year saw a plaid stitch in exciting colors on a sweater set called "My Bonnie". This, complete with a large matching beret with a jaunty feather, was to give a "North of the Border air" (see p. 294). Sparkle effects arrived. Glittering sequins could "add a touch of glamour to the dullest of sweaters": figures could be full or slim, though "with ever-growing emphasis on the full . . . whether the silhouette be full or slim, it is always fitted—modeled closely to the figure, accenting a small waistline and all natural curves". At last one could look "lovely" to go dancing or out to dinner on a Saturday night. Woman had become feminine, seductive and alluring. "It is the duty of every woman to look as lovely as she can. Beauty brings such pleasure and warms the hearts of us all. It has a tonic effect and makes us forget all the trivialities of everyday life."

The film star who embodied all this loveliness was the beautiful Veronica Lake. She inspired younger women to make up for the lost years, and gave them the "chocolate-box" beauty that they had longed for. Her romantic, sentimental image was typical of the Forties look. Hair was long, gleaming and well-groomed, curling in soft rolls on to the shoulder. Eyebrows were plucked into a high smooth curve. Eyes were dreamy and misty under a pair of long black lashes. Faces were clear, fresh and sparkling and complexions were set off by glittering earrings or a pearl necklace. Sweaters too became delicate and sentimental, with lacy trellis patterns and feather stitches. Colors had softened to rose pink, pale blue, white and yellow. Yellow daffodils were added to a sweater called "Daffy Down Dilly" (see p. 303). Or for Easter, chicks could make a charming decoration.

For the last three years of the Forties, the fresh, crisp look of a simple white blouse became popular. Over it, a cheerfully colored knitted bolero, waistcoat or low v-necked cardigan was worn. These were knitted in ribs and raised bobbles and cables, and other difficult stitches such as blackberry, bramble and tuft stitch. Rows of buttons and frills decorated the yoke, and bows and brooches could be added to give a youthful prettiness and sparkle. Fair Isle patterns were again the most popular everywhere. For casual and sports wear trousers became fashionable. In America, girls wore denim blue-jeans and pedal-pushers or, as in France and England, wide-bottomed slacks, culottes and shorts. For work, a smartly tailored full or narrow skirt with a matching jacket could be worn, in a fashionable black, navy or beige.

In 1947 Dior created the New Look, and by 1950 it had turned everything from square to round. Woman's figure became voluptuous, with emphasis on every curve. She had a "nipped in waist with rounded bosom and hips". Her skirt and frocks were "dressy", full and lengthened to the ankle. They were often circular cut and made with lots of material—brocade, net or paisley-patterned cotton. They had big side pockets, and a large cummerbund emphasised the waist. Padding helped to give the hips their rounded look and also made the waist look smaller. Underwear was pretty and frilly, and full petticoats were worn under the full skirt. The sweater was pretty too, with a small round neckline or collar and narrow sloping shoulders. It fitted closely at the waist, which needed to be a trim 23″–24″, and above clung to firmly rounded breasts which had to have "uplift". Often this was engineered by means of a brassière padded with foam rubber, known as a "gay deceiver". In the Fifties, enthusiasm for the time-consuming hand-knitted sweater waned. Knitted and crocheted sweaters gave way to the increasingly popular machine-knitted sweater set. The classic matching sweater set, or twin set, appeared in many exciting colors and was "so convenient to wear with everything".

The rounded look

The Tubular Look 1920-32

The early Twenties sweaters, suits and coats hang in a sack-like way to conceal the figure beneath and to give great freedom of movement. A youthful 'boyish' appearance is desired, with all femininity suppressed. The sweater is a baggy garment with a low round or v-neck which, with the sleeves and bottom edge, is finished with a lacy crocheted border. In the later Twenties the sweater becomes more fitted around the arms and hips, giving a 'tubular' appearance. By the early Thirties colors darken and stripes and floral borders appear. A knitted or crocheted 'cloche-hat' is worn to fit closely over the head, and undergarments are made as one-piece bodice and pants and called cami bockers.

"THE SOUTHERN MAID" WALTZ.—Selection Inside!

WOMAN'S WEEKLY

2ᵈ

A Scarf and Tam for Wintry Days

*T*HIS attractive Scarf is planned on "shawl" lines—quite the latest idea! It has two cosy pockets, and a narrow belt which keeps it snug to the figure.

The Tam is made to match, and it is very easy to knit.

NOV. 27, 1920.   Vol. XVIII. No. 474.

Knitted Tam and Scarf.

This cosy cape-scarf is ideal for cold weather, as it falls low over the shoulders, and at the same time wraps well over the chest. It adds utility to its attractions in the shape of two small pockets, and is kept in position with a knitted waistbelt.

THE TAMMY.

FOUR ounces of fawn " brush " wool for the crown and one ounce of brown for the band and pompons are required, with steel or bone needles, No. 10.

ABBREVIATIONS : K. knit ; p., purl ; tog., together.

Knit firmly, so that you will have a good surface for brushing ; and if you are a loose knitter, get No. 11 needles, which are one size thinner than the No. 10.

You can knit this tammy any size you like, as it begins with the band ; and this is worked shortways, so that it can be continued until the size of the head measurement is attained.

THE BAND.—Cast on 10 stitches and knit plain, backwards and forwards, until this strip measures about 19 inches, which will fit a fairly large head, as the ribs open out in wear and a certain amount of grip is advisable to keep the tammy well in position. Take the head measurement, and then allow this band a little smaller. At the end of the band cast off, leaving only one stitch.

Now hold this band with the length of knitting to the left and the one stitch at the top of the work, and on the long side of the strip pick up a loop at the end of every row of knitting, letting the loop already on the needle stand as the first stitch. Take note that a stitch is picked up at the end of every *row*, not every *ridge*. Join this into a round, as the ends of the band can be sewn on afterwards. Count the stitches, and in the next round increase here and there to bring the number up to 270, if you have not already that number on the needles. This is the number for a fairly full crown on a lady's tam ; for a child's, fewer stitches would be needed.

THE CROWN.—Now knit 20 plain rounds on three needles, and work with the fourth, just like a stocking.

TO DECREASE FOR THE CROWN.—1ST ROUND : * K. 8, k. 2 tog. ; repeat from * all round, k. 10 plain rounds.

12TH ROUND : * K. 7, k. 2 tog. ; repeat from * all round, k. 9 plain rounds.

22ND ROUND : * K. 6, k. 2 tog. ; repeat from * all round, k. 8 plain rounds.

31ST ROUND : * K. 5, k. 2 tog. ; repeat from *, k. 7 plain rounds.

39TH ROUND : * K. 4, k. 2 tog. ; repeat from *, k. 6 plain rounds.

46TH ROUND : * K. 3, k. 2 tog. ; repeat from *, k. 5 plain rounds.

52ND ROUND : * K. 2, k. 2 tog. ; repeat from *, k. 4 plain rounds.

57TH ROUND : * K. 1, k. 2 tog. ; repeat from *, k. 3 plain rounds.

61ST ROUND : K. 2 tog. all round, k. 2 plain rounds.

64TH ROUND : K. 3 tog. all round.

Break off the wool, leaving a length hanging, which thread in a darning-needle, draw through all the remaining stitches, and fasten off very securely, running in the ends on the wrong side of the tammy.

THE POMPON is made with a mixture of both wools wound over a 5-inch card. The strands are tied securely at one end and cut at the other, then trimmed into a nice round shape. Finally unravel the strands of wool, or brush them to make the pompon light and fluffy. You could make this after the scarf is finished, when you would be able to mix in more of the brown wool.

THE SCARF.

THIS is knitted on two of the No. 10 needles in rows of plain knitting, backwards and forwards, or you can knit one row and purl the back row. This will give a smoother surface on the right side for brushing, although it is inclined to curl when completed. This is easily remedied by placing a damp cloth on the *wrong* side of the work and pressing with a hot iron.

MATERIALS FOR SCARF.—For a scarf about 16 inches wide and 64 inches long you will require 14 ounces of the fawn wool and 2 ounces of the brown. The latter will allow for belt, pocket-tops, fringe, and some for the pompon on tammy.

Cast on 105 stitches and knit 64 inches as described above, slipping purlwise the first stitch of every row.

THE POCKETS.—Cast on 30 stitches with fawn and knit 56 rows. Join brown and knit 10 rows for the top band. Cast off. Sew on pockets at centre of each end of scarf, about 4½ inches up from the bottom.

THE BELT.—This is in brown wool. Cast on 6 stitches and increase 1 by knitting in the front and back of the second stitch in each row until there are 12 stitches on the needle. Now make a buttonhole, thus :

K. 4, k. 2 tog., pass wool twice round needle, k. 2 tog., k 4.

Next row completes the buttonhole. K. 5, k. 1 and purl 1 in the loop, k. 5.

A second buttonhole can be made 2 inches farther along ; the second buttonhole will allow the belt to be worn tighter or looser, as required. Now knit the length of belt according to waist measurement, then decrease off to 6 stitches by knitting together the second and third stitch of each row, and cast off. Measure the strip easily, and so that it is in a high-waisted position to get the prettiest effect. Sew buttons to correspond with buttonholes, or if you do not wish to make the buttonholes in the knitting, you can sew on snap fasteners.

THE FRINGE.—This is made with a mixture of both wools. Wind the wool round a piece of cardboard measuring about 5 inches and cut at one end. Take three of the strands—all one colour or mixed, as you like—double them, and pass the doubled end down through a stitch on the end of the scarf, from right side to wrong. A bone crochet hook will greatly help this operation. Draw through a little way, then pass the cut ends through the loop and draw up firmly. Repeat this all along the edge of scarf, setting the strands as closely together as the remnant of wool will allow. The garments are now ready for brushing, and after that operation the belt can be sewn in position on the scarf, so that it passes round the waist at the back and over the scarf in front.

HOW TO BRUSH.

TAKE care that your brush is the right one for wool-brushing. It should have little wires with hooks on, like a teazle, not the straight wires as on suede brushes. Hold the garment in the left hand and put a piece of wash-leather under the wool. Lift the brush with sharp staccato movements, at the same time let them be gentle, so that you just lift the pile. This pile can also be raised again after washing, when it will look like new.

IRISH CROCHET EDGING.

Suitable for edging fine lingerie, baby's clothes, etc.

ABBREVIATIONS : Tr., treble ; d.c., double crochet ; ch., chain.

Ardern's crochet cotton, No. 36, with a No. 8 hook, makes a narrow edging suitable for handkerchiefs and fine garments.

For the first row begin with 5 ch., then 1 tr. in the 1st stitch 5 ch. Turn.

2ND ROW : 1 tr. under 5 ch., 5 ch. Turn. Repeat the 2nd row twice. Now for the scallop, work 5 ch., miss the tr., and work 1 tr. under next 5 ch. that turned ; now 7 ch., 1 tr. under the same place, 5 ch., miss the next tr., 1 d.c. under the next 5 ch., 1 ch. Turn.

5TH ROW : In the loop of 5 ch. work 2 d.c., 4 ch., 2 d.c., 4 ch., 2 d.c. In the next loop of 7 ch., work 2 d.c., 4 ch., 2 d.c., 4 ch., 2 d.c. In the next loop work the same as the 1st loop of 5 ch., now 1 d.c. on the next tr., 5 ch., 1 tr. under 5 ch., 5 ch. Turn. Now repeat from the 2nd row for length required.

To join the scallops together, work 2 d.c. in 1st loop of 5 ch., then 1 ch., take out the hook, and insert it in the first little loop of previous scallop, and draw the dropped stitch through, then 3 ch., and work on as before.

To turn a corner, end the 5th row with 4 ch., 1 d.c. under 5 ch. * 4 ch. Turn, 1 d.c. under 4 ch. ; repeat from * twice. Now for scallop work 5 ch., miss 1 d.c., 1 tr., 7 ch., 1 tr. under next 4 ch. that turned, then 5 ch., miss 1 d.c., 1 d.c. under next 4 ch. Turn with 1 ch., and fill the three loops as for the other scallops, joining as before, end with 1 d.c. on the d.c., then 5 ch., 1 tr. under 4 ch. Turn with 5 ch., and work on as before for length required.

For the heading, work 1 d.c. under side of a tr., 3 ch., 1 tr. under the same tr., * 3 ch., 2 tr. under the next space along edge, and repeat from * all along.

At the corner put 2 groups of tr. together without ch. between.

A LONG, COMPLETE NOVEL BY OLIVER SANDYS: INSIDE!

WOMAN'S WEEKLY

JAN. 29. 1921. [Vol. XIX. No. 489.]

2d

Still Another Jumper!

In Knitting and Crochet this time!

Directions Inside...

Have You Made a Jumper Yet?

Every girl worthy of the name has made a jumper in knitting or crochet. Here's ever such an easy one, combining the simplest stitches of both those arts.

An Economical Jumper.

Three hanks of artificial silk were used for this jumper for a bust measure of 34 to 36 inches (or you can use three hanks of Star Sylko No. 3), with a pair of knitting needles No. 8, and a No. 9 bone crochet hook.

A JUMPER IN KNITTING AND CROCHET.

THIS little jumper is planned on the simplest lines with stocking web stitch (knitting front row and purling back) for the main part and crochet for the hip-band, neck, and lower part of sleeves.

ABBREVIATIONS: K., knit; p., purl; tog., together; ch., chain; d.c., double crochet; tr., treble.

FRONT.—Cast on 120 stitches and k. in stocking web for 10 inches.

Here the neck shaping begins on a plain row. Knit 50 stitches and pass them on a spare needle or a large safety pin. Cast off the following 20 stitches and knit plain the remaining 50 stitches. Work on one shoulder, leaving the other for a while. Purl back over the 50 stitches. Turn, k. 1, k. 2 tog., k. to end of row, p. back, continue decreasing in this manner on the neck edge, 1 stitch from the end of every plain row, until there are 10 decreasings, then continue without decreasing for 1½ inches. Now increase by knitting in the front and back of second stitch from the neck edge every plain row, until there are 50 stitches on the needle, then these stitches are put on to a spare needle.

Knit the other shoulder piece in the same manner, and after the last row, which finishes at the neck edge, cast on 20 stitches for back of neck, knit across the other 50 stitches, passing them all on one needle. Knit in stocking web for 10 inches, and cast off.

SLEEVES.—First fold the work and put a pin at the top of shoulder to measure centre of armhole. Pick up 100 stitches, 50 each side of the pin, then knit in stocking web for 4 inches. Now decrease 1 stitch at each end of work every 6th row until there are 94 stitches, then cast off loosely.

The other sleeve is done in the same manner

THE CROCHET BAND

ABBREVIATIONS: Tr., treble (cotton over the hook once); ch., chain; d.c., double crochet; sp., space, which is 2 ch., miss 2 st., 1 tr. in the next st. Take note that the tr. finishing a sp., bar, or lacet is counted in that sp., etc., and *not* in the group following.

A lacet is worked thus: 3 ch., miss 2 st., 1 d.c. in the next st., now 3 ch., miss 2 st., 1 tr. in the next stitch.

A bar is worked thus: 5 ch., then miss the lacet and work 1 tr. on the next tr.

Commence with 54 ch.

1ST ROW: 1 tr. in 4th ch. from hook, 1 tr. in each of next 2 stitches, 1 bar, 3 tr., 9 sp., 3 tr., 1 bar, 3 tr., 3 ch. Turn.

2ND ROW: Miss the 1st tr. over which the 3 ch. stands, 3 tr. on tr., 1 lacet, 3 tr., 9 sp., 3 tr., 1 lacet, 3 tr., 3 ch. Turn.

3RD ROW: 3 tr., 1 bar, 3 tr., 2 sp., 6 tr., 1 sp., 6 tr., 2 sp., 3 tr., 1 bar, 3 tr.

4TH ROW: 3 tr., 1 lacet, 3 tr., 2 sp., 6 tr., 1 sp., 6 tr., 2 sp., 3 tr., 1 lacet, 3 tr.

5TH ROW: 3 tr., 1 bar, 3 tr., 4 sp., 3 tr., 4 sp., 3 tr., 1 bar, 3 tr.

6TH ROW: 3 tr., 1 lacet, 3 tr., 4 sp., 3 tr., 4 sp., 3 tr., 1 lacet, 3 tr.

7TH ROW: 3 tr., 1 bar, 3 tr., 2 sp., 6 tr., 1 sp., 6 tr., 2 sp., 3 tr., 1 bar, 3 tr.

8TH ROW: 3 tr., 1 lacet, 3 tr., 2 sp., 6 tr., 1 sp., 6 tr., 2 sp., 3 tr., 1 lacet, 3 tr. Repeat from 1st row for length required.

This completes the pattern. In the original 6 patterns are worked for the front and 6 for the back. This is sewn on to the knitting and a ch. is made to thread through the top part of the trimming, to draw in the fulness if desired.

TRIMMING FOR THE NECK.—Make 24 ch.

1ST ROW: 1 tr. in the 4th ch. from hook and in each of the next 2 ch., 2 sp., 3 tr., 1 bar, 3 tr., 3 ch. Turn.

2ND ROW: Miss 1 tr., 3 tr., 1 lacet, 3 tr., 2 sp., 1 d.c. on each of last 3 tr. to contract this edge, 3 ch. Turn. Repeat these 2 rows for length required, making 3 tr. at the beginning of each repetition of the 1st row.

Sew the contracted edge of collar to neck-edge of jumper. Sew up sleeve and under-arm seams of jumper and the garment is completed.

THE LAST OF THE TRIANGLE INITIALS.

LETTER Y.

BEGIN with 112 ch.

1ST ROW: 1 tr. in the 9th st. from the hook; now 33 sp., then miss 3 st., 1 d.tr. in the next st., 4 ch. to turn always at this, the sloping side of triangle.

2ND ROW: Miss the 1st tr. and work 1 tr. on the next tr.; this makes a decrease of 1 sp. All the rows at this side begin in the same manner. Now 1 sp. and 3 tr. 16 times, 1 sp., 5 ch. to turn always at this, the straight side of triangle.

3RD ROW: 30 sp., 3 tr., 1 sp., now 1 d.tr. under the 4 ch. that turned, 4 ch. Turn.

4TH ROW: 1 tr., 1 sp., 3 tr., 21 sp., 6 tr., 4 sp., 3 tr., 1 sp.

5TH ROW: 6 sp., 3 tr., 21 sp., 3 tr., 1 sp., 1 d.tr.

6TH ROW: 1 tr., 1 sp., 3 tr., 20 sp., 6 tr., 3 sp., 3 tr., 1 sp.

7TH ROW: 3 sp., 15 tr., 18 sp., 3 tr., 1 sp., 1 d.tr.

8TH ROW: 1 tr., 1 sp., 3 tr., 16 sp., 9 tr., 2 sp., 3 tr., 1 sp., 3 tr., 1 sp.

9TH ROW: 7 sp., 21 tr., 10 sp., 3 tr., 1 sp., 1 d.tr.

10TH ROW: 1 tr., 1 sp., 3 tr., 3 sp., 3 tr., 2 sp., 12 tr., 3 sp., 6 tr., 6 sp., 3 tr., 1 sp.

11TH ROW: 8 sp., 3 tr., 1 sp., 3 tr., 6 sp., 6 tr., 3 sp., 3 tr., 1 sp., 1 d.tr.

12TH ROW: 1 tr., 1 sp., 3 tr., 3 sp., 3 tr., 8 sp., 3 tr., 6 sp., 3 tr., 1 sp.

13TH ROW: 8 sp., 3 tr., 7 sp., 3 tr., 3 sp., 3 tr., 1 sp., 1 d.tr.

14TH ROW: 1 tr., 1 sp., 3 tr., 9 sp., 6 tr., 6 sp., 3 tr., 1 sp.

15TH ROW: 9 sp., 3 tr., 8 sp., 3 tr., 1 sp., 1 d.tr.

16TH ROW: 1 tr., 1 sp., 3 tr., 7 sp., and 3 tr. twice, 1 sp.

17TH ROW: 9 sp., 3 tr., 2 sp., 3 tr., 3 sp., 3 tr., 1 sp., 1 d.tr.

18TH ROW: 1 tr., 1 sp., 3 tr., 3 sp., 6 tr., 8 sp., 3 tr., 1 sp.

19TH ROW: 10 sp., 3 tr., 3 sp., 3 tr., 1 sp., 1 d.tr.

20TH ROW: 1 tr., 1 sp., 3 tr., 3 sp., 3 tr., 7 sp., 3 tr., 1 sp. This finishes the initial. Now work on with spaces in centre of every row and borders as usual. This will bring you to the 30th row in which there will be 1 tr., then 1 sp. and 3 tr. twice, 1 sp.

31ST ROW: 2 sp., 3 tr., 1 sp., 1 d.tr.

32ND ROW: 1 tr., 1 sp., 3 tr., 1 sp.

33RD ROW: 2 sp., 1 d.tr.

34TH ROW: 1 tr., 1 sp., 3 ch. Turn and work 1 d.tr. under 4 ch. Fasten off.

WOMAN'S WEEKLY

2d

A Knitted
(MOSS STITCH)
Jumper
Crochet
Trimmed

Very simple directions for making this Jumper will be found on page 305.

MAR. 26, 1921. Vol. XIX No. 491.

Moss Stitch Jumper in Silk
(WITH CROCHET TRIMMINGS.)

Two simple knitting stitches and an easy bold crochet pattern make this delightful jumper. Any girl will be proud of it when she has made it herself.

ANOTHER jumper, and when you have knitted one from these directions, I think you will say that jumpers can go on for ever. You would say so if you could see the two jumpers I have here, worked from this identical pattern, one in amethyst and one in a lovely soft rose shade, so instead of sitting sighing and breaking the tenth commandment, as all the people in the office have done, set to work and knit one from these directions and tell your friends about it, so that they will not be wanting the directions after the book is out of print.

SIZE.

THE jumper illustrated and worked from the directions given, will fit a figure measuring 34 inches at the bust line, but these jumpers should never be tight-fitting, so if you want the 36 inches, you can use coarser needles without detriment to the work, as the original was done on rather fine needles for this kind of work. No. 6 or 7 needles would do for the larger size.

MATERIALS.

FOUR hanks of artificial silk were used for this jumper, with No. 9 needles, and a No. 1 steel crochet hook.

A WORD ABOUT NEEDLES AND HOOKS.

THESE must be perfectly smooth, and if of bone there must not be the slightest chip, or it will spell ruination for your silk. So aluminium or celluloid are the best materials, unless you are sure of an old and worn hook in any other material.

TO BEGIN THE WORK.

CAST on 120 st. for the back hip-line. With the needles mentioned above and average knitting, you will get 9 st. to the inch, and from this you can gauge the size of the jumper. You can add extra stitches here if you wish, but there must be an even number or you will get the moss stitch pattern wrong. The latter consists of k. 1, and p. 1, and the next row must be the reverse, p. 1 and k. 1. It is quite easy to keep this pattern correct after it is begun, because at the beginning of the row, if the stitch appears as a knitted one *on the side facing you*, it must be purled, and vice versa, so that there is always a knitted stitch over a purled one, and a purled stitch over a knitted one. Watch this carefully when you come to shape the neck.

Knit moss stitch until the work measures 9½ ins., which brings the work to the armhole.

THE SLEEVES.

CAST on 36 st., knit in pattern on these 36 st. and right across the row.

Next row: Cast on 36 st. for second sleeve and knit in pattern right across all the stitches. Continue on these stitches until the sleeve measures 7 ins. from the first row. Do not make the depth of the sleeve any less as a narrow armhole utterly spoils the appearance of a silk jumper.

THE SHOULDERS.

KNIT 82 st., cast off 28 for back of neck, k. 82 to end of row.
Next Row: K. back to neck, but increase one stitch by knitting in the back and front of the last stitch.
Knit back to cuff end.
Repeat the last two rows until there are 96 st. on this needle. Cut the silk, leaving a length hanging.
Rejoin silk at opposite shoulder and knit second front in the same way. This will complete the V neck.
Now knit across the stitches and across the second front joining by taking up the length of silk left hanging and knitting with the two threads.
Continue in pattern until the sleeve is the same depth as on back, making 14 ins. altogether. Now cast off 36 st. at beginning of next row, and cast off 36 at the beginning of next row, as this completes the two sleeves.

Continue knitting in pattern until you have as many rows on front as on back. Cast off.

KNITTED STRIPS FOR HEM OF JUMPER.

YOU will notice that the crochet band is inset, and there is a two-inch strip of moss stitch below the crochet. For these cast 118 st. and knit for a depth of 2 ins. You will require two strips this size.

CROCHET SLEEVE TRIMMING.

THIS is a little narrower than the hip-band, so special directions are given for it.
Begin with 32 ch.
1st Row: 1 tr. into 8th ch. from hook, 2 ch., miss 2 ch., 1 tr. in each of next 10 tr., 6 ch., miss 5 ch., 1 tr. into next chain (2 ch., miss 2, 1 tr. into next ch.) twice. Directions in brackets are always worked the number of times stated after the brackets. 5 ch., turn.
2nd Row: Miss first tr. over which 5 ch. stands, 1 tr. on second tr., 2 ch., 1 tr. on next tr., 6 ch., 1 tr. on each of first 2 tr. on block (2 ch., miss 2, 2 tr.) twice, 2 sp. of 2 ch. and 1 tr. each, 5 ch., turn.
3rd Row: 2 sp. over those below, the first one being formed by the 5 turning ch., 3 more trs. (last 2 over ch.), 2 ch., miss 2 tr., 4 tr., 6 ch., miss 6 ch., 2 sp. at end, 5 ch., turn.
4th Row: 2 sp., 3 ch., 1 d.cr. under all three chain bars below, 3 ch., 2 tr. on first 2 of group, 2 ch., miss 2 tr., 2 tr. under ch., 2 ch., miss 2 tr., 2 tr., 2 sp., 5 ch., turn.
5th Row: 2 sp., 10 tr., 6 ch. to span over bars, 2 sp., 5 ch., turn.
Now repeat from the first row of pattern, and this will reverse the block bringing it at the opposite side of the lace. Eight of the 10 tr. on first row will be worked under the 6 ch. which spans the bars.
Repeat these 10 rows until you have sufficient length to go round the cuff, then sew first and last rows together to form into a round, and along one side work the following edging.
1st Row: 5 ch., miss 1 sp., 1 d.cr. in next sp. ; repeat all round.
2nd Round: Into each loop all round work 1 d.cr., 4 ch., 2 d.cr., 4 ch., 2 d.cr., 4 ch., 1 d.cr.

CROCHET INSERTION FOR HIP-BAND.

BEGIN with 42 ch.
1st Row: 1 tr. in 8th ch. from hook, 2 ch., miss 2 ch., 1 tr. in each of the next 10 tr., 6 ch., miss 5 ch., 10 tr., 2 sp., 5 ch., turn.
2nd Row: 2 sp., 1 more tr. (2 ch., miss 2 tr., 2 tr.) twice, 6 ch., miss 5, 2 tr. on tr. ; repeat brackets twice, 2 sp., 5 ch., turn.
3rd Row: 2 sp., 3 tr. (2 under ch.), 2 ch., miss 2 tr., 4 tr., 6 ch., miss 6 ch., 4 tr. (last 2 under ch.), 2 ch., miss 2 tr., 2 tr. under ch., and 2 tr. on tr., 2 sp., 5 ch., turn.
4th Row: 2 sp., 1 more tr. (2 ch., miss 2 st., 2 tr.) twice, 3 ch., 1 d.cr. under the 3 ch. bars, 3 ch., 2 tr., and repeat brackets twice, 2 sp., 5 ch., turn.
5th Row: 2 sp., 9 tr. (making 10 with the tr. finishing the last sp.), 6 ch., 10 tr. (over tr. and spaces on second block), 2 sp., 5 ch., turn.
6th Row: 2 sp., 6 ch., miss 9 tr., 1 tr. at end of block, 8 under ch. and 1 on first tr. of next block, 6 ch., 1 tr. on last tr. of block, 2 sp., 5 ch., turn.
7th Row: 2 sp., 6 ch., 2 tr. (2 ch., miss 2 st., 2 tr.) twice, 6 ch., 2 sp. over sp., 5 ch., turn.
8th Row: 2 sp., 6 ch., 4 tr. (2 on tr. and 2 on ch.), 2 ch., miss 2 tr., 4 tr., 6 ch., 2 sp., 5 ch., turn.
9th Row: 2 sp., 3 ch., 1 d.cr. under the 3 ch. loops, 3 ch., 2 tr. (2 ch., miss 2 sp., 2 tr.) twice, 3 ch., 1 d.cr. under ch. loops, 3 ch., 1 tr., 2 sp., 5 ch., turn.
10th Row: 2 sp., 6 ch., 10 tr. across block, 6 ch., 2 sp., 5 ch., turn.

USE THIS MEASURE WHEN KNITTING YOUR JUMPER.

INCHES　1　2　3　4　5　6

THE ROSE MEDALLION CROCHET SERIAL.

Owing to lack of space the crochet serial has to be left out, but the tea cosy will be published next week.

FLORAL SPRAY CROCHET-SET BEGINS—*See inside*

WOMAN'S WEEKLY

EVERY TUESDAY · No 716 Vol. XXVIII · **JULY 11, 1925**

2D

Another Easy One!

It is made in One Piece!

And You Could Do it in a Day!

MADE IN A DAY

The Jumper on our Cover is composed of Simple Crochet loops

THIS quickly made tennis jumper is worked in crochet loops. It begins with a long length of chain at side seam, and is worked across the body instead of the usual way.

The length of chain (48 inches in model) folded in half at shoulder, gives length of jumper, 24 inches, and the width all round bust in model is about 44 inches without stretching. This is easily varied according to figure, by adding to or subtracting from the number of rows worked before beginning the square neck.

MATERIALS : Four hanks of Celanese Standard Twist and an Archer super bone crochet hook, No. 8, which has the size marked on it.

ABBREVIATIONS : Ch., chain; d.c., double crochet.

Make 288 ch.

1ST ROW : 1 d.c. in 6th ch., * 3 ch., miss 2 foundation ch., 1 d.c. in next; repeat from * all along ch., making 95 loops altogether, 3 ch. Turn.

2ND ROW : 1 d.c. in first loop of 3 ch. of last row, then 3 ch. and 1 d.c. in each loop to end of row.

Work 40 rows as 2nd row.

Mark the d.c. after the 47th loop from beginning of row; this is the top of shoulder. Work 41 loops only, then turn and work up and down on these 41 loops for 29 rows, ending at neck. Make 36 ch., and fasten off.

Leave 6 loops from the other side of the mark on shoulder, work a d.c. in 7th loop, work 30 rows, and with the last d.c. of last loop at neck, catch in the end of the 36 ch. made on front; work 12 loops across the 36 ch., then continue down front, and work 40 rows to match other side.

Sew up side seams, leaving 7 inches from top of shoulder for armhole.

Edge neck, armholes, and bottom of jumper as follows :

1ST ROW : * 1 d.c. in a loop, 1 d.c. on d.c.; and repeat from * all along.

2ND ROW : * 1 ch., miss 1 d.c. of last row, 1 tr. on next; repeat from *.

3RD ROW : 1 d.c. in every stitch.

PRESSING HIS SUIT

To spend ten guineas on your outfit isn't necessary to win your way to a girl's heart, says our contributor

I OFTEN wonder what originated that monstrous fable which would have us women believe that men are the modest, non-vain sex. Hark to the case of Lilith and Leslie.

Leslie was by way of being a walking fashion plate. His trousers habitually displayed a crease of almost painful exquisiteness. His jackets were miraculously "waisted." His coloured shirts and collars to match; his ties and socks also to match; and his dinky handkerchiefs made one harmonious whole of more than earthly perfection. He was a well-built stripling, carrying his clothes with an air, and when he appeared in public one could almost hear the bitterly envious comments of the less expensively clad menfolk.

And yet he was not happy. Why? Lilith!

"I'll tell you what it is," the poor lad confided to me, "Lilith—well, she surprises me. When I asked her how she liked my suit, she merely said : 'Oh! Is it a new suit? I hadn't noticed.' Bit galling after I'd spent ten guineas on the outfit. I wanted to please her."

"Listen, my lad," said I oracularly. "When you say you want to please her, what exactly do you mean? How much do you want to please her?"

He got rather red. Then he said bravely :

"I want her to marry me."

"Asked her yet?"

"I've—er—sounded her."

"Result, please?"

He turned a deeper red, which clashed horribly with that morning's symphony in grey, and replied, almost peevishly :

"Her exact words were, 'I'm far too shabby for your splendours, Leslie.'"

"My poor, poor innocent!" I laughed. "Do you imagine that any girl worth her salt—any girl worth marrying—will be influenced by a lover's clothes? She doesn't want sounding by a fop. She looks for flesh and blood and character. She wants a man, not a tailor's dummy."

"Dash it all," he protested, "one must smarten up for a lady."

"Years ago," I told him, "I read a burlesque advertisement which ran : THE SOAP FOR THE SMART SET. IF YOU ARE SMART ALREADY OUR SOAP WILL MAKE YOU SMART MORE."

"Funny!" he grunted sarcastically. "Go on."

"When you walk out with Lilith you make her smart with mortification. People look at you too much."

Positively he smirked with gratification. "They're jealous," he chuckled.

"That may be. But the net result is that Lilith thinks you promenade to show off your clothes, not because you like her."

He pondered gloomily. Then he said : "What do you advise?"

"Tone down your clothes, lad, and tone up your proposals. Be a bit more ardent, and dim your sartorial magnificence a trifle."

THE SEQUEL

DID he? Judge for yourself. When next he was along with Lilith he roughly dragged her to him, flung his arms round her, and demanded fiercely :

"You little wretch! Will you marry me?"

Their eyes met, and she saw in his a look that all girls long for. Something that was not laughter alone made her choke a little as she said :

"Leslie, Leslie, you'll spoil your beautiful clothes."

"Hang my beautiful clothes!" roared Leslie. "Will you, Lilith? Will you?"

And Lilith, vanquished, gently laid her pretty head against that marvellously tailored shoulder, the while she whispered "Yes."

Isn't it trim and tailored enough to please any man? And think how jolly to borrow it when occasion arises. You only have to fasten the buttons t'other way over.

A SLEEVELESS CARDIGAN

IT BUTTONS

I T'S just a matter of the buttons! Buttonholes are made in the knitting on both bands; the buttons are on a sateen strip which is attached to left front for a lady's wear, and to the right front for a man's wear, as he buttons over from left to right.

MATERIALS—Eight and a half ounces of 4-ply Second Quality Fingering in dark grey, and 2½ ounces in light grey, a pair of long bone knitting-needles No. 10, and two spare needles, six buttons, and a small strip of sateen for the button band.

SIZE AND TENSION.—Working at a tension to produce 7 stitches to the inch in width, the following measurements should be attained after light pressing : Length from shoulder to hem, 26 inches; width all round, including plain knitted bands, 41 inches.

ABBREVIATIONS.—K., knit ; p., purl ; tog., together; sl., slip; st., stitch. To decrease 1 at the beginning of a knitted row, k. the first st., then k. 2 tog. To decrease 1 at the end of a knitted row, work until 3 st. remain, then sl. 1, k. 1, pass the sl. st. over, k. the last st. Stocking-stitch is k. 1 row and p. 1 row alternately. Garter-stitch is produced by knitting every row plain.

The Pocket Linings

C AST on 35 st. in dark wool and work in stocking-stitch for 4 inches, the last row being a knitted row. Cut the wool leaving enough to sew three sides of pocket to

garment later. Slip these st. on a spare needle and work the second pocket lining in the same way.

Now cast on 258 st. in dark wool for all round the lower edge of garment.

K. 1 row into the back of cast-on stitches.

K. 11 more rows in garter-stitch and p. 1 row. Now work in the pattern as follows :

The Two-Colour Pattern

1st row : K. 3 dark, 2 light, * 4 dark, 2 light ; repeat from *, finishing with 1 dark.

2nd row : P. 2 dark, 2 light, * 4 dark, 2 light ; repeat from *, finishing with 2 dark.

3rd row : K. 1 dark, 2 light, * 4 dark, 2 light ; repeat from *, finishing with 3 dark.

4th row : P. 6 dark, 2 light, * 4 dark, 2 light ; repeat from *, finishing with 4 dark.

5th row : K. 5 dark, 2 light, * 4 dark, 2 light ; repeat from *, finishing with 5 dark.

6th row : P. 4 dark, 2 light, * 4 dark, 2 light ; repeat from *, finishing with 6 dark.

Work 4 rows all dark in stocking-stitch.

11th row : K. 1 dark, 2 light, * 2 dark, 2 light ; repeat from *, finishing with 3 dark.

12th row : P. 1 dark, 2 light, * 2 dark, 2 light ; repeat from *, finishing with 3 dark.

Repeat 11th and 12th rows once more.

Using dark wool, work 4 rows in stocking-stitch.

These 18 rows complete one pattern ; now work from the 1st row to the 15th row, inclusive.

Pocket Row

W ITH dark wool, p. 21, sl. the next 35 st. on a safety-pin, and, in place of these, p. 35 pocket-lining st. from spare needle, p. 146, sl. next 35 on a safety-pin, and in place of these p. 35 pocket-lining st.; p. remaining 21 st.

K. 1 row and p. 1 row all dark.

Now repeat the 18 pattern rows 4 times more, then work next pattern to the end of the 4th row.

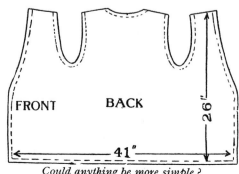

FRONT   BACK   26"   41"

Could anything be more simple ?

FOR SIR OR MADAM!

EITHER WAY

5th pattern row : K. 1, k. 2 tog., k. 60 in pattern. Now sl. these 62 st. on a spare needle for right front, cast off 6 st. for armhole ; k. next 120 st. in pattern and slip on a spare needle for back. Cast off 6 st., k. 60 st. in pattern, sl. 1, k. 1, pass the sl.-st. over, k. 1 (62 st. for left front).

The Left Front

WORK on these 62 st., beginning with the 6th pattern row.

At armhole end of work cast off 2 st. at beginning of every k. row for 5 decreasings, then decrease 1 st. at beginning of every k. row for 5 further decreasings. At the front edge (end of k. rows) decrease 1 st. at end of 2 following k. rows. Do not decrease at end of the next k. row. This will give 2 decreasings at front edge in every 6 rows. Take care to follow the pattern correctly while decreasing ; it is quite easy at this stage of the work with such a small pattern. After the armhole decreasings are completed, this end of row can be followed from the two-colour pattern given above.

Continue the front edge decreases until the st. are reduced to 24, then work to end of 14th row of next pattern and cast off.

The Right Front

JOIN wool on purl side of work at armhole end of 62 st. left for the right front, and work the 6th pattern row. Now work to correspond with left front, the armhole decreasings being at end of k. rows and front decreasings at beginning of k. rows.

The Back

JOIN wool on purl side of work to first of 120 st. left for back, and work the 6th pattern row. Continue in pattern, casting off 2 at beginning of every row for next 10 rows. Decrease 1 st. at each end of every k. row for 5 decrease rows. There should now be 90 st. Complete the pattern to end of 18th row, then work the 18 pattern rows twice more. Now work the first 6 pattern rows. Continue in pattern and cast off 5 st. at the beginning of each of the next 8 rows ; then cast off the remaining 50 st.

Pocket Tops

REJOIN the dark wool to 35 st. left on a safety-pin, k. 10 rows, and cast off.

Work the other pocket top in the same way.

The Garter-Stitch Borders

FOR neck and front strip, cast on 8 st. in dark wool and k. 4 rows garter-stitch.

    * *Next row :* K. 3, cast off 2, k. 3.
    Next row : K. 3, cast on 2, k. 3.

Please forgive us ! She looked so charming, and we were so interested in arranging the cardigan so that the pattern looked well —that nobody noticed she had fastened it up the wrong side over.

K. 24 rows, and repeat from * until 6 buttonholes have been worked.

Now k. for about 31 inches, then work 6 more buttonholes at intervals as before. Work 4 more rows and cast off.

For the armhole borders, cast on 8 st. in dark wool and k. in garter-stitch for about 19 inches, or enough to go round armhole, slightly stretching it. Cast off and work another piece in the same way.

To Make Up

PRESS all parts on the right side (except the neck and arm-hole garter-stitch strips), using a moderately hot iron over a damp cloth. Sew shoulder seams and sew pocket linings to wrong side and pocket tops to right side of garment. Join up the ends of the short strips and sew one to each armhole, putting the join at the under-arm and slightly stretching the band at that point. This will press out quite flat if a damp cloth be used. Pin centre of neck border to centre-back of neck, and pin in position at intervals down the fronts ; then sew neatly, stretching slightly at back of neck to give a good fit. Make a narrow strip of double sateen, about 16 inches long, and sew the buttons to this at equal distances to correspond with buttonholes. Pass the buttons through the buttonholes on the correct side (according to the wearer) and secure at the two narrow ends of the band.

Press all seams on the wrong side.

Long Sleeves-

Very simple, slender and trim is this Jumper with the long close-fitting sleeves. Worn over a white pleated crepe-de-Chine skirt it is suitable for afternoon or sports wear.

Very light in weight (only 4½ ounces with short sleeves) and the easiest possible knitting are two of the points which make this jumper an attractive piece of summer knitting. You can even begin it during the first few days of your holiday when "lazing" on the beach, and wear it before you come home, so easily and quickly is it done. The coloured bands give a bright note which can match a colour on the skirt, your headgear, or those little gay sandals which are so popular now.

Materials

For a short-sleeved jumper 3 ozs., and for long-sleeved jumper 4½ ozs. of Ladyship 2-ply Scotch Fingering in white, 1½ ozs. in lilac or other contrasting shade for either jumper, a pair of long bone knitting needles No. 9, and one spare needle and a stitch holder.

Tension and Measurements

Working at a tension of 7 sts. to the inch in width, the following measurements should be obtained after light pressing: Length from shoulder to hem, 25½ inches; length of sleeve, 18 inches; width all round, 40 inches.

Abbreviations

K., knit; p., purl; tog., together; s.s., stocking-stitch (k. 1 row, p. 1 row alternately); m.s., moss-stitch (k. 1, p. 1 st. alternately, every row the same on an odd number of stitches); sts., stitches.

Begin at Front Hem

Cast on 137 sts. in the coloured wool, k. 1 row into the back of sts., m.s. 21 rows, k. 1 row. Fasten off.
　　With white wool, do 12 rows of s.s., beginning with a k. row.
　　With lilac, k. 2 rows, m.s. 15 rows, and k. 1 row.
　　With white, 10 rows of s.s.
　　With lilac, k. 2 rows, m.s. 9 rows, and k. 1 row.
　　Beginning with a k. row, work s.s. all white for 15 inches, finishing with a p. row. This brings the work to the square neck line, and the sts. are here divided for the two shoulders.

　　Next row.—K. 37, and slip on a spare needle for left shoulder, k. next 63 and slip on a stitch holder, which will lock these sts. safely, and not be in the way as much as another spare needle. On the remaining 37 stitches, work 7 inches s.s., finishing at the neck end of a purl row.

The Coloured Yoke

With right side of work facing, join lilac to the beginning of a plain row on the 63 front sts., k. 2 rows, m.s. 9 rows.
　　Next row.—M.s. 9, k. 45, m.s. 9.
　　Next row.—M.s. 9, cast off 45; on remaining 9 work m.s. for 4½ inches, cut wool, which must be at neck end of row. Join wool to the other 9 sts. at neck end and work the same length, finishing at neck end of row. Now cast 45 sts.

Or Short!

For the tennis or river girl who likes short sleeves, here is another version of the same Jumper. Soft white wool with bands of laven-der-blue were the colours chosen for it.

on same needle for back yoke and m.s. and 9 sts. on first side of yoke (63 sts.).

Next row.—M.s. 9, k. 45 into back of sts., m.s. 9.

M.s. 9 rows across all sts., k. 1 row plain, then cut wool and slip sts. on a spare needle.

The Left Shoulder

JOIN white wool to 37 sts. for left shoulder at beginning of a p. row, and work s.s. to match right shoulder. After a plain row, k. the 63 back yoke sts., then k. the 37 right shoulder sts. all on the same needle, making 137 sts. altogether.

The Back

USING the white wool, work s.s. for 16 inches, finishing with a p. row.

With lilac, k. 2 rows, m.s. 9 rows, k. 1 row.

With white, k. 1 row and p. 1 row alternately 5 times (10 rows).

With lilac, k. 2 rows, m.s. 15 rows, k. 1 row.

With white, k. 1 row and p. 1 row 6 times (12 rows).

With lilac, k. 2 rows, m.s. 21 rows, k. 1 row and cast off.

Sleeve Bands

CAST on 9 sts. in lilac and work 12 inches in m.s.

The Long Sleeves

FOLD jumper at shoulder line and mark with a pin; measure 7 inches down each side of shoulder line and mark with pins. In this space, pick up 86 sts., that is, 43 at each side of shoulder. Using white wool work s.s. and at each end of every 6th row, k. 2 tog. until 46 sts. are left.

Work s.s. for 1 inch less than length of finished sleeve.

Work 1 inch of k. 1, p. 1 rib and cast off.

The Wrist Band

THIS is worked separately with lilac wool. Cast on 9 sts. and work 8 inches in m.s., cast off.

To Make Up the Jumper

FIRST press all parts lightly on the wrong side. Sew sides of yoke to shoulders and sew side seams for short-sleeved jumper, leaving 7 inches open at each side of shoulder line and sew the sleeve band to this.

For long-sleeved jumper, sew sleeve seam, then tack centre of wrist band to front of wrist, fold over and sew two buttons (cuff link fashion) to fasten wrist band together. One row of double crochet round neck will prevent this from stretching.

Now press the seams and final touches of sewing.

FOR
Autumn
Days—

You Have This Leaf-Brown Jumper With Its Many-Coloured Flower Embroidery

THIS jumper is knitted in a round. There are no side seams and no sleeve seams as the underarm part of sleeve is continued on some of the body stitches and the stitches for the upper part of sleeve are picked up round the armhole, after the shoulders have been grafted together. The one illustrated was worked in a fingering wool of a natural colour which makes a neutral background to throw up the varied colours of the posy.

MATERIALS : Twelve ounces of 2-ply Scotch Fingering, a set of four No. 9 bone needles pointed at both ends, and some odd lengths of gaily coloured wools for the embroidery.

TENSION AND MEASUREMENTS : Working at a tension of 6 stitches to the inch in width the measurements on the diagram are attained after light pressing.

To WORK : On each of three needles cast 80 stitches, making 240 in the round. Knit one plain round, putting the needle into the back of the stitches to give a neat edge.

Now do 12 rounds of moss-stitch, that is, in the first round k. 1 and p. 1 alternately, and on the next round reverse the order so that a purl stitch comes over a knitted one and vice versa. It is necessary to reverse with an even number of stitches.

Do 8 rounds of plain knitting when the openwork is reached.

THE OPEN PATTERN : *First round :* * K. 1, m. 1, k. 2 tog. ; repeat from * all round.

2nd round : K. plain.

3rd round : K. 2, * m. 1, k. 2 tog., k. 1 ; repeat from * all round. Knit one remaining stitch at end.

4th round : Knit plain.

5th round : K. 3, * m. 1, k. 2 tog., k. 1 ; repeat from * to end of round.

A little tassel of jade-green wool hangs down at the base of the embroidered V at the neck.

The whole design is worked in lazy-daisy and stem-stitches. You can use up any odd scraps of bright-coloured wools; it will only take a few inches of each colour.

The diagram on the left shows the correct measurements for the jumper when it is pressed and lying flat.

The jumper is knitted in a round. There are no side seams, as the underarm part of the sleeve is continued on some of the body stitches, and the stitches for the upper part of the sleeve are picked up round the armhole, after the shoulders have been grafted together.

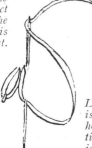

Lazy-daisy stitch is like button-holing, but the tip of the loop is held down by a tiny stitch.

19"

20"

25"

6th round : K. plain.

7th round : K. 2, * m. 1, k. 2 tog., k. 1 ; repeat from * all round, k. 1 stitch remaining.

8th round : K. plain.

9th round : * K. 1, m. 1, k. 2 tog. ; repeat from * all round.

10th round : K. plain. This finishes the fancy pattern.

K. 96 rounds of plain knitting to bring the work up to the armhole ; here the stitches must be divided equally on two needles, one for the front of jumper and one for the back, 120 on each side.

Now take 12 stitches at each side for the underarm piece, that is, 6 stitches from the end of front and back needle, at each end, and pass them on a safety pin at each end ; there are now 108 stitches on each needle.

THE FRONT : K. 12 rows of s s., that is, knitting on the front of the work and purling the back.

Left shoulder : K. 54 sts. and turn, leaving the remaining 54 stitches on a spare needle or stitch holder for the right shoulder. Purl back the 54 st. just knitted.

Next plain row : K. 50, k. 2 tog., k. 1. (This is the neck end and makes the first decrease for the neck slope.)

Purl back the next row.

Repeat the last two rows 21 times more, but always knitting one stitch less before the decrease on the plain rows, when there will be 32 stitches left for the shoulder ; cut the wool, leaving about 12 inches hanging and leave the stitches on the needle.

Right shoulder : Beginning at the centre front where the neck opening began, knit one row plain. On the next row purl 50, purl 2 tog., purl 1.

Continue this shoulder to match the left one exactly.

THE BACK : On the other 120 sts. k. s.s. for 56 rows, slipping the first stitch at the beginning of every plain row. Fasten off the wool securely, leaving the stitches on the needle. Those who do not wish to graft can cast off the sts. and sew shoulders in the ordinary way.

TO GRAFT THE SHOULDERS : This must be done before the sleeves are worked. Beginning where the wool is left at one shoulder end, place the two needles parallel, with the stitches of one needle right behind the other, and having threaded the wool into a bodkin, put the bodkin in first stitch of front row as if about to knit, slip stitch off needle, and draw wool through ; now put bodkin in second stitch of front needle, as if about to purl, draw wool through, but do not slip stitch off needle. Pass bodkin under first needle and put it in first stitch of back row as if about to purl, draw wool through, and slip

stitch off needle, put bodkin in second stitch of back needle as if about to knit, draw wool through, but do not slip off needle. You will see that the action of the front row is reversed on the back needle. Repeat until all the 32 front shoulder stitches are worked off, and do not draw the wool up tightly. Finally, pass wool through last stitch and fasten off very securely on wrong side.

Grafting can easily be remembered by the following little drill :

" Knit and slip off, purl and keep on. Purl and slip off, knit and keep on." although the " knit " and " purl " only indicates the position of the bodkin.

Now with a knitting needle and odd length of wool cast off the centre 44 stitches for the back of the neck, then graft the second shoulder stitches to the corresponding stitches of the back.

THE SLEEVES : Begin with the left sleeve. Pick up 36 stitches at each side of the armhole. On a third needle take the 12 stitches from the safety-pin. On this needle pass 15 stitches from each of

the other two, so that there will be 42 stitches on the underarm needle, and 21 stitches on each of the other two .

Knit in stocking web for 60 rounds.

FIRST DECREASE ROUND : On the underarm needle knit 1, knit 2 tog., k. 36, k. 2 tog., k. 1. Finish the round. K. 1 round plain. Repeat the decreasing on the underarm needle every second round, until there are only 60 sts. in the round.

Work the open pattern as at hem of jumper, then 3 rounds of plain knitting, 8 rounds of moss-stitch, and cast off.

Make the right sleeve in exactly the same way.

FINISHINGS : Work double crochet round the neck and cuffs, missing a stitch here and there on the knitting to keep the edge flat.

THE EMBROIDERED POSY.

THIS is a very simple design which the average embroiderer will be able to work right on the design without a pattern, by reference to the drawing on this page. Those who prefer a tracing can put a piece of tissue paper over the drawing and trace the design with a lead pencil. Tack the tracing in position on the jumper and work through it to the knitting. The paper will tear away easily when the work is finished.

The centre flower is worked in mauve, seven daisy-loop stitches forming the ring, then in the spaces between these stitches smaller daisy loops are worked in blue , the latter stitches are turned in the opposite direction. The two top daisies have a small centre of satin stitches, worked in grey with one bright red stitch in the centre of these. The petals of these daisies consist of the same daisy-loop stitches but worked closely together without any space at the centre and spread slightly at the outer edge to form the round. The leaf sprays above and below the daisies are worked in green and consist of daisy-loop stitches a little longer than those on the flowers. Below the centre flower make seven green stems fastening them below the flower with back stitches ; they consist of long loops about two inches long, which are cut at the end after being made quite secure at the top.

The straight stitches between the clusters of leaves and on the inner circle of centre flower, can be worked in stem or outline stitch. In stem stitch the thread is thrown over to the left of the needle, after inserting the latter in the material, and in outline stitch the thread goes over to the right. The latter keeps more to the outline than stem stitch.

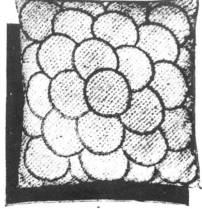

A SQUARE *of* HOUSE FLANNEL

Embroidered with old-gold circles makes such an effective cushion cover

Outline each circle in old-gold button-holing, making each stitch about a quarter of an inch deep.

Three-quarters of a yard of flannel will make the front of the cover with the same quantity of crash for the back.

CUT the flannel to an exact square. Draw round a tumbler or a saucer a three-and-a-half inch circle in the centre and pencil other circles round, as shown in the photograph above. Allow an inch margin all round for making up.

The button holing should be taken from left to right, always bringing the needle out on the line to keep the edge perfectly even.

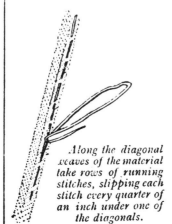

Along the diagonal xeaves of the material take rows of running stitches, slipping each stitch every quarter of an inch under one of the diagonals.

Embroider the design in buttonhole and running stitches, but do not take the needle right through the material or it will draw up and pucker The rows of running stitch should be a third of an inch apart across the circles.

When the embroidery is done, and the cover is made, bind it all round with two yards of fine gold cord.

A PULL-OVER OF GOOD LINE!

It retains a Smart Silhouette when the Wearer is in Motion as well as when she is in Repose

MATERIALS :—6 oz. of Paton's Super Scotch Fingering, 3-ply (or Beehive Shetland Floss)—the original was worked with 5 oz. of Dark Cedar and 1 oz. of Blue. Two No. 8 knitting needles.

MEASUREMENTS :—Length from top of shoulder to hem, 26 in. Width all round at underarm, 36 in.

ABBREVIATIONS :—K, knit plain ; p, purl ; tog., together ; C, Cedar ; B, Blue.

Work at a tension to produce seven stitches to the inch in width, measured over the plain knitting.

THE FRONT.

Using the Cedar wool, cast on 117 stitches.

1st row : K. 1, * p. 1, k. 1, repeat from * to the end of the row.

Repeat this row for 2 in.

THE TWO-COLOUR WAVE PATTERN.

1st row : Knit plain in Cedar.

2nd row : In Cedar. K. 1, purl to the last stitch, k. 1. Join in the Blue wool.

3rd row : K. 3C., * 3B., 3C., repeat from * to the end of the row.

4th row : K. 1C., * p. 1C., 5B., repeat from * to the last 2 stitches, p. 1C., k. 1C.

The bands at neck and arm-holes are in moss-stitch.

There is a border of the two-colour wave pattern. It is quite easy to knit in simple plain and purl stitches.

5th row : Knit plain in Blue.

6th row : K. 1, purl to the last stitch, k. 1 in Blue.

7th row : K. 3B., * 3C., 3B., repeat from * to the end of the row.

8th row : K. 1B., p. 1B., * 5C., 1B., repeat from * to the last stitch, k. 1B.

Fasten off the Blue wool.

Repeat these 8 rows three times. Proceed as follows :

1st row : Knit plain.

2nd row : K. 1, purl to the last stitch, k. 1. Repeat these two rows until the work measures 12 inches from the beginning, ending with a purl row.

This brings the work to the front opening, but before the stitches are divided, a little moss-stitch pattern is worked in the middle.

1st row : K. 58, p. 1, k. 58.

2nd row : K. 1, p. 56, k. 1, p. 1, k. 1, p. 56, k. 1.

3rd row : K. 56, (p. 1, k. 1) twice, p. 1, k. 56.

4th row : K. 1, p. 54, (k. 1, p. 1) three times, k. 1, p. 54, k. 1.

5th row : K. 54, (p. 1, k. 1) four times, p. 1, k. 54.

6th row : K. 1, p. 52, (k. 1, p. 1) five times, k. 1, p. 52, k. 1.

7th row : K. 52, (p. 1, k. 1) six times, p. 1, k. 52.

8th row : K. 1, p. 50, (k. 1, p. 1) seven times, k. 1, p. 50, k. 1.

9th row : K. 50, (p. 1, k. 1) eight times, p. 1, k. 50.

10th row : K. 1, p. 48, (k. 1, p. 1) nine times, k. 1, p. 48, k. 1.

Divide the stitches for the neck as follows :

1st row : K. 49, (k. 1, p. 1) four times, k. 2 tog., turn.

2nd row : (K. 1, p. 1) four times, k. 1, purl to the last stitch, k. 1.

3rd row : Knit plain to the last 8 stitches, (p. 1, k. 1) four times.

Repeat the 2nd and 3rd rows once, then the 2nd row once.

Keeping the continuity of the pattern, that is a k. over a p. st. and vice versa on the Moss-stitch border. Decrease once at the neck end of the needle in the next and every following 6th row (inside the Moss-stitch border) until 51 stitches remain, ending with the 2nd row.

This brings the work to the underarm and the Moss-stitch border at the arm-hole begins.

1st row : (K. 1, p. 1) three times, work in pattern to the end of the row. that is plain knitting up to the front border then Moss stitch as usual.

2nd row : Work in pattern to the last 7 stitches, (k. 1, p. 1) three times, k. 1.

3rd row : (K. 1, p. 1) four times, work in pattern to the end of the row.

4th row : Work in pattern to the last 9 stitches, (k. 1, p. 1) four times, k. 1.

5th row : (K. 1, p. 1) five times, knit plain to the last 11 stitches, k. 2 tog., (k. 1, p. 1) four times, k. 1.

6th row : (K. 1, p. 1) five times, purl to the last 11 stitches, (k. 1, p. 1) five times, k. 1.

7th row : (K. 1, p. 1) six times, work in pattern to the end of the row.

8th row : (K. 1, p. 1) five times, purl to the last 13 stitches, (k. 1, p. 1) six times, k. 1.

9th row : Cast off 4 stitches, (k. 1, p. 1) four times, work in pattern to the end of the row.

10th row : (K. 1, p. 1) four times, purl to the last 9 stitches, (k. 1, p. 1) four times, k. 1.

11th row : (K. 1, p. 1) five times, k. 1, k. 2 tog., knit plain to the last 11 stitches, k. 2 tog., (k. 1, p. 1) four times, k. 1.

Continue in this manner (still keeping a border of 9 stitches in Moss pattern at each end of the needle), whilst at the same time decreasing once at the beginning of the needle (armhole end) in every alternate row and at the neck end of the needle in every following 6th row, until 38 stitches remain.

Still decreasing at the neck edge in every 6th row, decrease once at the armhole edge in every 4th row until 34 stitches remain.

Continue decreasing at the neck edge in every 6th row until 28 stitches remain, then work 4 rows without decreasing.

Shape the shoulder line as follows :

1st row : Work in pattern to the last 9 stitches, turn.

2nd row : Work in pattern to the end of the row.

3rd row : Work in pattern to the last 18 stitches, turn.

4th row : Like the 2nd row.

5th row : Work in pattern across the row. Cast off.

RIGHT FRONT.

Go back to the last long row of front where the stitches were divided, and beginning at the neck end, proceed as follows :

1st row : (K. 1, p. 1) four times, k. 1, knit plain to the end of the row.

2nd row : K. 1, purl to the last 9 stitches, (k. 1, p. 1) four times.

Repeat these two rows, decreasing once at the beginning of the needle (inside the Moss-pattern border) in the 7th and every following 6th row until 51 stitches remain, ending with the 2nd row. Proceed as follows :

1st row : Work in pattern to the last

6 stitches, (p. 1, k. 1) three times.

2nd row : (K. 1, p. 1) three times, k. 1, work in pattern to the end of the row.

Work this front to match the first one, bearing in mind that the neck shaping is at the beginning of plain knitted rows, when the armhole border and shaping will fall at the opposite end.

THE BACK.

Using the Cedar wool, cast on 117 stitches.

Work as given for the front, until the work measures 18 inches from the beginning, end with a purl row. Here the underarm is reached and the Moss-stitch border at underarm is begun.

SPRAYS OF IRISH ROSES

Trim this Nightie Case of Mauve Organdie.

Crisp mauve organdie (1 yard of 44-inch) made this envelope-shaped nightdress case. The hem, faggoted to the flap with mauve Filo, was 1¾ inches wide. The crochet roses were stitched in graceful sprays at the corners.

TO CROCHET THE ROSES.

USING *two strands of Filo begin with 6 chain and make into a ring with a slip-stitch.*

1ST ROUND : Work 6 ch., 1 treble into the ring, then 3 ch. and 1 tr. into the ring four times, 3 ch. slip-stitch to 3rd of the 6 ch., making 6 loops in all.

2ND ROUND : Work 1 d.c., 2 tr., 2 d.tr. (thread twice round hook), 2 tr., 1 d.c. into each loop of 3 ch., making 6 petals in all.

Cut the thread and fasten off, then join two strands of green Filo at the back of the rose and work a chain about four inches in length. Fasten off.

The length of the chain for the stems should be varied with each rose to between two and four inches. For each spray work three mauve and four pink roses.

The roses are in mauve and pink with green stems.

1st row : (K. 1, p. 1) three times, knit plain to the last 6 stitches, (p. 1, k. 1) three times.

2nd row : (K. 1, p. 1) four times, purl to the last 8 stitches, (p. 1, k. 1) four times.

3rd row : (K. 1, p. 1) four times, knit plain to the last 8 stitches, (p. 1, k. 1) four times.

4th row : (K. 1, p. 1) five times, purl to the last 10 stitches, (p. 1, k. 1) five times.

5th row : (K. 1, p. 1) five times, knit plain to the last 10 stitches, (p. 1, k. 1) five times.

6th row : (K. 1, p. 1) six times, purl to the last 12 stitches, (p. 1, k. 1) six times.

7th row : (K. 1, p. 1) six times, knit plain to the last 12 stitches, (p. 1, k. 1) six times.

8th row : (K. 1, p. 1) seven times, purl to the last 14 stitches, (p. 1, k. 1) seven times.

9th row : Cast off 4 stitches, (k. 1, p. 1) four times, knit plain to the last 12 stitches, (p. 1, k. 1) six times.

10th row : Cast off 4 stitches, (k. 1, p. 1) four times, k. 1, purl to the last 9 stitches, k. 1, (p. 1, k. 1) four times.

11th row : (K. 1, p. 1) four times, k. 1, k. 2 tog., knit plain to the last 11 stitches, k. 2 tog., (k. 1, p. 1) four times, k. 1.

12th row : (K. 1, p. 1) four times, k. 1, purl to the last 9 stitches, (k. 1, p. 1) four times, k. 1.

Repeat the 11th and 12th rows five times.

Continue, keeping the Moss-pattern border at each end of the needle and decreasing once at each end of the needle in every 4th row, until 93 stitches remain.

Continue without shaping until the work measures 25½ inches from the beginning, ending with the 2nd row.

The Moss-stitch band at back of neck is worked in the following rows.

1st row : (K. 1, p. 1) four times, k. 11, (k. 1, p. 1) twenty-seven times, k. 12, (p. 1, k. 1) four times.

2nd row : (K. 1, p. 1) four times, k. 1, p. 10, (k. 1, p. 1) twenty-eight times, p. 9, k. 1, (p. 1, k. 1) four times.

3rd row : (K. 1, p. 1) four times, k. 11, (k. 1, p. 1) twenty-seven times, k. 11, turn, leaving the remaining stitches at end of row unworked to begin the shoulder slope.

4th row : P. 10, (k. 1, p. 1) twenty-eight times, p. 9, turn.

5th row : K. 11, (p. 1, k. 1) twenty-eight times, turn.

6th row : P. 1, (k. 1, p. 1) twenty-eight times, turn.

7th row : K. 2, (p. 1, k. 1) twenty-three times, turn.

8th row : (K. 1, p. 1) nineteen times, k. 1, turn.

9th row : Work in pattern to the end of the row.

10th row : Like the 2nd row. Cast off.

TO MAKE UP THE PULL-OVER.

With a damp cloth over the knitting press lightly on the wrong side, putting a thick blanket under the knitting. Sew up the side and shoulder seams.

A COMPLETE KNITTED OUTFIT for

**Neatness, Cosiness And a Slender Line Are The Three Essentials
Of The Knitted Jumper Suit. This Outfit Has All Three!**

KNITTED JUMPER

MATERIALS: 8 ozs. of Ladyship 4-ply Scotch Fingering in light shade and 2 ozs. in dark; a set of four long bone knitting needles, No. 9 with double points; a set of four steel knitting needles, No. 12 with double points; a buckle.

TENSION AND MEASUREMENTS.—Worked at a tension of 6¼ stitches to the inch in width with the No. 9 needles, the length of jumper from neck to hem is 22 inches, and 34 inches all round bust.

ABBREVIATIONS: K., knit; p., purl; tog., together; sl., slip; s.s., stocking stitch.

TO WORK.
The work proceeds in rounds, without side seams, as far as the underarm, so with light wool and No. 12 needles cast 284 stitches on three needles, 94 on first, 94 on second, and 96 on third needle, for all round lower edge. Work 12 rounds of single rib (k. 1 and p. 1 alternately). Change to No. 9 needles.

NEXT ROUND: K. 5, * k. 2 tog., k. 2, k. 2 tog., k. 4; repeat from * until 9 stitches from end of round, work these k. 2 tog., k. 2, k. 2 tog., k. 3. Now slip first stitch of third needle to end of second needle, making 76 stitches on each needle. * K. 1 round and p. 1 round twice in dark, k. 4 rounds in light; repeat from * until the third dark stripe is worked. K. 19 rounds light. Work for another three dark stripes. K. 82 rounds in light, or up to underarm.

NEXT ROUND: Cast off 4, k. the next 107 on to one needle for back, cast off 4, k. remaining 113 on to one needle for front.

THE FRONT.—Work on two needles in s.s. (p. 1 row and k. 1 row), casting off 2 stitches at the beginning of each of the next six rows. Now work 2 tog. at beginning of each of the next 14 rows (87 stitches). Work 4 rows in s.s.

NEXT ROW: (Wrong side facing worker) p. 2 tog., p. 19. Leave these 20 stitches on spare needle for right shoulder, cast off 45, p. 19 and p. 2 tog. for left shoulder.

THE SHOULDERS.—With dark wool * k. 4 rows; (k. 1 row and p. 1 row) twice in light; repeat from * for four dark stripes; work 3 light rows and leave these stitches to be grafted or cast off. Join wool to neck end of right shoulder stitches and work the same as given for left shoulder.

THE BACK.—Join wool to 107 back stitches at beginning of a k. row, work in s.s., casting off 2 stitches at beginning of each of the next 6 rows; work 2 tog. at the beginning of each of the next 12 rows (83 stitches). S.s. 22 rows.

NEXT ROW: K. 20 and leave on a spare needle for right shoulder, cast off 43. K. 20 for left shoulder. Work on the last 20 stitches for left shoulder (using dark wool) until the second dark stripe is finished, then leave for grafting or cast off. For right shoulder join wool to neck end of 20 stitches and work same as opposite shoulder. Cast off or leave stitches for grafting.

THE SLEEVES.—Using light wool and two No. 9 needles, cast on 13 stitches for sleeve top, k. 1 row. Work in s.s., casting on 2 stitches at beginning of every row until there are 73.

NEXT ROW: Cast on 3 stitches and p. to end.

NEXT ROW: Cast on 3 stitches and k. 21, making 24 for first needle; on a second needle k. 31; on a third needle k. remaining 24. Join in a round and k. in rounds, decreasing at underarm every eighth round by knitting 2 tog. at beginning of round, and at the end k. to within 2 stitches of the end, then sl. 1, k. 1, draw s.s. over knitted one. After the fifth decrease round there will be 19 stitches on first and third needles and 31 on second needle. K. 62 rounds, or length required,

less 2½ inches for coloured bands, as well as cuff. * With dark wool k. 1 round and p. 1 round twice, k. 4 rounds; repeat from * twice more.

NEXT ROUND: * K. 4, k. 2 tog.; repeat from * all round. Finish with k. 3; 58 stitches now on for cuffs. With No 12 needles and light wool, work 49 rounds of k. 1 and p. 1 rib, cast off.

THE BELT.—Cast on 10 stitches with dark wool and No. 12 needles, k. plain for length required and cast off.

TO MAKE UP.—First press all lightly on the wrong side. Graft front and back shoulders together, or sew cast off edges together. Sew sleeves into armholes and sew buckle to belt. Round neck edge, using light wool, work 5 rounds of double crochet with a No. 1 steel hook, working into the back loop of stitch. At the corners decrease by working three stitches into one, taking up one loop in the stitch before the corner, one at the corner and one after, and finally draw through all the three loops at once.

To finish, press neckband, seams and all joinings.

KNITTED SKIRT

MATERIALS: 6 ozs. of Ladyship 4-ply Scotch Fingering and a set of four No. 9 long bone knitting needles with double points.

Abbreviations and Tension as on Jumper.

The skirt measures 16 inches long and is 41 inches all round hem after very light pressing and measuring with pleats closed.

TO WORK.—Cast on 336 stitches, that is 112 stitches on each of three needles, for all round lower edge. Join in round and work 29 rounds in rib of k. 5 and p. 2 alternately. Work the first round into back of stitches for neatness.

RIDGE ROUND: * K. 1, p. 3, k. 1, p. 2; repeat from * all round. Rib 2 rounds as above, * p. the first stitch of next round on to end of last needle of last round. Rib 4 rounds as above, k. 5 and p. 2 (the rib is now moved one stitch to left all round). Repeat from last * three times more. P. the first stitch of next round on to end of last needle. Rib 2 rounds and work 1 ridge round. * Rib 2 rounds. * Before working last stitch on last round slip it on to first needle of next round, rib 4 rounds (the rib is now moved one stitch to right all round. Repeat from * three times more. Slip last stitch of last round on to first needle of next round before working it, rib 2 rounds. Now work the section between first ** and second ** to again reverse the slope. Rib 35 rounds.

NEXT ROUND: * K. 4, sl. 1, k. 2 tog., pass sl. stitch over; repeat from * all round. This leaves 80 stitches on each needle.

NEXT ROUND: * K. 2 tog., k. 8; repeat from * all round, leaving 72 on each needle.

K. 11 rounds and cast off.

Press the knitting and sew to edge of a lining bodice or a hip band

---

KNITTED SLEEVELESS CARDIGAN

MATERIALS: Seven ozs. of "Ladyship" 4-ply Scotch fingering in dark and 1 oz. in light shade; pair of long bone knitting needles No. 9, and 2 spare needles; 3 buttons.

MEASUREMENTS AND TENSION: Worked at a tension of

BIG GIRLS—AND LITTLE WOMEN!

A Prettily Striped Jumper, A Skirt That Gives Slenderness, And a Coatee For Extra Warmth

6½ stitches to the inch in width, the cardigan measures 24 inches from shoulder to hem and 35 inches round bust.

ABBREVIATIONS : As jumper.

TO WORK.—With dark wool cast on 29 stitches for a pocket lining. Work 37 rows in s.s., the last a k. row, cut wool end and slip these stitches on a spare needle. Work a second lining the same and put both aside for the present. For lower edge all round cast on 250 stitches in dark wool, k. 15 rows plain.

NEXT ROW: K 9 dark, with light k. until 9 remain, k. 9 dark. When changing from one wool to the other, pass the first wool over the second when knitting the first stitch of second colour. Take another ball for the second border of 9 sts., letting it hang at this end when not in use, but always twist over first stitch of fresh colour before dropping.

NEXT ROW: K. 9 dark, with light p until 9 remain, k. 9 dark. Repeat these two rows once more. K. plain 4 rows in dark. These last 8 rows are repeated three times more and in the meantime a button-hole is made on the dark border at end of the second row of second light stripe, thus : K. 3, cast off 3, k. 3. At beginning of next row complete the button-hole, thus : K. 3, cast on 3, k. 3.

Fasten off the light wool after the fourth light stripe, continue in dark altogether. K. 1 row.

NEXT ROW: K. 9, p. 18, k. 29, p. 138, k. 29, p. 18, k. 9. K. 1 row.

NEXT ROW: K. 9, p. 18, k. 29, p. 138, k. 29, p. 18, k. 3, cast off 3, k. 3.

NEXT ROW: K. 3, cast on 3, k. to end.

Work 3 more rows in s.s. with k. 9 at each end, and k. 29 at each pocket top on p. rows.

NEXT ROW: K. 27, cast off 29, k. 138, cast off 29, k. 27.

NEXT ROW: K. 9, p 18, p. 29 pocket lining stitches from spare needle, p. 138, p. 29 pocket lining stitches, p. 18, k. 9. Work 19 rows in s.s. with k. 9 at each end. On next 2 rows make a third buttonhole. Work 3 more rows as before.

*NEXT ROW: K. 9, k. 2 tog., k. until 11 from end, sl. 1, k. 1, pass sl.st. over, k. 9. Work 7 rows with k. 9 at each end of p. rows. Repeat from * until the tenth decrease row has been worked and you have 230 stitches.

NEXT ROW: K. 9 and p. 46, slip these 55 on a spare needle for left front, cast off 5, p. 110 and slip these on spare needle for back, cast off 5, p. 46 and k. 9, for right front.

RIGHT FRONT : This is continued in s.s. with k. 9 at end of p. rows. For armhole shaping cast off 2 at the beginning of each of the next 3 purl rows, then p. 2 tog. at beginning of the next 8 purl rows. At this end the shoulder now continues straight up without further shaping. The front decreases will continue within the k. 9 border on every eighth row as before for 7 more decreasings (34 stitches). Work 2 rows, then cast off 5 at beginning of the next five p. rows (shoulder end). K. 21 plain rows on remaining 9 stitches for half the strap at back of neck, and cast off.

THE BACK : Join to 110 stitches for back at beginning of a k. row and k. 1 row. Work in s.s. and cast off 2 at the beginning of each of the next 6 rows. Work 2 tog. at beginning of each of the next 14 rows (leaving 84 stitches). Work 29 rows in s.s., then cast off 5 sts. at the beginning of each of the next 8 rows. Cast off remaining stitches.

LEFT FRONT : Join to left front stitches at beginning of a k. row and k. 1 row. Work to match right front, the k. 9 border is at beginning of p. rows, while armhole shaping and shoulder shaping is at beginning of k. rows. The decreasing for front is worked before the k. 9 border on every eighth row.

TO MAKE UP : First press all lightly over a damp cloth. Sew pocket linings to wrong side of coat. Sew shoulder seams and back of trimming strip to back of neck. With a No. 1 steel hook work 3 rounds of double crochet on armhole, on the first row putting 1 d.c. into each knitted stitch. Press seams and crochet edges and sew buttons on left front.

The pullover is made on very simple lines that can easily be adapted for either a man or a girl.

Now is the TIME—

For Golf Or Walking This Pullover Is So Comfortable.

15*th and* 16*th rounds :* K. 2 mottle and 2 dark alternately.

17*th and* 18*th rounds :* K. 2 light and 6 dark alternately. Repeat the first 12 pattern rounds.

Next round : While working the 13th pattern round work as follows : K. 14, slip the next 30 st. on a spare needle for pocket top, and in place work 30 pocket-lining stitches from spare needle, work next 34 st., slip next 30 on spare needle, and in place work 30 pocket-lining stitches, work to end of round.

Work the 14th to 18th rounds in-

THIS pullover is constructed on very simple lines, with straight arm-hole and short·V neck, so that it is easily adaptable for either sex. The pattern is so simple (although it looks elaborate) that the beginner will not have any difficulty in following it, even on the short rows at the neck. Up to the armholes it is worked in rounds, and only two colours of wool are in operation at the same time. The colour not actually in use along the row is twisted once over the working thread, so that there are no loose threads at the back of the work.

MATERIALS : Templeton's " Ayr " " F " Fingering, 4-ply, in the following quantities : 6 oz. of mottle, 6 oz. light and 4 oz. dark ; 4 bone knitting needles No. 9, with double points, and four No. 10.

ABBREVIATIONS : K., knit plain ; p., purl ; tog., together ; s.s., stocking-stitch, which is k. on the front of the work and p. on the back.

TENSION AND MEASUREMENTS : Worked at a tension of 6 st. to the inch in width, the following measurements will be obtained after light pressing : From shoulder to hem, 25½ inches ; width all round body at underarm, 38 inches ; underarm-seam of sleeve, 20½ inches.

To Work

BEGIN with pocket linings and, using light wool and No. 9 needles, cast on 30 st. Work 30 rows in s.s., then cut wool and slip these stitches on a spare needle. Work a second lining exactly the same and put both aside for the present.

THE BODY OF PULLOVER : Begin at the lower edge, using mottle wool and No. 9 needles. Cast on 232 st., arranging 72 on the first needle, 88 on the second, and 72 on third needle. Join into a round and work 20 rounds of k. 2 and p. 2 alternately for the ribbed hip-band. It is now ready to begin the multi-colour pattern.

The Colour Pattern

FIRST *and* 2*nd rounds :* K. all light.

3*rd and* 4*th rounds :* K. 2 light and 2 mottle alternately all round.

5*th and* 6*th rounds :* K. 2 mottle and 2 dark alternately.

7*th and* 8*th rounds :* K. 2 dark and 2 mottle alternately.

9*th and* 10*th rounds :* K. 2 mottle and 2 light alternately.

11*th and* 12*th rounds :* K. all light.

13*th and* 14*th rounds :* K. 2 light and 6 dark alternately.

–for the COUNTRY

Made In Shades Of Brown And Fawn, The Perfect Autumn Colouring.

clusive. Repeat the 18 pattern rounds 4 times more, when armhole opening is reached.

Next round : With light wool cast off 2, k. 59 for left front; on a second needle k. 59 for right front; cast off 2, k. remaining 110 all on one needle for back. The work now proceeds in rows, so back or alternate rows will be purled, in pattern.

THE BACK.—Continue with 2nd pattern row, and on every row work items in reverse order to that given, for instance the 3rd and 4th rounds will be "2 mottle and 2 light alternately," which is simply continuing the pattern.

Repeat until the 18th row has been worked for the third time from the

Although the pattern looks elaborate, it is really very simple, and would not present any difficulty to a beginner.

armhole. Work the first 6 pattern rows, then cut threads and leave these stitches until fronts have been worked.

RIGHT FRONT.—Join light wool to beginning of purl row and continue with 2nd pattern row. K. 2 tog. at beginning (neck opening) of two k. rows out of every three (that is, 2 decreasings in every 6 rows) until 40 st. are left for shoulder. Work until 2 rows longer than back. Hold needle with these stitches in front of the matching 40 st. from end of back with the right sides of knitting together. K. tog. 1 from front and 1 from back needles and cast off at the same time.

LEFT FRONT.—Work as described for right front, except that decreasings are at end of k. rows instead of beginning.

THE NECK.—With mottle wool and No. 10 needles pick up 47 st. down left front of neck (taking 3 st. to every 4 rows) for first needle; on second needle pick up 47 st. at right-front neck; on third needle k. 30 back neck stitches. Work 1 round of k. 2 and p. 2 rib, then

work 6 rounds, decreasing at centre, front, thus: Sl. 1, k. 1 and pass sl.-stitch over on the last 2 st. of first needle, and k. 2 tog. at beginning of second needle in every round. Cast off rather loosely.

POCKET TOPS.—With mottle wool and No. 10 needles k. 8 rows and cast off.

Sleeves

WITH light wool and No. 9 needles cast on 88 st., 32 on first needle, 24 on second needle, and 32 on third needle. Join in to a round and work in pattern, decreasing on every 4th round. To decrease on first needle, k. 2, k. 2 tog., work to end of needle, work the 2nd needle to within 2 st. of end of 3rd needle, then sl. 1, k. 1, pass the sl.-stitch over. After the 5th decrease round, decrease every 8th round until 56 st. remain. Work for length required, then with No. 10 needles and mottle wool k. 1 round and k. 2 tog. at beginning of first and second needles, also at end of second and third needles (52 st.). Work 22 rounds of k. 2 and p. 2 rib, cast off.

TO MAKE UP.—Sew sleeves to armholes with join of rounds to under-arm. Sew pocket linings to wrong side of pullover, and darn in all ends. Press all, except ribbing, with a damp cloth over knitting.

Springtime HATS in Silken CROCHET

Quite Irresistible are these Dainty New Models—and so Becoming.

A New Pleated Cap (No. 1)

THIS cap is very smart worked in black silk, and the shaping and head fitting by deep tucks is quite an innovation. It is worked entirely in flat double crochet—that is, taking up both loops at the top of the stitch, so is very easy to work, and it proceeds in rounds without joining up at the end of the rounds.

Materials

9 balls (60 yards each) of Rickard's Sylvan Knitting (fine artificial silk), ¾ of a yard of ribbon 2 inches wide for the head-band; 1½ yards of ribbon 1 inch wide for trimming, and a No. 1 steel crochet hook.

Abbreviations

Ch., chain; d.c., double crochet; sl.st., slipstitch.

Size and Tension

Working at a tension of 10 st. to 1 inch in width, the following measurements will be attained after light pressing. Depth from centre of crown to lower edge, 8 inches; all round head measurement, 22 inches. This measurement can be regulated by the head-band and the fold of the tucks.

To Work

BEGIN at centre of crown with 4 ch., which join into a ring with a sl.st.

1st round : 7 d.c. into the ring. Now sew a piece of white cotton into the first d.c. to mark the beginning of the round as a guide for working the increases, as the rounds are not joined up.

2nd and 3rd rounds : 2 d.c. in each st. of previous round.

4th round : 1 d.c. in each st. all round.

5th round : * 1 d.c. in 1 st., then 2 d.c. in next st., and repeat from * all round.

6th round : 1 d.c. in each st. all round.

7th round : * 1 d.c. in each of 2 st., then 2 d.c. in the next, and repeat from * all round.

8th round : 1 d.c. in each st. all round.

Continue increasing on each alternate round, always with 1 st. extra before each increase on every successive increase round until there are eight st. in each section. From here increase in the same way, but with two rounds of single st. between the increase rounds, until there are 12 st. in each section.

From here increase in every 4th round until there are 16 st. in each section, after which work two rounds of 1 d.c. in each st.

The new Pleated Cap—an inspiration !

The shaping for the front trimming is now begun thus : * Work 2 st. into the first st. of the section, then 1 st. into each of the next 14 st., and 2 st. into the last st. of the section. Work the next section of 14 st. without alteration, then repeat from * three times more. Again work 2 st. into the first st. of next section, work the next 14 single st., then 2 d.c. into the last st. of the section. There will now be five sections with an increase at both ends, and a section between each of these without alteration. Now complete the round with single st.

Work two rounds of 1 d.c. in each st. The increased sections now have 18 st., and the others 16 as before.

On the next round increase in the first and last st. of the sections with 18 st., and work all others without increase. Work two rounds more of single stitches.

Continue in this way, increasing in the same sections on every third round until there are 46 st. in each of the increased sections. Work two rounds more of single stitches after the last increased round, and this completes the crochet.

Now make tucks on the increased sections, leaving 8 st. on each side of the tuck in each section, the tucks tapering to a point at the top. Press them a little under a slightly damp cloth. Pass the end of the narrow ribbon under the tuck and over the edge of the hat to the under side; pin here for the present. Carry the ribbon up to the centre of the crown, cut and secure at the top. Repeat this length of ribbon under each tuck, and in finishing the last piece fold the end over, secure at the fold and pass it across the centre top covering the cut ends of the other pieces of ribbon;

The close-fitting hat with side tabs gives a soft, caressing line.

Spring and the Urge for a New Hat are Somehow Inseparable! Here are Three Little Hints of Coming Fashion with Full Instructions How To Make Them.

(mark the first st. of this round with white cotton, as a guide for the new rounds).

3rd round : * 1 d.c. into 1 st., then 2 d.c. in the next and repeat from * all round.

4th round : * 1 d.c. into each of 2 st., then 2 d.c in the next and repeat from * all round.

5th round : * 1 d.c. in each of 3 st., then **2 d.c.** in the next and repeat from * all round.

again fold over at this side and secure with a few hemming stitches, and pass back to opposite side of circle, turn and hem down. Hem the end of narrow ribbons under the edge of hat on the inside, then with the wider ribbon make a band to fit the head and sew just inside. This band of ribbon may be allowed longer for a larger head measurement, and making the tucks smaller in proportion before sewing down.

Close-fitting Hat with Side Tabs (No. 2)

FOLLOW the directions given with the new pleated cap (No. 1) for materials, but only 8 balls of the silk and 1½ yards of 2-inch gros grain ribbon only ; size and tension, abbreviations, and description of stitch the same.

To Work

BEGIN with 4 ch., which join into a ring with a sl.st.
1st round : 8 d.c. into the ring.
2nd round : 2 d.c. into each st. of the previous round

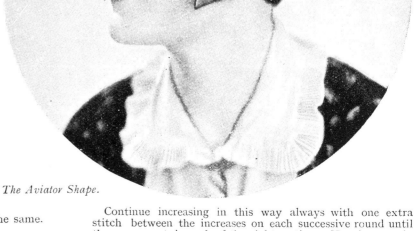

The Aviator Shape.

Continue increasing in this way always with one extra stitch between the increases on each successive round until there are 15 st. in each of the eight sections. Now increase in the same way on each alternate round until there are 20 st. in each section. From here increase in the same way on every third round until there are 27 st. in each section.

(Continued overleaf).

SPRINGTIME HATS IN SILK

(Continued from previous page.)

Now mark out three sections for the front and the three opposite sections for the back, leaving one section on each side for the ear tabs. Increases will now be made on the ear parts only at both ends of the section thus: Increase on the last st. of the back section, then 26 single d.c. and again an increase on the 27th st. Work 1 d.c. in each st. to the next ear section, then repeat as on first ear and finish the round. There are now two extra st. in each side section. Work a round of 1 d.c. in each st. Continue increasing in this way on both ear sections on every alternate round until there are 71 st. on each ear tab. Complete the round, finishing at the centre-back of the hat, and this finishes the main part.

The two ear tabs have now to be finished off separately. Each row is begun at the same end and the silk is cut at the end of the row, joining the silk on the second st. and working to within one st. of the end. Repeat this on every row until there are only 3 st. left, then work into these st. as one, and fasten off securely.

After working the second ear tab, join the silk to the centre-back of the hat and work 2 rows of d.c. all round, working st. into st. except at the points, where put 3 d.c. in the point st, and when working round the tabs carefully tuck in all the cut ends on the short rows, working the d.c. over them.

To Trim the Hat

In each section before the ear tabs were worked there were 27 st. Now fold the ear parts to form a tuck and sew from the top to the bottom, leaving 13 st. on each side of the tuck, so that these side sections will match the others. The tuck will be wide at the lower end and taper off at the top. Now press it flat in the form of a box pleat, pressing it well into shape over a damp cloth.

Fold the ribbon over to about 1½ inches wide and press; pass one end under the box pleat on the left side of the front close to the edge of the hat and pass along to the top of the pleat on the right side, and down to the lower edge of the pleat on the opposite side, passing the end under the pleat, and sew in position.

Sew the remainder of the ribbon just inside the lower edge for a head-band, and adjust this according to head measurement. Catch down the side of the ear pleats, just under the fold, and the hat is finished.

The Aviator Shape (No. 3)

Materials

One hank of Rickard's Sylvan Filo, a yard of ribbon to match the silk 1½ inches wide, ¼ yard of ribbon 2 inches wide for head-band, a yard of millinery wire and a No. 1 steel crochet hook. Abbreviations, description of working, size and tension as hat No. 1, except that the crown is half an inch deeper and the head measurement can be adjusted by arranging the wire to suit.

To Work

Make 5 ch. and join into a ring with a sl.st.

1st round : 10 d.c. into ring.

2nd round : 2 d.c. into each st. (mark first st. with white cotton for beginning of new rounds).

3rd round : * 1 d.c. into each of 2 st. then 2 d.c. in the next, and repeat from * all round.

4th round : 1 d.c. in each st.

5th round : * 1 d.c. in each of 3 st., then 2 d.c. in the next, and repeat from * all round.

6th round : * 1 d.c. into each of 4 st., then 2 d.c. in the next and repeat from * all round.

7th round : As *4th round*.

FRUITS
from the
SCRAP
BAG

Appliquéd on a Table Cloth.

First collect your odd scraps of silk and linen. Then draw on them circles of varying sizes round cups and coins or any other circular object. Group them on the corners of a square of linen, as shewn, and buttonhole them down with black silk.

Cut leaves from green material, appliqué these in the same way, and put in stems and other markings in stem-stitch. Turn up a hem, and edge it with coloured darning-stitches.

Arrange the fruits in groups as shown above.

8th round : * 1 d.c. into each of 5 st., then 2 d.c. in the next, and repeat from * all round.

9th round : * 1 d.c. into each of 6 st., then 2 d.c. in the next, and repeat from * all round.

Repeat the last round 3 times more.

13th round : As *4th round*.

14th round : * 1 d.c. into each of 9 st., then 2 d.c. in the next st. and repeat from * all round.

Repeat the last round 3 times more.

18th round : As *4th round*.

19th round : * 1 d.c. into each of 19 st., then 2 d.c. in the next and repeat from * all round.

Repeat the last two rounds until the work measures 8½ inches across the centre. From here continue in rounds of 1 d.c. in each st. for a depth of 3¼ inches, finishing at the centre-back of the hat, sl.st. to the next st., and cut the silk.

With pins mark out 7½ inches across centre-back and the same across centre-front, leaving 3½ inches on each side for the ear pieces : for these 35 st. will be required on each side.

With the right side of work facing do 35 d.c. for one ear piece ; cut silk Go back to beginning of last row and work across the 33 centre st., that is leaving one st. unworked at the beginning and end of row. Continue leaving one st. unworked at both ends in this way, cutting the silk at the end of each row, so that the work is done on the same side, until there are only 3 st. left, which work off as 1 d.c.

Work opposite ear piece in the same way.

The Edge

With double silk and beginning at the centre-back, work a row of d.c. all round over the wire ; put 3 d.c. into the st. at the point of the ear pieces, and bend the wire carefully here to form the shape of the edge. Work over the two ends of the wire for about two inches, where they meet at the back.

Make a flat bow with the ribbon to go across the front and sew this in position with fish-tail ends falling just past the ear pieces : in order to follow the shape of the hat fold the ribbon ends over behind the bow before bringing them down over the ear pieces. Make a head-band of the 2-inch wide ribbon and sew inside the edge of the hat, keeping the circle at the side by working along the first row of the ear pieces.

These hats may be worked in colours to tone with your new spring suit. Imagine any one of them in French Grey or Navy Blue or Deep Green.

The FLOWER BORDER CARDIGAN

A CHARMING DRESS NOVELTY WITH DETACHABLE SLEEVES!

A FASCINATING WOOLLIE THAT OFFERS A PLEASING VARIETY OF WORK—KNITTING AND THE SIMPLE WOOL EMBROIDERY THAT IS SO FASHIONABLE THIS AUTUMN

THE MODEL CARDIGAN, PHOTOGRAPHED, WAS KNITTED IN BEIGE WOOL WITH A FLOWER BORDER IN LOVELY NASTURTIUM COLOURING

INSTRUCTIONS FOR KNITTING AND EMBROIDERY OVERLEAF

On mild days wear your cardigan sleeveless; on cold ones slip-stitch the sleeves in place.

Actual size of Flower Border worked on the cardigan fronts.

An Embroidered Cardigan

MATERIALS.—As a sleeveless garment. 5¼ oz. Viyella Standard 3-ply knitting yarn, in natural. For sleeves, 3 oz. more of the same wool. One skein of embroidery wool in each of the following colours :— Green, black, orange, red, and terra cotta. Five buttons. No. 9 knitting needles.

Measurements.—Length from the top of the shoulders, 25 inches. Width all round, when closed, 37 inches. Round armhole, 15 inches. Length of sleeve from neck, including cuff, 27¼ inches.

Tension.—17 sts. to 2 inches in width.

The Back.—Begin at the lower edge by casting on 142 sts. and work in k. 1 and p. 1, rib for a depth of 4 inches, working into the backs of the sts. on the first row.

Change to stocking st. and continue in this until the work measures 17 inches from the beginning.

Shape the armholes by casting off 2 sts. at the beginning of each of the next 8 rows, then knitting 2 sts. tog. next to the edge st. at both ends of the needle on each of the next 9 knit rows (108 sts. remain).

Work without alteration on these sts. for a depth of 4½ inches, then shape the neck and shoulders.

1st row.—Knit to within 7 sts. of the end, turn. *2nd row.*—Slip the first st. and purl to within 7 sts. of the end, turn. *3rd row.*—Slip the first st. and knit to within 14 sts. of the end, turn. *4th row.*—Slip the first st. and purl to within 14 sts. of the end, turn. *5th row.*—Slip the first st., knit 27, cast off 24, then knit to within 1 sts. of the end, turn. *6th row.*—Slip the first st. and purl to neck. *7th row.*—Cast off 12 sts. and knit across the remainder. *8th row.*—Cast off. *9th row.*—Join the wool to the neck end of the opposite side and purl to within 21 sts. of the end, turn. *10th row.*—Slip the first st. and knit to neck. *11th row.*—Cast off 12 sts. and purl across the remainder. *12th row.*—Cast off.

The Right Front.—Cast on 86 sts. Work the ribbing in the same way as for the back, but after working a depth of 2 inches work a buttonhole by working 3 sts., then casting off the next 4 sts. and complete the row.

When working the next row cast on 4 sts. to take the place of those cast off on the previous row.

When the ribbing is the same depth as on the back change the main part to stocking st. Begin at the front edge and work 3 sts., cast off 4 sts. for a second buttonhole, then work 3 more sts. in the ribbing, and knit the remainder.

Keep the 10 sts. in the ribbing to the top of the front and continue working buttonholes at the same intervals till 5 have been worked.

Immediately after working the 5th buttonhole begin the front shaping. For the front shaping decrease next to the ribbing on every knit row till there are 24 decreases here. From here keep the front edge straight. When the side edge is the same depth as that of the back, shape the armhole by casting off 2 sts. at the beginning of each of the next 6 purl rows, then knitting 2 sts. tog. next to the edge st. on the same edge on each of the next 10 knit rows.

Continue quite straight on the remaining sts. till the armhole edge is 6 rows deeper than that of the back, then shape the shoulder.

1st row.—Working from the front edge work to within 7 sts. of the end, turn. *2nd row.*—Slip the first st. and work back to front. *3rd row.*—Work to within 14 sts. of the end, turn. *4th row.*—As 2nd row. *5th row.*—Work to within 21 sts. of the end, turn. *6th row.*—As 2nd row. *7th row.*—Work across all sts. *8th row.*—Cast off the 30 shoulder sts. and continue on the 10 sts. of the ribbing until this reaches to the centre of the back of the neck.

The Left Front.—Work this to match the right front with all shapings at opposite edges and without buttonholes.

For the Sleeveless Cardigan

The Armholes.—Pick up and knit through every loop and knot on the armhole edge. 132 sts. on the original. Work in k. 1, p. 1, rib for a depth of 8 rows, then cast off.

The Sleeves.—Begin at the top by casting on 44 sts. Knit into the backs of these sts. and cast on 2 sts. at the end of the row. Purl into the backs of the cast on sts. and complete the row, casting on 2 sts. again.

Continue in stocking st., casting on 2 sts. at the end of every row till there are 108 sts.

Work 4 rows without alteration, then on the next and every following 4th row decrease next to the edge st. at both ends of the needle till 100 sts. remain.

From here decrease in the same way on every 6th row till 60 sts. remain. Change to k. 1, p. 1, rib, work the same depth as on the lower edge of the cardigan, cast off.

To Complete the Cardigan.—If sleeveless, the garment is ready for pressing, after sewing the two edges of the ribbing together then sewing one edge to the neck.

If with sleeves the ribbing round the armholes will be omitted, and the tops of the sleeves sewn into the armholes.

Press work carefully avoiding all ribbing. Sew up the side seams, and also sleeve seams if these are made, press the seams and sew buttons on left front.

The Embroidery

The flowers are worked in "lazy daisy" stitch (*see* diagram below) round a centre of French knots. All the centres are black, the colours of the flowers red, terra cotta, red, orange, in rotation, the red being used for the biggest flower.

Work the stems in split-stitch and the leaves in satin-stitch. The irregular green stitches between the stems represent grass.

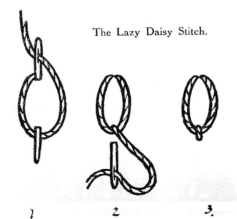

The Lazy Daisy Stitch.

1   2   3.

CAN YOU ADAPT YOURSELF ?

THE MISFIT

I AM told that there are animals whose fur changes from brown to white in those countries where there are months of snow. Nature makes them able to protect themselves by adapting themselves to their circumstances.

We can do it, too. Toe the line. Get into step. Fit in. It's not going to hurt us. It's going to help us.

You know the story of the small boy watching the march by of the new recruits, among whom was his recently joined-up brother.

"Oh, mum, they're all out of step but our Jock !"

Poor Jock was a "misfit." People who can't adapt themselves are a "misfit," a nuisance to themselves and to other folk. They are seldom happy and they are never a success.

After all, you adapt yourself to the weather. On a cold day you put on a pullover. When you are up against difficult people, put on an extra garment woven of good-humour and tolerance.

In an uphill climb spike your boots with courage and determination and stickability. But *never, never* turn round and run away.

THE FIRM STAND

BUT there come times to all of us when it would be *wrong* to adapt ourselves, when to do so would be to haul down all our standards of self-respect and the decent loyalties of life. We cannot afford to compromise with ugly things or wrong things, like injustice or cruelty or double dealing.

I have nothing but respect for the man who leaves his firm instead of adapting himself because he finds it is concerned in shady transactions ; or the girl who gives up her sweetheart because, in spite of her love and her help and her pleadings, he cannot or will not run straight.

That is where adapting yourself has to find its limit. That's where you no longer try to "mix."

But, apart from that, you should practise adapting yourself constantly. There are heaps of opportunities every moment of every day. In the home, in the office, in the shop.

Meet people half-way. Learn to give and take. Learn to make the best of things, circumstances, people, *as they are.* Cut your coat according to your cloth. Make the best of the homely serge instead of sighing for satin. Take the tools you've got and the materials you've got and make something beautiful out of them, however defective they seem to you to be.

Yes, facing reality and not running away from it but adapting ourselves to it is perhaps one of Life's greatest secrets of success.

There is Distinction HERE!

A Becoming Jumper of Most Uncommon Design.

I F you want to be smart and comfortable—here is the very garment to bring you your heart's desire.

Materials

O F Baldwin & Walker's 3-ply "Ladyship" Scotch Fingering 8 oz. of fawn, 1 oz. of dark brown, and 1 oz. of golden brown. A pair of long bone knitting needles No. 9, and a set of four No. 9 needles, with points at both ends.

Tension and Measurements

W ORKING at a tension of 8 st. to one inch in width, the following measurements are attained after light pressing. Length from top of shoulder to hem, 25 inches; width round bust line, 40 inches; length of sleeve seam, including cuff, 21½ inches.

ABBREVIATIONS : K., knit plain ; p., purl. ; st., stitch ; s.s., stocking-stitch ; tog., together.

The Front

W ITH fawn wool cast on 153 st. and work in single rib (k. 1 and p. 1 alternately) for 30 rows, working into the back of the st. on the first row. From here the work proceeds in s.s. Do two rows more in fawn.

1st *pattern row :* K. 150 st. in fawn and the last three st. in dark brown. When changing colours always twist the first colour over the second colour before working the first st. of the second colour : this will prevent a gap between the two colours.

On the next row purl 6 st. in dark brown—that is, 3 st. beyond the three brown of previous row, and complete the row in fawn.

Continue changing 3 st. from fawn to brown on every row until all st. are changed, but after working 14 rows in this way, begin the next shade at the same end the dark brown began. Work as usual to within the last 3 st. in dark brown, then change these to golden brown.

Continue changing 3 st. of fawn to dark brown and 3 st. of dark brown to golden brown until 14 rows of golden brown can be counted at the left side edge. On the next row begin to change the st. in golden brown to dark brown. Keep changing as usual towards the opposite side.

When another 14 rows in dark brown st. can be counted at the same left edge as other changes, begin to change the dark brown to fawn, still working the other changes as usual until the brown st. at the opposite end reach to the edge of the work.

Counting on the right side of the work from the right edge there will be 42 st. in brown, 42 in golden brown, 42 in nigger brown, and 27 in fawn. On the next row begin to change the st. back again, changing 3 st. of each

The horizontal line of the pattern has a very slimming effect.

shade back to the same shade as on previous row—that is, k. 3 fawn, then k. dark brown until 3 golden brown st. have been knitted, k. golden brown until 3 of the next lot of dark brown st. have been worked, then dark brown again until 3 of the fawn st. have been knitted, and finish the row in fawn.

Continue changing in this way until all the st. are in fawn again. The front is now completed in fawn wool, so continue quite straight until the whole work measures 17½ inches from the beginning or the length required up to the armhole.

The Front Opening

A T the beginning of the next row cast off 2 st. to begin the armhole shaping, k. 74, cast off 1 st., then k. the remainder. Pass the 74 st. of the opposite side on a stitch-holder or safety-pin.

RIGHT HALF OF FRONT

This is worked on the last 76 st. knitted. Cast off 2 st. at the beginning of each of the next 5 p. rows, and k. 2 st. tog. next to the edge st. on the same edge on each of the next 10 k. rows. This shaping is all at the armhole

There is Distinction Here!

(Continued from previous page.)

end. At the same time shape the front neck slope by decreasing next to the edge st. on the first and every following k. row until there are 24 decreases here. Continue quite straight on the remaining st. for 4 inches more.

To Shape the Shoulder.

Beginning at the neck edge work to within 8 st. of the end, turn.

2nd row : Slip the first st. and work back to front.

3rd row : Work to within 16 st. of the end, turn.

4th row : As 2nd row.

5th row : Work to within 24 st. of the end, turn.

6th row : As 2nd row.

7th row : Work across all st. and cast off.

Work the left front in the same way, but take care to reverse the shaping. The armhole shaping will be at the beginning of plain-knitted rows, and the front neck shaping at the end of knitted rows.

The Back

WITH fawn wool cast on 153 st. and work ribbing to match the front, then work in s.s. in fawn wool until there are as many rows as on front. Shape the armholes by casting off 2 st. at the beginning of each of the next 10 rows, then k. 2 st. tog. next to the edge st. at both ends of the needle on each of the next 10 k. rows.

Work quite straight on the remaining st. until the armhole edge is 6 rows less in depth than that of the front.

Now shape the neck and shoulders.

1st row : K. to within 8 st. of the end, turn.

2nd row : Sl. the first st. and purl to within 8 st. of the end, turn.

3rd row : Sl. the first st. and k. to within 16 st. of the end, turn.

4th row : P. to within 16 st. of the end, turn.

5th row : K. 25, cast off 29, then k. to within 24 st. of the end.

6th row : P. back to neck.

7th row : Cast off 10 st. and k. the remainder. Cast off.

Join the wool to the neck end of the opposite side, and p. to within 24 st. of the end; turn, and k. to neck. Cast off 10 st. and p. the remainder then cast off all st.

The Sleeves

BEGIN at the shoulder line by casting on 48 st. and k. into the back of these st. Cast on 2 st. at the beginning of the next row ; k. into the back of the cast on st. and p. the remainder. Continue casting on 2 st. at the beginning of each row until there are 112 st. on the needle. Work 4 rows without alteration.

On the next and every following 5th row decrease next to the edge st. at both ends of the needle until the st. are reduced to 64.

Now work the colour pattern as on front of jumper, but to a much smaller scale. Change the st. in sets of three, but instead of working 14 rows of nigger brown before beginning the golden brown, work 5 rows only, and after working 5 rows of golden brown begin changing these to the nigger brown. Work 3 rows, changing the nigger brown to fawn, then change the st. back again as on front. When the pattern is complete, work 1 row all across in fawn wool. Work 3 inches of single rib for cuff and cast off.

Work the second sleeve to match, and to do this it will be necessary to begin the pattern on the p. side of the work on this sleeve.

The Neck

FIRST sew the shoulders of the front and back tog. Holding the right side of the work towards you and using the set of four needles and the fawn wool, pick up and k. through every st. round the neck. There were 190 st. on the original. Work in single rib for 1 inch, decreasing at the lower front point on every row by working 3 st. tog., and decrease in the same way when casting off.

To Complete the Jumper

SEW the tops of the sleeves into the armholes on the wrong side.

Press this seam and all the work on the wrong side over a damp cloth and using a hot iron, then press lightly on the right side. Sew up the side and sleeve seams, then press these seams.

This jumper would look most effective in navy blue with the pattern in light blue and red, or on a grey ground with contrasting stripes. Wear a two-coloured necklace to match the pattern.

A Beret in Black and Gold

Made from Velvet Ribbon and Gold Lace.

This shows how the beret is begun.

To make this attractive beret, you will need four yards of gold lace insertion and four and a half yards of black velvet ribbon, both three-quarters of an inch wide.

Begin by whipping along one side of both velvet and insertion. Draw it up tightly at one end with the gathers getting less and less full along the rest of the whipping. Lay the velvet and insertion side by side, *with the edge of the insertion always just overlapping the velvet*, and continue sewing round and round, easing in the fullness as you go, drawing up the gathers or letting them out as you come to them. When the diameter of the beret is eleven or twelve inches—according to your taste and the size of your head—work a row or so with the material almost flat. Now decrease by whipping the *opposite* edge of velvet and insertion and drawing these up. Continue in this way round and round so that the underpart lies quite flat and until the edge fits the head.

Finish off by sloping in the edges. Cut a piece of velvet to fit the head, join it in a ring very neatly and bind the edge of the beret with it.

HAND-MADE HATS

These hand-worked hats are great favourites just now, and that is not to be wondered at, since they are so very serviceable and smart, and so *cheap* if made at home.

DESIGNED BY "*Finella*"

Which do you want—a " dressy " hat or a sports hat? This model could be used for either.

A SMART LITTLE HAT FOR A TAILORED SUIT

ABBREVIATIONS

In., inch ; d.c., double crochet ; st., stitch ; ch., chain.

MATERIALS

7 balls (60 yds.) of Rickard's Sylvan knitting silk in black, 2 balls of Rickard's Sylvan knitting silk in grey, ¾ of a yard of black ribbon, 2 ins. wide, for the head band, and a No. 16 Stratnoid crochet hook.

MEASUREMENTS

Round head band—22 ins. Can be arranged for a slightly smaller size or to 23 ins.

Depth from the centre of the crown to the edge of front—8 ins.

Depth from the centre of the crown to the lower edge of the back—9 ins.

TENSION

10 d.c. to 1 in. in width.

10 rows to 1 in. in depth.

THE beauty of the little hat lies in the fineness of the working and the closeness of the fitting. It is a good plan to practise the d.c. over a two-inch piece in order to get the exact tension. The silk can be used again for the hat itself if wound tightly round a book or any other article to stretch it.

BEGIN in the centre of the crown with 5 ch. joined into a ring.

1st round : 11 d.c. into the ring.

2nd round : 2 d.c. into every st. all round. Mark the end of the round with a coloured thread and carry this thread down the rows to the edge of the hat.

3rd round : 1 d.c. into every st. all round.

4th round : * 1 d.c. into 1 st., then 2 d.c. into the next, and repeat from * all round.

5th round : 1 d.c. into each st. all round.

6th round : * 1 d.c. into each of 2 sts., then 2 d.c. in the next, and repeat from * all round.

7th round : 1 d.c. in each st. all round.

8th round : * 1 d.c. into each of 3 sts., then 2 d.c. in the next, and repeat from * all round.

On looking at the work, it will be seen that there are 11 increase sts. and that as the work proceeds 1 st. extra is worked before these increases on each increase row. Continue in this way, increasing on alternate rows, till there are 17 sts. in each section. The next increase row will have increases in every 5th st. all round, and the next will have increases in every 6th st. all round, and so on. When there are 17 sts. in each section, increase in the same way, but on every 3rd row only till there are 21 sts. in each section. This will make 231 sts. all round, and at the correct tension the measurement will be 23 ins.

From here, work without alteration for a depth of 3¼ ins., finishing at the centre-back.

To make the hat fit well, a few decreases are now made across the centre-back.

On the next round, * work 1 d.c. in each of the next 5 sts., then miss 1 st. and repeat from * 4 times more, then continue round as usual, st. into st., to within 30 sts. of the centre-back ; then * miss 1 st., work 1 d.c. into each of the next 5 sts., and repeat from * 4 times more. Cut silk.

Now find the centre-front of the hat, then mark off 2 ins. on each side of the centre. This part is now left unworked for the front.

Join the silk to the mark on the left side of the hat and work all round the back to the mark on the opposite side of the front. Cut silk.

Go back to the beginning of the last row, leave the first 3 sts. unworked. Join the silk to the next st., and work all round to within 3 sts. of the end of the last row. Leave these unworked. Cut silk.

Repeat the last row 8 times more, leaving 3 sts. unworked on each successive row at both ends. Now join the silk to the centre-back and work 2 rows of d.c. all round, working st. into st. This completes the hat itself.

The Leaves.—With grey silk work 31 ch.

1st round : Miss the ch. next the hook, work 2 d.c. into the next ch., then 1 d.c. into each of the next 7 ch.,

Just the thing to wear with tweeds is this well-shaped hat, crocheted in real Shetland wool.

Pattern overleaf

1 tr. into each of the next 14 ch., 1 d.c. into each of the next 7 ch., then 3 d.c. into the last st. Turn and work down the opposite side of the ch., working 7 d.c., 14 tr., 7 d.c., then 2 d.c. into the last st., join to the first st. by a slip-st.

2nd round : 1 ch., then 2 d.c. into the first st., then 1 d.c. into each st. to the centre st. of the 3 d.c. at the point, and into this work 3 d.c., then continue down the opposite side in d.c. to the last st., and into this work 2 d.c. as before, then join by a slip-st. to the first st.

Repeat the last round 4 times more. Cut silk.

6 leaves in grey and 3 leaves in black are required for the trimming.

TO COMPLETE

Arrange the leaves in cascade fashion as illustrated on either the left or right side of the hat as best suits the wearer.

Join the ribbon into a band to fit the head and sew just inside the edge of the hat.

No pressing is required, except for the leaves which should be pressed lightly on the wrong side with a warm iron over a dry cloth.

Choose These for Chic!

A DAINTILY-SHAPED CAP TO WEAR WITH TWEEDS

MATERIALS

Two ozs. Paton and Baldwin's 2-ply Real Shetland wool, in brown, ¾ of a yard of 2-in. wide corded ribbon to match the wool, ¾ of a yard of soft silk, 2 ins. wide, ribbon for the head-band, a feather mount and a No. 14 Stratnoid crochet hook.

SIZE

Round the head—22 ins.
Depth from centre of crown to lower edge of front—8 ins.
Depth from centre of crown to lower edge of back—9½ ins.

TENSION

8 sts. to 1 in.

A very youthful "skull" cap is this little model made in brown with fawn stripes.

THE hat is worked in a short tr. stitch, as follows: Pass the wool over the hook, then through the st. below, and draw a loop through, as usual. There are now 3 loops on the hook. Pass the wool over the hook and draw through all 3 loops at once. These short trs. will be called sts. throughout the work.

Begin in the centre of the crown with 4 ch. joined into a ring.

1st round : 8 sts. into the ring.

2nd round : 2 sts. into each st. of the previous round. Mark the end of this round with a coloured thread and pass the thread down at the ends of the rounds as the work proceeds.

3rd round : As for the 2nd round.

4th round : 1 st. into each st. of the previous round.

5th round : * 1 st. into each of 2 sts., then 2 sts. into the next, and repeat from * all round.

6th round : As for the 5th round.

7th round : Work st. into st. all round

8th round : As for the 7th round.

Repeat the last 3 rounds till the work measures 6¾ ins. across the centre. On the next round work * 1 st. into each of 4 sts., then 2 sts. into the next, and repeat from * all round. From here work round and round without alteration for a depth of 3½ ins., finishing at the mark at the end of the rounds, slip-stitch to the next st., and cut wool. The mark at the end of the rounds is the centre-back.

Now count round and mark the centre-front. Join the wool to the 5th st. away from the centre st. towards the left side and work round the back to within 4 sts. of the centre-front on the opposite side. Cut wool. There are now 9 sts. left un-worked in the centre-front. Join the wool to the 7th st. from the beginning of the last row, and work all round to within 6 sts. of the end of the last row. Cut wool.

Repeat this last row twice more. Now join the wool to the 4th st. from the beginning of the last row, and work to within 18 sts. of the centre-back, miss 1 st., then work 1 st. into each of the next 4 sts., and repeat from * 7 times more, then miss 1 st., and continue round, st. into st. to within 3 sts. of the end of the last row. Cut wool. Join the wool to the 4th st. from the beginning of the last row and work st. into st. to within 3 sts. of the end of the last row. Cut wool.

Repeat the last row 6 times more. Now join the wool to the centre-back of the cap and work a row all round, working st. into st., join to the first st. by a slip-stitch, work 1 ch., then continue round once again, slip-stitch to the ch. at the beginning of the round, and cut wool.

Press the work on the wrong side with a hot iron over a damp cloth. Make a straight, stiff bow with the corded ribbon, and fish-tail the ends. Fix the bow in a slanting direction on the left side of the hat and the feather mount to come from under the knot of the bow towards the front. The arrangement of the bow and ribbon depends on the style that suits each individual. A smart effect should be attained.

With the soft silk ribbon make a band to fit the head and sew in position inside the hat. On the front this will be close to the edge, but at the back about an inch of the hat should be free below the band.

It might have come from Bond Street— but it need cost you only a few shillings.

A SMART SKULL CAP IN BROWN AND BEIGE

ABBREVIATIONS USED

Ch., chain ; d.c., double crochet ; st., stitch ; in., inch.

MATERIALS

7 balls of Rickards' Sylvan knitting silk in brown (60 yd. balls), 1 ball of the same silk in beige or fawn, ¾ of a yard of ribbon, 1½ ins. wide, in brown, for

And here we have the ever-popular beret, but this time it has the real French touch—the flat bow at the back and the ribbon head-band all round. This shape will suit any type of face, for it can be adapted so easily.

trimming, ¾ of a yard of ribbon, 2 ins. wide in brown, for the head-band, and a No. 16 Stratnoid crochet hook.

MEASUREMENTS

Depth from the centre of the crown to the lower edge—8½ ins.

Round head—22 ins. Can be made smaller by arranging the head-band.

TENSION

10 d.c. to 1 in. in width.

11 rows to 1 in. in depth.

The hat is worked entirely in d.c., working round and round except over the beige bands.

Begin in the centre of the crown with 5 ch. joined into a ring.

1st round : 11 d.c. into the ring.

2nd round : 2 d.c. into every st. of the previous round. Mark end of round.

3rd round : 1 d.c. into each st. of the previous round.

4th round : * 1 d.c. into 1 st., then 2 d.c. into the next, and repeat from * all round.

5th round : 1 d.c. into each st. of the previous round.

6th round : 2 d.c. into every 3rd st. of the previous round.

7th round : 1 d.c. in each st. of the previous round.

From here, increase on every alternate round with 1 st. extra before the increases on each successive increase round till there are 15 sts. before each increase.

Continue increasing in the same way, but with 2 rounds without alteration between the increase rounds instead of one, till there are 19 sts. before each increase. There will now be 220 sts. in the round.

Work round and round without alteration for a depth of 1 in., leaving the silk at the centre-back of the hat. Find the centre-front then mark 3½ ins. on each side of this centre, making 7 ins. for the centre-front of the hat.

With fawn silk work across this part st. into st., then cut silk.

Join the fawn silk on at the beginning of this row again and work another row across the same sts. Repeat this last row once more. Cut silk and leave this part.

Return to the brown silk at the back of the hat, and with this work 3 rounds over all sts., finishing at the centre-back.

Leave the brown silk hanging here.

Repeat the 3 rows in fawn and the 3 rounds in brown 6 times more, then work a further 5 rounds in brown and cut silk. Now mark off the centre 3 ins. at the front.

Leave this part and work from one side of this round the back to the opposite side of this part. Cut silk.

Go back to the beginning of the last row, leave 5 sts. of this row unworked, join the silk to the next st., and work over the last row to within 5 sts. of the end of the last row; leave these sts. unworked. Cut silk. Repeat this last row twice more.

Now work in the same way 4 times more, but instead of leaving 5 sts. unworked, leave 3 only at each end. After this work a further 8 rows, leaving 1 st. only at each end unworked on each row.

Now join the silk to the centre-back of the hat, and work 2 rounds, st. into st., all round. Cut silk and fasten off neatly.

Take 6 ins. of the narrow ribbon and fold one end to form a point. Sew this piece to the centre-front of the hat with the point projecting just below the edge. Take another piece 13½ ins. long, and make a point at both ends again by folding. Turn up the back of the hat about ½ an in., or as required for comfort. Sew one point of the ribbon over this turned-up edge, and pass the ribbon over the top to the striped part of the front. Sew the second point over the first ribbon here.

With the wider ribbon, make a band to fit the head and sew just inside the lower edge.

Note that no pressing is required. It is much better to leave all elasticity in the work rather than press it out

A SMART LITTLE TWEED CAP

MATERIALS

2½ ozs. of Paton & Baldwin's 2-ply Real Shetland wool in a mixture, 1 buckle, ¾ of a yard of ribbon about 2 ins. wide, for the head band, and a No. 14 Stratnoid crochet hook.

SIZE

Round head—22 ins.

Depth from the centre of the crown to the lower edge at back—8¾ ins.

The depth at the front is regulated by the tucks.

TENSION

8 d.c. to 1 in. in width.

9 rows to 1 in. in depth.

Begin in the centre of the crown with 5 ch. joined into a ring.

1st round : 7 d.c. into the ring.

2nd round : 2 d.c. into each st. of the previous round. Mark the end of this round with a coloured thread and carry this thread down the rows as the work proceeds.

3rd round : 2 d.c. into every st. of the previous round.

4th round : 1 d.c. into each st. of the previous round.

5th round : As for the 4th round.

6th round : * 1 d.c. into 1 st., then 2 d.c. into the next and repeat from * all round.

7th round : 1 d.c. into each st. of the previous round.

8th round : As for the 7th round.

9th round : * 1 d.c. into each of 2 sts., then 2 d.c. into the next and repeat from * all round.

Continue in this way, increasing on every 3rd round, with 1 st. more before the increases on each successive increase round till you have worked 1 d.c. into each of 11 sts., then 2 d.c. into the next. Work the next 2 rounds without alteration. On the next round, work 2 d.c. into every 26th st. all round. From here, continue quite straight for a depth of 3¼ ins., finishing the last round at the mark ; this mark forms the centre-back. On the next round, work 1 d.c. into each of 3 sts., work the next 2 sts. as 1, * 1 d.c. into each of 6 sts., work the next 2 sts. as 1, and repeat from * once more ; then work round without alteration to within 21 sts. of the mark. * work the next 2 sts. as 1,

then 1 d.c. into each of 6 sts., and repeat from * towards the mark, finishing with 1 d.c. into each of 3 sts. Repeat this last round once again, then work round and round without alteration for a depth of 1 in., finishing at the centre-back ; slip-st. to the next st. and cut wool.

The Buckle Tab.—Begin by working 15 ch.

On the first round, miss the ch. next the hook, then work 1 d.c. into each of the next 13 ch. 3 d.c. into the last ch., then work along the opposite side of the ch.—1 d.c. into each of 13 ch., 3 d.c. into the next which is the end st.

Continue round and round, always working 3 d.c. into the centre of the 3 d.c. at both ends, till 5 rounds have been worked, or till the work is wide enough to cover the bar of the buckle. Slip-st. to the next st. and cut wool.

Press the work on the wrong side with a hot iron over a damp cloth. Now form 3 pleats as shown in the centre-front. These pleats can be made to show as much or as little of the forehead as best suits the wearer. It is best to pin them in position first, and then try on the cap. If you can wear a hat well off the forehead, then the pleats can be formed rather deeply. The lower one should come to the edge of the cap. When arranged satisfactorily, press well with a hot iron over a damp cloth, then stitch securely from the back of the work. There must be no suggestion of sewing on the front of the cap. The edge of the upper pleat should be just covered by the buckle.

Sew the buckle to the centre-front, then pass the crocheted bar through.

With the ribbon, make a head-band to fit the head and sew just inside the cap.

THE NEW BERET

MATERIALS

2 ozs. Paton & Baldwin's 3-ply super Scotch fingering. The original was in shade No. 37, a mixture of black, grey and white. 1½ yards of Petersham ribbon 1½ ins. wide, ¾ of a yard of silk ribbon about 2 ins. wide for the head-band and a No. 14 Stratnoid crochet hook.

SIZE

Round the head-band—22 ins.

TENSION

9 sts. to 1 in.

The crochet work is in a short tr. worked in the following way : Wool over hook, then through the st. below draw a loop through, making 3 loops on the hook, now wool over hook and draw through all three loops at once. Throughout the work this will be called a stitch.

Begin in the centre of the crown by working 5 ch. and joining into a ring.

1st round : 7 sts. into the ring.

2nd round : 2 sts. into each st. of the previous round. Mark the end of this round with a coloured thread and pass this thread down the rows at the ends of the rounds as the work proceeds.

3rd round : 2 sts. into each st. of the previous round.

4th round : 1 st. into each st. of the previous round.

5th round : * 1 st. into 1 st. then 2 sts. into the next and repeat from * all round.

[Continued on next page]

HAND-MADE HATS

[Continued from previous page]

6th round : As for the 5th round.

7th round : 1 st. into each st. of the previous round.

8th round : * 1 st. into each of 3 sts., then 2 sts. into the next and repeat from * all round.

9th round : 1 st. into each st. of the previous round.

10th round : * 1 st. into each of 7 sts. then 2 sts. into the next and repeat from * all round.

Repeat the last 2 rounds till the work measures $7\frac{1}{4}$ ins. across the centre. Now increase in every 8th st. in the same way but on every 3rd round only, till the work measures 10 ins. across the centre. Now continue round and round without alteration till the work measures 15 ins. across the centre, finishing the last round at the mark at the end of the round. The edge is now decreased across the sides and back. Work * 1 st. into each of 4 sts. then miss the next st. and repeat from * all round to within 9 ins. of the mark, and across the remainder of the round work st. into st. till the mark is reached. Repeat this last round twice more. The edge of the work should now measure $22\frac{1}{2}$ ins. Work 2 rounds without further alteration.

To Complete the Beret

Press the work on the wrong side with a hot iron over a damp cloth. The straight 9 ins. of the work is the front, all the fullness being towards the back.

Cut off 24 ins. of the Petersham ribbon and with this make a band to fit the head comfortably. Press the seam open and slip-st. the edges down on the wrong side. Pin the join in the band to the centre-back of the hat. Sew the edge of the crochet just under the edge of the band on the wrong side without allowing the sts. to come through to the right side of the band.

Now pull the tammy crown back over the edge of the band at the back. Catch down here, and also on each side to keep in position.

With the remainder of the Petersham ribbon make a stiff bow and sew this to the back pulled-over part. Sew in the silk ribbon as a lining, close to the edge of the band.

THE END

FOR GARDENERS ALL

The Book For Which They Have Been Waiting.

IN this world there are one or two things of which we cannot speak slightingly.

No one in his senses, for instance, would speak slightingly of a girl to her infatuated sweetheart. Or of a garden to the gardener——

For gardeners are touchy.

No one's face lights up with such pleasure as the gardener's when you praise the noble hollyhocks which he has raised more by luck than good judgment.

For it is surprising how unscientific the gardener can be. Pottering round with his little trowel and his watering-can. Gathering wisdom from his mistakes. Searching wistfully for helpful hints from his neighbours.

It is for those who love their gardens that the " Popular Encyclopedia of Gardening " is being published, in 52 weekly parts.

Whatever Your Problem

IN this wonderful new book of reference there is nothing about gardening you cannot look up. Everything is arranged in alphabetical order.

From the most everyday things—transplanting seedlings, taking cuttings, grafting and budding, the whole of gardening is explained.

Full details are given of all the ordinary and the more strange and lovely flowers and plants.

Let us suppose that you have been given a Resurrection Plant; the Rose of Jericho is its other pretty name. A strange plant that returns to life after it has apparently been dead for a long time.

You can read all about it in the new Encyclopedia.

Or perhaps you are interested in your allotment. Exactly how to plan out a little plot of ground and cultivate it with vegetables is shown.

The Best Advice

WELL-KNOWN authorities on gardening have contributed to the " Popular Encyclopedia of Gardening." You may be sure that you are getting the very best information.

It is a complete and practical guide to every branch of gardening—and it cost only sixpence a week

The originality of this jumper lies in the choice of gold and green for the main colour-scheme. However, any colours could be substituted.

A Gay Spring Jumper—

Designed by "Finella"

Now that the bright Spring days are here once more, you will be longing for an outfit that is neither too light nor too warm.

ABBREVIATIONS USED :

In., inch ; st., stitch ; k., knit ; p., purl ; st.-st., stocking-stitch ; tr., treble ; ch., chain ; d.c., double crochet.

Stocking-stitch is knit one row, purl one row alternately.

A GAY SPRING JUMPER

MATERIALS

Nine ounces of Harrap's "Sirdar" crochet wool in gold, three ounces in soft green, three skeins each of D.M.C. in green, gold and brown (the green should be a lighter shade than the wool, and the gold thread should be the exact shade of the wool); a pair of No. 10 knitting needles and a No. 16 Stratnoid crochet-hook.

MEASUREMENTS

Length from the top of the shoulder—25½ ins.
Width all round—38 ins.
Length of sleeve from neck—28½ ins.
Length of sleeve seam—21½ ins.

TENSION

8 stitches to 1 inch.

THE BACK—Begin at the lower edge by casting on 152 sts. with the green wool and work in st.-st. for a depth of 4 ins., working into the backs of sts. on the 1st row.

Change to the gold wool and continue without alteration till the work measures 17 ins. from the beginning, then shape the armholes by knitting 2 sts. (or purling 2 sts.) tog. next to the edge st., at both ends of the needle on each of the the next 9 rows ; then decrease in the same way on each of the next 9 k. rows (116 sts. remain on the needle).

Continue quite straight on these sts. for a depth of 4½ ins., then shape the neck and shoulders :

1st row : K. to within 9 sts. of the end, turn.

2nd row : Slip the first st. and p. to within 9 sts. of the end, turn.

3rd row : Slip the first st., k. 32, cast off 32, then k. to within 18 sts. of the end, turn.

4th row : Slip the first st. and p. to neck.

5th row : Cast off 16 sts. and k. across the remainder.

6th row : Cast off.

7th row : Join the wool to the neck end of the opposite side and p. to within 18 sts. of the end, turn.

8th row : Slip the first st. and k. to neck.

9th row : Cast off 16 sts. and p. across the remainder.

10th row : Cast off.

The Front—Work this in the same way as for the back till the green border is completed. Leave this for the moment. With gold wool, cast on 32 sts. for the pocket back and work in st.-st. for the same number of rows as on the front, finishing at the end of a k. row. Cut the wool, push this piece of work along the needle, and work another piece in the same way, working an extra row so as to finish this piece at the end of a p. row.

You will now require the 4 needles. One will be used for the centre green sts. and one on each side for the gold sts.

Take up the front, work 24 sts. in gold, then across the centre 104 in green and across the last 24 in gold, using a second ball of wool for these last 24 sts. On the next row—a p. row—p. 24 sts. in gold, work across the sts. of a pocket back in gold, cast off 3 sts. of the green centre, then complete the remainder of the green part, and also the last 24 sts. in gold. On the following row, work across the 24 sts. in gold, then across the sts. of the second pocket back in gold ; leave this, and taking up the green wool, cast off 3 sts., then k. the remaining 98 sts. in green and the remainder in gold. Be careful to keep the parts separate for the pockets.

Continue in this way, keeping 56 sts. on each side in gold and casting off 3 sts. at the beginning of every row in the green centre until 30 sts. on each side have been cast off, then at the beginning of each of the next 2 rows on this part, cast off 2 sts. only.

This will make 32 sts. on each side for the pocket opening, and you will now have 56 sts. in gold, 40 in green, and 56 in gold.

On the next row, join up all sts. again to one needle, and p. 57 in gold, 38 in green, 57 in gold, twisting the wools round each other when changing colours in order to avoid a gap. Continue changing a st. on each side from green to gold till there are 20 sts. in the centre in green, then keep the sts. in this way and continue straight to the armhole. You will have 66 sts. in gold on each side with 20 in green in the centre.

Now shape the armhole by knitting 2 sts. tog. next to the edge st. at both ends of the needle on each of the next 9 rows.

The work is now divided for the front opening. Continue the armhole shaping as for the back, decreasing on each of the next 9 k. rows, but on the front work to the centre of the

A Smart Outdoor Jumper and Beret

Here are two attractive,
easy-to-make designs for the young wife
who is anxious to look her best.

Continued from overleaf

green panel only, and shape the front by decreasing next to the green sts. on every k. row till there are 22 decreases here.

From here continue quite straight till the armhole edge is 6 rows deeper than that of the back, then shape the shoulder.

1st row : Working from the front edge, work to within 9 sts. of the end, turn.

2nd row : Slip the first st. and work back to front.

3rd row : Work to within 18 sts. of the end, turn.

4th row : As for the *2nd row.*

5th row : Work across all sts.

6th row : Cast off the 26 shoulder sts. in gold and continue on the 10 sts. in green till there is a sufficient depth to reach to the centre of the back of the neck.

Leave these sts. on a pin for grafting, and join the wool to the neck edge of the opposite side ; complete this side to match the first and then graft the sts. of the border together.

Sew the shoulders of the back and front together, then sew the edge of the free border to the back of the neck.

The Sleeves—With gold wool cast on 46 sts. and work into the backs of these sts. on the first row, casting on 2 sts. at the end of the row.

On the next row work into the backs of the cast-on sts., then work the remainder, and cast on 2 sts. at the end of the row. Continue casting on 2 sts. at the end of every row till there are 114 sts. on the needle, always working into the backs of all cast-on sts.

Now work 6 rows without alteration, then on the next and every following 7th row, decrease next to the edge st. at both ends of the needle till there are 64 sts. on the needle, but when the sleeve measures 20 ins. from the top, change to the green wool and work the border as on the lower edge of jumper, then cast off.

Work a second sleeve in the same way.

To Complete the Jumper

Sew the tops of the sleeves into the armholes. Press out the work on the wrong and then on the right side with a hot iron over a damp cloth, then press again in the same way on the right side.

Work a row of d.c., working st. into st. across the upper edge of the pockets, using the green wool and work the same edging round the sleeve edges. Round the neck, beginning at the centre-back, work a row of d.c. all round, missing every 8th st. on the edge of the work.

Sew up the side and sleeve seams and sew down the side edges of the pocket backs.

Now work a row of d.c. all round the lower edge, working through the edges of the pocket backs when these are reached. Join by a slip-st., and work back in the opposite direction, then repeat the last row once more.

Now press out the seams and edges well on the wrong side.

The Embroidery—Three sts. only are employed: lazy-daisy st., French knots and satin st.

The flowers are in lazy-daisy st., and are worked in the gold thread, the centres being 1 in. from each other. They are worked all round the upper edge of the green border, up the fronts and round the neck. The centres of the flowers are completed with a French knot, these being in green and brown alternately.

A tiny leaf is worked close to each flower, in green for the flower with a green centre, and brown for the flower with a brown centre.

Work the same embroidery round the upper edge of the cuffs, then press the embroidery on the wrong side with a hot iron over a damp cloth.

If you decide to make yourself this neat and charming outfit, you will be delighted with it and will find it invaluable for outdoor wear.

A SMART OUTDOOR JUMPER AND BERET

Materials

Seventeen ounces of 4-ply Beehive soft knitting wool, an eighteen-inch Zip fastener, a pair of No. 10 knitting needles and a No. 14 Stratnoid crochet hook.

Measurements

Length from the top of the shoulder — 26½ ins.

Width all round body—40 ins.

Width round lower ribbing, without stretching —32 ins.

Length of sleeve from neck, including cuff—30 ins.

Length of sleeve seam, including cuff—21 ins.

Shoulder seam—4½ ins.

Tension

8 sts. to 1 in. in width.

The Back.—Begin at the lower edge by casting on 152 sts., and then work in k. 1, p. 1 rib for a depth of 4 ins., working into the backs of the sts. on the first row. Change to st.-st. and continue in this till the work measures 18½ ins. from the beginning.

Now shape the armholes by casting off 2 sts. at the beginning of each of the next 14 rows, then by decreasing next to the edge st. at both ends of the needle on each of the next 4 k. rows (116 sts. remain on the needle). Continue without further alteration on these sts. for a depth of 5 ins., then shape the shoulders and neck as follows:

1st row: K. to within 9 sts. of the end, turn.

2nd row: Slip the first st. and p. to within 9 sts. of the end, turn.

3rd row: Slip the first st. and k. to within 18 sts. of the end, turn.

4th row: Slip the first st. and p. to within 18 sts. of the end, turn.

5th row: Slip the first st., k. 29, cast off 20, then k. to within 27 sts. of the end, turn.

6th row: Slip the first st. and p. to neck.

7th row: Cast off 12 sts. and k. across the remainder.

8th row: Cast off.

9th row: Join the wool to the neck edge of the opposite side and p. to within 27 sts. of the end, turn.

10th row: Slip the first st. and k. to neck.

11th row: Cast off 12 sts. and p. across the remainder.

12th row: Cast off.

The Front.—Begin at the lower edge by casting on 172 sts., and work in the ribbing for the same number of rows as for the back, working into the backs of the sts. on the first row.

Change to st.-st. and k. across 64 sts. only, then pass the remaining sts. to a safety-pin for the moment. Continue on the 64 sts. on the needle for a depth of 3 ins.

On the next k. row, k. 17, then p. 1 and k. 1 alternately over the next 31 sts., and k. the last 16 sts. Continue with the 31 sts. in the ribbing, and the remainder in st.-st., till 10 rows have been worked. On the next row, k. 17, cast off 31, k. 16. Leave this part of the work for the moment.

Using a spare needle, cast on 31 sts. and work in st.-st. for the same number of rows as on the front of the coat above the ribbing of the lower border and finishing at the end of a k. row. Take up the front again, p. the first 16 sts. then across the sts. of the pocket back, then the remaining 17 sts. From here, work quite straight till the side edge is the same depth as on the back to the armhole.

At the beginning of each of the next 8 k. rows, cast off 2 sts., then decrease next to the edge st. on the same edge on each of the next 6 k. rows. Continue quite straight on the remaining sts. for a depth of 2¾ ins. On the next k. row, k. 20, k. 2 tog., k. 20. Work the next 3 rows without alteration.

On the next row, k. 19, k. 2 tog., k. 20, then work 3 rows without alteration. On the next row, k. 19 k. 2. tog., k. 19, then work 3 rows without alteration. On the next row, k. 18, k. 2 tog., k. 19, then work 3 rows without alteration. On the next row, k. 18, k. 2 tog., k. 18, then work 3 rows without alteration. On the next row, k. 17, k. 2 tog., k. 18, then work 3 rows without alteration.

Now shape the shoulder.

1st row: Working from the front edge, work to within 9 sts. of the end, turn.

2nd row: Slip the first st. and work back to front.

3rd row: Work to within 18 sts. of the end, turn.

4th row: As for the 2nd row.

5th row: Work to within 27 sts. of the end, turn.

6th row: As for the 2nd row.

7th row: Work across all sts.

8th row: Cast off.

The Second Front.—Holding the right side of the work towards you, join the wool to the first st. of those left behind, cast off 44 sts., then work across the remaining 64 sts. Complete this side of the front to match the first. Sew the shoulders of the back and fronts together.

The Sleeves.—Begin at the shoulder line by casting on 40 sts., k. into the backs of these sts. and cast on 2 sts. at the end of the row.

On the next row, p. into the backs of the 2 cast-on sts., p. across the remainder and cast on 2 sts. at the end of the row. Continue casting on 2 sts. at the end of every row till there are 116 sts. on the needle—always working into the backs of all cast-on sts.

Work the next 8 rows without alteration; then on the next and every following 8th row, decrease next to the edge st. at both ends of the needle till 106 sts. remain. From here, decrease in the same way on every 6th row till 66 sts. remain. Work a depth of 2 ins. without alteration, then change to the k.1, p. 1 rib, and work a depth of 4 ins. in this, then cast off.

Work the second sleeve in the same way.

Sew the tops of the sleeves into the armholes. Press out all st.-st. on the wrong and then on the right side with a hot iron over a damp cloth. Sew up the side and sleeve seams and press them. Sew the side edges and also lower edges of the pocket backs in position, then press these. Be careful not to allow the sts. to show through to the right side of the work.

The Crochet Front.—This is worked in a short tr. st.—just an ordinary tr. st. till the 3 loops are on the needle, then, instead of drawing the wool through 2 loops and again through 2 loops, draw through all 3 loops at once.

Holding the right side of the jumper towards you, work 1 short tr. into each cast-off st. in the centre-front (44 short trs. in all)—2 ch., turn. Work row upon row, working backwards and forwards and turning each row with 2 ch. for a depth of 4¼ ins. Now work across 22 sts. only and continue across these for a depth of 16 ins. and cut wool. The last row should finish next to the knitting.

Join the wool to the centre-front of the opposite side of the front, and work across the 22 sts. of this side for the same number of rows as on the first side—the last row should finish at the front edge. Now sew the edges of the crochet to the knitting edges, leaving 2¾ ins. of the knitting free at the top.

Now work in the crochet across the top of the last front piece, then up the side of the neck, missing every 10th stitch, working st. into st., across the back of the neck—missing every 10th st., down the second side of the neck as for the first, then across the sts. of the first front worked, 2 ch., turn. Work backwards and forwards across all sts. for a depth of 4¾ ins. On the next row, work across 22 sts. only, and continue across these sts. for a depth of 16¼ ins. Cut wool.

Join the wool to the 22nd st. from the opposite end of the collar, and work across 22 sts. at this side for the same number of rows as on the first side. The sts. for the sides and back of the neck are left unworked.

To Complete

Press the crochet on the wrong side. Fold down the collar to the inside, and sew the inside edge of this to the neck edge of the coat. Now sew the inner edges of the loose front pieces to the coat just over the sts. of the outer fronts. There is now a double front with the front edges free.

Place the Zip between these edges, and sew the crochet edges on both sides neatly over the Zip tape, leaving sufficient space for the Zip to run freely. Make a small tassel with wool and fix this to the Zip hook, to act as a puller.

THE BERET

Materials

Three ounces of 4-ply "Beehive" soft knitting in the same mixture as the jumper, three-quarters of a yard of ribbon, about 2 ins. wide, for the head band, a small feather mount and a No. 14 Stratnoid crochet hook.

Measurements

Round the head band—22 ins. This measurement can be regulated to fit any head (see directions). Depth from the centre of the crown to the edge, 9½ ins.

Tension

17 sts. to 2 ins in width.

The beret is made entirely in a short tr. stitch, which is worked as follows: Work in the same way as for the usual tr till the 3 loops are on the hook, then pass the wool over the hook and draw through all 3 loops at once, instead of through 2 loops at a time as for the ordinary tr

Begin in the centre of the crown with 5 ch. joined into a ring. For the first round, work 9 d.c. into the ring as a foundation.

Now proceed with the short tr. stitch, working * 1 short tr. into 1 st., then 2 into the next and repeat round and round from * till the circle measures 1½ ins. across.

Now work * 1 short tr. into each of 2 sts., then 2 into the next and repeat round and round from * till the circle measures 2½ ins. across.

Work * 1 short tr. into each of 7 sts., then 2 into the next and repeat from * till the circle measures 3½ ins. across.

Work * 1 short tr. into each of 11 sts., then 2 into the next and repeat from * till the circle measures 6 ins. across.

Work * 1 short tr. into each of 23 sts., then 2 into the next and repeat from * till the circle measures 10 ins. across.

From here continue round and round, working st. into st. till the work measures 15 ins. across.

The decreasing is now begun: To decrease, work 2 sts. as one in the following way: Draw a loop through a st. below as usual, making the 3 loops on the hook, then draw a loop through the

[Continued on next page]

next st. below, making 4 loops on the hook, then wool over hook and draw through all 4 loops at once. Work every 19th and 20th sts. tog. in this way, working round and round till the edge of the work measures 22 ins. round or the size required to fit the head. Mark the last decrease with a coloured thread. Now continue round and round without alteration till 3 rounds have been completed, slip-stitch to the next st. then cut wool.

To Complete

FASTEN in all ends of wool neatly on the wrong side. Press the work lightly on the wrong side with a warm iron over a dry cloth. With the ribbon, make a band to fit the head comfortably, and sew this just inside the edge of the beret.

Try on the beret and arrange two pleats at the front to form a V shape, and press these pleats a little. Arrange the little feather mount as shown. The pleated part can be worn at the side if this suits the wearer.

THE END

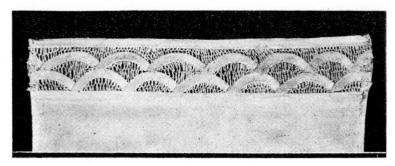

Making a MODESTY VEST

TAKE a piece of cream crêpe-de-Chine 9 inches by 27 inches wide. Cut off a piece about 10 inches long. Then from the remainder cut one straight strip ¾ inch wide, and some crossway strips also ¾ inch wide. Fold the strips in half lengthwise, seam them and turn them right side out.

Pin the piece of silk on to some strong brown paper. Immediately above the top edge draw half circles, using a penny as a guide, as shown in the photograph. Pin the crossway strips over the pencilled lines and faggot-stitch them to the vest, using two strands of cream-coloured " Filoselle " throughout, and taking long and short stitches to fit the curves of the circles. Mark a second row of half circles a little above the first row. Pin the crossway strips over the lines, and faggot-stitch them to the first row, as before.

Pin the straight strip to the paper about a quarter of an inch above the second row of curves, and faggot-stitch them together.

Remove the tackings from the vest and hem all round three sides of it neatly.

The Call of the SEA!

A Workmanlike Knitted Bathing Costume—but the Little Seagull Speaks of Feminine Grace!

THIS is a very easy garment to knit, and can be worked by any average knitter. The trunks are on practically straight lines; the two pieces, back and front (with skirt) are made separately and are afterwards sewn together.

Abbreviations

K., knit plain; p., purl; tog., together; inc., increase; dec., decrease; s.s., stocking-stitch (i.e. k. on front of work and p. back); st., stitch; N., navy; W., white for the two-colour work.

Materials

NINE ounces of Patons & Baldwins' 4-ply Crocus knitting yarn in navy, and 1 ounce of the same wool in white; a pair of bone knitting needles No. 10, and one spare needle.

Tension and Measurements

WORKING at a tension of 7 st. to the inch in width, the following measurements are attained after light pressing: Round bust, 26 inches; top of shoulder strap to hem of skirt, 30 inches; round hip part of skirt, 27 inches; length of trunk at side of leg, 12½ inches; round leg band with rib closed, 12 inches.

To Work

THE Front : For leg cast on 46 st. loosely with navy wool and work 10 rows of single rib (k. 1 and p. 1 alternately). Work in s.s. for another 5 inches, ending with a p. row. Fasten off wool and put these st. on a spare needle.

Work another leg in the same way, then k. the next row on second leg, and on the same needle continue the first leg-st., making 92 altogether. Work in s.s. for 6½ inches, ending with a p. row. Cut wool and leave these st. on a spare needle.

A bathing costume is such an important item of holiday kit that it should be chosen for its charm as well as its utility.

The Skirt

WITH navy wool cast on 92 st. loosely and work 6 rows in single rib, then work s.s. for 10½ inches, ending with a p. row. Place the needle with leg-st. behind the skirt-st. right side of each, facing worker. Now work one row, knitting together one st. from each needle to end of row.

Continue s.s., working 2 tog. at each end of every k. row until 74 st. remain. S.s. 12 rows for the waistline.

Now inc. one st. at each end of every k. row until there are 84 st. on the needle ; p. one row.

The Two-Colour Pattern

THE seagull is worked in s.s. like the rest, so the number of st. in each colour are given in the following directions. To avoid loose threads at the back, twist the working thread over the colour out of action before working each st.

1st row : K. 40 N., 2 W., 1 N., 2 W. 39, N
2nd row : P. 37 N., 7 W., 40 N.
3rd row : K. 38 N., 9 W., 37 N.
4th row : P. 40 N., 6 W., 21 N., 3 W., 14 N.

5th row : K. 11 N., 3 W., 1 N., 3 W., 19 N., 7 W., 1 N., 7 W., 32 N.

6th row : P. 29 N., 10 W., 6 N., 2 W., 16 N., 2 W., 1 N., 7 W., 11 N.

7th row : K. 9 N., 2 W., 1 N., 10 W., 18 N., 4 W., 2 N., 14 W., 24 N.

8th row : P. 20 N., 5 W., 2 N., 10 W., 2 N., 9 W., 13 N., 14 W., 9 N.

9th row : K. 8 N., 1 W., 1 N., 13 W., 1 N., 2 W., 8 N., 10 W., 3 N., 12 W., 1 N., 3 W., 21 N.

10th row : P. 24 N., 2 W., 1 N., 11 W., 5 N., 8 W., 6 N., 19 W., 8 N.

11th row : K. 11 N., 17 W., 1 N., 2 W., 1 N., 10 W., 2 N., 15 W., 25 N.

12th row : P. 30 N., 5 W., 1 N., 6 W., 4 N., 24 W., 14 N.

13th row : K. 16 N., 23 W., 1 N., 5 W., 6 N., 5 W., 28 N.

14th row : P. 26 N., 5 W., 11 N., 4 W., 1 N., 19 W., 18 N.

15th row : K. 19 N., 15 W., 2 N., 4 W., 13 N., 6 W., 25 N.

16th row : P. 25 N., 5 W., 16 N., 3 W., 2 N., 12 W., 21 N.

17th row : K. 22 N., 14 W., 19 N., 5 W., 24 N.

18th row : P. 24 N., 4 W., 21 N., 3 W., 2 N., 6 W., 24 N.

19th row : K. 25 N., 9 W., 23 N., 3 W., 24 N.

20th row : P. 23 N., 4 W., 24 N., 6 W., 27 N.

21st row : K. 57 N., 4 W., 23 N.

22nd row : P. 23 N., 4 W., 57 N.

Repeat 21st and 22nd rows once.

25th row : K. 57 N., 3 W., 24 N. Work 22nd row, then 21st row.

28th row : P. 24 N., 3 W., 57 N.

29th row : K. 58 N., 4 W., 22 N.

30th row : P. 21 N., 5 W., 58 N.

31st row : K. 59 N., 5 W., 20 N.

32nd row : P. 19 N., 6 W., 59 N.

33rd row : K. 60 N., 4 W., 20 N.

34th row : P. 17 N., 7 W., 60 N.

35th row : K. 61 N., 8 W., 15 N.

36th row : P. 14 N., 9 W., 61 N.

37th row : K. 62 N., 7 W., 15 N.

38th row : P. 12 N., 9 W., 63 N.

39th row : K. 64 N., 9 W., 11 N.

40th row : P. 12 N., 7 W., 65 N.

41st row : K. 66 N., 8 W., 10 N.

42nd row : P. 11 N., 6 W., 67 N.

43rd row : K. 68 N., 7 W., 9 N.

44th row : P. 10 N., 5 W., 69 N.

45th row : K. 71 N., 5 W., 8 N.

With all navy s.s. 7 rows.

Cast off 6 st. at beginning of each of the next 2 rows.

Work 2 tog. at each end of every k. row until 64 st. remain.

Next row : P. 22, cast off 20 st. loosely, p. 22.

For the shoulder, work s.s. on 22 st. and work 2 tog. at each end of every k. row until 12 st. remain. Dec. at each end of every 2nd k. row (that is, every 4th row) until 6 st. remain. Work in s.s. for 3 inches and cast off.

Join wool to neck end of 22 remaining shoulder-st., and work as given for first shoulder.

With navy wool pick up and k. 86 st. evenly round neck. K. two rows and cast off loosely.

The Back

WORK exactly as given for front, but all navy, no seagull design, then sew the corresponding shoulders together.

With navy wool pick up and k. 72 st. evenly round each armhole. K. 2 rows and cast off loosely.

The Gusset

WITH navy wool cast on 2 st. and work in s.s., inc. 1 st. at each end of every k. row until there are 42 st. on the needle, then work 2 tog. at each end of every k. row until the st. are reduced to 2 again, which cast off.

To Make Up

PRESS all parts on the wrong side, putting a damp cloth over the knitting. Sew up the side seams of the leg, skirt and bodice. Sew along the ribbed parts of the inside leg seam, then sew the gusset into the opening left. Darn in all ends and sew down with machine silk of the same colour. Press seams well.

A white seagull on a navy blue ground will look most distinguished.

Such an attractive little petal cluster decorates the crown.

There is Nonchalant Perfection—

Never Before was there Such Wonderful Scope—

and * fold the wrong side over obliquely so that the right-hand edge lies horizontally under the last row of d.c. sewn to the next strip. Let the end (wrong side facing) pass under the next strip to the left, then sew the narrow end of the first strip to the left-hand side of the second strip, as far as it will go, which should be half-way down the unsewn side. Now take the end of the second strip, to which the first has just been attached, and repeat from *. Do this with every strip, when there should be a band of diagonal triangles with folded edge

The Petal Cluster Cap

THIS becoming little cap will suit almost everyone, as its unusual brim forms a trimming that is not so trying as the bare cap.

MATERIALS

2 ounces of Patons & Baldwins 4-ply " Beehive " Super Fingering in green, and a No. 10 bone crochet hook.

To Work.

THE cap is composed of 12 strips of crochet, each 1¾ inches wide, so you can work as many strips as required. With the No. 10 hook make 13 ch.
1st row : 1 d.c. in the 3rd ch. from the hook, * 1 ch., miss 1 ch., 1 d.c. in the next ch., and repeat from * 4 times more, 2 ch., turn.
2nd row: * 1 d.c. under the ch. after the first st., 1 ch., and repeat from * to end, working the last d.c. under the 2 ch. at end of row, 2 ch., turn.
Repeat the 2nd row 44 times.
Now work off to a point, thus:

5 d.c. with 1 ch. after each, then decrease by merging 2 st. into 1, thus: draw the wool through next space, making 2 loops on the hook, draw the wool through the last space, making 3 loops, wool over and draw through all three loops at once, 2 ch., turn.
Work 2 rows more with 5 d.c. in each. Continue in this way, working 3 rows with 4 d.c. in each, 3 rows with 3 d.c., then 2 rows of 2 d.c., and in the last row make 1 d.c., through which draw the wool and fasten off.
Work 11 strips more in this way.
Now sew all these strips together, beginning at the point which will be the middle of the crown. Oversew them on the wrong side for 5½ inches down, leaving the rest hanging. Take the end of the first strip

The Petal Cluster

THIS is sewn at the top of the hat, * make 13 ch., 1 tr. in the 5th ch. from the hook, 1 tr. in each of the next 5 st., 1 s.tr. (the cotton over the hook as for ordinary tr., but draw through all the three loops with one action) in next st., 1 d.c. in last st. Now, without breaking off, repeat from * 5 times more, then pass the wool through the single ch. left at the top of each petal and draw up. Sew through this point to the centre of the cap, then catch down lightly along both edges of the petals. Press inside the hat with a warm iron.

The cap is made of separate strips afterwards joined and twisted to form the brim.

free on the right side of the cap and the end sewn down in a perpendicular line underneath.

—in these PRETTY CAPS

For Inexpensive and Youth-Giving Millinery.

The Shell Pattern Cap

THE Shell Pattern Cap takes 1½ ounces of Patons & Baldwins' 4-ply Soft Knitting Wool and a No. 9 bone crochet hook, for a head measurement of 20 inches.

To Work

MAKE 4 ch. and form into a ring by sl.st. to first st.

1st round : 7 d.c. into the ring.

2nd round : 1 d.c. in each of 7 d.c., working into the back loop only at the top of the st.

The Shell Pattern Cap—it is most becoming.

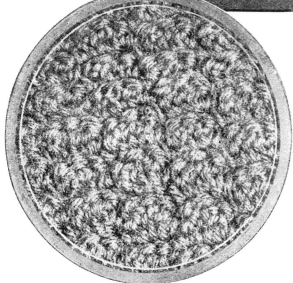

This is a circle showing the actual pattern.

3rd round : * 2 d.c. in each of the next 7 st. (count 14 d.c.) ; repeat from * twice more.

4th round : * 1 d.c., 1 tr., 1 d.c in the first st., miss 1 st., and repeat from * 13 times.

5th round : * 1 ch., 1 d.c., 1 tr., 1 d.c. in the top of the tr. on first group, and repeat from * in each of the next 13 groups.

6th round : Work the same group as in the 5th round, under the single ch. before each group, making 15 groups.

7th round : 1 ch., 1 d.c., 2 tr. and 1 d.c. in the single ch. before each group on previous round.

Work 2 rounds more as 7th round.

10th round : * 2 ch., 1 d.c., 3 tr., 1 d.c. in the single ch. before the group ; repeat from * all round.

Work 3 rounds more like the 10th round.

Now work 3 rounds more but put 3 tr. in the middle of each group and 3 ch. between the groups.

Work 17 rounds like the 10th round which completes the cap, but before fastening off try the cap on, to see whether more rounds are required, as heads vary so in depth.

GENERAL CROCHET AND KNITTING ABBREVIATIONS

Ch., chain; d.c., double crochet; tr., treble; sl., slip; st., stitch; k., knit plain; p., purl; tog., together; m.s., moss-st.

With a Touch of the MILITARY

Sheer Genius it Was to Combine a Suggestion of Military Smartness with this Irresistibly Feminine Crochet Cap and Cravat!

THIS smart little set of cap and cravat is carried out in royal blue and white in a simple double crochet

ABBREVIATIONS :
Ch., chain ; d.c., double crochet ; inc., increase ; sl.st., slipstitch.

MATERIALS :
Two ounces of Patons & Baldwin's 4-ply Super Fingering in white, and 2

ounces of the same wool in blue, will make both cap and cravat, using a No. 11 bone crochet hook

The Cap

WITH the blue wool make 5 ch., which form into a ring with a sl.st.
1st round : Into the ring work 5 d.c.
2nd round : 2 d.c. in each d.c.,

taking up both loops at the top of the st. throughout the cap.
3rd round : 2 d.c. in each d.c., counting 20 d.c. as the work proceeds. Tie a piece of white cotton to the first st. to denote the beginning of the rounds, as they are not joined at the end.
4th round : * 1 d.c. in first st., 2 d.c.

With a Touch of the Military

in the next to make an inc. of 1 st. Repeat from * all round.

5th round : 1 d.c. in each d.c.

6th round : Inc. in every 3rd d.c, 1 d.c. in the others.

7th round : Change to the white wool, and work 1 d.c.in each d.c.

8th round : Inc. in every 4th d.c.

9th round : 1 d.c. in each d.c.

10th round : Inc. in every 5th d.c.

11th round : 1 d.c. in each d.c.

12th round : Inc. in every 6th st.

Change to the blue wool, and from this point remember to change the colours after every 6 rows without further mention.

Continue working as given above—that is, increasing in alternate rounds, and in each successive inc. round work 1 d.c. more between the increases until the work measures 6¾ inches—in the cap illustrated to the end of the second blue band.

Work 18 rounds of 1 d.c. in each st. or according to the depth of the crown required. Fasten off.

The Chevron Trimming

WITH the white wool make 26 ch.

1st row : Miss the first ch. by the hook, then 1 d.c. in each st. to the end, making 25 d.c. altogether, 1 ch., turn. (This single ch. is used to facilitate turning and is not worked into at the end of rows.)

2nd row : Miss 1 d.c., 1 d.c. in each of 11 d.c., 3 d.c. in the next one, 1 d.c. in each of the next 10 d.c., miss 1, 1 d.c. in the last st., 1 ch., turn.

3rd row : Miss the first d.c., then 1 d.c. in each st. up to the middle one of the 3 worked in the centre st. of the last row, 3 d.c. in that st., then 1 d.c. in each d.c., but miss the one before the last.

Repeat the last row until there are 6 white, 6 blue, and 6 white rows, then fasten off.

Press the cap and the trimming with a hot iron over a damp cloth, then sew the trimming at one side of the cap.

The Cravat

WITH the blue wool make 40 ch.

1st row : 1 d.c. in the 2nd ch. from the hook, then continue 1 d.c. in each ch., making 39 d.c., 1 ch., turn. (This single ch. is for turning purposes only.)

2nd row : Miss 1 d.c., 1 d.c. in each of 18 d.c., 3 d.c. in the next d.c., 1 d.c. in each d.c., but miss the one before the last.

3rd row : Miss the 1st d.c., then 1 d.c. in each st. up to the centre one of the 3 worked in 1 st. ; then work 3 d.c. in that st., 1 d.c. in each d.c., but miss the one before the last.

Repeat the last row, changing the colour after every 6 rows. Cut the wool at each change of colour, and lay the cut end over the first few st. of the following row, so that it is covered with the d.c.

Repeat blue and white stripes until there are 23 stripes altogether, beginning and ending with a blue one. Fasten off and run in the end.

Press the scarf with a hot iron over a damp cloth.

For HOLIDAY-MAKERS !

Write to Barbara Mole, Our Holiday Expert

HIKING IN SCOTLAND

We are thinking of a walking tour in Scotland. Will you help with suggestions ?

I HAVE a list of twenty-five Walking Tour Itineraries in Scotland which not only give in the minutest detail the paths to follow right off the beaten track, so that you can easily find the nicest and best ways, but also particulars of accommodation to be found *en route*.

You need have no fear that a long day's trek will end you on a mountainside with only a stone wall for shelter !

These tours are planned for two weeks' duration, averaging about twelve miles a day, which is as much as one should attempt to manage on a long hike.

For instance, there is a planned walking tour of Loch Lomond and the Trossachs ; another from the Clyde to Oban ; Inveraray to Pitlochry ; the Isle of Skye ; North-West Scotland and Skye, and many others of equal attraction.

A copy of each tour, with all the details I have mentioned, costs 1s. 6d. I am sure one of these would help to make your holiday a great success.

*   *   *

LOG CABINS ON THE BEACH

Can you suggest somewhere in North Wales where my husband and I, with our little boy aged two and a half, could have a pleasant holiday on our own ?

THE first idea that comes to my mind is that you should hire a little beach hut. Right on the sands, fully equipped, where you would be able to cater for yourselves and enjoy a care-free holiday with every comfort and yet the joy of the open air—isn't that a delightful idea ?

To meet the demands of folk who love camping on their own, a great many caravan and little beach hut colonies are springing up by the beach at seaside resorts, such as between Rhyl and Prestatyn in North Wales ; on the sands by Clacton-on-Sea, and at various resorts along the South Coast and beauty spots in Devonshire.

Sweet Spring Bulbs

BULBS are long-suffering flowers. They are lifted, dried, and replanted annually with little regard to their welfare.

Many of the daffies are left in occupation of the same patch of soil year after year until they become massed together, and partly strangled for lack of room.

Yet in their friendly way they go on doing their best for us in all kinds of places.

Bulbs differ from seeds in that they contain food stores of their own sufficient to sustain them to the flowering stage even if they receive little in the way of nutriment from the soil. They can be grown in water or in fibre which contains little food value, but if you want to see what they really can achieve, treat them as friends and look after their comfort.

THE CHIEF ENEMY—DAMP !

THE chief enemy of all bulbs is damp. Even in wet gardens something can be done to keep them dry. When the hole is made for their reception trickle some sand into the bottom, then place the bulb upon it, and pour more sand around the sides. Sharp fine cinder ash will do as well.

Bulbs do not like manure in close proximity. Dig it in well below the roots. For the soil in their immediate surroundings bone meal is the best.

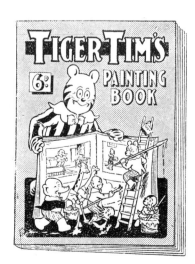

Jade-Green "Pretties"

Knitted in Shetland wool, these Cami-Bockers fit closely and warmly to the figure. They have Ribbon Shoulder-straps so that they can be worn with Day or Evening Dress

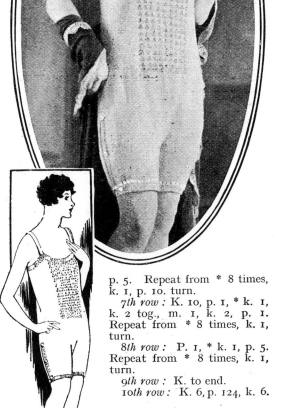

THIS little garment gives comfort without bulk, as it is worked in a fine wool which is accommodating to the figure, so the knitting does not require much shaping or too much extra width allowed for getting on and off.

There is an openwork panel, back and front, down to a low waist-line, but this can, of course, be made any length; those preferring more warmth may like to make a small yoke only by repeating the pattern row three or four times, or the extra busy girl who does not want to follow a pattern at all can work an easy ribbing for about two inches and do the rest in plain knitting.

The whole garment consists of three pieces only, the back and front (almost identical pieces), and a square gusset. The back and front pieces are both shaped at the sides, to make the latter shorter and give greater length at the centre of the garment; this allows for the extra " spring " required round the hip line. The fastening is down the side of the right leg only.

MATERIALS : 3½ ozs. of Shetland wool in a pale colour, less than ½ oz. of the same wool for the white stripe at top and knee bands, a pair of No. 9 bone knitting needles, 3 buttons, a stitch-holder, one yard of ribbon about one inch wide for shoulder straps, and 1½ yards of ½-inch elastic to thread through knee bands and at the underarms along the plain knitting.

SIZE AND TENSION : Working at a tension to produce 8 stitches to the inch in width the measurements on the diagram will be attained after light pressing only, and no stretching, so it

can be worn by figures varying from 34 to 38 inches bust measure, the latter size being worked with No. 8 needles.

ABBREVIATIONS . K., knit ; p., purl ; tog., together ; m., make by bringing the wool to the front of the needle ; s.s., stocking-stitch.

To KNIT : Begin at top of back with the main-coloured wool. Cast on 136 stitches, and do 20 rows of single ribbing (k. 1 and p. 1 alternately.) Leave coloured wool hanging.

21st row : With white wool, * k. 1, m. 1 (by passing wool over needle), k. 2 tog., k. 1. Repeat from * to end of row.

22nd row : All purl, and at end fasten off white wool.

23rd row : Take up coloured wool, k. 40, p. 1, * k. 1, k. 2 tog., m. 1, k. 2, p. 1. Repeat from * 8 times, k. remaining 41 sts.

24th row : K. 6, p. 35, * k. 1, p. 5. Repeat from * 8 times, k. 1, p. 34, k. 6.

25th row : K. 40, p. 1, * k. 2 tog., m. 1, k. 1, m. 1, slip 1, k. 1, pass the slipped st. over the knitted st., p. 1. Repeat from * 8 times, k. 41.

26th row : As 24th row.

27th row : K. 40, p. 1, * k. 5, p. 1. Repeat from * 8 times, k. 41.

28th row : As 24th row.

Repeat from 23rd to 28th row inclusive, 16 times more.

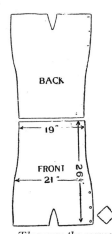

The low waist-line is now reached, and in the next 10 rows there is some shaping to make the sides a little shorter than the middle.

1st row of shaping : K. 40, p. 1, * k. 1, k. 2 tog., m. 1, k. 2, p. 1. Repeat from * 9 times, k. 31, turn, leaving 10 sts. un-knitted.

2nd row : P. 31, * k. 1, p. 5. Repeat from * 9 times, k. 1, p. 30, leaving 10 sts. unworked at this end.

3rd row : K. 30, p. 1, * k. 2 tog., m. 1, k. 1, m. 1, slip 1, k. 1, pass slipped st. over knitted st., p. 1. Repeat from * 8 times, k. 21, turn, again leaving 10 more sts. unworked.

4th row : P. 21, * k. 1, p. 5. Repeat from * 8 times, k. 1, p. 20, turn.

5th row : K. 20, p. 1, * k. 5, p. 1. Repeat from * 8 times, k. 11, turn.

6th row : P. 11, * k. 1,

p. 5. Repeat from * 8 times, k. 1, p. 10. turn.

7th row : K. 10, p. 1, * k. 1, k. 2 tog., m. 1, k. 2, p. 1. Repeat from * 8 times, k. 1, turn.

8th row : P. 1, * k. 1, p. 5. Repeat from * 8 times, k. 1, turn.

9th row : K. to end.

10th row : K. 6, p. 124, k. 6.

The Knicker Part

This begins here, and is worked in stocking-stitch, except for 6 sts. at the beginning of a plain row, and 12 sts. at end of row, which are worked in plain knitting on both sides, to produce garter stitch. The 12 stitches are for the under wrap on the side fastening.

1st row : * K. 2, m. 1 in next st. (by knitting first into front and then into back of same st.), thus making an increase. Repeat from * 13 times, k. 52, ** m. 1 in next st., k. 2. Repeat from ** 13 times. There should now be 164 sts.

2nd row : K. 6, p. 152, k. 6, and

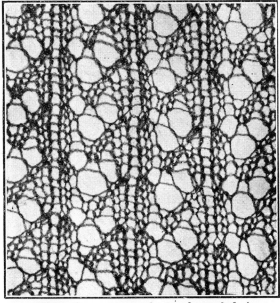

There is an openwork panel—worked in this pattern—at the back and front down to a low waist-line, but this, of course, can be made any length to suit the taste of the wearer.

BACK

19"

FRONT
21"

26"

These are the correct proportions when the cami-bockers are pressed out flat. The tiny gusset reinforces the legs.

3rd row : K. 164, cast on 6 sts. for opening at right side (170 sts.).

4th row : K. 12, p. 152, k. 6.

5th row : All knit.

Repeat last two rows until the work measures 7 inches from the beginning of the knicker part. Here the stitches are divided for the leg seams.

The Left Leg

1st row : K. 82, then turn, leaving remaining 88 sts. on holder for right leg.

2nd row : K. 6, p. 70, k. 6.

3rd row : All knit.

Repeat the 2nd and 3rd rows alternately until the leg seam is 5 inches, then drop coloured wool for the present without cutting and work 2 rows in white as described in 21st and 22nd rows at beginning of back.

Take up the coloured wool again and work 20 rows of single rib as at top of back. Cast off.

The Right Leg

On the remaining 88 sts., and beginning with the plain knitted side facing, knit plain.

2nd row : K. 12, p. 70. k. 6.

Continue this leg to match the left one, but remember always to knit 12 plain at the beginning of purl rows.

The Front

This is worked in the same manner as the back, with two slight differences. It is not necessary to cast on the 6 extra stitches given in the 3rd row of the knicker part ; simply continue the 6 garter-stitches, which wrap over the 6 cast-on stitches of back. On these 6 garter-stitches at this end of the row remember to make buttonholes ; on the original garment there are three, but more can be made if a closer fastening be preferred. Make the buttonholes thus : K. 3, cast off 3 sts., then continue row as usual ; on the return row cast 3 stitches on over those cast off, and this completes the buttonhole. The third (or last) buttonhole comes on the ribbed knee-band, and as this is folded over afterwards to make a double band two buttonholes must be worked on this ribbing, so that when it is folded over the two buttonholes lie over each other, and the edges are worked over with buttonhole silk. So make the first buttonhole as described above in this paragraph, on the 4th and 5th rows of the ribbing, and the second one on the 16th and 17th rows.

The Gusset

Cast on 21 st. and k. 27 rows. Cast off.

To Make Up

First press all pieces lightly on the wrong side, putting a slightly damp cloth over the knitting. Sew left side-seam from top to hem of knicker, on the wrong side.

Join right side from top as far as commencement of knicker part. Wrap the 6 sts. (cast on for side opening) under front part, and sew down.

Sew gusset in position, thus : Place one corner where the legs divide in front, and the opposite corner where the legs divide at back. Sew one side along front of right leg, the second side along front of left leg, and sew the other sides along back of left leg and back of right leg.

Make the seam joining back and front of left leg, and the corresponding seam of right leg.

Fold the ribbing at top in half, and make hem. Do the same at knicker edges, taking care when doing the right leg that the buttonholes on the knee band meet.

Insert elastic in top hem and in knee bands. Work buttonhole stitch round buttonholes, and sew buttons on back part of opening.

Sew shoulder-straps in position preferred, allowing them about 16 inches long, or according to individual measurement.

Each cosy measures three inches by three and a half, buttonholed all round in green wool with a little black hen appliquéd on the front.

BRIGHTER BREAKFASTS!

These jolly little egg-cosies in bright orange woolly cloth should deck the winter breakfast table

To make six of these gay little cosies, you will need a quarter of a yard of blanket-cloth, felt, or other woolly material, 36 inches wide ; two small scraps of black and green felt or serge ; a skein of green wool to match ; and a few strands of red filoselle or silko.

The big cosy on the left-hand side of the page is a quarter of an inch smaller than the finished cosy. Take a paper pattern of it by tracing it. Divide the width of the material into six, and fold each strip in half. Lay the pattern over and cut round it.

Buttonhole the Edge

Now take a needleful of green wool and buttonhole the pieces together in pairs, taking the stitches a little less than a quarter of an inch apart. Buttonhole across the base of the pieces, instead of making a hem.

The Appliqué

To appliqué the hen, trace over the design (given exact size) on to a scrap of black material. Cut this out exactly on the outline and buttonhole it neatly on to one side of the cosy with black cotton, indicating the feathers in the tail and the legs and claws in black cotton.

Transfer the grass patch on to the green material in the same way, and fasten it down as invisibly on the cosy as possible just under the hen's beak. Embroider the comb in red silk.

Trace over this design with carbon paper. It will show up quite well transferred on to the black material.

WHAT THEY ASK THE MATRON

We have persuaded the Matron of a big Welfare Centre, whose homely advice brings solace to dozens of mothers every week, to let us publish some of the queries just as they were brought to her, and the advice she gave the anxious mothers. That those who have little ones of their own will find the information invaluable we are confident.

THE EDITRESS.

A SORE TOOTH

My little boy has a sore tooth. He is four years old. I can see no signs of decay. Do you think at this age it is necessary to take him to the dentist?

A MOTHER should always take her child to the dentist when he complains of pain in a tooth, even if she can see no signs of decay. First teeth should be most carefully watched, for otherwise the second set may be defective.

A child who has a sore tooth and tries to bite on it is likely to avoid the pain, and either bolt the food or chew it on the other side of the mouth, which will make the jaw uneven.

From the age of two a child should be taken at least every six months to have his teeth inspected and cleaned.

* * *

LOW CEILINGS IN THE NURSERY

We are thinking of taking a flat at the top of a house where the rooms are rather low. Are low ceilings unhealthy in a nursery?

LOW ceilings are not unhealthy provided the rooms are not less than eight feet high.

The great necessity for children is plenty of *fresh* air. Try always to get a through draught, because stagnant air is bad air. Do all you can to keep the air moving. Even flapping a towel about will move the air.

* * *

THE BABY WHO CRIES AT NIGHT

My baby, aged four months, cries a good deal during the night although he takes his meals well and gains weight regularly. Can you suggest a reason?

SOMETIMES a baby will cry because he is tired of lying in one position.

A lift and a change of napkin are advisable. Be sure to keep the cot warm when he is removed.

Occasionally a baby cries because he is thirsty. If you give him a drink of cooled boiled water he will often fall asleep again.

* * *

BABY'S WEIGHT

I was alarmed recently to find that my baby, aged nine months, has not been putting on flesh at the same rate as the first six months. Why is this?

THIS is as it should be, and there is no cause for alarm.

A baby does not put on as much weight during the second half of the first year because his little muscles are more active. The first six months he mostly eats and sleeps.

You will now be able to judge your baby's progress better by his colour, brightness of eye and firm limbs than by weight alone.

The Buttercup Posy

Worked On A Crêpe-de-Chine Frock.

MORE simple embroidery! In fresh yellow, the buttercups are outlined in finest button-holing. The stems are back stitches, and the flower centres tiny green French knots.

The posy is tied with a bow of satin-stitch.

2 The Feminine Look 1932-35

Soft, loose-fitting sweaters characterize the change from the boyish-looking Twenties girl to the natural-looking feminine woman of the Thirties. Pretty pastel-colored sweaters with high waists, lacy puffed sleeves and capes are designed to flatter the natural curves of the figure and add height. Smart two-toned or striped sweaters and outfits are in brighter colors for the chic, well-dressed working girl.

The tri-colour scarf collar is a very gay affair.

The Correct Clothes Mean So Much Towards a Carefree Holiday.

TO WORK

Begin at the front waist-line, and with the beige thread and No. 12 needles cast on 140 sts. and work 32 rows of single rib (k.1, p. 1 alternately).

Change to No. 11 needles and begin the pattern.

1st row: With right side facing worker k. plain.

2nd row: K. 1, p. 1 alternately, (producing m.s. with the 4th row, when a p. is worked over a k. and vice versa).

3rd row: K. plain.

4th row: P. 1, k. 1 alternately.

Repeat these 4 rows until 102 rows have been worked above the waist ribbing, when the front neckline will be reached.

Divide the sts. for the shoulders thus: Work 66 in pattern, cast off 8 for the centre of the front neck, work 66 to end in pattern. Now pass the first 66 sts. on a spare needle or a stitch-holder with the point towards the neck. Continue the work on the last 66 sts.

THE RIGHT SHOULDER: The armhole shaping is also begun on this row.

1st row: Cast off 8 sts. at the beginning of this row, and work to neck, taking care to keep the pattern correct after casting off, but the pattern is so very easily seen that there is not the slightest difficulty.

2nd row: Cast off 3 sts. at the beginning of this row, work to armhole.

3rd row: Dec. 1 st. by taking 2 tog. at the beginning of the row and work to neck.

This jumper is knitted in a soft shade of beige and introduces a delightful colour scheme in its attractive scarf collar of red, blue and black.

MATERIALS:
6 1-oz. Kops of Knox's "Spider" Linen Jumper Thread size 0, shade No. 323 beige, 1 kop each of red, blue and black, a crochet hook No. 9, a pair of No. 12 and a pair of No. 11 long bone knitting needles.

ABBREVIATIONS:
K., knit plain; p., purl; st., stitch; dec., decrease; inc., increase; m.s., moss stitch; ch., chain; tr., treble.

TENSION AND MEASUREMENTS:
Worked at a tension of 8 sts. to the inch in width the following measurements are attained after light pressing; round the bust, 36 inches; length from shoulder to waist, 18 inches; underarm seam of sleeve, 2½ inches.

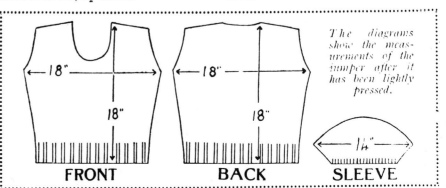

FRONT   BACK   SLEEVE

The diagrams show the measurements of the jumper after it has been lightly pressed.

A-Cruising We Will Go!

The Perfect Knitted Jumper for Days at Sea!

Repeat the last 2 rows 3 times more, which finishes the armhole shaping.

At the beginning of the next row cast off 3 sts. and work to armhole, and this will complete the neck shaping. There should now be 39 sts., on which continue in pattern until 66 rows can be counted from the first armhole row.

To slope the shoulder : * work to within 6 sts. of the end of the row (armhole end) turn and work back to neck. Repeat from * twice more, then cast off the remaining sts.

The Left Shoulder : Join the thread to the neck end of the first set of shoulder sts. and cast off 3 sts. for the first neck dec. This will come on the wrong side of the work and the first 8 sts. for the armhole shaping will

12 sts. will be decreased at each armhole, and 116 sts. left. Work on these sts. until you can count as many rows as on the armhole of the front, when the shoulder line will be reached.

To slope the back shoulders : Cast off 6 sts. at the beginning of each of

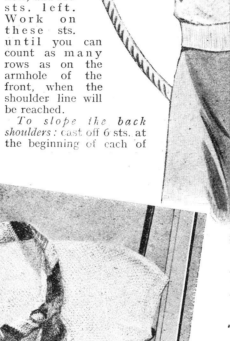

The jumper has such a pretty 'u' shaped neckline.

finishes the shaping of the top of the sleeve.

Work 12 rows in pattern on these sts., or if a little longer sleeve be desired more rows may be worked here. Work 10 rows of single rib and cast off.

Work the second sleeve in the same manner.

The Collar : With the No. 9 crochet hook and the blue thread make 34 ch:

1st row : 1 tr. in the 4th ch. from the hook, then 1 tr. in each st. to the end of the row. (This makes 32 tr. counting the 3 ch. at the beginning of the row, as 1 tr.)

2nd row : 2 tr. in the first st., 1 tr. in each st. to within 2 tr. of the end, take these last 2 sts. tog. thus : draw a loop through the top of the first tr., 2 loops on the hook, draw a loop through the last tr. when there will be 3 sts. on the hook, then work off these loops by twos as in the ordinary tr. so merging 2 sts. into 1, 3 ch., turn.

3rd row : Miss the first tr. over which the 3 ch. stands, 1 tr. into each st. taking up both loops at the top of the st. throughout the work.

Repeat the last 2 rows until there are 86 rows altogether, working 3 rows blue, 3 rows red, 3 rows beige, then one row of black, and repeat this order of colour to the end.

Now press all pieces on the wrong side, putting a damp cloth over the work and a thick blanket underneath.

To Make up the Jumper : With the beige linen thread sew up the shoulder seams on the wrong side, and beginning at the armhole end, sew through 1 k. st. on the front shoulder and one on the back, thereby taking up as many sts. from the back as there are on the front shoulder. Sew towards the neck on each shoulder. Now sew the top of the sleeves to the armholes, taking one st. from each piece at a time. Press these seams while the work is open.

Sew up the side and sleeve seams in one continuous line, in the same manner as described for the other seams, and press.

Sew the collar to the neck edge on the right side of the jumper as it folds over afterwards, and begin about 1½ inches up the left neck edge, from the centre front, and 11 inches from the end of the collar, sew right round to the centre front, so that the gap between the two ends is on the side of the neck. Tie over as desired □

be cast off on the right side at the beginning of the next row. Now work this shoulder to match the first.

THE BACK

Work exactly like the front up to the armholes, then cast off 8 at each side, then dec. 1 st. at the beginning of the next 8 rows, when

the next 10 rows, then cast off the remaining sts.

The Sleeves : Cast on 10 sts. and k. into the back of these sts. to set them. Now cast on 2 sts. at the beginning of each row until there are 78 sts. on, then cast on 9 st. at the beginning of each of the next 2 rows, to make 96 sts. altogether. This

With the NEW COWL Neck-line

A Sweetly Feminine Jumper—

measurements are attained after light pressing: round the bust, 37 inches, and from shoulder to edge of waist, 19½ inches. (Note that this material is very pliable and the expansion of the front collar will allow it to fall over a larger bust measurement, but the collar should not be dragged, it should fall in soft folds.)

To Work

BEGIN at the front edge by casting on 91 sts. and work in s.s. (k. on the right side and p. back) for 34 rows, when the lowest point of the neck line will be reached.

Next row : K. 45, m. 1, k. 1, m. 1, k. 45 to end of row.

Next row : P. back all the sts., including the two made loops, when there will be two extra sts.

Continued on page 66

The jumper looks so charming made in a pretty oyster shade.

A REAL summer jumper at last ! It is made with airy-fairy wings on the shoulders which just float away from the arm with every movement suggesting coolness and lightness itself.

MATERIALS :
Three skeins (two ounces each) of Darnley's Angel Yarn and a pair of No. 6 long bone knitting needles.

ABBREVIATIONS :
K., knit plain ; p., purl ; st., stitch ; m., make (by bringing the thread to the front of the needle so that it will pass over it when working the next st.) ; s.s., stocking-st.

IT *is very important that the tension of the work should be absolutely accurate, and it is advisable to practise until you get it right.*

TENSION AND MEASUREMENT :
Worked at a tension of 5 sts. to the inch in width, the following

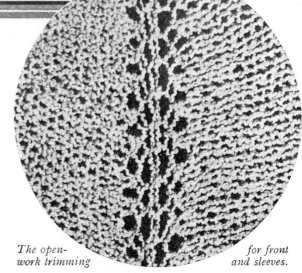

The open-work trimming   *for front and sleeves.*

A Cardigan for Tennis

It is So Easy to Knit!

Here's a gay, light-weight little coat to slip over your tennis frock.

MATERIALS :
3 ounces of Baldwin & Walker's "Ladyship" Scotch Fingering, 3-ply, in blue, also 1 ounce of white and about ¼ of an ounce of pink, so you may have some odd lengths that will work the beading of tr. sts. between the main part and the white bands ; also a pair of No. 11, and a pair of No. 7 long bone knitting needles, and a crochet hook No. 8.

ABBREVIATIONS :
K., knit plain ; p., purl ; st., stitch ; tog., together ; inc., increase ; dec., decrease ; m.s., moss-stitch, which is k. 1 and p. 1 alternately, and on successive rows a k. must always come over a purl and vice versa ; d.c., double crochet ; tr., treble ; d.tr., double treble.

The cardigan is of blue and white with a pretty beading of pink.

This photograph— *—shows the pink beading.*

TENSION AND MEASUREMENTS :
Worked at a tension of 11 sts. to 2 inches in width the coat is suitable for the average bust measurement of 34 to 36 inches ; it measures 7¾ inches across one half front just below the underarm, 18 inches across the back at the same place, 17 inches long from shoulder to hem, underarm seam of sleeve 3 inches.

To Work

Begin at the lower edge of the waist and cast on 220 sts. with blue wool and No. 11 needles for the main part of back and front, as there is no side seam.
Now work in single rib (k. 1, p. 1 alternately), inc. 1 st. at the beginning of the 3rd, 5th, 7th, 9th and 11th rows.
12th row : Rib until 18 sts. are left, cast off 7 for the buttonhole, and rib the remaining 11 sts.
13th row : Rib 11, cast on 7 sts. over those cast off, to complete the button-hole, and rib to end.

E

A CARDIGAN FOR TENNIS

Continue the rib, knitting 2 st. tog. at the beginning of the 15th, 17th, 19th, 21st and 23rd rows, when the sts. will be reduced to 220.

24th row : Cast off 20, rib 79 for left front and half of back, and slip these on a spare needle, cast off 4 sts., rib 13, and draw an odd length of wool through these for the centre back, cast off 4, rib 100, turn and cast off 21, which leaves 79 for the right side.

RIGHT SIDE.—Use No. 7 needles and work 10 rows in m.s.

On the next row k. 2 tog. at the beginning for front edge, and dec. in this way on every following 12th row, until 7 rows have been worked after the 5th dec. row (74 sts.).

Next row : M.s. 30 for one front, and slip the remaining 44 on a spare needle for the back.

RIGHT FRONT.—Cast on 8 sts. at the armhole end and m.s. 3 rows on all the sts. (38 sts.).

Next row : * K. 2 tog. at front edge, and inc. 1 at armhole end. M.s. 11 rows. Repeat from * until 5 rows have been worked after the 9th front dec. row, counting from the waist. Cast off.

RIGHT BACK.—Join the blue wool to the armhole end of the 44 back sts., and cast on 9. M.s. 6 rows on all sts. Continue m.s., inc. 1 st. at the armhole end of the next and every

following 12th row until 9 rows have been worked after the 3rd inc. row. Cast off.

LEFT SIDE.—Join the blue wool to the back end of the 79 left side sts., and with No. 7 needles m.s. 1 row. Now work as given for the right side, except that the front decreasings are worked by p. 2 tog. (with wrong side facing) instead of k. 2 tog. At the shoulder parts work 1 row less than on right side, which balances the extra row at the beginning of left side.

With the pink wool and crochet hook, join to waist edge of right front, and work 1 row of tr. at the front edge, shoulder, armhole, across top of back, and down the back edge. Take 1 tr. to every alternate row at row ends and on the cast-off edges miss every 5th st. To shape the corners work 2 tr., 1 d.tr., 2 tr., all into the corner st.

The White Straps

WITH the right side of work facing, use white wool and No. 7 needles, and k. 1 row on the 13 centre back sts. Work m.s. for 113 rows. Work 2 rows more, casting on 62 sts. at the beginning of each row (137 sts.), m.s. 8 rows more.

Next row : M.s. 57 and sl. on a spare needle for the right shoulder, cast off

23 sts. for the back of neck, m. s. 57 for the left shoulder.

LEFT SHOULDER : M.s. 12 rows. Cast off 44 sts. at the beginning of the next row (armhole end), which leaves 13 sts., and on these m.s. 120 rows and cast off.

RIGHT SHOULDER.—Join the white wool to the neck end of the right shoulder-st. and m.s. 11 rows. Cast off 44 at the beginning of next row, then on the remaining 13 sts. work 120 rows in m.s., and cast off.

With the white wool work 1 d.c. in each st. across the back of the neck.

To MAKE UP.—Press all parts except the ribbing, putting a damp cloth over the knitting and a thick blanket underneath.

Sew the back part of the white strap to the back and back shoulders, then sew fronts and front shoulders to the front parts of straps. Sew the waist edge of the front straps to the rib at the waist.

With white wool and No. 11 needles pick up and k. 62 sts. at the armhole edge. Rib 11 rows and cast off very loosely.

Work the second armhole in the same manner. Sew the underarm seams and press. Sew the button to the left-front waistband opposite the buttonhole. THE END

With the NEW COWL NECK-LINE

Continued from page 64

Repeat the last 2 rows 12 times more, on each repetition of the k. row, working 1 k. st. more before the first-made st., and 1 k. st. more after the second-made st., so that there will be 2 extra sts. on every k. row, when the armhole will be reached.

To shape the armhole * dec. at both ends of the row by k. tog. the second and third st. from the end, p. back the next row. Repeat from * 14 times more, all the time keeping up the centre " made " sts.

Next row : K. 27, turn, leaving the rest of the sts. for the present.

Work 3 rows more on these 27 sts. and cast off.

Join the thread to the first st. next to the shoulder just worked, and cast off the sts. to within 27 of the end. On these sts. work 3 rows more in s.s. to match the first shoulder, and cast off.

The Back

THIS is worked exactly like the front to the end of the armhole shaping (but without the " made " sts. at

centre), then cast off right across without working the short rows on the shoulder.

Shoulder Straps and Epaulettes

CAST on 21 sts. and work in single rib for 30 rows. Now work in s.s. like the front, making 1 st. before and after the centre st. for 30 rows, at the same time increasing 1 st. at both ends of every third row. Now work 2 rows of plain s.s. without any increase, and cast off all the sts.

Work the second shoulder strap in the same way.

The Sash

CAST on 26 sts. and work in single rib for 34 inches, or according to length of sash required to hang over. Short ends can be folded over and caught together with a scarf pin or small safety-pin.

To MAKE UP THE JUMPER.—First sew the shoulder straps to the front shoulders, beginning at the neck end and continue the sloping edge of the

epaulette to the armhole, to within about 1½ inches of the beginning of the armhole, which is left open.

Sew the back on in the same way, counting the same number of sts. from the arm end towards the neck, for the starting point for sewing, the intervening sts. between the two shoulder straps forming the back neckline. Now press this sewing and the whole of the work while it is open.

Sew up the side seams, leaving the left side seam open for about 3 inches at the waist. To sew on the sash, pin the centre of the sash to the right side seam, or if you prefer uneven ends adjust accordingly here. Now measure the size of waistband required and pin each half at the left side seam accordingly, then tack the two halves in position, easing on the back and front. Oversew the jumper on the wrong side, and press it. Round the neck and sleeve edge work a row of d.c., missing every fourth st.

THE END

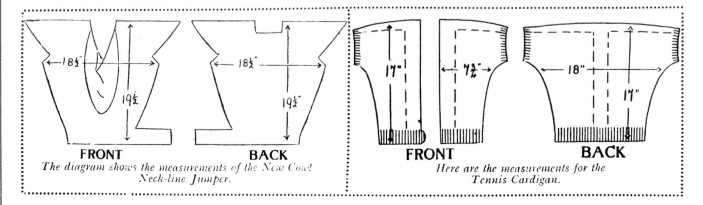

FRONT **BACK**
The diagram shows the measurements of the New Cowl Neck-line Jumper.

FRONT **BACK**
Here are the measurements for the Tennis Cardigan.

The MAGPIE SET

Such a Smart Out-fit of Jumper, Scarf and Cap!

It is chic without sleeves, but may be worn over a blouse.

Black and white is always smart, and this set of jumper, cap and cravat will prove ever-useful. The woollen jumper gives the little extra warmth for days not too warm, and at the same time allows for sleeveless freedom. It would look very smart worn over a white blouse for those who want sleeves.

Abbreviations:

Ch., chain; d.c., double crochet; tr., treble; sl., slip; st., stitch; k., knit; pl., plain; p., purl.

Materials:

For the jumper, 2½ ounces of 3-ply Super-fingering in black and 1½ ounces of white; for the cravat, ½ an ounce of each colour of the same wool; and for the cap, 1 ounce of black and ½ an ounce of white; one Stratnoid crochet hook No. 8, and one No. 11; also a pair of No. 8 Stratnoid knitting needles.

Tension and Measurements

Worked at a tension to produce 5 d.c. to the inch in width on the jumper with the No. 8 hook, the jumper measures 31 inches round the bust after light pressing, and is 17 inches long from shoulder to hem. This size is therefore suitable for the small figure of about 28 inches round the bust.

To Work the Jumper

Begin with 75 ch.

1st row : Miss the first ch., 1 d.c. in each ch. to the end, making 74 d.c.

Work 20 rows of d.c. on these st. altogether, taking up both loops at the top of the st. to produce flat d.c.

21st row : Work 32 d.c., turn without ch., working the last d.c. rather loosely. Work 34 rows more on these st., when the yoke line will be reached.

1st row of yoke slope : Miss the first d.c., then 1 d.c. in each st. to the end.

2nd row : 1 d.c. in each st. to within 2 of the end; here decrease by working 2 st. together, thus : Draw the wool

through the first st., making another loop on the hook; repeat in the second st., making 3 loops, then wool over and draw through all three loops.

Repeat the last 2 rows until there is only 1 st. left.

For the second half-front, go back to the last long row on the front and, beginning at the side edge, work as directed from the first short row of 32 d.c. This will leave 10 d.c. unworked in the middle of the row.

The Front Yoke

This begins with the little vest, for which, using the white wool, work 1 d.c. in each of the 10 d.c. left between the two half-fronts. Work 10 rows of flat d.c. on these st. Turn without ch. as on the first front edge. Now increase 1 st. at the beginning of the next row (by working 2 in 1 st.),

then at the beginning of every third row until 5 st. are added. These increases must come at alternate ends. Continue on these 15 st. until there are 35 rows altogether on this little front.

Still using the white wool, work 1 d.c. in the single d.c. on the last row of the point on left shoulder, then working down the curve put 1 d.c. at the end of each row, making 32 altogether, 1 d.c. in each st. across the top of the white front and 32 d.c. in the end of the rows of the second front, working the last into the single d.c. at the top of the point. Work 10 rows of d.c., increasing 1 st. at the beginning of each row, 89 st. altogether.

On the next 11 rows decrease 1 st. at the beginning of the row and 1 st. in a line with the first st. of the white vest, and 1 st. in a line with the last st. of the vest, then 1 d.c. in each st. to the end of

The MAGPIE SET

the row. When 11 rows have been worked in this way, there will be 33 st. less and 56 along the row, on which work 3 rows of d.c. and fasten off.

The Waistband

WITH No. 8 needles and the black wool, pick up a st. at the bottom of every d.c. on the foundation row and work 20 rows of single rib (k. 1 and p. 1 alternately), and cast off rather loosely.

The Back

BEGIN as directed for the front, but continue the long rows of d.c. until there are 66.

67th row : Work 17 d.c. only and turn. Now decrease 1 st. at the yoke edge of every row as described on the front, until there is only 1 st. left, draw wool through and fasten off. Now begin at the side edge of the last row and work the same small point at the opposite end, leaving 44 st. free in the middle.

The Back Yoke

WITH the right side facing worker and using the white wool, work 1 d.c. into the space at the end of the row, at the top of the little point, and continue down the end of the rows on this point, working 17 d.c. altogether, then 1 d.c. in each of the 44 st. across the middle of the back and 17 d.c. up the side of the second point, making 78 st., turn with 1 ch.

Work 10 rows more, increasing 1 st. at the beginning of each row (88 st.).

Now work 13 rows, decreasing 3 st. on each row, thus : One at the beginning of the row, one in a line with the 17th d.c. of the first row, which comes at the end of the little slope, and one on a line with the 17th st. from the opposite end. When these rows are finished there will be 49 st. along the row, on which work another row of d.c. and fasten off.

The Armlets

FIRST sew up the shoulder seam along the end of 14 rows from the neck edge. Now count down 40 rows from the first black row at the top of the little point, and mark that row with a small safety-pin. Work 26 d.c. along the end of these rows ; that will mean missing one here and there so that the 26 d.c. spread evenly over the end of 40 rows of d.c. Work 8 d.c. across the end of the white rows up to the shoulder seam, then repeat down the back 8 d.c. on the white rows and 26 d.c. along the end of 40 rows down the back (68 d.c. in the row).

Work 8 rows of d.c., decreasing 1 st. at the beginning of each row, and 1 st. in the centre on a line with the shoulder seam, then a final row of 1 d.c. in each st. and fasten off.

Work the second armlet in the same way.

Sew up the sides of the little vest with white wool, on the wrong side, then press all the work on the wrong side, putting a slightly damp cloth over it and a thick blanket underneath. Sew up the side seams on the wrong side and press these seams.

The Cap

THIS is worked with the No. 11 hook, beginning at the middle of the crown with the black wool. Make 4 ch. and form into a ring by sl.st. to the first st.

1st round : 5 d.c. into the ring. Do not sl.st. at the end of rounds, but mark the first st. with a piece of cotton to denote the beginning of the next round.

2nd round : 2 d.c. in each st., taking up both loops at the top of the st. throughout the work.

3rd round : 2 d.c. in each st.

4th round : * 1 d.c. in the first st., 2 d.c. in the next to increase a st., repeat from * all round.

5th round : 1 d.c. in each st.

6th round : Increase in every 3rd d.c.

7th round : 1 d.c. in each st.

8th round : Increase in every 4th d.c.

Continue in this way, increasing in every alternate round, each time working one st. more between the increases until the circle measures 7 inches across ; but after the 15th round fasten off the black wool and take up the white. There will be 11 rounds of white before the black is taken up again.

Work three rounds of 1 d.c. in each st., then do another increase round, putting one d.c. more between the increases than in the last increase round. This round determines the head measurement, which should be about 20 inches. This will, of course, stretch further, or it can be contracted by working the tr. band shorter.

From now proceed with rounds of 1 d.c. in each st. and after the 11 white rounds work 32 rounds of black, or according to depth of crown required. This must be the full depth, as the white band turns over to the outside of the cap.

The White Band

WITH the No. 8 hook make 15 ch., then 1 tr. in the 4th ch. from the hook, 11 tr. more ; turn with 3 ch., * miss the first tr. over which the 3 ch. stands, 1 tr. in each remaining st. to the end of the row, taking up both loops at the top of the st., and repeat from * until the band is long enough to go round the cap, and if you want the cap to grip the head, make it one inch shorter than the edge of the cap and stretch on in sewing. Oversew to the edge of cap on the right side, sew the first and last row of tr. together, then turn the band over the right side of cap, and press well in position.

The Cravat

WITH No. 8 hook and black wool make 41 ch.

1st row : Miss the first ch., then 40 d.c. along the row, working the last st. fairly loosely so as to turn on that st. without any ch.

2nd row : 2 d.c. in the first st., then 1 d.c. in each st. up to the last, which leave unworked ; there will still be 40 d.c. along the row.

3rd row : 1 d.c. in each st. of the previous row.

Repeat the last two rows 9 times more, but finish the last row with 3 ch.,

and join on the white wool.

** The 3 ch. will stand for the first tr., then put 1 tr. in the first d.c., this will make the increase of 1 st. ; then 1 tr. in each st. along the row, except the last one, 3 ch., turn. Miss the first tr., then 1 tr. in each st. to the end of the row. Repeat from ** once more, and fasten off the white wool.

Change to black wool and begin to decrease at one edge, thus : * 2 d.c. in first st. as usual, then 1 d.c. into each st. until within 4 st. of the end, then work the first 2 st. as 1 d.c. and the last 2 st. as 1 d.c., turn without ch. ; miss the first d.c. and work 1 d.c. in each st. to end of this row. Repeat from * until there are only 15 d.c. in the row, but after 10 rows of black change to white, and continue with white wool until further notice. Work back to the straight edge, putting 1 d.c. into each st.

Work the 2nd and 3rd rows 26 times.

The shaping of the opposite end of the cravat is now begun and the edge which has been kept straight must now be sloped. The slope will be on the opposite edge to the other end.

** 2 d.c. in the first st., then 1 d.c. in each st. except the last, turn without ch. and work 1 d.c. in each st. up to end, then 1 extra d.c. in the last st. Repeat from ** until there are 40 d.c. in the row, but change from white to black wool when you have 30 d.c. in the row, so that the last 10 rows are black.

Work the 4 tr. rows and the 21 rows of black d.c., as at the beginning, and fasten off.

How To Join Wools

To Help You When Knitting Up

AFTER knitting the stitches required with the first colour, place the second colour behind the next stitch to be knitted, on the left-hand needle, leaving about 3 inches hanging below the stitch, and hold it in this position with the forefinger of the left-hand. Pass the first colour over the second one, then knit the first stitch with the second colour. (For further security the end of the new colour may be tied to the main length with a single knot to prevent the wool slipping.)

When working a mingled pattern in alternate colours, let the wool out of action, lie behind the single stitch.

SO COMPLETELY FEMININE!

SO COMPLETELY FEMININE !

The Young Girl Looks Her Sweetest In a Butterfly Collar.

IT is the sweetest little woolly you ever saw—and the butterfly revers are knitted, too !
The moss-stitch pattern is easy to do.

MATERIALS : 4 oz. of " Greenock " Scottish Fleece (from the Scotch Wool & Hosiery Stores) in white and an oddment of green, or other colour preferred for the tiny edging round the collar. A pair of No. 7 and a pair of No. 6 long bone knitting needles, and a No. 1 steel crochet hook.

ABBREVIATIONS : K., knit ; p., purl ; st., stitch ; m.s., moss-stitch ; d.c., double crochet ; ch., chain ; tr., treble ; sl.-st., slip-stitch.

TENSION AND MEASUREMENTS : Worked at a tension of 6 sts. to the inch in width, the measurements on the diagram are attained after pressing.

TO WORK

BEGIN at the front waistline, and using No. 7 needles cast on 95 sts. Work 16 rows of single rib (k. 1, p. 1 alternately).
Change to No. 6 needles and proceed in m.s. (k. 1, p. 1 alternately, but on succeeding rows the k. must come over a p. and vice versa). Work 60 rows when the armhole will be reached For a longer jumper more rows may be worked here before shaping the armhole.

To SHAPE THE ARMHOLES : Cast off 8 sts. at the beginning of each of the next 2 rows, then decrease 1 st. at the beginning of each of the next 6 rows, when 11 sts. will be decreased at each armhole, 73 sts. on.

THE NECK OPENING : Work 36 sts. in m.s. and leave these on a spare needle for the left shoulder. Cast off 1 st. at the centre of the neck, work m.s. on the remaining 36 sts.

THE RIGHT SHOULDER : Working on the last set of sts. decrease 1 st. at the neck end of every 4th row, until 6 sts. are decreased away. On the remaining sts. work until 35 rows can be counted along the neck edge, then cast off. Join the wool at the neck edge of the first set of sts. and work the left shoulder to correspond.

THE BACK : Work as directed for the front until the armhole shaping is finished, after which work straight up for 20 rows more.
To slope the shoulders cast off 5 sts. at the beginning of each of the next 10 rows and decrease 1 st. at the beginning of the next 3 rows, then cast off the remaining sts.

THE SHOULDER PIECES : Cast on 24 sts. with the No. 7 needles and work single rib for 4 inches. Cast off 12 sts. at the beginning of the next row, after which cast off 1 st. at the same end of every alternate row, until the sts. are reduced to 3. Cast off.
Work the second shoulder strap in the same way, as it is reversible.

THE BUTTERFLY COLLAR

THIS is a large collar spreading over the full width of the front, but it works off to nothing at the shoulder seam, and does not go round the back.
Cast on 60 sts. with No. 6 needles and work 8 rows in m.s. Now increase 1 st. at the beginning of each of the next 8 rows. Cast on 11 sts. at the beginning of the next 2 rows (90 sts. on). Work 10 rows straight on these sts.
Here the sts. are divided for the V neck. Work 45 sts.
On the next row decrease 1 st. by taking 2 tog. according to the pattern, at the neck end. (This is done on

every 4th row at the neck end.) Work to the end of the row and turn. *At this end of the row (outside edge) decrease 1 st. on alternate rows until there are 5 decreases on this edge. Work 2 rows, keeping the outside edge straight, then work 10 rows increasing 1 st. on alternate rows on the outside edge, at the same time decreasing as before at the neck edge. Repeat from * once more.
Now decrease 1 st. on every alternate row at the neck edge and on every row at the outside edge, until the sts. are reduced to 5, and cast off.

THE SLEEVES

BEGIN at the arm-band by casting on 60 sts. with No. 7 needles and work single rib for 6 rows. Change to No. 6 needles and inc. in every alternate st., making 90 sts., on which work m.s. for 5 inches.
To shape the top of the sleeve cast off 10 sts. at the beginning of the next 2 rows, then cast off 2 sts. at the beginning of each of the next 10 rows. Cast off the remainder.
Work the second sleeve in the same manner.

TO MAKE THE JUMPER

FIRST press all pieces on the wrong side, putting a damp cloth over the knitting ; press lightly and do not drag, as the knitting is fairly loose. Now sew the front shoulders to the straps, the shorter side of the latter being towards the front ; ease the front a little. Sew the sloping back shoulders to the opposite edge of the strap, beginning at the armhole in each case. Now stitch the collar to the right side of the jumper, putting one end of it to the back point of the left shoulder strap, and oversew to the corresponding point on the opposite shoulder.

EDGING THE COLLAR

ROUND the edge of the collar and the back of the neck work with the green wool and crochet hook, putting 1 d.c. in each k. st., but to avoid fluting through loose working, miss a st. here and there if found necessary. At the end of the round work * 6 ch., sl.-st. back into the 3rd ch. to form a picot, 3 ch., miss 1 d.c. along the first row, 1 d.c. in the next st. and repeat from * all round.
The centre front of the collar is drawn up and kept in position with a little crochet strap, which work as follows : Work chain-st. for a length of 3½ inches, 1 tr. into the 5th ch. from the hook, * 2 ch., miss 2 ch., 1 tr. in the next st. ; repeat from * to the end, turn and work d.c. all round this little piece, and fasten off.
Sew one end of it about 1 inch below the V on the front of the jumper, pass the strap over the centre of the collar, and sew the opposite end, just over the neck edge, on the wrong side. Now press the seams first worked, and this edging.
Sew the sleeves into the armholes easing round the top, and press, taking only 1 st. at a time from each side, so that this seam is quite flat. Sew up the sleeves and side seams in one continuous line, in the same manner, to produce a flat seam, and press.

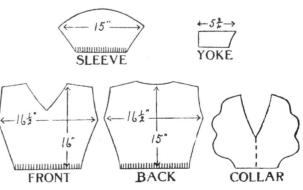

Work to these measurements.

AN INTERESTING NECKLINE

Just above is a photograph showing
the stitches in detail

An Interesting NECKLINE!

A Jumper Which Has New Features Without Being Too Short Waisted

3RD ROW : 41 medium, 1 light, 94 medium.

4TH ROW : P. all medium.

5TH ROW : 40 medium, 1 light, 1 medium, 1 light, finish the row in medium.

6TH ROW : As 4th row. Each alternate row will be worked in the same way unless stated otherwise. When working these rows keep the light wool to the purl side of the work.

7TH ROW : 41 medium, 1 light, 1 medium, and 1 light.

9TH ROW : 40 medium (1 light, 1 dark) twice, 1 light, and finish medium.

It will be noticed that the right side of the two-colour piece is kept straight, but the opposite edge gradually widens, forming an oblique line from the ribbing to the shoulder. The 11th row will therefore have 3 light st. like the 9th row, and the 13th and 15th row will have 4 light st. There are two rows with the same number of light st. because one row begins with a light green and, the next 2-colour row with a medium green, so that the colours on both edges of the diagonal piece are alternated.

Continue the two-colour piece as described above, with the plain colour each side, until 78 rows have been worked above the ribbing, when the underarm will be reached. There should be 19 light green st. across the diagonal front.

THIS jumper is worked in two shades of green. The main part in the darker shade, while the diagonal front and lower sleeves have alternate stitches in light green.

The ribbing is worked on the coarser needles, to give more spring on the hips than usual, but the finer needles (No. 10) may be used for this, if preferred.

The jumper is all knitted in stocking-stitch, plain knitting on the front of the work and purl at the back.

MATERIALS : Patons & Baldwins'"Azalea" crochet wool was used for the original, in the proportion of 7 ounces of the medium green shade and 1 ounce of the lighter shade, with a pair of needles, No. 10 and No. 8.

ABBREVIATIONS : K., knit plain ; p., purl ; s.s., stocking-stitch ; st., stitch or stitches ; tog., together ; inc., increase. Directions in brackets are worked the number of times stated after the brackets.

TENSION AND MEASUREMENTS : Worked at a tension of 7 st. to the inch in width, with the No. 10 needles the following measurements are attained after light pressing : Round bust, 38 inches ; length from shoulder to hem, 19¼ inches ; underarm seam of sleeve with cuff, 20½ inches.

THE FRONT : Begin at the front waistline by casting on 136 st. with the No. 8 needles, and work a ribbing of k. 2 and p. 2 for 4 inches.

Change to No. 10 needles and work 6 rows of s.s. finishing with a purl row.

The two-colour diagonal front is now begun. (See previous page for How to join the Wools.)

1ST ROW : K. 40 medium green, join on light green and k. 1, passing the first colour over the second before working the first st. of the second colour, k. 95 medium green.

2ND ROW : P. all medium.

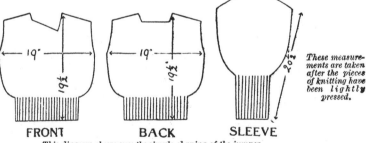

FRONT   BACK   SLEEVE

These measurements are taken after the pieces of knitting have been lightly pressed.

This diagram shows you the simple shaping of the jumper and the proportions to follow

To shape the armholes, cast off 2 st. at the beginning of each of the next 12 rows, at the same time continuing the diagonal line of the front. There will be 112 st. left on which work 22 rows straight, when the neck line will be reached.

THE LEFT SHOULDER

WORK 42 st. in the same order as before, turn and work back to armhole. Work 40 rows more on these st., keeping both edges straight, when the back neck-line will be reached. Cut and fasten off both wools.

Return to the neck edge, and on the remaining st. work in the same order of pattern, decreasing 1 st. at the neck edge of each of the next 28 rows, and keeping the two-colour edge straight at the arm side ; the only slope will be on the neck edge. When 28 st. have been decreased at the neck edge continue in the same pattern on the remaining stitches, until there are as many rows on this part above the armhole shaping, as there are on the opposite shoulder. Finish at the neck end with a purl row, then cast on 24 st. for the back of the neck.

Continued on page 77

"The pinafore jumper speaks for itself"

For pattern see p. 97

73

"A knitted moss-stitch jumper (crochet-trimmed)"

For pattern see p. 22

"A clever trimming with crocheted rings"

For pattern see p. 100

"A man's swimming suit"

For pattern see p. 96

Continued from page 72

using the light and medium wool alternately, then work across the first shoulder stitches.

Work 13 rows more, with medium wool at the beginning and end of needles, and the centre st. (comprising bands at side of neck and the back neck st.) in the two-colour pattern. Fasten off the light wool.

Work 26 rows in the one colour, keeping both edges straight, then work 22 rows more, increasing 1 st. at the beginning only, of each row. Continue straight down on these st. until as many rows as on the front side seam can be counted, not measured. Finish off with the ribbing to match the front, changing to No. 8 needles for this part.

THE SLEEVES

BEGIN at the wrist and with No. 8 needles and medium green wool, cast on 40 st. and work in rib to match the waist. Inc. 1 st. at the beginning and end of the 12th row, and every following 12th row until there are 56 st. on, taking the extra st. gradually into the rib pattern.

Now change to No. 10 needles and work 1 row plain, inc. in every 4th st. (by k in the front and back of st.) until 14 st. are added. Work 11 rows more, inc. 1 st. at both ends of each p. row when 12 st. will be added.

On the next row the two-colour pattern will begin, so take the light wool and work 1 st. light and 1 medium alternately. Repeat these rows 12 times more, inc. 1 st. at both ends of every 4th row, when there will be 74 st. Fasten off the light wool and continue the medium shade for 60 rows more, or the length required for the underarm seam, bearing in mind that they stretch in wear.

To shape the top of the sleeve cast off 6 st. at the beginning of each of the next 4 rows, then cast off 2 st. at the beginning of each row until only 20 remain. Cast off all.

Work the second sleeve to match.

TO MAKE UP THE JUMPER

FIRST sew in any ends, paying particular attention to the two-colour work. Now press the knitting on the wrong side, putting a damp cloth over the work and a thick blanket underneath to emboss the colour work. Sew in the sleeves taking 1 st. from each piece at a time to make a flat line, then press this seam while the work is open. Stitch up the underarm and sleeve seams in one continuous line, and press.

SIMPLE CUTWORK MOTIFS

For a Linen Duchess Set or Dainty Guest Towels.

A runner and three mats make up the duchess set.

First outline the design with tiny stitches, working the bars as you come to them. Take the thread across the bar, make a back stitch— then buttonhole over the thread, not through the material. Buttonhole round the design and cut away the material beneath the bars.

Who Likes a Pretty NEGLIGEE?

An Enchanting Cross-Over Design

Pale mauve, with white wool for the trimmings, makes the daintiest dressing jacket, especially when knitted in a light lace stitch, with Irish crochet for the white roses. The pattern is very easy too, consisting of two identical rows of pattern, separated by a plain knit row and a purl row.

MATERIALS: 4 ozs. of Greenock 2-ply Super Fingering No. 241, lilac, and 1 oz.

of white; a pair of knitting needles No. 11 and No. 7, and two spare needles; a bone crochet hook No. 13 and No. 9.

ABBREVIATIONS: K., knit; p., purl; tog., together; m., make (by bringing the wool to the front of the needle);

st., stitch; ch., chain; sl., slip; st., stitch; d.c., double crochet; tr., treble; inc., increase; directions in brackets are worked the number of times stated immediately after the brackets.

TENSION AND MEASUREMENTS: Worked at a tension of 11 stitches to 2 inches in width the following measurements are attained after light pressing: 18 inches across the back at the underarm; 12 inches across each front at the dip of the scallop, but when the revers are folded over there is an actual bust measurement of 34 inches. Length from centre of shoulder line to edge of waist 17 inches; underarm seam of sleeve without scallops 12 inches.

To Work

Begin with the sleeves at the flounce, which is worked short ways.

Cast on 18 sts. with No. 7 needles and work in lace pattern as follows:

1st row: With right side facing k. plain.

2nd row: K. 3, * m. 1, k. 2 tog., repeat from * until 3 remain, k. 3.

3rd row: Cast on 2 sts. to increase the scallop, then work as second row.

4th row: K. plain.

Repeat these 4 rows once more, casting on 2 sts. at the beginning of the 1st and 3rd row which gives 24 sts.

Repeat the 4 rows straight 3 times (note that the 3rd row without inc. is worked like the 2nd row). Repeat the 1st and 2nd row, then cast off 2 sts. at the beginning of the 3rd row, work 4th row, then work 4 pattern rows again, casting off 2 sts. at the beginning of the 1st and 3rd row. There are again 18 sts. on the row and 28 rows worked. Repeat these 28 rows 4 times more, which completes the flounce. Beginning at the scallop end, cast off until only 1 st. remains.

Now pick up and k. 70 sts. from the row-ends at straight edge of flounce for the upper part of the sleeve. Continue in pattern, beginning with 2nd row (the 2nd and 3rd rows now begin and end with k. 1 instead of k. 3) until the 18th pattern has been completed, or more if a longer sleeve be desired.

TO SHAPE THE TOP OF THE SLEEVE: Cast off 2 sts. at the beginning of every row until only 14 sts. remain, then cast off all.

Work the second sleeve in the same manner.

THE LEFT FRONT AND TIE.—Begin at the lower edge and with No. 7 needles and lilac wool cast on 190 sts. K. 6 rows, casting on 2 sts. at the beginning of 3rd and 5th row for tie end. Work 2nd pattern row, casting on 2 sts. at the beginning (196 sts.) and k. 3 border at each end. Work 15 rows straight in pattern with k. 3 border, beginning with 3rd row and ending with the 1st row. Work 4 rows more, casting off 2 sts. at the beginning of 1st and 3rd of these rows.

Next row: Cast off 2 sts., k. 153, * m. 1, k. 2 tog., repeat from * until 3 remain, k. 3.

Next row: K. 3 (m. 1, k. 2 tog.) 17 times, k. 153.

Next row: Cast off 150, k. 40. Cut the wool and leave the sts. on a spare needle.

THE BACK WAIST.—With No. 11 needles and lilac wool cast on 120 sts. Work 30 rows of single rib (k. 1 and p. 1 alternately). Cut wool and leave until needed.

THE RIGHT FRONT AND TIE.—With

A close up photograph showing the scalloped edge and one of the roses.

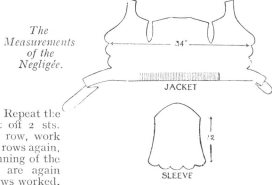

The Measurements of the Negligée.

lilac wool and No. 7 needles cast on 88 sts. and k. 7 rows, casting on 2 sts. at the beginning of 3rd, 5th and 7th row, which gives 94 sts. Work 17 rows in pattern with a k. 3 border at both ends. Beginning with a 2nd row and ending with a 2nd row. Cast off 2 sts. and work the 3rd pattern row. K. 2 rows, casting off 2 sts. at the beginning of the 2nd row.

Next row: K. 3 (m. 1, k. 2 tog.) 17 times, k. 53.

Next row: Cast off 2, k. 51 (m. 1, k. 2 tog.) 17 times, k. 3. K. 1 row.

Next row: Cast off 48 (k. 9, inc. 1 by knitting into back and front of next stitch) 4 times (44 sts.); on the same needle work the back waist sts. thus: (k. 9, inc. 1 as before) 12 times (132 sts. more), and still on the same needle work the left front sts. thus: (inc. 1 as before, k. 9) 4 times (44 sts. more). This gives a total of 220 sts. on the same needle for all round the jacket. Work the 2nd pattern row with k. 3 at each end.

Continue in pattern, beginning with the 3rd row and keep k. 3 at each end, at the same time shape the rever scallops as follows: * Cast on 2 sts. at the beginning of each of the next 8 rows. Work the next 12 rows straight, then cast off 2 at the beginning of each of the next 6 rows. Work 2 rows straight, thus completing 28 rows from the * for one scallop. Repeat these 28 rows once more making a second scallop, then work 7 rows of the 3rd scallop up to the armhole (242 sts.).

Next row: (the 2nd pattern row and 8th row of 3rd scallop) cast on 2 (making 244 sts. on left-hand needle), k. 3 (m. 1, k. 2 tog.) 35 times, k. 3, slip these 74 sts. on a spare needle for left front, cast off 2 for first underarm, k. 1 (m. 1, k. 2 tog.) 45 times k. 1, slip these

92 sts. on a spare needle for the back, cast off 2, k. 1 (m. 1, k. 2 tog.) 35 times, k. 3. The last 74 sts. are for the right front.

THE RIGHT FRONT.—Continue in pattern with k. 3 at scallop end and k. 1 at armhole end (keeping straight at scallop end), until 12 rows are worked, and at the same time cast off 1 st. at the beginning of alternate rows (armhole end) for 6 decreasings (68 sts.). Continue with borders as before, with 2 more decreasings at armhole end, then work straight at this end, and at neck end shape all the time by casting off 2 sts. at beginning of 1st and 3rd row in every 6 rows. Continue neck decreasings until 38 sts. remain, on which work 6 rows to shoulder.

TO SLOPE THE SHOULDER: Cast off 6 sts. at the beginning of next row and every following alternate row (armhole end) until only 14 sts. remain. Work 19 rows in pattern with k. 3 border at both ends for collar, then cast off 3 sts. at the inside neck edge of alternate rows until 5 remain. Cast off.

THE BACK.—Join lilac wool to right armhole end of the back st. Work the 3rd pattern row with k. 1 at each end. Continue in pattern, casting off 1 st. at the beginning of each of the next 16 rows. There are now 76 sts. on which work 32 rows in pattern with k. 1 at each border.

TO SLOPE THE BACK SHOULDERS: Cast off 6 sts. at the beginning of each of the next 8 rows. Cast off the remaining stitches.

THE LEFT FRONT.—Join the lilac wool to the armhole end of the remaining sts. and work 3rd pattern row with k. 3 at scallop end. Continue as given for right front.

TO MAKE UP.—Sew the cast-off ends of collar together for the centre back and sew the front shoulders to the back shoulders on the wrong side and sew the collar to the centre back of neck en the right side.

With white wool and No. 9 hook work 3 rows of d.c. round rever and collar edges, putting 1 d.c. into each k. st. on the first row. On the 2nd and 3rd row increase by putting 2 d.c. in the 1st and last d.c. of the 8 d.c. over the straight rows on each scallop, and dec. by missing 1 d.c. at the centre of the dip between the scallops. Work 3 rows of 1 d.c. in each st. at each sash end, using white wool and a No. 9 hook. Work 3 rows in white at the scalloped edge of sleeve flounce as on the front.

Sew the sleeve seams and press on a sleeve board, then sew sleeves into armholes.

Sew the waist band together at left side, and at right side sew about half an inch at each edge (so that a slot is left open for the belt).

THE ROSES.—With white wool and No. 13 hook, make 6 ch. and sl. st. to the 1st ch.

1st round: 1 ch., into the ring work (3 tr. and 1 d.c.) 6 times.

2nd round: (2 ch., 1 d.c. into next d.c. on last row) 6 times.

3rd round: Into each ch. loop on last round work 1 d.c., 5 tr. and 1 d.c. and fasten off. Work 17 roses more.

Sew one rose to each scallop and one on each sash end.

This jacket is not pressed but the scalloped edges should be pressed under a damp cloth to prevent any tendency to curl.

Can You Crochet a TOQUE?

Here is an Irresistible Little Model with a Border of Knitted Leaves.

These three photographs show the pretty toque from every angle.

THIS little cap can be adjusted to any size required. The shaped brim gives extra measurement, and it is actually $23\frac{1}{2}$ inches inside head measurement, but as the leaves are worked separately and sewn on, this again can be adjusted to size. As a rough guide the original cap was worked at a tension of 6 d.c. to the inch in width.

ABBREVIATIONS :
Ch., chain ; d.c., double crochet ; st., stitch ; sl., slip ; k., knit plain ; p., purl ; m., make.

MATERIALS :
3 ounces of Fleming Reid's "Greenock" 4-ply Super-Fingering, a No. 11 bone crochet hook, and a pair of No. 14 steel knitting needles for the leaves.

TO WORK :
BEGIN in the centre of the crown with 5 ch., and form into a ring with a sl.st.

1st round : 5 d.c. into the ring.

Now work 2 rounds of 2 d.c. in each st., taking up both loops at the top of the st. to make flat d.c. Do not join up at the end of each round, but tie a piece of cotton to the first st. of one round to denote the beginning. If you catch up this piece of cotton at the beginning of each round, it will form a good guide.

4th round : * 1 d.c. in the 1st st., 2 d.c. in the next st. ; repeat from * all round.

5th round : 1 d.c. in each st. Every alternate round is worked in this way, so will not be repeated.

6th round : * 1 d.c. in each

80

of first 2 sts., 2 d.c. in the next st. Repeat from * all round

8th round : 1 d.c. in each of first 3 st., 2 d.c. in the next st. ; repeat from * all round.

10th round : 1 d.c. in each of 4 sts., 2 d.c. in the next, and repeat from * all round.

Continue in this way, increasing on every alternate round, and on each increase round, working 1 st. more between the increases until the work measures 7 inches across.

(These rounds may be varied here for different sizes.)

Now work 3 rounds of 1 d.c. in each st. followed by a round increasing in every 14th st. to give a little expansion on the bend of the head.

Work 20 rounds more, putting 1 d.c. in each st., or according to the depth of cap required ; the shaped brim gives another 2 inches on the widest part.

THE BRIM : This is continued right on without cutting the wool.

1st row : Work 1 d.c. in each st. until within 6 sts. of the end, 1 ch., turn. This ch. is not worked into at the end of rows, as it is only intended to facilitate turning.

2nd row : Miss the first d.c., 1 d.c. in each st. until within 1 st. of the end of the last row.

Repeat the 2nd row 13 times more.

Here the work reverts to rounds again, so work one round putting a d.c. in every st. of last round, and 1 in the end of the rows on the little slope, 1 in each of the 6 sts., missed on the last round of crown and 1 in the end of rows on the second slope.

Work 4 rounds more, putting 1 d.c. in each st., and fasten off.

THE LEAVES : Cast on 3 sts. and k. plain.

K. 2 rows more, increasing 1 st. at the end of the row.

Next row : K. 2, p. 1. k. 2.

Next row : K. 2, m. 1, (by bringing the wool to the front of the needle) k. 1, m. 1, k. 2.

Next row : K. 2, p. 3. k. 2.

Next row : K. 3, m. 1, k. 1, m. 1, k. 3.

Next row : K. 2, p 5, k. 2.

Repeat the last 2 rows until there are 17 sts. in the row, always k. the first 2 and last 2 sts. to keep the little garter-st. edge. Note that on every front row there will be one st. more to k. before the first " made " st., and 1 st. more

after the second one.

After the 17 sts. are gained work the back row, then work 2 rows more on these sts.

Now begin the decrease rows to shape the top of the leaf. On the front of the work, k. until the st. before the centre one, sl. 1, k. 2 tog., and draw the sl. st. over, k. to end of row.

Next row : Purl, keeping the 2 border sts. at each edge.

Repeat the last 2 rows until the sts. are reduced to 5.

Next row : K. 2, p. 1, k. 2.

Next row : K. 2, k. 2 tog., k 1.

Decrease in the same way on the next row, when the sts. will be reduced to 3 ; finally k 2 tog., k. 1, pass the sl.st. over, draw the wool through the last st., and fasten off

There are 17 leaves round the hat illustrated, but make as many as you will require to arrange in a double row round the brim.

Before sewing on the leaves press them lightly, but do not flatten them, as they are sewn round the edge, and are set a little full at the centre. Press the inside of the cap before sewing on the leaves.

GREY WOOL JUMPER

MATERIALS : 10 ozs. of Patons and Baldwins 3-ply Super Scotch fingering in grey, 1 oz. each in royal blue and white, one pair of No. 11 " Stratnoid " knitting needles, and one pair of No. 9 ; a silk scarf and ½ yard of narrow elastic.

Measurements : Length from shoulder at neck edge, 20 inches ; width all round under the arm, 34 inches ; length of sleeve seam, 10 inches.

Tension : One stripe of pattern to 1½ inches in width, and 8 rows to 1 inch in depth.

Abbreviations : K. = knit ; p. = purl ; sts. = stitches ; w.fd. = wool forward ; tog. = together ; rep. = repeat.

Always work into the back of all cast-on sts. to produce firm edges, and when changing from one colour to the other in the ribbing always knit a plain row for the first row.

The Back

Begin at the lower edge. Cast on 110 sts., using grey wool and No. 11 needles, and work 8 rows in k. 1, p. 1 rib in grey, * 2 rows in white, 2 rows in blue, 2 rows in grey. Rep. from * once more, then continue in the rib in grey until the ribbing measures 5 inches from the beginning. Now change to No. 9 needles and the following pattern :—

1st row—* K. 1, w.fd., k. 2, k. 2 tog. twice,

Continued on page 83

Madame— When You Walk

And when you take a walk, here's the bag that holds your powder puff and cigs., and, like the rest of the set, it is in royal blue and white

*I*T'S no use, we really must begin to think about autumn things— and it's not so hard when you see such an attractive set as the one illustrated here. Cap, cravat, bag and cuffs in softest white and royal blue wool, and designed specially for the day when there's a "nip" in the air.

The cap is one of the most becoming shapes—rather "tammy-ish," pulled well down on one side and revealing your pretty waves on the other, with a flat bow perched on the top. The cravat you'll simply love. It has a "dickey" front that is kept neatly in place with a tiny knitted waistbelt. Long ends form the cravat, which can be worn in various attractive ways.

Of course, there's a bag to match—a very useful shape, too. It has a wooden handle and a lining made slightly smaller all round than the bag, so that when full the knitting won't stretch into ungainly shapes. To complete the set there are cuffs to match. Just the thing to cheer up a rather plain frock.

Photos: **LENARE**

MATERIALS.—3 ounces of Paton's 2-ply Super Scotch Fingering in white and 1½ ounces of the same wool in royal blue. A pair of No. 10 Stratnoid knitting pins, a No. 8 crochet hook made by the same firm, and a fancy wooden handle for the handbag, 3 press fasteners.

Measurements.—Hat : Head-band, 21 inches. Depth from centre of crown to lower edge, 7½ inches. *Fancy Front :* Depth down centre front, including collar, 16½ inches. Width at widest part, 11 inches. *Scarf :* Length, 42 inches. *Cuffs :* Depth at lowest point, 8 inches; width at wrist, 6 inches. *Handbag :* Depth of bag down centre, without handle, 10 inches. Width at widest part, 13½ inches.

Tension.—7 stitches in width and 10 rows in depth to 1 inch.

Abbreviations.—K., knit; p., purl; sts., stitches; inc., increase; dec., decrease; tog., together; rep., repeat; s.-s., stocking-stitch; d.c., double crochet; ch., chain; B., Blue; W., White.

Always knit into the back of each cast-on stitch.

The Hat

This is made in five sections as follows : For one section cast on 38 sts. with blue wool and k. 6 rows in s.-s. (alternate rows of plain and purl). Change and join on W. and work 4 rows s.-s. in W. These 10 rows form the pattern, making one blue and one white stripe. Rep. these 10 rows and dec. 1 st. at both ends of needle on the 13th row, and then on every k. row following until 1 st. remains. Fasten off. Make 4 more pieces in this way.

To Make Up Hat

Join the five sections together, with points in the centre. Then work 1 row of d.c. in W. round edge of hat, working into every alternate stitch. Continue in d.c., working round and round, stitch into stitch, until the brim is 3 inches in depth. Fasten off. For the bow : Cast on 30 sts. in W., and k. in s.-s. for 14 inches. Cast off. Work 4 rows of d.c. at each end of this strip and 1 row along each side. Fasten off.

Press hat and strip carefully under a damp cloth. Try on hat, tack down right side of crown to brim, twist strip into a single bow, and fasten on to left side of hat.

The Fancy Front

Using B. wool, cast on 180 sts. Work in s.-s., dec. 1 st. in centre of row, and inc. 1 st. at end of each row, knitting 6 rows in B. and 4 rows in W. alternately. Work in this way for 16 rows (*i.e.,* 2 stripes in B. and 1 stripe in W.). Then cast off 12 sts. at beginning of next 2 rows for neck shaping. K. 1 row without dec.; dec. 1 st. at both ends of next row; k. another row without dec., and dec. 1st. at both ends of following row. Continue in this way until 36 rows have been knitted altogether, then k. 10 rows in W., still dec. as before. Cast off.

Now, commencing in centre, sew together the two halves of the last row

of W., forming a shield-shaped piece. Edge sides with 9 rows of d.c. in W. wool, and finish shoulders with 2 rows of d.c. in W. wool.

The Scarf Piece

Cast on 60 sts. in B. wool, and work in s.-s., dec. 1 st. in centre of each row. K. 12 rows in B., 6 rows in W., and 4 rows in B., then continue in W. only until 20 sts. remain. Now continue dec. 1 st. in centre and inc. 1 st. at the end of each row until scarf measures 16 inches. Then continue to dec. 1 st. in centre and also dec. 1 st. at both ends of each row, until 1 st. remains. Fasten off. Work a second piece in the same manner, but continue until scarf measures 26 inches. Then fasten off.

The Belt

Cast on 26 sts. in W., and work in s.-s. for 28 inches. Cast off. Fold in two lengthwise, and close with a row of d.c.

To Make Up Front

Carefully press each piece under a damp cloth. Sew together the two pieces forming the scarf. Then arrange the join of scarf to come at the right-hand edge of neck, and sew one edge of scarf to the neck edge of front. Join one end of belt to the point on front, and fasten with 3 press studs.

The Cuffs

Cast on 80 sts. in B., and work in s.-s., dec. 1 st. in the centre of each row. Work 6 rows in B. and 4 rows in W. alternately for 30 rows (*i.e.,* 3 alternate B. and W. stripes). When 50 sts. remain on needle, continue in W., dec. 1 st. in centre and inc. 1 st. at the end of each row for 20 rows; then dec. 1 st. at beginning, 1 st. in centre, and 1 st. at the end of each row, until 1 st. remains. Fasten off. Using W. wool, sew up seam and edge wide end with 3 rows and narrow end with 1 row of d.c. Press carefully under a damp cloth.

The Handbag

Cast on 100 sts. in B. wool and k. in s.-s., dec. 1 st. in the centre of each row. On the 7th row, change to W. wool and k. 4 rows. Beginning with the 11th row, k. 6 B. rows. Beginning with the 17th row, k. 4 rows in W. Beginning with the 21st row, work 6 rows in B. Beginning with the 27th row, k. 6 rows in W. Beginning with the 33rd row, k. 6 rows in B., and beginning with the 39th row, k. 4 rows in W. Continue with W., dec. 1 st. in the centre and inc. 1 st. at the end of each row. After 19 rows, dec. 1 st. in centre and 1 st. at both ends of each row until only 1 st. remains. Fasten off. With the exception of the part of bag to be sewn to handle, edge the remainder of bag with 7 rows of d.c. Make another piece in the same way.

To Make Up Handbag

Join together the edges of the two sections (except those edges to be sewn to the handle) with 3 rows of d.c. Then carefully press under a damp cloth. Sew free edges neatly to the hinged handles, and finish off the inside of bag with a suitable lining.

Grey Wool Jumper

Continued from page 81

k. 2, w.fd., k. 1. *2nd row*—P. These 2 rows form the pattern and are repeated throughout the jumper. Continue in pattern until the work measures 14 inches from the beginning, then shape the armholes as follows :—

Cast off 4 sts. at the beginning of the next 2 rows, then cast off 2 sts. at the beginning of the next 6 rows—90 sts. remain. Continue in pattern until the armholes measure 6½ inches on the straight. Cast off.

The Front

Cast on 120 sts., using grey wool and No. 11 needles, and work exactly like the back until the armholes are shaped and 100 sts. remain. Now begin the neck opening as follows :—

Work 40 sts. in pattern, cast off 20, work 40 sts. in pattern. Now continue on these two sets of 40 sts., using two balls of wool, until the armholes measure 6½ inches, then at the beginning of every row (armhole edges) cast off 6 sts. until all are cast off.

The Sleeves

Begin at the lower edge. With No. 9 needles and grey wool cast on 150 sts.

K. 2 rows plain, then change to the pattern for 9 inches. *Next row*—* K. 1, k. 2 tog. Rep. from * to end—100 sts. remain. Change to No. 11 needles and work 3 rows in k. 1, p. 1 rib. Still working in the rib work 2 rows white, 2 rows blue, 2 rows grey, 2 rows white, 2 rows blue, then continue in grey, still working in the rib, but cast off 2 sts. at the beginning of every row until 30 sts. remain. Cast off.

Now pick up the 20 sts. cast off at the front neck, using grey wool and No. 11 needles, and k. 4 plain rows, then decrease 1 st. at both ends of every row until 1 st. remains. Cut wool. Pick up the centre 20 sts. on the back neck and work on these in the same way.

Press the work on both sides with a warm iron and damp cloth. Join the shoulders, sew in the sleeves and press the seams. Join up the side and sleeve seams and press them. Sew down the two little tabs at the neck by the points, then slot the scarf through to tie in front. Insert a piece of elastic through the pattern at the sleeve edges.

chic underlined

WOOL LACE PARTY "PRETTIES"

backless and clinging, and as frivolous as chiffon

DANCES and other gaieties are apt to entail diaphanous frocks in totally unsuitable weather! The fascinating "step-ins" opposite ('wool next to the skin,' though they don't look it!) are specially designed to end those agonising decisions between silk "beneaths" and a consequent cold next day and *warm*, but bulgy and uninspiring woollens.

It takes astonishingly little time to crochet and join up the lacy circles that form this adorable garment —in fact two people working at it together, one crocheting and one stitching, could finish the whole thing in an afternoon.

The shell pink and black of the original is specially planned for wearing under a black frock. Pale turquoise and black would be lovely, too. Under light-coloured dresses you will prefer to have the cami-knickers all one colour, or else to substitute white as the contrast.

●

MATERIALS: Of "Beehive" (or Paton's Super) Scotch Fingering, 2-ply, 3 ozs. of pink, No. 245½, and 3 ozs. of black (if made in one colour, 5 ozs. is sufficient). A No. 5 "Inox" crochet hook. Four medium size press studs. ¾ yd. of narrow black satin ribbon.

MEASUREMENT: Width of garment at under-arm, 34 inches.

N.B.—*This will fit a slightly larger or slightly smaller size, as the lacy material stretches or clings as required.*

TENSION: Each circle should measure, pressed, 3 inches in diameter.

FRONT

BACK

ABBREVIATIONS:—ch.=chain; s.s.= slip stitch; tr.=treble.

THE CIRCLES

Wind wool 5 times round the left fore-finger and slip off. IST ROUND: s.s. into the ring just made, 3 ch., 14 tr. into ring, s.s. into top of the 3 ch.

2ND ROUND: 3 ch., 3 tr. on next tr., * 1 tr. on each of the next 2 tr., then

● Assembling the circles is very simple. The pink ones have been numbered in columns to give you extra guidance in their arrangement.

3 tr. in next tr., repeat from * 3 times, 1 tr. on next tr., s.s. into top of the 3 ch.

3RD ROUND: 3 ch., * 3 tr. on next tr., 1 tr. on next tr., repeat from * to end of round, s.s. into top of the 3 ch. Fasten off the wool, running the end in neatly.

You will need 47 of these circles in black and 56 in pink.

MAKING UP

The diagrams show you how the circles are assembled. Take a large, uncrumpled sheet of brown paper and pin them into position on it.

Beginning with the back, first pin the centre column of five—two black and three pink—and you will then find it quite easy to fit in first the remaining pink circles, and then the black ones. Stitch the circles together by the stitches which form the chain edge to them. Begin the front similarly with the centre column —one black and five pink.

Unpin front and back and press on the wrong side with a hot iron and damp cloth. Place back to front, right sides together, and seam up the sides (there will be turnings of about ¾ inch where the scallops at the edge are widest). Sew press studs round the opening between the legs. Cut two 12 inch ribbon shoulder straps and sew on firmly.

F

A Featherweight Set for Restful Moments and a Smart Wool Front to wear with your Autumn Suit

KNIT *this smart two-coloured front to wear with your autumn suit. The fashionable high neck is so snug on chilly days.*

MATERIALS.—1 oz. of Paton's two-ply Super Scotch Fingering in yellow and ½ oz. of the same wool in royal blue; a pair of No. 10 Stratnoid knitting needles and a No. 8 Stratnoid crochet hook; 7 press fasteners and 3 fancy buttons.

Measurements.—Depth from neck edge, 14 in.; width across, 8 in.

Abbreviations.—K., knit; p., purl; sts., stitches; inc., increase; dec., decrease; tog., together; rep., repeat; Y., yellow; B., blue.

Tension.—7½ stitches in width and 9 rows in depth to 1 in. Always knit into the back of each cast-on stitch.

Stitches.—Stocking-stitch is alternative rows of plain and purl. D.C. is double crochet.

FOR working this design two balls of each colour should be wound, to allow for changes in the colours. When changing from the yellow to blue wool, or vice versa, the two wools should be twisted once round each other, so as to avoid gaps in the work where colour changes occur.

Cast on 50 sts. in B.

1st row.—K. 5 Y., 45 B. *2nd row.*

—P. 44 B., 6 Y. *3rd row.*—K. 7 Y., 43 B. *4th row.*—P. 42 B., 8 Y. *5th row.*—K. 9 Y., remainder B. *6th row.*—P. 40 B., 10 Y. *7th row.*—K. 11 Y., remainder B. *8th row.*—P. 38 B., 12 Y. *9th row.*—K. 13 Y., 37 B. *10th row.*—P. Inc. 1 st. at beginning and end of row. 37 B., 15 Y. *11th row.*—K. 1 B., 15 Y., remainder B. *12th row.*—P. 35 B., 15 Y., then 2 B. *13th row.*—K. 3 B., 15 Y., remainder B. *14th row.*—P. 33 B., 15 Y., 4 B. *15th row.*—K. 5 B., 15 Y., remainder B. *16th row.*—P. 31 B., 15 Y., then 6 B. *17th row.*—K. 7 B., 15 Y., remainder B. *18th row.*—P. 29 B., 15 Y., 8 B. *19th row.*—K. 9 B., 15 Y., remainder B. *20th row.*—P. Inc. 1 st., beginning and

end of row—28 B., 15 Y., 11 B. 21st row.
—K. 10 B., 15 Y., remainder B. 22nd row.
—P. 1 Y., 29 B., 15 Y., then 9 B. 23rd row.
—K. 8 B., 15 Y., 29 B., 2 Y. 24th row.—
P. 3 Y., 29 B., 15 Y., 7 B. 25th row.—
K. 6. B., 15 Y., 29 B., 4 Y. 26th row.—
P. 5 Y., 29 B., 15 Y., then 5 B. 27th row.
—K. 4 B., 15 Y., 29 B., 6 Y. 28th row.—
P. 7 Y., 29 B., 15 Y., 3 B. 29th row.—K.
2 B., 15 Y., 29 B., then 8 Y. 30th row.—
P. Inc. 1 st. beginning and end of row—
10 Y., 29 B., 15 Y., 2 B. 31st row.—K.
1 B., 15 Y., 29 B., 11 Y. 32nd row.—P.
12 Y., 29 B., 15 Y., fasten off B. wool.

33rd row.—K. 14 Y., 29 B., 13 Y.
34th row.—P. 14 Y., 29 B., 13 Y. 35th row.
—K. 12 Y., 29 B., 15 Y. 36th row.—P.
1 B., 15 Y., 29 B., 11 Y. 37th row.—
K. 10 Y., 29 B., 15 Y., 2 B. 38th row.—
P. 3 B., 15 Y., 29 B., 9 Y. 39th row.—K.
8 Y., 29 B., 15 Y., 4 B. 40th row.—P. Inc.
1 st. at beginning and end of row—
6 B., 15 Y., 29 B., 8 Y. 41st row.—K. 9 Y.,
27 B., 15 Y., 7 B. 42nd row.—P. 8 B.,
15 Y., 25 B., 10 Y. 43rd row.—K. 11 Y.,
23 B., 15 Y., 9 B. 44th row.—P. 10 B.,
15 Y., 21 B., 12 Y. 45th row.—K. 13 Y.,
19 B., 15 Y., 11 B. 46th row.—P. 12 B.,
15 Y., 17 B., 14 Y. 47th row.—K. 15 Y.,
15 B., 15 Y., 13 B. 48th row.—P. 14 B.,
15 Y., 15 B., 16 Y. 49th row.—K. 17 Y.,
11 B., 15 Y., 15 B. 50th row.—P. (inc. 1 st.
at beginning and end of row), 17 B., 15 Y.,
9 B., 19 Y. 51st row.—K. 18 Y., 9 B.,
15 Y., 18 B. 52nd row.—P. 19 B., 15 Y.,
9 B., 17 Y. 53rd row.—K. 16 Y., 9 B.,
15 Y., 20 B. 54th row.—P. 21 B., 15 Y.,
9 B., 15 Y. 55th row.—K. 14 Y., 9 B.,
15 Y., 22 B. 56th row.—P. 23 B., 15 Y.,
9 B., 13 Y. 57th row.—K. 12 Y., 9 B.,
15 Y., 24 B. 58th row.—P. 25 B., 15 Y.,
9 B., 11 Y. 59th row.—K. 10 Y., 9 B.,
15 Y., 26 B. 60th row.—P. (inc. 1 st. at
beginning and end of row), 28 B., 15 Y.,
9 B., 10 Y. 61st row.—K. 9 Y., 9 B., 15 Y.,
then 29 B. 62nd row.—P. 30 B., 15 Y.,
9 B., 8 Y. 63rd row.—K. 7 Y., 9 B.,
15 Y., 31 B. 64th row.—P. 32 B., 15 Y.,
15 B., and fasten off Y. wool.

65th row.—K. 14 B., 15 Y, 25 B., 8 Y.
66th row.—P. 9 Y., 25 B., 15 Y., 13 B.
67th row.—K. 14 B., 15 Y., 23 B., 10 Y.
68th row.—P. 11 Y., 23 B., 15 Y., 13 B.
69th row.—K. 13 B., 15 Y., 22 B., then
12 Y. 70th row.—P. (inc. 1 st. at beginning
and end of row), 14 Y., 21 B., 15 Y., 14 B.
71st row.—K. 14 B., 15 Y., 20 B. 15 Y.
72nd row.—P. 16 Y., 19 B., 15 Y., 14 B.
73rd row.—K. 14 B., 15 Y., 18 B., 17 Y.
74th row.—P. 18 Y., 17 B., 15 Y., 14 B.
75th row.—K. 14 B., 15 Y., 16 B., 19 Y.
76th row.—P. 20 Y., 15 B., 15 Y., 14 B.
77th row.—K. 14 B., 15 Y., 14 B., 21 Y.
78th row.—P. 22 Y., 13 B., 15 Y., 14 B.
79th row.—K. 14 B., 15 Y., 12 B., 23 Y.
80th row.—P. (inc. 1 st. at beginning and
end of row), 25 Y., 11 B., 15 Y., 15 B.
81st row.—K. 15 B., 15 Y., 10 B., 26 Y.
82nd row.—P. 25 Y., 11 B., 15 Y., 15 B.
83rd row.—K. 15 B., 15 Y., 12 B., 24 Y.
84th row.—P. 23 Y., 13 B., 15 Y., 15 B.
85th row.—K. 15 B., 15 Y., 14 B., 22 Y.
86th row.—P. 21 Y., 15 B., 15 Y., 15 B.
87th row.—K. 15 B., 15 Y., 16 B., 20 Y.
88th row.—P. 19 Y., 17 B., 15 Y., 15 B.
89th row.—K. 15 B., 15 Y., 18 B., 18 Y.
90th row.—P. (inc. 1 st at beginning and
end of row), 18 Y., 19 B., 15 Y., 16 B.
91st row.—K. 16 B., 15 Y., 20 B., 17 Y.
92nd row.—P. 16 Y., 21 B., 15 Y., 16 B.
93rd row.—K. 16 B., 15 Y., 22 B., 15 Y.

94th row.—P. 14 Y., 23 B., 15 Y., 16 B.
95th row.—K. 16 B., 15 Y., 24 B., 13 Y.
96th row.—P. 12 Y., 25 B., 15 Y., 16 B.
97th row.—K. 16 B., 15 Y., 26 B., 11 Y.
98th row.—P. 10 Y., 27 B., 15 Y., 16 B.
99th row.—K. 16 B., 15 Y., 28 B., 9 Y.
100th row.—P. (inc. 1 st. at beginning
and end of row), 9 Y., 29 B., 15 Y., 17 B.
101st row.—K. 17 B., 15 Y., 30 B., 8 Y.
102nd row.—P. 9 Y., 29 B., 15 Y., 17 B.
103rd row.—K. 17 B., 15 Y., 28 B., 10 Y.
104th row.—P. 11 Y., 27 B., 15 Y., 17 B.
105th row.—K. 17 B., 15 Y., 26 B., 12 Y.
106th row.—P. 13 Y., 25 B., 15 Y., 17 B.
107th row.—K. 17 B., 15 Y., 24 B., 14 Y.
108th row.—P. 15 Y., 23 B., 15 Y., 17 B.
109th row.—K. 17 B., 15 Y., 22 B., 16 Y.
110th row.—P. 17 Y., 21 B., 15 Y., 17 B.
111th row.—K. 17 B., 15 Y., 20 B., 18 Y.
112th row.—P. 19 Y., 19 B., 15 Y., 17 B.
113th row.—K. 17 B., 13 Y. Cast off
10 sts. for neck, 9 B., 20 Y. 114th row.

—P. 19 Y., 11 B. 115th row.—K. Cast off
3, 8 B., 18 Y.

Continue to knit right shoulder as
follows :—116th row.—P. 17 Y., 10 B.
117th row.—K. Cast off 3, 7 B., then 16 Y.
118th row.—P. 15 Y., 9 B. 119th row.—
K. Cast off 2, knit 7 B., then 14 Y.
120th row.—P. 13 Y., 9 B. 121st row.—
K. 10 B., 12 Y. 122nd row.—P. 11 Y.,
11 B. 123rd row.—K. 12 B., 10 Y.
124th row.—P. 9 Y., 13 B. 125th row.—
K. 14 B., 8 Y. 126th row.—Cast off.

Now proceed to work left shoulder as
follows :—114th row.—P. Cast off 3, 9 Y.,
17 B. 115th row.—K. 17 B., 10 Y. 116th
row.—P. Cast off 3, 6 Y., 17 B. 117th
row.—K. 17 B., 7 Y. 118th row.—P.
Cast off 2, 4 Y., 17 B. Continue, working
the same number of stitches to the row
until 126th row is reached, and cast off.

The Collar.—Cast on 30 sts. in Y. wool.
Knit in stocking-stitch for a length of
13 ins. Cast off. Fold in two lengthwise,
and close with 1 row of d.c.

The Belt.—Cast on 40 sts. in Y. wool.
Work in stocking-stitch for 28 ins. Fold
in two lengthwise and close with 1 row
of d.c.

To Complete Front.—Sew collar to
front, leaving opening on the right side,
this should be made to close by means of
press fasteners. Sew belt on to front,
so as to close on right side with press
fasteners. Press carefully under a damp
cloth, then sew on the three fancy buttons
for trimming.

*THE model is
in royal blue
and yellow, but
use any two col-
ours that suit
your dress
scheme.*

A JUMPER for the Well-Dressed Woman

Excellent Style in Every Line. A Woolly That Will Appeal to the Knitter of Good Taste.

DIAGONAL lace stripes give a very smart touch to this new jumper, and they are carried out in a very simple pattern.

MATERIALS :
5 ozs. Copley's 2-ply " Excelsior " Super Shetland wool, and a pair each of No. 10 and No. 12 bone knitting needles.

TENSION AND MEASUREMENTS :
Worked at a tension of 8 sts. to the inch in width the following measurements are attained after light pressing.

Width all round at underarm 35 inches (as these measurements are taken without any stretching this jumper can be worn over an actual bust measurement of 32 to 34 inches, according to how close-fitting you like to wear your jumper). Length from top of shoulder to edge of waist, 19 inches. Length of sleeve-seam, including cuff, 19 inches.

ABBREVIATIONS :
K., knit ; p., purl ; st., stitch ; tog., together ; inc., increase ; s.s., stocking stitch (k. on right side and p. back) ; m. 1 (by bringing wool to front of needle). Directions in brackets are worked the number of times stated after brackets.

The Front

Begin at the lower edge and using the No. 12 needles cast on 116 sts.

Work 46 rows of single rib (k. 1 and p. 1 alternately), working into the back of the sts. on the first row.

On the next row p. 6 sts., inc. in the next st. by purling in the back of the st., then, before passing it off the left-hand needle, p. in the front of the same st. ; * p. 5, inc. in the next st., and repeat from * as far as the last 7 sts. P. these. There are now 134 sts.

Change to No. 10 needles and work s.s. for 41 rows more, finishing at the end of a p. row.

Now work as follows :

1st row : K. 66, m. 1, k. 2 tog., k. the remaining 66 sts.

2nd row : P. this and every alternate row.

3rd row : K. 64, * m. 1, k. 2 tog. and repeat from * twice more, k. the remaining 64 sts.

5th row : K. 62, * m. 1, k. 2 tog. and repeat from * 4 times more, then k. the remaining 62 sts.

7th row : K. 60, * m. 1, k. 2 tog. and repeat from * 6 times more, then k. the remaining 60 sts.

9th row : K. 58, * m. 1, k. 2 tog., and

repeat from * 3 times more, k. 2, ** m. 1, k. 2 tog., and repeat from ** 3 times more, then k. the remaining 58 sts.

11th row : K. 56, * m. 1, k. 2 tog. and repeat from * 3 times more, k. 6, ** m. 1, k. 2 tog. and repeat from ** 3 times more, then k. the remaining 56 sts.

Continue in this way, working 2 sts. less in s.s. at the beginning of k. rows, and always keep 8 sts. in each lace insertion ; there will consequently be 4 sts. more to k. plain between the insertion, on the centre point, and also 2 sts. less to k. plain after the second insertion, to match the beginning of the row. When there are 26 sts. in the centre in s.s. p. the next row as usual when the point of two stripes (open and solid) will be completed.

On the next row k. 44, * m. 1, k. 2 tog. and repeat from * 3 times more, k. 14, m. 1, k. 2 tog., k. 14, ** m. 1, k. 2 tog. and repeat from ** 3 times more, then k. the remaining 44 sts.

In this way a new V point is begun as on the first pattern row, but with the lace st. and s.s. stripe on each side changing as usual. The lace st. stripe always consists of 8 sts., and the s.s. stripe of 14 sts., so this is an easy guide to keeping the pattern correct.

P. the next row as usual, then continue

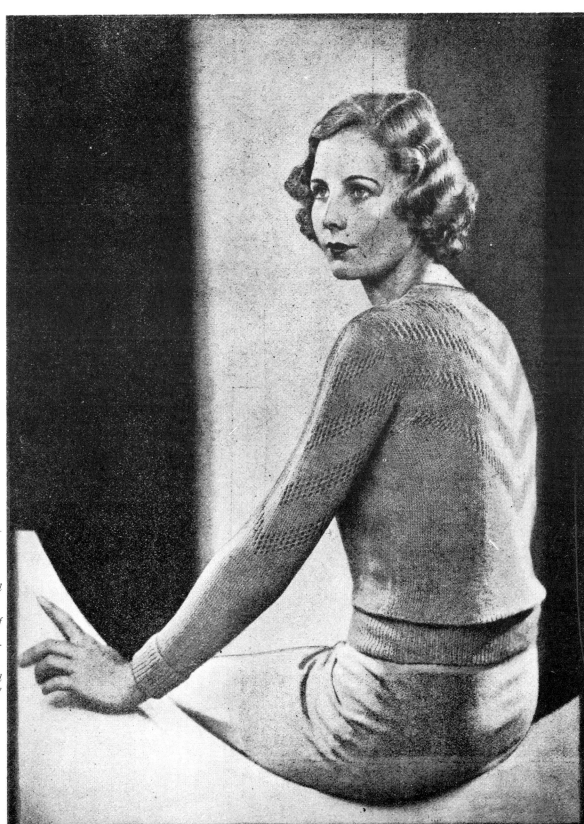

How charming she looks! Those who knit their own jumpers will appreciate the flattering lines of the lace stitch insertions—the attention to pretty detail in the lovely bow.

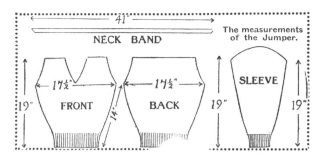

the pattern gradually building up 2 rows of insertion on each half, with the plain stripe of 14 sts. between, until there are 84 rows of s.s. above the ribbing up to the armhole.

To Shape the Armholes

Cast off 3 sts. at the beginning of each of the next 6 rows, then dec. 1 st. at both ends of needle on each of next 2 rows, still changing the sts. as usual, and beginning another V point in the centre by repeating the pattern as before.

On the next row k. 2 tog., k. 1, * (m. 1, k. 2 tog.) 4 times, k. 14 and repeat from * once more, then m. 1, k. 2 tog., 4 times, k. 1 (55 sts.). Now pass the 56 sts. of the opposite side on a safety pin or spare needle. On the next row p. 2 tog., then p. to within the last 2 sts., p. these tog. (53 sts.).

Next row : K. 2 tog., k. 1 (m. 1 and k. 2 tog.) twice, k. 14 and continue across the row, changing the sts. as usual, ending with a lace st. stripe, then k. 2.

Next row : P. 2 tog., then p. across the remainder.

Next row : (M. 1, k. 2 tog.) twice, k. 14, then continue as usual, changing the sts., ending with k. 3.

On the following row p. 2 tog., and p. across the remaining sts.

On the next row m. 1, k. 2 tog., k. 14 and continue across the row as usual, ending k. 4.

Continue in this way, keeping the armhole edge straight and still decreasing on every purl row at the neck edge until there are 19 decreases on the neck edge, at the same time keeping the diagonal lace pattern as usual.

Work 13 rows straight up to the shoulder-line, then cast off straight across.

Join the wool to the front edge of the opposite side and k. 1, then * (m. 1, k. 2 tog.) 4 times, k. 14 and repeat from * once more, (m. 1, k. 2 tog.) 4 times, k. 1, k. 2 tog.

On the next row p. 2 tog., then p. across as far as the last 2 sts., p. these tog.

Now complete this side to match the first, but with all shaping at opposite edges.

The Back

WORK this in exactly the same way as the front up to the underarm.

To Shape the Armholes.—Cast off 3 sts. at the beginning of each of the next 6 rows, then decrease at both ends of the needle on each of the next 5 rows (106 sts. remain).

Work straight on these sts. (keeping the diagonal lace insertion as on the front) until the armhole edge is 5 rows less in depth than that of the front.

To Shape the Neck.—1st row : With wrong side facing, p. 44, cast off 18, p. 44.

2nd row : Work back to neck in pattern.

3rd row : Cast off 10 sts., and p. across the remainder.

4th row : Work back to neck. Cast off.

Join the wool to the neck edge of the opposite side, k. 2 tog., m. 1, k. 2 tog.,

k. 14, and complete the row in pattern. P. back to neck.

Cast off 10 sts. and work across the remainder. Cast off.

The Sleeves

USING No. 12 needles, cast on 66 sts. and work 46 rows of single rib. P. the next row.

Change to No. 10 needles and work in s.s. increasing next to the edge st. at both ends of the needle on the next and every following 6th row until there are 88 sts. on the needle.

Work 3 rows straight.

Change to the insertion pattern as on the back of the jumper.

The first pattern row will have k. 43, k. 2 tog., m. 1, k. 43.

Now continue in the pattern as for the back of the jumper but with fewer sts. in s.s. on each side of the centre pattern, and still increasing on both ends of the needle as before, until there are 106 sts. on the needle.

Work 9 rows straight, still keeping the diagonal pattern, when the full length of the sleeve seam will be attained.

To Shape the Top of the Sleeve.— Cast off 2 sts. at the beginning of every row till 50 sts. remain, keeping the pattern right to the top of the sleeve.

Work a second sleeve in the same manner.

The Tie

USING No. 12 needles, cast on 1 st. P. 1 and k. 1 into this st.

On the next row k. 1 and p. 1 into the first st., then k. the remaining sts.

Continue in the ribbing, increasing in the edge st. on the same edge on every row and keeping the opposite edge straight until there are 11 sts. on the needle.

Work quite straight in single rib on these sts. for a depth of 40 inches. Now decrease at the opposite edge to that on which the increases were made at the beginning of the tie until all the sts. are worked off.

To Make Up the Jumper.—First press all the pieces on the wrong side, putting a damp cloth over the knitting. Sew the front and back shoulders together, then sew the top of the sleeves into the armholes and press these seams while the work is open.

Now sew up the side and sleeve seams in one continuous line, and press these seams.

Pin the centre of the tie to the centre back of the neck, and sew one edge of this to the neck edge, finishing at the front V point with a bow.

GOOD THINGS FOR THE PARTY

Coffee Soufflés

INGREDIENTS :
1 tablespoonful coffee essence.
2 ozs. castor sugar.
1½ gills milk. 2 eggs.
¼ oz. gelatine. ¼ gill water.
Coloured coffee candy.
Ten paper soufflé cases.

SEPARATE the eggs.

Beat up the yolks and add the sugar and whisk them for a minute.

Heat the milk and add it slowly. Turn the mixture into the top of a double boiler.

Cook it over hot water until it thickens, keeping it stirred, and being careful not to let it curdle. Take it off the heat. Stir in the coffee essence and let the custard get cold.

Dissolve the gelatine in a saucepan with the water and strain it into the custard. Leave it until it begins to set, then whisk the egg whites to a stiff froth and fold them in lightly.

Fill the soufflé cases with the prepared mixture, and when it is just set, sprinkle with coloured coffee candy.

N.B.—*These soufflé cases cost 3½d. per dozen, and have coloured rims of either red, green, pink or yellow.*

CONCENTRATE On the SLEEVES!

These Great Big Affairs Are Wonderfully Becoming

SLEEVES must be extravagant to be fashionable to-day. These are very becoming ones, you will find.

The jumper is knitted in just plain and purl.

MATERIALS: Nine ounces of Patons & Baldwin's 4-ply Super Scotch Fingering wool, a pair of No. 9 and No. 6 knitting needles, and a No. 11 bone crochet hook. Two chromium buttons.

TENSION AND MEASUREMENTS.— Worked at a tension of 6 stitches to the inch in width, the following measurements are attained after light pressing:

Width round bust at the underarm, 35 inches; length from shoulder to edge of waist, 16½ inches; side seam, 12 inches; sleeve seam, including long cuff, 21 inches.

ABBREVIATIONS: K., knit plain; p., purl; st., stitch; tog., together; ch., chain; dec., decrease; inc., increase.

TO WORK

BEGIN at the lower edge of the front, and cast on 96 sts. with No. 9 needles, k. into the back of the sts. on the 1st row, then work 58 rows in a rib of k. 4 and p. 4 alternately.

Change to No. 6 needles, and k. 9 rows—or more rows may be worked here for a longer jumper—before making the front opening.

10TH ROW: K. 62, put the remaining 34 sts. on to a stitch-holder for the left front.

THE RIGHT FRONT

WORK 29 rows on the 62 sts. up to the armhole.

To SHAPE THE ARMHOLE: Cast off 3 sts. at the

beginning of the next row, and the next 2 alternate rows at the armhole end.

On the next row k. 2 tog. at both ends of the row.

NEXT ROW: K. 2 tog. at armhole end of row.

Repeat last 2 rows until the sts. are reduced to 39.

* NEXT ROW: K. 2 tog. at neck end of row.

NEXT ROW: K. 2 tog. at armhole end

On the next row k. 2 tog. at both ends of row. Repeat from * once more.

Now k. 2 tog. at the neck end of every row until only 27 sts. remain. Then dec. (at the neck edge only) on every 3rd row, until only 24 sts. remain. Continue without further decreasing for 12 rows up to the shoulder line.

To SLOPE THE SHOULDER: Work to within 8 sts. of the armhole end of the row, turn and work back to neck edge. Work to within 16 sts. of the end of the row, turn and work back. K. 1 row plain. Cast off.

THE LEFT FRONT

BEGINNING at the front edge of the 34 sts. left on the stitch-holder, cast on 5 sts., and work to match the right front to the end of the 5th row of the armhole shaping, which gives 9 sts. cast off in sets of three.

On the next row k. 2 tog. at the end of row, then k. 1 row plain.

The exact shaping and measurements of the jumper

Continue knitting 2 tog. at armhole edge on alternate rows for the next 6 rows, when 26 sts. will remain.

K. 2 rows plain.

NEXT ROW: K. 2 tog. at armhole edge. Repeat the last 3 rows once more, leaving 24 sts. on the needle.

Continue straight until there are as many rows as on the right shoulder, then slope the shoulder in exactly the same way.

THE BACK

WITH No. 9 needles cast on 96 sts., and work in ribbing as for front. Change to No. 6 needles, and dec. to 94 sts. by k. 2 tog. at beginning and end of the next row. Now continue working to match the front until there are as many rows as on the front to the armhole.

To SHAPE THE ARMHOLE: Cast off 3 sts. at beginning of each of the next 4 rows. Cast off 2 sts. at beginning of next 2 rows.

NEXT ROW: K. 2 tog. at beginning and end of row. (76 sts.).

NEXT ROW: K. plain.

Notice the modern Sleeves, the high Waistline, and the pretty Neck !

Repeat the last 2 rows 3 times more when 70 sts. will remain. K. 2 rows plain.

NEXT ROW : K. 2 tog. at beginning and end. Repeat last 3 rows once more, leaving 66 sts. on needle. Continue without further alteration for 18 rows more.

NEXT ROW : K. 24, cast off 18.

On the remaining 24 sts. shape the left shoulder thus :

K. to within 8 sts. of the armhole edge. Turn and k. back. Repeat these 2 rows once more, leaving 16 sts. from the armhole on the 1st row. K. 1 plain row. Cast off.

Join the wool at the neck end of the first shoulder sts., and work exactly like the left shoulder.

Concentrate on the Sleeves

THE SLEEVES

WITH No. 9 needles cast on 48 sts. and k. into the back of the sts. to make a neat edge. Work 20 rows of rib to match the waist.

NEXT ROW : Inc. by k. into the back and front of the 2nd st. from each end of the next row, and every 5th row, until there are 80 sts. on the needle. Continue without further increasing for 28 rows more, which finishes the cuff.

NEXT ROW : K. plain.

2ND ROW : K. 1, inc. in every st. except the last, which k. plain (158 sts.). Change to No. 6 needles, and k. 42 rows for the full length of the sleeve seam.

TO SHAPE THE ARMHOLE : Cast off 4 sts. at the beginning of each of the next 4 rows, then k. 2 tog. at each end of every alternate row until 14 sts. more have been decreased from each side, leaving 114 sts. on the needle. Now k. 2 tog. at each end of the next 7 rows (100 sts. remain).

NEXT ROW : K. 2 tog., k. 24, k. 2 tog. Continuing on these 26 sts. only, k. 2 tog. at each end of the next 5 rows (16 sts.). Cast off.

* Join wool to the next st. along the main row, and cast off next 8 sts., then on the next 28 sts. work another point like the first one. Repeat from * once.

This completes one sleeve. Work the second sleeve in exactly the same way.

THE NECK BAND

WITH No. 9 needles cast on 216 sts., and k. into the back of the sts. on the 1st row. Work 4 rows of rib to match the cuffs, and cast off.

TO MAKE UP THE JUMPER

PRESS all the pieces with a hot iron and a damp cloth over the wrong side of the knitting, only touching the ribbing lightly. Sew up the shoulder seams on the wrong side.

Fold each point at the top of the sleeves in half, and oversew the edges as invisibly as possible on the right side. Sew the points for about 6½ inches down the sleeve, beginning at the base of the slope on the top edge of the point and running off to nothing. Now sew the top of the sleeves into the armholes, placing the centre point on the shoulder seam.

Oversew the neck band to the wrong side of the neck and front opening, beginning at the lower edge of the right front ; mitre at the corner of the neck and slightly stretch the band round the curve of the neck. Sew down the end under the right front and sew the right side opening over the left at the lower edge.

Press all these seams while the work is open, then sew up the side and sleeve seams in one continuous line and press. Crochet 2 ch. loops on right side for the fastening, and attach buttons to the left side.

To prevent the weight of the cartridge pleats from dragging the shoulders a strip of prussian binding can be sewn inside, if you wish, along the shoulder seams.

Beautiful 8 Page ART SUPPLEMENT FREE

Two little feathers adorn the top of the crown.

In Town— The NEW Crochet HAT!

It Has An Adjustable Brim.

can, however, be made from these directions as explained in the working.

To Work

BEGIN with 2 ch.

1st round : 9 d.c. into first ch.

2nd round : 2 d.c. into each st. taking up both loops at the top of the st., making 18 d.c.

On this hat the increases are evenly marked, so put a piece of white cotton in the first st. to mark the beginning of the round, then it is only necessary

Continued on page 96

THE last word in smartness, yet simple enough for the beginner in crochet work. There is only one stitch to learn after the foundation chain, and that is double crochet.

ABBREVIATIONS : ch., chain ; d.c., double crochet ; st., stitch. Directions in brackets are worked the number of times stated immediately after the brackets.

MATERIALS : 2 ounces of Patons and Baldwins' 3 ply Super-fingering and a No. 0 steel crochet hook.

SIZE AND TENSION : Worked at a tension of 7 d.c. to the inch in width this cap will have a head measurement of 21 inches, after following the instructions below. A hat of any measurement

Made in royal blue with one blue feather and one white one the hat looks most distinctive.

A BERET *for* Country Walks!

It is Worked in Tufted Crochet.

THIS beret is worked in an attractive stitch, which is very simple after a little practice, and it has the great advantage of being adaptable to any size. A beret for a small child can be made from the same directions, as well as one for the largest head.

Abbreviations as page 26.

MATERIALS: 3 ounces of "Greenock" 2-ply crochet wool (obtainable only at any of the branches of the Scotch Wool and Hosiery Stores), and a No. 0 steel crochet hook.

It is such a becoming cap and can be worn at different angles to suit individual taste.

The beret can be made in any size.

To Work

BEGIN at the centre of the crown with 4 ch., and sl.st. to the first st. to form a ring.

1st round : 8 d.c. into the ring.

2nd round : Into each d.c. work a tuft as follows : draw up the st. on the hook to about quarter of an inch (wool over hook, insert the hook into the first d.c. and draw the wool through to the same height as the previous loop) 3 times, 1 ch. to close the tuft. Do not join the end of the round, but put a piece of white cotton in the first st. as a guide to counting the rounds.

3rd round : * 2 tufts in the first st., 1 tuft in the next st., and repeat from * all round, making 12 tufts.

In Town—the New Crochet Hat

Continued from page 94

to count carefully the sts. between the increases.

Work two rounds of 1 d.c. in each st.

5th round : 2 d.c. into every 3rd d.c., working 1 d.c. on each intervening st. always.

6th round : 1 d.c. in each st.

7th round : 2 d.c. into every 4th st.

8th round : As 6th round.

9th round : 2 d.c. into every 5th st., making 6 increase points in the round.

Now continue working in this way, increasing over the increase stitches of previous round (on each successive round working 1 d.c. more before the increase) until the 27th round is worked, with 2 d.c. into every 23rd st.

More or less increase rounds may be worked here according to size of hat required, as the outer edge of this piece determines the head measurement.

Now work 35 rounds of d.c. without alteration for the full depth of the crown.

The Brim

This is worked in rows, that is turning at the end of every row, still taking up both loops of the stitch. Work 23 rounds in this way and fasten off. Sew up the end of the rows on the brim, and turn up at the depth required.

Make a fold in the crown about ¾ of an inch wide, so that the folded edge comes just below the last increase round of the crown. Catch on the wrong side of the cap, making a st. in a d.c. on one side of the fold, miss 3 d.c. on the opposite edge of the fold and make another st. there. Continue in this way all round.

Put a damp cloth on the inside of the cap and press the fold and brim well.

Run two quills through the d.c. near the centre top of the cap.

❅   ❅   ❅

A Beret for Country Walks

Continued from page 95

4th round : As 3rd round, 18 tufts.

5th round : As 3rd round, but work two separate tufts between the increases, 24 tufts.

6th round : On this round make 8 increases in the round. These need not be evenly spaced, provided 4 are worked on each half of the circle, as the increases should not be in a definite line.

7th round : Work only 4 increases in this round at fairly equal distances apart.

Repeat the last 2 rounds until the flat circle measures 8½ inches in diameter, or according to the size of beret required.

It may be necessary to vary the shaping in these rounds, as nearly everyone works tufted crochet at a slightly different tension, so if the work is inclined to flute, work a round with 4 increases instead of 8, or if the work is inclined to curl you are working more tightly than required; this is easily remedied with a few more increases in the round.

The head measurement can be made any size by varying the increase rounds, and any depth by working more of the straight rounds which follow this part, and making a tighter or looser d.c. band as required.

Next 6 rounds : Work one tuft after every tuft of the previous round.

Next 4 rounds : * Work 15 tufts, miss the next one and repeat from * until 4 rounds more have been worked.

The Head-Band.—This is worked in flat d.c., taking up both loops at the top of the stitch. On the first round work 2 d.c. into every space between the tufts, then work 7 rounds of d.c., putting 1 d.c. into each st. of the previous round. The change of stitch is enough to make a close-fitting band, but decreases, by missing a d.c. here and there for a tighter head-band.

A MAN'S SWIMMING SUIT

Materials: 7 oz. Sirdar Sunshine Bathing Wool in deep red, 4 oz. Sirdar Sunshine Bathing Wool in navy. 1 pair No. 12 Stratnoid knitting needles. 2 buttons. **Abbreviations :** k., knit ; p., purl ; st., stitches ; m., make ; inc., increase ; dec., decrease ; tog., together. **Measurements :** Length, shoulder to hem, 30 in. ; across chest, 15 in. ; hips, 15 in. ; waist, 12 in. ; **Tension :** 7 stitches to the inch.

The Front.—Cast on 62 sts. with deep red wool. Knit into back 1st row loosely and rib for 10 rows in k. 1—p. 1. Change to stocking-stitch (1 row plain, 1 row purl) and work 44 rows. Slip this on to a safety-pin. Knit another piece the same. Then join the two pieces together, giving 124 sts. on needle. Work 25 rows in stocking-stitch. **Next row :** * k. 2, slip 1 k. 1. Pass slip stitch over knitted one. Knit to within 4 sts. from end of row. K. 2 tog., k. 2.* Then k. 3 rows stocking-stitch without shaping. Repeat from * to * until 94 sts. on pin. Now work 20 rows without decrease. Join on blue wool and increase as follows : K. 3. M. 1 by knitting into front and back of stitch. Knit to within 3 sts. from end of row, m. 1,

k. 3. The next 3 rows without increase. Repeat these 4 rows until 110 sts. on pin, but after 15 rows of blue, join on red with a plain row. P. 1 row. Join on blue. Work 5 rows. Join on red. Work 1 row. Join on blue. Work 5 rows. Join on red. Work 15 rows. Join on blue. Work 5 rows. **Next row :** k. 4, p. 102, k. 4. **Next row :** Knit. **Next row :** K. 6, p. 98, k. 6. **Next row :** Cast off 2 sts., k. to end of row. **Next row :** Cast off 2 sts., k. 4, p. 98, k. 4. **Next row :** K. 3, slip 1, pass st. over, knit to within 5 sts., k. 2 tog., k. 3. **Next row :** K. 4, p. to within 4, k. 4. Repeat the last 2 rows until 86 sts. on pin. **Next row :** K. 4, p. 33, k. 12, p. 33, k. 4. **Next row :** K. 3, slip 1, k. 1, pass st. over. Knit to within 5 sts., k. 2 tog., k. 3. **Next row :** K. 4, p. 29, k. 18, p. 29, k. 4. **Next row :** K. 3, slip 1, k. 1, pass st. over. Knit to within 5. K. 2 tog., k. 3. **Next row :** K. 4, p. 26, k. 5. Slip on to a large safety-pin. Then cast off 12, k. 5, p. 26, k. 4 for the other shoulder. **Next row** (one shoulder only) : Cast off 2 sts., k. 4, purl to within 4 sts., k. these. Now continue to k. 4

each end of every purl row and dec. 1 st. each end of every knit row at armhole edge until 18 sts. remain. Work until armhole measures 9½ ins., then k. 8 rows stocking-stitch. Go to other side and k. the same.

The Back.—This is made exactly as front, but make 2 buttonholes at left strap, before finishing 8 rows stocking-stitch. K. 4. Cast off 4. K. 2. Cast off 4. K. 4. **Next row :** Cast on the sts. cast off.

Gusset.—Cast on 2 and knit in stocking-stitch, increasing every knit row 1 each end until 38 sts. Then cast off 1 each end every plain row until all sts. cast off.

To make up.—Sew up side seams. (See that stripes match perfectly.) Sew in gusset. Sew up inner leg seam. Press thoroughly with warm iron and damp cloth. Work button-holes. Sew on buttons.

The buckled straps over the white top give it a very jaunty and nautical air.

The PINAFORE JUMPER Speaks for Itself !

It is Quite the Most Novel and Attractive of the New Spring Knitting Designs.

Blue and white carries out this smart jumper, with a touch of red on the spots of the scarf, to complete the popular trio of colours. The buckled straps over the white top give a very jaunty and nautical air, so you will love this jumper for holidays. You can, of course, adopt your own colour scheme and tone with a tweed skirt.

Materials : Three ounces of Baldwin & Walker's " Ladyship " 3-ply Scotch Fingering in blue and 4 ounces of the same wool in white, a small ball or a few odd lengths of red wool for the spots, a pair each of knitting needles No. 12 and No. 8, and a bone crochet hook No. 13 or a steel hook No. oo (the coarsest size in steel hooks), and a pair of buckles.

Tension and Measurements : Worked at a tension of 6½ stitches to the inch in width on the blue pinafore part (and 6 sts. to the inch on the light lace part, as it is an open pattern), the following measurements are attained

after light pressing : Round the bust, 38 inches (19½ inches across the front and 18½ inches across the back) at the top of the blue part, just under the points ; length of front from shoulder seam to lower edge, 20 inches ; length of back from shoulder seam to lower edge, 19 inches ; side seam, 12 inches ; sleeve seam, 4 inches.

Abbreviations : K., knit ; p., purl ; tog., together ; inc., increase (by working into the back and front of the same st.) ; sl., slip ; st., stitch ; m., make (by bringing the wool to the front of the needle) rib is k. 2 and p. 2 alternately ; directions in brackets are worked the number of times stated immediately after the brackets ; ch., chain ; d.c., double crochet ; tr., treble.

To Work the Pinafore Front

Begin at the lower edge of the front and, using No. 12 needles, cast on 108 sts. with the blue wool. Rib 32 rows.

Next row : Inc. in the first st., k. 1, inc. in the next st. (rib. 6, inc. in the next st.) 15 times, giving 125 sts. altogether. Change to No. 8 needles and work in the following pattern :

1st row : With the right side facing k. plain.
2nd row : All purl.
3rd row : All knit.
4th row : K. 1, * p. 1, k. 1 ; repeat from * to end.
5th row : All knit.
6th row : All purl.
7th row : All knit.
8th row : P. 1, * k. 1, p. 1 ; repeat from * to end.

Repeat these 8 rows 7 times more, then work 3 rows more in pattern.

Next row : With the wrong side facing, k. 13, pattern 41, k. 17, pattern 41, k. 13 (when working the back of the jumper k. 8 at each end instead of 13).
K. one row.

Next row : Cast off 11 sts., k. 4 (including the one on the needle after casting off), p. 37, k. 4, cast off 13, k. 4, p. 37, k. 4, cast off 11, and fasten off. (On the back of the jumper cast off 6 sts. at the beginning and end instead of 11.)

There are now two sets of 45 sts. for the points to which the shoulder straps are afterwards fastened.

To work the points, join the wool to the beginning of 45 sts. with the right side facing the worker.

1st row : K. 2 tog., k. until 2 sts. remain, k. 2 tog.
2nd row : K. 2 tog., k. 3, work in pattern until 5 remain, k. 3, k. 2 tog.

Repeat these 2 rows until 13 sts. remain ; cast off.

Work the second point in the same way.

The Back : Work the waist rib as on the front.

Navy Blue and White is Always Smart and it is Particularly Suitable for this New Jumper. The Dash of Red Introduced by the Spots on the Scarf Will Give You the Popular Tri-colour Effect.

The scarf can be attached to the back of the neck or worn loose just when it is wanted.

Next row : Rib 3, (inc. in the next st., rib. 14) 7 times. There are now 115 sts.

Change to No. 8 needles and work as given for the front (bearing in mind the special points where the back directions vary from the front, and which are specially bracketed in the front directions) until the back point is reduced to 13 sts. Now work 137 rows straight, but k. 2 as a border at each end of the wrong side rows and the 9 middle sts. in pattern. Now mitre the end by working 2 sts. tog. at each end of the next row (with right side facing) and every following alternate row, until all are worked off.

Work the second strap in the same manner.

The Lace Back : With white wool and No. 8 needles, cast on 115 sts. and work in the following pattern :

1st row : With the right side facing, k. plain.

2nd row : All purl.

3rd and *4th row :* K. 2, * m. 1, k. 2 tog. ; repeat from * to end, finishing with k. 1.

Repeat these 4 rows twice more up to the armhole.

To shape the armhole cast off 2 sts. from the beginning of each of the next 6 rows, after which cast off 1 st. from the beginning of the following 12 rows, which leaves 91 sts.

Work 34 rows up to the shoulder-line.

To slope the shoulders cast off 6 sts. from the beginning of each of the next 8 rows. Cast off the remaining 43 sts. for the back neck.

The Lace Front : With No. 8 needles and white wool, cast on 123 sts. and work the lace pattern for 12 rows to armhole.

To shape the armhole cast off 2 sts. from the beginning of the next 14 rows, then cast off 1 st. from the beginning of the following 4 rows ; this leaves 91 sts.

Work 23 rows straight up to the neck-line, ending with the first pattern row.

Next row : With the wrong side facing p. 41, and sl. these sts. on a spare needle for the right shoulder, cast off 9, p. 41 (including the 1 st. on the needle after casting off) for the left shoulder.

The Left Shoulder : Continue in pattern, casting off 2 sts. from the beginning of alternate rows (neck end) 4 times, then cast off 1 from the beginning of alternate rows (neck end) 4 times, which leaves 29 sts. Work 4 rows, then cast off 6 sts. from the beginning of the next row and every alternate row (armhole end) 4 times, and finally cast off the remaining 5 sts.

The Right Shoulder : Join the wool to the neck end and work 1 row, then follow the directions as given for the left shoulder.

The Sleeves : With white wool and No. 12 needles, cast on 92 sts. and rib 10 rows.

Next row : P. 2 tog., (p. 7, p. 2 tog.) 10 times, which leaves 81 sts.

Now with No. 8 needles work the lacy pattern for 24 rows.

To shape the top of the sleeve : *Continue in the same pattern, casting off 4 sts. from the beginning of the 1st and 2nd pattern rows, and cast off 2 sts. from the beginning of the 3rd and 4th pattern rows ; repeat from * until 21 sts. remain. Cast off.

Work the second sleeve in the same manner.

The Scarf : With No. 8 needles and white wool, cast on 37 sts. and k. 24 rows.

Now work the following pattern :

1st row : With the right side facing all knit.

2nd row : K. 4, p. until 4 remain, k. 4.

3rd and 4th rows : K. 4, * m. 1, k. 2 tog., repeat from * until 3 sts. remain, k. 3.

Repeat these 4 rows 4 times more, then continue in the same pattern, working 2 sts. tog. at each end of the next row (that is the 3rd and 4th st. from each end of row) and every following 8th row until there are 29 sts. left. Work the 4 pattern rows 38 times (beginning with the 2nd pattern row and ending with the 4th pattern row). Continue in pattern, increasing 1 st. in the 4th st. from each end of the next row and every following 8th row, until there are 37 sts. on the needle, ending with the 1st pattern row.

The back view of the jumper is plain, but it has a very becoming line.

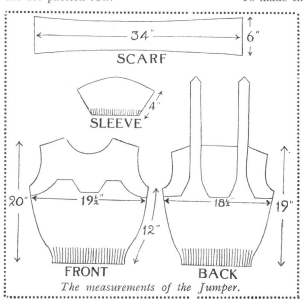

SCARF   34"   6"

SLEEVE   4"

FRONT   BACK

20"   19½"   18½"   19"

12"

The measurements of the Jumper.

Work 21 rows more, in pattern, ending with the 2nd pattern row. K. 24 rows plain and cast off loosely.

The Spots : For the large spots using red wool and crochet hook, make 4 ch. and sl.-st. into the end ch., work 4 ch., then into the ring work 12 tr. and fasten off. Work 5 spots more exactly the same. To make the small spots begin as for the large spots and after the sl.-st. make 2 ch., and work 8 d.c. into the ring and fasten off. Work 15 spots in the same manner. Sew half the spots of each size to each end of the scarf, as seen in the illustration, or arrange them according to individual fancy. Sew them with running sts. of the same red wool, just inside the chain edge of the last round.

To Make Up : First press all pieces with a damp cloth over the wrong side of the work, taking care that the rib is not stretched. Tack the cast-on edge of the white top to the wrong side of the blue piece (taking care that

the right side of both pieces is facing the same way) with the edge of the white wool on a level with the row that has a little ridge of knitting at the side seam. Now, using the blue wool, sew the two pieces together, taking the needle through one white st. and one blue st. for every hemming st., except at the centre, where take two blue to one white twice, to dispose of the two extra blue stitches.

Join the back white piece to the blue in the same manner at the corresponding position. Sew the shoulder seams, beginning at the armhole end, and taking 1 st. from each side at a time. With white wool work 2 rows of flat d.c. round the neck, putting 1 d.c. in each k. st. on the first row. Sew the top of the sleeves to the armholes and press all these seams and the neck while the work is open. Now sew the sleeve and side seams in one continuous line and press. Sew one buckle to each point on the pinafore front, by over-casting the bar of the buckle and putting the needle through one k. st. at a time. Adjust the straps to the right position in wear and pass the end of the straps through the buckles and the point through the centre of one of the knitted stitches.

Sew the scarf to the back of the neck if preferred for indoor wear, or leave unattached for outside wear only.

A Clever Trimming
WITH CROCHET RINGS

THE main part of this jumper is knitted, but the little white rings round the neck and sleeves are worked in crochet.

Pretty in any two-colour scheme!

Our model was made up in golden-fawn and white.

You can adapt the jumper to any size, and the number of rings can be altered accordingly.

MATERIALS.—Five ounces of Sirdar Crochet wool in fawn and 2 ounces in white; a pair each of knitting needles, No. 10 and No. 8; a No. 9 bone crochet hook.

ABBREVIATIONS.—K., knit plain; p., purl; tog., together; st., stitch; m., make (by bringing the wool to the front of the needle); inc., increase; dec., decrease; ch., chain; d.c., double crochet; tr., treble; d.tr., double tr. (wool twice round the hook, then work off the loops in twos as in ordinary tr.). Directions in brackets are worked the number of times stated immediately after the brackets.

TENSION and MEASUREMENTS.—Worked at a tension of 6 sts. to the inch in width on the fancy pattern knitting, the following measurements are attained after pressing: Round the bust, 36 inches; front length, 16½ inches; side seam, 10 inches; sleeve seam, 8 inches; full width at top of sleeve, 15 inches.

To work the back

WITH No. 10 needles cast on 100 sts. in fawn, and work in a rib of k. 2 and p. 2 alternately for 25 rows. (For a larger bust measurement add a number of stitches that will divide by 4.)

Change to No. 8 needles and work a purl row in which inc. 10 sts. at equal distances along the row by knitting into the front and back of each of these stitches (110 sts. on).

1ST ROW OF PATTERN: K 2, * m. 1, k. 2 tog., k. 2; repeat from * to the end of row.

2ND ROW (and all even numbered rows). All purl.

3RD ROW: K. 2, * k. 2 tog., m. 1 k. 2; repeat from * to the end.

4TH ROW: Purl.

These four rows form one pattern, so repeat them 11 times more, then work the first 2 rows again, when the armholes will be reached. (If a bigger jumper is being made and more length is required, work it here before shaping the armholes.)

To shape the armholes, cast off 5 sts., then repeat from * in the 3rd row.

NEXT ROW: Cast off 5 sts. and p. to end.

Continue in pattern, taking 2 sts. tog. at the beginning and end of the next 4 rows, so the 3rd row of armhole (equivalent to the 1st row of the pattern) will be worked thus: K. 2 tog., k. 1, m. 1, k. 2, then repeat from * in 1st row until within 2 sts. of the end of the row, k. 2 tog.

4TH ROW: All purl, decreasing at both ends.

5TH ROW: K. 2 tog., k. 2, then repeat from * in 3rd row to within 2 sts. of the end, k. 2 tog.

6TH ROW: All purl, dec. 1 st. at each end. There should now be 92 sts.

Now work 15 rows straight without alteration, up to the back neck-line. (Take care to keep the pattern correct at the beginning of right side rows, but it can be seen very plainly now as the k. 2 rib comes straight up the work.)

NEXT ROW: P. 34, p. 2 tog., cast off 20, when there will be 1 st. on the right hand needle, p. 2 tog., p. 33, making 35 sts. at this end.

RIGHT BACK SHOULDER: 1ST ROW: In pattern and k. 2 tog. at the end. (Slip the other 35 sts. on a spare needle.)

2ND ROW: Cast off 3 sts. and p. to end.

Repeat the last 2 rows until 22 sts. remain on the needle, after which dec. 1 st. at the neck end of each row until 6 sts. remain, on which work 1 inch and cast off.

Join the wool to the opposite shoulder sts. at the centre of the back, and work the left shoulder to match.

The front

WORK from the back directions, but begin with 102 sts. and inc. to 114. Change to No. 8 needles and work 15 rows. (More rows may be worked here for a larger size.)

NEXT ROW: P. 46, cast off 22 centre sts. and p. 45 more, making 46 with the one on the needle after casting off.

THE LEFT FRONT: Work back on the last 46 sts. in pattern, taking the last 2 sts. tog. and slip the other 46 sts. on a stitch-holder.

2ND ROW: Cast off 3 sts. and p. to end (42 sts. on needle).

3RD ROW: In pattern taking the last 2 sts. tog.

Repeat the last 2 rows once more.

Now continue in pattern, decreasing 1 st. every 4th row at the inside edge only, keeping the side seam straight until the sts. are reduced to 30. Work on 30 sts. without further decrease until there are as many rows on the side seam up to the armhole as on the corresponding part of the back, ending with a purl row.

To shape the front armhole cast off 5 sts. and work in pattern to end.

NEXT ROW: Purl.

Cast off 1 st. at the beginning of the next 4 rows, then work back to centre edge.

* At the beginning of the next row take 2 tog. (centre edge) and p. to end of row. Work the next 3 rows in pattern without any dec. and repeat from * until 6 sts. remain. Work on 6 sts. in pattern for 4 rows and cast off.

Join the wool at the centre edge of the sts. on the spare needle and work the right half of front to match, remembering to reverse the front by working the inside edge decreases at the beginning of right side rows, and begin the armhole shaping on the wrong side, when the rest will follow suit. Press the back and front with a hot iron and a damp cloth over on the wrong side of the work. Join both shoulder seams, then work d.c. all round the centre opening, back and front, putting just enough stitches to allow the edge to lie quite flat, and do not fasten off the fawn wool.

The rings

Take a fresh ball of fawn wool and the crochet hook, and work as follows: 4 ch. and sl.st. to first st. to form a ring, 4 ch. to stand for 1 tr. and 1 ch., 1 tr. into the ring, ★ 1 ch., 1 tr. into the ring and repeat from ★ 12 times more, 1 ch., sl.st. to the top of 4 ch. at the beginning to join; fasten off. Join the white wool where the fawn was fastened off, 4 ch., to stand for a d.tr. Work 2 d.tr. more under the first 1 ch. between 2 tr. of previous round, then 3 d.tr. under every space of 1 ch. and join with a sl.st. to the top of 4 ch. at the beginning of the round, and fasten off.

Work a second ring, but when 7 groups of 3 d.tr. have been worked, take out the hook and sl. it through the corresponding d.tr. of the previous ring, draw the st. through and make a close ch. (this joins the rings together), finish the round on the second ring and fasten off. Continue working and joining the rings in this way until there are enough to go all round the centre opening (17 on the jumper illustrated), then press with a hot iron and damp cloth over the wrong side.

Now join the rings to the jumper as follows: Holding the jumper with the right side facing, take up the wool that was left hanging after the first round of d.c. on the inside edge and put 1 d.c. in a d.c. on that edge, take up the rings and work, ★ 1 d.c. in the 7th d.tr. from the side join, 4 d.c. along the row, miss 3 white d.tr. on the ring, 1 d.c. on the next white d.tr., 1 d.c. in the same place along the row, miss 3 white d.tr., 1 d.c. in the next white d.tr., 1 d.c. in the same place along the row as the last d.c., 4 d.c. along the row, 1 d.c. in the same place as the last d.c., miss 4 white d.tr. on the ring, 1 d.c. in the next st., 2 ch., 1 d.c. in the corresponding st. on the next ring, 1 ch., 1 d.c. in the same st. along the row that already has 2 d.c. in it, 3 d.c. along the row, miss 4 white d.tr., 1 d.c. in the next d.tr., 4 d.c. along the row and repeat from ★ until all the rings are joined on this edge and fasten off.

THE TOP ROW: Begin with the ring which is on a level with the left shoulder seam, count 7 d.tr. to the left from the side join, and in the space after that st. put 1 d.c. ★ 3 ch., miss 3 d.tr., 1 d.c. between the next 2 sts., 3 ch., miss 3 d.tr., wool over hook, insert hook between 2 sts., draw through two loops, wool over hook, insert hook through the corresponding st. on the next ring, draw through two loops only, wool over hook, draw through all the loops on the hook, (3 ch., miss 3 d.tr., 1 d.c. between the next 2 sts.) twice, then repeat from ★ all round and fasten off.

At the back, the rings follow the higher neckline.

THE NECK FILLING: Hold the work with the right side facing, then using fawn wool and No. 8 needles, pick up and k. 28 sts. along the top of the three centre rings, from the ch. and d.c. sts., turn and p. to the end and here pick up 2 sts. more along the ch., turn and work the first row of the pattern and at the end pick up 2 sts. more along the chain sts., turn and p. back and again pick up 2 sts. more along the row at this end. Remember to keep the right side rows in pattern after picking up more sts. Continue in this way working in pattern, taking up 1 st. more from the ch. at the end of each row, until there are 52 sts. on the needle, ending with a pattern row.

Change to No. 10 needles and continue along the row, taking up one thread of every alternate st. up the side of the neck to the right shoulder seam. (If every alternate st. contracts the knitting, pick up several consecutive sts. here and there, as every knitter varies), turn and p. back along these sts. and over the 52 centre sts., then pick up along the opposite side of the neck up to the left shoulder seam to correspond with the first side. Continue in rib pattern on the right side working k. 2 and p. 3, and on the wrong side of the work k. 3 and p. 2 all along. Work 12 rows more in this ribbing and cast off loosely.

Now pick up the stitches round the back of the neck and work the ribbing in the same way.

The sleeves

WORK six rings as described for the jumper, joining to form a circle when they are finished.

Work on both the long edges as instructed for the top row of the rings on the jumper, but putting 3 ch. between all the sts. so that the row is not contracted; it should be quite straight.

For the knitted part of the sleeve cast on 78 sts. and work in fancy pattern, casting on 2 sts. at the beginning of each of the next 10 rows, when there will be 98 sts. on the needle. Continue in pattern taking 2 tog. at both ends of every 8th row until 90 sts. remain; work 6 rows more, then cast off.

With No. 10 needles cast on 80 sts. and work 12 rows in rib to match the ribbing at the neck and cast off loosely. Work the pieces for the second sleeve in the same manner, then press them all on the wrong side.

Sew the ribbing to one edge of the rings and the sleeve piece to the other edge.

To make up the jumper

WORK a row of d.c. round the armhole to strengthen it, but do not contract the edge; sew the top of the sleeve to this row, and press this seam while the work is open. Join the side and sleeve seams in one continuous line, and press. Sew up the short seams of knitting at the sides of the neck.

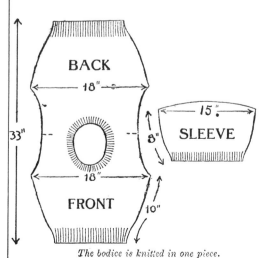

BACK

18"

33"

SLEEVE

15"

8"

FRONT

18"

10"

The bodice is knitted in one piece.

Hasn't it a graceful line on the shoulders?

It Will Always—

This Is One Of Our Prettiest Confections !

bust, 18 inches from the shoulder to the lower edge of the front, and 12 inches on the side seam.

TO WORK THE FRONT

BEGIN at the waist edge, using No. 10 needles, and cast on 90 sts.

Work 20 rows of single rib (k. 1 and p. 1 alternately).

Change to No 8 needles and proceed in s.s., increasing 1 st. at the beginning and end of the 5th, 11th, 17th, 23rd and 29th rows, making a total of 100 sts. On these continue straight until the 66th row above the rib is completed, or in any other length until the armhole is reached.

To shape the armhole cast off 8 sts. at the beginning of each of the next 2 rows, after which dec. 1 st. at the beginning of the next 4 rows (80 sts. on).

THE YOKE. 1st Row: K. 2 tog., k. 24, (m. 1, k. 2 tog.) 14 times, k. 24, k. 2 tog.

2ND ROW: P. 25, k. 28, p. 25.

3RD ROW: K. plain, decreasing 1 st. at the beginning and end of the row.

4TH ROW: All purl.

5TH ROW: K. 2 tog., k. 10, (m. 1, k. 2 tog.) 26 times, k. 10, k. 2 tog. (74 sts. on).

6TH ROW: P. 11, k. 52, p. 11.

7TH ROW: K. plain.

8TH ROW: Purl (74 sts.).

9TH ROW: K. 1, (m. 1, k. 2 tog.) 36 times, k. 1.

10TH ROW: K. plain.

11TH ROW: K. plain.

12TH ROW: Purl.

13TH ROW: Cast on 2 sts., k. 1, * m. 1, k. 2 tog. ; repeat from * to the last st., which k. plain (76 sts.).

14TH ROW: Cast on 2 sts. and k. to end of row.

Work the next 2 rows in s.s., beginning with a k. row (78 sts. on).

17TH ROW: Cast on 4 sts., k. 1, (m. 1, k. 2 tog.) 18 times, cast off 12, leaving 1 st. on the right hand needle, (m. 1, k. 2 tog.) 16 times.

THE RIGHT SHOULDER : Cast on 4 sts. and k. back to neck, when there will be 37 sts. for the right shoulder. Pass the first 37 sts. on a spare needle or a stitch-holder for the present.

Work 2 rows more in s.s. to finish this pattern.

NEXT PATTERN. 1st Row: K. 1, * m. 1, k. 2 tog. to end of row.

2ND ROW: K. plain.

3RD ROW: K. plain.

HERE'S a jumper you can make at the last minute for your holidays ! Don't you love the pretty bertha effect ? It is so delightfully feminine.

MATERIALS : Three ounces of Patons & Baldwins' 2-ply Super Fingering and a pair each of No. 10 and No. 8 knitting needles, a No. 12 bone crochet hook or a No. 00 steel hook.

ABBREVIATIONS : K., knit plain, p., purl ; m., make (by bringing the wool to the front of the needle) ; tog., together ; st., stitch ; inc., increase ; dec., decrease ; s.s., stocking st. (k. on the right side and p. back) ; directions in brackets are worked the number of times stated immediately after the brackets ; ch., chain ; d.c., double crochet ; tr., treble.

TENSION AND MEASUREMENTS : Working at a tension of 6½ sts. to the inch in width on the plain knitting with the No. 8 needles, the jumper measures 33 inches round the

Be Your Friend!

And It's Simple Enough For Your Holiday Knitting.

4TH ROW: Purl all.

Repeat the last pattern 4 times more.

To slope the shoulder, work the first row of the last pattern.

NEXT ROW: Cast off 5 sts. and k. to end of row.

NEXT ROW: K. plain.

NEXT ROW: Cast off 2, and p. to end.

NEXT ROW: K. 1, then m. 1 and k. 2 tog. to the end of the row.

NEXT ROW: Cast off 5 and k. to end.

NEXT ROW: K. plain.

NEXT ROW: Cast off 2 and p. to end.

NEXT ROW: K. 1, then m. 1 and k. 2 tog. to the end of the row, k. 1 at end.

NEXT ROW: Cast off 5 and k. to end.

NEXT ROW: K. plain.

Cast off on the wrong side.

THE LEFT SHOULDER: Join the wool at the neck end of the first shoulder sts. and, beginning with the second row of the pattern (plain k. row), work to shoulder end. Continue working to match the first shoulder, but note that the sloping of the shoulder will begin on the right side of the work, instead of the wrong side.

THE BACK

CAST on 90 sts. and work as front until the armhole shaping is finished, when there will be 80 sts. on.

Continue in s.s. for 18 rows more.

NEXT ROW: K. 20 (m. 1, k. 2 tog.) 20 times, k. 20.

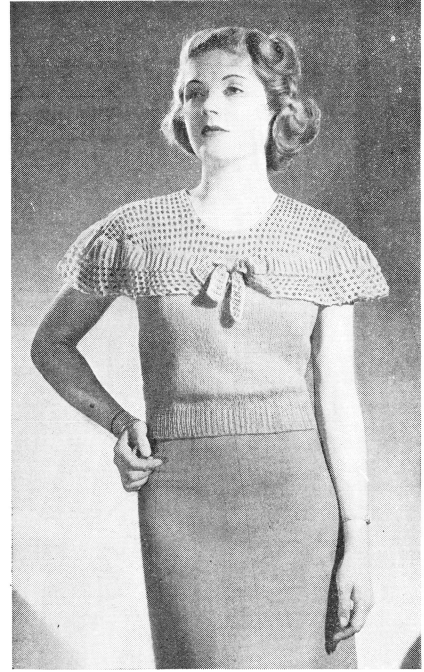

The main part of the knitting is ordinary stocking stitch.

NEXT ROW: P. 20, k. 40, p. 20.

K. one row and p. one row.

Now continue in the open-work pattern from the 1st row, casting on 2 sts. at the beginning of each of the next 8 rows, when there will be 96 sts. on and 3 rows of open pattern altogether, counting the 1st row with 20 holes in the middle.

Repeat the 4 pattern rows on these 96 sts. 3 times more, when the back-neckline will be reached.

RIGHT BACK SHOULDER: On the next row divide the sts. for the two shoulders thus: K. 1, (m. 1, k. 2 tog.) 20 times, leaving the remaining 55 sts. on a spare needle.

Continue on the first shoulder thus: * cast off 2 sts. and k. to end, turn. Cast off 7 sts. from the shoulder end and k. back to neck. Repeat from * twice more, keeping the pattern correct. Cast off the remaining 14 sts.

Continued on page 106

52"

3½"

18" **16½"** **12"** **FRONT**

16½" **BACK** **18"**

These are the separate pieces of the knitting.

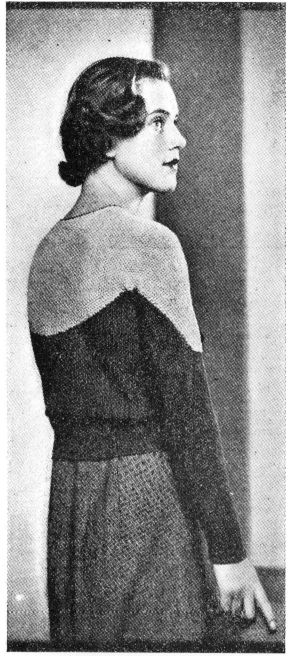

The yoke is prettily curved at the back.

IT'S VERY CAPTIVATING!

The Yoke, In Lighter Wool, Is Knitted In Moss Stitch, While The Bodice Is In Stocking Stitch.

TO WORK THE FRONT

BEGIN at the lower edge and with No. 12 needles and dark wool cast on 120 sts.

Work 45 rows in single rib.

Change to No. 9 needles and work 20 rows in s.s., beginning with a k. row for the right side of the work.

On the next row the pointed yoke in the light wool is begun. Note that this is worked in m.s. throughout in the light wool and the dark sts. at each side are worked in s.s. with the dark wool, so in the following directions only the number of light and dark sts. will be given. When working the first light st. always twist the dark wool over the light wool before working the first light st. to avoid a gap between the two colours. Do this at every change of colour.

On the next 4 rows work 59 dark, 2 light, 59 dark.

NEXT 4 ROWS : 58 dark, 4 light, 58 dark.
NEXT 4 ROWS : 57 dark, 6 light, 57 dark.
NEXT 3 ROWS : 56 dark, 8 light, 56 dark.
NEXT 3 ROWS : 55 dark, 10 light, 55 dark.
NEXT 3 ROWS : 54 dark, 12 light, 54 dark.
NEXT 3 ROWS : 53 dark, 14 light, 53 dark.
NEXT 2 ROWS : 52 dark, 16 light, 52 dark.
NEXT 2 ROWS : 51 dark, 18 light, 51 dark.
NEXT 3 ROWS : 50 dark, 20 light, 50 dark.
NEXT 2 ROWS : 49 dark, 22 light, 49 dark.
NEXT 2 ROWS : 48 dark, 24 light, 48 dark.
NEXT 2 ROWS : 47 dark, 26 light, 47 dark.
NEXT 2 ROWS : 46 dark, 28 light, 46 dark.
NEXT 2 ROWS : 45 dark, 30 light, 45 dark.
NEXT 2 ROWS : 44 dark, 32 light, 44 dark.
NEXT 2 ROWS : 43 dark, 34 light, 43 dark.
NEXT ROW : 42 dark, 36 light, 42 dark.
NEXT ROW : 41 dark, 38 light, 41 dark.
NEXT 2 ROWS : 40 dark, 40 light, 40 dark.
NEXT ROW : 39 dark, 42 light, 39 dark.
NEXT 2 ROWS : 38 dark, 44 light, 38 dark.
NEXT ROW : 37 dark, 46, light, 37 dark.

Now work 7 rows with 1 stitch less in dark wool on each side of the centre light sts. and consequently 2 light sts. more on each row, when the armholes will be reached.

To shape the armholes, cast off 10 sts. and work 19 dark, including the

---

A JUMPER with a lighter yoke is so becoming! In brown and creamy beige our model is a very feminine affair.

MATERIALS : Two ounces of Baldwin & Walker's 3-ply "Ladyship" Scotch Fingering in a light shade and 5 ounces of the same wool in a dark shade, two No. 9 and two No. 12 bone knitting needles, a No. 12 bone crochet hook, 1 large button, and 3 small ones to match.

ABBREVIATIONS : K., knit plain; p., purl; st., stitch; tog., together; s.s., stocking stitch (k. on the right side and p. back); m.s., moss st. (k. 1 and p. 1 alternately, and on successive rows a k. must come over a purl, and vice versa); single rib is k. 1 and p. 1 alternately.

TENSION AND MEASUREMENTS : Worked at a tension of 7 sts. to the inch in width on the plain s.s., the following measurements are attained after pressing : Round the bust at the underarms, 35 inches ; length from shoulder to hem, 17 inches, side seam 12½ inches, sleeve seam with cuff 19½ inches.

BACK — 17½

34″

FRONT — 17½ — 12½″

SLEEVE — 19½

This is how the pieces of knitting are shaped.

1 st. on the needle after casting off, 62 light, 29 dark.

Cast off 10 sts., 18 dark, 64 light, 18 dark.

NEXT ROW: 17 dark, 66 light, 15 dark, and take 2 tog. for a decrease.

NEXT ROW: 15 dark, 68 light, 14 dark and take 2 tog.

NEXT ROW: 13 dark, 72 light, 11 dark and take 2 tog.

NEXT ROW: 10 dark, 76 light, 9 dark and take 2 tog.

NEXT ROW: 9 dark, 78 light, 7 dark and take 2 tog.

NEXT ROW: 6 dark, 82 light, 5 dark and take 2 tog.

NEXT ROW: 5 dark, 84 light, 3 dark and take 2 tog.

NEXT ROW: 3 dark, 86 light, 2 dark, and take 2 tog.

NEXT ROW: 2 dark, 88 light, take 2 tog. with dark wool, then fasten off the dark wool.

NEXT ROW: Work 89 in m.s. and dec. on the last 2 sts.

On the next row the neck opening is begun. Continue with all light wool and inc. at the shoulder end, (by working into the back and front of the end st.) on every row, the first row being as follows: m.s. 44 (including inc.), take 2 tog. and turn, leaving the remaining 50 sts. on a spare needle for the right shoulder.

Could you picture a more feminine jumper?

A close-up of the jumper to show you the details.

THE LEFT SHOULDER: Dec. on every other row at the neck edge 12 times more, remembering to inc. at the shoulder edge on every row, then work 22 rows with the neck edge straight, or until there are 80 sts. On these sts. work 10 rows with both edges straight, then slip them on a spare needle.

Join the wool at the neck edge of the sts. left on the spare needle, and work the right shoulder exactly the same.

THE BACK

THIS is continued right on the work.

1ST ROW OF BACK: M.s. 80, cast on 26 for the back of the neck, m.s. 80 (186 sts.).

Work 6 rows straight, after which dec. 1 st. at both ends of every row until 90 sts. remain.

Now take two balls of dark wool and begin the dark sts. at each side as detailed below for the back of the jumper.

Continued overleaf

It's Very Captivating

Continued from page 105

With dark wool inc. in the first st., work 88 light, inc. in the last st. with dark wool.

NEXT ROW : 2 dark, 88 light, 2 dark.

NEXT ROW : K. 1, inc., 1 dark, 86 light, 1 dark, inc., 1 dark.

NEXT ROW : 4 dark, 86 light, 4 dark.

NEXT ROW : K. 1, inc. in the next st., 3 dark, 84 light, 3 dark, inc., k. 1.

NEXT ROW : 6 dark, 84 light, 6 dark.

NEXT ROW : K. 1 inc. in the next st., 5 dark, 82 light, 5 dark, inc., k. 1.

NEXT ROW : 9 dark, 80 light, 9 dark.

NEXT ROW : K. 1, inc., 7 dark, 80 light, 7 dark, inc., k. 1.

NEXT ROW : 11 dark, 78 light, 11 dark.

NEXT ROW : 12 dark, 76 light, 12 dark and cast on 10.

NEXT ROW : 23 dark, 74 light, 13 dark and cast on 10. (This row finishes the back armhole shaping.)

NEXT 2 ROWS : 24 dark, 72 light, 24 dark.

NEXT ROW : 25 dark, 70 light, 25 dark.

NEXT ROW : 26 dark, 68 light, 26 dark.

NEXT ROW : 27 dark, 66 light, 27 dark.

NEXT ROW : 28 dark, 64 light, 28 dark.

NEXT ROW : 29 dark, 62 light, 29 dark.

NEXT ROW : 30 dark, 60 light, 30 dark.

NEXT ROW : 32 dark, 56 light, 32 dark.

NEXT ROW : 33 dark, 54 light, 33 dark.

NEXT ROW : 34 dark, 52 light, 34 dark.

NEXT ROW : 35 dark, 50 light, 35 dark.

NEXT ROW : 37 dark, 46 light, 37 dark.

NEXT ROW : 39 dark, 42 light, 39 dark.

NEXT ROW : 40 dark, 40 light, 40 dark.

NEXT ROW : 42 dark, 36 light, 42 dark.

NEXT ROW : 44 dark, 32 light, 44 dark.

NEXT ROW : 47 dark, 26 light, 47 dark.

NEXT ROW : 50 dark, 20 light, 50 dark.

NEXT ROW : 55 dark, 10 light, 55 dark.

Fasten off the light wool.

With dark wool work 60 rows in s.s.

Change to No. 12 needles and work 45 rows in single rib. Cast off.

THE SLEEVES

WITH No. 12 needles and dark wool, cast on 56 sts. and work 60 rows in single rib.

Change to No. 9 needles and proceed in s.s., increasing at both ends of the 9th and every 8th succeeding row until there are 76 sts. Work 3 rows more.

NEXT ROW : K. 33, cast off 10 sts., k. 33, including the st. left on the needle.

NEXT ROW : P. 31, take 2 tog., and continue in this way, decreasing on every alternate row at the centre opening, and increase at the seam as previously directed 5 times more. Work 7 rows without increase, but dec. at each end of every row until all the sts. are worked off.

Join the wool to the wrong side of the first set of 33 sts. and work to match the first half of sleeve top.

The second sleeve is the same.

TO MAKE UP THE JUMPER

PRESS all the knitting except the ribbing, with a hot iron and a damp cloth over the wrong side of the work. Fit the yoke to the opening at the top of each sleeve, and oversew the sleeve and yoke together on the wrong side. Press these seams, then join up the side and sleeve seams.

Work a row of double crochet in dark wool round the neck and press.

Sew a small button at each point on the sleeves, and a large button with a small one underneath on the front point.

Beauty Advice !

Write to the Beauty Expert, c/o " Woman's Weekly," The Fleetway House, Farringdon Street, London, E.C.4, Enclosing a Stamped, Self-Addressed Envelope for a Personal reply.

A ROLL OF FAT ABOVE HER WAIST

To my great disgust, I have developed an ugly roll of fat above my waist. Can you tell me how to get rid of it, as quickly as possible ?—CONSTANT READER.

IF you will let me have your address, I will send you two exercises which I guarantee will break up your roll of fat in a few weeks, providing you sit and stand erectly. If you slump you will undo all their good work.

* * *

DISGUISE FOR " RED VEINS "

Can I do anything to disguise red veins on my face ?—JANET.

YOU will find green powder quite a satisfactory disguise. I can recommend a very hard-wearing brand, which costs only 1s. a box.

* * *

PAINFULLY FLAT-CHESTED

I am painfully flat-chested. Do you think massage with olive oil really helps ?—MUCH-TOO-FLAT.

CERTAINLY, though it is a slow-but-sure business. I would also advise you to go through a few simple deep breathing, arm-flinging exercises morning and evening. As you fling your arms outwards inhale, as you bring them back to your sides exhale.

Meantime, an uplift brassière will make you look rounder.

* * *

UNDERARM TOILETTE

Would you tell me if it is quite safe to use a deodorant. As it is, I ruin all my frocks.—HESITATING (Yorks).

YOU can set your fears at rest. By using a deodorant you are merely diverting the perspiration to other channels where it can escape more readily.

A well-known deodorant is actually a doctor's prescription. You need have no doubts, my dear.

It Will Always Be Your Friend !

Continued from page 103

Join the wool to the last long row at the neck edge and cast off 14 sts. for the centre back of neck, and continue the first row of the pattern to the shoulder end, then work off this shoulder to match the first, beginning with cast off 7 at the shoulder end.

THE BERTHA

CAST on 12 sts. with No. 8 needles.

1ST ROW : K. plain.

2ND ROW : Purl.

3RD ROW : K. 1, (m. 1, k. 2 tog.) 5 times, inc. by working in the front and back of the last st.

4TH ROW : K. plain.

5TH ROW : K. plain, increasing in the last st.

6TH ROW : Purl.

Repeat the last 4 rows until there are 20 sts. on the needle. (Note that the item between the brackets in the 3rd row must be worked as far as it will go after the increases, always increasing in the last st.)

Now work 105 repeats of the pattern on these 20 sts., after which dec. 1 st. on every alternate row, at the same edge on which the increases were made, until 12 sts. remain ; cast off.

THE BOW : Make 13 ch.

1ST ROW : 1 tr. into the 4th ch. from the hook, then 1 tr. in each ch. to the end, 3 ch., turn.

2ND ROW : Miss the first tr. over which the 3 ch. stands, then 1 tr. on each tr., 3 ch., turn.

Repeat the last row until there are 65 rows. Fasten off.

TO MAKE UP THE JUMPER

FIRST press all the knitting with a damp cloth over the wrong side of the work. Join the shoulder seams, beginning at the armhole end and taking only 1 st. from each side at a time.

Now arrange the bertha round the yoke, so that it follows the line of the open holes on the back and the front, allowing a little fullness over the shoulders and putting one corner of the straight edge one and a half inches away from the centre front of the jumper. Pin the opposite corner one and a half inches away from the centre front, on the other side, leaving a gap of three inches at the centre.

Sew on with little running stitches all along the plain edge of the bertha through the plain part just below the open yoke, after which gather up the two sloping edges of the bertha and sew along the three inches at the centre front.

Gather the two narrow ends to the centre and sew in position ; tie the crochet bow and catch in the centre. Join the side seams and press flat.

Work a row of d.c. round the neck and round the outer edge of the bertha, putting 3 d.c. in each space, and 1 d.c. on the st. between the spaces.

Tie the crochet bow, and sew it to the front.

Out-of-Doors GIRL

This Modern Sports Jumper with Becoming

Scarf Collar has some very

Smart Points about it

BACK view of jumper, showing diagonal yoke.

MATERIALS.—6 oz. Patons' 3-ply Super Scotch Fingering in cobalt blue and 2 oz. in white. A pair each of No. 10 and No. 13 Stratnoid knitting needles.

Measurements.—Length from shoulder to lower edge, 20 in.; width all round under-arms, 36 in.; length of sleeve seam, 19 in.

Abbreviations.—K., knit; p., purl; st., stitch; inc., increase; dec., decrease; tog., together; rep., repeat; patt., pattern; rem., remain; cont., continue; beg., beginning; st.-st., stocking-stitch—k. 1 row, p. 1 row, alternately; garter-st., garter-stitch—plain knitting in every row; two rows make one ridge; wl., wool; B., blue; W., white.

Tension.—7 stitches to 1 in. in width. Always knit into the backs of all cast-on stitches to produce firm edges.

THE FRONT

Begin at the lower edge. Using No. 13 needles, cast on 100 sts. in blue wl. and work in a k. 1, p. 1 rib for 3 in.

Next row.—*K. 4, k. twice into next st., rep. from * to end-(120 sts.). *Following row.*—Purl. Change to No. 10 needles and work 20 rows in st.-st., then beg. the white design. You will require 3 balls of blue and two balls of white for the patt.

Note.—Take care when changing from one colour to the other to twist the wools once, to avoid gaps in the knitting.

Join in a ball of white wl., k. 13 W., join in a ball of blue and k. 94 B., join in another ball of white and k. 13 W.

Row 2.—P. 13 W., k. 14 B., p. 66 B., k. 14 B., p. 13 W.

Row 3.—(K.) 1 B., 13 W., 92 B., 13 W., 1 B. *Row 4.*—K. 1 B., p. 13 W., k. 14 B., p. 64 B., k. 14 B., p. 13 W., k. 1 B.

Row 5.—(K.) 2 B., 13 W., 90 B., 13 W., 2 B. *Row 6.*—K. 2 B., p. 13 W., k. 14 B., p. 62 B., k. 14 B., p. 13 W., k. 2 B.

Row 7.—(K.) 3 B., 13 W., 88 B., 13 W., 3 B. *Row 8.*—K. 3 B., p. 13 W., k. 14 B., p. 60 B., k. 14 B., p. 13 W., k. 3 B.

Row 9.—(K.) 4 B., 13 W., 86 B., 13 W., 4 B. *Row 10.*—K. 4 B., p. 13 W., k. 14 B., p. 58 B., k. 14 B., p. 13 W., k. 4 B.

Now cont. in this manner, working 1 st. more in B. in garter-st. at both sides of work every 2 rows, and 1 st. fewer on both sides of the B. st.-st. piece in the centre, taking care to keep the W. stripe design correct, until the following row is reached :—

K. 32 B., p. 13 W., k. 14 B., p. 2 B., k. 14 B., p. 13 W., k. 32 B. This completes the pointed centre-piece in st.-st.

Row 67.—(K.) 33 B., 13 W., 28 B., 13 W., 33 B. *Row 68.*—K. 33 B., P. 13 W.,

THE model is knitted in cobalt blue with a white stripe, but vary the colour scheme to match your autumn suit.

k. 28 B., p. 13 W., k. 33 B. *Row 69.*—(K.) 34 B., 13 W., 26 B., 13 W., 34 B.

Row 70.—K. 34 B., p. 13 W., k. 26 B., p. 13 W., k. 34 B. *Row 71.*—(K.) 35 B., 13 W., 24 B., 13 W., 35 B. *Row 72.*—K. 35 B., p. 13 W., k. 24 B., p. 13 W., k. 35 B. *Row 73.*—(K.) 36 B., 13 W., 22 B., 13 W., 36 B. *Row 74.*—K. 36 B., p. 13 W., k. 22 B., p. 13 W., k. 36 B.

Continued overleaf

Out-of-Doors Girl

Continued from page 107

Row 75.—(K.) 37 B., 13 W., 20 B., 13 W., 37 B. *Row* 76.—K. 37 B., p. 13 W., k. 20 B., p. 13 W., k. 37 B. *Row* 77.—(K.) 38 B., 13 W., 18 B., 13 W., 38 B.

Row 78.—K. 38 B., p. 13 W., k. 18 B., p. 13 W., k. 38 B. *Row* 79.—(K.) 39 B., 13 W., 16 B., 13 W., 39 B. *Row* 80.—K. 39 B., p. 13 W., k. 16 B., p. 13 W., k. 39 B. *Row* 81.—(K.) 40 B., 13 W., 14 B., 13 W., 40 B. *Row* 82.—K. 40 B., p. 13 W., k. 14 B., p. 13 W., k. 40 B. *Row* 83.—(K.) 41 B., 13 W., 12 B., 13 W., 41 B.

Row 84.—K. 41 B., p. 13 W., k. 12 B., p. 13 W., k. 41 B. *Row* 85.—(K.) 42 B., 13 W., 10 B., 13 W., 42 B. *Row* 86.—K. 42 B., p. 13 W., k. 10 B., p. 13 W., k. 42 B.

Now shape armholes : *Row* 87.—Cast off 5, k. 37 B., 13 W., 8 B., 13 W., k. 43 B. *Row* 88.—Cast off 5, k. 37 B., p. 13 W., k. 8 B., 13 W., k. 38 B. *Row* 89.—K. 2 tog. B., then k. 37 B., 13 W., 6 B., 13 W., k. in B., until 2 rem., k. 2 tog. *Row* 90.—K. 2 tog. B., k. 36 B., p. 13 W., k. 6 B., p. 13 W., k. in B., until 2 rem., k. 2 tog.

Row 91.—K. 2 tog. B., k. 36 B., 13 W., 4 B., 13 W., k. in B., until 2 rem., k. 2 tog. *Row* 92.—K. 2 tog. B., k. 35 B., p. 13 W., k. 4 B., p. 13 W., k. in B., until 2 rem., k. 2 tog. (102 sts. remain). *Row* 93.—(K.) 37 B., 13 W., 2 B., 13 W., 37 B. *Row* 94.—K. 37 B., p. 13 W., k. 2 B., p. 13 W., k. 37 B. *Row* 95.—(K.) 38 B., 26 W., 38 B. *Row* 96.—K. 38 B., p. 26 W., k. 38 B.

Now continue in this way, knitting 1 st. more in B. at both sides of work, and 1 st. fewer on both sides of the white centre-piece until the following row is reached.

Next row:—K. 50 B., 2 W., 50 B. Then work 3 rows in B. in garter-st. right across all sts. Now divide for front opening as follows : *Next row.*—K. 51, and slip the remaining 51 sts. on to a spare needle for the present. Continue on the first set in garter-st. for 15 rows, then shape neck as follows :—Cast off 5 sts. at neck edge and finish row. Work back to neck. From here, knit 2 sts. tog. on every row at neck edge, until 32 sts. remain. Work 10 rows more without shaping. Cast off.

Go back to the other 51 sts., slip them on to a No. 10 needle, point towards centre front, join on wl. and work up this side to correspond with the other.

THE BACK.—Work the back in the same way as the front, but omitting the front opening and continuing in patt. until point of white stripe is reached. Then continue right across all sts. in B. in garter-st. for 30 rows. Cast off.

The Sleeves

WITH No. 13 needles cast on 50 sts. in B. wl. and work in k. 1, p. 1 rib for 3 ins. Change to No. 10 needles and work in st.-st., inc. 1 st. at both ends of needle on the 11th row and on every following 10th row until sleeve measures 19 ins. from the beg. Shape top by knit 2 sts. tog. at both ends of needle on every row till all sts. are worked off.

THE SCARF-COLLAR.—With No. 10 needles cast on 2 sts. in blue wl. Work in st.-st., inc. 1 st. at both ends of needle on every row until there are 26 sts. on needle. Continue in st.-st. until collar measures 50 ins. from the beg. Then k. 2 tog. at both ends of needle on every row until 2 sts. remain. Cast off.

MAKING UP.—Press all pieces on the wrong side under a damp cloth with a hot iron. Sew up shoulder seams and press. Sew tops of sleeves into armholes and press. Then sew up underarm and side seams. Fold the centre portion of scarf in two and neatly sew both edges together round neck edge, leaving the two ends open. PRESS ALL SEAMS.

Tea Time

Continued from page 109 ▷

Row 3.—K. 2, p. 1, * k. 4, p. 1, rep. from * to end. *Row* 4.—P. 1, * k. 1, p. 2, k. 1, p. 6, rep. from * ending with p. 3. *Row* 5.—K. 4, * p. 2, k. 8, rep. from * ending with k. 2. *Row* 6.—All p.

Rep. 18th patt. 6 times (7 patts. altogether), then shape front opening thus :—On neck edge, cast off 9 sts. and finish row in patt. Turn, and work back in patt. to neck edge. From here, k. 2 sts. tog. at neck edge on every row until 26 sts. rem. Then continue in patt. without decreasing, until there are 28 patts. from the beg. Cast off.

Left Front

TRANSFER from spare needle on to a No. 9 needle (point towards centre of work) 39 sts., and slip the first 18 sts. (to form centre front strip) on to a spare needle for the present and work on the remaining 39 sts. for left front as follows :—With wrong side of work towards you join on wool, and cast on 10 sts., k. into the backs of these 10 sts., then p. rem. of row.

18th Pattern. Row 1.—K. 7, * p. 2, k. 8, rep. from * ending p. 2. *Row* 2.—* P. 2, k. 1, p. 6, k. 1, rep. from * ending k. 1, p. 6. *Row* 3.—K. 1, * k. 4, p. 1, rep. from * ending k. 3. *Row* 4.—P. 4, * k. 1, p. 2, k. 1, p. 6, rep. from * ending p. 1. *Row* 5.—K. 2, * p. 2, k. 8, rep. from * ending k. 5. *Row* 6.—All purl.

Rep. 18th patt. 6 times more, finishing at neck edge. Then cast off 10 sts. at neck edge and finish row in patt. Now finish to correspond with right front and cast off.

FRONT CENTRE STRIP.—Pick up the 18 sts. left on spare needle, and work in moss-st. for 3½ ins., then work a button-hole thus :—K. 6 sts., cast off 6 (1 st. left on needle), k. 5.

Next row.—Cast on 6 sts. to replace those cast off in previous row. K. 2 rows more in moss-st. Cast off.

The Sleeves

(Both alike, each worked in 2 separate parts.)

1st part of Sleeve.—Beginning at the lower edge, with No. 9 needles and blue wool, cast on 42 sts. Work into the backs of sts. on first row.

Next row.—All p. Now continue patt. as follows : *Row* 1.—K. 5, * p. 2, k. 8, rep. from * ending k. 5. *Row* 2.—P. 4, * k. 1, p. 2, k. 1, p. 6, rep. from * ending p. 4. *Row* 3.—K. 3, * p. 1, k. 4, rep. from * ending k. 3. *Row* 4.—* P. 2, k. 1, p. 6, k. 1, rep. from * ending p. 2. *Row* 5.—K. 1, p. 1, * k. 8, p. 2, rep. from * to end. *Row* 6.—All p. These 6 rows complete one patt.

2nd Pattern. Row 1.—Inc. 1 st. into 1st st., k. 4, * p. 2, k. 8, rep. from * ending with p. 2, k. 4, inc. 1 st. into last st. *Row* 2.—P. 5, * k. 1, p. 2, k. 1, p. 6, rep. from * ending with p. 5. *Row* 3.—* K. 4, p. 1, rep. from * ending k. 4. *Row* 4.—P. 3, * k. 1, p. 6, k. 1, p., 2 rep. from * ending k. 1. *Row* 5.—K. 1, * p. 2, k. 8, rep. from * ending with p. 2, k. 1. *Row* 6.—All p.

3rd Pattern. Row 1.—K. 6, * p. 2, k. 8, rep. from * ending k. 6. *Row* 2.—Inc. 1 st. into 1st st., p. 4, * k. 1, p. 2, k. 1, p. 6, rep. from * ending with k. 1, p. 2, k. 1, p. 4, inc. 1st into last st. *Row* 3.—K. 5, * p. 1, k. 4, rep. from * ending k. 5. *Row* 4.—K. 2, * p. 2, k. 1, p. 6, k. 1, rep. from * ending with k. 1, p. 1. *Row* 5.—K. 2, * p. 2, k. 8, rep. from * ending with p. 2, k. 2. *Row* 6.—All p.

4th Pattern. Row 1.—K. 7, * p. 2, k. 8, rep. from * ending with k. 7. *Row* 2.—* k. 1, p. 2, k. 1, rep. from * ending with p. 6. *Row* 3.—Inc. 1 st. into 1st st. * k. 4, p. 1, rep. from * ending with k. 4, inc. 1st into the last st.

Row 4.—P. 2, * k. 1, p. 2, k. 1, p. 6, rep. from * ending with p. 2. *Row* 5.—K. 3, * p. 2, k. 8, rep. from * ending with k. 3. *Row* 6.—All p.

5th Pattern. Row 1.—* K. 8, p. 2, rep. from * ending with k. 8. *Row* 2.—P. 7, * k. 1, p. 2, k. 1, p. 6, rep. from * ending with k. 1. *Row* 3.—K. 1, * p. 1, k. 4, rep. from * ending with p. 2.

Row 4.—Inc. 1 st. into 1st st., p. 1, * k. 1, p. 2, k. 1, p. 6, rep. from * ending with k. 1, p. 2, k. 1, p. 1, inc. 1st into last st. *Row* 5.—K. 4, * p. 2, k. 8, rep. from * ending with p. 2, k. 4. *Row* 6.—All p.

6th Pattern. Row 1.—K. 9, * p. 2, k. 8, rep. from * ending with p. 1. *Row* 2.—K. 2, * p. 6, k. 1, p. 2, k. 1, rep. from * ending k. 2. *Row* 3.—K. 2, * p. 1, k. 4, rep. from * ending p. 1, k. 2.

Row 4.—P. 3, * k. 1, p. 2, k. 1, p. 6, rep. from * ending p. 3. *Row* 5.—Inc. 1 st. into 1st st., k. 3, * p. 2, k. 8, rep. from * ending with p. 2, k. 3, inc. 1 st. into last st. Continue in patt. inc. 1 st. at both ends of needle on every 7th row, and working extra sts. into patt. as they become due until there are 82 sts. Cast off.

2nd part of Sleeve.—With No. 9 Needles cast on 124 sts. and commence the lace patt. as follows :—

Row 1.—K. 1, * wl. fwd., sl. 1, k. 1, and p. s. s. o., rep. from * ending with k. 1.

Row 2.—All p.

Row 3.—K. 2, * wl. fwd., sl. 1, k. 1, and p. s. s. o., rep. from * ending with k. 2. *Row* 4.—All p. These 4 rows complete the lace pattern.

Note.—The k. st. of one row becomes a sl. st. in the next row, and the sl. st. a k. st.).

Rep. this patt. for 3 ins., ending on a last row of patt.

Next row.—Dec. to 82 sts., thus : * k. 1, k. 2 tog., rep. from * to end.

Following row.—All p.

Now work 3 complete patts. as for back of jumper, then k. 2 tog. at both ends of every row, keeping patt. correct whilst shaping, until 5 sts. rem. Cast off.

THE SCARF.—With No. 9 Needles cast on 32 sts. in white wool and work in the lace pattern (as sleeve frill) for 26 ins. Cast off.

MAKING UP.—Carefully press out all the pieces under a damp cloth with a hot iron. Sew up all the seams. Sew the 1st part of sleeve neatly under the frill, and seam up the sleeve, leaving 3½ ins. open at the wrist. Work 1 row d.c. around the lower edge of sleeve, making 3 button-hole loops along one side of the slit. Work 1 row of d.c. round the edge of front opening, making a button-hole loop at the top right side.

Press all seams and sew on buttons to correspond with button-hole loops. Sew scarf double round neck edge, leaving the ends loose. Cross these, and keep in place with the moss-stitch strap, which buttons to neck.

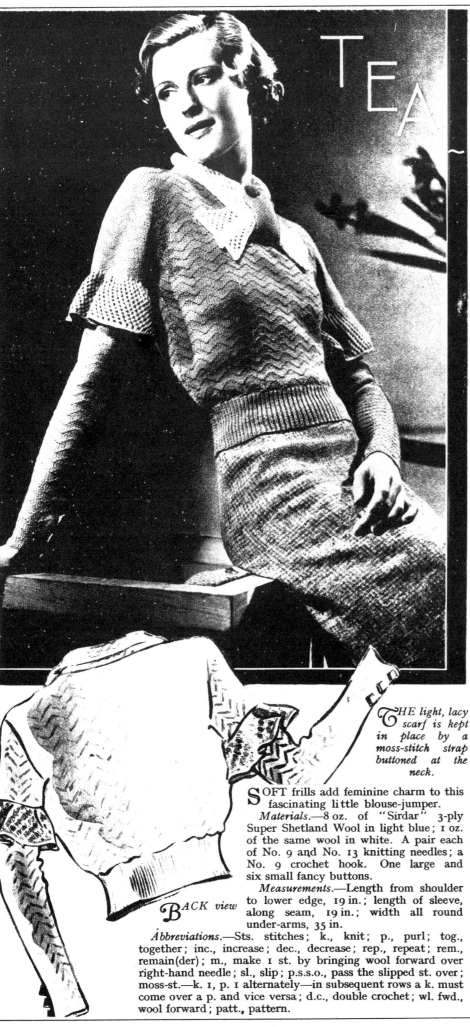

TEA~TIME

◁ Continued on previous page

Elbow Frills and a Lace-Stitch Scarf Collar add Feminine Charm to this Fascinating little Blouse Jumper

THE light, lacy scarf is kept in place by a moss-stitch strap buttoned at the neck.

SOFT frills add feminine charm to this fascinating little blouse-jumper.

Materials.—8 oz. of "Sirdar" 3-ply Super Shetland Wool in light blue; 1 oz. of the same wool in white. A pair each of No. 9 and No. 13 knitting needles; a No. 9 crochet hook. One large and six small fancy buttons.

Measurements.—Length from shoulder to lower edge, 19 in.; length of sleeve, along seam, 19 in.; width all round under-arms, 35 in.

Abbreviations.—Sts., stitches; k., knit; p., purl; tog., together; inc., increase; dec., decrease; rep., repeat; rem., remain(der); m., make 1 st. by bringing wool forward over right-hand needle; sl., slip; p.s.s.o., pass the slipped st. over; moss-st.—k. 1, p. 1 alternately—in subsequent rows a k. must come over a p. and vice versa; d.c., double crochet; wl. fwd., wool forward; patt., pattern.

BACK view

THE BACK

Begin at the lower edge of the back. With No. 13 needles, cast on 100 sts. in blue wool and work in a k. 1, p. 1 rib for 3 in.

Next row.—* K. 9, inc. 1 st. into the next st., rep. from * to end (110 sts).

Following row.—All p., inc. 1 st. into first and last sts. (112 sts.).

Now change to No. 9 needles and start patt. as follows :—

Row 1.—K. 5, * p. 2, k. 8, rep. from * ending row with k. 5, instead of k. 8.

Row 2.—P. 4, * k. 1, p. 2, k. 1, p. 6, rep. from * ending with p. 4 instead of p. 6. *Row 3.*—K. 3, * p. 1, k. 4, rep. from * ending with k. 3 instead of k. 2.

Row 4.—* P. 2, k. 1, p. 6, k. 1, rep. from * ending with p. 2, instead of k. 1.

Row 5.—K. 1, p. 1, * k. 8, p. 2, rep. from * to end. *Row 6.*—All p. These 6 rows complete one patt.

Work 16 complete patts., and the first 4 rows of the 17th, then :—

Row 5.—Shape armholes, thus : Cast off 8 sts., then k. 1, p. 2, * k. 8, p. 2, rep. from * to end. *Row 6.*—Cast off 8 sts. all p. from rem. of row (96 sts.)

18th pattern, Row 1.—K. 7, * p. 2, k. 8, rep. from * ending with p. 2, k. 7.

Row 2.—*P. 6, k. 1, p. 2, k. 1, rep. from * ending with p. 6. *Row 3.*—P. 1, * k. 4, p. 1, rep. from * to end.

Row 4.—P. 1, * k. 1, p. 2, k. 1, p. 6, rep. from * ending with p. 1.

Row 5.—K. 2, * p. 2, k. 8, rep. from* ending with p. 2, k. 2. *Row 6.*—All p.

Rep. 18th patt. until 26 patts. from beginning have been worked. Cast off.

THE FRONT

Work as for back until 16 patts. and the first 4 rows of 17th patt. have been completed, then :—

Row 5.—Shape armhole, thus : Cast off 8 sts., k. 1, p. 2, * k. 8, p. 2, rep. from * to end. *Row 6.*—Cast off 8 (1 st. left on needle), so p. 38 sts. Slip the remaining 57 sts. on to a spare needle for the present, and work right front, thus :—

Turn the work, and with right side of work towards you, cast on 9 sts.

18th pattern, Row 1.—Work into the backs of the 9 cast-on sts., then : * p. 2, k. 8, rep. from * ending with k. 7.

Row 2.—* P. 6, k. 1, p. 2, k. 1, rep from * ending with k. 1, p. 1.

109

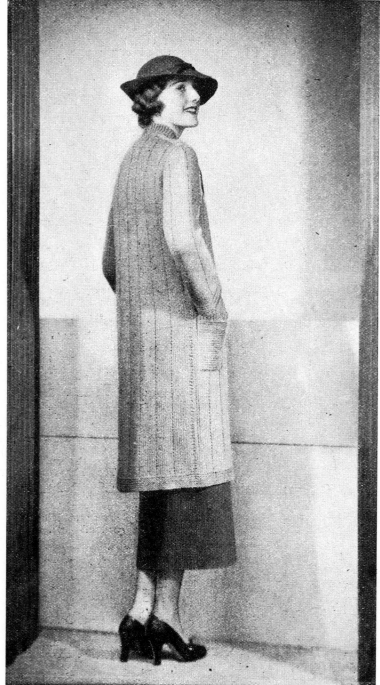

The broad stripes give the coat a very slimming effect — which is most becoming.

A SWAGGER COAT—

Hand-Knitted

Designed for an Extra-Thick Wool it is Very Quickly Made.

To Work the Back

Begin at the lower edge and, using No. 3 needles, cast on 65 sts. K. 11 rows for border.

Now work the pattern as follows:

1st row: With the right side facing, all knit.

2nd row: K. 1, * p. 7, k. 1, repeat from * to end.

Repeat these 2 rows 72 times more to armholes.

To Shape the Armholes: Cast off 1 st. at the beginning of the next 10 rows, which leaves 55 sts. Work 26 rows straight up to the shoulder-line.

To Slope the Shoulders: Cast off 5 sts. at the beginning of the next 8 rows. Cast off the remaining sts.

The Left Front.—Begin at the lower edge and cast on 44 sts. with the No. 3 needles. K. 11 rows for the border.

Now work in pattern as follows:

1st row: With right side facing, all knit.

2nd row: (for left front only): k. 4 for front border, * p. 7, k. 1, repeat from * to end.

(On the right front the 2nd row is reversed and worked as follows: * k. 1, p. 7, repeat from * until 4 sts. remain, k. 4 front border.)

Repeat these 2 rows until there are as many rows up to the armhole as on the back. (On the right front work one row more.)

Here is the coat ideal for the country tramp, as it combines cosiness without weight and is just the right length. The broad stripes give a smart and slim effect, which suits all figures.

Materials: 1½ lb. of W.B. "Kwiknit" wool in blue, a pair of knitting needles No. 3 and No. 5, and two large buttons. (The nearest equivalent to the size of this wool is Double Knitting wool.)

Tension and Measurements: Worked at a tension of 4 sts. to the inch in width with the No. 3 needles, the following measurements are attained after pressing: across each front at the underarm, 12 inches; across the back at the same place, 17 inches; front and back length from shoulder to hem, 38 inches; side seam, 30 inches; sleeve seam, 17 inches.

Abbreviations: K., knit plain; p., purl; tog., together; inc., increase (by working into the back and front of the same st.); st., stitch; dec., decrease (by taking 2 sts. tog. according to pattern).

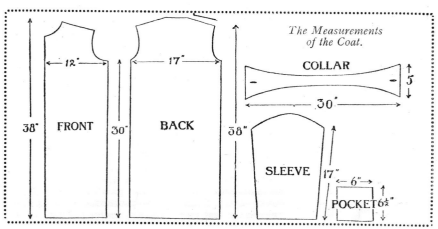

The Measurements of the Coat.

FRONT — 12" — 38"

BACK — 17" — 30" — 38"

COLLAR — 30" — 5

SLEEVE — 17"

POCKET — 6" — 6½"

The cravat collar is very neat and cosy and gives a charming finish to the coat.

A SWAGGER COAT
Hand-Knitted

Continued

To Shape the Front Armhole : Cast off 2 sts. at the beginning of the next row, and every alternate row (arm end) 4 times, then cast off 1 st. at the beginning of alternate rows (arm end) 5 times, which leaves 31 sts. Work 12 rows in pattern with k. 4 border at the front end to the neck.

To shape the neck cast off 3 sts. from the beginning of the next row and following alternate rows (neck end) 3 times, after which cast off 1 st. from the beginning of alternate row (neck end) 3 times, which leaves 19 sts.

Work 2 rows up to the shoulder line.

To slope the shoulder, cast off 5 sts. from the beginning of the next row and two following alternate rows (arm end) then cast off the 4 remaining sts.

THE RIGHT FRONT.—Work as given for the left front, with alterations as stated.

THE SLEEVE.—Begin at the top and using No. 3 needles, cast on 15 sts. Work one row thus : P. 7, k. 1, p. 7.

Now work the following increase pattern :

1st row (and every odd row) : With right side facing, inc. in the first st., k. until 1 st. remains, inc. in the last st.

2nd row : P. 1 and k. 1 in the 1st st., p. 7, * k. 1, p. 7, in following patterns repeat from *, inc. in the last st.

4th row : K. 1 and p. 1 in the first st., p. 1, k. 1, * p. 7; k. 1, repeat from * until 2 remain, p. 1, inc. in the last st.

6th row : K. 1 and p. 1 in the 1st st., p. 3, k. 1, * p. 7, k. 1, repeat from * until 4 remain, p. 3, inc. in the last st.

8th row : K. 1 and p. 1 in the 1st st., p. 5, k. 1, * p. 7, k. 1, repeat from * until 6 remain, p. 5, inc. in the last st.

Repeat these 8 rows until there are 47 sts. on the needle. Cast on 3 sts. at the beginning of each of the next 2 rows, making 53 sts. altogether for the full width of the sleeve. Work 6 rows straight. To slope the sleeve seam take 2 sts. tog. at each end of the next row, and every following 8th row, until the sts. are reduced to 43. Work 43 rows, then k. 11 rows and cast off.

Work the second sleeve in the same manner.

THE POCKETS.—With No. 3 needles cast on 27 sts. and work the two pattern rows as given on the left front 17 times (34 rows).

Cast off and work the second pocket in the same manner.

THE TIE COLLAR.—With No. 5 needles cast on 20 sts. and k. 9 rows. For the buttonhole k. 7 rows on the first 10 sts. then sl.-st. down the end of this row (by bringing the wool through each st. with a crochet hook to avoid cutting the wool), then on the second set of 10 sts. k. 7 rows.

Now work on all the sts. and dec. on the next row (by taking tog. the 3rd and 4th st. from each end) and every following 6th row until only 10 sts. remain. K. 131 rows.

Now inc. in the third st. from each end of the next row and every following 6th row until the 5th inc. row is worked with 20 sts. Work the buttonhole as before, then on all the sts. k. 9 rows and cast off.

To Make Up the Coat

FIRST press all with a damp cloth over the wrong side of the work. Sew the shoulder seams, taking only 1 st. from each side at a time, then sew the top of the sleeves into the armholes and press these seams while the work is open. Join the side and sleeve seams, putting the sleeve to the side seam in one continuous line and press. Sew the pockets to the right side of the coat, placing them so that the k. 4 border forms the top edge. Sew the edge of the collar to the wrong side of the neck, beginning at the first inc. row of the collar, for half an inch only, then leave a gap of 1½ inches to form a slot, and continue sewing round the neck edge to within 2 inches of the opposite end of the collar ; leave a similar gap for the second slot and sew the collar to the last half inch of the neck, leaving this end of the tie long enough to pass round the other end. Press all seams and sew one button on each front, 5½ inches down from the shoulder at the second broad stripe, in position to meet the tie buttonholes.

To fasten the tie collar in wear, draw the left end through the right neck slot from the inside, and fasten to the right-front button. Draw the right tie end through the left neck slot from underneath, and over the opposite part of the collar which is buttoned down, then underneath in a tying motion, and fasten this end to the left front button.

Three crochet roses are the perfect touch!

THE ROSE JUMPER

In Soft "Embroidery" With A Velvety Finish.

THIS graceful jumper is worked in a cotton which is as soft and silky as velvet. It is most fashionable for "special-occasion" jumpers, you'll discover.

MATERIALS: Five balls of Clark's "Anchor" Soft Embroidery in one of the many pretty colours in which this cotton is made, a pair of knitting needles No. 8 and No. 11, a crochet hook No. 11.

TENSION AND MEASUREMENTS: Worked at a tension of 6 sts. to the inch in width, the following measurements are attained after light pressing: Across the back at the underarms, 18 inches; across the front at the same point, 19½ inches (bear in mind that this pattern is very elastic and will easily stretch to 40 inches bust measure); length from shoulder fold to lower edge, 19 inches; side seam, 12 inches; sleeve seam, 13 inches.

ABBREVIATIONS: K., knit; p., purl; st., stitch; tog., together; m., make (by bringing the wool to the front of the needle); inc., increase (by working into the back and front of the same st.); single rib is k. 1 and p. 1 alternately; ch., chain; sl., slip; d.c., double crochet; tr., treble; d.tr., double treble (cotton twice round the hook).

TO WORK THE BACK

WITH No. 11 needles, cast on 104 sts. and work 28 rows of single rib, increasing 1 st. on the last row, which gives 105 sts. for the pattern.
Change to No. 8 needles and work in pattern as follows:
1st Row: (With right side facing) All knit.

2ND Row: All purl.
3RD and 4TH Row: * K. 2, m. 1, k. 2 tog.; repeat from * until there is 1 st. left, k. 1.
5TH Row: All knit.
6TH Row: All purl.
7TH and 8TH Row: K. 4, * m. 1, k. 2 tog., k. 2; repeat from * until there is only 1 st. left, k. 1 (this makes k. 3 at the end).
Repeat these 8 rows 6 times more, then work 4 rows more up to the armhole.
TO SHAPE THE ARMHOLE: Take 2 sts. tog. at each end of the next 17 rows, ending with an all k. row.
* NEXT ROW: P. without decreasing.
Work 2 sts. tog. at each end of the next 3 rows. Repeat from * until there are 37 sts. left. Work 2 rows and cast off.

THE FRONT

WITH No. 11 needles, cast on 108 sts. for the waist edge and rib 27 rows.
NEXT ROW: With wrong side facing, rib 8, * inc. in the next st., rib 19; repeat from * to end, which gives 113 sts. for the pattern part.
With No. 8 needles, work the 8 pattern rows 7 times, then 4 rows more.
TO SHAPE THE ARMHOLE: Cast off 3 sts. at the beginning of each of the next 2 rows, * work 2 sts. tog. at each end of the next 3 rows, then work one row without decreasing. Repeat from * until there are 55 sts. left. Cast off.

THE SLEEVES

WITH No. 8 needles, cast on 25 sts. for the neck edge and k. one row.
NEXT ROW: K. 1, p. 23, k. 1.
Now work in the following inc. pattern.

Continued on page 116

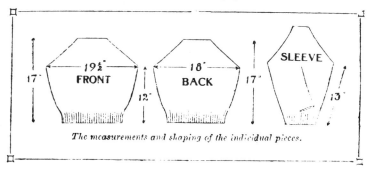

The measurements and shaping of the individual pieces.

PRETTY ENOUGH FOR PARTIES!

On the left :
THE ROSE JUMPER.

On the right :
THE FRILLY JUMPER.   Instructions on opposite page.

THE FRILLY JUMPER

This Is Worked With Silky Cotton In A Diagonal Openwork Pattern With Lacy Frills.

A FRILLY jumper is pretty for parties. This one is very charming with its fluting frills and dainty lace stitch.

MATERIALS: Three balls of Clark's "Anchor" Stranded Cotton, a pair of knitting needles No. 9 and No. 11, and a spare needle; four small clips.

TENSION AND MEASUREMENTS: Worked at a tension of 6½ sts. to the inch in width, the following measurements are attained after light pressing: round the bust, 39 inches; shoulder fold to lower edge, 18 inches; side seam, 13 inches.

ABBREVIATIONS: K., knit plain; p., purl; tog., together; m., make (by bringing the wool to the front of the needle); sl., slip; inc., increase (by working into the front and back of the same st.); st., stitch; single rib is k. 1 and p. 1 alternately; p.s.s.o., pass sl.st. over. Directions in brackets are worked the number of times stated after the brackets.

TO WORK THE JUMPER

BEGIN at the back waist edge by casting on 108 sts. with No. 11 needles. Work 35 rows in single rib.

NEXT ROW: With wrong side facing, inc. in the 1st st., rib 11, (inc. in the next st., rib 11) 8 times, which gives 117 sts.

Change to No. 9 needles and work in pattern as follows:

1ST ROW: With the right side facing, * k. 5, (m. 1, k. 2 tog.) twice; repeat from * to end.

2ND ROW (and every even-numbered row): All purl.

3RD ROW: K. 4, (m. 1, k. 2 tog.) twice, * k. 5, (m. 1, k. 2 tog.) twice; repeat from *, ending with k. 1.

5TH ROW: K. 3, (m. 1, k. 2 tog.) twice, * k. 5,

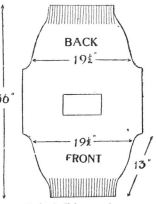

BACK
19½"

36"

19½"
FRONT

13"

Knitted all in one piece.

(m. 1, k. 2 tog.) twice; repeat from *, ending with k. 2.

7TH ROW: K. 2, (m. 1, k. 2 tog.), twice, * k. 5, (m. 1, k. 2 tog.) twice; repeat from *, ending with k. 3.

9TH ROW: K. 1, (m. 1, k. 2 tog.) twice, * k. 5, (m. 1, k. 2 tog.) twice; repeat from *, ending with k. 4.

11TH ROW: * (m. 1, k. 2 tog.) twice, k. 5; repeat from * to end.

13TH ROW: K. 1, m. 1, k. 2 tog., k. 5, * (m. 1, k. 2 tog.) twice, k. 5; repeat from * until there is only 1 st. left, k. 1 (this makes k. 6 at the end).

15TH ROW: M. 1, k. 2 tog., k. 5, * (m. 1, k. 2 tog.) twice, k. 5; repeat from * until 2 sts. are left, m. 1, k. 2 tog.

17TH ROW: K. 6, * (m. 1, k. 2 tog.) twice, k. 5; repeat from * until 3 sts. are left, m. 1, k. 2. tog., k. 1.

18TH ROW: All purl.

Repeat these 18 rows until 62 rows have been worked in pattern.

Continue in the same pattern but now inc. 1 st. at each end of the next 9 rows, which gives 135 sts. including the short sleeves.

Work 37 rows in pattern to the back of the neck.

NEXT ROW: With right side facing, work 45 sts. for the right shoulder (as 1st pattern row), and slip these on a spare needle, cast off 45 for the back of the neck, pattern 45 for the left shoulder, including the 1 on the needle after casting off.

THE LEFT SHOULDER: Work 35 rows in pattern, ending with the 18th pattern row; fasten off the thread and leave these sts. on a spare needle until needed.

THE RIGHT SHOULDER: Join the thread to the neck end of the right front sts., and work 36 rows in pattern, beginning with the second pattern row and ending with the 1st row, then with the same needle cast on 45 sts. for the front of the neck. Now work in the 1st row of the pattern on the 45 left-shoulder sts., passing them on to the same needle, which gives 135 sts. for the front.

A brilliant clip finishes each corner of the square neck so prettily.

Continued overleaf

The Rose Jumper

Continued from page 113

Continued from page 113

1ST and 2ND ROW : * K. 2, m. 1, k. 2 tog. ; repeat from * until there is only 1 st. left, k. 1.

3RD ROW : Inc. in the first st., k. until there are only 2 sts. left, inc. in the next st., k. 1.

4TH ROW : Inc. in the first st., p. until there is 1 st. left, inc. in the last st.

Repeat these 4 rows until there are 73 sts. on the needle, on which work 26 rows in pattern without alteration.

Continue in pattern, increasing 1 st. at each end of next row and every following 4th row until the 10th inc. row has been worked with 93 sts., on which work 3 rows more. Now build the edge up as follows : K. 89, turn, leaving 4 sts. unworked ; p. 85, turn, leaving 4 sts. unworked at this edge ; pattern 81, turn, p. 2 tog., pattern 75, turn ; k. 2 tog., k. 71, turn ; p. 69, turn ; pattern 65, turn ; p. 2 tog., pattern 59, turn ; k. 2 tog., k. 55, turn ; p. 53, turn ; pattern 49, turn ; p. 2 tog., pattern 43, turn ; k. 2 tog., k. 39, turn ; p. 3, cast off 31 knitwise, p. 3, turn, leaving 25 sts., k. 3. There are now 28 sts. on each needle.

With the right side facing. k. the left-hand sts. to right-hand needle, which gives 56 sts. on the same needle.

With No. 11 needles rib 19 rows and cast off loosely.

Work the second sleeve in the same manner.

TO MAKE UP THE JUMPER

FIRST press all except the rib with a damp cloth over the wrong side of the work. Join the sloping edges of the sleeve tops to the corresponding parts of the back and front, sewing the last 4 rows on the back to the 3 end sts. of the sleeve top.

Arrange four half-inch tucks equidistant on the front neck edge, and tack them in place.

With the crochet hook work 2 rows of d.c. round the neck edge, leaving the sts. on the tucks free. Work 1 row of d.c. on the poke edge of the sleeve, if you intend to leave it free from the cuff as worked ; do not work the d.c. if you intend to gather it to the cuff. Join the sleeve and side seams in one continuous line, taking only 1 st. from each side at a time and press the seams.

THE ROSES

WITH crochet hook make 6 ch. and form a ring by slip-stitching to the first st.

1ST ROUND : * 4 ch., 1 d.c. into the ring ; repeat from * 5 times more.

2ND ROUND : * Into the first ch. loop, on the last row work 1 d.c., 6 tr. and 1 d.c. ; repeat from * 5 times more, sl.st. to back of first d.c. on round.

3RD ROUND : 2 ch., * 1 tr. into the original ring at the back of the next petal, between 2 d.c. on the 1st round, 3 ch. ; repeat from * 5 times more, and sl.st. to top of the first tr. on the round.

4TH ROUND : * Into the next ch. bar on the last row work 1 d.c., 2 tr., 5 d.tr., 2 tr., 1 d.c. ; repeat from * 5 times more Fasten off.

Work two more roses in the same manner, then sew them to the front of the neck, between the tucks.

The Frilly Jumper

Work 21 rows in pattern, beginning with the 2nd pattern row, after which take 2 sts. tog. at each end of the next 9 rows, which leaves 117 sts.

Work 62 rows in pattern, then change to No. 11 needles and work thus : * P. 2 tog., k. 1, (p. 1, k. 1) 5 times ; repeat from * to end, which gives 108 sts. for the waist.

With No. 11 needles, work 35 rows in single rib and cast off.

THE FRONT NECK FRILL

WITH No. 9 needles cast on 92 sts. and k. 3 rows. (Do not work into the back of the sts. on the first row.)

4TH ROW : K. 2, p. until there are 2 sts. left, k. 2.

5TH ROW : K. 2, * m. 1, k. 2, k. 2 tog., sl. 1, k. 1, p.s.s.o., k. 2, m. 1, k. 2 ; repeat from * to end.

6TH ROW : K. 2, p. until there are 2 sts. left, k. 2.

Repeat the 5th and 6th row 4 times more.

NEXT ROW : K. 1, now k. 2 tog. until there is only 1 st. left, k. 1 (47 sts.).

With No. 11 needles work in pattern as follows :

1ST ROW : (Wrong side facing) K. 2, p. 1, * k. 1, p. 1 ; repeat from * until there are 2 sts. left, k. 2.

2ND ROW : K. 3, p. 1, * k. 1, p. 1 ; repeat from * until there are 3 sts. left, k. 3.

Repeat these 2 rows twice more and cast off loosely.

Work a second frill exactly the same for the back of the neck.

THE SHOULDER FRILLS

WITH No. 9 needles, cast on 82 sts and work as given for the front frill until ready to work the decrease row. The decrease row is k. 2 tog. along the whole row, which leaves 41 sts. With No. 11 needles work the two rib rows 3 times, and cast off loosely.

Work a second shoulder frill in the same manner.

THE SLEEVE FRILLS

WITH No. 9 needles, cast on 152 sts. and work as given for the lace part of the front neck frill until 14 rows are worked.

NEXT ROW : * K. 1, k. 2 tog. ; repeat from * until 2 sts. are left, k. 2 (102 sts.).

With No. 11 needles rib 3 rows and cast off.

Work a second arm frill in the same manner.

TO MAKE UP THE JUMPER

FIRST press all the knitting with a damp cloth over the wrong side of the work, taking care that the rib is not stretched.

Sew the frills to the neck edge or join them on with a row of d.c. worked with a No. 12 hook. Stitch the arm frills to the armhole end, then join the side and sleeve seams in one line, taking only 1 st. from each side at a time.

Press all seams and edges.

Wear a clip at each corner of the neck.

THERE ARE THREE WAYS YOU CAN WEAR IT

There are THREE WAYS *You Can* WEAR IT!

*This Clever Ensemble Has
a Pointed Yoke to Both
Jumper and Skirt*

THE highest achievement in knitting, combining perfect line and fit, is represented here. It is well within the scope of the average knitter, but it is not meant for the beginner.

MATERIALS.—One lb. four ounces of " Greenock " 4-ply Super Fingering, (obtainable only at any of the branches of the Scotch Wool and Hosiery Stores) (12 ounces for the skirt and belt, and 8 ounces for the jumper), a pair of No. 12 and No. 9 knitting needles, a waist-length of $\frac{3}{4}$-inch wide elastic, 8 buttons ($\frac{3}{4}$-inch diameter) to match the wool.

ABBREVIATIONS.—K., knit ; p., purl ; st., stitch ; tog., together ; sl., slip ; dec., decrease ; inc., increase ; p.s.s.o., pass sl. st. over ; s.s., stocking st. (k. on the right side and p. back).

TENSION AND MEASUREMENTS.— Worked at a tension of $6\frac{1}{2}$ sts. to the inch in width on the No. 9 needles, the skirt measures 38 inches round the hip-line (including the button-wrap), 48 inches round the hem, and 35 inches long from the top of the waist edge to the hem.

The jumper measures $18\frac{1}{2}$ inches across the back at the underarm ; $9\frac{1}{2}$ inches at the same point across each front ; length of front and back from shoulder seam to lower edge, $18\frac{1}{2}$ inches ; side seam 9 inches ; sleeve seam 19 inches.

To Work the Skirt

BEGIN at the waist, and, using No. 12 needles, cast on 135 sts. K. the first row through the back of the sts. Work 10 rows in s.s., beginning with a k. row which will be the right side of the work.

Next row : K. 33, turn, leaving the rest of the row unworked for the present.

Next row : * P. 2 tog., p. to the end of the row.

Next row : K. until within 2 sts. of the end of the row, k. 2 tog.

Repeat the last 2 rows from * until

The dress can be worn with the jumper tucked inside, and a belt ; or as a jumper and skirt.

A JUMPER—
A DRESS—
or a NEAT
SPORTS-SUIT

*The Buttons Go Right
Down the Front to Give
a Long Slender Line*

there is only 1 st. left ; draw the wool through and fasten off.

Join the wool to the next st. along the row and * k. 2 tog., k. 65, k. 2 tog.

Next row : P. 2 tog., p. to within 2 sts. of the end of the row, p. 2 tog.

Repeat the last 2 rows from * until the sts. are reduced to 3, then p. 2 tog., p. 1, turn and k. 2 tog. and fasten off.

Join the wool to the next st. along the row (which is the first of the last 33), k. to the end of the row.

Next row : * P. to within 2 sts. of the end of the row, p. 2 tog.

Next row : K. 2 tog., k. to the end of the row.

Repeat from * until there is only 1 st. left, draw the wool through and fasten off.

Now, holding the work with the right side facing, begin at the top of the point on the right-hand edge and pick up a st. in the first loop on the sloping side and continue taking up sts. down this side until there are 33, pick up one st. at the dip of the slope, then 33 sts. up the next slope, 1 st. at the top, and 33 down the next slope, 1 st. at the dip of the slope and 33 up the next slope, making 135 sts. on the needle as at the beginning.

Change to No. 9 needles and p. one row.

Now begin the crossway pattern.

1st row : * K. 1 in the front and back of the first st., k. 30, sl. 1, k. 1, p.s.s.o., k. 1, k. 2 tog., k. 30, k. in the front and back of the next st., k. 1, repeat from * once more, but omit the last k. 1.

2nd row : P. 135 sts. and count them to make sure that you have the same number on which the previous row was worked.

Repeat these 2 rows 23 times more, making 48 rows worked.

* On the next row inc. 1 st. at the beginning and end of the row additional to the inc. which is already in the pattern, as this must give 2 sts. more on the row. Work the rest of the row in exactly the same way as before.

A soft bow finishes the neckline. It can either be knitted or be of silk to match the outfit.

Work 7 rows more on these sts., bearing in mind the extra st. in the first and last section of the row. As the lines of the pattern are now well defined there should not be any difficulty in keeping the stitches correct, after the increases.

Repeat the last 8 rows 18 times more, or according to length of skirt desired, measuring on the side edge of the piece of knitting. Bear in mind that the knitting will drop in wear, so it is advisable to make it about 6 inches shorter than actually wanted.

To fill in the crossway corners, work as follows : * With the right side of the work facing, cast off 5 sts., then k. in the usual pattern to the end of the row.

Cast off 5 sts. at the beginning of the next row and p. to end.

Repeat from * 4 times more.

Now continue to work in the same way, but casting off only 2 sts. at the beginning of each row until all the sts. are cast off. At the same time remember to carry on the same pattern, with the decreases and increases respectively at each side of the centre st. on each rib. Draw the wool through the last st. and fasten off.

THE RIGHT FRONT.—Cast on 74 sts. and work s.s. rows as on the back. Now work off the first 33 sts. exactly as on the back.

Join the wool to the next st. along the row and work another piece, taking off the first st. next to the centre st., to begin the opposite slope, and continue like the second slope on the back yoke until there are 7 sts. left after the last decrease. Turn and p. these sts., then pick up 33 sts. down the side of the first slope, taking up the loops from the back of the st., so that a ridge will not be left on the right side of the knitting, p. 1, p. 33 up the second slope, making 74 sts. as at the beginning. Now work in the same crossway pattern as on the back, but there will be more sts. after the centre rib to the front edge, and the first buttonhole must be made on the 18th and 19th row by knitting to within 9 sts. of the edge of the row, then cast off 7 and k. 2. On the next row cast on 7 over those cast off to finish the buttonhole. Work 7 buttonholes more down the front at intervals of 22 rows, and inc. at the opposite edge of the row, exactly as on the back, additional to the increases which form the pattern at the beginning of the row.

When there are as many rows as on

the back, fill in the crossway piece by casting off 4 sts. at the beginning of right side rows 4 times, and 2 sts. only at the beginning of p. rows, keeping the rib intact as before. After this point cast off 2 sts. at the beginning of each row until they are all worked off.

THE LEFT FRONT.—Cast on 81 sts. (7 more than on the right front) to allow for a little under-wrap. Proceed as on the right front, but when beginning to work off the triangular pieces on the yoke, dec. at the end of the first set of

The ensemble as a jumper-suit.

sts. until there are 14 sts. left. Leave these on the needle until wanted, and with another ball of wool work up the second slope until all the sts. are taken off. Pick up from the right side, beginning with the needle that holds the 14 sts., so that when finished there will again be 81 sts. as before. Continue in the crossway pattern, working the same extra increases at the end of the needle to form the slope on the side seam. When the full length is attained fill in the hem by casting off 4 sts. at the beginning of the first 10 rows, then take off 2 at a time as before.

To Make Up the Skirt

PRESS very lightly on the wrong side. Sew the waist elastic at both edges to the top of the skirt, easing the skirt a little to fit the elastic. Cover the elastic with a strip of silk or ribbon, and sew the hooks and snap fastener in position. Sew the buttons opposite the buttonholes about 1½ inches from the edge of the skirt. Finally whip round the edge of the buttonhole with the same wool and draw in a little to close the buttonhole neatly.

The Belt

WITH No. 12 needles, cast on 17 sts. and k. one row through the back of the sts.

1st row of pattern : Inc. in the 1st st., k. 5, sl. 1, k. 1, p.s.s.o., k. 1, k. 2 tog., k. 5, inc. in the last st.

2nd row : All p. (17 sts.).

Repeat these two rows for the length of belt required, less 1½ inches straight and the mitred point.

Before the mitre make a buttonhole by working on one half of the sts. for 10 rows, preserving the same pattern as before, after which cast off the centre st. and work on the other half. Work three-quarters of an inch straight (casting on the centre st. again on the first row), then mitre the point by decreasing 1 st. at the beginning and end of the right side rows as well as the decrease at each side the centre st., until all the stitches are worked off. Purl the back row as usual.

The Jumper

BEGIN at the shoulder-line for which cast on 135 sts., using No. 9 needles.

Now follow the directions for the back,

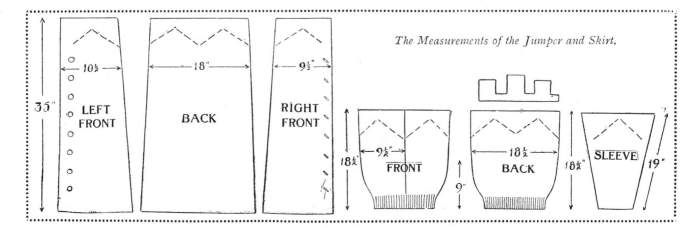

The Measurements of the Jumper and Skirt.

LEFT FRONT — 10½" — 35"

BACK — 18"

RIGHT FRONT — 9½"

FRONT — 9½" — 18½"

BACK — 18½" — 18½" — 9"

SLEEVE — 19"

but without the extra increases at the side seam, until there are 76 of the crossway pattern rows worked. To fill in the corners, cast off 2 sts. at the beginning of every row, otherwise carry out the pattern as usual in the middle of the work, until all the sts. are worked off.

The Waist-band.—With No. 12 needles pick up 114 sts. along the cast-off edge (that is, missing a st. here and there at equal intervals) and work 4 rows of single rib.

Change to No. 9 needles and work 28 rows of single rib. Purl one row on the right side of the work, and cast off on the wrong side.

THE LEFT FRONT.—Cast on 81 sts. for the shoulder-line, then work exactly as the left front of the skirt until there are as many rows as on the back of the jumper, counting along the side edge.

To finish off the cross way corners, work as before, but cast off 5 sts. 4 times at the beginning of right side rows, after which cast off 2 sts. at this end, and cast off 2 sts. at the beginning of every wrong side row. Now put this piece aside until the opposite front is worked.

THE RIGHT FRONT.—Cast on 74 sts. and work the pointed yoke and the crossway pattern exactly as on the right front of the skirt, until there are the same number of rows at the side seam as on the opposite front, but button-holes must be made in the meantime. The first buttonhole should be made at the end of the third row of the cross-way pattern, by working until 9 sts. are left, then cast off 7 and k. 2 exactly as on the back. Cast on 7 sts. on the next row, over those cast off to complete the buttonhole. Two buttonholes more are worked at intervals of 22 rows. Finish off the front like the right front of the skirt.

The Front Waist-band.—Hold the two fronts with the right side facing and wrap the right front over the left at the lower edge for the width of 7 sts., and pin in position. Still holding the right side facing take the No. 12 needles, pick up 124 sts. (knitting through the two fronts at the centre), and work 4 rows in single rib. Change to No. 9 needles and finish exactly as on the back waist-band.

The Sleeves

BEFORE these can be worked it is necessary first to join the shoulder seams with the same wool. Beginning at the shoulder end, join 40 sts. on each side taking 1 st. from each side at a time. Press these seams.

Now pin the work out flat with the right side uppermost. Measure up from the waist edge 9 inches and put pin No. 1 at this point; this represents the side seam. Measure the same distance from the opposite edge of the waist-band and put pin No. 2. Now with the No. 12 needles pick up and k. 40 sts. up to the shoulder seam, one st. at the seam, and 40 sts. down the other side to the second pin, making 81 sts.

Change to No. 9 needles and work 9 rows more in s.s.

On the next row k. 38, k. 2 tog., turn and p. back. Continue in this way until there are only 7 sts. left, and leave the ball of wool hanging. Work on the remaining half of the row in the same way, leaving 7 sts. Fasten off the wool on this side. Take up the sts. exactly as on the back pattern, when there will be 81 again.

Now work 44 rows in the crossway pattern, that is, increasing at both ends and decreasing at each side of the centre st., which is the one picked up on a level with the shoulder seam.

* On the next row, dec. 1 st. at both ends, after increasing the st. which keeps the diagonal pattern, and work the same pattern at the centre of the sleeve.

Work 3 rows in the usual pattern.

Repeat from * until there are 15 dec. rows and 51 sts. left. Work 5 rows in pattern without further alteration, or according to length of sleeve desired.

Now fill in the crossway piece by casting off 2 sts. at the beginning of each row until all are worked off.

Work the second sleeve the same.

The Collar

WITH the No. 9 needles cast on 114 sts., and k. 1 row into the back of the sts.

Next row : P. 15, k. 25, p. 8, k. 33, p. 8, k. 25.

Next row : P. 25, k. 8, p. 33, k. 8, p. 25, k. 15.

Repeat the last 2 rows twice more.

Next row : Cast off 15 sts. and work in pattern as usual.

Next row : P. 10, p. 2 tog., turn and k. back.

Repeat the last 2 rows until there is only 1 st. left, draw the wool through and fasten off.

Join the wool to the centre st. on the wrong side, p. 2 tog., and p. to end of row, then finish this half to match the first, keeping the last st. on the needle.

Now pick up the sts. round the edge of the V-piece as on the back yoke until there are 25 sts. as before.

Work 12 rows of the crossway pattern, then fill in the corners by casting off 2 sts. at the beginning of each row, working the centre pattern as usual.

Hold the work with the right side facing and, beginning at the next st. along the main line, cast off the 8 p. sts. and on the next 33 sts. work another tab like the first one, but longer owing to more sts. at the beginning.

Cast off the next 8 sts., then work the third tab on the remaining 25 sts.

THE TIE : Cast on 13 sts. and k. 10 rows plain, then work in the diagonal pattern for 14 inches. Work 10 rows more, increasing at both ends of the plain rows, additional to the increase in the first st. Finish off the end by casting off 2 sts. at the beginning of each row, with the usual dec. at the centre.

Work the second piece exactly the same and sew together at the s.s. ends.

To Make Up the Jumper

FIRST press all pieces with a damp cloth over the wrong side of the knitting.

Sew the collar to the right side of the jumper so that when it is turned over the right side of the crossway pattern with the ribs will be uppermost. Put the edge of the first tab about one inch from the front edge of the right front and the straight piece with 15 sts. will come to the edge on the opposite end of the neck. Sew snap fasteners where required at the neck.

Join up the sleeve seams and press on a sleeve-board. Sew on three buttons.

The scarf can be knotted prettily at the back.

Which Way Will You Wear It?

With the Scarf in a Soft Double Knot at the Back —Or Loosely Looped in the Front?

ABBREVIATIONS: K., knit ; p., purl ; tog., together ; inc., increase (by working into the back and front of the same stitch) ; st., stitch ; s.s., stocking-stitch (k. on the right side and p. back) ; rib is k. 2 and p. 2 alternately.

This is the stitch used for the main part of the Jumper.

THIS delightful jumper is knitted in a most attractive all-over diamond pattern, which sets off the stocking-stitch scarf.

MATERIALS : 7 ounces of Sirdar 3-ply Super Shetland wool in light grey ; 1 ounce in darker grey ; and one ounce in coral. A pair each of knitting needles No. 8 and No. 11, and two spare needles ; one button ; and a No. 10 crochet hook.

TENSION AND MEASUREMENTS : Worked at a tension of 6½ sts. to the inch in width the following measurements are attained after light pressing : Round bust, 38 inches ; shoulder to lower edge, 20 inches ; underarm side measurement, 13 inches ; sleeve seam, 19 inches.

To Work the Jumper

BEGIN at the waist with grey wool and No. 11 needles, and cast on 206 sts. Work 33 rows in rib.

Next row : Inc. in first st., * rib 8, inc. in next st., repeat from * until 7 sts. remain, rib 6, inc. in last st. There are now 230 sts.

With No. 8 needles, work in pattern as follows :

1st row (and every odd row) : With right side facing, all k.

2nd row : P. 3, k. 4, * p. 6, k. 4 ; repeat from *, ending with p. 3.

4th row : (P. 2, k. 2) twice, * p. 4, k. 2, p. 2, k. 2 ; repeat from * until there are 2 sts. left, p. 2.

6th row : P. 1, k. 2, p. 4, k. 2, * p. 2, k.2, p. 4, k. 2 ; repeat from * until 1 st. remains, p. 1.

8th row : K. 2, p. 6 * k. 4, p. 6 ; repeat from *, ending with k. 2.

10th row : As 6th row.

12th row : As 4th row.

These 12 rows complete one pattern. Repeat them 5 times more, then work 2 rows of the next pattern. (That is, 74 rows in pattern.)

On the next row the sts. are divided for the two fronts and back, thus : With right side facing, k. 58 for right front, and slip on to a spare needle ; cast off 2 for the underarm, k. 110 for back and slip on to a spare needle, cast off 2 for the second underarm, k. 58 for left front.

Take care to keep the pattern correct after the division of the sts. ; but this should be easy by now as the pattern is solid, and the diamond shape clearly marked. (Beginners can work

The Jumper is equally charming with the scarf worn this way.

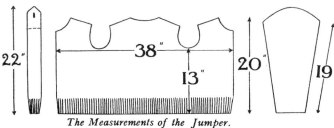

22″

38″

13″

20″

19

The Measurements of the Jumper.

s.s. on front and back yokes and sleeves with a smart effect.)

The Left Front.—Continue in pattern, casting off 2 sts. at the beginning of alternate rows (armhole end) 9 times, which leaves 40 sts. Work 24 rows straight up to the neckline.

To Shape the Neck.—Cast off 3 sts. at beginning of next row and following alternate row (neck end) for 2 decreases,

WHICH WAY WILL YOU WEAR IT?

then cast off 2 from beginning of alternate rows (neck end) for 3 times, then cast off 1 from beginning of alternate rows (neck end) for 3 times, which leaves 25 sts.

Work 4 rows more to the shoulder.

To Slope the Shoulder.—Cast off 6 sts. at the beginning of alternate rows (armhole end) until there is 1 st. left. Draw the wool through and fasten off.

The Back.—Join light grey wool to left arm end of the back sts., and work 1 row.

To Shape the Back Armholes.—Cast off 2 sts. at the beginning of each of the next 2 rows, then cast off 1 at the beginning of the following 16 rows. There are now 90 sts. on which work 33 rows up to the back neckline.

Next row : With wrong side facing, pattern 37 and leave these on a spare needle for left back shoulder, cast off 16, pattern 37 for right back shoulder.

Right Back Shoulder.—Cast off 6 sts. at the beginning of next and every alternate row from armhole end, and, at the same time, cast off 4 sts. from beginning of alternate rows (neck end) until there is 1 st. left. Fasten off.

Left Back Shoulder.—Join light grey wool to neck end of the left back shoulder sts. and work 1 row. Then work as given for right back shoulder.

The Right Front.—Join light grey wool to the arm end of right front sts. and work as given for left front.

The Front Panel.—With coral wool and No. 11 needles, cast on 14 sts. and rib 34 rows. With No. 8 needles, work 121 rows in s.s., ending with a k. row. K. plain 1 row more (to reverse right side of s.s. for the tab top). Continue in reversed s.s. for 19 rows, beginning and ending with a p. row.

For the buttonhole, work 5 rows on the first 7 sts. of the row, then on the the second set of 7 sts. work 5 rows. On all sts. work 5 rows, ending with a p. row. Now work 2 tog. at each end of next and every following alternate row until all are worked off.

Work 2 rows of double crochet with dark grey wool on the two long sides, and tab end of this strip.

The Sleeves.—Begin at the top and, with No. 8 needles, cast on 24 sts. Work one row thus : K. 4, * p. 6, k. 4 ; repeat from *. Now work thus :

1st row (and every odd row) : With right side facing, inc. in first st., k. until 1 remains, inc. in last st.

2nd row : Inc. in 1st st., k. 1, p. 2, * k. 2, p. 2, k. 2, p. 2 ; repeat from * until 2 remain, k. 1, inc. in last st.

4th row : Inc. in 1st st., k. 2, p. 4, k. 2, * p. 2, k. 2, p. 4, k. 2 ; repeat from * until there is 1 st. left, inc. in last st.

6th row : Inc. in 1st st., k. 3, p. 6, * k. 4, p. 6 ; repeat from * until 4 remain, k. 3, inc. in last st.

8th row : Inc. in 1st st., k. 2, p. 2, k. 2, * p. 4, k. 2, p. 2, k. 2 ; repeat from * until there is 1 st. left, inc. in last st.

10th row : Inc. in 1st st., p. 1, k. 2, p. 4, k. 2, * p. 2, k. 2, p. 4, k. 2 ; repeat from * until 2 sts. are left, p. 1, inc. in last st.

12th row : Inc. in 1st st., k. 4, * p. 6, k. 4 ; repeat from * until there is 1 st. left, inc. in the last st.

14th row : Inc. in 1st st., p. 1, k. 2, p. 2, k. 2, * p. 4, k. 2, p. 2, k. 2 ; repeat from * until there are 2 sts. left, p. 1, inc. in last st.

16th row : Inc. in 1st st., p. 2, * k. 2, p. 4, k. 2, p. 2 ; repeat from *, inc. in last st.

18th row : Inc. in 1st st., p. 1, k. 4, * p. 6, k. 4 ; repeat from * until there are 2 sts. left, p. 1, inc. in last st.

20th row : Inc. in 1st st., (p. 2, k. 2) twice, * p. 4, k. 2, p. 2, k. 2 ; repeat from * till 3 sts. remain, p. 2, inc. in last st.

22nd row : Inc. in 1st st., k. 1, p. 2, * k. 2, p. 4, k. 2, p. 2 ; repeat from * till 2 sts. remain, k. 1, inc. in last st.

24th row : Inc. in 1st st., p. 2, k. 4, * p. 6, k. 4 ; repeat from *, p. 2, inc. in last st.

26th row : Inc. in 1st st., p. 3, k. 2, p. 2, k. 2, * p. 4, k. 2, p. 2, k. 2 ; repeat from * until 4 sts. are left, p. 3, inc. in last st.

28th row : Inc. in 1st st., k. 2, p. 2, k. 2, * p. 4, k. 2, p. 2, k. 2 ; repeat from * till 1 st. remains, inc. in last st. (80 sts.).

Work 6 rows straight, beginning with the 1st row of the pattern, as on the body of the jumper.

(Those who prefer short sleeves should stop at the 24th row and work 1 inch of rib. The cuff is made in the same way as given below for the long sleeve jumper, but about three inches longer.)

To Slope the Seam.—Work 2 sts. tog. at each end of next row, and every following 8th row, until the 7th dec. row is worked ; now decrease at each end of every 10th row until 48 sts. remain, work 9 rows more. Cast off.

The Cuffs.—With coral wool and No. 8 needles, cast on 17 sts. and work striped pattern as follows :

** Work 12 rows s.s. (with k. 4 border at beginning of p. rows) in coral, then 2 rows light grey, 2 rows coral, 2 rows light grey, 2 rows dark grey, 2 rows coral, 2 rows dark grey. Repeat from ** twice more. Cast off. Work a second cuff in the same manner.

The Scarf.—With coral wool, cast on 30 sts. with No. 8 needles, and k. 22 rows. Now work in s.s. with a border of k. 4 at each end of every p. row in the following colours :

*** With light grey wool 2 rows, 2 rows coral, 2 rows light grey, 2 rows dark grey, 2 rows coral, 2 rows dark grey, 16 rows coral ; repeat from *** 11 times more, then work 12 rows more in the narrow bands of colour, then 23 rows of garter-st. in coral, cast off.

The Neck Edge.—With light grey wool pick up and k. 102 sts. round the neck with right side of jumper facing. Rib 5 rows and cast off. Press the edge.

To Make Up.—First press all pieces with a damp cloth over the wrong side. Sew the shoulder seams. Join the sleeve seams and stitch the sleeves into the armholes. Sew the ends of the cuffs and set to sleeve edges. Join the front panel to centre front of jumper with rib at the waistline, and allow the reversed s.s. to turn over and the crochet border to overlap at the sides.

Sew the button to correspond with the buttonhole to under part of the panel.

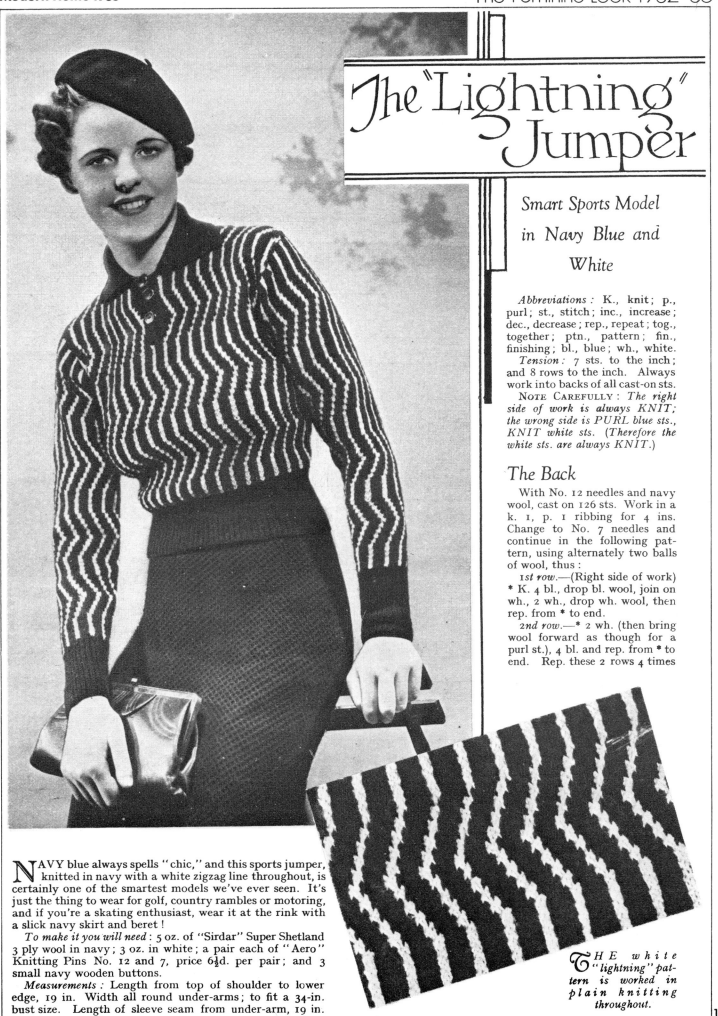

The "Lightning" Jumper

Smart Sports Model in Navy Blue and White

Abbreviations : K., knit; p., purl; st., stitch; inc., increase; dec., decrease; rep., repeat; tog., together; ptn., pattern; fin., finishing; bl., blue; wh., white.

Tension : 7 sts. to the inch; and 8 rows to the inch. Always work into backs of all cast-on sts.

NOTE CAREFULLY : *The right side of work is always KNIT; the wrong side is PURL blue sts., KNIT white sts. (Therefore the white sts. are always KNIT.)*

The Back

With No. 12 needles and navy wool, cast on 126 sts. Work in a k. 1, p. 1 ribbing for 4 ins. Change to No. 7 needles and continue in the following pattern, using alternately two balls of wool, thus :

1st row.—(Right side of work) * K. 4 bl., drop bl. wool, join on wh., 2 wh., drop wh. wool, then rep. from * to end.

2nd row.—* 2 wh. (then bring wool forward as though for a purl st.), 4 bl. and rep. from * to end. Rep. these 2 rows 4 times

NAVY blue always spells "chic," and this sports jumper, knitted in navy with a white zigzag line throughout, is certainly one of the smartest models we've ever seen. It's just the thing to wear for golf, country rambles or motoring, and if you're a skating enthusiast, wear it at the rink with a slick navy skirt and beret !

To make it you will need : 5 oz. of "Sirdar" Super Shetland 3 ply wool in navy ; 3 oz. in white ; a pair each of "Aero" Knitting Pins No. 12 and 7, price 6½d. per pair ; and 3 small navy wooden buttons.

Measurements : Length from top of shoulder to lower edge, 19 in. Width all round under-arms; to fit a 34-in. bust size. Length of sleeve seam from under-arm, 19 in.

THE white "lightning" pattern is worked in plain knitting throughout.

THE LIGHTNING JUMPER

more (ten rows in all). *11th row.*—3 bl., then 2 wh. 4 bl. to end. *12th row.*—1 bl., then 2 wh. 4 bl. to end. *13th row.*—2 bl., then 2 wh. 4 bl. to end. *14th row.*—2 bl., then 2 wh. 4 bl. to end. *15th row.*—1 bl., then 2 wh. 4 bl. to end. *16th row.*—3 bl., then 2 wh. 4 bl. to end. *17th row.*—2 wh. 4 bl. to end. *18th row.*—4 bl. 2 wh. to end. *19th row.*—1 wh., then 4 bl. 2 wh. to end. *20th row.*—1 wh., then 4 bl. 2 wh. to end. *21st row.*—2 wh. 4 bl. to end. *22nd row.*—4 bl. 2 wh. to end. *23rd row.*—1 bl., then 2 wh. 4 bl. to end. *24th row.*—3 bl., then 2 wh. 4 bl. to end. *25th row.*—2 bl., then 2 wh. 4 bl. to end. *26th row.*—2 bl., then 2 wh. 4 bl. to end. *27th row.*—3 bl., then 2 wh. 4 bl. to end. *28th row.*—1 bl., then 2 wh. 4 bl. to end. *29th row.*—4 bl. 2 wh. to end. *30th row.*—2 wh. 4 bl. to end.

Now rep. these last 2 rows 4 times more, and then continue from 11th to 30th rows (inclusive) once more.

Now shape for armholes thus:—*1st row.*—Cast off 2 sts., 1 bl., then 2 wh. 4 bl. to end. *2nd row.*—Cast off 2 sts., 3 bl., then 2 wh. 4 bl. to end. *3rd row.*—Cast off 2 sts., 1 wh., then 4 bl. 2 wh. to end. *4th row.*—Cast off 2 sts., 1 bl., then 2 wh. 4 bl. to end. *5th row.*—Cast off 2 sts., 3 bl., then 2 wh. 4 bl. to end. *6th row.*—Cast off 2 sts., 1 wh., then 4 bl. 2 wh. to end. *7th row.* Cast off 2 sts., 1 bl., then 2 wh. 4 bl. to end. *8th row.*—Cast off 2 sts., 3 bl., then 2 wh. 4 bl. to end.

There should now be 110 sts. on needle. *9th row.*—1 bl., then 2 wh. 4 bl. to end. *10th row.*—1 wh., then 4 bl. 2 wh. to end. *11th row.*—2 wh., 4 bl. to end. *12th row.*—2 wh. 4 bl. to end. *13th row.*—1 wh., then 4 bl. 2 wh. to end. *14th row.*—1 bl., then 2 wh. 4 bl. to end. *15th row.*—4 bl. 2 wh. to end. *16th row.*—2 bl., then 2 wh. 4 bl. to end. *17th row.*—3 bl., then 2 wh. 4 bl. to end. *18th row.*—3 bl., then 2 wh. 4 bl. to end. *19th row.*—4 bl. 2 wh. to end. *20th row.*—2 bl. then 2 wh. 4 bl. to end. *21st row.*—1 wh., then 4 bl. 2 wh. to end. *22nd row.*—1 bl., then 2 wh. 4 bl. to end. *23rd row.*—2 wh. 4 bl. to end. *24th row.*—2 wh. 4 bl. to end. *25th row.*—1 bl., then 2 wh. 4 bl. to end. *26th row.*—1 wh., then 4 bl. 2 wh. to end. *27th row.*—2 bl., then 2 wh. 4 bl. to end. *28th row.*—4 bl., 2 wh. to end.

Rep. these last 2 rows 4 times more. Then rep. from 9th to 16th rows (after armhole shaping) inclusive, once more.

Then shape for shoulders thus: Next row work as 17th row to within last 12 sts., turn, and p. 1 bl., then 2 wh. 4 bl. back to within last 12 sts., turn. Next row work as for 19th row to within last 24 sts., turn, and 2 wh. 4 bl. back to within last 24 sts., turn. Next row work as 21st row to within last 36 sts., turn, and 1 wh., then 4 bl. 2 wh. to within last 36 sts., turn. Next row k. wh. sts. over wh. and bl. over bl. sts. (as on previous row). Next row cast off all sts., using navy wool.

The Front

With No. 12 needles and navy wool, cast on 132 sts. Work as for back up to 8th row after armhole shaping. (116 sts. on needle.) Continue thus: *9th row.*—1 bl., then 2 wh. 4 bl. until you have worked 58 sts. Put remaining 58 sts. on spare needle, and continue on first set thus:

10th row.—Cast on 6 sts. in bl. for placket. (These 6 sts. must be k. plain in every row at front edge.) K. back on these 6 sts., p. 1 bl., then 2 wh. 4 bl. to end. *11th row.*—2 wh. 4 bl. to end, fin. 8 bl. *12th row.*—K. 6 bl. p. 2 bl., then 2 wh. 4 bl. to end. *13th row.*—1 wh., then 4 bl. 2 wh. to end, fin. 9 bl. *14th row.*—K. 6 bl. p. 3 bl., then 2 wh. 4 bl. to end. *15th row.*—4 bl. 2 wh. to end, fin. 10 bl. *16th row.*—K. 6 bl. p. 4 bl., then 2 wh. 4 bl. to end. *17th row.*—3 bl., then 2 wh. 4 bl. to end, fin. 11 bl. *18th row.*—K. 6 bl. p. 5 bl., then 2 wh. 4 bl. to end. *19th row.*—As 15th. *20th row.*—As 16th. *21st row.*—As 13th. *22nd row.*—As 14th. *23rd row.*—As 11th. *24th row.*—As 12th. *25th row.*—1 bl., then 2 wh. 4 bl. to end, fin. 7 bl. *26th row.*—K. 6 bl. p. 1 bl., then 2 wh. 4 bl. to end. *27th row.*—2 bl., then 2 wh. 4 bl. to end, fin. 6 bl. *28th row.*—K. 6 bl. (wool forward as though for a p. st.), then 2 wh. 4 bl. to end. Rep. 27th and 28th rows 4 times more.

37th row.—1 bl., then 2 wh., 4 bl. to end, fin. 7 bl. *38th row.*—Cast off 6 sts., then 2 wh. 4 bl. to end. *39th row.*—2 wh. 4 bl. to end.

40th row.—Cast off 4 sts. (using navy wool), 3 bl., then 2 wh. 4 bl. to end. *41st row.*—1 wh., then 4 bl. 2 wh. to end. *42nd row.*—Cast off 4 sts., 2 wh. 4 bl. to end. *43rd row.*—4 bl. 2 wh. to end. *44th row.*—Cast off 4 sts., 3 bl., then 2 wh. 4 bl. to end. *45th row.*—3 bl., then 2 wh. 4 bl. to end, k. last 2 sts. tog. *46th row.*—4 bl. 2 wh. to end. *47th row.*—2 bl., then 2 wh. 4 bl. to end, k. last 2 sts. tog. Next row cast off all sts.

Now join navy wool to centre front neck opening of other 58 sts. and continue thus: *1st row.*—K. 9 bl., then 2 wh. 4 bl. to end. *2nd row.*—1 wh., then 4 bl. 2 wh. to end, fin. p. 3 bl. k. 6 bl. *3rd row.*—8 bl., then 2 wh. 4 bl. to end. *4th row.*—2 wh. 4 bl. to end, fin. p. 2 bl. k. 6 bl. *5th row.*—7 bl., then 2 wh. 4 bl. to end. *6th row.*—1 bl., then 2 wh. 4 bl. to end, fin. p. 1 bl. k. 6 bl. *7th row.*—4 bl., cast off 2 sts., 1 bl., then 2 wh. 4 bl. to end. *8th row.*—2 bl., then 2 wh. 4 bl. to within last 4 sts., these work thus: k. 2 bl., cast on 2 sts. (in place of those cast off on previous row), k. 2 bl. *9th row.*—7 bl., then 2 wh. 4 bl. to end. *10th row.*—1 bl., then 2 wh. 4 bl. to end, fin. p. 1 bl. k. 6 bl. *11th row.*—8 bl., then 2 wh. 4 bl. to end. *12th row.*—2 wh. 4 bl. to end, fin. p. 2 bl. k. 6 bl. *13th row.*—9 bl., then 2 wh. 4 bl. to end. *14th row.*—1 wh., then 4 bl. 2 wh. to end, fin. p. 3 bl. k. 6 bl. *15th row.*—K. 4 bl., cast off 2, k. 5 bl., then 2 wh. 4 bl. to end. *16th row.*—4 bl. 2 wh. to within last 4 sts., these work thus: k. 2 bl., cast on 2, k. 2 bl.

17th row.—11 bl., then 2 wh. 4 bl. to end. *18th row.*—3 bl., then 2 wh. 4 bl. to end, fin. p. 5 bl. k. 6 bl. *19th row.*—As 17th. *20th row.*—As 18th. *21st row.*—As 17th. *22nd row.*—As 18th. *23rd row.*—K. 4 bl., cast off 2, 6 bl., then 2 wh. 4 bl. to end. *24th row.*—3 bl., then 2 wh. 4 bl. to within last 4 sts., work these thus: k. 2 bl., cast on 2, k. 2 bl. *25th row.*—Cast off 6 sts., 3 bl., then 2 wh. 4 bl. to end. *26th row.*—4 bl. 2 wh. to end. *27th row.*—Cast off 4 sts., 4 bl. 2 wh. to end. *28th row.*—1 wh., then 4 bl. 2 wh. to end. *29th row.*—Cast off 4 sts., 1 wh., then 4 bl. 2 wh. to end. *30th row.*—2 wh. 4 bl. to end. *31st row.*—Cast off 4 sts., 2 wh. 4 bl. to end. *32nd row.*—1 bl., then 2 wh. 4 bl. to end. *33rd row.*—K. first 2 sts. tog., 4 bl. 2 wh. to end. *34th row.*—2 bl., then 2 wh. 4 bl. to end. *35th row.*—K. first 2 sts. tog., 2 bl., then 2 wh. 4 bl. to end. *36th row.*—Cast off all sts.

The Sleeves

With No. 12 needles and navy wool, cast on 68 sts. Work in a k. 1, p. 1 ribbing for 4 ins. Change to No. 7 needles and continue inc. in ptn., thus:

1st row.—K. twice into first st., 2 bl., then 2 wh. 4 bl. to end, k. twice into last st. *2nd row.*—2 wh. 4 bl. to end. *3rd row.*—4 bl. 2 wh. to end. *4th row.*—As 2nd. *5th row.*—K. twice into first st. 3 bl., then 2 wh. 4 bl. to end, k. twice into last st. *6th row.*—1 bl., then 2 wh. 4 bl. to end. *7th row.*—1 wh., then 4 bl. 2 wh. to end. *8th row.*—1 bl., then 2 wh. 4 bl. to end. *9th row.*—K. twice into first st., then 4 bl. 2 wh. to end, k. twice into last st. *10th row.*—2 bl., then 2 wh. 4 bl. to end. *11th row.*—1 wh., then 4 bl. 2 wh. to end. *12th row.*—3 bl., then 2 wh. 4 bl. to end. *13th row.*—K. twice into first st. 3 bl., then 2 wh. 4 bl. to end, k. twice into last st. *14th row.*—1 wh., then 4 bl. 2 wh. to end. *15th row.*—4 bl. 2 wh. to end. *16th row.*—2 wh. 4 bl. to end. *17th row.* K. twice into first st. 2 bl., then 2 wh. 4 bl. to end, k. twice into last st. *18th row.*—2 bl., then 2 wh. 4 bl. to end. *19th row.*—3 bl., then 2 wh. 4 bl. to end. *20th row.*—3 bl., then 2 wh. 4 bl. to end.

21st row.—K. twice into first st. 3 bl., then 2 wh. 4 bl. to end, k. twice into last st. *22nd row.*—3 bl., then 2 wh. 4 bl. to end. *23rd row.*—2 wh. 4 bl. to end. *24th row.*—2 bl., then 2 wh. 4 bl. to end. *25th row.*—K. twice into first st., then 2 wh. 4 bl. to end, k. twice into last st. *26th row.*—2 bl., then 2 wh. 4 bl. to end. *27th row.*—3 bl., then 2 wh. 4 bl. to end. *28th row.*—1 bl., then 2 wh. 4 bl. to end. *29th row.*—K. twice into first st. 2 bl., then 2 wh. 4 bl. to end, k. twice into last st. *30th row.*—1 bl., then 2 wh. 4 bl. to end. *31st row.*—1 wh., then 4 bl. 2 wh. to end. *32nd row.*—1 bl., then 2 wh. 4 bl. to end. *33rd row.*—K. twice into first st., then 4 bl. 2 wh. to end, k. twice into last st. *34th row.*—2 bl., then 2 wh. 4 bl. to end.

35th row.—2 wh. 4 bl. to end. *36th row.*—2 bl., then 2 wh. 4 bl. to end. *37th row.*—K. twice into first st., 1 wh., then 4 bl. 2 wh. to end, k. twice into last st. *38th row.*—3 bl., then 2 wh. 4 bl. to end. *39th row.*—2 wh. 4 bl. to end. *40th row.*—4 bl. 2 wh. to end. *41st row.*—K. twice into first st. 4 bl. 2 wh. to end, k. twice into last st. *42nd row.*—2 wh. 4 bl. to end. *43rd row.*—1 wh., then 4 bl. 2 wh. to end. *44th row.*—1 bl., then 2 wh. 4 bl. to end. *45th row.*—K. twice into first st. 3 bl., then 2 wh. 4 bl. to end, k. twice into last st. *46th row.*—3 bl., then 2 wh. 4 bl. to end. *47th row.*—4 bl. 2 wh. to end. *48th row.*—4 bl. 2 wh. to end.

49th row.—K. twice into first st. *50th row.*—4 bl. 2 wh. to end. *51st row.*—K. twice into first st. 2 wh. 4 bl. to end, k. twice into last st. *52nd row.*—4 bl. 2 wh. to end. *53rd row.*—3 bl., then 2 wh. 4 bl. to end. *54th row.*—3 bl., then 2 wh. 4 bl. to end. *55th row.*—K. twice into first st. 3 bl., then 2 wh. 4 bl. to end, k. twice into last st. *56th row.*—3 bl., then 2 wh. 4 bl. to end. *57th row.*—2 wh. 4 bl. to end. *58th row.*—2 bl., then 2 wh. 4 bl. to end. Rep. 57th and 58th rows 4 times more.

67th row.—1 wh., then 4 bl. 2 wh. to end. *68th row.*—3 bl., then 2 wh. 4 bl. to end. *69th row.*—4 bl. 2 wh. to end. *70th row.*—4 bl. 2 wh. to end. *71st row.*—3 bl., then 2 wh. 4 bl. to end. *72nd row.*—3 bl., then 2 wh. 4 bl. to end. *73rd row.*—1 wh., then 4 bl. 2 wh. to end. *74th row.*—2 bl., then 2 wh. 4 bl. to end. *75th row.*—2 wh. 4 bl. to end. *76th row.*—2 wh. 4 bl. to end. *77th row.*—1 bl., then 2 wh. 4 bl. to end. *78th row.*—1 bl., then 2 wh. 4 bl. to end.

79th row.—As 74th. *80th row.*—As 75th. *81st row.*—As 72nd. *82nd row.*—As 73rd. *83rd row.*—As 69th. *84th row.*—As 70th. *85th row.*—1 wh., then 4 bl. 2 wh. to end. *86th row.*—3 bl., then 2 wh. 4 bl. to end. *87th row.*—2 wh. 4 bl. to end. *88th row.*—2 bl., then 2 wh. 4 bl. to end. Rep. 87th and 88th rows 4 times more. Then rep. from 67th to 78th rows inclusive.

Now shape for top of sleeve thus: *1st row.*—Cast off 2, 5 bl., then 2 wh. 4 bl. to end. *2nd row.*—Cast off 2, 3 bl., then 2 wh. 4 bl. to end. *3rd row.*—Cast off 2, 4 bl. 2 wh. to end. *4th row.*—Cast off 2, 2 wh. 4 bl. to end. *5th row.*—Cast off 2, 3 bl., then 2 wh. 4 bl. to end. *6th row.*—Cast off 2, 3 bl., then 2 wh. 4 bl. to end. *7th row.*—Cast off 2, 2 bl., then 2 wh. 4 bl. to end. *8th row*—Cast off 2, 2 wh. 4 bl. to end. *9th row.*—Cast off 2, 1 bl., then 2 wh. 4 bl. to end. *10th row.*—Cast off 2, 3 bl., then 2 wh. 4 bl. to end.

11th row.—Cast off 2, 1 wh., then 4 bl. 2 wh. to end. *12th row.*—Cast off 2, 1 bl., then 2 wh. 4 bl. to end. *13th row.*—Cast off 2, 3 bl., then 2 wh. 4 bl. to end. *14th row.*—Cast off 2, 1 wh., then 4 bl. 2 wh. to end. *15th row.*—Cast off 2, 1 bl., then 2 wh. 4 bl. to end. *16th row.*—Cast off 2, 3 bl., then 2 wh. 4 bl. to end. *17th row.*—Cast off 2, 1 wh., then 4 bl. 2 wh. to end. *18th row.*—Cast off 2, 1 bl., then 2 wh. 4 bl. to end. Next row cast off all sts.

The Collar

With navy wool and No. 12 needles, cast on 140 sts. Work in a k. 1, p. 1 ribbing for 4 ins. Cast off.

To Make Up Jumper

Press all parts with a hot iron and a damp cloth. Sew side, shoulder and sleeve seams. Sew sleeves into armholes. Halve collar, place centre to centre back neck, and oversew to neck edge. Sew three buttons on left placket to correspond with buttonholes. Press all seams with hot iron and a damp cloth.

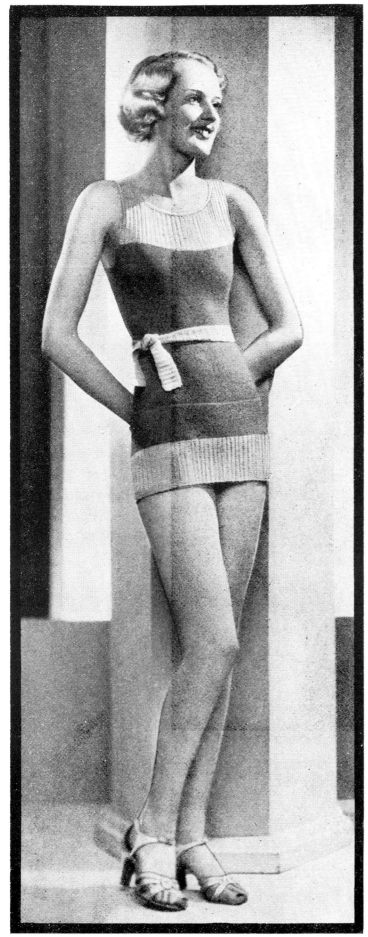

The neckline is quite high in front, but the back has a fairly low "V" for sun bathing.

SEA-WAVES *and* SUNNY DAYS A*head!*

Hand-Knitted and Very Trim—the Perfect Swimming-Suit

A VERY easy fancy rib, with stocking-stitch, makes this swimming-suit, so it is very easy to follow. It is worked closely on No. 11 needles, so two sizes larger can be made by using needles No. 10 and 9 respectively throughout.

MATERIALS : 5 ounces of Wolsey "Sportsman" 4-ply Lido wool in light blue, and 4 ounces of the same wool in a deeper shade ; a pair of "Aero" knitting needles No. 11 and one spare needle.

TENSION AND MEASUREMENTS : Worked at a tension of 8 sts. to the inch in width on the s.s., the following measurements are attained after light pressing : Round the bustline and under-arms, 29 inches ; round the hips at the top of the skirt, 29 inches ; length from shoulder seam to edge of skirt, 27 inches ; length of trunk at side seam, 7 inches ; round leg rib without stretching, 14 inches.

ABBREVIATIONS : K., knit plain ; p., purl ; tog., together ; sl., slip ; inc., increase (by working into the back and front of the same stitch) ; p.s.s.o., pass slip-stitch over ; st., stitch ; s.s., stocking-stitch (k. on the right side and p. back), directions in brackets are worked the number of times stated immediately after the brackets ; single rib is k. 1 and p. 1 alternately.

To Work the Trunks

FOR the first leg, using light wool, cast on 58 sts. loosely, then work 7 rows in single rib.

Now build up the inside edge as follows : K. 5, turn, p. 5, k. 10, turn, p. 10, k. 15, turn, p. 15, k. 20, turn, p. 20, k. 25, turn, p. 25, k. 30, turn, p. 30, k. 35, turn, p. 35, k. 40, turn, p. 40, k. 45, turn, p. 45, k. 50, turn, p. 50.

On all sts. work 24 rows in s.s., ending with a p. row. Cut the wool end and leave these sts. on a spare needle for the present.

For the second half of the leg cast on 58 sts. with light wool and work 7 rows in single rib. Work 1 row plain, then build up the inside edge as follows :

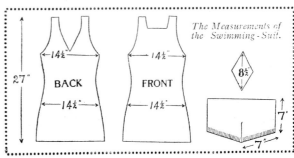

The Measurements of the Swimming-Suit.

27" — BACK — 14½" — 14½"

FRONT — 14½" — 14½"

8½"

7" — 7"

Although It is So Smart, the Bathing Suit is Very Simple to Make. It is Knitted in an Easy Fancy Rib, with Stocking-Stitch

P. 5, turn, k. 5,
p. 10, turn, k. 10,
p. 15, turn, k. 15,
p. 20, turn, k. 20,
p. 25, turn, k. 25,
p. 30, turn, k. 30,
p. 35, turn, k. 35,
p. 40, turn, k. 40,
p. 45, turn, k. 45,
p. 50, turn, k. 50.
On all sts. work 24 rows s.s., ending with a k. row, then on the same needle k. the 58 first half leg sts., which gives 116 sts. on the same needle with the long edges in the centre. Work 33 rows s.s., ending with a p. row. Cut the wool and leave these sts. on a spare needle until the skirt has been worked.

To Work the Skirt

Begin at the lower edge by casting on 118 sts. with light wool, then work in pattern as follows :

The suit looks very attractive made in two shades of blue.

1st row (wrong side facing) : K. 1, * p. 2, k. 1, repeat from * to end.
2nd row : All knit.
Repeat these 2 rows until 39 rows have been worked, ending with a wrong side row.
Change to dark wool and k. 1 row, taking 2 sts. tog. at each end (116 sts.).
Work 29 rows more in s.s., ending with a p. row.
Now join the skirt and knickers as follows :
Hold the needle with knicker sts. at the back of the skirt needle sts. (right side of both pieces facing the worker),* take 1 st. from skirt needle, and 1 st. from knicker needle, and k. these together. Repeat from * to end, which gives 116 sts. on the same needle.
The Hip Shaping.—** Work 3 rows in s.s.
Decrease row : K. 3, sl. 1, k. 1, p.s.s.o., k. until 5 remain, k. 2 tog., k. 3.
Repeat the last 4 rows from ** until the 13th decrease row has been worked with 90 sts.

A close-up photograph of the ribbing stitch.

Work 21 rows in s.s. (NOTE.—The back of the suit is worked the same to this point.)

Now begin the increases for the bodice.

***Increase row*: K. 3, inc. in next st., k. until 4 remain, inc. in next st., k. 3.

Work 3 rows in s.s.

Repeat the last 4 rows from *** until the 10th increase row has been worked with 110 sts.

Work 14 rows s.s. to armhole, ending with a knit row.

Next row: K. 5, p. until 5 remain, k. 5.

Knit 1 row.

Next row: K. 6, p. until 6 remain, k. 6.

To Shape the Armhole: Next row: Cast off 4, k. to end.

Next row: Cast off 4, k. 3, p. 40, leave these 43 sts. on a spare needle for the right front, cast off 16 loosely, p. 40, k. 3 (43 for left front).

Left Front.—*1st row* (right side facing): K. 3, sl. 1, k. 1, p.s.s.o., k. to end.

2nd row: Cast off 5 (neck end), p. until 3 remain, k. 3.

Repeat these 2 rows until all are worked off.

The Right Front.—Join the dark wool to the centre edge of right front sts., k. until 5 remain, k. 2 tog., k. 3.

Next row (wrong side facing): K. 3, p. to end.

Next row: Cast off 5, k. until 5 remain, k. 2 tog., k. 3.

Repeat the last 2 rows until all are worked off.

The Front Yoke

USING light wool, pick up and k. 92 sts. from the right side of front neck edge.

* Work 3 rows in pattern as on skirt border, but every wrong side row should begin and end with k. 3 to give a plain border.

Next row: K. 3, sl. 1, k. 1, p.s.s.o., k. until 5 remain, k. 2 tog., k. 3.

Repeat the last 4 rows from last * until the 3rd decrease row is worked and 86 sts. remain.

Work 21 rows more in pattern, ending with a wrong side row.

Next row: K. 23, k. 2 tog., (k. 1, k. 2 tog.) 13 times, k. 22.

Next row (wrong side facing): Pattern 17, k. 38, pattern 17.

K. 1 row.

Next row (wrong side facing): Pattern 16, k. 40, pattern 16.

Next row: K. 19 for left shoulder, cast off 34, k. 19 for right shoulder.

RIGHT FRONT SHOULDER.—*Next row* (wrong side facing): Work in pattern with 3 plain sts. at each end to keep a plain border.

Next row: K. 3 (neck end), sl. 1, k. 1, p.s.s.o., k. to end.

Repeat these 2 rows until 11 sts. remain

Work 12 rows straight and cast off.

LEFT FRONT SHOULDER.—Join the light wool to the neck end and work as follows:

Next row (wrong side facing: Work in pattern with k. 3 border at each end.

Next row: K. until 5 remain, k. 2 tog., k. 3.

Repeat these 2 rows until 11 sts. remain. Work 12 rows on these sts. and cast off.

The Back

THIS is worked in exactly the same way as the front until the waist-line is reached and 21 rows worked in s.s.

Next row: K. 3 inc. in next st., k. until 4 remain, inc. in next st., k. 3.

Work 3 rows straight in s.s.

Now begin the V-shape in light wool as follows:

1st row (right side facing): With dark wool k. 3, inc., k. 41, now take the light wool and place it behind the next st. on the left-hand needle leaving about 3 inches hanging below. Hold the wool in position with the forefinger of the left hand, pass the dark wool over the light once, leave the dark wool hanging, then k. 2 sts. with light, with a second ball of dark wool k. 41, inc. in the next st., k. 3. (Remember to twist the wool out of action over the working colour at each change of wool.)

2nd row: P. 45, dark, 4 light, 45 dark.

3rd row: K. 44 dark, 6 light, 44 dark.

4th row: P. 43 dark, with light wool p. 2, (k. 1, p. 2) twice, p. 43 dark.

5th row: K. 3, dark inc. in next st., k. 38, with light wool k. 10, with dark wool k. 38, inc. in next st., k. 3.

6th row: P. 42 dark, with light p. 1, k. 1, (k. 1, p. 2), three times, p. 1, with dark wool p. 42.

7th row: K. 41 dark, 14 light, 41 dark.

8th row: P. 40 dark, with light p. 3, k. 1, (p. 2, k. 1) 3 times, p. 3, p. 40 dark.

Continue on this plan with light coloured centre sts. in pattern (each row will have 2 extra sts. in light wool, and one less in dark wool on either side) and the ends in dark s.s. inc. in the 4th st. from each end of next and every following 4th row until the 10th inc. row is worked with 110 sts. (66 light sts. in the centre).

Work 10 rows more with 2 extra light sts. in pattern as before. These rows will end with a right side row with 12 dark at each end and 86 light in the centre.

Next row (wrong side facing): P. 11 dark, pattern 42 light, k. 4, pattern 42, p. 11 dark.

Next row: K. 10 dark, 90 light, 10 dark.

Next row: P. 9 dark, with light pattern 43, k. 6, pattern 43, p. 9 dark.

On the next row the sts. are divided for the neckline.

RIGHT BACK SHOULDER.—*1st row*: K. 8 dark, 47 light, pass the remaining 55 sts. on a spare needle for the left shoulder.

2nd row: With light wool k. 3, pattern 45, with dark wool p. 2, k. 5.

3rd row: K. 6 dark, with light wool k. until 5 remain, k. 2 tog., k. 3.

4th row: With light wool k. 3, pattern until 5 remain, k. 5 dark.

5th row: With dark wool cast off 4, with light wool k. until 5 remain, k. 2 tog., k. 3.

Now use all light wool as follows (both back shoulders are the same from here):

* *Next row* (wrong side facing): K. 3, pattern until 3 remain, k. 3.

Next row: K. 3, sl. 1, k. 1, p.s.s.o., k. until 5 remain, k. 2 tog., k. 3.

Repeat these last 2 rows until 27 sts. remain.

Now work straight at the armhole end, but continue with the neck end decreases until 17 sts. remain.

Work 3 rows straight in pattern.

Next row: Work in pattern, decreasing at the neck end as before.

Repeat these last 4 rows until 11 sts. remain.

Work 14 rows straight and cast off.

LEFT BACK SHOULDER.—Join the light wool to neck end and work as follows:

1st row: K. 47 light, 8 dark.

2nd row: With dark wool k. 5, p. 2, pattern 45, k. 3 light.

3rd row: With light wool k. 3, sl. 1, k. 1, p.s.s.o., k. until 6 remain, k. 6 dark.

4th row: K. 5 dark, pattern in light until 3 remain, k. 3.

5th row: With light wool k. 3, sl. 1, k. 1, p.s.s.o., k. until 4 remain, cast off 4 with dark wool.

Now work as given on right back shoulder from *.

The Gusset

WITH light wool cast on 3 sts. and p. these. Continue in s.s., inc. at each end of next and every following 3rd row until there are 33 sts. on the row. Work 3 rows straight.

Continue in s.s., taking 2 sts. tog. at each end of next, and every following 3rd row, until 3 sts. remain. Cast off.

The Belt

WITH light wool cast on 242 sts. and work as follows:

1st row (wrong side facing): K. 3, p. 2, * k. 1, p. 2, repeat from * until 3 remain, k. 3.

2nd row: All knit.

Repeat these 2 rows until 15 rows are worked altogether. Cast off loosely.

To Make Up the Suit

FIRST press all pieces with a damp cloth over the wrong side of the work. Join the side and shoulder seams, and sew the inside leg edge of the ribbed border only.

The gusset is then stitched into the opening thus left.

Darn in all ends and press the seams carefully.

Press the belt, and wear tied round the costume at the natural waistline.

Continued from page 132

next 2 rows, 1 st. at the beginning of the next 4 rows, when there will be 48 sts. left, on which work 5 patterns more without dec.

NEXT ROW: Sl. 1, k. to end.

NEXT ROW: Sl. 1, p. 13, k. 20, p. 14.

Repeat these 2 rows twice.

NEXT ROW: Sl. 1, k. 16 for the right back shoulder, cast off 14 sts. for the middle of the neck, leaving 17 sts. for the left shoulder.

THE LEFT SHOULDER: K. 17.

NEXT ROW: Sl. 1, p. 13, k. 3.

Repeat these 2 rows once more and cast off loosely.

THE RIGHT SHOULDER: Join to the neck end of the first set of 17 sts. and beginning with the second row, work to match the first shoulder.

THE SLEEVES

BEGIN at the wrist, for which cast on 28 sts. loosely. K. in pattern as on the front for 5 patterns.

Now inc. at the beginning and end of the 1st row of each pattern until there are 60 sts., on which work two patterns more, or according to length of sleeve seam required.

To shape the top of the sleeve, cast off 6 sts. at the beginning of the next 2 rows, cast off 3 sts. at the beginning of the next 2 rows, then dec. 1 st. at the beginning of the next 26 rows. Cast off the remaining 16 sts. loosely.

THE BOWS

USING the No. 15 steel needles, cast on 1 st. and k. into the front and back of this st., after which inc. at the beginning of each row until there are 20 sts. on the needle.

NEXT ROW: K. 2 tog. 10 times.

NEXT ROW: K. plain.

NEXT ROW: K. 2 tog. 5 times.

NEXT ROW: K. plain.

NEXT ROW: K. into the front and back of each st.

NEXT ROW: K. plain.

Now dec. at the beginning of each row until 1 st. remains, draw the wool through this st. and fasten off.

TO MAKE UP THE JUMPER

FIRST press all pieces very lightly, putting a damp cloth over the wrong side of the work. Join the shoulder seams, taking 1 st. from the back and front together, then sew the top of the sleeves to the armholes, and press these seams while the work is open.

Join the side and sleeve seams in one continuous line, taking only 1 st. from each side at a time to ensure a flat seam, and press.

Finally, add the four little bows, sewing them to the left side of the panel as you see in the photograph.

KNIT yourself this delightful slim-line all-in-one and you'll keep out wintry chills without adding an inch to your figure— a great asset in these days of "slinky" frocks

Knit these Slimline Undies

WE know you'll love this soft cosy all-in-one, to wear next to your skin this winter. It's a mere feather-weight, but beautifully warm; and will cost you less than half-a-crown to make. You will need :—

4 oz. of Harrap's "Sirdar" 2 ply Super Shetland Wool; a pair each of No. 10 and No. 12 knitting needles; a No. 12 bone crochet hook; 1 yard of ½-inch width ribbon for shoulder straps; and 1⅛ yards of a narrower width for threading through the top of the cami; seven small press fasteners.

Measurements.—From the top to the lower edge of centre front, 21 inches. Width all round under arms (unstretched), 30 inches, stretches to 34 inches.

Tension.—7 stitches in width to 1 inch when using No. 10 needles.

Abbreviations.—K., knit; p., purl; st., stitch; dec., decrease; inc., increase; tog., together; rep., repeat; st.-st., stocking-stitch, alternate k. and p. rows; cont., continue; beg., beginning.

Knit into the backs of all cast-on sts. to make firm edges.

THE BACK.—Using the No. 10 needles begin by casting on 32 sts. K. 8 rows in st.-st. Then, at the beg. of every row cast on 3 sts. (always k. into the backs of the cast on sts.) until there are 128 sts. on needle. Cont. on these sts. in st.-st., without alteration, for 8 inches. Then begin shaping for the back thus : With the right side of work towards you, k. to within 12 sts. from end of row, turn (always slipping the first st. after turning).

2nd row.—P. to within 12 sts. from end of row, turn.
3rd row.—K. to within 18 sts. from end of row, turn.
4th row.—P. to within 18 sts. from end of row, turn.
5th row.—K. to within 24 sts. from end of row, turn.
6th row.—P. to within 24 sts. from end of row, turn.
7th row.—K. to within 30 sts. from end of row, turn.
8th row.—P. to within 30 sts. from end of row, turn.
9th row.—K. to within 36 sts. from end of row, turn.
10th row.—P. to within 36 sts. from end of row, turn.
11th row.—K. to within 42 sts. from end of row, turn. *12th row.*—P. to within 42 sts. from end of row, turn. *13th row.*—K. to end of row. *14th row.*—P. to end of row.

Change to No. 12 needles and work in a k. 2, p. 2 ribbing for 2 inches.

Change back to No. 10 needles and cont. in st.-st. for 4 inches. *Next row.*—* k. 14, k. 2 tog., rep. from * to end of row, leaving 120 sts. Then start the fancy patt. thus : *1st row.*—Slip 1, k. 2, * m. 1 (by bringing wool forward as though to purl); k. 2 tog., k. 1 and rep. from * to the end. Cont. always working like this patt. row for 2½ inches. Then work 3 rows in moss-st. thus. *Next row.*—K. 1, p. 1 alternately to end of row. *Next row.*—P. 1, k. 1 alternately to end of row. *Next row.*—K. 1, p. 1 alternately to end of row. Cast off at a medium tension.

THE FRONT.—Work this in the same way as for the back, but *without* the back shaping.

TO COMPLETE THE GARMENT.—Press both pieces of knitting on the wrong side under a damp cloth with a warm iron. Do not press the *ribbing*. Join up the side seams and press. Now hold the cami-knickers in the left hand with the right side towards you. Take a No. 12 knitting needle in the right hand and, using it like a crochet hook, pick up and draw through 144 loops on to the needle along the sloping edge of the legs. P. the next row. Then work in the fancy patt. for 1¾ inches and finish off with 3 rows in moss-st. Cast off at a medium tension. At the lower edge of the front and back flap work 2 rows of double crochet. Then sew a narrow piece of white ribbon just inside the edge of the flap on the wrong side and sew on the press fasteners. Sew 2 more press fasteners to each of the tiny leg seams to fasten. Divide the wider ribbon in half and sew a piece to the front and back of the top part. Thread the narrower ribbon through the top. Press all seams.

ON the right you see a close-up of the pretty lace-stitch used for the cami-top and the leg bands. It is very simple to knit; and you must admit the result is adorably dainty!

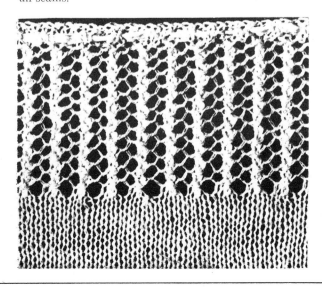

It's Simple and— It's Charming!

The Narrow Panel Has A Wonderfully Slimming Effect.

HERE is such a pretty little jumper for the beginner; it's chiefly plain knitting with one pair of needles for both the fine and the coarse row.

For the average size of 34 to 36 inches bust measurement use No. 6 needles.

MATERIALS.—4 ounces of Golden Eagle 3-ply Standard Fingering, or any 3-ply Fingering of good make, and a pair of knitting needles No. 8, steel needles No. 15 for the bows.

ABBREVIATIONS.—K., knit plain; p., purl; st., stitch; tog., together; dec., decrease; inc., increase.

TENSION AND MEASUREMENTS.—Worked at a tension of 5 sts. to the inch in width the following measurements are attained after light pressing. Across the front at the under-arms, 17 inches; across the back at the same place, 13 inches; length, from shoulder to lower edge, 19 inches; side seam, 13 inches; sleeve seam, 19 inches. (The back may be worked like the front, with the exception of the higher back neck-line, and no panel for a larger bust measurement.)

TO WORK THE FRONT

CAST on 84 sts. loosely and k. one row, then k. a second row, winding the wool twice round the needle before knitting each st.

NEXT ROW: Sl. 1, and k. to the end of the row, working into one twist of each st. and letting the second twist fall from the needle.

Now proceed with the pattern:

1ST ROW: With the right side facing, sl. 1, k. all sts., winding the wool twice round the needle for each st. (All the k. rows are worked in this way throughout the jumper.)

2ND ROW: Sl. 1, p. to the end of the row, working into 1 twist only on each st.

3RD ROW: As 1st row.

4TH ROW: As 2nd row.

5TH ROW: As 1st row.

6TH ROW: Sl. 1, k. to end of row, making the double loops as usual for a k. row; this one is on the wrong side of the work and produces the ridge at the top of each pattern on the right side.

Repeat these 6 rows 4 times more, decreasing 1 st. at each end of the first row of each pattern (by knitting 2 tog.). 76 sts. now on.

Work one pattern more without decreasing.

K. two patterns more, inc. 1 st. (by knitting into the back and front of the same st.) at both ends of the first row of each pattern (80 sts.).

Now begin the plain panel.

1ST ROW: Inc. in the first st., k. 27, p. 1, k. 22, p. 1, k. 27, inc. 1 in the last st. (82 sts.).

2ND ROW: Sl. 1, p. 28, k. 1, p. 22, k. 1, p. 29.

3RD ROW: Sl. 1, k. 28, p. 1, k. 22, p. 1, k. 29.

Repeat the 2nd and 3rd row once more.

6TH ROW: Sl. 1, k. 29, p. 22, k. 30.

Repeat these 6 rows once more (84 sts.).

Now repeat the pattern of 6 rows 5 times more, but without inc. or dec.

TO SHAPE THE ARMHOLE.—Cast off 6 sts. at the beginning of the next 2 rows, then 2 sts. at the beginning of the next 4 rows, after which dec. 1 st. at the beginning of the next 6 rows (58 sts.).

Work 5 rows of another pattern without inc., then on the next row, sl. 1, k. across all the sts.

NEXT ROW: Sl. 1, k. to the end of the row.

NEXT ROW: Sl. 1, p. 13, k. 30, p. 14.

Repeat the last 2 rows twice more up to the front neck-line.

NEXT ROW: Sl. 1, k. 16, cast off 24 sts. loosely for the front of the neck.

THE RIGHT SHOULDER

THIS is continued on the 17 remaining sts.

1ST ROW: K. 17.

2ND ROW: Sl. 1, p. 13, k. 3.

3RD ROW: K. 17.

4TH ROW: Sl. 1, p. 13, k. 3.

5TH ROW: K. 17.

6TH ROW: Sl. 1, p. 16.

Repeat these 6 rows 3 times more, then cast off loosely.

THE LEFT SHOULDER

JOIN the wool to the neck end of the first set of 17 sts. Repeat from the 2nd row of the right shoulder and work to correspond.

THE BACK

CAST on 60 sts. loosely, and k. plain.

NEXT ROW: Sl. 1, k. all sts., twisting the wool round the needle twice for each st.

NEXT ROW: Sl. 1, k. to end.

Now work the same pattern as on the front, and dec. 1 st. at the beginning and end of the 1st row of 5 patterns (50 sts.).

Now inc. at both ends of the 1st row of each pattern for 5 patterns more (60 sts.), then work for another 5 patterns without inc. up to the armhole.

To shape the armhole, cast off 4 sts. at the beginning of the

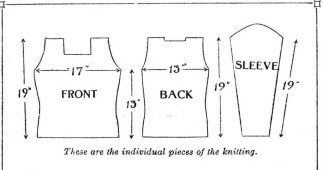

These are the individual pieces of the knitting.

Continued on page 130

3

The Fitted Tailored Look 1935-37

The sweater becomes longer and fits closely to the figure with a belt defining a smaller waist. The higher neckline has to be varied and interesting—it is cowled, scalloped or rolled or has large lapels and a neck-tie. Unusual petal and sun-ray collars are a flattering feature. For smartness, buttons, buckles, broaches and clips are fastened to the sweater, and for the sports-sweater a neat pattern in an original stitch gives distinction. For a more feminine appearance, decoration in the form of frills, ruffs, lacy stitches or sequins may be added. Sleeves are long and fitted or bloused. Underwear and the backless bathing-suit are shaped closely to the figure.

Crochet A "Cobweb" Jumper!

Never Have We Had A More Enchanting Jumper Than This—It Will Make Every Woman Look Her Best!

THIS is our masterpiece in crochet! A lovely cobweb jumper.

Without the jabot it is just a simple little crochet jumper which any beginner can work, and the jabot is quite easy, too.

MATERIALS : Eight half-ounce balls of Copley's 2-ply Fine " Cobweb " wool in natural, or one of the pretty colours in which this wool is made ; an " Aero " crochet hook No. 11, and a pair of " Aero " knitting needles No. 10. A ready-made belt to tone in colour.

TENSION AND MEASUREMENTS : Worked at a tension of 7 sts. to the inch in width, the following measurements are attained after light pressing : Across the back at the under-arms, 19 inches ; across the front, 19 inches ; front length shoulder seam to lower edge, 23 inches ; back length shoulder seam to lower edge, 21 inches ; side seam, 15 inches ; sleeve seam, 6 inches. (Note that as this wool is so light and lacy this jumper is adaptable to the average figure of 34 to 36 inches bust measure by using a crochet hook one size smaller. A little extra width will fall softly to the figure.)

ABBREVIATIONS : K., knit ; p., purl ; ch., chain ; sl., slip ; st., stitch ; d.c., double crochet ; tr., treble ; d.tr., double treble (wool twice round the hook, and work off the loops in twos as for ordinary tr.). Directions in brackets are worked the number of times stated after the brackets.

TO WORK THE BACK

WITH the crochet hook, make 129 ch. for the waistline.

NEXT ROW : 1 tr. into the 5th ch. from the hook, 124 tr. more, making a row of 126 tr., counting the 3 turning ch. as 1 tr. and it is treated as such throughout the work, by working into the third ch., as in the top of a tr.

NEXT ROW : 3 ch., miss the first tr., over which the 3 ch. stands, 1 tr. on 2nd tr. of last row, 124 tr. more, always working into both loops at the top of the st. on the last row, 3 ch., turn.

Repeat the last row 26 times more to the armhole, making 1 ch. at the end of last row.

To SHAPE THE ARMHOLE : Sl.st. along the top of the sts. to the third tr. on last row, 3 ch., 1 tr. on next tr. of last row, 120 tr. more, 1 ch., turn.

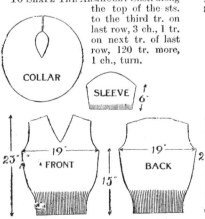

COLLAR

SLEEVE 6"

23"   19"
FRONT

19"   21"
BACK

15"

The pieces of the jumper laid out flat.

Repeat this armhole row 7 times more, each row having 4 tr. less, that is 2 less at the beginning by slipstitching over 2 tr. and 2 left unworked at the end of the row. The last row has therefore 94 tr. altogether.

Work 14 rows more on these sts. to shoulder.

To SLOPE THE BACK SHOULDERS : Sl.st. along to the 7th tr. on the last row, 1 ch., 6 d.c., 69 tr., 6 d.c., turn.

NEXT ROW : Sl.st. along to the next tr., 6 d.c., 58 tr., 6 d.c. Fasten off.

THE FRONT

WORK as on the back until the armhole decreases are finished and there are 94 tr. along the row. Work 4 rows more on these sts.

FIRST FRONT SHOULDER : 1ST ROW : 3 ch., 1 tr. on 2nd tr. of last row, 44 tr. more, making 46 sts., counting the first 3 ch. as 1 tr., 1 ch., turn.

Continue in tr., decreasing 2 sts. at the neck end *only* of every row by sl.st. as at the armhole at the beginning of a row, and by leaving 2 sts. unworked at the end of a row, until 10 rows more are worked, the last with 26 tr.

Work 3 rows more on these sts., ending with 1 ch., turn.

NEXT ROW : Sl.st. along to 7th tr. from the arm end, 6 d.c., 13 tr., turn.

NEXT ROW : 3 ch., 6 tr., 6 d.c., and fasten off.

SECOND FRONT SHOULDER : Miss 2 tr. in centre front of neck and sl.st. to the 3rd tr., 3 ch., 45 tr., turn.

Work 10 rows more, decreasing 2 tr. at the neck end of each one, the last row having 26 sts. Work 3 rows more on these sts.

NEXT ROW : 3 ch., 12 tr., 6 d.c., turn.

NEXT ROW : 12 d.c., 7 tr., fasten off.

THE SLEEVE

BEGIN at the top and make 30 ch.

NEXT ROW : 1 d.c. into the 4th ch. from the hook, miss one foundation ch., 1 tr. in the next ch., 24 tr. more, (work 1 tr. into the base of the last tr.) 3 times, turn.

INCREASE ROW : 6 ch., 1 d.c. into the 4th ch. from the hook, miss one foundation ch., 1 tr. in next ch., 30 tr. more (in each repeat there will be 6 tr. more to work at this point), (1 tr. into the base of the last tr.) 3 times, turn.

Repeat the increase row 8 times more, the last row having 78 tr. in the centre.

NEXT ROW : 3 ch., 1 tr. on the 2nd tr. of last row, 82 tr. more, turn.

Repeat the last row 14 times more.

FOR THE LONG SLEEVES : Continue in this manner, dec. 1 st. at each end of every 5th row until the width desired is attained. Continue straight on these sts. for length required, and fasten off. Then, using No. 10 needles and double wool, work a two-inch cuff of k. 2 and p. 2 rib.

Fasten off and work the second sleeve in the same manner.

THE ARM BANDS : With No. 10 needles and using the wool double, pick up and k. 84 sts. Work 12 rows of k. 2 and p. 2 rib., then cast off rather loosely.

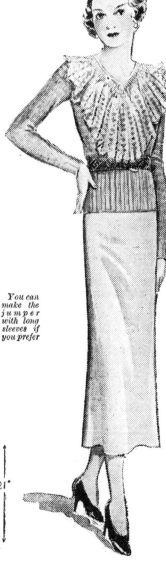

You can make the jumper with long sleeves if you prefer

The delicate jabot, like a soft fall of lace, is the prettiest ever seen.

THE WAIST RIB

WITH No. 10 needles, pick up and k. 120 sts. from the waist edge, using the wool double.

Work 55 rows in k. 2 and p. 2 rib. Cast off fairly loosely. Work the back and front waist the same.

THE JABOT

WITH the crochet hook, make 126 ch.

1st Row : 1 tr. into the 5th ch. from the hook (1 ch., miss one foundation ch., 1 tr. in the next ch.) 30 times,

Crochet A "Cobweb" Jumper!

Continued

2 ch., 1 tr. in the same st., (1 ch., 1 tr. in 2nd foundation ch.) 30 times, 1 tr. more, 3 ch., turn.

2ND Row : 1 tr. on 2nd tr. of last row, 1 ch., 1 tr. into next space, 1 ch., miss 2 tr. on the last row, into the next ch. space work 1 tr., then (1 ch. and 1 tr. in the same space) 3 times, * 1 ch., miss 1 space, 1 tr. in the next space on the last row, (1 ch., 1 tr. in the next space) 3 times, 1 ch., miss one space, 1 tr. into the next space, (1 ch. and 1 tr. in the same space) 3 times more, repeat from * twice more. Repeat from * once more, but work the last item 7 times more in the same place, to make the centre scallop. Now repeat from first * 4 times more, then 1 ch., 1 tr. in the end space, 1 ch., 2 tr. on end, 3 ch., turn.

3RD Row : 1 tr. on 2nd tr., 1 tr. between next 2 tr., 1 ch., * miss 1 space on last row, (1 tr. in next space, 1 ch., 1 tr. in the same space, 1 ch.) 3 times, miss 1 space on last row, (1 tr. in next space, 1 ch.) 3 times ; repeat from * 8 times more, in the 4th repeat the first bracket is worked 7 times, and at the end of the last repeat work the last 3 tr. without ch. between, 3 ch., turn.

4TH Row : 3 ch., 1 tr. on second tr. of last row, * 1 ch., miss 1 space on last row, (1 tr. in the next space, 1 ch., 1 tr. in the same space, 1 ch.) 5 times, miss 1 space, 1 tr. in the next space, 1 ch., 1 tr. in the following space ; repeat from * 3 times more. Again repeat from *, but this time work d.tr. inside the brackets and work the bracket item 13 times. Repeat from first * 4 times and omit the ch. between the last 2 tr., turn.

5TH Row : 3 ch., 1 tr. on the 2nd tr. of the last row, * (miss 1 space, 2 tr. in the next space, 2 ch., 2 tr. in the same space) 5 times, miss 1 space, 1 tr. in the next space ; repeat from * twice more. Now repeat from * with d.tr. instead of tr. in the groups. Work the middle scallop in the same way, but repeat the bracket item 13 times. Repeat once more from * with d.tr. instead of tr., then repeat from first * 3 times more, ending with 1 tr. more at end of row, 3 ch., turn.

6TH Row : 1 tr. on second tr., * (2 tr. in next 2-ch. loop, 2 ch., 2 tr. in same loop) 5 times, 1 tr. on single tr. on last row. Now work group over group on the next 5 scallops (including the middle one), but working d.tr. instead of tr. Work the two remaining scallops with tr. as at the beginning of the row, and remember to work the tr. over the single tr. between each scallop. End with 1 tr. more in the last st., 3 ch., turn.

7TH Row : 1 tr. on 2nd tr., * (3 tr. in next ch. loop, 2 ch., 3 tr. in the same loop) 5 times, 1 tr. on next single tr. Now repeat these groups over the groups of the previous row and the 1 tr. on single tr., but working d.tr. instead of ordinary tr. until the last group is reached. Here work tr. as at the beginning of the row and end with 1 tr. more, 3 ch., turn.

8TH Row : As last row, but work d.tr. every time and fasten off the wool.

9TH Row : Join with a sl.st. to single d.tr. between the 1st and 2nd scallop, 3 ch. Work 2 rows more the same as the last row, but omit the end scallops, only 7 scallops being worked on the 9th and 10th rows. Fasten off.

11TH Row : Join with a sl.st. to the single d.tr. between 2nd and 3rd scallop from shoulder, 3 ch. Work two rows similar to last two rows, except that there are 4 d.tr. in each group, instead of 3, also two scallops are left unworked at each end.

13TH Row : Join to single d.tr. between the 3rd and 4th scallops, 3 ch., work the same as the last row, but only over the 3 centre scallops.

14TH Row : 3 ch., work over all the groups on the last row, but with 5 d.tr. in each group. Fasten off.

15TH Row : Join to a single tr. at the beginning of centre scallop, 3 ch., work the same as the last row over the centre scallop only. Fasten off.

¶ THE OUTER EDGE.—Join to the shoulder edge and work round the outer edge of the jabot as follows : 3 ch., * 1 d.c. in next ch. loop, (5 ch., 1 d.c. in the same loop) 3 times, 3 ch., 1 d.c. between next two tr. groups, 3 ch. ; repeat from * until two scallops are worked over. Now for the next scallop work the bracket item 4 times, and work 4 ch. at either side of single d.c. Over the 3 centre scallops work 5 ch. at each side of single d.c. and complete the remaining scallops to match the first half.

TO MAKE UP THE JUMPER

PRESS lightly all pieces except the rib over a thin cloth. Join the shoulder seams, beginning at the armhole end and sew through 1 st. from the back and front together. Set the sleeves into the armholes, and press.

Stitch the jabot to the neck, catching each narrow end down with running stitches along the shoulder seam on each side. Finish the neck with 3 rows of d.c. On the first row, work through a chain on the jabot as well as the neck edge.

Join the sleeve and side seams in one continuous line, then press.

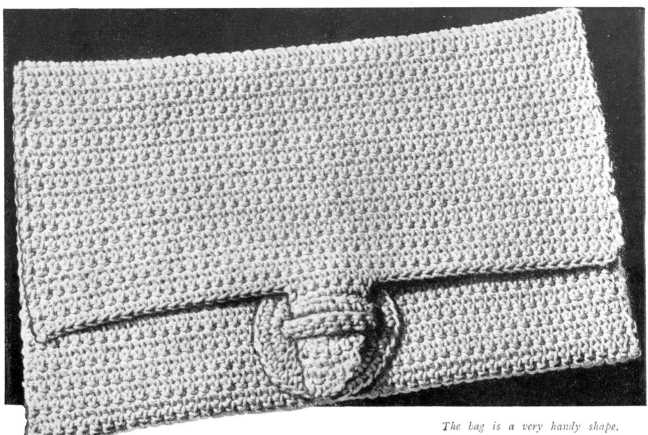

The bag is a very handy shape.

AND HERE *are the* Latest ACCESSORIES!

*Crochet Them in the Gayest Colours
to Match Your Summer Outfit*

Now that there are such lovely shades in macramé string, there is no excuse for not having your accessories to match your summer frock, especially when the string is firm enough for a handbag. This one is worked in the simplest stitch—double crochet.

MATERIALS.—*Two ¼-lb. balls of Strutt's macramé string No. 5 will make this bag and belt, and leave some over for those who want to add a few more rows to bag or belt ; and a No. 0 steel crochet hook was used for firmness.*

TENSION AND MEASUREMENTS.—*Worked at a tension of 5½ sts. to the inch in width the bag measures 9 inches wide* and 6 *inches deep when made up. The belt is* 36 *inches by* 1½ *inches.*

ABBREVIATIONS.—*Ch., chain ; d.c., double crochet ; st., stitch ; sl., slip.*

The Bag

Make 51 ch.
    1st row: Miss the first 2 ch., which will stand for 1 d.c., 1 d.c. in each remaining ch., making 49 d.c. more, 2 ch., turn.
    2nd row : Miss the first d.c., 1 d.c. in each st., taking up both loops at the top of each st. on the previous row, 1 d.c. in each st. across the row and 1 d.c. in the top of the ch. at the beginning of the row, 2 ch., turn.

Repeat the second row until there are 98 rows worked ; fasten off and run the end of the string through the middle of the sts.

THE TAB.—Join the string with a sl.st. into the 22nd d.c. from the end of the row, there make another ch. for the first d.c., then 7 d.c. more, 2 ch., turn.

Work 4 rows more in d.c. as on the main part of the bag.

On the next row make 6 d.c. 2 ch., turn.

Work 3 rows more on these 6 d.c.

On the next row make 4 d.c., cut the end and fasten off.

Continued overleaf

Note the clever buckle fastening of the belt.

A String Belt and Bag to Go With Every Dress —Why Not? They Are So Delightfully Simple to Make

THE BUCKLE.—Make 4 ch. and sl.st. to first st. to form a ring.

1st round : Into the ring work 7 d.c. Do not join each round, but put a piece of cotton in the first st. to indicate the beginning of the round.

2nd round : * 2 d.c. in the first st., 1 d.c. in the next st. and repeat from * all round.

3rd round : Work 2 d.c. in every third st. and 1 d.c. in each of the others.

4th round : 2 d.c. in every 5th st.

5th round : As 4th round and fasten off.

THE BAR.—Make 10 ch., leaving about 8 inches of the string at the beginning of the ch., and make 3 rows of d.c. as at the beginning of the bag ; fasten off, leaving about 8 inches of string.

Using the cut ends of the string attached to the bar, sew one narrow end to the 3rd round of d.c. on the base of the buckle, then sew the opposite end of the bar on the other half of the third round, exactly opposite, and fasten off.

TO MAKE UP THE BAG.—Count 34 rows up from the straight end of the bag, and turn up at that end ; sew down the two sides with the macramé string. Stitch the buckle at the centre of the bag just above the lower fold, for which use sewing silk double, in the same colour as the string, and put a hemming st. through each st. of the crochet. Pass the tab under the bar of the buckle to close the bag.

The Belt

MAKE 190 ch. for the full length of the belt, and work one row of d.c. as at the beginning of the bag.

* On the next row decrease 1 st. at the end of the row by leaving the last st. unworked, 2 ch., turn.

Next row : 1 d.c. on each st. as usual. Repeat from * twice more, then work one row more in d.c. and fasten off.

THE BELT BUCKLE.—Make the first 5 rounds like the bag buckle.

6th round : As 5th round.

7th round : Increase in every 6th st.

8th round : Increase in every 8th st.

9th round : Increase in every 10th st.

10th round : 1 d.c. in each st. and fasten off.

THE BAR.—Make 14 ch., leaving an end of string to attach the bar as before. Work 4 rows of d.c. as described at the beginning of the bag. Cut the end and draw through the last st. Sew by the cut ends over the centre of the buckle base, in this case touching the ends of the 6th round. Sew the straight end of the belt at the centre back of the buckle.

They give new individuality to your holiday woollies.

Here you see the jumper worn with just a little vestee.

We

Present—

THE

PINAFORE

JUMPER !

**A Fascinating Little Woolly
For Sports, For The Office,
Or For The Home !**

ABBREVIATIONS

K., knit; p., purl; tog., together; inc., increase (by working into the back and front of the same stitch); st., stitch; m.s., moss-stitch (k. 1 and p. 1 alternately, and on subsequent rows the sts. are reversed); single rib is k. 1 and p. 1 alternately to end.

MATERIALS

SEVEN ounces of Sirdar 3-ply Super Shetland Wool; a pair each of " Aero " knitting needles No. 8 and No. 11, and one short spare needle.

TENSION AND MEASUREMENTS

WORKED at a tension of 7½ sts. to the inch on the m.s., the following measurements are attained after light pressing : Across the back and front at the underarms, 18 inches ; front length from shoulder to edge, 19½ inches : back length 18½ inches ; side seam, 13 inches ; sleeve seam, 19 inches.

TO TWIST THE CABLE

A CABLE is made on 4 sts. as follows : slip the first 2 sts. from the point of the left-hand needle on to a spare needle, and leave these at the front of the work, k. the next 2 sts., then pass the 2 spare-needle sts. back to the left-hand needle and k. these 2 sts. (You will notice that the 1st and 2nd set of stitches exchange places

This is a close-up of the fascinating stitch in which the jumper is made.

Woman's Weekly 1935

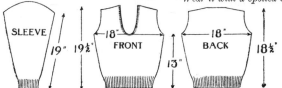

Wear it with a spotted scarf, or over a silk blouse.

to give the cable twist.) Directions in brackets are worked the number of times stated immediately after the brackets.

TO WORK THE BACK

USING No. 11 needles, cast on 108 sts. and work 29 rows in single rib.

INCREASE ROW : Wrong side facing. (Rib 4, inc. in next st., rib 3, inc. in next st.) 12 times. 132 sts. now on.

Change to No. 8 needles and work in pattern as follows :

1ST ROW. Right side facing. (K. 1, p. 1) twice, k. 4, * (k. 1, p. 1), 4 times, k. 4 ; repeat from * until 4 remain, (k. 1, p. 1) twice.

2ND ROW : (P. 1, k. 1) twice, p. 4, * (p. 1, k. 1) 4 times, p. 4 ; repeat from * until 4 remain, (p. 1, k. 1) twice.

3RD ROW : (K. 1, p. 1) twice, cable, * (k. 1, p. 1) 4 times, cable : repeat from * until 4 remain, (k. 1, p. 1) twice.

4TH ROW : As 2nd row.

Repeat these 4 pattern rows twice more. (This makes 12 rows in pattern with a stripe of 8 m.s. and a cable in between.)

13TH Row : All knit.

14TH Row : All purl.

15TH Row : Work all in cables.

16TH Row : All purl.

Repeat these 16 pattern rows 3 times more, then 14 rows of the next pattern to armhole (78 rows in pattern).

TO SHAPE THE ARMHOLES : Continue in pattern, casting off 2 sts. at the beginning of each of the next 20 rows. (92 sts.)

Work 36 rows straight in pattern to shoulder. By this time the pattern will be quite plainly seen, so that it can easily be kept correct after decreasing. After all the decreases are made the pattern will begin and end with m.s. 8 instead of m.s. 4.

TO SLOPE THE SHOULDERS : Cast off 7 sts. at the beginning of each of the next 8 rows. Cast off the remaining sts.

THE FRONT

WORK from the back instructions until 77 rows in pattern have been worked to armhole (ending with the 13th pattern row).

On the next row the sts. are divided for the neck.

NEXT ROW : P. 63 sts. for right front and darn these on an odd length of wool and leave until needed, cast off 6, p. 63 for left front (including the 1 st. left on needle after casting off).

THE LEFT-FRONT SHOULDER

** CONTINUE in pattern (working on right-side rows as far as the pattern will go), casting off 2 sts. at the beginning of each of the next 9 rows (4 decreases at neck edge, and 5 decreases at the armhole end).

Continue in pattern, casting off 2 at the beginning of alternate rows (armhole end) for 5 times more, and also work 2 sts. tog. at the beginning of every 4th row (neck end) for 3 times (32 sts.).

Continue straight at the armhole end, but now work 2 sts. tog. at the beginning of every 6th row (neck end) until 28 sts. remain.

Work 22 rows straight on these sts. to shoulder.

TO SLOPE THE SHOULDER : Cast off 7 sts. at the beginning of next and every following alternate row (armhole end) until all are worked off.

THE RIGHT-FRONT SHOULDER

JOIN the wool to the neck end of right-front shoulder sts. and work 1 row. Continue from ** on left front shoulder.

THE FRONT NECK EDGE

WITH right side of work facing, and using No. 11 needles, pick up and k. 125 sts. from all round the neck edge. Work 3 rows in single rib, and cast off loosely.

THE SLEEVES

WITH No. 8 needles cast on 22 sts. and p. 1 row. Continue in inc. pattern as follows :

1ST ROW (right side facing) : Inc., (k. 1, p. 1) 4 times, * k. 4, (k. 1, p. 1) 4 times ; repeat from * in following patterns, inc. in last st.

2ND ROW : Inc., p. 1, (p. 1, k. 1) 4 times, * p. 4, (p. 1, k. 1)

4 times ; repeat from * in following patterns until 2 remain, p. 1, inc.

3RD ROW : Inc., k. 2, m.s. 8, * cable, m.s. 8 : repeat from * in following patterns until 3 remain, k. 2, inc.

4TH ROW : Inc., p. 3, m.s. 8, * p. 4, m.s. 8 : repeat from * in following patterns until 4 remain, p. 3, inc.

5TH ROW : Inc., k. 4, * m.s. 8, k. 4 ; repeat from * until 1 remains, inc. in last st.

6TH ROW : Inc., k. 1, p. 4, * m.s. 8, p. 4 ; repeat from * until 2 remain, p. 1, inc.

7TH ROW : Inc., k. 1, p. 1, cable, * m.s. 8, cable ; repeat from * until 3 remain, k. 1, p. 1, inc.

8TH ROW : Inc., k. 1, p. 1, k. 1, p. 4, * m.s. 8, p. 4 ; repeat from * until 4 remain, p. 1, k. 1, p. 1, inc.

9TH ROW : Inc., m.s. 4, k. 4, * m.s. 8, k. 4 ; repeat from * until 5 remain, m.s. 4, inc.

10TH ROW : Inc., m.s. 5, p. 4, * m.s. 8, p. 4 ; repeat from * until 6 remain, m.s. 5, inc.

11TH ROW : Inc., m.s. 6, cable, * m.s. 8, cable ; repeat from * until 7 remain, m.s. 6, inc.

12TH ROW : Inc., m.s. 7, p. 4, * m.s. 8, p. 4 ; repeat from * until 8 remain, m.s. 7, inc.

13TH ROW : Inc. in the 1st st., k. until 1 remains, inc.

14TH ROW : Inc. in the 1st st., p. until 1 remains, inc.

15TH ROW : Inc., k. 2, work in cable pattern until 3 remain, k. 2, inc.

16TH ROW : As 14th row.

Repeat the 5th to the 12th row inclusive, and then the 1st to the 4th row inclusive (78 sts.). Work from the 13th to 16th row again (86 sts.).

NEXT ROW : Inc., m.s. 4, k. 4, * m.s. 8, k. 4 ; repeat from * until 5 remain, m.s. 4, inc. (88 sts.)

Work 3 rows straight in pattern, beginning with 2nd pattern row. (NOTE.—These rows will begin and end with m.s. 6.)

Continue in pattern, taking 2 sts. tog. at each end of next and every following 8th row until 56 sts. remain.

Work 3 rows more.

NEXT ROW : Change to No. 11 needles, * k. 2 tog., p. 1, (k. 1, p. 1) 7 times ; repeat from * twice more, k. 2 tog., p. 1, k. 1, p. 1.

Now work 29 rows in single rib on these 52 sts. Cast off fairly loosely.

Work a second sleeve in the same manner.

THE COLLAR

WITH No. 11 needles. Cast on 155 sts. and work in following rib.

1ST ROW : (right side facing) P. 1, * k. 1, p. 1 ; repeat from * to end.

2ND ROW : P. 2, k. 1, * p. 1, k. 1 ; repeat from * until 2 remain, p. 2.

Repeat these 2 rows until 24 rows have been worked. Cast off fairly loosely.

TO MAKE UP THE JUMPER

FIRST press all pieces, except the rib, with a hot iron and a damp cloth over the wrong side of the work. Sew the shoulder seams, beginning at the armhole end, and taking only one stitch from each side at a time to ensure a flat seam. Set the sleeves into armholes and press this seam while the work is open.

Stitch the collar to neck edge, beginning at the centre back, after marking the centre of the collar, and sew down each side of the neck as far as the collar will go.

Press all seams while the work is open. Join the sleeve and side seams in one continuous line and press.

Are You LOOKING for a FRESH NOTE?

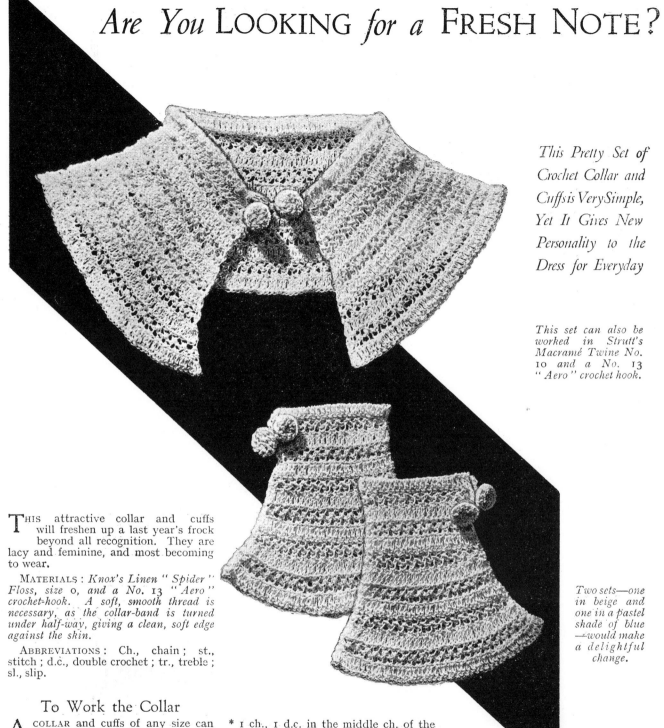

This Pretty Set of Crochet Collar and Cuffs is Very Simple, Yet It Gives New Personality to the Dress for Everyday

This set can also be worked in Strutt's Macramé Twine No. 10 and a No. 13 "Aero" crochet hook.

THIS attractive collar and cuffs will freshen up a last year's frock beyond all recognition. They are lacy and feminine, and most becoming to wear.

MATERIALS : Knox's Linen "Spider" Floss, size 0, and a No. 13 "Aero" crochet-hook. A soft, smooth thread is necessary, as the collar-band is turned under half-way, giving a clean, soft edge against the skin.

ABBREVIATIONS : Ch., chain ; st., stitch ; d.c., double crochet ; tr., treble ; sl., slip.

Two sets—one in beige and one in a pastel shade of blue —would make a delightful change.

To Work the Collar

A COLLAR and cuffs of any size can be made according to the foundation chain.

For the neck edge of the collar, make 93 ch.

1st row : 1 tr. in the 4th ch. from the hook, then 1 tr. in each st. to the end of the row, making 90 tr. altogether. The 3 ch. at the beginning of the row also counts as 1 tr. throughout the work, so there will be 91 sts. on this row, 3 ch., turn.

2nd row : Miss the tr. over which the 3 ch. stands and the next tr., 1 d.c. in the third tr., * 3 ch., miss 1 tr., 1 d.c. in the next tr., taking up the back loop of the st. only ; repeat from * to the end of the row, 3 ch., turn.

3rd row : 1 d.c. in the middle ch. of the loop, taking up 1 thread only,

* 1 ch., 1 d.c. in the middle ch. of the next loop as before ; repeat from * to the end of the row, finishing with 1 ch., 1 d.c. in the end ch., 3 ch., turn.

4th row : 1 tr. in every st. (ch. and d.c.) across the row, 3 ch., turn.

Repeat the 2nd to the 4th row, inclusive, 5 times, but to shape the collar increases must be made on every repetition of the 4th row, which is the tr. row, thus : On the first repetition work 2 tr. in every sixth st., and the next 2 rows will increase automatically.

On the second repetition, increase in every fifth st., and on the third repetition increase in every sixth st.

On the fourth repetition, increase in every fifth st., and on the fifth repetition increase in every sixth st., and this is the last row of the collar.

The Cuffs

BEGIN at the wrist with 46 ch., and proceed exactly as on the collar, working 9 rows without any increase.

On the next tr. row increase in every fifth st., and continue in the same pattern with increases as on the collar until there are 3 tr. rows more ; but always put 2 tr. in the first and last st. of the increase rows, in addition to the other increases.

The crochet button-links make a charming finishing touch to the collar and cuffs.

The Button-Links

MAKE 4 ch. and sl.-st. to the first ch. to form a round. Work 6 d.c. into the ring, * 1 d.c. in the next st., 2 d.c. in the next st.; repeat from *, working round and round without joining, until the little circle is big enough to cover the button mould.

Now work 2 rounds of 1 d.c. in each st., after which miss every alternate d.c. until the hole is nearly closed. Slip in the button mould before the opening is too small, and finally cut the thread, pass it into an embroidery needle and close up.

Work a second cover in the same way, but after closing up the hole leave enough thread to make a crochet ch. as the link between the two buttons. Pass the end of this chain through an open stitch on each side of the cuff opening, then fasten this end to the middle of the first button.

Work another pair of links in the same way.

"WINTER WOOLLIES"—in ADVANCE

*The Vest has the Prettiest Opera Top, and Instructions
are Given for Making It in Stock Size and Outsize*

STOCK SIZE

HERE is a beautifully shaped vest with a pretty opera top. Instructions are given for two sizes —for the average figure and the not-so-slim.

MATERIALS : Three ounces of Patons & Baldwins' 2-ply " Nonshrink " vest wool in white ; a pair each of " Aero " knitting needles, No. 8 and No. 11 ; 1 yard of ribbon for shoulder straps and 1¼ yards of narrow ribbon ; an " Aero " crochet hook No. 13.

TENSION AND MEASUREMENTS : *Worked at a tension of 7 sts. to the inch on the No. 8 needles, the following measurements are attained after light pressing— top to hem, 25 inches ; round bust, 28 inches ; round skirt below decreases, 31 inches.*

ABBREVIATIONS : *K., knit ; p., purl ; tog., together ; inc., increase (by working into the back and front of the same st.) ; sl., slip ; st., stitch ; single rib is k. 1 and p. 1 alternately ; s.s., stocking-stitch (k. on the right side and p. back) ; directions in brackets are worked the number of times stated immediately after the brackets ; p.s.s.o., pass. sl.st. over.*

CROCHET ABBREVIATIONS : *Ch., chain; sl.st., slip-stitch ; d.c., double crochet ; tr., treble.*

To Work

BEGIN at the back and with the No. 8 needles cast on 110 st. for the lower edge. Work 30 rows of single rib.

Now work 8 rows in s.s.

* *Next row* (decrease row) : K. 2, sl. 1, k. 1, p.s.s.o., k. until 4 sts. remain, k. 2 tog., k. 2.

Work 7 rows in s.s.

Repeat the last 8 rows from * until 90 sts. remain, ending with 7 rows of s.s.

Change to No. 11 needles and work 40 rows of s.s. for the waist.

Change to No. 8 needles and work 6 rows of s.s.

* * *Next row* (increase row) : K. 2, inc. in the next st., k. until 3 sts. remain, inc. in the next st., k. 2. Work 5 rows of s.s., then repeat the last 6 rows from * * until the 5th increase row has been worked (100 sts. on).

Now begin the Insertion Pattern.

1st row (wrong side) : K. 2, * sl. 1, k. 1 ; repeat from * to end.

2nd and every right side row : All knit.

3rd row : All purl.

5th row : P. 2, * k. 1, (sl. 1, k. 1) 5 times, p. 5, k. 2, p. 2, k. 1, sl. 1, k. 2, sl. 1, k. 1, p. 2, k. 2, p. 5, k. 1, (sl. 1, k.1) 5 times, p. 4 ; repeat from * once, ending with p. 2 instead of p. 4.

7th row : P. 3, * k. 1, (sl. 1, k. 1) 5 times, p. 9, k. 1, p. 2, k. 1, p. 9, k. 1, (sl. 1, k. 1) 5 times, p. 6 ; repeat from *, ending with p. 3 instead of p. 6.

9th row : K. 1, * p. 3, k. 1, (sl. 1, k. 1) 8 times, p. 3, k. 2, p. 3, k. 1, (sl. 1, k. 1) 8 times, p. 3, k. 2 ; repeat from *, ending with k. 1.

11th row : P. 1, * k. 1, p. 9, k. 1, (sl. 1, k. 1) 5 times, p.6, k. 1. (sl. 1, k. 1) 5 times, p. 9, k. 1, p. 2 ; repeat from *, ending with p. 1 instead of p. 2.

13th row : K. 1, * sl. 1, k. 1, p. 2, k. 2, p. 5, k. 1, (sl. 1, k. 1) 5 times, p. 4, k. 1 (sl. 1, k. 1) 5 times, p. 5, k. 2, p. 2, k. 1, sl. 1, k. 2 ; repeat from *, ending with k. 1 instead of k. 2.

15th row : All purl.

17th row : K. 2, * sl. 1, k. 1 ; repeat from * to end.

19th row : All purl.

Cast off loosely.

THE FRONT : Work this in exactly the same way as the back.

To Make Up

FIRST press the two pieces of knitting putting a damp cloth over the wrong side of the work, then sew up the side seams.

THE TOP EDGE : With the crochet hook and white wool, work one round of d.c. all round the top.

2nd round : Make 7 ch., sl.st. to 4th ch. from hook, 1 tr. into the 2nd st.

on the last round, * 4 ch., sl.st. to 4th ch. from hook, miss 1 st. on the last round, and work 1 tr. in the next st. ; repeat from * all round and fasten off.

Sew the shoulder straps in place, press the seams and edges, and thread the narrow ribbon through the fancy edging.

OUTSIZE VEST

MATERIALS : Four ounces of Patons & Baldwins' 2-ply " Nonshrink " vest wool in white ; a pair of " Aero " knitting needles No. 8 ; an " Aero " crochet hook No. 13. For the shoulder straps allow 1 yard of ribbon, and 2 yards of narrow ribbon. (For making two vests 7 ounces of wool is enough, and three vests can be made from 10 ounces.)

TENSION AND MEASUREMENTS : *Worked at a tension of 7 sts. to the inch, the following measurements are attained after light pressing—round the bust, 30 inches ; round skirt below decreases, 34 inches ; length from top to hem, 28 inches.*

ABBREVIATIONS : *As given for the Stock Size Vest.*

To Work

BEGIN at the back and with No. 8 needles cast on 118 sts. for the lower edge. Work 30 rows in single rib. Then work 40 rows in s.s.

* *Next row* (decrease row) : K. 2, sl. 1, k. 1, p.s.s.o., k. until 4 sts. remain, k. 2 tog., k. 2.

Work 7 rows in s.s.

Repeat the last 8 rows from * until the 10th decrease row has been worked, with 98 sts. on the needle.

Work 33 rows in s.s. for the waist.

* * *Next row* (increase row) : K. 2, inc. in the next st., k. until 3 sts. remain, inc. in the next st., k. 2.

Work 7 rows in s.s.

Repeat the last 8 rows from * * until there are 104 sts. on the needle. Then work 6 rows of s.s., ending with a k. row.

8 times, p. 3, k. 2, p. 3, k. 1, (sl. 1, k. 1) 8 times, p. 3, k. 2 ; repeat from * until 1 st. remains, k. 1.

11th row : K. 4, * p. 9, k. 1, (sl. 1, k. 1) 5 times, p. 6, k. 1, (sl. 1, k. 1) 5 times, p. 9, k. 4 ; repeat from * to end.

13th row : K. 3, * sl. 1, k. 1, p. 2, k. 2, p. 5, k. 1, (sl. 1, k. 1) 5 times, p. 4, k. 1, (sl. 1, k. 1) 5 times, p. 5, k. 2, p. 2, k. 1, sl. 1, k. 2 ; repeat from * until 1 st. remains, k. 1.

15th row : All purl.

17th row : K. 2, * sl. 1, k. 1 ; repeat from * to end.

19th row : All purl.

Next row : Cast off loosely.

THE FRONT : Work this in exactly the same way as the back.

To Make Up

FIRST press the knitting, putting a damp cloth over the wrong side of the work. Sew the side seams together.

THE TOP EDGE : With crochet hook work 1 row of d.c. all round the top edge, sl.st. to 1st d.c. of round.

2nd round : Make 7 ch., sl.st. to 4th ch. from hook, * miss 1 d.c. on last round, and work 1 tr. into the next d.c. on last round, 4 ch., sl. st. to 4th ch. from hook ; repeat from * all round.

Fasten off.

Press the seams and edge. Sew the shoulder straps in place and thread the narrow ribbon through the fancy edging.

✻　　✻　　✻

ANOTHER DELICIOUS APPLE RECIPE

Spanish Apple Pudding

INGREDIENTS :

1 lb. cooking apples
2 ozs. Valencia raisins
2 ozs. butter
3 ozs. Barbados sugar
2 ozs. desiccated coconut
¼ level teaspoonful ground cloves
½ lb. self-raising flour
½ level teaspoonful ground cinnamon
2 ozs. castor sugar
2 ozs. margarine
1 egg　　　　Milk

PEEL and quarter the apples, remove the cores and slice them thickly.

Put them into a buttered pie-dish, sprinkle them with the Barbados sugar mixed with the ground cloves, and dot them with the butter cut into small pieces. Cover them and cook them gently in the oven.

When they are about half cooked, lightly mix in the coconut and stored raisins, and finish cooking the apples. Let them cool slightly.

Sift the flour with the ground cinnamon, rub in the margarine and add the castor sugar. Stir in the beaten egg and a little milk as required. Put this mixture on the top of the apples, and bake the pudding in a moderately hot oven for about half an hour.

Continue in the insertion pattern as follows :

1st row (wrong side) : K. 2, * sl. 1, k. 1 ; repeat from * to end.

2nd and every right side row : All knit.

3rd row : All purl.

5th row : P. 4, * k. 1, (sl. 1, k. 1) 5 times, p. 5, k. 2, p. 2, k. 1, sl. 1, k. 2, sl. 1, k. 1, p. 2, k. 2, p. 5, k. 1, (sl. 1, k. 1) 5 times, p. 4 ; repeat from * to end.

7th row : P. 5, * k. 1, (sl. 1, k. 1) 5 times, p. 9, k. 1, p. 2, k. 1, p. 9, k. 1, (sl. 1, k. 1) 5 times, p. 6 ; repeat from *, ending with p. 5 instead of p. 6.

9th row : K. 3, * p. 3, k. 1, (sl. 1, k. 1)

A Cosy Little Set for the Cold Days

MATERIALS REQUIRED: 7 ounces of Templeton's Baby Wool, shade 2551, pink; 1 pair of Stratnoid knitting needles, size 9; 1 Stratnoid crochet hook, size 3; ¾ yard of white elastic, ¼ inch wide.

ABBREVIATIONS: k. = knit; p. = purl; tog. = together; sl. = slip; inc. = increase; dec. = decrease; rep. = repeat.

TENSION: 13 sts. to 2 inches.

MEASUREMENTS: VEST—Length, 28 inches; width around under arms, 32 inches unstretched. KNICKERS—Side leg, 16½ inches; waist, 26 inches unstretched. (Both small women's size.)

The Vest

Commence at the bottom of the vest front, casting on 116 sts., and work as follows:—

1st row.—p. 1, for the seam st., then k. 2, p. 1, to end of row.

2nd row.—k. 1, then p. 2, k. 1, to end of row.

3rd and 5th rows.—As 1st row.

4th row.—As 2nd row.

6th row.—(Right side facing you), purl.

These 6 rows complete the pattern.

Rep. for depth of 14 inches.

Now change to k. 1, p. 1, rib knitting twice into the last st. on the 1st row, to make sts. equal, and work for 3 inches in depth.

Now work for the yoke as follows :—

1st row.—With right side facing you, purl seam st. (then k. 3 tog., k. 1, p. 1, k. 1, all into the front of the next st.). Rep. to last st., p. 1.

2nd row.—k. 1, purl to the last st., k. 1.

3rd row.—Purl seam st. (then k. 1, p. 1, k. 1, all into the front of the next st., k. 3 tog.). Rep. to end of row, purl the seam st.

4th row.—Knit the seam sts., and purl the rest. These 4 rows complete the pattern.

Work in pattern for 5 inches in depth. Now shape for top of yoke, e.g. with the right side of work facing you. Cast off 3 sts. at the beginning of the 1st row, work to centre front, turn and k. 2 tog., work to the last 2 sts., k. 2 tog.

Next row in pattern. Rep. the last 2 rows until 9 sts. left. Work on these 9 sts. for 7 inches for the shoulder-strap. Fasten off work at other side-front to correspond. *The back is worked exactly as the front.*

To Make Up

Press both parts to size and shape very lightly, using a damp cloth and warm iron. Stitch together with the wool. With the crochet hook and wool work a picot edging around yoke and straps with 5 d.c., then 5 ch. into last st. Rep. all round. Press lightly.

The Knickers

Commence at top of right side, casting on 118 sts., and rib in k. 1, p. 1, for 2½ inches in depth. Now change to pattern st., and shape as follows, increasing 1 st. at each end of every 4th row :— With the right side facing you, work 20 sts. Turn and work back, slipping the 1st st. at this and every turn. Continuing in pattern, work a second shaping to 30 sts. and back ; a third shaping to 40 sts. and back ; a fourth shaping to 50 sts. and back ; a fifth shaping to 60 sts. and back ; a sixth shaping to 70 sts. and back ; a seventh shaping to 80 sts. and back.

Now continue right across and in pattern, still increasing at each end of every 4th row, until there are 140 sts. on needle.

Continue in pattern *without* increasing until 4 inches on the straight are completed and front seam, shortest side, measures 15 inches and the shaped longest side measures 16½ inches.

Now shape for the legs : p. 1, then k. 2 tog., at beginning of next row, then work in pattern to the last 3 sts., k. 2 tog., p. 1.

2nd row.—Knit the seam sts. and pattern the rest.

Rep. these 2 rows until 120 sts. are on needle and ending on the wrong side. On the next row commence the pattern st. and work for 2 inches in depth. Then cast off loosely.

Work the left side to correspond, using same sts. and measurements as in right, only commencing the shapings for the back from left side instead of right.

The Gusset

Cast on 31 sts. and work in pattern for same depth as width to form a square. Cast off.

To Make Up

Press both parts and gusset to size and shape, using a damp cloth and warm iron. Then sew up seams and put in gusset, stitching it to the four 4-inch sides at lower part of knickers. Press. With crochet hook and pink wool work picot edging round the legs as on vest. Join the elastic in a round, then stitch this to waist with a row of double crochet worked very closely together. Give final light press.

Designed by "Dorette"

The yoke fastens at the back with tiny diamanté buttons.

This One For Parties!

It Is Knitted In Silk And Has Such An Air!

HERE'S a silk jumper for a change ! With a skirt of silk material to tone or contrast with the jumper, you are just right for afternoon affairs and homely evening parties.

MATERIALS

SIX hanks (2 ounces each) of " Knopsyl," an artificial silk composed of twisted strands of uneven thickness, but those who prefer a smooth fabric made from silk without the " knops " should use 6 ounces of Copley's Art. Crêpe Silk, and a pair each of No. 1 and No. 7 " Aero " knitting needles.

TENSION AND MEASUREMENT

WORKED at a tension of 4 sts. to the inch in width on the s.s. with the No 4 needles the following measurements are attained after light pressing : Round the bust, 37 inches ; length from shoulder fold of the yoke to the lower edge, 19 inches ; side seam, 12 inches ; sleeve seam, 18 inches.

TO WORK THE FRONT

BEGIN at the lower edge and cast on 70 sts. with the No. 7 needles and work 22 rows in single rib (k. 1 and p. 1 alternately).

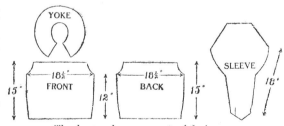

The shape and measurements of the jumper.

Change to the No. 1 needles and work 32 rows in s.s. up to the armhole.

(As workers vary when using silk and big needles, more or less rows may be worked here before shaping the armholes, according to the length of side seam required for individual measurements.

TO SHAPE THE ARMHOLES.—Take tog. the second and third st. from the beginning of each of the next 6 rows, after which work 6 rows in s.s. when the yoke line will be reached. Cast off straight across.

Such pretty sleeves, with flattering points over the hands.

THE BACK

This is worked exactly the same as the front.

THE YOKE

WITH No. 7 needles cast on 20 sts., * k. 20, turn and p. 20 sts., then k. 8, turn and p. 8, k. 16 turn and p. 16, repeat from * until the work measures 38 inches on

the lower edge of the yoke, then k. one row across all the sts. and cast off.

THE SLEEVES

BEGIN at the top and using the No. 1 needles, cast on 32 sts., then k. one row into the back of the sts.

Now work in s.s., increasing 1 st. at the beginning of

every row until there are 56 sts. on the needle, after which cast on 2 sts. at the beginning of the next 4 rows. On these 64 sts. k. straight for 7 inches.

Change to No. 7 needles and decrease on the next row by knitting every 3rd and 4th st. tog., when 48 sts. will remain.

Next Row : P. 48 sts.

Next Row : K. 1 (k. 2 tog., k. 1, k. 2 tog., k. 1, k. 2 tog.), k. to within 9 sts of the end of the row, then repeat the part in brackets at the beginning of the row, when 42 sts. will remain.

* Work 19 rows more on these sts., then on the next row decrease 1 st. at the beginning and end of the row. Repeat from * twice more when 36 sts. will remain.

Next Row : K. 8, turn and p. back. Repeat these 2 rows on the 8 sts. only until there are 16 short rows, then cast off.

Now join the silk to the 9th st. along the row, where the narrow strip began, and work 16 rows on these 28 sts., after which cast off 3 sts. at the beginning of each row until 1 remains, draw the wool through this st. and fasten off securely. This gives a finishing point to the sleeve.

Work the second sleeve in the same manner, until the opening at the wrist is reached. On this sleeve the narrow strip will be worked on the last 8 sts. instead of the first 8, and the remainder of the sleeve finished on the first 28 sts. of the row.

TO MAKE UP THE JUMPER

FIRST press all pieces lightly with a moderately hot iron and a *dry* cloth over the wrong side of the work. The jumper buttons up the back, so measure from one end of the lower edge of the yoke (that will be the centre-back when made up) 6½ inches from that end, put a small safety-pin at that point ; from this pin measure a further 5½ inches along the lower edge of the yoke and put in a 2nd safety-pin ; from this second pin measure 14 inches and mark with a third safety-pin. From the 3rd pin measure 5½ inches and put in another safety-pin. This will leave 6½ inches for the remainder of the back.

Now sew the front and back of the jumper to the respective parts of the yoke. The front will be sewn to the 14 inches between the 2nd and 3rd safety-pins ; one half of the back is sewn to the first measurement of 6½ inches at one end of the yoke, and the remaining half of the back to the last measurement of 6½ inches. This leaves 2 divisions measuring 5½ inches each, into which the cast-on edge at the top of the sleeve is sewn to the yoke, and the remaining part of the sleeve is sewn straight down to the first row of the armhole shaping. Very lightly press these seams while the work is open, then sew the sleeve and side seams in one long line and press.

To finish off the neck edge begin at the lower end of the left side opening and work 1 d.c. into each st. all round, but when working on the opposite side of the opening, make the buttonhole loops by working 4 ch., miss 3 sts. on the knitted edge, and work 1 d.c. in each st. to the centre of the yoke, then make another buttonhole, and work d.c. until within 4 sts. of the lower edge of the yoke, where make another buttonhole. Finish off the sleeve opening in the same way, and make 2 buttonholes on one side of the opening. Sew on buttons to correspond.

FUN AT SCHOOL

Naughty Roley Robin Has An Idea

It was Miss Thrush who opened it. Richard gave the message and Miss Thrush was just going off to the waiting-room when Mr. Rook stopped her.

Mr. Rook hadn't forgotten the date !

"Ask the visitor to come here," said Mr. Rook.

Richard went off rather dolefully.

But when Miss Thrush heard of Mr. Rook's suspicions she said that she hadn't the heart to disappoint the children. She hurried after Richard and burst into the waiting-room in front of the watching pupils.

"You little rascals," said Miss Thrush when she saw the notice. "And now no more fooling, but run off to your class-rooms and try and be good."

THE three little Robins set off bright and early for school on the morning of April 1st. They were hoping to make an April Fool of one of their teachers before lessons began. Under Roley's arm was tucked a square of cardboard and on it was written in large letters : APRIL 1st. HA ! HA !

At school Roley told his plan to the other little early-comers. He would put the board in the waiting-room, then someone was to run off to Miss Owl's study and say that there was a visitor waiting to see one of the teachers.

It was decided that little Richard Robin should take the message. Richard hurried off and tapped at the study door.

It was April 1st!

K

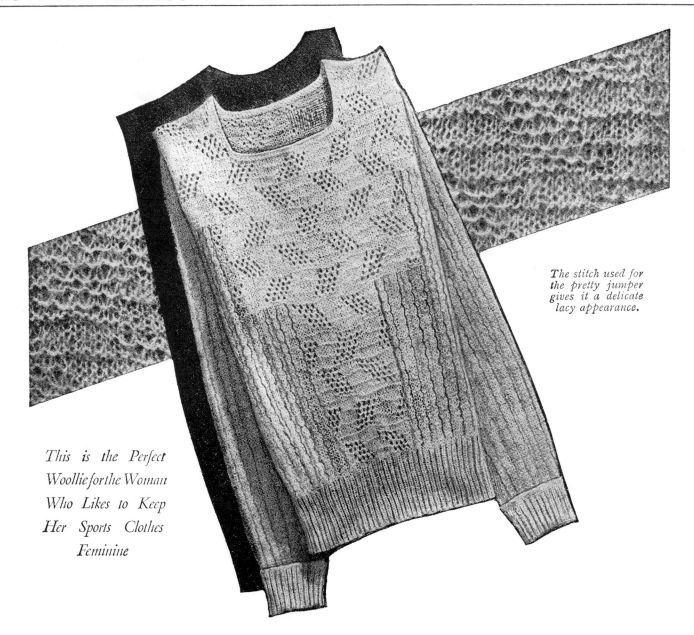

This is the Perfect Woollie for the Woman Who Likes to Keep Her Sports Clothes Feminine

The stitch used for the pretty jumper gives it a delicate lacy appearance.

Simple ELEGANCE *in* Cobwebby WOOL

KNITTED in fine, soft wool, this jumper has a special charm of its own.

MATERIALS.—*Four ½-ounce balls of Copley's Fine 2-ply " Cobweb" wool in cactus shade No. 164 ; a pair each of No. 8 and No. 11 "Aero" knitting needles and a spare needle ; also a No. 14 "Aero" crochet hook.*

TENSION AND MEASUREMENTS.— *Worked at a tension of 7 sts. to the inch in width on the No. 8 needles, the following measurements are attained after light pressing : Round the bust, 38 inches ; front length from shoulder seam to lower edge, 19 inches ; back length, 18 inches ; side seam, 13 inches ; sleeve seam, 18 inches.*

ABBREVIATIONS.—*K., knit plain ; p., purl ; tog., together ; inc., increase (by working into the back and front of the same st.) ; sl., slip ; single rib is k. 1 and p. 1 alternately ; st., stitch. Directions in brackets are worked the number of times stated immediately after the brackets.*

To Work

BEGIN at the lower edge of the back, and using No. 11 needles, cast on 116 sts. on which rib 31 rows.

Next row (wrong side) : Rib 4, (inc. in the next st., rib 6) 16 times, which gives 132 sts. on the row.

Change to No. 8 needles and work in the main pattern as follows :

1st row (right side) : P. 1, k. 2, * p. 2, k. 2 ; repeat from *, ending the row with p. 1.

2nd row : K. 1, p. 2, * k. 2, p. 2 ; repeat from *, ending the row with k. 1.

3rd and 4th rows : Work both as 1st row.

Repeat these 4 rows 17 times more to armhole.

(Note that this simple little pattern is in "2 and 2" rib, with the sts. reversed on every 4th row, so this is very easy to keep correct after casting off the sts.)

To shape the armhole, cast off 2 sts. at the beginning of the next 18 rows,

then work 2 sts. tog. at the beginning at each of the next 2 rows, which leaves 94 sts.

Work two rows more, then another row in the same pattern, taking 2 sts. tog. at the centre, which leaves 93 sts.

K. the next row plain with the wrong side facing.

The Yoke Pattern

1st row (and every odd row) : With the right side facing, all knit.

2nd row : P. 4, k. 1, (sl. 1, k. 1) 4 times, * p. 7, k. 1, (sl. 1, k. 1) 4 times ; repeat from * 5 times to end of row.

4th row : K. 4, sl. 1, (k. 1, sl. 1) 3 times, * k. 9, sl. 1, (k. 1, sl. 1) 3 times ; repeat from * until 2 sts. remain, k. 2.

6th row : P. 2, k. 1, (sl. 1, k. 1) 4 times, * p. 7, k. 1, (sl. 1, k. 1) 4 times repeat from * until 2 sts. remain, p. 2.

8th row : K. 2, sl. 1, (k. 1, sl. 1) 3 times, * k. 9, sl. 1, (k. 1, sl. 1) 3 times ; repeat from * until 4 remain, k. 4.

10th row : K. 1, (sl. 1, k. 1) 4 times,

Worn with sparkling clips the jumper is all ready for the afternoon.

The measurements of the jumper.

*p. 7, k. 1, (sl. 1, k. 1) 4 times ; repeat from * until 4 remain, p. 4.

12th row : All k.

14th row : K. 1, p. 7, * k. 1, (sl. 1, k. 1) 4 times, p. 7 ; repeat from * until 5 remain, k. 1, (sl. 1, k. 1) twice.

16th row : Sl. 1, k. 9, * sl. 1, (k. 1,

A NEW JUMPER—AND ONE
WHICH WILL CHARM!

sl. 1) 3 times, k. 9; repeat from * until 3 remain, sl. 1, k. 1, sl. 1.

18th row: K. 1, sl. 1, k. 1, p. 7, * k. 1, (sl. 1, k. 1) 4 times, p. 7; repeat from * until 3 sts. remain, k. 1, sl. 1, k. 1.

20th row: Sl. 1, k. 1, sl. 1, k. 9, * sl. 1, (k. 1, sl. 1) 3 times, k. 9; repeat from * until 1 st. remains, sl. 1.

22nd row: K. 1, (sl. 1, k. 1) twice, p. 7, k. 1, * (sl. 1, k. 1) 4 times, p. 7, k. 1; repeat from * to end.

24th row: All knit on 93 sts.

Now repeat from the 1st to the 8th row of this pattern which brings the work up to the shoulders.

To Shape the Shoulders: *1st row* (and every odd row): With the right side facing, cast off 6 sts. and k. to end (87 sts.).

2nd row: Cast off 6, leaving 1 st. on the right-hand needle, sl. 1, k. 1, * p. 7, k. 1, (sl. 1, k. 1) 4 times; repeat from * and at the end work the pattern as far as the sts. go.

4th row: Cast off 6, and k. to end.

6th row: Cast off 6, which will leave 1 st. on the right-hand needle, p. 5, * k. 1, (sl. 1, k. 1) 4 times, p. 7; repeat from *.

8th row: Cast off 6 sts. (now 1 on right-hand needle), k. 1, * sl. 1, (k. 1, sl. 1) 3 times, k. 9; repeat from * to end.

Cast off the remaining sts.

The Front

WITH No. 11 needles cast on 116 sts. and work 31 rows in rib.

Next row (wrong side): Rib 3, inc. in the next st., (rib 6, inc. in the next st.) 16 times, which gives 133 sts. on the row.

On the next 59 rows work 52 sts. at each end of every row in the main pattern and 29 sts. in the centre in the yoke pattern. The yoke pattern on 29 sts. works out exactly as given in the Back Yoke Directions, working once only from the *. For beginners the details are given below.

1st row (right side): P. 1, k. 2, (p. 2, k. 2) 12 times, p. 1; this gives 52 sts. in the main pattern; k. 29 in centre for yoke pattern; p. 1, k. 2, (p. 2, k. 2) 12 times, p. 1; this gives 52 in main pattern. Every right side row is the same.

2nd row: K. 1, p. 2, (k. 2, p. 2) 12 times, k. 1; which gives 52 in the main pattern, p. 4, k. 1, (sl. 1, k. 1) 4 times, p. 7, k. 1, (sl. 1, k. 1) 4 times; this gives 29 in the yoke pattern. K. 1, p. 2, (k. 2, p. 2) 12 times, k. 1; which gives 52 in the main pattern.

4th row: P. 1, k. 2, (p. 2, k. 2) 12 times, p. 1, which gives 52 in the main pattern, k. 4, sl. 1, (k. 1, sl. 1) 3 times, k. 9, sl. 1, (k. 1, sl. 1) 3 times, k. 2, which gives 29 in the yoke pattern; p. 1, k. 2, (p. 2, k. 2) 12 times, p. 1, which gives 52 in the main pattern.

As these 4 rows have set the main pattern it will not be given in detail on the following rows.

6th row: Work 52 in main pattern; p. 2, k. 1, (sl. 1, k. 1) 4 times, p. 7, k. 1, (sl. 1, k. 1) 4 times, p. 2, work 52 in main pattern.

8th row: Work 52 in main pattern; k. 2, sl. 1, (k. 1, sl. 1) 3 times, k. 9, sl. 1, (k. 1, sl. 1) 3 times, k. 4, then 52 in main pattern.

10th row: Work 52 in main pattern; k. 1, (sl. 1, k. 1) 4 times, p. 7, k. 1, (sl. 1, k. 1) 4 times, p. 4, then 52 in main pattern.

12th row: Work 52 in main pattern, k. 29, then 52 in main pattern.

14th row: Work 52 in main pattern; k. 1, p. 7, k. 1, (sl. 1, k. 1), 4 times, p. 7, k. 1, (sl. 1, k. 1) twice, then 52 in main pattern.

A wide belt and a dashing scarf give it the correct "country" atmosphere.

16th row : Work 52 in main pattern ; sl. 1, k. 9, sl. 1 (k. 1, sl. 1) 3 times, k. 9, sl. 1, k. 1, sl. 1, then 52 in main pattern.

18th row : Work 52 in main pattern, k. 1, sl. 1, k. 1, p. 7, k. 1, (sl. 1, k. 1) 4 times, p. 7, k. 1, sl. 1, k. 1, then 52 in main pattern.

20th row : Work 52 in main pattern ; sl. 1, k. 1, sl. 1, k. 9, sl. 1, (k. 1, sl. 1) 3 times, k. 9, sl. 1, then 52 in main pattern.

22nd row : Work 52 in main pattern ; k. 1, (sl. 1, k. 1) twice, p. 7, k. 1, (sl. 1, k. 1) 4 times, p. 7, k. 1, then 52 in main pattern.

24th row : Work 52 in main pattern, k. 29, then 52 in main pattern.

Repeat these 24 rows once, then work from the 1st to the 11th row inclusive, giving 59 rows after the waist rib.

Next row (wrong side) : Work 36 in the main pattern, k. 61, then 36 in the main pattern.

For the next 12 rows work the centre 61 sts. in the yoke pattern (that is, repeating from the * in that pattern twice more, after working once), and 36 at each end in the main pattern, beginning with the 13th row of the yoke pattern and ending with the 24th row of the yoke pattern. Work from the back yoke instructions, each row beginning with 36 sts. in the main pattern, then work the yoke pattern over 61 sts., ending with 36 in the main pattern. This brings the work to the armhole.

To Shape the Armhole : Continue with the centre 61 sts. in the yoke pattern and cast off 2 sts. at the beginning of the next 20 rows, which leaves 93 sts., ending with the 20th row of the yoke pattern.

Work 3 rows more, still keeping 61 sts. in the centre in yoke pattern.

Next row : With wrong side facing all knit.

Now work entirely in yoke pattern, beginning with the first row until 23 rows have been worked to the neck.

Next row (wrong side) : K. 29 for the right shoulder, and leave these on a spare needle, cast off 35, k. 29 (including 1 st. on the needle after casting off) for the left shoulder.

THE LEFT SHOULDER : Continue in yoke pattern, beginning with the 1st row, until 18 rows have been worked, then cast off 6 at the beginning of the next row and every following alternate row (arm end) until all are worked off.

THE RIGHT SHOULDER : Join the wool to the neck end of the right shoulder sts. and work in yoke pattern until 19 rows have been worked, beginning with the 1st row.

To Slope the Shoulder : 1st row : Cast off 6 sts., 1 on right hand needle, k. 5, sl. 1, (k. 1, sl. 1) 3 times, k. 10.

2nd row (and every even row) : With right side facing all knit.

3rd row : Cast off 6, (1 on right-hand needle), sl. 1, (k. 1, sl. 1) 3 times, k. 1, p. 7, k. 1.

5th row : Cast off 6 sts. and k. to end.

7th row : Cast off 6 sts. and p. to end. Cast off.

The Sleeves

WITH No. 8 needles cast on 26 sts. and work the next row thus : K. 2, * p. 2, k. 2, and repeat from *.

Continue in the increase pattern as follows :

1st row (right side) : Inc. in the first st., k. 1, p. 2, * k. 2, p. 2 ; repeat from * until 2 sts. remain, k. 1, inc. in the last st.

2nd row : Inc. in the first st., p. 2, * k. 2, p. 2 ; repeat from * until 1 st. remains, inc. in the last st.

3rd row : Inc. in the first st., p. 1, k. 2, * p. 2, k. 2 ; repeat from * until 2 remain, p. 1, inc. in the last st.

4th row : Inc. in the first st., p. 2, * k. 2, p. 2 ; repeat from * until 1 st remains, inc. in the last st.

Repeat these 4 rows until there are 90 sts. on the needle, then work 4 rows more in the same pattern but without inc.

Continue in the same pattern, taking 2 sts. tog. at each end of the next row, and every following 4th row, until 80 sts. remain, then work 2 sts. tog. at each end of every 8th row until 56 sts. remain.

Change to No. 11 needles, rib 28 rows, and cast off.

Work the second sleeve in the same manner.

To Make Up the Jumper

FIRST press all the pieces on the wrong side very lightly, putting a damp cloth over the work and a thick blanket underneath. Sew the shoulder seams with the same wool, beginning at the arm end and taking only 1 st. from each side at a time. Set the sleeves into the armholes, then press these seams while the work is open.

With the No. 14 crochet hook, work 3 rows of double crochet round the neck edge. Sew the sleeve and side seams in one long line, press the remaining seams and the neck edge.

PLAN for a MORNING ROOM

CARPENTER, *face it so that its windows*
  Will catch the first sunlight over the hills ;
  Windows to open to the morning ;
Windows with bright, clean panes, and sills
Wide enough for a potted primrose ;
Deep enough for a cage to swing
Between the frills of the ruffled curtains,
Where a golden-throated bird may sing.

I want this room to be clean and simple,
It must be cheerful and gay and bright :
A pivot of mornings for a family ;
A magnet to draw them home at night.
Paint it with golden paints—with colours
That will hold the warmth and light of the sun.
How can I wait until it is finished !
Carpenter, when can the work be done ?

GRACE NOLL CROWELL

Finished with a SCARF~

A Pretty Jumper in Lace Stitch with Peasant Sleeves.

Abbreviations : K., knit; p. purl; st., stitch; sts., stitches; dec., decrease or decreasing; inc., increase or increasing; wl. fwd., wool forward; tog., together; sl., slip; p.s.s.o., pass slipped stitch over; rep., repeat; ptn., pattern; cont., continue; beg., beginning; ins., inches.

Tension : 11 sts. to 2 ins. in width and 8 rows to 1 in. in depth.

Note : Always work into backs of cast on sts.

The Back.

Cast on 96 sts., using No. 12 needles, and work in a k. 1, p. 1 rib for 40 rows. Change to No. 8 needles and work ptn. as follows :

1st row : K. 1, * wl. fwd., k. 1. Rep. from * to end. *2nd row :* K. 1 * drop wl. fwd., off left-hand needle, k. 1. Rep. from * to end. *3rd and 4th rows :* K. These 4 rows make one ptn. Rep. them 16 times more.

THE graceful little cowl scarf is detachable, and the jumper is equally becoming with or without it.

THIS cosy and alluring little jumper is specially good to wear with a coat and skirt—the scarf that finishes off the neckline fills in the opening of the coat so nicely. Note the new peasant sleeves, which are gathered into tiny cuffs. The jumper is worked in a simple lace-stitch, and even if you are a beginner you will have no difficulty in following the pattern.

Materials : 8 ozs. "Golden Eagle" Merino Wool, 3-ply. Two pairs of "Stratnoid" knitting needles Nos. 8 and 12. Three buttons about the size of a shilling and two press fasteners.

Measurements : Length from shoulder to lower edge, 20 ins. Width all round under arms, 36 ins. Length of sleeve seam, including cuff, 18½ ins.

Shape Armholes : 1st row.—Cast off 3 sts., work as 1st ptn. row from * to last 3 sts., k. 3. 2nd row.—Cast off 3 sts., work as 2nd ptn. row from * to end. Now cont. in ptn., dec. 1 st. at each end of every 1st, 3rd and 4th pattern rows until 70 sts. remain. Cont. without dec., until there are 11 ptns. from beg. of armhole, ending with a 4th row of ptn.

Shape Shoulders : 1st row.—Cast off 3 sts., work as 1st ptn. row from * to last 5 sts., then wl. fwd., sl. 1, k. 1, p.s.s.o., k. 3. 2nd row.—Cast off 3 sts., work as 2nd ptn. row to last 2 sts., drop wl. fwd., off left-hand needle, sl. 1, drop wl. fwd., off left-hand needle, k. 1, p.s.s.o. 3rd and 4th rows.—Cast off 3 sts., k. to last 2 sts., k. 2 tog. Rep. last 4 rows until 22 sts. remain. Cast off.

The Front

Cast on 100 sts., using No. 12 needles, and work exactly as for back until the armholes are reached.

Shape Armholes.—Cast off 3 sts. at beg. of next 2 rows as for back armholes. 3rd row.—K. 2 tog., k. 42, sl. 1, k. 1, p.s.s.o., k. 1, turn. Slip the remaining 47 sts. for right shoulder on to a spare needle and leave for the present. Cont. on the 45 sts. for left shoulder as follows : Work in the ptn., dec. 1 st. at armhole edge on every 1st, 3rd and 4th ptn. rows until 11 more sts. have been taken off the armhole edge ; *and, at the same time,* dec. 1 st. at neck edge on every 3rd ptn. row until 24 sts. remain.

Cont. without dec., until there are 13½ ptns. from beg. of armhole, finishing after a 2nd ptn. row. Shape shoulder by casting off 3 sts. at beg. of every 3rd and 1st ptn. rows and dec. 1 st. at end of every 4th and 2nd row until all sts. are cast off.

Go back to the remaining 47 sts. for right side, re-join wool at centre edge, k. 1, k. 2 tog., k. to last 2 sts., sl. 1, k. 1, p.s.s.o. Now shape armhole and front as for left side until shoulder is reached, then shape the shoulder by dec. 1 st. at end of 3rd and 1st rows, and casting off 3 sts. at beg. of 4th and 2nd rows until all sts. are cast off.

The Sleeves (both worked alike)

Begin at lower edge. Cast on 130 sts. on No. 8 needles and k. 1 row **. Rep. the four ptn. rows 3 times, then work the first 2 ptn. rows once. ** Decrease 10 times on the next row as follows : *Next row.*—K. 5, * k. 2 tog., k. 11. Rep. from * to end, finishing k. 6 instead of

k. 11 (120 sts.) K. one row. Rep. from ** to ** once. *Next row.*—K. 5, * k. 2 tog., k. 10. Rep. from * to end, finishing k. 5. Now cont. in this way, dec. 10 times on every 16th row following (always a 3rd ptn. row) by working 1 st. less between the decreasings on every dec. row until 90 sts. remain.

Cont. without dec. until there are 23 ptns. from the beg., ending with a 4th row of ptn. *Next row.*—As 1st ptn. row. *Next row.*—K. 1, * drop wl. fwd., off left-hand needle, k. 1, rep. from * 5 times more, ** drop wl. fwd. off left-hand needle, sl. 1, drop wl. fwd., k. 1, p.s.s.o., drop wl. fwd., k. 1. Rep. from ** 25 times more, then rep. from * to * at beg. of row to the end. (64 sts.) Cont. in the ptn., inc. 1 st. at each end of every alternate 3rd ptn. row until there are 70 sts. Work a few more rows without inc., until there are 30 ptns. from beg., or length required, finishing after a 4th ptn. row. Shape top by dec. 1 st. at each end of every row until 8 sts. remain. Cast off.

The Cuffs.—Cast on 44 sts., using a pair of No. 8 needles and k. 6 rows. Cast off.

The Scarf Collar.—Cast on 140 sts., using a pair of No. 8 needles and k. 3 rows. Cont. in the 4 ptn. rows, and dec. 1 st. at each end of every 1st, 3rd and 4th rows until all sts. are decreased. Now pick up and draw through all the sts. down one of the sloping sides. K. 2 rows, inc. 1st at each end of both rows. Cast off. Work in the same manner down the other side. Join corner neatly.

To Complete Jumper

Press lightly on both sides with a warm iron over a damp cloth. Join shoulders. Using a No. 12 needle, pick up and draw through 3 out of every 4 sts. up the right side of neck and every st. along back of neck. Using the 8 needles, k. 6 rows, dec. 1 st. at bottom of V on last 4 rows. Cast off. Work down the left side in the same way. Join neatly on left shoulder and at V. Gather lower edges of sleeves to fit cuffs and oversew cuffs to sleeves. Sew sleeves into armholes. Join side and underarm seams, leaving about 2 ins. free above cuffs. Press seams. Fasten cuffs with press studs, catching the sleeve together over join of sleeve to neaten. Fold over the two ends of scarf and catch with a button. Sew another button on the point to weight it. Slip over head and arrange in folds. If preferred, instead of using buttons, tie a small knot at back of neck and fasten point of jumper with a pin. Sew a button to V of jumper, or if preferred, wear a clip when jumper is worn without a scarf.

A Little House

AND this I should call Heaven—
A little house apart,
Up the road, or down the road . . .
If it held your heart.

A fire-bright room for winter,
A wind lost in a tree,
Three words you have whispered
That made a world for me.

For it is most mysterious,
That Heaven comes from this ;
The thrill of arms close-clinging,
The wonder of your kiss.

HELEN WELSHIMER

Your jumper fits snugly at the waist.

A Wide Collar Is Most Becoming

Quite a New Zigzag Pattern Is Used For This Woolly

MATERIALS

SEVEN ounces of " Sirdar " 3-ply Super Shetland Wool ; a pair each of Stratnoid knitting pins No. 9 and No. 11; 17 small fancy buttons ; a Stratnoid crochet hook No. 13.

TENSION AND MEASUREMENTS

WORKED at a tension of 7 sts. to the inch in width on No. 9 pins, the following measurements are attained after light pressing : Round the bust, 38 inches ; front length from shoulder seam to lower edge, 19 inches ; back length, 18 inches ; side seam, 12 inches ; sleeve seam, 18½ inches.

ABBREVIATIONS

K., knit ; p., purl ; tog., together ; inc., increase (by working into the back and front of the same stitch) ; s.s., stocking-stitch (k. on the right side and p. back). Directions in brackets are worked the number of times stated immediately after the brackets.

CROCHET ABBREVIATIONS

CH., chain ; sl.st., slip-stitch ; d.c., double crochet.

TO WORK

BEGIN at the back and using No. 11 pins, cast on 106 sts. for the lower edge. Knit 8 rows.
    NEXT ROW : All purl.
(K. 5 rows and p. 1 row) 5 times.
    NEXT ROW (right side facing) : Inc., (k. 4, inc) 21 times, which gives 128 sts.
    NEXT ROW : All purl.

Change to No. 9 pins, and work in pattern as follows :
    1ST ROW (right side facing) : P. 30, k. 4, p. 60, k. 4, p. 30.
2ND ROW (and every even-numbered row) : All purl.
3RD ROW : P. 26, k. 12, p. 52, k. 12, p. 26.
5TH ROW : P. 22, k. 20, p. 44, k. 20, p. 22.
7TH ROW : P. 18, k. 12, p. 4, k. 12, p. 36, k. 12, p. 4, k. 12, p. 18.
9TH ROW : P. 14, k. 12, p. 12, k. 12, p. 28, k. 12, p. 12, k. 12, p. 14.
11TH ROW : P. 10, k. 12, (p. 20, k. 12) 3 times, p. 10.
13TH ROW : P. 6, k. 12, p. 28, k. 12, p. 12, k. 12, p. 28, k. 12, p. 6.

The collar, waist and sleeves are a different pattern—so pretty!

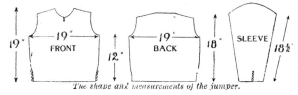

The shape and measurements of the jumper.

15TH ROW : P. 2, k. 12, p. 36, k. 12, p. 4, k. 12, p. 36, k. 12, p. 2.

17TH ROW : K. 10, p. 44, k. 20, p. 44, k. 10.

19TH ROW : K. 6, p. 52, k. 12, p. 52, k. 6.

21ST ROW : K. 2, p. 60, k. 4, p. 60, k. 2.

22ND ROW : All purl.

Continued overleaf

A Wide Collar Is Most Becoming

Continued

Repeat from the 1st to the 22nd row twice more, then from the 1st to the 6th row again, which completes **72 rows** in pattern.

73RD ROW : P. 18, k. 28, p. 36, k. 28, p. 18.

75TH ROW : P. 14, k. 36, p. 28, k. 36, p. 14.

77TH ROW : P. 10, k. 44, p. 20, k. 44, p. 10.

79TH ROW : P. 6, k. 52, p. 12, k. 52, p. 6.

81ST ROW : P. 2, k. 60, p. 4, k. 60, p. 2.

82ND ROW : All purl.

TO SHAPE THE ARMHOLES : Continue in s.s. only and cast off 2 sts. at the beginning of each of the next 12 rows, then work 2 sts. tog. at the beginning of each of the following 6 rows (98 sts.).

Work 40 rows straight in s.s. to shoulders.

TO SLOPE THE SHOULDERS : Cast off 7 sts. at the beginning of each of the next 8 rows. Cast off the remaining sts.

THE FRONT

THIS is worked exactly the same as the back until the armhole shaping is finished and 98 sts. remain.

Work 10 rows straight on these sts. in s.s.

THE LEFT-FRONT SHOULDER

THIS is worked on the first 49 sts., the remaining 49 being passed on to a spare needle or stitch-holder for the right shoulder.

Work 19 rows in s.s.

** TO SHAPE THE NECK : Cast off 3 sts. at the beginning of next row, and every following alternate row (neck end) 3 times, then cast off 2 sts. at the beginning of alternate rows (neck end) 3 times. Finally work 2 sts. tog. at the beginning of alternate rows (neck end) for 2 decreases, which leaves 32 sts.

Work 6 rows straight on these sts. to shoulder.

TO SLOPE THE SHOULDER : Cast off 7 sts. at the beginning of next row and every alternate row (armhole end) until 11 sts. remain, then turn and cast off.

THE RIGHT-FRONT SHOULDER

JOIN the wool to neck end of right-front sts. and work 20 rows in s.s. Then shape the neck as from ** on Left-Front directions.

THE SLEEVES

WITH No. 9 pins cast on 22 sts. and p. 1 row.
Continue in increase pattern as follows :

1ST AND 2ND ROWS : Inc., k. until 1 remains, inc.

3RD AND 4TH ROWS : Inc., p. until 1 remains, inc.

Repeat these 4 rows until there are 84 sts., which finishes the increases.

Work 9 rows straight (without increases), after which take 2 sts. tog. at each end of next row and every following 8th row until 48 sts. remain.

Work 7 rows straight in pattern.

Now divide the sts. for the wrist, putting 24 sts. on an odd length of wool for the second half, and leaving 24 on the working needle for the first half.

FIRST HALF OF WRIST : With No. 11 pins work as follows :
(K. 5 rows and p. 1 row) 5 times.
K. 7 rows plain and cast off.

Work the second half in the same manner.

Work a second sleeve exactly the same.

THE COLLAR

WITH No. 11 pins cast on 40 sts. and k. 8 rows.
NEXT ROW : All purl.
(K. 5 rows and p. 1 row) 16 times.
K. 7 rows plain and cast off.

Work a second collar piece in the same manner.

THE FRONT NECK-EDGE

WITH the crochet hook work 1 row of d.c. all round the small front opening, finishing at the right-front neck-edge, make 6 ch. (for button loop), turn and sl.st. to the 3rd d.c. from hook, sl.st. to next d.c., turn and work 1 d.c. in the ch. loop, and fasten off.

THE WRIST OPENING

AT the underarm edge of each wrist opening, work a row of d.c., missing every 4th k. st., and fasten off.

On the upper edge of each wrist opening work 1 row of d.c. as described on the opposite edge, 1 ch., turn.

NEXT ROW : Work 4 d.c. on 4 d.c. of previous row, * 5 ch., miss 2 d.c., 4 d.c. on next 4 sts. ; repeat from * to end, ending with 1 d.c. at the wrist edge.

Work 1 row of d.c., putting 4 d.c. in each loop and 1 d.c. on each d.c.

TO MAKE UP THE JUMPER

FIRST press all pieces with a hot iron and a damp cloth over the wrong side of the work. Join the shoulder seams, taking 1 st. from each side at a time, and sew the collar to the neck. Set the sleeves into armholes and press these seams. Join the sleeve and side seams in one continuous line, leaving the striped waistband open at each side.

THE WAISTBAND OPENING

THIS is worked exactly as for the wrist openings.
Sew four buttons to each wrist, and side fastenings of jumper, and one at the front of neck.

□ □ □

Special Spring-time Woollies

—

COMING SOON

SCOTT

ACCESSORY *for Your* SPRING SUIT

THIS pretty jumper is knitted in fine wool, the main part is in garter-stitch, with the openwork pattern for the front panel, collar and bow.

MATERIALS : *6 ounces of W.B. Rosedale 2-ply Fingering ; a pair each of " Aero " knitting pins No. 9 and No. 11 ; one spare pin.*

TENSION AND MEASUREMENTS : *Worked at a tension of 7½ sts. to the inch in width on No. 9 pins the following measurements are attained after light pressing : Across the back at the underarms, 17 inches ; across the front, 18 inches ; side seam, 12 inches ; sleeve seam, 19 inches ; back length from shoulder seam to lower edge 17 inches ; front length, 18½ inches.*

ABBREVIATIONS : *K., knit ; p., purl ; tog., together ; sl., slip ; inc., increase (by working into the back and front of the same stitch) ; m., make (by bringing the wool to the front of the pin) ; p.s.s.o., pass slipped stitch over ; st., stitch ; single rib is k. 1, and p. 1 alternately. Directions in brackets are worked the number of times stated after the brackets. Mock cable is worked on 6 sts. as follows : * Insert the right-hand pin into the 5th st. from point of the left-hand pin, and slip this st. over the 4 end sts. and off the point of the pin, then repeat from * once. This has taken the original 5th and 6th st. over the 4 end sts. which are worked as follows : K. 1, inc. in each of next 2 sts., k. 1.*

The Back

BEGIN at the back and using No. 11 pins cast on 116 sts. for the lower edge.

Work 30 rows in single rib.

Increase Row : K. 8, inc., (k. 13, inc.) 7 times, k. 9, which gives 124 sts. on the row.

Change to No. 9 pins and k. 97 rows in garter-st.

To Shape the Armholes : Continue in garter-st., casting off 2 sts. at the beginning of each of the next 8 rows, then work 2 sts. tog. at the beginning of each of the following 14 rows which leaves 94 sts.

K. 46 rows straight on these sts. to shoulder.

To Slope the Shoulders : Cast off 6 sts. at the beginning of each of the next 8 rows. Cast off the remaining sts.

The Front

WITH No. 11 pins cast on 116 sts. and work 30 rows in single rib.

Increase row (right side facing) : K. 1, (inc. k. 5) 19 times, inc. which will give 136 sts. on the row.

Next row (wrong side facing) : Change to No. 9 pins and k. 55, p. 6, (k. 4, p. 6) twice, k. 55.

Now continue in pattern as follows :

1st row (right side facing) : K. 51, m. 1, sl. 1, k. 1, p.s.s.o., k. 2 tog., m. 1, (k. 6, m. 1, sl. 1, k. 1, p.s.s.o., k. 2 tog., m. 1) 3 times, k. 51.

2nd row : K. 55, p. 6, (k. 4, p. 6) twice, k. 55.

Repeat the 1st and 2nd row once more.

5th row : K. 51, m. 1, sl. 1, k. 1, p.s.s.o., k. 2 tog., m. 1, (mock cable on

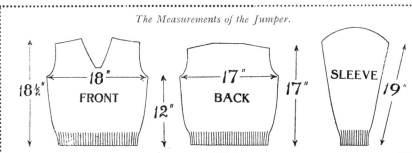

The Measurements of the Jumper.

FRONT 18″ 18½″ 12″

BACK 17″ 17″

SLEEVE 19″ 17″

the next 6 sts., m. 1, sl. 1, k. 1, p.s.s.o., k. 2 tog., m. 1) 3 times, k. 51.

6th row : As 2nd row.

Repeat these 6 rows twice more, which will complete 18 rows with 3 cable stripes in the centre.

Continue with 5 stripes as follows :

19th row : K. 41, m. 1, sl. 1, k. 1, p.s.s.o., k. 2 tog., m. 1, (k. 6, m.1 sl. 1, k. 1, p.s.s.o., k. 2 tog., m. 1) 5 times, k. 41.

ACCESSORY
for Your
SPRING SUIT

The cuffs and waist of the jumper are worked in single ribs, the main part is garter-stitch. It would look very attractive knitted in a soft shade of grey.

Cast off 2 sts. from the beginning of alternate rows (armhole end) for 5 times more, and then continue straight at this end; there will now be k. 11 (garter-st.) at the armhole end. At the same time shape the neck edge by working 2 sts. tog. at the end of every 4th row until 33 sts. remain.

Work 13 rows straight on these sts.

To Slope the Shoulder : Cast off 7 sts. at the beginning of next 3 alternate rows (armhole end) then cast off 6 sts. at the same end of following 2 alternate rows. Fasten off.

The Sleeves

WITH No. 9 pins cast on 18 sts. and k. 1 row.

Continue in garter-st. inc. at each end of every row until there are 90 sts. which finishes the increases.

K. 5 rows straight on these sts.

Continue in garter-st. taking 2 sts. tog. at each end of next row and every following 10th row until 56 sts. remain. K. 2 rows on these sts.

Next row (wrong side facing) . Change to No. 11 pins and work as follows : K. 2 tog., * p. 1, k. 1 ; repeat from * until 2 remain, p. 2 tog.

Work 33 rows more in single rib and cast off.

Work a second sleeve in the same manner.

The Collar

WITH No. 9 pins cast on 32 sts. and k. 10 rows.

Now continue in pattern as follows :

1st row (right side facing) : K. 4, m. 1, sl. 1, k. 1, p.s.s.o., k. 2 tog., m. 1, (k. 6, m. 1, sl. 1, k. 1, p.s.s.o., k. 2 tog., m. 1) twice, k. 4.

2nd row : K. 8, p. 6, k. 4, p. 6, k. 8.

Repeat these 2 rows once more.

5th row : K. 4, m. 1, sl. 1, k. 1, p.s.s.o., k. 2 tog., m. 1, (mock cable, m. 1, sl. 1, k. 1, p.s.s.o., k. 2 tog., m. 1) twice, k. 4.

6th row : As 2nd row.

Repeat these 6 rows 75 times more. Work 2 rows more of next pattern. K. 9 rows plain and cast off.

To Make up the Jumper : First press all pieces with a hot iron, and a damp cloth, over the wrong side of the work. Sew the shoulder seams and set the sleeves into the armholes, then press these seams while the work is open. Join the sleeve and side seams in one continuous line, and press. Sew the collar to the right side of the neck, leaving about 2 inches of the neck edge free at the centre front, and tie in a bow at the front.

20th row : K. 45, p. 6, (k. 4, p. 6) 4 times, k. 45.

Repeat the 19th and 20th row once.

23rd row : K. 41, m. 1, sl. 1, k. 1, p.s.s.o., k. 2 tog., m. 1, (mock cable, m. 1, sl. 1, k. 1, p.s.s.o., k. 2 tog., m. 1) 5 times, k. 41.

24th row : As 20th row.

Repeat from the 19th to the 24th row 8 times more.

Continue with 7 centre stripes thus :

73rd row : K. 31, m. 1, sl. 1, k. 1, p.s.s.o., k. 2 tog., m. 1, (k. 6, m. 1, sl. 1, k. 1, p.s.s.o., k. 2 tog., m. 1) 7 times, k. 31.

74th row : K. 35, p. 6, (k. 4, p. 6) 6 times, k. 35.

Repeat the 73rd and 74th row once more.

77th row : K. 31, m. 1, sl. 1, k. 1, p.s.s.o., k. 2 tog., m. 1, (mock cable, m. 1, sl. 1, k. 1, p.s.s.o., k. 2 tog., m. 1) 7 times, k. 31.

78th row : As 74th row.

Repeat from the 73rd to 78th row 3 times more which completes 96 rows in pattern to armholes. (136 sts.)

To Shape the Armholes : Continue in pattern as now set, but shape at the armhole end by casting off 2 sts. from the beginning of each of the next 8 rows, which leaves 120 sts.

On the next row the sts. are divided for the neck opening as follows : Cast off 2 (1 st. on right-hand needle), work in pattern on 56 sts. and leave these 57 sts. on a spare needle. For the left front shoulder, cast off 2 sts in centre. Work pattern on 59 sts. for right front shoulder.

The Right Front Shoulder : Continue in same pattern and shape at both ends as follows : Cast off 2 sts. at the beginning of every alternate row (armhole end) for 6 times more (10 decreases at the arm end altogether), and then continue straight at this end, which will give a border of 11 sts. in garter-st. at the armhole end of every row. At the same time shape the neck by working 2 sts. tog. at the beginning of every 4th row until 33 sts. remain.

(NOTE.—After casting off the sts. remember to keep the pattern correct, but as the design is in straight stripes it is easily seen.)

Work 14 rows straight in pattern to shoulder.

To Slope the Shoulder : Cast off 7 sts. at the beginning of next 3 alternate rows (armhole end), then cast off 6 sts. at the armhole end of following 2 alternate rows. Fasten off.

The Left Front Shoulder : Join the wool to the neck end of spare needle sts. and shape at both ends as follows :

Crochet flowers in a contrasting shade make the charming trimming.

TWO SHADES *of* GREY!

THIS becoming little hat would be charming in grey with the ribbon band and the crochet flowers in a paler tone.

MATERIALS : *Four ounces of Patons & Baldwins' "Totem" knitting wool in dark grey, and 1 ounce of the same wool in light grey, a No. 11 Stratnoid crochet hook, some millinery wire, and 1 yard of silk corded ribbon.*

To Make the Hat

BEGIN at the centre of the crown and make 3 ch.
   1st round : 2 d.c. into the second ch. from the hook, 4 d.c. in the next ch., then 2 d.c. into the other side of the ch., which has the first 2 d.c. worked into it. This will form a round of 8 d.c. Do not join up any of the rounds, but put a coloured thread in the first st., as a guide to the beginning of rounds. Work flat d.c. throughout, that is taking up both loops at the top of the st.
   2nd round : 2 d.c. into each d.c. of previous round.
   3rd round : * 2 d.c. into the first d.c., 1 d.c. in each of the next 2 sts. ; repeat from * to the end of the round.
   4th round : * 2 d.c. into the first st., 1 d.c. into each of the next 3 sts. ; repeat from * to the end of the round.

ABBREVIATIONS : *Ch., chain ; d.c., double crochet ; tr., treble ; d.tr., double treble (wool twice round the hook and work off the loops in twos as for ordinary tr.) ; sl., slip ; st., stitch ; inc., increase.*

TENSION AND MEASUREMENTS : *Worked at a tension of 6 d.c. to the inch in width the hat has a head measurement of 21 inches without stretching. This can be regulated by the ribbon head lining, and the hat can also be made any size by varying the circular crown.*

Now continue to inc. in this way with 1 extra d.c. between each inc. until 15 rounds are worked, or if you are a loose worker continue until the diameter of the piece is 5 inches. The work should be quite flat if worked closely, but if it should flute through loose working, do a round of 1 d.c. in each st.
   Now count the d.c. in the round, and exactly halfway, put a pin, work 1 d.c. in each st. up to that pin, make 10 ch., then 1 d.c. in each remaining st. to the end of the round, there make 10 ch., which should be opposite the 10 ch. loop on the other half of the circle.
   Next round : 1 d.c. in each st. and in each of the 10 ch. on the loops.
   Work 25 rounds of 1 d.c. in *every* d.c. of the previous round.
   This makes the full depth of the crown, so if a deeper hat be wanted, more rounds should be worked here, before shaping the brim.

The Brim

NOW holding the hat in the same position as when working the last round, count up to the 32nd d.c. and put a small safety-pin in that st., make 1 ch. to use as a turning ch. only, turn and work in the opposite direction, putting 1 d.c. in each st. round the hat up to the st. marked with a pin, make one turning ch., turn.
   Work 2 rows more with 1 d.c. in each st. of previous row and 1 turning ch.
   4th row : 2 d.c. in the first st., then 1 d.c. in each st. to the end, where put an additional d.c. in the last ch., 1 ch., turn.
   Work 11 rows more like the 4th row.
   Now take the millinery wire and place it along the top of the last row of sts. Work 2 d.c. in each st and over the wire at the same time ; this will spread the edge of the brim. At the end turn down the wire and work about 3 d.c. on the edge, then cut away the surplus wire. At the beginning of this row turn in the end of the wire and work over it with the dark grey wool along the edge to cover the wire.

The Flowers

MAKE 7 ch. and sl.st. to the first ch. to form a ring. Put 1 d.c. into the loop, then 3 tr., 2 d.tr. (wool over the hook twice and work off the loops in twos as for ordinary tr.), 1 triple tr. at the point (wool round the hook 3 times), 2 d.tr., 3 ordinary tr., 1 d.c. and cut the wool, leaving a length over, by which to sew the flower to the ribbon. Mount the flower with the wrong side of the crochet uppermost.
   Work 9 more of these flowers, or as required, and sew them to the ribbon.
   To Make Up the Hat : First press inside the crown, putting a damp cloth over the wool, and press the brim, spreading it a little close to the wire. Turn up the brim at the back and catch each point to the crown. Form a pleat with the 10 d.c. into the loop at each side of the hat, sew it down along the top edge, then in an oblique line tapering to a point towards the front of the hat. Pass the hat-band under the two points at the back and form a flat bow.

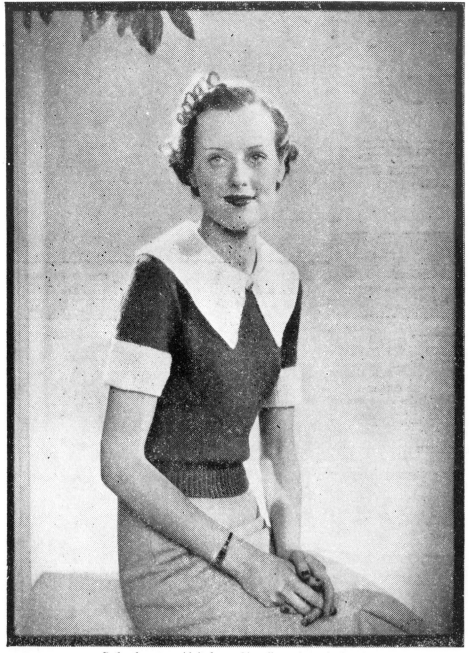

Rather demure—with its large white collar and turn-back cuffs.

You Can Make

It Is Perfectly
Simple In
Stocking-stitch
And Single
Ribbing.

TENSION AND MEASUREMENTS

*W*ORKED at a tension of 6 sts. to the inch in width on No. 9 knitting pins, the following measurements are attained after light pressing : Round the bust, 40 inches ; front length from shoulder seam to lower edge, 19 inches ; back length, 18 inches ; side seam, 14 inches ; sleeve seam of short sleeve, 5 inches.

MATERIALS

*S*IX ounces of Sirdar 3-ply Super Shetland Wool in navy blue, and one ounce each of the same wool in light blue, and in white for the frilly jabot and cuffs. For the plain collar and cuffs you will need 2 ounces of the same wool in white. A pair each of No. 9 and No. 13 Acro knitting pins.

ABBREVIATIONS

K., KNIT ; p., purl ; tog., together ; inc., increase (by working into the back and front of the same stitch) ; st., stitch ; Directions in brackets are worked the number of times stated immediately after the brackets. S.s., stocking-stitch (k. on the right side and purl back). Single rib is k. 1 and p. 1 alternately.

THE BACK

*W*ITH No. 13 pins, cast on 100 sts. and work 36 rows in single rib, after which the work proceeds in s.s. until otherwise stated.

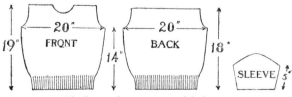

The shape and measurements of the jumper.

INCREASE ROW : * K. 4, inc. ; repeat from * to end. (120 sts.)

Purl one row.

Change to No. 9 pins and work 80 rows in s.s., ending with a purl row.

TO SHAPE THE ARMHOLES.—Cast off 3 sts. at the beginning of each of the next 6 rows, then k. 2 tog. at the beginning of each of the next 12 rows, when 90 sts. will remain.

It Either Way

A Beginner Can Make It—The Jabot Is Worked Only In Garter-stitch

A frilly affair—with a gay striped jabot in three pretty colours.

Work 36 rows straight on these sts. to shoulder.

Cast off straight across.

THE FRONT

THIS is worked exactly the same as the back until the armhole shaping is finished and 90 sts. remain.

Work 22 rows straight on these sts., when the neckline will be reached.

On the next row divide the sts. for the neck and shoulders, thus:

Work 40 sts. and leave these on a spare needle for the Left-Front shoulder; cast off 10 sts. and k. to end.

Take 2 sts. tog. at the neck end of every row until 28 sts. remain. Work 11 rows straight on these sts. to shoulder. Cast off straight across.

On the spare pin sts. work the Right-Front Shoulder to match the first shoulder.

THE SLEEVES

BEGIN at the top and, using navy blue wool and No. 9 pins, cast on 10 sts. Work in s.s., inc. one st. at both ends of every row until there are 78 sts. Work 2 rows straight on these sts., then slope the sleeve seam by taking 2 sts. tog. at each end of next row and every following 8th row until 68 sts. remain. Cast off.

LONG SLEEVES.—For a long sleeve take 2 sts. tog. at each end of every 8th row until 50 sts. remain. Work 10 rows straight. Change to No. 13 pins and work 36 rows in s.s. and cast off.)

Work a second sleeve in the same manner.

THE STRIPED JABOT

WITH No. 13 pins and navy blue wool, cast on 130 sts. Work 10 rows in single rib.

INCREASE ROW: All knit, working into the back and front of every stitch. (260 sts.)

Change to No. 9 pins and begin the stripes as follows:

With light blue wool knit 4 rows. Leave the wool hanging.

** With white wool knit 2 rows.

With navy blue wool knit 4 rows.

With light blue wool knit 2 rows.

With navy blue wool knit 2 rows.

Repeat these 10 rows from ** twice more.

Now work 4 rows in light blue, 2 rows white, and 6 navy blue. Cast off.

THE STRIPED CUFFS

WITH No. 13 pins cast on 70 sts. and work 6 rows in single rib. Change to No. 9 pins and work the 10 stripe pattern rows from ** on the jabot twice.

YOU CAN MAKE IT EITHER WAY
Continued

Now work 4 rows light blue, 2 rows white, and 6 rows navy blue. Cast off. Work a second cuff in the same manner.

THE WHITE COLLAR

WITH No. 13 pins cast on 130 sts. and work as follows : K. 5, then work single rib until 5 remain, k. 5.
Repeat this row 5 times more.
Change to No. 9 pins and work as follows :
1st Row : * K. 4, inc.: repeat from * until 5 remain, k. 5. (155 sts.)
2nd Row : K. 5, p. until 5 remain, k. 5.
3rd Row : All knit.
Repeat the 2nd and 3rd row 14 times more, then work 9 rows in plain knitting. Cast off loosely.

THE CUFFS

WITH No. 13 pins cast on 68 sts. and work 5 rows of single rib. Change to No. 9 pins and work 24 rows in s.s., then work 10 rows plain and cast off.
Work a second cuff in the same manner.

TO MAKE UP THE JUMPER

FIRST press all pieces, except the rib, with a hot iron over a damp cloth.
Join the shoulder seams, taking 1 st. from each side at a time and press. Set in sleeves, and press while the work is open. Join the sleeve and side seams in one long line and press. Work 3 rows of double crochet all round the neck edge, on the first row, missing every 5th st. and on succeeding rows put 1 d.c. in each st. Stitch the collar and cuffs in position, on the right side of jumper and turn over.
If you are having the jabot instead of collar, fold the strip in half and join the cast-on edge of the ribbing. Across the top of the jabot, that is at the end of the knitting rows, work a row of d.c., putting 1 d.c. in the end of each row, missing every 4th row, to keep the edge flat. Sew the jabot to the jumper up the centre line of single rib, and catch the two top points in position, seen in the illustration.

◻   ◻   ◻

A TWEED SKIRT

Can you tell me how to dry clean a light brown tweed skirt at home? It is rather grubby.—TERESE.

YOU could clean your tweed skirt by brushing it well with fig dust, cedar dust and naphthalene, and using a very stiff brush.
Fig dust can be obtained from a corn-chandlers, and tins of cedar dust and napthalene already mixed are sold by any chemist.

Sleek and smooth and utterly ship-shape —this cap and jumper !

THIS little cap is so quickly made, you can have one to match every jumper or cardigan !
MATERIALS : 2 ounces of W. B. Rosedale Fingering 3-ply and a set of No. 11 "Aero" knitting pins; also a length of silk corded ribbon according to head measurement, and about 1 inch wide.
This cap measures 20 inches round the head, but it can be made any size according to the number of stitches cast on at the beginning, and this again can be varied by the ribbon head-band and the expansion of the rib.

To Work the Cap

CAST 48 sts. on each of 3 pins and, working with the 4th pin, k. 4 and p 4 alternately all round.
Repeat this round until 38 have been worked altogether.

Next 2 rounds : K. 1 and p. 1 alternately all round.
Next 2 rounds : P. 1 and k. 1 alternately all round.
Repeat the last 4 rounds 11 times more.
Next round : Work in pattern over 72 sts., then turn and work back over these 72 sts., leaving the remaining 72 sts. on the two needles.
Next row : Decrease 1 st. at the beginning and end of the row.
Work 1 row without shaping and

BE CLEVER—AND WEAR
THIS SET
Quite the Best Type of Knitted Woollies

take care to keep the pattern correct after decreasing.

Repeat the last 2 rows until the sts. are reduced to 12, after which decrease at both ends of every 6th row, until 2 sts. remain, slip 1 st. over the other, draw the wool through the remaining st. and fasten off.

Work on the remaining 72 sts. in the same manner.

To make up the cap sew the ribbon into a round, then with the same wool run the face edge of the cap to one edge of the ribbon, overlapping the latter about ¼ of an inch. Now turn this edge under to the wrong side of the cap so that about 1 inch of the knitting is turned with the ribbon. Press in position putting a slightly damp cloth over the knitting. Tie the two points of the cap in a knot to form two " ears," securing at the centre with a few stitches.

The Jumper

HERE is the " country jumper " you are looking for, and it is the perfect companion to the cap shown on the facing page.

MATERIALS : *9 ounces of W.B. Rosedale Fingering wool in 3-ply, or eight ounces of the same wool if you are not working the belt. A pair each of No. 11 and No. 9 " Aero " knitting pins and a buckle for the belt.*

TENSION AND MEASUREMENTS: *Worked at a tension of 7½ sts. to the inch in width on No. 9 pins the following measurements are attained after pressing : Round the bust, 37 inches ; front length from shoulder seam to lower edge, 23 inches ; back length, 21 inches ; side seam, 15 inches ; sleeve seam, 19 inches.*

ABBREVIATIONS : *K., knit ; p., purl ; tog., together ; inc., increase (by working into the back and front of the same stitch) ; st., stitch ; m.s., moss-stitch (k. 1 and p. 1 alternately, and on subsequent rows the sts. are reversed) ; s.s., stocking-stitch (k. on the right side and p. back). To " pick up 1 " work knitwise under the horizontal thread lying between 2 sts. of the row below. Single rib is k. 1 and p. 1 alternately. Directions in brackets are worked the number of times stated after the brackets.*

To Work

BEGIN at the back and, using No. 11 pins, cast on 128 sts.

1st row : (right side facing) * P. 3, k. 1 ; repeat from * to end.

2nd row : * K. 3, p. 1 ; repeat from * to end.

Repeat these 2 rows until 66 rows have been worked.

Increase row (right side facing) : K. 9, inc. in the next st., (k. 17, inc.) 6 times, k. 10. (135 sts.)

Change to No. 9 pins and work 71

rows in s.s., beginning and ending with a p. row.

On the next row begin the V-yoke in m.s. as follows :

1st row (right side facing) : K. 67, p. 1, k. 67.

2nd row : P. 66, k. 1, p. 1, k. 1, p. 66.

3rd row : K. 65, p. 1, (k. 1, p. 1) twice, k. 65.

4th row : P. 64, m.s. 7, p. 64.

5th row : K. 63, m.s. 9, k. 63.

6th row : P. 62, m.s. 11, p. 62.

To Shape the Armholes : Continue in pattern, working 2 sts. more in m.s. on every row, and cast off 2 sts. at the beginning of each of the next 16 rows, then work 2 sts. tog. at the beginning of each of the following 4 rows, which leaves 99 sts.

Continue in the same pattern until the whole row is worked in m.s. Then work 19 rows more in m.s. up to the shoulder line.

The jumper has a ribbed belt to match the collar and cuffs. Notice, too, the pretty line of the moss-stitch pattern at the tops of the sleeves.

To Slope the Shoulders : Cast off 7 sts. at the beginning of each of the next 8 rows, then cast off 5 sts. at the beginning of 2 following rows, which leaves 33 sts.

Next row (right side facing) : With No. 11 pins work 18 rows in single rib, decreasing 1 st. at the end of the last row to reduce the sts. to 32. Work 20 rows in waist rib pattern, and cast off loosely.

The Front

THIS is worked exactly the same as the back until the armhole decreases are finished and 99 sts. remain.

Continue as on the back for 32 rows more.

THE LEFT FRONT SHOULDER : M.s. 45, turn, m.s. 45, m.s. 43, turn, m.s. 43, m.s. 41, turn, m.s. 41., m. s. 39, turn,

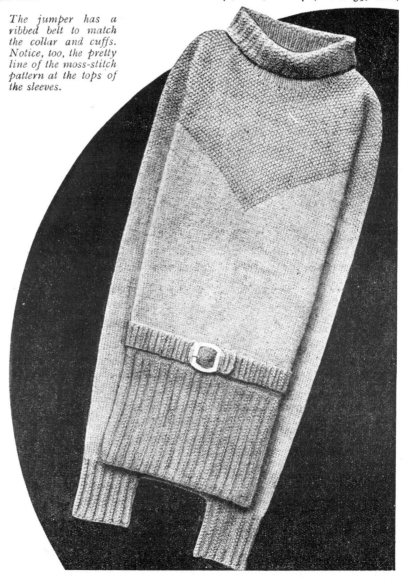

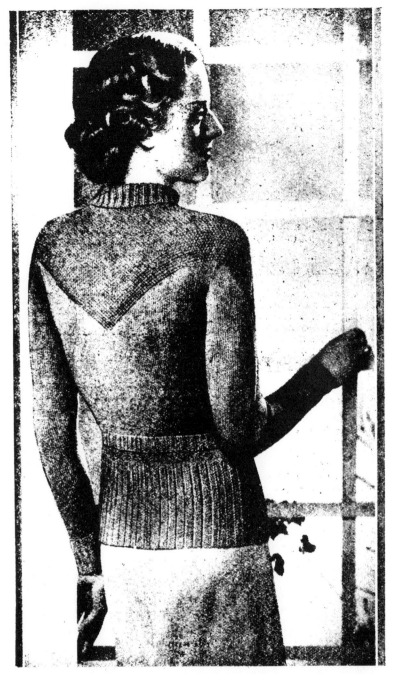

The yoke forms a point at the back as well as the front.

With Moss-Stitch YOKE and POLO COLLAR—

Two of the most interesting Features of this Attractive Jumper

The Sleeves

WITH No. 9 pins cast on 21 sts. for the top of the sleeve.

Next row (wrong side facing) : K. 1, * p. 1, k. 1 ; repeat from * to end.

Continue in increase pattern as follows :

1st row (right side facing) : Inc., p. 1, * k. 1, p. 1 ; repeat from * until 1 remains, inc.

2nd row : Inc., k. 1, * p. 1, k. 1 ; repeat from * until 1 remains, inc.

3rd row : As 1st row.
4th row : As 2nd row.
5th row : Inc., k. 1, m.s. 25, k. 1, inc.
6th row : Inc., p. 2, m.s. 25, p. 2, inc.
7th row : Inc., k. 4, m.s. 23, k. 4, inc.
8th row : Inc., p. 5, m.s. 23, p. 5, inc.
9th row : Inc., k. 6, m.s. 23, k. 6, inc.
10th row : Inc., p. 8, m.s. 21, p. 8, inc.
11th row : Inc., k. 9, m. s. 21, k. 9, inc.
12th row : Inc., p. 10, m.s. 21, p. 10, inc.

Repeat from the 7th to 12th row, which gives an increase at each end of every row to be worked in s.s., while the m.s. in the centre is reduced by 2 sts. on every 3 rows.

Continue in this manner until there are 87 sts. on the pin.

Next 3 rows : S.s. 41, m.s. 5, s.s. 41.
Next 3 rows : S.s. 42, m.s. 3, s.s. 42.
Next row : P. 43, k. 1, p. 43.

Continue in s.s taking 2 sts. tog. at each end of next row, and every following 8th row, until 53 sts. remain. Work 5 rows more in s.s., taking 2 sts. tog. at the end of last row (52 sts.).

Change to No. 11 pins and work in waist rib for 32 rows. Cast off loosely.

Work a second sleeve in the same manner.

THE BELT : With No. 11 pins cast on 232 sts. and work in waist rib for 12 rows. Cast off.

Sew the buckle to the belt, passing the prong through a space between two of the stitches.

m.s. 39, m.s. 37, turn, m.s. 37, m.s. 35, turn, m.s. 35.

On the remaining 33 sts. work 10 rows in m.s.

TO SLOPE THE SHOULDER : Continue in m.s., casting off 7 sts. at the beginning of next row, and the 2 following alternate rows (armhole end), then cast off 6 sts. at the beginning of the next 2 alternate rows (armhole end).

THE RIGHT FRONT SHOULDER : Slip a No. 9 pin through 21 sts. at neck end, then join on wool and work the remaining 45 sts. in m.s. for the right front shoulder. Continue as for left front shoulder to end.

There are now 33 sts. left on the pins for the front neck.

THE FRONT COLLAR : With No. 11 pins pick up and k. 17 sts. along the end of the rows on left front, then with the same pin work the spare pin sts. as

follows (k. 2, pick up and k. 1) 6 times, k. 4, inc. in next st., k. 4, (pick up and k. 1, k. 2) 6 times, pick up and k. 17 from the right front neck, which will give 80 sts. With No. 11 pins work 18 rows in single rib, then work 20 rows in waist rib and cast off loosely.

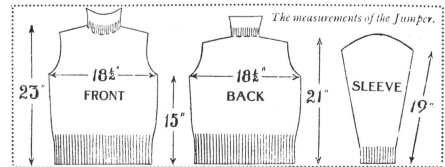

The measurements of the Jumper.

23" — FRONT — 18½" — 15"

BACK — 18½" — 21"

SLEEVE — 19"

To MAKE UP THE JUMPER : First press all pieces with a hot iron over a damp cloth. Beginning at the armhole end. Sew the shoulder and collar seams

One of the newest Spring designs—it is ideal for country wear.

in one line taking 1 st. from each side at a time. Sew the sleeves into the armholes and press. Join the sleeve and side seams and press.

—IN SIMPLE KNITTING FOR THE EARLY SUMMER

Elbow-length sleeves are very youthful and becoming.

A Special Design

Worked Chiefly In Moss-Stitch

THE BACK

CAST on 107 sts. and work in m.s. throughout, except the cuffs.

Work 9 rows straight.

Inc. 1 st. at both ends of the next row.

Repeat these 10 rows 7 times more, when there will be 123 sts. Work 2 rows more to armholes.

To SHAPE THE ARMHOLES.—Cast off 3 sts. at the beginning of each of the next 6 rows, then k. 2 tog. at the beginning of each of the following 14 rows when 91 sts. will remain.

Work 58 rows straight on these sts. to the shoulder-line and cast off straight across.

MATERIALS

EIGHT ounces of Patons and Baldwins "Pagoda" crêpe; a pair each of No. 10 and No. 11 knitting pins, and a Milward's Phantom crochet hook No. 11.

TENSION AND MEASUREMENTS

WORKED at a tension of 7 sts. to the inch in width on No. 10 pins, the following measurements are attained after light pressing : Across the back at the underarms, 18 inches ; across each front at the same place, 10 inches (making a total bust measurement of 38 inches when fastened) ; front length from shoulder seam to lower edge of basque, 20 inches ; back length, 19 inches ; side seam, 12 inches ; sleeve seam, with cuff, 13 inches.

ABBREVIATIONS

K., KNIT ; p., purl ; st., stitch ; tog., together ; inc., increase (by working into the back and front of the same stitch) ; m.s., moss-stitch (k. 1 and p. 1 alternately and on subsequent rows k. over p. and p. over k) ; ch., chain ; d.c., double crochet.

THE FRONT

CAST on 65 sts. and work 9 rows in m.s.

NEXT ROW : Inc. in the first st., then work m.s. to end. Repeat these last 10 rows 7 times more, when there will be 73 sts.

Work 3 rows straight on these sts. to armhole.

To SHAPE THE ARMHOLES : Continue in pattern, casting off 3 sts. at the beginning of next row, and following 2 alternate rows, when 64 sts. will remain. Work 1 row, then take 2 sts. tog. at the armhole end of next row and the next 6 alternate rows, when 58 sts. will remain.

Work 36 rows straight on these sts. to neck.

To SHAPE THE NECK : Cast off 10 sts. at the beginning of the next row (neck end), then work 2 sts. tog. at the same end of every row until 29 sts. remain.

Work 16 rows straight on these sts. to the shoulder-line, then cast off straight across.

Work the second front in the same way.

TO WEAR
in the
EVENINGS!

**It Has All The New Points, A Becoming
Basque, And Full Soft Sleeves**

*Knitted in a fine silky wool, with crystal
buttons, the jumper is perfect for parties.*

THE BACK BASQUE

CAST on 99 sts. for the upper edge and work
10 rows in m.s.
1st INCREASE ROW : m.s. 4,* inc. in the
next st., m.s. 8, repeat from * until 5 remain,
inc., m.s. 4 (110 sts.).
Work 9 rows straight in m.s.
2ND INCREASE ROW : M.s. 5, * inc., m.s. 9,
repeat from * until 5 remain, inc., m.s. 4 (121
sts.).
Work 9 rows in m.s.
3RD INCREASE ROW : M.s. 5, * inc., m.s. 10,
repeat from * until 6 remain, inc., m.s. 5 (132
sts.).
Work 9 rows in m.s.
4TH INCREASE ROW : M.s. 6, * inc., m.s. 11,
repeat from * until 6 remain, inc., m.s. 5
(143 sts). Continue straight on these sts. for
14 rows more. Cast off.

THE FRONT BASQUE

CAST on 61 sts. and work 10 rows in m.s.
1ST INCREASE ROW : M.s. 5, * inc.,
m.s. 9, repeat from * until 6 remain,
inc., m.s. 5 (67 sts.).
Work 9 rows in m.s.
2ND INCREASE ROW : M.s. 6, * inc., m.s. 10,
repeat from * until 6 remain, inc., m.s. 5
(73 sts.).
Work 9 rows in m.s.
3RD INCREASE ROW : M.s. 6, * inc., m.s. 11,
repeat from * until 7 remain, inc., m.s. 6 (79 sts.).
Work 9 rows in m.s.
4TH INCREASE ROW : M.s. 7, * inc., m.s. 12,
repeat from * until 7 remain, inc., m.s. 6
(85 sts.).
Work 14 rows straight on these sts. Cast off.
Work a second piece in the same manner.

THE SLEEVES

BEGIN at the top and cast on 26 sts.
Work 1 row into the back of these sts.
NEXT ROW : K. 1, inc. in each of the
remaining 25 sts. (51 sts.)

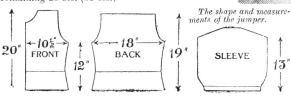

*The shape and measure-
ments of the jumper.*

20"   ←10½"→ FRONT   ←18"→ BACK   19"   SLEEVE   13"

12"

Continue in increase pattern as follows :
1st Row : Inc., p. 1, * k. 1, p. 1, repeat from * until 1 st.
remains, inc.
2ND ROW : Inc., k. 1, * p. 1, k. 1, repeat from * until 1 st.
remains, inc.

Continued on page 179

Note the pretty V at the back of the neck.

VARIATION on the CROSS-OVER LINE !

It is Knitted in a Ribbed Pattern

beginning of each of the next 14 rows, then work 2 sts. tog. at the beginning of each of the following 4 rows, when 89 sts. will remain.

Work 15 rows straight in pattern.

On the next row the sts. are divided for the back yoke opening.

Next row (with wrong side facing) : Work 44 sts. in pattern for the left back shoulder, and leave these on a spare needle for the present, cast off 1 st., pattern 44 sts. for the right back shoulder (including the 1 st. on the needle after casting off).

THE RIGHT BACK SHOULDER : Continue in pattern, taking 2 sts. tog. at the neck end of every row until 26 sts. remain. Continue with the neck end decreases, and at the same time slope the shoulder by casting off 7 sts. at the beginning of next row and every following alternate row (armhole end) until all are worked off.

THE LEFT BACK SHOULDER : Join the wool to the neck end of the spare pin sts. and work in pattern, taking 2 sts. tog. at the neck end of every row until 25 sts. remain. Continue with the neck decreases and, at the same time, cast off 7 sts. at the beginning of next row, and every following alternate row (armhole end) until all are worked off.

The Front

WITH No. 11 pins cast on 121 sts. and work 55 rows in pattern as on back waist.

On the next row the sts. are divided for the two fronts and vest. Pattern 37 sts. and darn these on an odd length of wool for the right front, pattern the next 47 sts. and darn these on an odd length of wool for the vest fronts, pattern the remaining 37 sts. for the left front.

THE LEFT FRONT : With No. 8 pins, work in pattern as follows :

1st row (right side facing) : P. 1, seam end, * k. 3, p. 1 ; repeat from * until 4 remain, k. 4 (front end).

(Continued on page 172)

THE panelled front of this attractive jumper is designed in a cross-over style that is so becoming to wear.

MATERIALS : *Seven ounces of "Green-ock" 3-ply Super-fingering (obtainable only at any of the branches of the Scotch Wool and Hosiery Stores), a pair of Stratnoid knitting pins, No. 11 and No. 8.*

TENSION AND MEASUREMENTS : *Worked at a tension of 6½ sts. to the inch in width on No. 8 pins the following measurements are attained after light pressing : Across the back at the underarms, 18½ inches ; across the front at the underarms, after the fronts are sewn in position, 19½ inches ; front length from shoulder seam to lower edge, 20 inches ; back length, 20 inches ; side seam, 14 inches ; sleeve seam, 19 inches.*

ABBREVIATIONS : *K., knit ; p., purl ; tog., together ; inc., increase (by working into the back and front of the same stitch) ; st., stitch. Directions in brackets are worked the number of times stated immediately after the brackets.*

To Work the Back

BEGIN at the lower edge, and using No. 11 pins, cast on 121 sts.

1st row (right side facing) : P. 1, * k. 3, p. 1 ; repeat from * to end.

2nd row : K. 2, p. 1, * k. 3, p. 1 ; repeat from * until 2 remain, k. 2.

These 2 rows form Ridge Pattern, so repeat them until 56 rows have been worked.

As an aid to keeping the pattern correct, note that the middle st. of the " k. 3 " after the * on every row is the plain knitted st. that runs continuously along the top of the ridge, with a p. st. on each side of it on the row below. This is a great help when shaping the armhole and neck.

Change to No. 8 pins and work 72 rows more in the same pattern.

TO SHAPE THE ARMHOLES : Continue in pattern, casting off 2 sts. at the

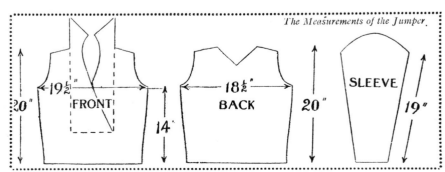

The Measurements of the Jumper

20"   19½"   FRONT   14   18½"   BACK   20"   SLEEVE   19"

The little vest-front gives the becoming cross-over line. A large brooch fastened on it gives a distinctive touch. Make it now—you can never have too many woollies in early summer.

VARIATION ON THE CROSS-OVER LINE

Continued

2nd row : K. 2, front end, p. 1, * k. 3, p. 1 ; repeat from * until 2 remain, k. 2.

Repeat these 2 rows until 72 rows have been worked on No. 8 pins to armhole.

** To Shape the Armhole : Continue in pattern, casting off 2 sts. at the beginning of next row and every following alternate row (armhole end) 7 times, then work 2 sts. tog. at the beginning of alternate rows (armhole end) for 2 decreases, which will leave 21 sts.

Work 45 rows straight in pattern to shoulder.

To Slope the Shoulder : Cast off 7 sts. at the beginning of next row and every following alternate row (armhole end) until all are worked off.

The Right Front : Join the wool to the centre end of 37 right front sts., and with No. 8 pins work in pattern as follows :

1st row (right side facing) : K. 4, front end, p. 1, * k. 3, p. 1 ; repeat from * to end.

2nd row : K. 2, p. 1, * k. 3, p. 1 ; repeat from * until 2 remain, k. 2.

Repeat these 2 rows until 73 rows have been worked on No. 8 pins. Then work from ** on left front to end.

The Right Front Vest : With wrong side of work facing, slip a No. 11 pin through the 47 centre front sts. (so that the pin point is towards the left arm end of row). With No. 8 pins work as follows.

Next row (right side facing) : Pick up and k. 2, by working twice into the horizontal thread lying between 2 sts. on the row below, pattern 47, pick up and k. 2 from wrong side of right front edge (51 sts. now on).

Next row (wrong side facing) : P. 1, * k. 3, p. 1 ; repeat from * until 2 remain, k. 2, front end.

To slope the lower edge, work as follows :

Next row (front end) : K. 4, p. 1, k. 3, p. 1, turn, k. 2, p. 1, k. 3, p. 1, k. 2.

Next row : Begin at the front end and work in pattern for 6 sts. farther along the row, then on the last row turn and work back. (*Note.*—Always keep the k. 2 border at the front end.)

Repeat from * 5 times more, always working 6 sts. more on every row, then work 2 rows on all the sts.

*** *Next row* (right side facing) : Work in pattern until 2 remain, k. 2 tog.

Pattern 3 rows.

Repeat the last 4 rows once more.

Next row : Pattern until 2 sts. remain, k. 2 tog.

Work 1 row more.

Repeat these 10 rows from *** until 13 sts. remain.

Work 11 rows straight.

Continue in same pattern inc. in the 4th st. from the neck end of next row and every following alternate row (every right side row) until there are 23 sts. on the row. Continue in pattern, taking 2 sts. tog. at the neck end of every row until all are worked off.

The Left Front Vest : Using No. 8 pins, cast on 51 sts. for the lower edge.

Next row (right side facing) : K. 2, p. 1, * k. 3, p. 1 ; repeat from * until 4 remain, k. 4 (front end).

Now slope the front edge as follows :

Next row : K. 2, front end, p. 1, k. 3, p. 1, k. 2, turn, p. 1, k. 3, p. 1, k. 4, front end.

* *Next row* : K. 2, front end, p. 1 (k. 3, p. 1), repeat brackets until 6 sts. are worked beyond the turn on previous row, turn and pattern until 4 remain, k. 4.

Repeat from * 4 times more, then work 3 rows on all the sts, remembering to keep the k. 2 border at the front end.

**** *Next row* (right side facing) : K. 2 tog., seam end, pattern to end.

Work 3 rows.

Repeat the last 4 rows once more.

Next row : K. 2 tog., pattern to end.

Pattern 1 row.

Repeat the last 10 rows from **** until 13 sts. remain. Work 11 rows straight.

Continue in pattern increasing in the 4th st. from the neck end of next row and every following alternate row (every right side row) until there are 23 sts. on the pin. Continue in pattern, taking 2 sts. tog. at neck end of every row until all are worked off.

The Sleeves

WITH No. 8 pins, cast on 23 sts. for the top of the sleeve.

Next row : K. 3, * p. 1, k. 3 ; repeat from * to end.

Continue in inc. pattern as follows :

1st row : Inc., p. 1, * k. 3, p. 1 ; repeat from * until 1 remains, inc.

2nd row : Inc., k. 3, * p. 1, k. 3 ; repeat from * until 1 remains, inc.

3rd row : Inc., k. 2, p. 1, * k. 3, p. 1 ; repeat from * until 3 remain, k. 2, inc.

4th row : Inc., k. 1, p. 1, * k. 3, p. 1 ; repeat from * until 2 remain, k. 1, inc.

Repeat these 4 rows until there are 87 sts. on the pins.

Work 6 rows straight in pattern.

Continue in pattern, taking 2 sts. tog. at each end of next row and every following 8th row until 57 sts. remain.

Change to No. 11 pins, and work in the same pattern, taking 2 sts. tog. at each end of every 8th row for 2 decrease rows more, which will leave 53 sts. Work 24 rows straight in same pattern, then cast off.

Work a second sleeve the same.

To Make Up the Jumper

FIRST press all pieces with a hot iron and a damp cloth over the wrong side of the work. Join the sloping edge of the right front vest to the edge of the right front, matching row for row, and so that the k. 2 border of the right front overlaps the right side of the vest. Sew the lower edge of the left front vest at centre-front waistline behind the corresponding sts. of the opposite vest, and join the seam edge to left front of jumper, as on the right front.

Join the shoulder seams, beginning at the armhole end, and taking 1 st. from each side at a time, then join the decreased edges of the vest together at the centre back, and sew into the V opening on the back of the jumper. Set the sleeve into armholes, and press all these seams while the work is open. Join the sleeve and side seams in one long line, and press.

WITH SPECIAL APPEAL!

Cheese and Apple Salad

INGREDIENTS :

4 *eating apples*
4 *tablespoonfuls coarsely grated cheese*
1 *dessertspoonful lemon juice*
1 *tablespoonful salad oil*
1 *dessertspoonful cream*
Salt, pepper, mustard
Heart of a lettuce

CHOOSE good medium-sized apples, about four to the pound.

Wipe them and cut off a slice from the top, then with a corer remove the core without cutting quite through to the base.

Scoop out the apple very carefully and chop it up. A curved grape fruit knife is the best to use for scooping out the apple, and use a stainless knife when chopping it.

Grate the cheese on the coarse side of the grater, and mix with the chopped apple.

Mix the oil and lemon juice on a plate, season with salt, pepper and a little made mustard, then stir in the cream very gradually.

Mix this dressing with the apple and cheese and use to fill up the apple shells.

Replace the top slice and stalk, and arrange on individual plates surrounded with lettuce leaves.

Sausage Snacks

INGREDIENTS :

6 *ozs. breakfast sausage*
3 *tomatoes*
1 *hard-boiled egg*
Gherkins
Mixed mustard

SKIN the sausage and cut it in thick slices, then spread with mixed mustard. Dip the tomatoes into boiling water, then take out and remove the skin, chill, and slice thickly.

Season the slices with pepper and salt and arrange one on each piece of sausage. Top with a slice of hard-boiled egg, then with a small piece of gherkin. Serve with a plain lettuce salad.

"Knit these slimline undies"

For pattern see p. 130

"An interesting neckline"

"It's very captivating"

For pattern see p. 72

For pattern see p. 104

"This one for parties"

For pattern see p. 148. One of the sweaters has been knitted with sleeves exactly double the size given in the pattern, to show how the patterns can be adapted.

"To wear on sunny shores"

For pattern see p. 182

It is dashing with a striped knitted tie.

Something ENDEARING To Wear With YOUR SUIT

TENSION AND MEASUREMENTS

WORKED at a tension so that one pattern of 16 sts. measures $1\frac{3}{4}$ inches in width the following measurements are attained after light pressing : Round the bust, 33 inches ; length from shoulder fold to lower edge, 21 inches ; side seam, $13\frac{1}{2}$ inches ; sleeve seam, 5 inches.

TO WORK THE BACK

BEGIN at the lower edge by casting on 146 sts. with the No. 10 pins, and work 30 rows in single rib. Always sl. the first st. of every row to make a neat edge.

Change to No. 8 pins and begin the pattern:

1ST ROW : Sl. 1, * k. 2 tog., k. 5, inc. in each of the next 2 sts., k. 5, k. 2 tog. ; repeat from * until 1 st. remains, k. 1.

2ND ROW : All p.

Repeat these 2 rows 3 times more, then work the first row again.

10TH ROW : All k. on the wrong side, so this makes the ridge running between the patterns on the right side.

These 10 rows form one pattern.

Repeat the pattern 8 times more to the armholes.

TO SHAPE THE ARMHOLES.—Cast off 8 sts., 1 st. on pin, * inc., k. 5, (k. 2 tog.) twice, k. 5, inc., and repeat from * until 9 sts. remain, then inc., k. 5, k. 2 tog., k. 1.

NEXT ROW : Cast off 8 sts. and p. to end of row.

Now dec. 1 st. at both ends of the next 8 rows, when 16 sts. will have been taken

THIS is such a fascinating pattern, and if the beginner works a small piece before beginning the jumper, she will find the set of the pattern quite simple to follow. For this purpose cast on 34 sts., which give two patterns and two end sts., and work the 10 rows of the pattern as given at the beginning of the back.

MATERIALS

FIVE ounces of Patons' (or Beehive) Super Scotch Fingering, 2-ply in natural shade (6 ounces will make long sleeves), $\frac{1}{2}$-ounce of the same wool in navy blue, and $\frac{1}{4}$-ounce in pale coral or the nearest to that tone ; a pair of No. 10 and No. 8 Stratnoid knitting pins.

ABBREVIATIONS

K., KNIT plain, p., purl ; st., stitch ; tog., together ; inc., increase (by working into the back and front of the same st.), single rib is k. 1 and p. 1 alternately. Directions in brackets are worked the number of times stated after the brackets. Sl., slip.

A close-up of the stitch itself.

**An Easy "Wave" Pattern With
A Dainty Scalloped Collar**

**It Is Knitted In A Pretty
Soft Wool**

away at each armhole, and the pattern will continue without a break, with 1 st. over at each end (114 sts. on).

Continue straight on these sts. until 13 complete patterns can be counted above the waist ribbing, then work 3 rows more to the neckline.

On the next row the sts. are divided for the two shoulders, thus : P. 34 and leave these sts. on a stitch-holder for the left shoulder, p. 46, and pass these 46 sts. on a piece of spare wool for the back of the neck. This will leave 1 st. on the pin, p. the remaining 33 sts., making 34 altogether for the Right Shoulder.

Continue straight on these sts., beginning with the 5th row, until there are 4 repetitions of the 10th row of the pattern on the shoulder (this is seen clearly by the raised ridge on the right side).

Work the 1st row of the next pattern, then at the beginning of the following row cast on 24 sts., p. these sts. and p. to the end of the row (58 sts.).

Continue on these sts. until the 10th row of the pattern has been worked twice more, that is, making 2 ridges more on the right side of the work. On the pattern rows which finish at the front edge there will be half a pattern and one edge st., so when working the last repetition of the 10th row, k. 2 sts. tog. at the neck end, to take away the edge st., which will not be required when all the front sts. are worked.

Now work the 1st row of the next pattern, then leave these 57 sts. on a stitch-holder, securing the ball with the sts., and leave for the present.

THE LEFT SHOULDER.—Join the wool to the neck edge of the Left Shoulder sts. on the stitch-holder (leaving the back neck sts. still on the length of wool) and work as opposite shoulder, but work 1 row less, so as to end with the 10th row of the pattern at the neck edge. Then cast on 24 sts., making 58 altogether.

Continue on these sts. until 2 patterns more are worked to match the opposite front, but finish with the 10th row of the pattern at the neck edge, knitting the last 2 sts. tog., and fasten off the wool (57 sts.).

(Remember when working the pattern rows that there is half a pattern at the beginning of the row, so this row will begin with sl. 1, inc., k. 5, k. 2 tog., then as from * in the first pattern row.)

Now continue

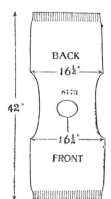

Open at the neck the jumper will be more becoming to some of us.

with the pin which holds the Right Shoulder sts. and work across the second shoulder, following the 1st row of the pattern, when there will be 114 sts. on the pin.

Continue in pattern on these sts., increasing 1 st. at both ends of the next 8 rows, after which cast on 8 sts. at the beginning of the next 2 rows. This adds 16 sts. at each end, forming a complete repeat of the pattern, 146 sts. altogether, including 2 end sts.

Continue in pattern on these sts. until there are as many rows, counting at the side seam edge, as on the back to the armholes.

Change to No. 10 pins and work the hip ribbing to match the back.

THE COLLAR

HOLDING the work with the wrong side facing and using No. 10 pins, pick up and k. 130 sts. from the neck edge, and when taking up the sts. at the top of

Continued from page 169

To Wear Under Your Suit

the two points of the front at the neck opening turn back these points and pick up the sts. in a straight line; the points can be sewn down at the back afterwards. Work 8 rows in single rib.

Change to No. 8 pins, and k. plain to end of row.

1ST ROW OF THE PATTERN: Sl. 1, * k. 2 tog., k. 5, inc. in each of the next 2 sts., k. 5, k. 2 tog.; repeat from * until 1 st. remains, k. 1.

2ND ROW: All p.

Repeat the last 2 rows 3 times more, then work the 1st row again.

NEXT ROW: K. plain.

Repeat the 1st and 2nd row 3 times more, then cast off loosely.

THE SLEEVES

CAST on 34 sts. and p. 1 row, then begin the inc. pattern for the top of the sleeve.

1ST ROW: As 1st row of pattern on the back.

2ND ROW: K. 1 and p. 1 in the first st., p. until 1 st. remains, then p. 1 and k. 1 in the last st.

3RD ROW: Sl. 1, k. 1, then repeat from * in the 1st row, until 2 sts. remain, k. 2.

4TH ROW: As 2nd row.

5TH ROW: Sl. 1, k. 2, then repeat from * in the 1st row until 3 sts. remain, k. 3.

6TH ROW: As 2nd row.

7TH ROW: Sl. 1, k. 3, then repeat from * in the 1st row until 4 sts. remain, k. 4.

8TH ROW: As 2nd row.

9TH ROW: Sl. 1, k. 4, then repeat from * in the 1st row until 5 sts. remain, k. 5.

10TH ROW: Inc. in the 1st st., k. until 1 st. remains, inc. in the last st. (44 sts.).

Continue working in this way, increasing 1 st. at both ends of every wrong side row, when there will be 1 st. extra to k. at the beginning and end of each right side row, until there are 16 extra sts. at each end, then the 1st row will repeat exactly as the 1st row of the pattern on the back.

Inc. on the next row as before, and continue as on the inc. pattern above until there are 82 sts. altogether. There will be half a pattern at the beginning and end of the row, but the pattern is so very clearly seen now, that there will not be any difficulty in getting it correct.

Now continue straight on these sts., working from the 3rd row of this pattern, then one complete pattern of 10 rows more and 9 rows of the next pattern.

*** Long sleeves may be continued from here.

For the short sleeve band work 13 rows of single rib and cast off loosely.

*** To work long sleeves continue in pattern, decreasing 1 st. at the beginning and end of every 10th row until the width of sleeve desired is obtained, then continue on this width for the length of sleeve desired, finishing with a little cuff of single rib.

THE TIE

WITH No. 10 pins and navy blue wool, cast on 30 sts., and k. plain throughout.

1ST ROW: K. 1, k. 2 tog., k. to end of row.

2ND ROW: K. 1, increase in the next st., and k. to the end of the row.

Repeat these 2 rows until there are 30 rows in blue.

* Work 8 rows in natural and 8 rows in coral, and 14 rows in blue; repeat from * once.

Now begin the decreases for the neck band as follows: K. 1, k. 2 tog., * k. 6, k. 2 tog.; repeat from * twice more, k. 2.

NEXT ROW: K. 1, inc. in the next st., * k. 5, k. 2 tog., and repeat from * twice more, k. 3.

Repeat the last 2 rows until 12 sts. remain.

Work as before on these 12 sts. for about 6 inches, or enough to go half-way round the neck, and cast off or leave the sts. for grafting.

Work a second piece exactly the same, then join at the centre of the narrow strip.

TO MAKE UP THE JUMPER

FIRST press all very lightly. Set the sleeves into the armholes, sewing the little points at the top of the sleeve on the inside of the shoulder; sew the sleeve and side seams in one line and press.

Problem Corner For Gardeners

IMPROVING A CLAY SOIL

Can you please tell me how to improve clay soil?

CLAY soil should always be dug in the autumn, and the surface should be left rough and lumpy so that the winter frosts can break it up thoroughly. During the digging, ashes, grit, or sand should be added, and lime should be applied freely.

DESTROYING NETTLES

I have had a few chickens in a run in my tiny orchard, and the site is now covered with nettles. How can I rid myself of them?

NETTLES always come where chickens have had a run. Why, I have never been able to fathom. Keep them cut very short, and they will gradually die out.

TO WEAR IN THE EVENINGS!

Repeat these 2 rows until there are 135 sts.

Continue straight on these sts. for 108 rows more.

1ST DECREASE ROW: M.s. 6, * k. 2 tog., m.s. 9, repeat from * until 8 remain, m.s. 8 (124 sts.).

Work 3 rows straight in m.s.

2ND DECREASE ROW: M.s. 6, * k. 2 tog., m.s. 8, repeat from * until 8 remain, m.s. 8 (113 sts.).

Work 3 rows straight in m.s.

3RD DECREASE ROW: M.s. 5, * k. 2 tog., m.s. 7, repeat from * until 9 remain, m.s. 9 (102 sts.).

Work 3 rows straight in m.s.

4TH DECREASE ROW: M.s. 4, * k. 2 tog., m.s. 6, repeat from * until 10 remain, m.s. 10 (91 sts.).

Work 10 rows straight in m.s. Cast off.

Work a second sleeve in the same manner.

THE SLEEVE BANDS

CAST on 14 sts. and work 12 inches in single rib.

1ST BUTTONHOLE ROW: Rib 5, cast off 4, rib to end.

2ND BUTTONHOLE ROW: Work in rib, casting on 4 sts. over those cast off to complete the buttonhole.

Continue in rib, working 2 sts. tog. at both ends of every row until 1 st. remains. Fasten off.

TO MAKE A SHORT PUFF SLEEVE

WORK the top of the sleeve as instructed above until there are 135 sts.

Work 30 rows in m.s. on these sts.

On the next row decrease by knitting together every 4th and 5th st. Change to No. 11 pins, work 12 rows in single rib, and cast off loosely.

THE COLLAR

CAST on 27 sts. and work entirely in m.s. for 200 rows.

Cast off.

TO MAKE UP THE JUMPER

PRESS all pieces with a hot iron over a damp cloth on the wrong side of the work. Join the shoulder seams, beginning at the armhole end and taking 1 st. from each side at a time. Slightly gather the sleeve tops and set into armholes; press these seams. Oversew the back basque to edge of back on the wrong side and the small basques to each front. Stitch the collar to the neck edge, then gather in the narrow ends at the front of neck. Make buttonloops by putting 1 d.c. into the first st. on the edge above the basque. * 6 ch., miss 4 rows of knitting, 1 d.c. in each of the next 3 sts., and repeat from * to the neck edge.

Sea and Sun Suit

MATERIALS.—7 ozs. of nigger brown, and 4 ozs. of "sand" Patons & Baldwins "Diana" Swim Wool, 1 pair "Aero" knitting needles, No. 12; 1 button.

Knitted in Flattering Tones of Light Sunburn and Deep Bronze

Measurements.— From shoulder to edge, 29 inches. To fit a 34-36-inch bust measurement.

Abbreviations.—K., knit; p., purl; sts., stitches; tog., together; beg., beginning; inc., increase; dec., decrease; patt., pattern.

Tension.—8 sts. to 1 inch in width. K. into the back of all cast-on sts.

Knickers : Front.—With brown wool and No. 12 needles cast on 66 sts. Rib 1 inch in k. 1, p. 1.

Then shape leg as follows : 1*st row.*—Rib 6, turn, rib back. 3*rd row.*—Rib 12, turn, rib back. 5*th row.*—Rib 18, turn, rib back. 7*th row.*—Rib 24, turn, rib back. 9*th row.*—Rib 30, turn, rib back. 11*th row.*—Rib 36, turn, rib back.

Continue in this way 6 sts. more each time until all sts. are on one needle. Then purl 1 row.

Now continue in the following patt. : 1*st row.*—*K. 3, p. 3, repeat from * to end. 2*nd row.*—*P. 3, k. 3, repeat from * to end. Repeat these 2 rows for 2 inches. Break off wool and place on a spare needle.

Work another half leg (with shaping at opposite edge). Then work across both sets of sts. and continue in patt. for 3½ inches. Then k. 2 tog. at beg. and end of next and every 6th row following until 112 sts. on needle. When short edge of knickers measures 12 inches, rib 1 inch in k. 1, p. 1. Cast off in rib.

Make back exactly the same.

Gusset.—With brown wool and No. 12 needles cast on 2 sts., work in patt., increasing 1 st. each end of every alternate row (by k. twice into first and last sts.) until 36 sts. Work 4 rows without inc. Then dec. 1 st. each end of every alternate row (by k. tog.) until 2 sts. remain. Cast off.

Top : Left Half.—With nigger brown wool and No. 12 needles cast on 112 sts. and work throughout in stocking st. Work 24 rows. Change to "sand" wool. Work 6 rows.

*T*HIS jolly suit for gay days in the sea and sun is designed to leave your back free to acquire a lovely tan.

31*st row*.—Cast off 16. K. to end (96 sts.). Continue on these 96 sts. dec. 1 st. at the same edge as the cast off sts. every 4th row until 78 sts. remain and work measures 10 ins. from start, working stripes of nigger brown and sand alternately of 24 rows each colour.

Then dec. 1 st. each end of every row, until 42 sts. remain. Then at straight edge cast off 3 sts. every alternate row, until 21 sts. remain. Then at this edge dec. 1 st. every row until 12 sts. remain.

Continue in nigger brown wool only. Rib 6½ ins. (or length required) in k. 1, p. 1. Point end by dec. 1 st. each end of every row until 4 sts. remain. Cast off.

Right half of top.—Work as for left half with shaping at opposite edges, starting with " sand " wool and ending with " sand " wool (you thus reverse the order of stripes), and on this side when neck strap measures 6½ ins. (or length required) make a buttonhole. thus : Rib 3. Cast off 6. Rib 3. On the returning row, rib 3. Cast on 6. Rib 3. Then make point as other side.

To make up.—Press under a damp cloth with warm iron. Sew the two half fronts together, making stripes match, in opposite colours. Sew seams of knickers. Sew in gusset. Sew top to knickers. Sew on button to strap.

Pattern overleaf THE NEWEST SWIM-SUIT is in CROCHET

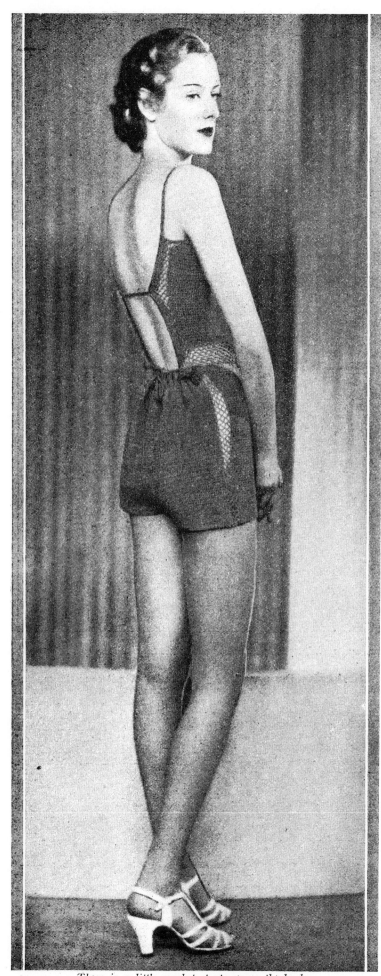

There is a little crochet strap across the back.

To Wear on SUNNY SHORES—

Backless—and So Chic!

The simplest crochet stitches are used for this attractive bathing costume.

MATERIALS : *7 ounces of Patons & Baldwins' Crocus Non-shrink Knitting wool, 4-ply, and a No. 14 "Aero" Crochet hook.*

TENSION AND MEASUREMENTS : *Worked at a tension of 7 d.c. to the inch in width, the following measurements are attained after light pressing : Across the top piece at the bust line 23 inches, all round hips 34 inches, front length without straps 24 inches.*

ABBREVIATIONS : *Ch., chain ; d.c., double crochet ; sl., slip ; st., stitch.*

To Work the Trunks

BEGIN at the back waist-line and make 116 ch.

1st row : 1 d. c. into the 3rd ch. from the hook, 1 d.c. into each st. to the end of the row, 2 ch., turn.

2nd row : Miss the first d.c. over which the 2 ch. stands, 1 d.c. in each st. to the end, taking up both loops at the top of the st., 2 ch., turn.

Repeat the 2nd row until 54 rows are worked altogether.

Next row : Work 57 d.c., 2 ch., turn, leaving the rest of the row unworked.

Work 14 rows more on these 57 d.c. for one half leg, and fasten off.

Work on the remaining d.c. for the second half leg.

The Front of Trunks : Work a second piece in exactly the same manner.

The Gusset : Make 18 ch., and work in exactly the same way as the two larger pieces until 18 rows of d.c. have been worked. Sew this gusset in position, setting it cornerwise between the two leg pieces of the front trunks, and the second half of it between the two leg pieces of the back trunks.

The Bodice

THIS is worked on the front only, so join the wool to the first d.c. of the first row at the waist edge, * 5 ch., miss 2 d.c. along the row, 1 d.c. in the next st., and repeat from * to the end of the row, 5 ch., turn.

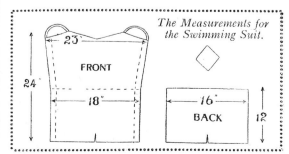

The Measurements for the Swimming Suit.

—The Newest SWIM-SUIT is in Crochet

The Openwork Panels Are Very Decorative

Work 8 rows of chain loops as described on previous page, putting the d.c. in the centre of each loop on the previous row.

Next row : 3 ch., 1 d.c. in the centre of the first loop, * 2 ch., 1 d.c. in the next loop, and repeat from * to the end of the row.

Next row : Work 1 d.c. in each st., that is d.c. and ch., 2 ch., turn.

Work 39 rows of d.c., increasing 1 st. at both ends of every 4th row, by working 2 d.c. into the st. before the end one.

On the next row work d.c. across half of the sts., then turn without one.

Next row : Sl.st. over 2 d.c., then 1 d.c. in each st. to the centre one, miss the centre st., then 1 d.c. in each st. to the end of the row.

Repeat the last row until 3 d.c. remain ; on these 3 sts. work a strap 9 inches long and fasten off.

Work a second front point and strap on the remaining d.c.

The Openwork Side Panels

These are worked on the front of the suit and the back of the trunk part only is joined to the last row of loops. Begin with a d.c. in the end of the first row at the lower edge of the suit, * 5 ch., miss the end of one row, 1 d.c. at the end of the next row and repeat from * all along the edge of the trunk, and when working over the openwork at the waist put 1 d.c. in each chain loop, then continue along the bodice as on the trunk ; at the end turn with 5 ch.

Next row : 1 d.c. in the first loop of 5 ch., * 5 ch., 1 d.c. in the next loop and repeat from * to the end of the row.

Work 2 rows more like the last row.

Next row : Beginning at the lower edge, work 2 ch., 1 d.c. in the end of the last row on the back of the trunks, * 2 ch., 1 d.c. in the next loop on the openwork panel, 2 ch., miss 1 row on the back of the trunks, 1 d.c. in the next st., and repeat from * until all the back piece is joined. Now continue along the front, putting 3 d.c. in each ch. loop, at the end turn with 2 ch., miss the first d.c., 1 d.c. in each st. to the end of the row. Work 2 rows more like the

last one and fasten off. Sew the end of the shoulder strap to the end of the last 4 rows.

Work a second openwork panel in exactly the same way on the opposite side of the suit.

The Back Strap

This spans across the centre of the back to keep the bodice in place.

Make 6 ch., then miss 2 ch. and work 3 d.c. along the row. Continue rows of 3 d.c. and 2 ch. until the strap is about 4 inches long, then sew the short ends in position to each side of the bodice.

THE GIRDLE : Make three lengths of crochet chain, each one yard long, plait together and run through the stitches along the top of the trunks at the back, beginning at the right hand side, then across the front in the row just under the open work, bringing the end out at the right side. Finish each end with a small tassel.

✻　　✻　　✻

GAMES for the GARDEN

A Reader's Query

I should like one or two good outdoor games to amuse my young people and their friends. I have a garden of the average size. We are tired of clock-golf and croquet.

Tenikoit is one of the most popular games of the moment, being an adaptation of deck-tennis played with a rubber ring over a net, well known to all "cruisers." It is really an excellent game and very fast.

Miniten is a miniature tennis game, and can be played over a Tenikoit net. It is a good game where there is not enough room for a full-sized tennis court. It has all the strokes exactly as in tennis and requires as much strength owing to the particular construction of the bats.

Another exciting game is Corballo, evolved from the old Basque game of "Pelota." The apparatus consisting of basket throwers and a ball. You can get come excellent fun with this even without a marked-out court, and it may be played in summer or winter.

✻　　✻　　✻

"That day, when you asked me if I were Frances Ferrier, I said I was because—silly and impossible as I suppose you will think it is—I wanted to know you."

Michael's eyes wavered, but he did not look at her.

"You wanted to know me ; I think I realised that. It is not the first time I have been invited to form an unconventional friendship."

"I know—but this—was something different," she said.

"How different?"

She held her secret for a moment longer, then suddenly she let it go :

"Different because—you see I had fallen in love with you." She drew a quick breath. "You may laugh if you like," she added proudly.

(Another long instalment of " Owner Gone Abroad " in the July number of WOMAN AND HOME, *on sale on June 19th.)*

A Sleeveless Coat in "Ramada" Wool

THIS charming and useful little sleeveless coat is made in a diagonal rib pattern which is very simple to work but most effective (a close-up of the knitting is shown on the next page), and the fashionable wide revers are worked in moss-stitch.

MATERIALS REQUIRED :—6 ounces of "Ramada" 4-ply Wool, shade No. R 2134 (pink) ; 1 pair of No. 9 Stratnoid knitting needles ; 3 buttons for fastening.

TENSION :—7 sts. to 1 inch in width.   SIZE :—34 inches round under arms.

ABBREVIATIONS :—k. = knit ; p. = purl ; st. = stitch ; rep. = repeat ; inc. = increase ; dec. = decrease ; tog. = together.

The Back

Cast on 112 sts., and work in the following pattern :—

1st row.—*k. 4, p. 4, and rep. from * to end.

2nd row.—k. 3, * p. 4, k. 4, and rep. from * to within 5 sts. of end, p. 4, k. 1.

3rd row.—p. 2, * k. 4, p. 4, and rep. from *, ending k. 4, p. 2.

4th row.—k. 1, * p. 4, k. 4, and rep. from *, ending p. 4, k. 3.

5th row.—* p. 4, k. 4, and rep. from * to end.

6th row.—p. 3, * k. 4, p. 4, and rep. from *, ending k. 4, p. 1.

7th row.—k. 2, * p. 4, k. 4, and rep. from *, ending p. 4, k. 2.

8th row.—p. 1, * k. 4, p. 4, and rep. from * ending k. 4, p. 3.

These 8 rows form the pattern and are repeated throughout.

Continue until work measures 2½ inches, then dec. by taking 2 sts. tog. (being careful always to keep continuity of pattern) at beginning and end of the next row, and every following 4*th row* (3 rows straight between each dec. row) until sts. are reduced to 100. From here, work 1½ inches straight, then *inc.* by working twice into the first and last st. of the next row, and every following 6*th row* (5 rows straight between each inc. row) until sts. number 112.

Work a few more rows straight until side seam measures 13 inches, then shape for armholes by casting off 10 sts. at beginning of the next 2 rows, then continue to shape armhole by taking 2 sts. tog. at beginning and end of the next 6 rows (80 sts. remain). From here, work straight until armhole is 7½ inches measured round its edge, then shape shoulders by casting off 8 sts. at beginning of the next 6 rows.

Cast off remaining sts. for back of neck.

Left Front

Cast on 64 sts. and work exactly as given for back until work measures 2½ inches, ending at completion of an *even* row of pattern, then commence to dec. by taking 2 sts. tog. at *beginning* of the next row, and every following 4*th row*, until sts. are reduced to 58. Work 1½ inches straight, again ending at completion of an *even* numbered row, then commence to *inc.* by working twice into the first st. of the next row, and every following 6*th row*, until you have made 6 inc. rows at this side. When these inc. are commenced, *dec.* by taking 2 sts. tog. at centre-front edge (opposite edge to the dec. and inc. of side seam) on the next row, and every following 6*th row*, until you have 3 dec. rows at centre front, then continue to shape front slope by taking 2 sts. tog. at this side on every 4*th row*, until further directions are given.

When side seam inc. are finished, work straight at this edge until work measures same as that of back up to armhole, ending at completion of an *even* numbered row, then shape armhole by casting off 10 sts. at beginning of the next row, then take 2 sts. tog. at armhole edge on the next 6 rows. Continue front slope dec. until sts. are reduced to 24, then work straight until armhole measures 8 inches round edge; shape shoulder by casting off 8 sts. at beginning of the next 3 rows, starting from armhole edge.

Right Front

This is worked exactly the same as the left, all shapings coming on *same* side of work as shapings of left front, then, when the right front is reversed to the *wrong* side, the stripes of each front will run towards each other, as shown in photograph.

The only difference in the two fronts is that buttonholes are made on this right front, these being made at beginnings of the *even* numbered rows, working the first one 1 inch from the cast-on edge, then two more, each 1 inch apart from each other.

Work the buttonholes thus : Work in pattern over 3 sts., cast off 4 sts., pattern to end. *Next row.*— Pattern, casting on 4 sts. over those cast off in previous row.

The Revers

With right side of left front towards you, and starting from shoulder, pick up 79 sts. down from shoulder to end of the front edge slope.

1st row.—k. 1, p. 1 to within 1 st. of end, k. 1. *2nd row.*—k. 1, p. 1 to within 1 st. of end, k. 1 (these 2 rows form moss-stitch). Now, always keeping continuity of moss-stitches by knitting over a purled st. and purling over a knitted st., dec. by taking 2 sts. tog. on every row at *waist* edge, and 2 sts. tog. on every *alternate* row at shoulder edge, until all sts. are worked off.

Work a second rever in same way on right front.

To Complete Coat

Press lightly with a warm iron over a damp cloth. Join shoulder seams. Next, with right side of work towards you, pick up 101 sts. round one armhole, and work 9 rows in moss-stitch, taking 2 sts. tog. at beginning and end of the last 4 rows. Cast off. Repeat round second armhole.

Press shoulder seams, then sew up side seams. Sew buttons opposite buttonholes, and the coat will be ready for you to wear.

THERE can be no question that the strawberry is the queen of our English fruits, and the hall-mark of summer. The large firm berries are most delicious soaked in a little lemon juice, sprinkled with castor sugar and served with plenty of fresh cream. The smaller berries, or the cheaper fruit if there are plenty about, make many delightful dishes which but enhance their royal reputation.

Queen of Fruits

of two eggs and three ounces of castor sugar to the purée. Dissolve half an ounce of gelatine in two or three tablespoonfuls of hot water, and add it to the fruit with a teaspoonful of lemon juice, and the stiffly-whipped whites of the eggs. Use a few drops of cochineal for colouring, and then turn the mixture into a soufflé case, with a band of stiff paper tied round the outside of the case, so that it stands up above it. Leave the soufflé to set, and serve in the case, decorated with a few large strawberries and a piping of cream.

Strawberry Trifle

Dissolve a pint packet of Chivers' Strawberry Jelly in hot water, pouring half of it over a sponge ring placed in the bottom of a glass dish, and leave the remainder to set. Make a pint of vanilla custard, from Bird's Custard

Powder, set it aside to cool, and in the meantime mash three-quarters of a pound of strawberries to a pulp. Sweeten with two ounces of castor sugar, add a tablespoonful of lemon-juice, and put this mixture into the hole in the centre of the sponge cake. Pour the custard round the outside, and decorate the trifle with the rest of the jelly, coarsely chopped, and a few strawberries. This is enough for seven or eight people.

Strawberry Foam

Dissolve half an ounce of leaf gelatine in a gill of water, and then stir in two ounces of sugar and a pound of strawberries, crushed to a pulp. Add the beaten whites of two eggs, and whisk the whole in a cool place until it stiffens, and then pile it pyramid-fashion in a glass dish. This is enough for four or five people.

Strawberry Soufflé

Rub a pound of strawberries through a hair sieve, and add the beaten yolks

Strawberry Tartlets

Line some small greased tartlet tins with short-crust pastry, and bake until they are golden-brown. When cold, fill them up with small strawberries which have been allowed to soak in castor sugar and lemon juice. Make a syrup of a little sugar and water, adding some strawberry flavouring and some cochineal. Allow to cool before pouring over the fruit. When the tartlets are cold and ready for table, put a small portion of cream on each.

M

The jumper fastens at the back with two pretty buttons.

A JUMPER with SUN-RAY RIBBING

This Round Neck is Finished with the Prettiest Pointed Edge

Repeat these 2 rows until 34 rows have been worked.

Now begin the main ribbed pattern as follows :

1st row (right side facing) : P. 2, * k. 2, inc., k. 3, p. 3 ; repeat from *, ending with p. 2 instead of p. 3 (121 sts.).

Change to No. 8 pins and work as follows :

2nd row : K. 2, p. 7, * k. 3, p. 7; repeat from * until 2 remain, k. 2.

3rd row : P. 2, k. 7, * p. 3, k. 7; repeat from * until 2 remain, p. 2.

4th row : K. 2, p. 7, * k. 3, p. 7; repeat from * until 2 remain, k. 2.

5th row : Work in rib as now set inc. at each end (123 sts.).

6th row : P. 1, k. 2, p. 7, * k. 3, p. 7; repeat from * until 3 remain, k. 2, p. 1.

7th row : K. 1, p. 2, k. 7, * p. 3, k. 7; repeat from * until 3 remain, p. 2, k. 1.

8th row : As 6th row.

9th row : In same rib inc. 1 st. at both ends of the row (125 sts.).

10th row : P. 2, k. 2, p. 7, * k. 3, p. 7; repeat from * until 4 remain, k. 2, p. 2.

11th row : K. 2, p. 2, k. 7, * p. 3, k. 7; repeat from * until 4 remain, p. 2, k. 2.

12th row : As 10th row.

13th row : In same rib inc. 1 st. at both ends of the row (127 sts.).

14th row : P. 3, k. 2, p. 7, * k. 3, p. 7; repeat from * until 5 remain, k. 2, p. 3.

15th row : K. 3, p. 2, k. 7, * p. 3, k. 7; repeat from * until 5 remain, p. 2, k. 3.

16th row : As 14th row.

17th row : In rib as now set inc. at both ends of the row (129 sts.).

18th row : P. 4, k. 2, p. 7, * k. 3, p. 7; repeat from * until 6 remain, k. 2, p. 4.

19th row : K. 4, p. 2, k. 7, * p. 3, k. 7; repeat from * until 6 remain, p. 2 k. 4.

20th row : As 18th row.

21st row : In same rib inc. at both ends of the row (131 sts.).

22nd row : P. 5, k. 2, p. 7, * k. 3, p. 7; repeat from * until 7 remain, k. 2, p. 5.

23rd row : K. 5, p. 2, k. 7, * p. 3, k. 7; repeat from * until 7 remain, p. 2, k. 5.

24th row : As 22nd row.

THE clever arrangement of the ribbing gives an attractive ray effect to this pretty jumper. Notice, too, the charming pointed edging of the neck.

MATERIALS : *4 ounces of Lister's "Lavenda" 2-ply Scotch Fingering, a pair of No. 8 and No. 11 Stratnoid knitting pins ; 2 fancy buttons.*

TENSION AND MEASUREMENTS : *Worked at a tension of 7½ sts. to the inch in width on No. 8 pins, the following measurements are attained after light pressing : Round the bust, 35 inches ; length from shoulder fold to lower edge, 19 inches ; side seam, 12 inches ; short sleeve seam, 6 inches.*

ABBREVIATIONS : *k., knit ; p., purl ; tog., together ; st., stitch ; inc., increase (by working into the back and front of the same stitch) ; sl., slip ; p.s.s.o., pass the slipped stitch over the knit st. Directions in brackets are worked the number of times stated immediately after the brackets.*

To Work

BEGIN at the front and using No. 11 pins cast on 109 sts. for the waist edge, and work in rib as follows :

1st row (right side facing) : P. 2, * k. 2, p. 2, k. 2, p. 3 ; repeat from * ending with p. 2 instead of p. 3.

2nd row : K. 2, * p. 2, k. 2, p. 2, k. 3 ; repeat from *, ending with k. 2 instead of k. 3.

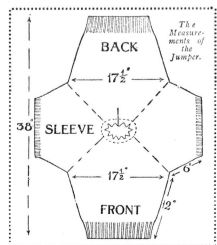

The Measurements of the Jumper.

BACK

17½"

38" SLEEVE

17½"

6"

2"

FRONT

If you'd like it in Pink—choose coral with white buttons.
Wear a two-piece of heavy natural tussore. A matching coral-pink hat trimmed with white petersham ribbon. White shoes and handbag. Wear coral-pink gloves of fine suede.

If you'd like it in White—choose glass buttons for the yoke.
Wear a white linen-tweed skirt. A matching linen hat, trimmed with dark green ribbon. White court shoes with green leather trimming. Dark green gloves. Carry a green and white handbag.

A JUMPER With SUN-RAY RIBBING

25th row: Inc., k. 4, p. 2, k. 5, k. 2 tog., * p. 3, k. 5, k. 2 tog.; repeat from * until 7 remain, p. 2, k. 4, inc. (121 sts.).

26th row: P. 6, k. 2, p. 6, * k. 3, p. 6; repeat from * until 8 remain, k. 2, p. 6.

27th row: K. 6, p. 2, k. 6, * p. 3, k. 6; repeat from * until 8 remain, p. 2, k. 6.

28th row: As 26th row.

29th row: Work in rib as now set, inc. at both ends (123 sts.).

30th row: K. 1, p. 6, k. 2, p. 6, * k. 3, p. 6; repeat from * until 9 remain, k. 2, p. 6, k. 1.

Work 2 rows more in same rib without increases.

33rd row: Inc., at both ends of row (125 sts.).

34th row: (K. 2, p. 6) twice, * k. 3, p. 6; repeat from * until 10 remain, k. 2, p. 6, k. 2.

Work 2 rows more in same rib without increase.

37th row: Work in rib as now set, inc. at both ends (127 sts.).

38th row: P. 1, (k. 2, p. 6) twice, * k. 3, p. 6; repeat from * until 11 remain, k. 2, p. 6, k. 2, p. 1.

Work 2 rows more in same rib.

41st row: Work in same rib increasing at both ends (129 sts.).

42nd row: P. 2, (k. 2, p. 6) twice, * k. 3, p. 6; repeat from * until 12 remain, k. 2, p. 6, k. 2, p. 2.

Work 2 rows more in same rib.

45th row: Work in same rib, increasing at both ends (131 sts.).

46th row: P. 3, (k. 2, p. 6) twice, * k. 3, p. 6; repeat from * until 13 remain, k. 2, p. 6, k. 2, p. 3.

Work 2 rows more in same rib.

49th row: Inc., k. 2, (p. 2, k. 6) twice, * p. 1, p. 2 tog., k. 6; repeat from * until 13 remain, p. 2, k. 6, p. 2, k. 2, inc. (122 sts.).

50th row: P. 4, k. 2, * p. 6, k. 2; repeat from * until 4 remain, p. 4.

Work 2 rows more in the same rib.

Continue in rib as now set inc. at each end of next row and every following 4th row until 5 more increase rows have been worked and there are 132 sts. on the pins.

70th row: P. 1, k. 2, * p. 6, k. 2; repeat from * until 1 remains, p. 1.

This brings the work to the underarm.

Work 2 sts. tog. at each end of the next 2 rows (128 sts.).

73rd row: P. 1, * sl. 1, k. 1, p.s.s.o., k. 4, p. 2; repeat from *, ending with p. 1, instead of p. 2 (16 decreases and 112 sts. left).

74th row: K. 1, * p. 5, k. 2; repeat from *, ending with k. 1, instead of k. 2.

Work 10 rows more in same rib without decreases.

85th row: P. 1, * k. 3, k. 2 tog., p. 2; repeat from *, ending with p. 1 instead of p. 2 (16 decreases and 96 sts. left).

86th row: K. 1, * p. 4, k. 2; repeat from *, ending with k. 1 instead of k. 2.

Work 10 rows more in same rib.

97th row: P. 1, * sl. 1, k. 1, p.s.s.o., k. 2, p. 2; repeat from *, ending the last repeat with p. 1 instead of p. 2 (80 sts.).

98th row: K. 1, * p. 3, k. 2; repeat from *, ending the last repeat with k. 1 instead of k. 2.

Work 10 rows more in the same rib. When making the sleeves note that 6 rows only are worked here.

109th row: P. 1, * k. 1, k. 2 tog., p. 2; repeat from *, ending the last repeat with p. 1 instead of p. 2.

110th row: K. 1, * p. 2, k. 2; repeat from * until 1 remains, k. 1.

Work 10 more rows in the same rib (6 rows only when working the sleeve).

121st row: P. 1, k. 2, * p. 2 tog., k. 2; repeat from * until 1 remains, p. 1.

122nd row: K. 1, * p. 2, k. 1; repeat from * to end.

Work 7 rows more in the same rib.

Cast off, and at the same time work together every 2nd and 3rd st.

The Back

THIS is worked the same as the front until the 97th row has been worked with 80 sts. Work 5 rows more. Now divide the sts. for the back opening, leaving 40 sts. on the working pin, and the remaining sts. on an odd length of wool for the present.

The Half Backs.—Work 6 rows more in the same rib on the 40 working pin sts. Then work from the 109th to the 122nd row. Work 17 rows straight in rib as now set. Cast off, working tog. every 2nd and 3rd st.

Join the wool to the back neck edge of the spare pin sts. and work in the same manner.

The Sleeves

WITH No. 11 pins cast on 73 sts. for the arm edge, and work 16 rows in rib as on the front waist-band. Work the wide ribs exactly as given for the jumper, beginning with the 1st row and finishing with the 26th row, when there will be 85 sts. on the pins.

Continue in pattern as follows:

27th row: In rib as now set, increasing at each end of the row (87 sts.).

28th row: K. 1, p. 6, k. 2, p. 6, * k. 3, p. 6; repeat from * until 9 remain, k. 2, p. 6, k. 1.

29th row: Inc. at each end (89 sts.).

30th row: (K. 2, p. 6) twice, * k. 3, p. 6; repeat from * until 10 remain, k. 2, p. 6, k. 2.

31st row: In same rib, increasing at each end (91 sts.).

32nd row: P. 1, (k. 2, p. 6) twice, * k. 3, p. 6; repeat from * until 11 remain, k. 2, p. 6, k. 2, p. 1.

Work 2 sts. tog. at each end of the next row, then work 1 row.

Repeat the last 2 rows once more (87 sts.).

37th row: (right side facing) P. 1, k. 6, p. 2, k. 6, * p 1, p. 2 tog., k. 6; repeat from * until 9 remain, p. 2, k. 6, p. 1 (80 sts.).

38th row: K. 1, p. 6, * k. 2, p. 6; repeat from * until 1 remains, k. 1.

Work 10 rows more in the same rib.

Work as on the front from the 73rd to the 122nd row inclusive, but take special note of the instructions in brackets, where the number of rows is altered for the sleeves.

Cast off, working tog. every 2nd and 3rd st.

Work a second sleeve in the same manner.

THE BUTTON-BAND: With No. 11 pins pick up and k. 30 sts. from the row ends of the right back opening (3 sts. from every 4 rows). K. 4 rows straight, and cast off loosely.

THE BUTTONHOLE BAND: With No. 11 pins, and beginning at the lower edge, of the left side, pick up and k. 11, cast on 3, miss 4 rows pick up and k. 12, cast on 3, miss 4 sts. from row ends, k. 1 (30 sts.).

K. 4 rows and cast off loosely.

The Neck Edge

SEW the raglan sleeves to back and front of jumper. With No. 11 pins and right side facing pick up and k. 108 sts. from all round the neck edge. K. 7 rows.

** On the first 9 sts. k 2 rows. Continue on the same sts., working tog. the 2nd and 3rd st. from each end of next row and following alternate row. K. 1 row.

Next row: K. 1, k. 3 tog., k. 1. K. 1 row, k. 3 tog., and fasten off.

Repeat from ** for 11 times more. Darn in all ends.

TO MAKE UP THE JUMPER.—First press all pieces with a hot iron and a damp cloth over the wrong side of the work. Join the sleeve and side seams and press. Stitch two buttons to the right half back opposite the button-holes.

A back-view of the jumper

A BEWITCHING PETAL-COLLAR

*Flower-Like and Youthful
—A Jumper You Will
Love to Wear*

Materials

Four ounces of W.B. Rosedale 2-ply Fingering in medium shade, and 1 ounce of the same wool in white ; a pair of " Aero " knitting pins No. 8 and a set of four No..11 " Aero " pins ; an " Aero " stitch-holder which keeps the sts. secure with a spring and cap over the pin.

Tension and Measurements

Worked at a tension of 7 sts. to the inch in width on No 8 pins, the following measurements are attained after light pressing : round the bust 37 inches ; front length from shoulder seam to lower edge, 19 inches ; back length, 18 inches ; side seams, 13 inches ; sleeve seam, 19 inches.

* * *

Abbreviations

K., *knit* ; p., *purl* ; st., *stitch* ; tog., *together* ; inc., *increase (by working into the back and front of the same st.)* ; *to* "pick up 1" *is to work knitwise into the thread that lies horizontally between the 2 sts. on the previous row* ; rib. *is k. 2 and p. 2, alternately. Directions in brackets are worked the number of times stated immediately after the brackets.*

To Work the Back : With No. 11 pins and medium wool cast on 112 sts. and work in rib as follows :

1st row : (Right side facing) P. 1, k. 2, * p. 2, k. 2 ; repeat from * until 1 remains, p. 1.

2nd row : K. 1, p. 2, * k. 2, p. 2 ; repeat from * until 1 remains, k. 1.

Repeat these 2 rows until 36 rows have been worked.

Increase row : (Right side facing) Inc., k. 5, inc., (k. 6, inc.) 15 times (129 sts. now on).

Change to No. 8 pins and p. one row, then work in pattern as follows :

1st row : (Right side facing) P. 2 tog., pick up 1, k. 5, * pick up 1, p. 3 tog., pick up 1, k. 5 ; repeat from * until 2 remain, pick up 1, p. 2 tog.

2nd row (and every even-numbered row) : (Wrong side facing) All purl.

3rd row : As 1st row.

5th and 7th rows : K. 3, * pick up 1, p. 3 tog., pick up 1, k. 5 ; repeat from * ending the last repeat with k. 3 instead of k. 5.

8th row : All purl.

Repeat these 8 rows for 9 times more to armholes.

Part of the pretty fancy-stitch shown in detail.

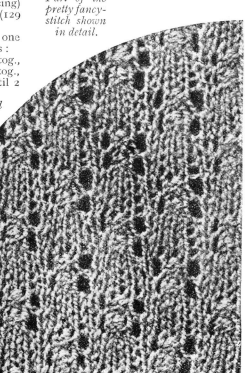

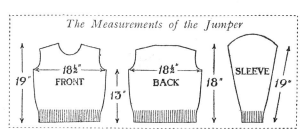

The Measurements of the Jumper

19" 18½" FRONT 13" 18½" BACK 18" SLEEVE 19"

Knit it in any pretty shade

To Shape the Armholes: 1st row: (Right side facing) K. 2 tog., k. 5, * pick up 1, p. 3 tog., pick up 1, k. 5; repeat from * until 2 remain, k. 2 tog.

2nd (*and every even-numbered row*): P. 2 tog., p. until 2 remain, p. 2 tog.
3rd row: K. 2 tog., k. 3, pick up 1, p. 3 tog., pick up 1, * k. 5, pick up 1,

p. 3 tog., pick up 1 ; repeat from * until 5 remain, K.3, K.2., tog.

A BEWITCHING PETAL COLLAR

4th row : As 2nd row.

Repeat these 4 rows 3 times more, then the 1st and 2nd rows again, when 93 sts. will remain.

Next row: (Right side facing) K. 5, * pick up 1, p. 3 tog., pick up 1, k. 5 ; repeat from * to end.

Next row : All purl.

Now continue in pattern as follows : purling every wrong side row.

1st and 3rd rows : K. 1, * pick up 1, p. 3 tog., pick up 1, k. 5 ; repeat from *, ending the last repeat with k. 1.

5th and 7th rows : K. 5, * pick up 1, p. 3 tog., pick up 1, k. 5 ; repeat from * to end.

8th row : All purl.

Repeat these 8 rows 3 times more, then 4 rows more to shoulders.

To Slope the Shoulders : Continue in same pattern, casting off 6 sts. at the beginning of each of the next 8 rows, then cast off the remaining sts.

THE FRONT.—This is worked exactly the same as the back until the 8th straight pattern row has been worked after the armhole decreases are finished.

Repeat these 8 rows once more, then 7 rows more to neck.

To Shape the Neck : Next row : (Wrong side facing) P. 43 and pass these sts. on to the stitch-holder until needed for the right shoulder, cast off 7 sts. (1 st. on pin), p. to end (43 sts. for Left Front Shoulder).

THE LEFT FRONT SHOULDER.—Continue in pattern as follows.

1st row : K. 1, * pick up 1, p. 3 tog., pick up 1, k. 5 ; repeat from * until 2 remain, k. 2 tog. (neck end).

2nd row (and every wrong side row) : P. 2 tog., p. to end.

3rd row : K. 1, * pick up 1, p. 3 tog., pick up 1, k. 5 ; repeat from *, ending the last repeat with k. 3, k. 2 tog. (neck end).

5th row : * K. 5, pick up 1, p. 3 tog., pick up 1 ; repeat from * until 7 remain, k. 5, k. 2 tog. (neck end).

7th row : * K. 5, pick up 1, p. 3 tog., pick up 1 ; repeat from * until 5 remain, k. 3, k. 2 tog.

8th row : P. 2 tog., p. to end.

Repeat the 1st to the 5th row when 30 sts. will remain.

Work 11 rows straight in pattern, as on back shoulders, beginning with the 6th row, but note that there will be 1 st. extra to pattern at the neck end.

To Slope the Shoulder : Continue in pattern casting off 6 sts. at the beginning of next row and every following alternate row (armhole end) until all are worked off.

THE RIGHT FRONT SHOULDER.—Join the wool to neck end of Right Front sts. and work in pattern as follows :

1st row : K. 2 tog., * k. 5, pick up 1, p. 3 tog., pick up 1 ; repeat from * until 1 remains, k. 1.

2nd row (and every even-numbered row) : (Wrong side facing) P until 2 remain, p. 2 tog. (neck end).

3rd row : K. 2 tog., k. 3, pick up 1, p. 3 tog., pick up 1, * k. 5, pick up 1, p. 3 tog., pick up 1, repeat from * until 1 remains, k. 1.

5th row : K. 2 tog., k. 5, * pick up 1, p. 3 tog., pick up 1, k. 5 ; repeat from * to end.

7th row : K. 2 tog., k. 3, * pick up 1, p. 3 tog., pick up 1, k. 5 ; repeat from * to end.

8th row : As 2nd row.

Repeat from the 1st to the 5th of these rows, when 30 sts. will remain.

Now work 12 rows straight in pattern, beginning with the 6th row of back shoulder pattern, but note that there will be 1 st. extra in pattern at the neck end of every row.

To Slope the Shoulder : Continue in pattern, casting off 6 sts. at the beginning of next row and every following alternate row until all are worked off.

THE SLEEVES.—With medium wool and No. 8 pins cast on 23 sts. and purl 1 row.

Continue in increase pattern as follows :

1st row : (Right side facing) Inc., k. 1, pick up 1, p. 3 tog., pick up 1, * k. 5, pick up 1, p. 3 tog., pick up 1 ; repeat from * until 2 remain, k. 1, inc.

2nd row (and every wrong side row) : Inc., p. until 1 remains, inc.

3rd row : Inc., k. 3, pick up 1, p. 3 tog., pick up 1, * k. 5, pick up 1, p. 3 tog., pick up 1 ; repeat from * until 4 remain, k. 3, inc.

4th row : As 2nd row.

Repeat these 4 rows until there are 87 sts. on the row ending with the 4th row.

Now work in pattern as follows :

1st row : K. 2, * pick up 1, p. 3 tog., pick up 1, k. 5, repeat from * until 2 remain, k. 2.

2nd row (and every even-numbered row) : All purl.

3rd row : As 1st row, ending the last repeat with k. 2.

5th and 7th rows : As 1st row, beginning and ending with k. 6.

8th row and every following 8th row : (Wrong side facing) P. 2 tog., p. until 2 remain, p. 2 tog.

9th and 11th rows : As 1st row, beginning and ending with k. 1.

13th and 15th rows : As 1st row, beginning and ending with k. 5.

17th and 19th rows : As 1st row, beginning and ending with k. 8.

21st and 23rd rows : As 1st row, beginning and ending with k. 4.

25th and 27th rows : As 1st row, beginning and ending with k. 7.

29th and 31st rows : As 1st row, beginning and ending with k. 3.

33rd and 35th rows : As 1st row, beginning and ending with k. 6.

37th and 39th rows : As 1st row, beginning and ending with k. 2.

41st and 43rd rows : As 1st row, beginning and ending with k. 5.

45th and 47th rows : As 1st row, beginning and ending with k. 1.

49th and 51st rows : As 1st row, beginning and ending with k. 4.

53rd and 55th rows : As 1st row, beginning and ending with k. 8.

57th and 59th rows : As 1st row, beginning and ending with k. 3.

61st and 63rd rows : As 1st row, beginning and ending with k. 7.

64th row : P. 2 tog., p. until 2 remain, p. 2 tog.

Repeat these 64 rows once more when 55 sts. will remain, then work from the 1st to the 7th row again.

Next row : (Wrong side facing) Change to No. 11 pins and work as follows : P. 13, (p. 2 tog., p. 12) 3 times (52 sts.).

Work 32 rows in rib as at waist and cast off. Work a second sleeve in the same manner.

THE NECK EDGE.—Join the back and front shoulders, beginning at the armhole end and taking 1 st. from each side at a time. Press these seams.

Using a set of four No. 11 pins pick up and knit 120 sts. from all round the neck edge (40 sts. on each of three pins). Work 2 rows in single rib. Leave these sts. on the pins and work the petals as follows :

THE PETALS.—Slip a No. 11 pin through the 1st 15 neck sts. and work in pattern as follows, using two balls of white wool and one of medium.

1st row : (Wrong side of jumper facing) K. 4 white, twist the white wool over the medium and with medium wool increase, k. 5, inc. With the second ball of white wool twist the medium over the white and k. 4, white (17 sts.).

2nd row : K. 4 white, p. 9 medium, k. 4 white.

3rd row : K. 4 white, with medium wool k. 3, pick up 1, p. 3 tog., pick up 1, k. 3, k. 4 white.

Repeat the 2nd and 3rd row, until 20 rows have been worked altogether.

21st row : K. 4 white ; with medium wool k. 3, k. 3 tog., k. 3 ; k. 4 white.

Next 3 rows : K. 4 white, s.s. 7 medium, k. 4 white.

25th row : K. 4 white ; k. 2, k. 3 tog., k. 2 medium, k. 4 white.

Next 3 rows : K. 4 white, s.s. 5 medium, k. 4 white.

29th row : K. 4 white ; with medium wool, k. 1, k. 3 tog., k. 1 ; k. 4 white.

Next 3 rows : K. 4 white ; s.s. 3 medium, k. 4 white.

33rd row : K. 4 white ; with medium wool, k. 3 tog., k. 4 white.

34th row : K. 4 white ; p. 1 medium, k. 4 white. Fasten off the medium.

Next 2 rows : All knit in white wool.

37th row : K. 3, k. 3 tog., k. 3. Knit 3 rows.

41st row : K. 2, k. 3 tog., k. 2. Knit 1 row.

43rd row : K. 1, k. 3 tog., k. 1. Knit 1 row.

Knit 3 tog. Draw wool through and fasten off.

Work 7 petals more in the same way, when all the neck band sts. will be used.

Make up the jumper in the usual way.

✻   ✻   ✻

The little turn-down collar is very youthful.

Frilly Sleeves

**A Pretty Jumper
In An Easy Stitch**

MATERIALS

NINE ounces of Golden Eagle "Suede"; a pair each
of No. 9 and No. 13 "Aero" knitting pins. One
button.

TENSION AND MEASUREMENTS

WORKED at a tension of 7 sts. to the inch in width on No. 9
pins, the following measurements are attained after
light pressing: Round the bust, 35 inches; front
length from shoulder seam to lower edge, 20 inches; back length,
18½ inches; side seam, 15 inches; sleeve seam 13 inches.

Beginners are advised to cast on 22 sts. and work the
first 4 rows of the back pattern until they are familiar with it
when the rest will be easy.

THE BACK

WITH No. 13 pins cast on 100 sts. and work 30 rows in
single rib.
INCREASE ROW: * rib 4, inc., repeat from * to end.
(120 sts.)
NEXT ROW: Inc. in the first st., p. until 1 remains, inc.
(122 sts.)
Change to No. 9 pins and work in pattern as follows:
1ST ROW: K. 1, * m. 1, sl. 1, k. 3, p.s.s.o. the 3 k. sts.,
repeat from * until 1 remains, k. 1.

A photograph of the actual stitch.

2ND ROW: All p.
3RD ROW: K. 3, * m. 1, sl. 1, k. 3, p.s.s.o., repeat from *
until 3 remain, k. 3.
4TH ROW: All p.
These 4 rows comprise one pattern.
Repeat the 4 pattern rows 23 times more to armhole.
(24 patterns above the waist rib.)
TO SHAPE THE ARMHOLES.—1ST ROW: Cast off 5 (1 st. on

pin), k. 3, * m. 1, sl. 1, k. 3, p.s.s.o., repeat from * until 1 remains, k. 1.

2ND ROW: Cast off 5 sts., p. to end.

3RD ROW: K. 2 tog., (1 st. on pin), * m. 1, sl. 1, k. 3, p.s.s.o., repeat from * until 2 remain, k. 2 tog.

4TH ROW: P. 2 tog., p. until 2 remain, p. 2 tog.

Repeat the 3rd and 4th row twice more when 102 sts. will remain.

Continue straight on these sts. for 42 rows more.

Cast off straight across.

THE FRONT

WORK exactly the same as the back until the armhole shaping is finished and 102 sts. remain.

Continue straight

The shape and measurements of the jumper.

on these sts. for 4 rows more. On the next row the sts. are divided for the neck opening as follows: Work 51 sts., turn, and leave the remaining 51 sts. on a spare pin until needed for the Right Front Shoulder.

THE LEFT FRONT SHOULDER.—Continue straight on the remaining 51 sts. for 16 rows more to neck.

To SHAPE THE NECK.—Cast off 5 sts. at the neck end of the next row and work in pattern to end.

Continue in pattern, taking 2 sts. tog. at the neck end of every row until the sts. are reduced to 36.

Work 12 rows more on these sts. then cast off straight across.

THE RIGHT FRONT SHOULDER.—Join the wool to the neck end of the spare pin sts. and work exactly the same as the Left Front Shoulder.

THE SLEEVES

BEGIN at the top by casting on 14 sts. and k. one row into the back of the sts., then begin the pattern.

1ST ROW: K. into the front and back of the 1st. to inc. 1, * m. 1, sl. 1, k. 3, p.s.s.o. the 3 k. sts., repeat from * until 1 st. remains, inc. in that st. as at the beginning of the row.

2ND ROW: Inc. in the 1st st. by knitting in the front and purling into the back of the st., p. until 1 st. remains, p. in the front of that st. and k. into the back.

3RD ROW: Inc. into the 1st st., * m. 1, sl. 1, k. 3, p.s.s.o. the 3 k. sts., and repeat from * until 1 st. remains, inc. into that st.

4TH ROW: Inc. into the 1st st., p. until 1 st. remains, inc.

Repeat these 4 rows until there are 82 sts. altogether, which will end with the 2nd row of the pattern.

Work 14 rows more in the lattice pattern for the top part of the sleeve.

(Those who would like a short sleeve can now work a ribbed arm band in single rib with the No. 13 pins.)

To continue the long sleeves:

NEXT ROW: K. into the front and back of every st., making 164 altogether.

NEXT ROW: All p.

Now begin the open pattern on the puffs.

1ST ROW: * k. 1, m. 1, repeat from * until 1 st. remains, k. 1.

2ND ROW: K. 1, drop the made st. over the point of the left-hand pin, repeat from * until 1 st. remains, k. 1. K. 2 rows plain.

These 4 rows form the puff pattern, so repeat them 17 times more, then repeat the first 2 rows again.

NEXT ROW: K. 2 sts. tog. along the whole row when there will again be 82 sts.

NEXT ROW: K. 3, then k. 2 tog. until 3 sts. remain, k. 3 (44 sts. now on).

Change to No. 13 pins and work 24 rows of single rib for a double wristband, but if a single one be preferred, work only 12 rows. Cast off loosely.

Work a second sleeve in the same manner.

THE COLLAR

WITH No. 13 pins cast on 120 sts. and work as follows:

1ST ROW: K. 6, work single rib until 6 sts. remain, k. 6.

Repeat this row 5 times more.

NEXT ROW: K. 6, work m.s. until 6 sts. remain, k. 6.

Repeat the last row 43 times more.

K. 8 rows plain and cast off loosely.

TO MAKE UP THE JUMPER

FIRST press all pieces with a hot iron over a damp cloth on the wrong side of the work. Join the shoulder seams, beginning at the armhole edge and taking 1 st. from each side at a time, and sew the top of the sleeves to the armholes. Join the collar to the neck edge on the right side of the jumper and press all these seams while the work is open. Turn up the ribbed cuff to form a double band and sew the edge in position on the wrong side of the sleeve. Join the sleeve and side seams in one long line and press. Work a row of double crochet all round the slit at the front of the neck. Sew a button to the left front and make a button loop of crochet chain on the right front.

To wear about the house, this becoming peasant-sleeved jumper — knitted mainly in moss-stitch and stocking-stitch.

Peasant-Sleeved Jumper

Materials.—4 oz. Carter and Parker's 3-ply Wendy Wool, navy; 3 oz. same wool light blue; a pair each of No. 8 and No. 13 "Stratnoid" knitting pins; one button.

Measurements.—Length to top of shoulder, 18 in.; length of sleeve along seam, 22 in.; width all round under arms, 38 in. (To fit a 34 in. bust).

Abbreviations.—Sts., stitches; k., knit; p., purl; tog., together; rep., repeat; rem., remain (-s, -ing, -der); inc., increase (-ing); dec., decrease (-ing).

For Moss-st., k. 1, p. 1 alternately, working second row so that the k. st. comes over p. st. in previous row, and p. st. over k.

THE BACK.—With No. 13 needles cast on 100 sts. in light blue wool, and work in a k. 1, p. 1 rib. for 3 inches. *Next row.*—Inc. to 120 sts. by knitting into the front and back of every 5th st.

Now change to No. 8 needles and work 48 rows in moss-st.

Cast off 5 sts. at the beginning of each of the next 8 rows, then k. 2 tog. at both ends of every row, until 20 sts. rem. Work 3 rows without further alteration, then inc. 1 st. at both ends of every row until there are 90 sts.

Work 1 more row. Cast off.

THE FRONT.—Work as back, until 20 sts. rem. Work one more row on these 20 sts. *Next row.*—Moss-st. for 10 sts., turn the piece.

Leave the rem. 10 sts. on a spare needle for the present, and work the left side thus : Cast on 5 sts. (for the under-lap) and work into the backs of these, then moss-st. to end of row.

Next row.—Inc. one st. into first st., moss-st. rem. of row. *Following row.*—Moss-st. until 1 st. rem., inc. one st. into last st. Rep. the last 2 rows until there are 27 sts. then :—

SHAPE NECK.—Thus : cast off 10 sts., moss-st. until 1 st. rem., inc. 1 st. into last st.

Next row.—Inc. 1 st. into first st., moss-st. until

2 sts. rem., k. 2 tog. *Following row*—K. 2 tog., moss-st. until 1 st. rem., inc. one st. into last st.

Rep. the last 2 rows until 23 sts. rem., then—keeping the neck edge straight—continue to inc. on the outer edge every row, until there are 28 sts. Work 12 more rows without further alteration. Cast off.

The Right Side.—Pick up the 10 sts. from spare needle (point of No. 8 needle held towards centre of work), join in the wool and work 2 rows without alteration. *Next row*—Work moss-st. until 1 st. rem., inc. one st. into last st. *Following row*—Inc. one st. into first st., moss-st. to end.

Rep. the last 2 rows until there are 28 sts.

Next row—Cast off 5 sts., moss-st. until 1 st. rem., inc. one st. into last st. *Following row*—Inc. one st. into first st., moss-st. until 2 sts. rem., k. 2 tog. *Next row*—K. 2 tog., moss-st. until 1 st. rem., inc. one st. into last st.

Rep. the last 2 rows until 23 sts. rem., then—keeping the neck edge straight—continue to inc. one st. on the outer edge every row until there are 28 sts. Work 12 more rows without further alteration. Cast off.

The Side Panels.—With No. 8 needles cast on 5 sts. in navy wool, then :—*Row 1*—All k. *Row 2*—All p. *Row 3*—All k. *Row 4*—Cast on 5 sts., work into the backs of these, p. rem.

Rep. rows 3 and 4 twice (8 rows in all). *Row 9*—All k., but inc. one st. into last st. *Row 10*—Inc. 1 st. into first st., p. rem. Rep. the last 2 rows until there are 42 sts. on needle, then :—

Shape arm-hole.—*Row 1* (with right side of work towards you). Cast off 3 sts., all k. until 1 st. rem., inc. one st. into last st. *Row 2*—Inc. 1 st. into first st., all p. to end. Rep. these 2 rows twice, then :—

Row 7—K. 2 tog., all k. until 1 st. rem., inc. one st. into last st. *Row 8*—Inc. one st. into first st., all p. to end. *Row 9*—K. 2 tog., all k. to end. *Row 10*—All p. *Row 11*—As Row 9. *Row 12*—K. 2 tog., p. to end. *Row 13*—K. 2 tog., k. until 2 sts. rem., k. 2 tog. *Row 14*—K. 2 tog., p. to end. Rep. rows 13 and 14 twice, then :—*Next row*—All k., k. tog. the last 2 sts. *Following row*—K. 2 tog., p. to end. Rep. the last 2 rows until 1 st. rem. Fasten off.

Work a second similar piece in precisely the same way. Work two more similar pieces, but reverse the inc. and dec. (4 pieces in all.)

The Sleeves (*Two alike*).—Commence at the top end of sleeve. With No. 8 needles cast on 10 sts. in navy wool, and work in stocking-st. (k. 1 row, p. 1 row alternately), but inc. one st. at both ends of every row until there are 78 sts.

Work 4 more rows without further inc., then k. 2 tog. at both ends of the next row, and likewise every following 10th row, until 58 sts. rem.

Work 8 more rows, then :—

Next row—K. 3, then inc. one st. into every st. until 3 sts. rem., k. 3 (110 sts.).

Now proceed to work : * 10 rows in garter-st. (all k.), then 8 rows in stocking-st. Rep. from * twice more (three times in all). Next row—K. 2 tog. for the entire row (55 sts.).

Now change over to No. 13 needles, and work in a k. 1, p. 1 rib for 24 rows. Cast off loosely.

If a straight, narrow sleeve is preferred, continue to k. 2 tog. at both ends of every 10th row, until the sleeve seam measures 15 ins., then change to No. 13 needles and work in single rib for 3 ins. Cast off.

The Collar.—With No. 8 needles cast on 120 sts. in light blue wool, and work in single rib for 2 ins. Cast off.

The Cord.—Take 8 strands of the navy wool, each about 4 yards long, then twist tightly (either fasten one set of ends to some fixed object, or get someone to hold them). When well twisted, slip the loop of a large key or similar weight over one set of ends, keeping the cord taut, slide the weight to centre of cord, bring the two sets of ends together and allow the weight to twirl one half of the cord around the other. When the weight has ceased twirling cut off, and secure the ends with a knot, allowing a short length to unravel and form a tassel at each end.

To Make-up.—Neatly sew in the side panels to front and back, and sew tops of sleeves into arm-holes, then carefully press open the work under a damp cloth with a warm iron. Work a row of double-crochet round the edges of front-opening, working a loop at the top of right front. Sew up side and sleeve seams in one operation. Sew the collar double round neck edge, and pass the cord through. Sew a button on top corner of left front opening, and press all seams.

A Well fitting Jumper

A close rib and openwork diagonal stripes are combined in this pretty and practical short-sleeved jumper

Materials : 3 oz. Briggs's 3-ply Rosedale fingering in brown, same amount in green. 1 pair No. 10 needles. 1 pair No. 11. **Measurements :** Length from top of shoulders, 19 in. Will fit a figure with a bust measurement of 32 to 34 in. **Tension:** 7 stitches to an inch on No. 10 needles. **Abbreviations :** K., knit ; p., purl ; m.s.k.p.o., make 1, slip 1, knit 1, pass the slipped stitch over ; dec., decreasing ; tog , together.

The Front.—Cast on 96 sts. with brown wool and No. 10 needles. Work in ribbing of k. 2, p. 2 for 44 rows, working the first row into the back of each st. to get a firm edge. Change to No. 11 needles, continue in ribbing for another 44 rows. Now change again to No. 10 needles and increase 1 at both ends of every 10th row until there are 104 stitches on. These 128 rows altogether will measure about 11 in. Now begin in green and brown on the right side of work. (The ribbing is all brown and the pattern all green.) **Row 1 :** Green, k. 6, wool forward to make 1, slip 1, k. 1, pass the slipped stitch over the knitted one (in future this will be referred to as m.s.k.p.o.), k. 4. Change to brown, twisting colours together to avoid

a gap, rib 80. Join on another length of green, k. 12. **Row 2 :** P. 7, make 1 by putting wool right round needle, p. 2 tog., p. 4, rib 78, p. 13. **Row 3 :** K. 7, m.s.k.p.o., k. 5, rib 76, k. 14. **Row 4 :** P. 8, m. 1, p. 2 tog., p. 5, rib 74, p. 15. **Row 5 :** K. 8, m.s.k.p.o., k. 6, rib 72, k. 16. **Row 6 :** P. 9, m. 1, p. 2 tog., p. 6, rib 70, p. 17. **Row 7 :** K. 9, m.s.k.p.o., k. 7, rib 68, k. 18. **Row 8 :** P. 10, m. 1, p. 2 tog., p. 7, rib 66, p. 19. **Row 9 :** K. 10, m.s.k.p.o., k. 8, rib 64, k. 20. **Row 10 :** P. 11, m. 1, p. 2 tog., p. 8, rib 62, p. 21. **Armhole** (right side) : Cast off 5, k. 6, m.s.k.p.o., k. 6, m.s.k.p.o., k. 1, rib 60, k. 22. **Next row :** Cast off 5, p. 7, m. 1, p. 2 tog., p. 6, m. 1, p. 2 tog., p. 1, rib 58, p. 18. **Next row :** Cast off 4, k. 3, m.s.k.p.o., k. 6, m.s.k.p.o., k. 2, rib 56, k. 19. **Next row :** Cast off 4, p. 4, m. 1, p. 2 tog., p. 6, m. 1, p. 2 tog., p. 2, rib 54, p. 16. Now continue, but keep the side edges straight thus, **Row 1 :** K. 4, m.s.k.p.o., k. 6, m.s.k.p.o., k. 3, rib 52, k. 17. **Row 2 :** P. 5, m. 1, p. 2 tog., p. 6, m. 1, p. 2 tog., p. 3, rib 50, p. 18. **Row 3 :** K. 5, m.s.k.p.o., k. 6, m.s.k.p.o., k. 4, rib 48, k. 19. **Row 4 :** P. 6, m. 1, p. 2 tog., p. 6, m. 1, p. 2 tog., p. 4, rib 46, p. 20. **Row 5 :** K. 6, m.s.k.p.o., k. 6, m.s.k.p.o., k. 5, rib 44, k. 21. **Row 6 :** P. 7, m. 1, p. 2 tog., p. 6, m. 1, p. 2 tog., p. 5, rib 42, p. 22. **Row 7 :** K. 7, m.s.k.p.o., k. 6, m.s.k.p.o., k. 6, rib 40, k. 23. **Row 8 :** P. 8, m. 1, p. 2 tog., p. 6, m. 1, p. 2 tog., p. 6, rib 38, p. 24. **Row 9 :** K. 8, m.s.k.p.o., k. 6, m.s.k.p.o., k. 7, rib 36, k. 25. **Row 10 :** P. 9, m. 1, p. 2 tog., p. 6, m. 1, p. 2 tog., p. 7, rib 34, p. 26. **Row 11 :** K. 1, m.s.k.p.o., k. 6, m.s.k.p.o., k. 6, m.s.k.p.o., k. 8, rib 32, k. 27. **Row 12 :** P. 2, m. 1, p. 2 tog., p. 6, m. 1, p. 2 tog., p. 6, m. 1, p. 2 tog., p. 8, rib 30, p. 28. **Row 13 :** K. 2, m.s.k.p.o., k. 6, m.s.k.p.o., k. 6, m.s.k.p.o., k. 6, m.s.k.p.o., k. 1, rib 28, k. 29. **Row 14 :** P. 3, m. 1, p. 2 tog., p. 6, m. 1, p. 2 tog., p. 6, m. 1, p. 2 tog., p. 1, rib 26, p. 30. **Row 15 :** K. 3, m.s.k.p.o., k. 6, m.s.k.p.o., k. 6, m.s.k.p.o., k. 2, rib 24, k. 31. **Row 16 :** P. 4, m. 1,

p. 2 tog., p. 6, m. 1, p. 2 tog., p. 6, m. 1, p. 2 tog., p. 6, m. 1, p. 2 tog., p. 2, rib 22, p. 32. **Row 17 :** K. 4, m.s.k.p.o., k. 6, m.s.k.p.o., k. 6, m.s.k.p.o., k. 6, m.s.k.p.o., k. 3, rib 20, k. 33. **Row 18 :** P. 5, m. 1, p. 2 tog., p. 6, m. 1, p. 2 tog., p. 6, m. 1, p. 2 tog., p. 6, m. 1, p. 2 tog., p. 3, rib 18, p. 34. **Row 19 :** K. 5, * m.s.k.p.o., k. 6. Repeat from * twice, then m.s.k.p.o., k. 4, rib 16, k. 35. **Row 20 :** P. 6, m. 1, p. 2 tog., p. 6, m. 1, p. 2 tog., p. 6, m. 1, p. 2 tog., p. 6, m. 1, p. 2 tog., p. 4, rib 14, p. 36. **Row 21 :** K. 6, * m.s.k.p.o., k. 6. Repeat from * twice, m.s.k.p.o., k. 5, rib 12, k. 37. **Row 22 :** P. 7, * m. 1, p. 2 tog., p. 6. Repeat from * twice, m. 1, p. 2 tog., p. 5, rib 10, p. 38. **Row 23 :** K. 7, * m.s.k.p.o., k. 6. Repeat from * 3 times, rib 8, k. 39 **Row 24 :** P. 18, * m. 1, p. 2 tog., p. 6. Repeat from * 3 times, rib 6, p. 40. **Row 25 :** K. 8, * m.s.k.p.o., k. 6. Repeat from * twice, then m.s.k.p.o., k. 7, rib 4, k. 41. **Row 26 :** P. 9, * m. 1, p. 2 tog., p. 6. Repeat from * twice, then m. 1, p. 2 tog., p. 7, rib 2, p. 42. **Row 27 :** K. 1, * m.s.k.p.o., k. 6. Repeat from * 3 times, m.s.k.p.o., k. 8, to centre. Continue to the end in green, breaking off brown and joining the end of brown securely (86 stitches on). **Row 28 :** P. 2, * m. 1, p. 2 tog., p. 6. Repeat from * 3 times, m. 1, p. 2 tog., p. to the end of row. **Row 29 :** K. 2, * m.s.k.p.o., k. 6. Repeat from * 3 times, m.s.k.p.o., k. to end. **Row 30 :** P. 3, * m. 1, p. 2 tog., p. 6. Repeat from * 3 times, m. 1, p. 2 tog., p. to the end of row. **Row 31 :** K. 3, * m.s.k.p.o., k. 6. Repeat from * 3 times, m.s.k.p.o., k. to end. **Row 32 :** P. 4, * m. 1, p. 2 tog., p. 6. Repeat from * 3 times, m. 1, p. 2 tog., p. to the end. **Row 33 :** K. 4, * m.s.k.p.o., k. 6. Repeat from * 3 times, m.s.k.p.o., k. to end. **Row 34 :** P. 5, * m. 1, p. 2 tog., p. 6. Repeat from * 3 times, then m. 1, p. 2 tog., p. to the end. **Row 35 :** K. 5, * m.s.k.p.o., k. 6. Repeat from * 3 times, then m.s.k.p.o., k. to end of row. **Row 36 :** P. 6, * m. 1, p. 2 tog., p. 6. Repeat from * 3 times, then m. 1, p. 2 tog., p. to the end. **Row 37** (neck) : K. 6, * m.s.k.p.o., k. 6. Repeat from * twice, then m.s.k.p.o., k. 3, p. 16, k. 35 to the end. **Row 38 :** P. 7, * m. 1, p. 2 tog., p. 6. Repeat from * twice, then m. 1, k. 2 tog., k. 2. Cast off 16, k. 3, p. to end (35 stitches on each half). Now work up both shoulders at the same time, decreasing 6 sts. on each side, and keeping the 3 edge sts. in garter stitch thus : **Row 1** (shoulder) : K. 7, m.s.k.p.o., k. 6, m.s.k.p.o., k. 6, m.s.k.p.o., k. 6, m.s.k.p.o., k. 2. Join on another length of wool and knit plain across the other set of stitches. **Row 2 :** P. 8, * m. 1, p. 2 tog., p. 6. Repeat from * twice, m. 1, k. 2 tog., k. 1. Continue across, k. 3, p. to the end. **Row 3 :** K. 8, * m.s.k.p.o., k. 6. Repeat from * twice, ending the row k. 3. Continue across the other set all knit. **Row 4 :** P. 9, * m. 1, p. 2 tog., p. 6. Repeat from *

Continued

once, then m. 1, p. 2 tog., p. 5, k. 3 at the end of the row. Continue across, k. 3, p. to end. **Row 5 :** K. 1, * m.s.k.p.o., k. 6. Repeat from * twice, then m.s.k.p.o., k. 8. K. right across the other side. **Row 6 :** P. 2, * m. 1, p. 2 tog., p. 6. Repeat from * twice, m. 1, p. 2 tog., p. 4, k. 3. Continue across, k. 3, p. to the end. **Row 7** (1st decreasing) : There is no need to continue giving the pattern in detail as it is so easy to follow, so the rows will be given thus : Work across in pattern until you have 4 open patterns, then k. 2, slip 1, k. 1, pass slipped one over to reduce one, k. 3. Continue across, k. 3, k. 2 tog., k. to end. **Row 8 :** P. in pattern for 4 open stripes, ending p. 2, k. 3. Continue across, k. 3, p. to end. **Row 9** (2nd decreasing) : Work 4 open patterns across, ending slip 1, k. 1, pass the slipped stitch over, k. 3. Continue across, k. 3, k. 2 tog., k. to end. **Row 10 :** P. in pattern 3 open stripes, then p. 8, k. 3. Continue across, k. 3, p. to the end. **Row 11** (3rd decreasing) : Pattern across, ending k. 6, slip 1, k. 1, pass slipped stitch over, k. 3. Continue across, k. 3, k. 2 tog., k. to end. **Row 12 :** P. in pattern, ending p. 6, k. 3. Continue across, k. 3. p. to end. You have now 32 sts. on each half. Continue working in pattern across both halves on 32 sts. and keeping the 3 in garter stitch at the neck edges. When you have worked another 15 rows, decrease at each neck end as before, just inside the border stitches on knit rows. Work 1 row without decreasing, decrease again, 1 row without, and decrease again, making 29 sts. on each half. Cast off.

The Back.—This is exactly like the front up to the 36th row before the neck, then you continue in pattern until the inner open stripes meet in the centre. Carry on in pattern until the next two inner stripes meet in the centre. After this work in pattern on 29 sts. at each end and garter stitch on centre 28 sts. in every row for 8 rows. Cast off.

Left Sleeve.—Cast on 20 sts. in green wool and No. 10 needles. P. 1 row into the back threads. **Row 1 :** K. 6, m.s.k.p.o., k. 6, m.s.k.p.o., k. 4. **Row 2 :** Cast on 1 st., p. to the end, purling twice into the last stitch. **Row 3 :** K. 8, m.s.k.p.o., k. 6, m.s.k.p.o., k. 4. **Row 4 :** Cast on 1 st., p. to the end, purling twice into last stitch. (All even rows are the same.) **Row 5 :** K. 2, m.s.k.p.o., k. 6, m.s.k.p.o., k. 6, m.s.k.p.o., k. 4. **Row 7 :** K. 4, *m.s.k.p.o., k. 6. Repeat from *, ending m.s.k.p.o., k. 4. One more even row. Repeat the pattern from the 1st row, with extra repeats when necessary, of course, until you have 76 sts. on. Work on 76 sts. for 7 in. and cast off.

Right Sleeve.—Cast on 20 sts. and work a plain row into the back threads. **Row 1 :** P. 6, m. 1, p. 2 tog., p. 6, m. 1, p. 2 tog., p. 4. **Row 2** (and all even rows) : Cast on 1, k. along, knitting twice into the last stitch. This has given you a start, now follow the pattern as for the other sleeve, but purl all odd rows and knit even ones.

Cuffs.—With green wool and No. 11 needles cast on 17 sts. and work garter stitch for 9 in. Cast off. Press and join into a ring.

To make up.—Press all the patterned parts with a hot iron over a damp cloth on the wrong side. Press the ribbing, but lightly. Join the shoulders by a narrow running seam, open out and press well. Join the sleeves into the armholes in the same manner and press well; then join up the sides and underarms. Gather the lower sleeve edges and stitch on the cuffs. Press the seams.

These Pictures Make Good Entertainment

This Week's Films

" LOVE IS NEWS "

Steve Leyton	Tyrone Power
Toni Gateson	Loretta Young
Martin J. Canavan	Don Ameche
Judge Hart	Slim Summerville
Cyrus Jeffrey	Dudley Digges
Eddie Johnson ..	Walter Catlett
Count André de Guyon	George Sanders
Mrs. Flaherty.. ..	Jane Darwell

SHE was an heiress, and enchantingly lovely. He was a newspaper reporter—and she could have liked him if he hadn't brought her hated publicity. However, she very neatly turned the tables and brought *him* a taste of publicity, too !

" TOPPER "

Marion Kerby ..	Constance Bennett
George Kerby	Cary Grant
Cosmo Topper ..	Roland Young
Mrs. Topper	Billie Burke
Wilkins	Alan Mowbray
Casey	Eugene Pallette
Elevator Boy	Arthur Lake
Mrs. Stuyvesant ..	Hedda Hopper

THEY were so gay and crazy a couple that they made exceedingly gay ghosts—and had a quite extraordinary effect upon a staid and pompous business man of their acquaintance. A lot of fantastic fun you will enjoy.

" COMMAND PERFORMANCE "

The Street Singer ..	Arthur Tracy
Susan	Lilli Palmer
Joe	Mark Daly
The Manager	Finlay Currie
The Journalist ..	Jack Melford

HE sang his way to fame and adulation—but had to run away from both to find his heart's happiness, in the peace of the country—and in the beauty of a gipsy girl.

" THERE GOES MY GIRL "

Jerry	Gene Raymond
Connie	Ann Sothern
Whalen	Richard Lane
Bum..	Alec Craig
Actress	Maxine Jennings
Dunn	Gordon Jones
Faraday	Charles Coleman

CYNICS may " gloom " that no one is indispensable—but you won't believe it from this picture, which shows the quite desperate (if flattering !) lengths to which an Editor went to prevent his best girl reporter from marrying a reporter on a rival paper !

SUPPLEMENT of SPECIAL QUICK KNITTING—INSIDE!

WOMAN'S WEEKLY

SEPTEMBER 19, 1936   No. 1,298 Vol. L   EVERY TUESDAY   **2ᵈ**

Quickly Knitted, New and Exciting!

The jumper back is easy to shape.

Made So Quickly!

A Pet Of A Jumper In Easy Knitting

MATERIALS

NINE ounces of Sirdar "Supreme" wool; a pair each of "Aero" knitting pins No. 3 and No. 10. Six buttons.

TENSION AND MEASUREMENTS

WORKED at a tension of 4½ sts. to the inch in width on No. 3 pins, the following measurements are attained after light pressing : across the back at the underarms 18 inches ; across each front at the same place, 10 inches (making a total bust measurement of 36 inches when fastened) ; front length from shoulder seam to lower edge, 21 inches ; back length, 19 inches ; side seam 14 inches ; sleeve seam, 8 inches.

ABBREVIATIONS

K., KNIT ; p., purl ; st., stitch ; tog., together ; inc., increase (by working into the front and back of the same stitch) ; dec., decrease. Directions in brackets are worked the number of times stated after the brackets. Single rib is k. 1 and p. 1 alternately.

TO WORK THE BACK

WITH No. 10 pins cast on 80 sts. and work 30 rows in single rib.
Change to No. 3 pins and work in pattern as follows :
1ST ROW : K. 2, p. 2 ; repeat from * to end.

2ND ROW : All purl.
3RD ROW : K. 3, * p. 2, k. 2 : repeat from * until 1 remains, p. 1.
4TH ROW : All purl.
Repeat these 4 pattern rows 15 times more to armholes (64 rows above the waist rib).
TO SHAPE THE ARMHOLES : Continue in pattern, casting off 3 sts. at the beginning of each of the next 6 rows, then work 2 sts. tog. at the beginning of each of the following 6 rows, when 56 sts. will remain.
Work 28 rows straight on these sts.
Cast off straight across.

THE FRONT

WITH No. 10 pins cast on 80 sts. and work 30 rows in single rib.
Change to No. 3 pins and work as follows :

THE LEFT HALF FRONT

PATTERN 36 sts. as on back, and leave remaining 44 sts. on a stitch-holder until needed for Right Half Front.
NEXT ROW : Cast on 8 sts. and work into the back of these sts., purl to end of row (44 sts. for Left Half Front).

Continue in pattern on these sts., beginning with the 3rd row of back pattern for 62 rows more (64 rows above the waist rib), to armhole.
** TO SHAPE THE ARMHOLE AND NECK.—Cast off 3 sts. at the beginning of the next row and every following alternate row (armhole end) 3 times, then take 2 sts. tog. at the armhole end of every alternate row 3 times, when the armhole shaping will be finished. At the same time slope the neck edge by working 2 sts. tog. at the neck end of every third row until

Full puff sleeves and a V neck-line are most becoming.

1ST BUTTONHOLE ROW: Pattern 6, cast off 2 sts., pattern to end.

2ND BUTTONHOLE ROW: Work in pattern, casting on 2 sts. over those cast off on previous row to complete the buttonhole.

Work 8 rows more in pattern.

Repeat the last 10 rows 4 times more, then the 2 buttonhole rows again.

Work 1 row more.

Shape the neck and armholes as from ** on Left Half Front to end.

THE SHORT SLEEVES

BEGIN at the top and with No. 3 pins cast on 26 sts.

1ST ROW: * K. 2, p. 2; repeat from * to end of row.

2ND ROW: Inc. in the 1st st., purl until 1 st. remains, inc.

3RD ROW: Inc., k. 3, * p. 2, k. 2; repeat from * to the end of the row, but inc. in the last st.

4TH ROW: As 2nd row.

5TH ROW: Inc. in the 1st st., * p. 2, k. 2 repeat from * until 3 sts. remain, p. 2, inc. in the last st.

Repeat from the 2nd row until there are 80 sts. altogether.

Continue in pattern for 32 rows more.

NEXT ROW: Decrease as follows: * k. 2, k. 2 tog., and repeat from * to the end of the row, when 60 sts. will remain.

Change to No. 10 pins and work 12 rows in single rib. Cast off.

Work the second sleeve in the same manner.

LONG SLEEVES

WORK the top of the sleeve exactly as given for the short sleeve, then decrease 1 st. at the beginning and end of every 6th row until the width desired for the forearm is attained. Continue for length of sleeve required on these sts., less 2 inches for the cuff, which finish in single rib on No. 10 pins.

TO MAKE UP THE JUMPER

FIRST press all pieces with a hot iron over a damp cloth on the wrong side of the work. Join the shoulder seams, beginning at the armhole end and taking 1 st. from each side at a time. Stitch the underlap of the Left Half Front just under the Right Front on to the ribbing.

With a No. 9 crochet hook work 1 row of double crochet all round the neck edge.

Set the sleeves into armholes and press these seams while the work is open. Join the sleeves and side seams in one long line and press. Stitch buttons to the Left Front opposite the buttonholes.

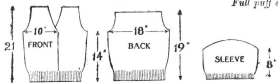

The shape and measurements of the jumper.

20 sts. remain, beginning the next shaping on the first row as the armhole shaping.

Work 10 rows straight on these sts. and cast off.

THE RIGHT HALF FRONT

WITH a No. 3 pin and point towards the centre of the work, pass the 44 sts. from the spare pin.

Work 10 rows in pattern as on back.

The shoulder band and sleeve top in one fits trimly.

One of the Prettiest!

In A Fascinating Roll Stitch

MATERIALS

*S*IX ounces of " Greenock." 2-ply Super Fingering (obtainable only from any branch of SCOTCH WOOL & HOSIERY STORES) ; a pair each of Stratnoid knitting pins, No. 10 and No. 12. A Stratnoid crochet-hook No. 13 ; three wooden button-moulds.

TENSION AND MEASURE-MENTS

*W*ORKED at a tension of 8 sts. to the inch in width on No. 10 pins the following measurements are attained after light pressing : Round the bust, 36 inches ; length from shoulder fold to lower edge, 19 inches : side seam, 13 inches ; sleeve seam, 20 inches.

ABBREVIATIONS

K, knit ; p., purl ; st., stitch ; tog., together ; inc., increase (by working into the back and front of the same stitch) ; sl., slip ; dec., decrease. Directions in brackets are worked the number of times stated immediately after the brackets. Single rib is k. 1 and p. 1 alternately. S.s., stocking-stitch (k. 1 row and p. 1 row alternately).

TO WORK THE BACK

*W*ITH No. 12 pins cast on 120 sts. and work 47 rows in single rib.

INCREASE ROW : * K. 5, inc., repeat from * to end (140 sts.). Now work the main pattern as follows : Work the first 3 rows in s.s., beginning with a purl row. (Note that in this special design the purl side of the s.s. is the right side of the jumper.)

4TH ROW : K. 7, * p. 6, k. 12 ; repeat from * until 7 remain, p. 6, k. 1.

Work 3 rows in s.s., beginning with a purl row.

8TH ROW : K. 7, * (pick up the first purl st. of the group of 6 on the 3rd row with the right-hand pin, then knit the 1st st. on the left-hand pin and slip the picked-up st. over, and off the pin) 6 times, k. 12 ; repeat from * until 7 remain, work the bracketed item as before, then k. 1.

Work 3 rows in s.s, beginning with a purl row.

12TH ROW : K. 1, * p. 6, k. 12 ; repeat from * until 13 remain, p. 6, k. 7.

A photograph of the actual stitch.

Isn't it fun?—The sloping roll pattern.

Work 3 rows in s.s., beginning with a purl row.
16TH Row : K. 1, work from * to * as on the 8th row, ending the last repeat with k. 7, instead of k. 12.
Work 3 rows in s.s., beginning with a purl row.
20TH Row : K. 13, * p. 6, k. 12 ; repeat from * until 1 remains, k. 1.
Work 3 rows in s.s., beginning with a purl row.
Continued overleaf

24TH ROW : K. 13, work from * to * as on the 8th row, until 1 remains, k.1.

These 24 rows form one pattern.

Change to No. 10 pins and work the 24 pattern rows 4 times more to the armholes.

TO SHAPE THE ARMHOLES : Continue in pattern as now set, casting off 5 sts. at the beginning of each of the next 2 rows. Then work 2 sts. tog. at both ends of the next 5 rows. Finally, take 2 sts. tog. at the beginning only of each of the next 10 rows when 110 sts. will remain.

Work 27 rows straight on these sts. to the shoulders.

TO SLOPE THE SHOULDERS : Continue in pattern, casting off 12 sts. at the beginning of each of the next 6 rows. Cast off the remaining sts.

THE FRONT

THIS is worked exactly the same as the back until the armhole shaping is finished and 110 sts. remain, then work one row more. On the next row the sts. are divided for the neck opening as follows : Pattern 55 sts. and leave these on a stitch-holder until needed for the Left Front Shoulder.

Pattern the remaining 55 sts. for the Right Front Shoulder.

THE RIGHT FRONT SHOULDER

WORK straight in pattern as now set for 25 rows more to neck.

** TO SHAPE THE NECK : Cast off 6 sts. at the beginning of the next row. Work 1 row back to neck. Continue in pattern, taking 2 sts. tog. at the beginning of next row and the following 12 alternate rows (neck end), when 36 sts. will remain.

Work 2 rows more on these sts.

TO SLOPE THE SHOULDER : Cast off 12 sts. at the beginning of next row and every following alternate row (armhole end) until all are worked off.

THE LEFT FRONT SHOULDER

JOIN the wool to the neck end of the Left Front Shoulder sts., and work 24 rows in pattern to neck.

Continue as from ** on Right Front Shoulder, to end.

THE SLEEVES

WITH No. 12 pins cast on 68 sts. and work 46 rows in single rib.

Knit 1 row.

Work the 24 rows in pattern as on the back.

Change to No. 10 pins and continue in pattern, increasing 1 st. at both ends of the next row and every following 8th row until there are 110 sts. (By this time the pattern can be so plainly seen that it is easily kept correct after increasing).

More rows can be worked here if a longer sleeve is desired.

TO SHAPE THE SLEEVE TOP : Continue in pattern, casting off 5 sts. at the beginning of each of the next 4 rows : then work 2 sts. tog. at the beginning of each of the following 24 rows. (66 sts.).

Cast off 21 sts. at the beginning of the following 2 rows when 24 sts. will remain for the shoulder-strap. Work 42 rows straight in pattern on these sts. Cast off.

Work a second sleeve in the same manner.

TO MAKE UP THE JUMPER

FIRST press all pieces with a hot iron over a damp cloth on the wrong side of the work, with a thick blanket underneath. Join the shoulder seams of front and back to the corresponding part of the sleeve top, then stitch the shaped edges of the sleeves into armholes.

THE NECK-BAND

NOW work the neck-band thus : Holding the work with the wrong side facing, join the wool to the lower edge of the neck opening on the Left Front. Work double crochet along this edge, missing a knitted st. here and there if necessary to keep the edge flat. Continue the double crochet all round the neck edge and down the opposite side of the neck opening.

2ND ROW : 1 d.c. in the first d.c., * 8 ch., miss about half an inch of the d.c. edge of the first row, 2 d.c. along the edge, and repeat from * once, 8 ch.

Without turning, continue along the neck edge and work 1 d.c. in each d.c. of previous row to the opposite corner of the neck. Turn and work another row of d.c. on the neck edge only, and fasten off.

Press this edging and the sleeve seams while the work is open, then sew up the side and sleeve seams in one line, and press.

¤   ¤   ¤

GOOD HINTS !

All The Little Points That Housewives Want To Know

WHEN THE LIGHT FLARES

One of our big electric lamps which lights a central pendant in our living-room has begun to behave very strangely. Now and then it goes out and there comes a kind of miniature lightning flash in the globe. The light is a vivid blue and does not last for more than a fraction of a second. If I shake the lamp the ordinary light then comes on again. What is the matter, please, and is there any danger ?

THE most serious part of the matter is that the filament inside the lamp has broken and the lamp is virtually done for. By accident the broken ends of the filament have lodged on each other and give the proper light. When they part from vibration in the room the blue flashes are formed at the broken ends.

I'm afraid you cannot count on much more light from this bulb ; it may give out at any moment. I wonder how it got broken ? Perhaps during cleaning, which should be done with the light on.

*   *   *

WASHING HAIR BRUSHES

How can one clean a tortoiseshell without making the back of the brush and the handle wet ?—K. N.

RUB the back of the brush and the handle very sparingly with vaseline before the brush is washed. Afterwards the tortoiseshell can be polished.

It is easier to wash your brushes in borax and water. This is less likely to splash the backs than soap and water, and is just as good.

*   *   *

INK ON THE WALL

Could you tell me of anything that will remove an ink stain from a cream distempered wall ?

I THINK your best plan would be to scrape off the distemper and to size the scraped place. Then distemper over again to match the surroundings.

You can tint the distemper yourself and judge the effect until you get the precise shade by trying it on a waste piece of smooth wood. Get white distemper and a little burnt umber, and raw and burnt sienna powdered paint.

*   *   *

CLEANING OXYDISED SILVER.

Do you know of any inexpensive method of taking the stains off oxydised silver articles ?—D. B.

Every now and then the light goes out and there is a miniature lightning flash in the globe

VARIOUS remedies are available. You may use the juice of a freshly cut lemon, weak ammonia, or even turpentine. The main point is to watch that no hard rubbing is given to the oxydised silver "skin," otherwise you will rub it off.

A mixture of turpentine, rotten-stone, and soft soap makes a useful polish for this class of ware.

You Must Make This One!

It's such a fascinating pattern to work and to wear, and the instructions are very simple. Designed by "Finella"

A FAIR-ISLE JUMPER?

MATERIALS

Four shades of Sirdar 3-ply Super Shetland wool, the original was worked in the following : 7 oz. of fawn (Shade No. 210), 1 oz. of green (Shade No. 260) 1 oz. of brown (Shade No. 264), 2 oz. of rust (Shade No. 226) ; a pair each of Nos. 9, 10 and 11 " Aero " knitting pins ; and a leather belt.

MEASUREMENTS

Round bust, 34 ins. ; length from shoulder to lower edge, 21½ ins. ; sleeve seam with cuff turned back, 18 ins.

TENSION

On No. 9 needles over Fair-Isle pattern, 15 sts. to 2 ins. in width, 8 rows to 1 in. in depth. NOTE : To achieve correct measurements this tension is essential. Tight knitters should use No. 8 needles.

ABBREVIATIONS

St., stitch ; k., knit ; p., purl ; inc., increase ; dec., decrease ; tog., together ; st.-st., stocking-stitch ; f., fawn ; g., green ; r., rust ; b., brown.

THE *Back.*—With No. 9 needles and f. wool, cast on 130 sts. and work 6 rows in k. 1, p. 1 rib. Change to st.-st. and work 4 rows. Then, still working in st.-st., commence pattern, thus :

1st row : 1 b., * 3 f., 2 b. ; repeat from * to end, ending 3 f., 1 b.

2nd row : 1 f., * 1 b., 1 f., 1 b., 2 f. ; repeat from *, ending 1 f. instead of 2.

3rd row : 2 f., * 1 b., 4 f. ; repeat from *, ending 1 b., 2 f.

4th row : As 2nd row.

5th row : As 1st row.

Then, in f. only, work 5 rows of st.-st.

11th row : 1 f., * 3 r., 3 f., 1 g., 3 f. ; repeat from *, ending 2 f. instead of 3.

12th row : 1 f., * 3 g., 1 f., 2 r., 1 f., 2 r., 1 f. ; repeat from *, ending 2 r.

13th row : * 2 r., 1 f., 2 r., 5 g. ; repeat from * to end.

14th row : As 12th row.

15th row : * 2 r., 1 f., 2 r., 2 f., 1 g., 2 f. ; repeat from * to end.

16th row : * 2 f., 1 g., 2 f., 2 r., 1 f., 2 r. ; repeat from * to end.

17th row : * 2 r., 1 f., 2 r., 1 f., 3 g., 1 f. ; repeat from * to end.

18th row : * 5 g., 2 r., 1 f., 2 r. ; repeat from * to end.

19th row : * 2 r., 1 f., 2 r., 1 f., 3 g., 1 f. ; repeat from * to end.

20th row : 2 f., * 1 g., 3 f., 3 r., 3 f. ; repeat from *, ending 1 f.

Work 6 rows of plain f. in st.-st., repeat first 5 rows of pattern, then work 5 more rows in plain f. st.-st.

37th row : * 6 f., 1 r., 6 f., 1 g., 3 f., 5 r., 3 f., 1 g. ; repeat from * to end.

38th row : 1 f., * 1 g., 3 f., 3 r., 3 f., 1 g., 6 f., 3 r., 6 f. ; repeat from *, ending 5 f.

39th row : 4 f., * 5 r., 6 f., 1 g., 3 f., 1 r., 3 f., 1 g., 6 f. ; repeat from *, ending 2 f.

40th row : 3 f., * 1 g., 5 f., 1 g., 6 f., 3 r., 1 f., 3 r., 6 f. ; repeat from *, ending 3 f.

41st row : 2 f., * 3 r., 3 f., 3 r., 6 f., 1 g., 1 f., 1 g., 1 f., 1 g., 6 f. ; repeat from *, ending 4 f.

42nd row : 5 f., * 3 g., 6 f., 3 r., 2 f., 1 r., 2 f., 3 r., 6 f. ; repeat from *, ending 1 f.

43rd row : 1 f., * 3 r., 1 f., 3 r., 1 f., 3 r., 4 f., 7 g., 4 f. ; repeat from *, ending 3 f.

Now work backwards from 42nd to 37th row inclusive. Work 5 rows in plain f. st.-st. These 54 rows complete the pattern.

Repeat the first 50 rows once more ; then, still keeping to pattern, cast off 6 sts. at beginning of next 2 rows. Dec. 1 st. at both ends of next 2 rows.

Now start pattern from 1st row again and dec. 1 st. at each end of first 4 rows. Work 44 more rows without further dec.

Shape shoulder by casting off 10 sts. at beginning of next 6 rows. Cast off.

THE *Front.*—Work exactly as for back, but when pattern is being repeated for second time work only the first 49 rows. On 50th row (a plain f. row) work first half of sts. on to a spare needle, finish row. Then, working only on left side of front, continue thus :

51st row : Cast off 6, work to end.

52nd row : Work 2 tog., work to end.

53rd row : Work 2 tog., work to end.

54th row : Work 2 tog., work to last 2, work 2 tog.

Now commence pattern again, decreasing at beginning of 1st and 3rd rows and both ends of 2nd and 4th rows. Work 38 more rows, decreasing 1 st. at beginning only of every p. row. Work 6 more rows without further dec.

Shape shoulder by casting off 10 sts. at beginning of next 3 rows which commence at armhole edge. Fasten off.

Return to right side of front and work to match, but with all shapings reversed.

THE *Sleeves.*—With No. 10 needles and f. wool, cast on 60 sts. and work 4 ins. in k. 1, p. 1 rib. Change to No. 9 needles and work 2 rows of st.-st., then work first 5 rows of pattern as for back. On following 5 rows of plain colour inc. both ends of 2nd and 5th rows (64 sts.).

Next row : 3 f., * 3 r., 3 f., 1 g., 3 f. ; repeat from *, ending 1 r.

Next row : 2 r., 1 f., * 3 g., 1 f., 2 r., 1 f., 2 r., 1 f. ; repeat from *, ending 1 g.

Continue for next 8 rows of pattern, always allowing for these extra sts., then work 6 rows of plain f. st.-st., increasing at both ends of 3rd and 6th rows (68 sts.). Work first 5 rows of pattern again, the 1st row being worked thus : * 3 f., 2 b ; repeat from *, ending 3 f.

Work 5 rows of plain f., increasing at both ends of 2nd and 5th rows (72 sts.).

Start next pattern group (37th row) thus : 2 r., 3 f., 1 g. (then work complete pattern as given for back, ending 6 f.).

Complete the 13 rows of this pattern group, always allowing for extra sts. at either end. Then work 5 rows of plain f. st.-st., increasing at both ends of 2nd and 5th rows (76 sts. and 54 rows from end of ribbing).

Work 54 more rows of pattern, increasing in exactly the same way as on first 54 rows, giving 92 sts. Then work 4 more rows without further inc.

Now work 12 rows, decreasing 2 sts. at each end of every row. Then dec. 1 st. at each end of every row until 16 sts. remain. Cast off.

TO MAKE UP

Press work well on wrong side with a hot iron over a damp cloth, stretching out to correct measurements.

With No. 11 needles and f. wool, pick up 80 sts. along one side of V neck (on right side of work). Work 9 rows of k. 1, p. 1 rib, decreasing 1 st. on every row at base of V. Cast off, working k. sts. knitwise and p. sts. purlwise. Work ribbing on other side of neck to match. Across back of neck, pick up 44 sts. in same way ; work 9 rows of ribbing. Cast off.

Join shoulder seams. Sew sleeves into armholes ; then sew up side and sleeve seams.

JUST RIGHT *for* CHRISTMAS!

A Pretty Jumper Worked In Fine Wool, And Threaded With Glittering Sequins

THE waist, neck and armbands are knitted in single rib, and the rest of the jumper is in crochet, including the attachment of the sequins.

MATERIALS

FOUR ounces of "Greenock" 2-ply Super Fingering (obtainable only from branches of SCOTCH WOOL & HOSIERY STORES), a pair of "Stratnoid" knitting pins, No. 11; a "Stratnoid" crochet hook, No. 8; 1,980 sequins, measuring 5/16ths of an inch in diameter.

TENSION AND MEASUREMENTS

THE tension must be judged on the first row of crochet above the knitted rib, and if this is worked so as to produce 2 groups and a half to the inch in width, the following measurements will be attained after light pressing : Round the bust, 35 inches; front length from shoulder seam to lower edge, 21 inches; back length, 20 inches; side seam, 13 inches; sleeve seam, 5 inches.

ABBREVIATIONS

K., KNIT; p., purl; st., stitch; tog., together; single rib is k. 1 and p. 1 alternately; ch., chain; sl.st., slip stitch; tr., treble; s.ch., sequin chain, worked thus: bring a sequin along wool and close to back of hook, then work ordinary ch. Always work into both loops at the top of the st. on last row. Directions in brackets are worked the number of times stated after the brackets.

TO WORK THE BACK

FOR the waistband cast on 106 sts. with No. 11 pins and work 32 rows in rib. Cast off loosely.

Pass about 300 sequins on a half-ounce ball of wool. These are pushed along the wool and brought up to the hook as needed. It is important that there should not be any knots on the wool.

Work the crochet pattern as follows:

1st Row (right side): Join the wool with a sl.st. to the first st. along the cast-off edge, 5 ch., 1 tr. into the same st., 1 ch., 1 tr. into the same st., * miss 2 sts. on the knitting, then into the next st. work 1 tr. 1 ch. and 1 tr. making a group, miss 3 sts. on the knitting, 1 group into the next st., repeat from * to the end, making 31 groups altogether, 5 ch., turn.

2nd Row : * 1 tr. into the next space between 2 groups, 1 s.ch., 1 tr. in the same place, and repeat from * to the end of the row, working the last group in the space between the last group of previous row and the turning ch., 5 ch., turn. There should be 31 groups on this row.

3rd Row (without sequins) : * 1 group in the space between 2 sequin groups of the previous row; repeat from * putting the last group in the space before the turning ch. at the end. Count and make sure that you have the same number of groups as on the first row; 5 ch., turn.

(The last 2 rows form the pattern, consisting of one right side row without sequins and one wrong side row with sequins.)

Repeat the 2nd and 3rd row twice more, then the 2nd row again.

9th Row : This is worked like the 3rd row, but increase one group at the beginning and end of the row, thus : Work one group into the 5th ch. from the hook (that is on the turning chain), then work groups across the row, between the groups of previous row, and increase at the end by working 2 groups in the end space, 5 ch., turn. There should be 33 groups on this row.

Now repeat the 2nd and 3rd row, increasing on the 17th and 26th row, as on the 9th row, until there are 14 rows of sequins, when the armhole will be reached.

To Shape the Armholes. 1st Armhole Row : Sl.st. along to 6th tr. (that is, insert the hook in every st. whether ch. or tr. and draw the wool through that st. and the loop on the hook in one movement) ; 5 ch., work the first group after the 4th group, then work in pattern as before until within 4 groups of the end of the row ; leave these 4 groups free, 5 ch., turn (29 groups).

2nd Armhole Row : Miss the first group, then work in pattern until one group remains, 5 ch., turn. (There will be 28 groups now as you are working between the groups of last row, not right over the groups.)

Work 3 rows more like the 2nd armhole row as far as decreases are concerned at the beginning and end of the row, but remember always to alternate the plain rows and the sequin rows (25 groups)

Work 12 rows in pattern without decreases, when the back neck-line will be reached.

LEFT BACK SHOULDER

WORK in pattern until there are 7 groups completed, 5 ch., turn.

Work 3 rows more on these 7 groups and fasten off.

RIGHT BACK SHOULDER

JOIN the wool to the armhole end of the last long row and work 4 rows of 7 groups to match the opposite shoulder.

THE FRONT

WORK same as for the back until 6 rows have been worked after the armhole shaping. Now work the two shoulders on 7 groups only, but work 14 rows on each shoulder.

THE SLEEVES

WITH No. 11 pins cast on 60 sts. and rib 16 rows. Cast off loosely. Thread 296 sequins on the wool ; join to last cast-off st. with crochet hook, 5 ch., 1 tr. into same last row st., which makes the first group. * Miss 1 st., 1 group into the next st., and repeat from *, getting 30 groups along the row. Now work a sequin row, getting 29 sequin groups along the row. Repeat the last 2 rows 3 times more for the length of the sleeve seam.

To shape the top of the sleeve, decrease one group at the beginning of each row, until 21 rows more are worked, then fasten off.

Work the second sleeve in the same manner.

Now sew the shoulder seams, beginning at the armhole end and taking 1 st. from each side at a time.

THE BACK NECK

WITH No. 11 pins pick up and k. 51 sts. from the straight edge between the shoulders. Rib 1 row, then continue in rib, taking 2 sts. tog. at each end of next row and every following alternate row until 39 sts. remain, then cast off.

Work the front neck in the same way on the same number of sts., then work each side of the neck in the same way. Sew the 4 corners together to form a mitre.

THE FRILL

HOLD the jumper with the neckband nearest the worker and the right side of work facing. With crochet hook join the wool to the right half of a k. st. at the lower edge of the ribbed yoke, 5 ch., 1 tr. into the left half of next k. st., * 2 ch., miss the purl st. and put 1 tr. into right half of next k. st., 5 ch., 1 tr. into opposite half of the same st. and repeat from * all round the edge of the yoke. At the end, sl.st. to the top of the first 5 ch. Work the same frill at each armband.

TO MAKE UP THE JUMPER

THE rib can be pressed on wrong side very lightly, but do not press the crochet parts or the sequins will be spoiled. Sew the sleeves into the armholes, easing the fullness on the straight piece along the top of the sleeve, then sew the side seams in one line, passing the needle through one st. from each side at a time, so that a flat seam is ensured.

The shape and measurements of the jumper.

21" — FRONT 17½"

17½" — BACK — 20"

13"

SLEEVE 5"

4

Smart Suits and Puffed Sleeves 1937-40

Day wear becomes formal in appearance with well-tailored knitted suits, gowns, tunics and dresses. These are smart and heavier-looking, with more material used in a flared skirt, a cape or a bustle-effect. The 'Tyrolean' peasant look is popular, with small embroidered flowers decorating the sweater. For the office, sports or at home, numerous 'pretty' lacy stitches and deep cable patterns are used for the fashionable sweater, and for evening wear or parties, elegant fully puffed sleeves are worn high on the arm.

COSSACK SET

MATERIALS *Required.—The Coat :* 12 oz. Patons & Baldwins "Kanastra" wool ; 4 oz. Patons & Baldwins 4-ply Super Scotch fingering wool ; 2 wood button moulds ; 6 press fasteners.

The Cap : 2 oz. "Kanastra" wool ; 1 oz. 4-ply Super Scotch fingering ; a fancy feather.

The Muff : 4 oz. "Kanastra" wool ; a piece of sheet cotton-wool ; a piece of lining material ; a pair each of No. 3, No. 7, and No. 10 "Stratnoid" knitting pins.

Measurements (after pressing).—The Coat : Length to top of shoulder, 25 in. ; length of sleeve, along seam, 17 in. ; width all round, under arms (when fastened), 34 in.

The Cap : To fit 20-22-in. head.

The Muff : All round at widest point, 26 in. ; width, 14 in. ; depth, 13 in.

Abbreviations.—Sts., stitches ; k., knit ; p., purl ; tog., together ; rep., repeat ; rem., remain(s)(ing)(der) ; inc., increase (ing).

Tension.—Work to produce 6 sts. and 9 rows to 1 in. in the 4-ply fingering wool, using No. 7 needles.

K. into back of all cast-on sts. to produce firm edges.

The Back (Three Pieces)

(1) *Lower Flare.*—With No. 3 needles and "Kanastra" wool, cast on 60 sts. and work in garter-st. throughout, as follows : Knit 10 rows, then : *Row 11.*—K. 4, * inc. into next st. (by knitting into the front and the back of the st.—likewise every time there is an inc.), k. 4, rep. from * to end, finishing row k. 5 instead of k. 4.

Knit 7 more rows, then rep. from rows 11 to 18, inclusive, three times more, finishing each of the 3 inc. rows, k. 1, k. 5, k. 1, respectively (4 times in all). Work 4 more rows. Cast off.

(2) *Centre Back.*—With No. 7 needles and 4-ply wool, cast on 75 sts. and work in stocking-st. throughout, inc. one st. at both ends of every 10th row, until there are 89 sts. Work 6 more rows, then :

Shape Armholes, thus.—Cast off 3 sts. at the beginning of each of the next 4 rows, then k. 2 tog. at both ends of every row until 69 sts. rem. Cast off.

(3) *Back Yoke.*—With No. 3 needles and "Kanastra" wool, cast on 47 sts. and work straight in garter-st. for 5½ in. Cast off.

The Left Front (Two Pieces)

(1) *Flare, Front Edging, and Yoke—all in one piece.*—With No. 3 needles and "Kanastra" wool, cast on 50 sts. and work in garter-st. throughout, as follows : Knit 4 rows, then : *Row 5.*—* K. 8, k. 2 tog., rep. from * to end. Knit 9 more rows. *Row 15.*—* K. 7, k. 2 tog., rep. from * to end. Knit 9 more rows. *Row 25.*—* K. 6, k. 2 tog., rep. from * to end. Knit 9 more rows. *Row 35.*—* K. 5, k. 2 tog., rep. from * to end (30 sts.). Knit 8 more rows. *Row 44.*—Cast off 18 sts., k. rem. of row (12 sts.). Work

*T*HE "Kanastra" wool used for this jaunty set gives the fashionable astrakhan effect. The deep blue quill in the cap matches the suède belt.

Flared Jacket, Peaked Cap and Muff all to Match—and Very Dashing in Smoke Grey

straight on these 12 sts. (for the edging) without alteration until the piece measures 16½ in. from beginning.

Now, on the same edge as 18 sts. were cast off, cast on 15 sts. (27 sts. on the needle). Work straight on these 27 sts. (for the yoke) for 4 in. more, then on the edge opposite to that on which 15 sts. were cast on (the straight edge), commence to *shape front neck, thus :* Cast off 5 sts. at the beginning of the first row, then on the same edge k. 2 tog. every row until 14 sts. rem.

Continue to work on these 14 sts. without further alteration for 2 in. Cast off.

(2) *Centre.*—With No. 7 needles and 4-ply wool, cast on 47 sts. and work in stocking-st. throughout, as follows : Work 9 rows, then : *Row 10.*—All p. until 1 st. rem., inc. (armhole edge). Rep. row 10 every following 10th row until there are 54 sts. Work 6 more rows, then : *Shape armhole thus :* *Row 1.*—Cast off 3 sts., k. rem. of row. *Row 2.*—P. Rep. these 2 rows once. *Row 5.*—K. 2 tog., k. rem. of row. *Row 6.*—P. until 2 sts. rem., k. 2 tog. Rep. the last 2 rows once more. Cast off.

The Right Front (Two Pieces)

(1) *Flare, Front Edging, and Yoke—all in one piece.*—Work the first piece in "Kanastra" wool exactly as the first piece of left front.

(2) *Centre.*—Work in 4-ply wool to match the second piece of left front, but inc. 1 st. on armhole edge at the end of row 11 (instead of at the end of row 10, as in left front), and rep. row 11 every following 10th row until there are 54 sts. Work 6 more rows, then *shape armhole*, as in left front (except that a k. row will now be a p. row and *vice-versa*).

The Sleeves (Two Alike)

With No, 3 needles and "Kanastra" wool, cast on 24 sts. and work in garter-st. throughout as follows : Work straight for 3 in. Inc. 1 st. at both ends of next row, and likewise every following 8th row, until there are 48 sts. Continue to work without further alteration until the piece measures 17 in. from the beginning, then :

Shape top thus.—K. 2 tog. at both ends of the next row and likewise every following 3rd row, until 28 sts. rem., then : *Row 1.*—K. 12, k. 3 tog., k. 11, k. 2 tog. *Row 2.*—K. 11, k. 3 tog., k. 9, k. 2 tog. *Row 3.*—K. 9, k. 3 tog., k. 8, k. 2 tog. *Row 4.*—K. 8, k. 3 tog., k. 6, k. 2 tog. *Row 5.*—K. 6, k. 3 tog., k. 5, k. 2 tog. *Row 6.*—K. 5, k. 3 tog., k. 3, k. 2 tog. *Row 7.*—K. 3, k. 3 tog., k. 2, k. 2 tog. *Row 8.*—K. 2, k. 3 tog., k. 2 tog. *Row 9.*—K. 2 tog., k. 2 tog., pass the first st. over ; fasten off.

The Collar.—With No. 3 needles and "Kanastra" wool, cast on 10 sts. and work in garter-st. to the length required (to fit individual neck). Cast off.

To Cover the Wood Button Moulds.— With No. 3 needles and "Kanastra" wool, cast on 16 sts. and work in garter-st. for 3 in. Cast off. Work a second similar piece.

Fold the piece in two, then neatly gather over the wood mould and fasten off securely.

To Make Up and Finish.—Carefully press the three pieces worked in 4-ply wool only on the wrong side under a damp cloth with a warm iron. Sew up side seams and press. Join the first piece of back (lower flare, worked in "Kanastra") to the first portions (flared) of left and right fronts by a neat seam. Sew the third piece of back (yoke) to the top of second back piece (centre, worked in 4-ply). Neatly sew the two front edgings (worked in "Kanastra") over the two pieces of front worked in 4-ply wool, and the "Kanastra" yoke to the top edge ;

SEE how the jacket flares full from a fitted waist. It is so designed that you can wear it without the belt if you like.

then sew the "Kanastra" trimming around the lower edge. Seam up the shoulders ; sew up sleeve seams and sew sleeves neatly into armholes, then sew collar piece around neck edge. Lightly press all seams and the trimming. Sew press fasteners along front and sew on the two covered buttons to the right front, as shown on the model.

The Cap (Two Pieces)

(1) *Crown.*—With No. 10 needles and 4-ply wool, cast on 120 sts. and work in a k. 1, p. 1 rib for 1 in. Continue in stocking-st., working straight for 24 rows, finishing on a p. row, then : *Shape top, thus.*—*Row 1.*—* K. 10, k. 2 tog., rep. from * to end. Rows 2 to 8 as row 1   *Continued overleaf*

from * to end. *Row* 9—* K. 6, k. 2 tog., rep.
from * to end. *Row* 11—* K. 5, k. 2 tog., rep.
from * to end. *Row* 13—* K. 4, k. 2 tog., rep.
from * to end. *Row* 15—* K. 3, k. 2 tog., rep.
from * to end. *Row* 17—* K. 2, k. 2 tog., rep.
from * to end. *Row* 19—* K. 1, k. 2 tog., rep.
from * to end. *Row* 21—K. 2 tog. along the
entire row *Row* 22—As Row 21. Cast off.

(2) *Trimming*—With No. 3 needles and
" Kanastra" wool, cast on 34 sts. and work in
garter-st. for 18½ins. Cast off.

To Make Up and Finish.—Carefully press the
crown piece on the wrong side under a damp
cloth, with a hot iron. Sew up the seam and
make a little tuck on one side of the crown
piece to make it fit snugly to the head. Join
together the two short ends of the second piece,
then neatly sew one edge all around to edge of
crown. Fold in the top edge for about 1½ins.,
and sew on feather as shown in illustration

THE MUFF

With No. 3 needles and " Kanastra" wool
cast on 40 sts. and work in garter-st.
throughout, as follows : Knit 6 rows, then :
Row 7—K. 4, * inc. into next st., k. 9, rep. from *
twice more, then inc. 1 st., k. 5. K. 5 more rows,
then *Row* 13—K. 4, * inc. into next st., k. 8, rep.
from * 3 times more, then inc. 1 st., k. 3. K. 5
more rows. *Row* 19—K. 4, * inc. into next st.,
k. 7, rep. from * 4 times more, then inc. 1 st., k. 4.
K. 5 more rows. *Row* 25—K. 3, * inc. into next
st., k. 6, rep. from * until 3 sts. remain, inc. 1 st.,
k. 2. K. 5 more rows. *Row* 31—K. 2, * inc.
into next st., k. 5, rep. from * until 1 st. rem.,
inc. 1 st., into last. K. 5 more rows. *Row* 37—
K. 1, * inc. into next st., k. 4, rep. from * until
3 sts. rem., inc. 1 st., k. 2 (89 sts.).

Continue to work in garter-st. without further
alteration, until the piece measures 9ins. from the
beginning, then : *Row* 1—K. 1, * k. 2 tog., k. 4,
rep. from * until 4 sts. rem., k. 2 tog., k. 2.
K. 5 more rows. *Row* 7—K. 2, * k. 2 tog., k. 5,
rep. from * until 2 sts. rem., k. 2 tog. K. 5 more
rows. *Row* 13—K. 3, * k. 2 tog., k. 6, rep. from
* until 4 sts. rem., k. 2 tog., k. 2. K. 5 more rows.
Row 19—K. 4, * k. 2 tog., k. 7, rep. from * until
6 sts. rem., k. 2 tog., k. 4. K. 5 more rows.
Row 25—K. 4, * k. 2 tog., k. 8, rep. from * until
5 sts. rem., k. 2 tog., k. 3. K. 5 more rows.
Row 31—K. 4, * k. 2 tog., k. 9, rep. from * twice
more, then k. 2 tog., k. 5 (40 sts.). K. 6 more
rows. Cast off.

To Make Up and Finish.—Join together the
two longer edges, then line carefully with the
cotton-wool and cover this neatly with the lining,
taking care to finish off with a neat stitch around
the edges of openings.

DIAGRAMS OF COSSACK SET

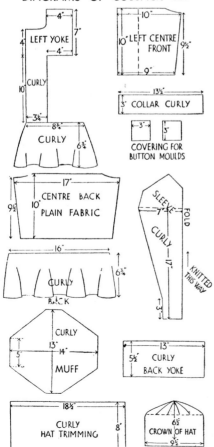

The dressing-gown is girdled with a wide knitted sash tied loosely in front.

On In a MOMENT

Quickly Knitted in Thick Soft Wool This Charming Dressing-Gown is the Cosiest Thing

ON big needles and of thick wool this lovely dressing-gown is soon knitted.

MATERIALS : *2 lbs. of Sirdar " Knitfast " wool ; a pair of " Aero " knitting pins, No. 2 ; and an " Aero " crochet hook, No. 10 ; 3 large buttons.*

TENSION AND MEASUREMENTS : *Worked at a tension of 3 sts. to the inch in width, the following measurements are attained after light pressing : Across the back at the under-arms, 20 inches ; across each front at the same place, 18 inches (this allows for a wrap-over of 10 inches, which gives a complete bust measurement of 46 inches when fastened). Length from neck to lower edge, 49 inches ; side seams, 43 inches ; sleeve seam, 19 inches.*

ABBREVIATIONS : *K., knit ; p., purl ; st., stitch ; tog., together ; inc., increase (by working into the back and front of the same stitch). Directions in brackets are worked the number of times stated immediately after the brackets.*

To Work the Back

CAST on 80 sts. and work 1 row into the back of the sts. to give a neat edge.
Continue in pattern as follows :

1st *Pattern.*—1st row : * K. 4, p. 4 ; repeat from * to end.
Repeat this row 9 times more.

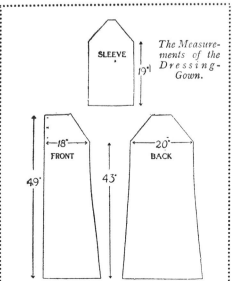

SLEEVE
19"1

The Measurements of the Dressing-Gown.

18"
FRONT

49"

43"

20"
BACK

A cravat is worn at the throat.

COLOUR-SCHEMES

If you'd like it in Blue — choose Powder Blue (Shade No. 553). Have Buttons to tone. Wear Matching Blue Mules. A Cherry-Red Silk Scarf.

If you'd like it in Pink — choose a soft Rose Pink (Shade No. 550). Have Pink Buttons. Wear Midnight-Blue Velvet Mules. A Matching Blue Velvet Cravat.

2nd Pattern.—1st row : K. 2, * p. 4, k. 4 ; repeat from *, ending the last repeat with k. 2 instead of k. 4.

2nd row : P. 2, * k. 4, p. 4 ; repeat from *, ending the last repeat with p. 2 instead of p. 4.

Repeat these 2 rows 4 times more.

3rd Pattern.—1st row : * P. 4, k. 4 ; repeat from * to end.

Repeat this row 9 times more.

4th Pattern.—1st row : P. 2, * k. 4, p. 4 ; repeat from *, ending the last repeat with p. 2 instead of p. 4.

2nd row : K. 2, * p. 4, k. 4 ; repeat from *, ending the last repeat with k. 2 instead of k. 4.

Repeat these 2 rows 4 times more.

Now repeat the 1st and 2nd patterns once more (60 rows in pattern).

1st Decrease Pattern.—Decrease row : P. 1, p. 2 tog., p. 1, * k. 4, p. 4 ; repeat from * until 4 remain, k. 1, k. 2 tog., k. 1 (78 sts.).

Next row : P. 3, * k. 4, p. 4 ; repeat from * until 3 remain, k. 3.

Repeat the last row 8 times more.

2nd Decrease Pattern.—Decrease row : K. 1, k. 2 tog., k. 2, * p. 4, k. 4 ; repeat from * until 9 remain, p. 4, k. 2, k. 2 tog., k. 1. (76 sts.).

Next row : * P. 4, k. 4 ; repeat from * until 4 remain, p. 4.

Next row : * K. 4, p. 4 ; repeat from * until 4 remain, k. 4.

Repeat the last 2 rows 3 times more, then the 1st row again.

3rd Decrease Pattern.—Decrease row : K. 1, p. 2 tog., p. 3, * k. 4, p. 4 ; repeat from * until 6 remain, k. 3, k. 2 tog., p. 1 (74 sts.).

Next row : K. 1, * p. 4, k. 4 ; repeat from * until 1 remains, p. 1.

Repeat this row 8 times more

4th Decrease Pattern.—Decrease row : P. 1, p. 2 tog., * k. 4, p. 4, repeat from * until 7 remain, k. 4, p. 2 tog., p. 1 (72 sts.).

Next row : K. 2, * p. 4, k. 4, repeat from * until 6 remain, p. 4, k. 2.

Next row : P. 2, * k. 4, p. 4 ; repeat from * until 6 remain, k. 4, p. 2.

Repeat the last 2 rows 3 times, then the 1st row again.

5th Decrease Pattern.—Decrease row : K. 1, k. 2 tog., k 1, * p. 4, k. 4 ; repeat from * until 4 remain, p. 1, p. 2 tog., p. 1 (70 sts.).

Next row : K. 3, * p. 4, k. 4 ; repeat from * until 3 remain, p. 3.

Repeat the last row 8 times more.

6th Decrease Pattern.—Decrease row : P. 1, p. 2 tog., p. 2, * k. 4, p. 4 ; repeat from * until 9 remain, k. 4, p. 2, p. 2 tog., p. 1. (68 sts.).

Next row : * K. 4, p. 4 ; repeat from * until 4 remain, k. 4.

Next row : * P. 4., k. 4 ; repeat from * until 4 remain, p. 4.

Repeat the last 2 rows 3 times more, then the first of these rows again.

7th Decrease Pattern.—Decrease row : P. 1, k. 2 tog., k. 3, * p. 4, k. 4 ; repeat from * until 6 remain, p. 3, p. 2 tog., k. 1 (66 sts.).

Next row : P. 1, * k. 4, p. 4 ; repeat from * until 1 remains, k. 1.

Repeat this row 8 times more.

8th Decrease Pattern.—Decrease row : K. 1, k. 2 tog., * p. 4, k. 4 ; repeat from * until 7 remain, p. 4, k. 2 tog., k. 1 (64 sts.).

Next row : P. 2, * k. 4, p. 4 ; repeat from * until 6 remain, k. 4, p. 2

Next row : K. 2, * p. 4, k. 4 ; repeat from * until 6 remain, p. 4, k. 2.

Repeat these 2 rows 3 times more, then the 1st of these rows again.

9th decrease Pattern.—Decrease row : P. 1, p. 2 tog., p. 1, * k. 4, p. 4 ; repeat from * until 4 remain, k. 1, k. 2 tog., k. 1 (62 sts.).

Next row : P. 3, * k. 4, p. 4 ; repeat from * until 3 remain, k. 3.

Repeat this row 8 times more.

Now work the second decrease pattern rows once more (60 sts.).

Continue straight in pattern as follows :

17th Pattern.—Next row : K. 2, * p. 4, k. 4 ; repeat from * until 2 remain, p. 2.

Repeat this row 9 times more.

18th Pattern.—Next row : * P. 4, k. 4 ; repeat from * until 4 remain, p. 4.

Next row : * K. 4, p. 4 ; repeat from * to end until 4 remain, k. 4.

Repeat these 2 rows 4 times more—to armholes.

To Shape the Armholes.—Continue in pattern as follows :

1st decrease row : P. 1, k. 2 tog., k. 3, * p. 4, k. 4 ; repeat from * until 6 remain, p. 3, p. 2 tog., k. 1.

2nd row : P. 1, * k. 4, p. 4 ; repeat from * until 1 remains, k. 1.

3rd row : K. 1, k. 2 tog., k. 2, * p. 4, k. 4 ; repeat from * until 5 remain, p. 2, p. 2 tog., p. 1.

4th row : * K. 4, p. 4 ; repeat from * to end.

5th row : K. 1, k. 2 tog., k. 1, * p. 4, k. 4 ; repeat from * until 4 remain, p. 1, p. 2 tog., p. 1.

6th row : K. 3, * p. 4, k. 4 ; repeat from * until 3 remain, p. 3.

7th row : K. 1, k. 2 tog., * p. 4, k. 4 ; repeat from * until 3 remain, p. 2 tog., p. 1.

8th row : K. 2, * p. 4, k. 4 ; repeat from * until 2 remain, p. 2.

9th row : K. 1, p. 2 tog., p. 3, * k. 4, p. 4 ; repeat from * until 6 remain, k. 3, k. 2 tog., p. 1.

10th row : K. 1, * p. 4, k. 4 ; repeat from * until 1 remains, p. 1.

11th row : P. 1, p. 2 tog., * k. 4, p. 4 ; repeat from * until 3 remain, p. 2 tog., p. 1.

12th row : K. 2, * p. 4, k. 4 ; repeat from * until 6 remain, p. 4, k. 2.

13th row : P. 1, k. 2 tog., k. 3, * p. 4, k. 4 ; repeat from * until 10 remain, p. 4, k. 3, k. 2 tog., p. 1.

14th row : K. 1, * p. 4, k. 4 ; repeat from * until 5 remain, p. 4, k. 1.

15th row : K. 1, k. 2 tog., k. 2, * p. 4, k. 4 ; repeat from * until 9 remain, p. 4, k. 2, k. 2 tog., k. 1.

16th row : * P. 4, k. 4 ; repeat from * until 4 remain, p. 4.

17th row : K. 1, k. 2 tog., k. 1, * p. 4, k. 4 ; repeat from * until 8 remain, p. 4, k. 2 tog., k. 1.

18th row : P. 3, * k. 4, p. 4 ; repeat from * until 7 remain, k. 4, p. 3.

19th row : K. 1, k. 2 tog., * p. 4, k. 4 ; repeat from * until 7 remain, p. 4, k. 2 tog., k. 1.

20th row : P. 2, * k. 4, p. 4 ; repeat from * until 6 remain, k. 4, p. 2.

21st row : P. 1, p. 2 tog., p. 1, * k. 4, p. 4 ; repeat from * until 4 remain, k. 1, k. 2 tog., k. 1.

22nd row : P. 3, * k. 4, p. 4 ; repeat from * until 3 remain, k. 3.

23rd row : P. 1, p. 2 tog., * k. 4, p. 4 ; repeat from * until 3 remain, k. 2 tog., k. 1.

24th row : P. 2, * k. 4, p. 4 ; repeat from * until 2 remain, k. 2.

25th row : P. 1, k. 2 tog., k. 3, * p. 4, k. 4 ; repeat from * until 6 remain, p. 3, p. 2 tog., k. 1.

26th row : P. 1, * k. 4, p. 4 ; repeat from * until 1 remains, k. 1.

27th row : K. 1, k. 2 tog., k. 2, * p. 4, k. 4 ; repeat from * until 5 remain, p. 2, p. 2 tog., p. 1.

28th row : * K. 4, p. 4 ; repeat from * to end.

29th row : K. 1, k. 2 tog., k. 1, * p. 4, k. 4 ; repeat from * until 4 remain, p. 1, p. 2 tog., p. 1.

30th row : K. 3, * p. 4, k. 4 ; repeat from * until 3 remain, p. 3.

31st row : P. 1, p. 2 tog., p. 2, * k. 4, p. 4 ; repeat from * until 9 remain, k. 4, p. 2, p. 2 tog., p. 1.

32nd row : * K. 4, p. 4 ; repeat from * until 4 remain, k. 4.

33rd row : P. 1, p. 2 tog., p. 1, * k. 4, p. 4 ; repeat from * until 8 remain, k. 4, p. 1, p. 2 tog., p. 1.

34th row : K. 3, * p. 4, k. 4 ; repeat from * until 7 remain, p. 4, k. 3.

35th row : P. 1, p. 2 tog., * k. 4, p. 4 ; repeat from * until 7 remain, k. 4, p. 2

tog., p. 1.

Cast off remaining 24 sts.

The Right Front

CAST on 56 sts. and work 1 row into the back of the sts. to give a neat edge.

Now work the first 4 patterns as on the back (40 rows).

Repeat these 4 patterns 3 times more, then the 1st and 2nd patterns again, when the armhole will be reached.

To Shape the Armhole.—1st row : P. 3, cast off 3 for buttonhole (1 st. on pin), k. 1, * p. 4, k. 4 ; repeat from * until 8 remain, p. 4, k. 1, k. 2 tog., k. 1.

2nd row : P. 3, * k. 4, p. 4 ; repeat from * to end of row, casting on 3 sts. over those cast off to complete the buttonhole, and ending with k. 3.

3rd row : * P. 4, k. 4 ; repeat from * until 7 remain, p. 4, k. 2 tog., k. 1.

4th row : P. 2, * k. 4, p. 4 ; repeat from * until 4 remain, k. 4.

5th row : * P. 4, k. 4 ; repeat from * until 6 remain, p. 3, p. 2 tog., k. 1.

6th row : P. 1, * k. 4, p. 4 ; repeat from * until 4 remain, k. 4.

7th row : * P. 4, k. 4 ; repeat from * until 5 remain, p. 2, p. 2 tog., p. 1.

8th row : K. 4, p. 4 ; repeat from * until 4 remain, k. 4.

9th row : * P. 4, k. 4 ; repeat from * until 4 remain, p. 1, p. 2 tog., p. 1.

10th row : K. 3, * p. 4, k. 4 ; repeat from * to end.

11th row : P. 2, * k. 4, p. 4 ; repeat from * until 9 remain, k. 4, p. 2, p. 2 tog., p. 1.

12th row : * K. 4, p. 4 ; repeat from * until 2 remain, k. 2.

13th row : P. 2, * k. 4, p. 4 ; repeat from * until 8 remain, k. 4, p. 1, p. 2 tog., p. 1.

14th row : K. 3, * p. 4, k. 4 ; repeat from * until 6 remain, p. 4, k. 2.

15th row : P. 2, k. 1, cast off 3 (1 st. on pin), p. 3, * k. 4, p. 4 ; repeat from * until 7 remain, k. 4, p. 2 tog., p. 1.

16th row : K. 2, * p. 4, k. 4 ; repeat from * casting on 3 sts. over those cast off on previous row and ending the row with p. 1, k. 2.

17th row : P. 2, * k. 4, p. 4 ; repeat from * until 6 remain, k. 3, k. 2 tog., p. 1.

18th row : K. 1, * p. 4, k. 4 ; repeat from * until 6 remain, p. 4, k. 2.

19th row : P. 2, * k. 4, p. 4 ; repeat from * until 5 remain, k. 2, k. 2 tog., k. 1.

20th row : * P. 4, k. 4 ; repeat from * until 6 remain, p. 4, k. 2.

21st row : * K. 4, p. 4 ; repeat from * until 6 remain, k. 3, k. 2 tog., p. 1.

22nd row : K. 1, * p. 4, k. 4 ; repeat from * until 4 remain, p. 4.

23rd row : * K. 4, p. 4 ; repeat from * until 5 remain, k. 2, k. 2 tog., k. 1.

24th row : * K. 4, p. 4 ; repeat from * until 4 remain, p. 4.

25th row : * K. 4, p. 4 ; repeat from * until 4 remain, k. 1, k. 2 tog., k. 1.

26th row : P. 3, * k. 4, p. 4 ; repeat from * to end.

27th row : * K. 4, p. 4 ; repeat from * until 3 remain, k. 2 tog., k. 1.

28th row : P. 2, * k. 4, p. 4 ; repeat from * to end.

29th row : K. 3, cast off 3 for buttonhole (1 st. on pin), p. 1, * k. 4, p. 4 ; repeat from * until 10 remain, k. 4, p. 3, p. 2 tog., k. 1.

30th row : P. 1, * k. 4, p. 4 ; repeat from *, casting on 3 sts. over those cast off to complete the buttonhole.

31st row : P. 1, * k. 4, p. 4 ; repeat from * until 7 remain, k. 3, p. 2 tog., p. 1.

32nd row : K. 2, * p. 4, k. 4 ; repeat from * until 6 remain, p. 4, k. 2.

33rd row : P. 2, * k. 4, p. 4 ; repeat from * until 6 remain, k. 3, k. 2 tog., k. 1.

34th row : K. 1, * p. 4, k. 4 ; repeat from * until 6 remain, p. 4, k. 2.

Cast off the remaining sts.

Continued overleaf

The Left Front

THIS is worked the same as the Right Front, but without the buttonholes, making it up on the opposite side.

The Sleeves

CAST on 48 sts. and work 1 row into the back of the sts. to give a neat edge.

Now work the first 4 patterns as on the back (40 rows).

Repeat these 4 patterns once more.

To Shape the Sleeve Top.—Continue in decrease pattern as follows :

1st row : Cast off 3 (1 st. on pin) * p. 4, k. 4 ; repeat from * until 4 remain, p. 4.

2nd row : Cast off 3 (1 st. on pin) * p. 4, k. 4 ; repeat from * until 1 remains, p. 1.

3rd row : P. 1, p. 2 tog., p. 2, * k. 4, p. 4 ; repeat from * until 5 remain, k. 2, k. 2 tog., k. 1.

4th row : * P. 4, k. 4 ; repeat from * to end.

5th row : P. 1, p. 2 tog., p. 1, * k. 4, p. 4 ; repeat from * until 4 remain, k. 1, k. 2 tog., k. 1.

6th row : P. 3, * k. 4, p. 4 ; repeat from * until 3 remain, k. 3.

7th row : P. 1, p. 2 tog., * k. 4, p. 4 ; repeat from * until 3 remain, k. 2 tog., k. 1.

8th row : P. 2, * k. 4, p. 4 ; repeat from * until 2 remain, k. 2.

9th row : P. 1, k. 2 tog., k. 3, * p. 4, k. 4 ; repeat from * until 6 remain, p. 3, p. 2 tog., k. 1.

10th row : P. 1, * k. 4, p. 4 ; repeat from * until 1 remains, k. 1.

11th row : K. 1, k. 2 tog., * p. 4, k. 4 ; repeat from * until 7 remain, p. 4, k. 2 tog., k. 1.

12th row : P. 2, * k. 4, p. 4 ; repeat from * until 6 remain, k. 4, p. 2.

13th row : K. 1, p. 2 tog., p. 3, * k. 4, p. 4 ; repeat from * until 6 remain, p. 3, p. 2 tog., k. 1.

14th row : P. 1, * k. 4, p. 4 ; repeat from * until 5 remain, k. 4, p. 1.

15th row : P. 1, p. 2 tog., p. 2, * k. 4, p. 4 ; repeat from * until 5 remain, p. 2, p. 2 tog., p. 1.

16th row : * K. 4, p. 4 ; repeat from * until 4 remain, k. 4.

17th row : P. 1, p. 2 tog., p. 1, * k. 4, p. 4 ; repeat from * ending the last repeat with p. 1, p. 2 tog., p. 1 instead of p. 4.

18th row : K. 3, * p. 4, k. 4 ; repeat from * until 7 remain, p. 4, k. 3.

19th row : P. 1, p. 2 tog., * k. 4, p. 4 ; repeat from * until 7 remain, k. 4, p. 2 tog., p. 1.

20th row : K. 2, * p. 4, k. 4 ; repeat from * until 6 remain, p. 4, k. 2.

21st row : K. 1, k. 2 tog., k. 1, * p. 4, k. 4 ; repeat from * until 4 remain, p. 1, p. 2 tog., p. 1.

22nd row : K. 3, * p. 4, k. 4 ; repeat from * until 3 remain, p. 3.

23rd row : K. 1, k. 2 tog., * p. 4, k. 4 ; repeat from * until 3 remain, p. 2 tog., p. 1.

24th row : K. 2, * p. 4, k. 4 ; repeat from * until 2 remain, p. 2.

25th row : K. 1, p. 2 tog., p. 3, k. 4, p. 4, k. 3, k. 2 tog., p. 1.

26th row : K. 1, * p. 4, k. 4 ; repeat from * until 1 remains, p. 1.

27th row : P. 1, p. 2 tog., p. 2, k. 4, p. 4, k. 2, k. 2 tog., k. 1.

28th row : * P. 4, k. 4 ; repeat from * to end.

29th row : P. 1, p. 2 tog., p. 1, k. 4, p. 4, k. 1, k. 2 tog., k. 1.

30th row : P. 3, k. 4, p. 4, k. 3.

31st row : K. 1, k. 2 tog., k. 2, p. 4, k. 2, k. 2 tog., k. 1.

32nd row : P. 4, k. 4, p. 4.

33rd row : K. 1, k. 2 tog., k. 1, p. 4, k. 1, k. 2 tog., k. 1.

34th row : P. 3, k. 4, p. 3.

Cast off loosely.

Work a second sleeve in the same manner.

THE BELT.—Cast on 8 sts. and work the first 4 patterns as on back for 6 times. Cast off.

TO MAKE UP THE DRESSING-GOWN.— First press all pieces with a hot iron over a damp cloth on the wrong side of the work. Join the sloping edges of sleeve tops to corresponding portions of back and fronts and press these seams. Join the sleeve and side seams in one long line.

Work 1 row double crochet all round the front edge and neck. Sew buttons to the left front allowing about ten inches for wrapover.

"A HAPPY HOUSE"

I HOPE my house will have a doorstep fair and clean, and free of any gossip or anything that's mean. I hope the stairs will lead to nights of peace and rest. I hope at least one room harbours a happy guest.

I hope my fireside will be a place for friends to come and gather round after their journey ends. I hope however small my rooms and house may be, that they will give folk cheer, and prove a sanctuary.

I hope the red-roofed porch will shelter folk from rain, and those who care to use it will often come again. I hope a bird will build beneath its roof and rest, then I will feel my house is wonderfully blest.

JEAN MORTON.

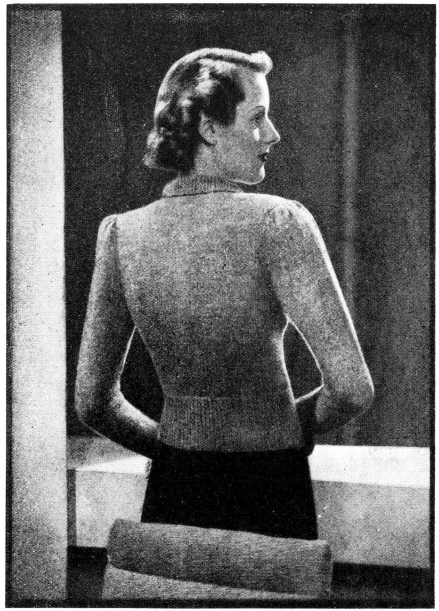

The quite plain back has a very tailored air

WE MUST Have a TYROLEAN TOUCH

A Jumper Embroidered with the Gayest of Little Flowers — Scarlet Daisies with Bright Green Leaves

THIS charming jumper-cardigan knitted in stocking-stitch has the fronts embroidered with gay little flowers. The result is most attractive, as you can see.

Materials

Seven ounces of " Beehive " Shetland Floss in beige ; 3 skeins of embroidery wool, red, yellow and green ; 1 pair each of knitting pins No. 9 and No. 11 ; and 12 small buttons.

Abbreviations

K., knit ; p., purl ; st., stitch ; s.s., stocking stitch (k. plain on the right side and purl back) ; inc., increase (by knitting into the front and back of the same st.) ; dec., decrease.

Tension and Measurements

Worked at a tension of 6½ sts. to the inch in width, the following measurements are attained after light pressing : Across the back at the underarms, 17 inches ; across each front at the same place, 10 inches, making a bust measurement of 36 inches when fastened ; length of back and front from shoulder seam to lower edge, 18 inches ; side seam, 12 inches ; sleeve seam, 19 inches.

The Back

Begin at the lower edge by casting on 100 sts.
Work 34 rows in single rib (k. 1, and p. 1 alternately) working into the back of the sts. on the first row. Now work 42 rows in s.s., after which inc. 1 st. at the beginning and end of the next row and every following 4th row,

until 5 inc. rows have been worked here (110 sts.). Work 3 rows more to the armholes.

To Shape the Armholes : Cast off 10 sts. at the beginning of each of the next 2 rows, after which dec. 1 st. at the beginning *only* of the next 6 rows (84 sts.). Work 44 rows in s.s. to the shoulder line.

To Slope the Shoulders : Cast off 9 sts. at the beginning of the next 6 rows, then cast off the remaining sts.

RIGHT FRONT.—Cast on 60 sts. and work 2 rows of single rib as on the Back.

3rd row : K. 1, p. 1, cast off 3 sts., and work in single rib to the end.

4th row : Work in single rib, casting on 3 sts. over those cast off to complete the buttonhole.

Work 8 rows in single rib.

Repeat last 10 rows twice more, then work another buttonhole on the next 2 rows, which makes 34 rows of rib as on the back.

Next row : (K. 1, p. 1) 5 times for the single rib border, which is maintained to the neck-line, k. to end.

Next row : P. to last 10 sts., rib to end.

Repeat the last 2 rows 4 times more, then work 2 rows with a buttonhole.

Repeat the last 12 rows twice more.

Work 6 rows more in the pattern as now set, that is s.s. on the main part with a single rib border on 10 sts. at the front edge. Inc. 1 st. at the end of the next row. Work 3 rows more.

On the next row begin another buttonhole and inc. 1 st. at the end of the row.

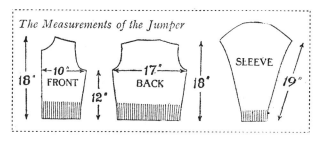

The Measurements of the Jumper

FRONT 18" 10" 12"

BACK 17" 18"

SLEEVE 19"

Work the next row in pattern and finish the buttonhole.

Repeat the last 12 rows, inc. 1 st. at the end of every fourth row, until there are 5 increases, then work 2 rows more in s.s. still keeping the ribbed border, to the armhole (65 sts.).

To Shape the Armhole : Cast off 10 sts., p. to last 10 sts., rib 10.

Work 6 rows more, decreasing 1 st. at the end of the next and each alternate row (52 sts.).

On the next 2 rows work another buttonhole, then continue in s.s. and rib until 2 buttonholes more have been worked, that is 24 rows to the neck-line.

To Shape the Neck : Cast off 17 sts., k. to end.

Next row : All purl.

Work 16 rows more in s.s., dec. 1 st. at the neck end of every alternate row.

K. one row more to the shoulder-line.

To Slope the Shoulder : * Cast off 9 sts., p. to neck edge, turn, and k. back. Repeat from * until all sts. are worked off. Cast off.

THE LEFT FRONT.—Cast on 60 sts. and work 34 rows of single rib as on opposite front.

Now begin the main pattern.

1st row : K. to last 10 sts., then k. 1 and p. 1 alternately to the end.

2nd row : (K. 1 and p. 1) 5 times, p. to end.

Repeat the last 2 rows 20 times more. Work 20 rows more increasing 1 st. at the beginning of the next and every following 4th row, until 5 increases have been made (65 sts.).

To Shape the Armhole : Cast off 10 sts., k. to the last 10 sts., rib to end.

Next row : (K. 1, p. 1) 5 times, p. to end.

Work 6 rows more, decreasing 1 st. at the beginning of the next and each alternate row (52 sts.). Work 27 rows more to the neck-line.

To Shape the Neck : Cast off 17 sts. and p. to end.

Work 16 rows more, dec. 1 st. at the end of the next and each alternate row (27 sts.).

To Slope the Shoulder : Cast off 9 sts. at the beginning of the next row and each alternate row (armhole end) until all the sts. are worked off.

LONG SLEEVES.—Cast on 50 sts. and work 24 rows of single rib as at waist.

Now work in s.s. as follows : K. 20, k. twice into each of the next 10 sts., k. 20.

Next row : All purl (60 sts.).

Work 50 rows in s.s. then work 34 rows more increasing 1 st. at each end of the next row and every following 4th row (78 sts.). (** Short sleeve reference.)

Work 34 rows of s.s., increasing 1 st. at each end of every alternate row (112 sts.). More rows may be worked here without increases for a longer sleeve.

To Shape the Sleeve Top : Cast off 12 sts. at the beginning of the next 2 rows, then work 28 rows more, decreasing 1 st. at each end of the next and every alternate row (60 sts.).

Next row : K. 2 tog. to the end of the row, then p. one row and cast off.

Work a second sleeve the same.

SHORT SLEEVES.—Cast on 66 sts. with No. 11 pins and work 1 inch in single rib, then continue from ** short sleeve reference, on long sleeve directions.

THE COLLAR.—Cast on 120 sts. and k. into the back of the sts. on the 1st row.

Work 8 rows in single rib, then work 14 rows more, increasing 1 st. at the beginning of each row. Cast off.

TO MAKE UP.—Press all pieces on the wrong side over a damp cloth, avoiding the rib.

THE EMBROIDERY.—This consists of rows of lazy-daisies set alternately 3 on the 1st row and 2 on the 2nd, making 7 rows in all to the shoulders.

When all the sprays are finished on both fronts, place the two pieces with the flowers downwards over a thick, soft blanket and press.

Set the sleeves into the armholes, arranging the fullness at the top, and press these seams while the work is open. Sew the collar on the right side and turn over. Sew sleeve and side seams in one line and press. Sew buttons on left front to correspond with buttonholes.

ALL OUR "KNITTEDS" are EMBROIDERED this SEASON

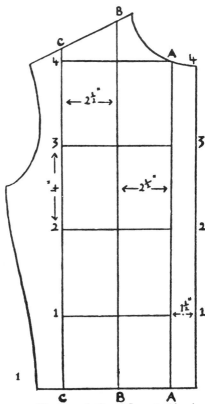

The lines A, B and C are tacking in white cotton parallel with the front, and lines 1, 2, 3 and 4 are parallel with the ribbing at the bottom.

Where the lines cross and in the centre of each little oblong a flower is embroidered, the stalks all turning towards the centre front.

How to Arrange the Flowers on Our Tyrolean Jumper

THE flowers on this jumper are evenly spaced by lines of white tacking-cotton and this is most easily done after pressing but before the garment is made up.

Spread one front on a table and tack a straight line 1½ inches from the front edge and parallel with it as in Line A (Diagram 1).

Tack two more lines B and C (keeping straight with the knitting), and 2½ inches between the lines. Next 1 inch from the ribbing at the bottom tack a line parallel with the bottom and at right angles to the others (Line 1). Lines 2, 3 and 4 are 4 inches apart, and parallel to Line 1.

Now embroider the flowers so that the centre of each flower comes where the lines cross. Six other flowers come one in the middle of each oblong.

It is best to embroider the petals of the flowers first and the centre afterwards and then the stalk and leaves. See that the stalks slant towards the middle of the jumper on both fronts. Do not let the embroidery wool pierce the tacking cotton. Finally, remove the tacking threads.

✳　　　　✳　　　　✳

HOW TO EMBROIDER THE FLOWERS WITHOUT A TRANSFER

First work a lazy-daisy loop upwards in red.

Then work a red lazy-daisy loop downwards to the left.

The next red loop is worked downwards to the right.

The next loop, also red, goes upwards to the left, between the first two stitches.

The last red loop is embroidered upwards to the right. This completes the petals.

Make a yellow French-knot in the centre. Take up a tiny piece of the material. Twist the wool round and round the needle-point. Pull the wool through, holding the wool down with the left thumb, and the wool will form a knot.

Next work a slightly curved stem in stem-stitch, in green.

A lazy-daisy loop should be worked upwards to the left for one leaf in green.

And the last leaf is another lazy-daisy loop worked upwards to the right.

o

EMBROIDERED with TINY FLOWERS

Embroidered Jumpers will be this Season's "Irresistibles." They may be gaily besprinkled with multi-coloured wool flowers or more restrained in tone as in this enchanting design which has its yoke and sleeves embroidered with little sprigs of White Heather.

Full directions for knitting this pretty "Salzburg" Jumper will be found on **facing page**

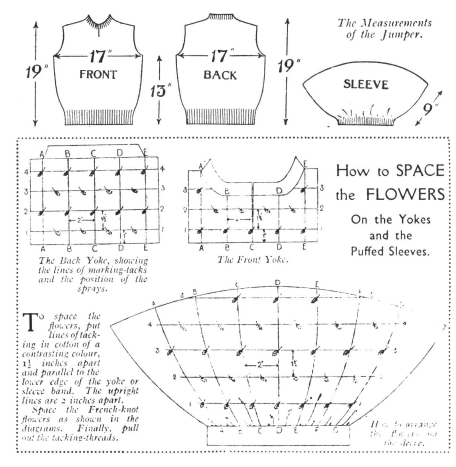

The Measurements of the Jumper.

19" — 17" FRONT — 13" — 17" BACK — 19" — SLEEVE — 9"

How to SPACE the FLOWERS

On the Yokes and the Puffed Sleeves.

The Back Yoke, showing the lines of marking-tacks and the position of the sprays.

The Front Yoke.

To space the flowers, put lines of tacking in cotton of a contrasting colour, 1½ inches apart and parallel to the lower edge of the yoke or sleeve band. The upright lines are 2 inches apart. Space the French-knot flowers as shown in the diagrams. Finally, pull out the tacking-threads.

How to arrange the flowers on the sleeve.

EMBROIDERED *with* TINY FLOWERS

A Lovable Jumper with the Salzburg Touch

THE big " balloon " sleeves and the demure square yoke are decorated with sprigs of white heather—an enchanting jumper and one you will love wearing !

MATERIALS.—*Eight ounces of " Greenock " 3-ply Super Fingering (obtainable only from branches of SCOTCH WOOL & HOSIERY STORES) ; a pair of No. 10 and No. 13 Stratnoid knitting pins ; 3 skeins white and 2 skeins green embroidery cotton ; 1 yard of black velvet ribbon.*

TENSION AND MEASUREMENTS.—*Worked at a tension of 7 sts. to the inch in width on the No. 10 pins, the following measurements are attained after light pressing : Width all round at the underarm, 34 inches ; front and back length from shoulder seam to lower edge, 19 inches ; side seam, 13 inches ; sleeve seam, 9 inches.*

ABBREVIATIONS.—*K., knit ; p., purl ; m., make ; st., stitch ; tog., together ; inc., increase ; s.s., stocking-stitch (knit plain on the right side and purl back).*

Directions in brackets are worked the number of times stated immediately after the brackets.

The Back

USING No. 13 pins cast on 105 sts. for the lower edge. Work 32 rows in single rib (k. 1 and p. 1 alternately).

Change to No. 10 pins and continue in s.s., increasing at each end of every 8th row 4 times (113 sts.), then work straight until there are 86 rows in s.s. to the armholes.

To Shape the Armholes : Cast off 8 sts. at the beginning of the next 2 rows and dec. 1 st. at each end of the next 4 rows. (89 sts.)

THE YOKE.—This begins on the next row and is worked thus :

K. 20, p. 49, k. 20.

Next row : P. 20, * p. twice into the next st., p. 1 ; repeat from * 23 times more, k. 1, p. 20. (113 sts.)

Next row : K. 20, p. 1, k. 71, p. 1, k. 20.

Next row : P. 20, k. 1, p. 71, k. 1, p. 20.

Repeat the last 2 rows 25 times more to the shoulder-line.

To Slope the Shoulders : Cast off 7 sts. at the beginning of the next 8 rows. Slip the remaining 57 sts. on a spare pin.

The Front

WORK exactly the same as the back until 14 rows have been worked on the yoke, after the increase row. On the next row divide the sts. thus : K. 56 and slip the remaining 57 sts. on a spare pin. On the first 56 sts. work 18 rows more in s.s.

To Shape the Neck : Work 21 sts. and slip them on a spare pin, finish the row, then dec. at neck edge of the next 8 rows. Work 10 rows more without shaping to the shoulder-line.

To Slope the Shoulder : Cast off 9 sts. at the beginning of the next row and the next 2 alternate rows (armhole edge).

Join the wool to the first of the remaining 57 sts. (neck end) and k. 2 tog. at the beginning of the row to reduce to 56 sts., then work to correspond with the opposite side. Note that the neck shaping will begin on a right side row and the shoulder shaping on a wrong side row.

THE NECK BAND.—First join the shoulder seams, beginning at the armhole end and taking 1 st. from each side at a time. Now holding the right side of the work facing, and using No. 13 pins, work across the sts. on the right front in single rib, then pick up 17 sts. at the side of the neck, work across the sts. on the spare pin for the back of the neck, pick up 16 sts. on the opposite side and lastly work across the sts. on the left front. (132 sts.)

Work 4 rows in single rib. On the next row make slots for the ribbon thus : (K. 1, p. 1) twice, * m. 1 (by bringing the wool to the front of the pin, then over it and to the front again), p. 2 tog., (k. 1, p. 1) 3 times ; repeat from * to end of row.

Work 4 rows more in single rib and cast off.

The Sleeves

USING No. 13 pins cast on 70 sts. and work 20 rows in single rib. On the next row inc. by knitting 3 times into every st. that is, k. into the back, front and back again (210 sts. altogether).

Change to No. 10 pins and work 52 rows in s.s.

To shape the top of the sleeve, take 3 sts. tog. at each end of the next 38 rows, after which work 1 row, taking 3 sts. together all along the row, then turn and cast off.

Make another sleeve in the same manner.

TO MAKE UP.—First press all pieces (except the rib) with a hot iron over a damp cloth on the wrong side.

Outline the yoke with a row of double crochet working into a loop of the knit stitch preceding the purl lines at the side of the neck and into the purl sts. of the ridge on the front and back.

Before sewing up the jumper, embroider the sprigs of white heather over the yoke and sleeves. (Instructions and diagrams for the embroidery are given on page 75.)

Now sew the sleeves into the armholes, easing the fullness round the top, then sew the sleeve and side seams in one line and press.

To make a French-knot, take up a tiny piece of the material. Twist the cotton round and round the needle-point. Draw the needle through, holding the cotton down with the left thumb, and the cotton will form a knot.

To work stem-stitch take up a little of the material with the needle, throw the thread over to the right and draw it through. Take up a little more material, bringing the needle out a little to the left above the last stitch, so that the stitches overlap slightly.

White French-knots are grouped on each side of the green stalk.

To Wear With A Summer Suit

A Trim Pretty Jumper Knitted In Lustre Suede

MATERIALS

*E*IGHT *ounces " Golden Eagle" 3-ply Lustre Suede ; a pair each of " Aero" knitting pins No. 10 and No. 13 ; 4 buttons.*

TENSION AND MEASUREMENTS

*W*ORKED *at a tension of 8 sts. to the inch in width on the moss-stitch the following measurements are attained after light pressing : Round the bust, 34 inches ; front length from shoulder seam to lower edge, 20 inches ; back length, 19 inches ; side seams, 13 inches ; sleeve seam without cuff, 6 inches.*

ABBREVIATIONS

K., *KNIT ; p., purl ; st., stitch ; tog., together ; inc., increase (by working into the back and front of the same stitch) ; dec., decrease ; m., make (by bringing the wool to the front of the pin and over it) ; single rib is k. 1 and p. 1 alternately ; m.s., moss-stitch (k. 1 and p. 1 alternately, and on subsequent rows the sts. are reversed). Directions in brackets are worked the number of times stated immediately after the brackets.*

TO WORK THE BACK

*W*ITH No. 13 pins cast on 110 sts. and work 37 rows in single rib.

INCREASE ROW : Rib 9, * inc., rib 5 ; repeat from * until 5 remain, inc., rib 4. (127 sts.)

Change to No. 10 pins and work in pattern as follows :

1ST ROW : K. 6, * m. 1, k. 3 tog., m. 1, k. 11 ; repeat from * until 9 remain, m. 1, k. 3 tog., m. 1, k. 6.

2ND ROW and every even numbered row : (Wrong side facing.) All purl.

3RD ROW : K. 5, * m. 1, k. 2 tog., k. 1, k. 2 tog., m. 1, k. 9 ; repeat from * until 10 remain, m. 1, k. 2 tog., k. 1, k. 2 tog., m. 1, k. 5.

5TH ROW : K. 4, * m. 1, k. 2 tog., m. 1, k. 3 tog., m. 1, k. 2 tog., m. 1, k. 7 ; repeat from *, ending the last repeat with k. 4 instead of k. 7.

7TH ROW : K. 3, * (m. 1, k. 2 tog.) twice, k. 1, (k. 2 tog., m. 1) twice, k. 5 ; repeat from *, ending the last repeat with k. 3 instead of k. 5.

9TH ROW : K. 2, * (m. 1, k. 2 tog.) twice, m. 1, k. 3 tog., (m. 1, k. 2 tog.) twice, m. 1, k. 3 ; repeat from *, ending the last repeat with k. 2 instead of k. 3.

11TH ROW : K. 1, * (m. 1, k. 2 tog.) 3 times, k. 1, (k. 2 tog., m. 1) 3 times, k. 1 ; repeat from * to end.

13TH ROW : As 9th row.

15TH ROW : As 7th row.

17TH ROW : As 5th row.

19TH ROW : As 3rd row.

20TH ROW : All purl.

These 20 rows complete one pattern.

Work 3 complete patterns more (4 in all), then 12 rows of the next pattern.

TO SHAPE THE ARMHOLES.—Continue entirely in m.s. for yoke and cast off 3 sts. at the beginning of each of the next 6 rows, then work 2 sts. tog. at both ends of each of the next 7 rows, when 95 sts. will remain.

Work 57 rows straight on these sts.

Cast off straight across.

THE FRONT

*T*HIS is worked exactly the same as the Back until the armhole shaping is finished and 95 sts. remain.

Work 1 row more.

On the next row the sts. are divided for the front opening as follows : Pattern 42 sts. for Left Front Shoulder, then slip the remaining 53 sts. on a stitch-holder until needed for the Right Front Shoulder.

THE LEFT FRONT SHOULDER

*C*ONTINUE in m.s., casting on 11 sts. at the beginning of the next row for underlap. (53 sts.)

Work 33 rows more on these 53 sts.

** TO SHAPE THE NECK. Cast off 11 sts. at the beginning of the next row (neck end), then continue in m.s., taking 2 sts. tog. at the neck end of each of the next 13 rows when 29 sts. will remain.

Work 19 rows straight on these sts.

Cast off.

THE RIGHT FRONT SHOULDER

*J*OIN the wool to the 53 Right Front Shoulder sts., and beginning at the centre end work 10 rows in m.s.

1ST BUTTONHOLE ROW : M.s. 5, cast off 3, m.s. to end.

2ND BUTTONHOLE ROW : Work in m.s., casting on 3 sts. over those cast off to complete the buttonhole.

*** Work 8 rows straight, then repeat the 2 buttonhole rows. Repeat from *** once more.

Work 2 rows more.

Continue from ** To Shape the Neck on Left Front to end.

THE SLEEVES

*W*ITH No. 10 pins begin at the top by casting on 69 sts. Work in m.s., increasing at both ends of every row until there are 85 sts. on the pins. Work 2 rows, then continue in m.s., increasing at both ends of next row and every following 3rd row until there are 129 sts. on the pins. Continue in m.s., decreasing 1 st. at the beginning of every row until 75 sts. remain. Work 4 rows. Cast off.

Work a second sleeve in the same manner.

THE LONG SLEEVES

*T*HESE are worked exactly the same as for short sleeves until 75 sts. remain. Continue on these sts., decreasing at both ends of every 10th row until 65 sts. remain. Work straight on these sts. for length of sleeve desired. Cast off.

Work a second sleeve in the same manner.

The photo shows the diamond pattern.

THE NECK BAND

WITH No. 10 pins cast on 6 sts. and work in m.s. as follows :
  1st Row : M.s. 6.
  2nd Row : M.s. until 1 remains, inc.
  3rd Row : Inc., m.s. to end.

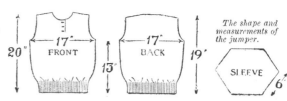

The shape and measurements of the jumper.

The diamond pattern is so charming—and don't you like the pretty little cuffs?

Repeat the last 2 rows until there are 12 sts. (7 rows from the beginning).

1st Buttonhole Row : M.s. 4, cast off 3, m.s. to end.

2nd Buttonhole Row : M.s. 5, cast on 3 over those cast off to complete the buttonhole, m.s. 4.

10th Row : M.s. 12.
11th Row : K. 2 tog., m.s. to end.
12th Row : M.s. until 2 remain, k. 2 tog.

Repeat the last 2 rows until 6 sts. remain. (16 rows from the beginning.)

These 16 rows form one vandyke point.

Work the 16 rows eight times more, omitting the buttonholes on the 8th and 9th rows.

Cast off.

THE SLEEVE BANDS

CAST on 9 sts. and work in vandyke pattern as for the neck band, but note that there will now be 15 sts. on the pins after the increases, instead of 12. Work 6 vandyke points in all. Cast off.

Work a second band in the same way.

THE SHOULDER PADS

WITH No. 10 pins cast on 46 sts. and work four inches in single rib. Cast off.

Work a second pad in the same way.

TO MAKE UP THE JUMPER

FIRST press all pieces with a hot iron over a damp cloth. Join the shoulder seams, beginning at the armhole end and taking 1 st. from each side at a time. Stitch the neck band to neck edge with the buttonhole on right front edge. Set the sleeves into armholes, first making three darts of one inch (one at each end and one in the middle of the straight edge at the top of the sleeve) to give the square shoulder line. Roll the pieces of single rib widthwise, forming shoulder pads one inch wide. Stitch these under the sleeve top at the centre, passing the sts. up and down through one long edge of the pad, and through the top sleeve seam. Stitch the sleeve bands to the wrong side of sleeve edge. Join the sleeve and side seam in one line and press. Sew buttons to the left front.

A LACY CHEVRON-PATTERN of INFINITE CHARM

This Softly-Feminine Little. Jumper Will Delight You

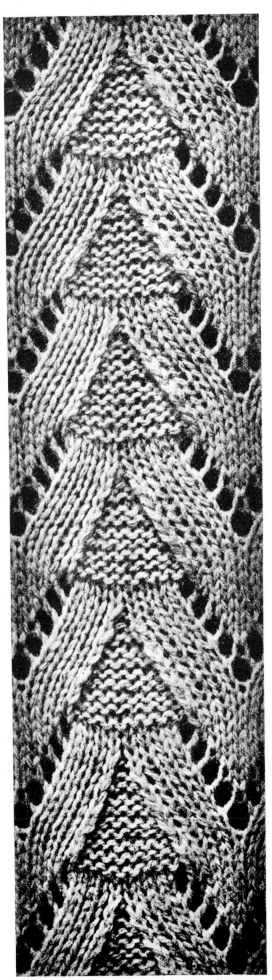

A close-up photograph of the lacy stitch.

THE lacy chevron pattern is fascinating to do, and every row of the shaping is given so that it can be followed quite easily.

MATERIALS: 8 ounces of " *Greenock* " *Super Fingering,* 3-*ply (obtainable only from SCOTCH WOOL & HOSIERY STORES), a pair each of Stratnoid knitting pins No. 9 and No. 13.*

TENSION AND MEASUREMENTS: *Worked at a tension of 7 sts. to the inch in width on No. 9 pins the following measurements are attained after light pressing : Round the bust, 34 inches ; front length from shoulder seam to lower edge, 18 inches ; back length, 17 inches ; side seam, 12 inches ; sleeve seam, 19 inches.*

ABBREVIATIONS: *K., knit ; p., purl ; st., stitch ; tog., together ; inc., increase (by working into the back and front of the same stitch) ;* dec., decrease ; sl., slip ; m., make *(by bringing the wool to the front of the pin) ;* p.s.s.o., *pass the slipped stitch over. Single rib is k. 1, and p. 1 alternately. Directions in brackets are worked the number of times stated immediately after the brackets.*

To Work the Back

WITH No. 13 pins cast on 100 sts. and work 35 rows in single rib.

Increase row : * rib 4, inc., repeat from * until 10 remain, rib. 10 (118 sts.).

Change to No. 9 pins and work in main pattern as follows :

1st row : K. 1, p. 3, * k. 8, p. 9; repeat from *, ending the last repeat with p. 4 instead of p. 9.

2nd row : K. 4, * p. 8, k. 9; repeat from *, ending the last repeat with k. 4 instead of k. 9.

❋   ❋   ❋

If you'd like it in Blue—Choose Turquoise Blue (Shade No. 263). Have a Wine-Red Angora Woollen Skirt. Wine-Red Shoes. A Paste Clip.

THREE

CHARMING

COLOUR SCHEMES

If you'd like it in Brown—Choose Chestnut-Brown (Shade No. 124.) Have a Brown Wool Crepe - de - Chine Skirt. Brown Oxfordettes. Lime-Green Belt.

If you'd like it in White—Choose Snow-White (Shade No. 93). Have a Navy-blue Flannel Coat and Skirt. Navy Blue Shoes and Belt.

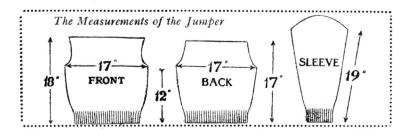

The Measurements of the Jumper

The neck-line is high and slightly "cowled." Wear it with one clip as shown, or with one at each side, which ever suits you better.

3rd row : K. 1, p. 2, * k. 2 tog., k. 3, m. 1, k. 3, sl. 1, k. 1, p.s.s.o., p. 7 ; repeat from *, ending the last repeat with p. 3 instead of p. 7.

4th row : K. 3, * p. 9, k. 7 ; repeat from *, ending the last repeat with k. 3 instead of k. 7.

5th row : K. 1, p. 1, * k. 2 tog., k. 3, m. 1, k. 1, m. 1, k. 3, sl. 1, k. 1, p.s.s.o. p. 5 ; repeat from * until 2 sts. remain, p. 2.

6th row : K. 2, * p. 11, k. 5 ; repeat from *, ending the last repeat with k. 2 instead of k. 5.

7th row : K. 1, * k. 2 tog., (k. 3, m. 1)

twice, k. 3, sl. 1, k. 1, p.s.s.o., p. 3 ; repeat from *, ending the last repeat with p. 1 instead of p. 3.

8th row : K. 1, * p. 13, k. 3 ; repeat from *, ending the last repeat with k. 1 instead of k. 3.

9th row : * K. 2 tog., k. 3, m. 1, k. 5, m. 1, k. 3, sl., 1, k. 1, p.s.s.o., p. 1 ; repeat from * until 15 remain, k. 2 tog.,

k. 3, m. 1, k. 5, m. 1, k. 3, k. 2 tog.

10th row : K. 1, p. 14, * k. 1, p. 15 ; repeat from * to end.

11th row : K. 4, * m. 1, k. 7, m. 1, k. 4, k. 2 tog., k. 3 ; repeat from * until 11 remain, m. 1, k. 7, m. 1, k. 2, k. 2 tog.

12th row : All purl.

These 12 rows comprise one pattern.

Repeat the 12 pattern rows 5 times more to armholes.

To Shape the Armholes.—1st armhole row : Cast off 5 (1 st. on pin) k. 6, * p. 9, k. 8 ; repeat from * until 4 remain, p. 4.

2nd armhole row : Cast off 5 (1 st. on pin), p. 6, * k. 9, p. 8 ; repeat from *, ending the last repeat with p. 7 instead of p. 8

3rd armhole row : Cast off 5 sts. (1 on pin), * sl. 1, k. 1, p.s.s.o., p. 7, k. 2 tog., k. 3, m. 1, k. 3 ; repeat from * to end.

4th armhole row : Cast off 5 (1 st. on pin), p. 2, * k. 7, p. 9 ; repeat from * until 9 remain, k. 7, p. 2.

5th armhole row : K. 1, * sl. 1, k. 1, p.s.s.o., p. 5, k. 2 tog., k. 3, m. 1, k. 1, m. 1, k. 3 ; repeat from * until 11 remain, sl. 1, k. 1, p.s.s.o., p. 5, (k. 2 tog.) twice.

6th armhole row : P. 2, * k. 5, p. 11 ; repeat from * until 7 remain, k. 5, p. 2 tog.

7th armhole row : P. 5, * k. 2 tog., (k. 3, m. 1) twice, k. 3, sl. 1, k. 1, p.s.s.o., p. 3 ; repeat from * until 3 remain, k. 1, k. 2 tog.

8th armhole row : P. 2, * k. 3, p. 13 ; repeat from * until 5 remain, k. 3, p. 2 tog.

9th armhole row : P. 3, * k. 2 tog., k. 3, m. 1, k. 5, m. 1, k. 3, sl. 1, k. 1, p.s.s.o., p. 1 ; repeat from * until 3 remain, k. 1, k. 2 tog.

10th armhole row : P. 2, * k. 1, p. 15 ; repeat from * until 3 remain, k. 1, p. 2 tog.

11th armhole row : P. 1, * k. 2 tog., k. 3, m. 1, k. 7, m. 1, k. 4 ; repeat from *, ending the last repeat with m. 1, k. 2, k. 2 tog., k. 3 tog. after the k. 7.

12th armhole row : K. 2 tog., p. until 2 remain, k. 2 tog. (84 sts.).

Work 3 complete patterns more as at beginning of back, then cast off straight across.

The Front

THIS is worked exactly the same as the back until the armhole shaping is finished and 84 sts. remain.

Work 1 complete pattern more on these sts.

To Shape the Cowl Neck.—Work in inc. pattern as follows :

1st neck row : K. 1, p. 3, * k. 8, p. 9 ; repeat from *, ending the last repeat with p. 4 instead of p. 9.

2nd neck row : Inc., k. 3, * p. 8, k. 9 ; repeat from * until 12 remain, p. 8, k. 3, inc.

3rd neck row : K. 1, p. 3, * k. 2 tog., k. 3, m. 1, k. 3, sl. 1, k. 1, p.s.s.o., p. 7 ; repeat from *, ending the last repeat with p. 4 instead of p. 7.

4th neck row : Inc., k. 3, * p. 9, k. 7 ; repeat from * until 13 remain, p. 9, k. 3, inc.

5th neck row : K. 1, p. 3, * k. 2 tog., k. 3, m. 1, k. 1, m. 1, k. 3, sl. 1, k. 1, p.s.s.o., p. 5 ; repeat from *, ending the last repeat with p. 4 instead of p. 5.

6th neck row : Inc., k. 3, * p. 11, k. 5 ; repeat from * until 15 remain, p. 11, k. 3, inc.

7th neck row : K. 1, p. 3, * k. 2 tog., (k. 3, m. 1) twice, k. 3, sl. 1, k. 1, p.s.s.o., p. 3 ; repeat from *, ending the last repeat with p. 4 instead of p. 3.

8th neck row : Inc., k. 3, * p. 13, k. 3 ; repeat from * until 1 remains, inc.

9th neck row : K. 3, p. 1, * k. 2 tog., k. 3, m. 1, k. 5, m. 1, k. 3, sl. 1, k. 1, p.s.s.o., p. 1 ; repeat from * until 3 remain, k. 3.

10th neck row : Inc., p. 2, * k. 1, p. 15 ; repeat from * until 4 remain, k. 1, p. 2, inc.

11th neck row : K. 9, * m. 1, k. 7, m. 1, k. 4, k. 2 tog., k. 3 ; repeat from * until 16 remain, m. 1, k. 7, m. 1, k. 2,

k. 2 tog., k. 5.

12th neck row : Inc., p. until 1 remains, inc.

13th neck row : K. 1, * p. 9, k. 8 ; repeat from * until 10 remain, p. 9, k. 1.

14th neck row : Inc., * k. 9, p. 8 ; repeat from * until 10 remain, k. 9, inc.

15th neck row : K. 3, * p. 7, k. 2 tog., k. 3, m. 1, k. 3, sl. 1, k. 1, p.s.s.o. ; repeat from * until 10 remain, p. 7, k. 3.

16th neck row : Inc., p. 2, * k. 7, p. 9 ; repeat from * until 10 remain, k. 7, p. 2, inc.

17th neck row : K. 5, * p. 5, k. 2 tog., k. 3, m. 1, k. 1, m. 1, k. 3, sl. 1, k. 1, p.s.s.o. ; repeat from * until 10 remain, p. 5, k. 5.

18th neck row : Inc., p. 4, * k. 5, p. 11 ; repeat from * until 10 remain, k. 5, p. 4, inc.

19th neck row : K. 2, m. 1, k. 3, sl. 1, k. 1, p.s.s.o., * p. 3, k. 2 tog., (k. 3, m. 1) twice, k. 3, sl. 1, k. 1, p.s.s.o. ; repeat from * until 10 remain, p. 3, k. 2 tog., k. 3, m.1, k. 2.

20th neck row : Inc., p. 6, * k. 3, p. 13 ; repeat from * until 10 remain, k. 3, p. 6, inc.

21st neck row : K. 4, m. 1, k. 3, sl. 1, k. 1, p.s.s.o., * p. 1, k. 2 tog., k. 3, m. 1, k. 5, m. 1, k. 3, sl. 1, k. 1, p.s.s.o. ; repeat from * until 10 remain, p. 3, k. 2 tog., k. 3, m. 1, k. 2.

22nd neck row : Inc., p. 8, * k. 1, p. 15 ; repeat from * until 10 remain, k. 1, p. 8, inc.

23rd neck row : K. 6, * m. 1, k. 4, k. 2 tog., k. 3, m. 1, k. 7 ; repeat from * until 15 remain, m. 1, k. 4, k. 2 tog., k. 3, m. 1, k. 4, k. 2 tog.

24th neck row : Inc., p. until 1 remains, inc.

25th neck row : K. 7, * p. 9, k. 8 ; repeat from *, ending the last repeat with k. 7 instead of k. 8.

26th neck row : Inc., p. 6, * k. 9, p. 8 ; repeat from *, ending the last repeat with p. 6, inc. instead of p. 8.

27th neck row : K. 4, m. 1, k. 3, sl. 1, k. 1, p.s.s.o., * p. 7, k. 2 tog., k. 3, m. 1, k. 3, sl. 1, k. 1, p.s.s.o. ; repeat from * until 16 remain, p. 7, k. 2 tog., k. 3, m. 1, k. 4.

28th neck row : Inc., p. 8, * k. 7, p. 9 ; repeat from *, ending the last repeat with p. 8, inc., instead of p. 9.

29th neck row : * K. 2 tog., k. 3, m. 1, k. 1, m. 1, k. 3, sl. 1, k. 1, p.s.s.o., p. 5 ; repeat from *, omitting the p. 5 at the end of the last repeat.

30th neck row : Inc., p. 10, * k. 5, p. 11 ; repeat from *, ending the last repeat with p. 10, inc., instead of p. 11.

31st neck row : * K. 2 tog., (k. 3, m.1) twice, k. 3, sl. 1, k. 1, p.s.s.o., p. 3 ; repeat from *, omitting the p. 3 on last repeat.

32nd neck row : Inc., p. 12, * k. 3, p. 13 ; repeat from *, ending the last repeat with p. 12, inc., instead of p. 13.

33rd neck row : * K. 2 tog., k. 3, m. 1, k. 5, m. 1, k. 3, sl. 1, k. 1, p.s.s.o., p. 1 ; repeat from *, omitting the p. 1 at the end of the last repeat.

34th neck row : Inc., p.14, * k. 1, p. 15 ; repeat from *, ending the last repeat with p. 14, inc., instead of p. 15.

35th neck row : K. 5, * m. 1, k. 7, m. 1, k. 4, k. 2 tog., k. 3 ; repeat from * until 12 remain, m. 1, k. 7, m. 1, k. 5.

Cast off loosely.

The Sleeves

WITH No. 13 pins begin at the wrist by casting on 50 sts. Work 34

rows in single rib. Change to No. 9 pins and work in pattern as on back for 7 rows. This sets the position of the pattern which is kept intact to top of sleeve. Continue in pattern, increasing 1 st. at both ends of the next row and every following 8th row until there are 78 sts. on the pins, working all the extra sts. in s.s. at each end of the row.

Work on these sts. until 10 complete patterns have been worked.

To Shape the Sleeve Top.—Keep the pattern correct in the centre and take 2 sts. tog. at both ends of every row until 52 sts. remain.

Now work in dec. pattern as follows :

1st row : (3rd row of pattern)k 2 tog , p. 2, * k. 2 tog., k. 3, m. 1, k. 3, sl. 1, k. 1, p.s.s.o., p. 7 ; repeat from *, ending the last repeat with p. 2, k. 2 tog. instead of p. 7.

2nd row : K. 2 tog., k. 1, * p. 9, k. 7 ; repeat from * until 12 remain, p. 9, k. 1, k. 2 tog.

3rd row : K. 3 tog., * k. 3, m. 1, k. 1, m. 1, k. 3, sl. 1, k. 1, p.s.s.o., p. 5, k. 2 tog. ; repeat from * until 10 sts. remain, k. 3, m. 1, k. 1, m. 1, k. 3, sl. 1, k. 2 tog., p.s.s.o.

4th row : P. 2 tog., p. 9, k. 5, p. 11, k. 5, p. 9, p. 2 tog.

5th row : K. 2 tog., k. 4, m. 1, k. 3, sl. 1, k. 1, p.s.s.o., p. 3, k. 2 tog., (k. 3, m. 1) twice, k. 3, sl. 1, k. 1, p.s.s.o., p. 3, k. 2 tog., k. 3, m. 1, k. 4, k. 2 tog.

6th row : P. 2 tog., p. 8, k. 3, p. 13, k. 3, p. 8, p. 2 tog.

7th row : K. 2 tog., k. 3, m. 1, k. 3, sl. 1, k. 1, p.s.s.o., p. 1, k. 2 tog., k. 3, m. 1, k. 5, m. 1, k. 3, sl. 1, k. 1, p.s.s.o., p. 1, k. 2 tog., k. 3, m. 1, k. 3, k. 2 tog.

8th row : P. 2 tog., p. 7, k. 1, p. 15, k. 1, p. 7, p. 2 tog.

9th row : K. 2 tog., k. 2, m. 1, k. 4, k. 2 tog., k. 3, m. 1, k. 7, m. 1, k. 4, k. 2 tog., k. 3, m. 1, k. 2, k. 2 tog.

10th row : P. 2 tog., p. until 2 remain, p. 2. tog.

11th row : K. 2 tog., p. 9, k. 8, p. 9, k. 1, k. 2 tog.

12th row : K. 2 tog., k. 9, p. 8, k. 9, p. 1.

13th row : P. 2 tog., p. 7, k. 2 tog., k. 3, m. 1, k. 3, sl. 1, k. 1, p.s.s.o., p. 7, p. 2 tog.

14th row : K. 2 tog., k. 6, p. 9, k. 6, k. 2 tog.

15th row : P. 2 tog., p. 4, k. 2 tog., k. 3, m. 1, k. 1, m. 1, k. 3, sl. 1, k. 1, p.s.s.o., p.4, p. 2 tog.

16th row : K. 2 tog., k. 3, p. 11, k. 3, k. 2, tog.

17th row : P. 2 tog., p. 1, k. 2 tog (k. 3, m 1) twice, k. 3, sl. 1, k. 1, p.s.s.o., p. 1, p. 2 tog.

18th row : K. 2 tog., p. 13, k. 2 tog.

19th row : K. 2 tog., k. 3, m. 1, k. 5, m 1, k. 3, sl. 1, k. 1, p.s.s.o.

20th row : P. 2 tog., p. 11, p. 2 tog. (13 sts.).

Cast off.

Work a second sleeve in the same manner.

TO MAKE UP THE JUMPER.—First press all pieces with a hot iron over a damp cloth on the wrong side of the work. Join the shoulder seams, beginning at the armhole end and taking 1 st. from each side at a time until about 4 inches has been joined, leaving the rest for the middle of the neck to form the cowl. Set the sleeves into armholes, and press these seams while the work is open. Join the sleeve and side seams in one long line and press.

"A jumper with sunray ribbing"

For pattern see p. 186

"The frilly sleeves give charm"

For pattern see p. 192

"Such flattering puffed sleeves"

For pattern see p. 240

"It cannot fail to please"

For pattern see p. 244

The perfect jumper for informal entertaining.

TO GREET *the* NEW SEASON

A Very Feminine Jumper with Three Demure Little Bows

A N easily knitted jumper in a pretty fancy wool. The lines are both becoming and slimming.

Materials

Twelve ounces of Anny Blatt " NEW BOUCLETTE " yarn ; ¾ yard of 2-inch Petersham ribbon to match ; a pair each of " Aero " knitting pins, No. 10 and No. 12 ; an " Aero " crochet hook, No. 12.

Tension and Measurements

Worked at a tension of 7 sts. to the inch in width on No. 10 pins, the following measurements are attained after light pressing : Across the back at the underarms, 19 inches ; across each front at the same place, 10½ inches (making a total bust measurement of 40 inches) ; front and back length from shoulder seam to lower edge, 22 inches ; side seam, 15 inches ; sleeve seam, 19 inches.

Abbreviations

K., knit ; p., purl ; st., stitch ; tog., together ; inc., increase (by working into the back and front of the same stitch) ; dec., decrease ; s.s., stocking-stitch (k. on the right side and purl back) ; single rib is k. 1 and p. 1 alternately.

To Work the Back

With No. 10 pins, cast on 102 sts. and work 48 rows in s.s., working into the back of the sts. on the 1st row to give a neat edge.

Continue in s.s., increasing at both ends of the next row and every following 6th row until 8 increase rows have been worked and there are 118 sts.

Work 5 rows straight on these sts., then continue in s.s., increasing at both ends of the next row and every following 7th row until 5 more increase rows have been worked and there are 128 sts. on the pins.

Work 13 rows straight on these sts. to armholes (138 rows).

To Shape the Armholes.—Continue in s.s., casting off

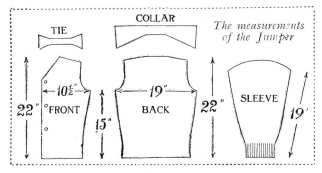

229

As Vivid or Pastel as You Choose

Knit It to Match or in Bright Contrast to Your Skirt

8 sts. at the beginning of each of the next 2 rows; then work 2 sts. tog. at both ends of the next row and following alternate row, when 108 sts. will remain.

Work 64 rows straight on these sts. to shoulders.

To Slope the Shoulders: Cast off 12 sts. at the beginning of each of the next 6 rows. Cast off the remaining sts.

The Right Front

With No. 10 pins, cast on 54 sts. and work 48 rows straight in s.s., working into the back of the sts. on the 1st row to give a neat edge.

Continue in s.s., increasing at the end of the next row and every following 6th row until 4 increase rows have been worked (58 sts.). P. 1 row.

1st buttonhole row: K. 4, cast off 4, k. to end.

P. 1 row and k. 1 row, passing the wool across the buttonhole, but do not draw up.

Next row: All purl, casting on 4 sts. over those cast off on 1st buttonhole row.

Work 49 rows straight on these sts., increasing at the end of the next row and every following 6th row until there are 67 sts. on the pins.

Now work a second buttonhole as before. Work 12 rows straight to armhole (1 row more here on Left Front).

To Shape the Armhole: Cast off 8 sts., p. to end.

K. 1 row.

Continue in s.s., taking 2 sts. tog. at the beginning of next row and following alternate row (armhole end), when 57 sts. will remain.

Work 12 rows straight on these sts., then work a third buttonhole as before. Work 6 rows more in s.s., when the neck-line will be reached.

To Shape the Neck: Continue in s.s., taking 2 sts. tog. at the neck end of next row and every following alternate row until 22 decrease rows have been worked. P. 1 row and k. 1 row to shoulder.

To Slope the Shoulder: Cast off 12 sts. at the beginning of next row and following alternate row.

Work 1 row. Cast off.

The Left Front

This is worked exactly the same as the Right Front, but the increases will now be worked at the beginning of k. rows, and the buttonholes will be begun at the end of the row. The armhole shaping is now begun on a k. row.

The Sleeves

Begin at the top and, using No. 10 pins, cast on 56 sts. Work 1 row into the back of the sts. Continue in s.s., increasing 1 st. at both ends of the next 8 rows (72 sts.).

Now increase at both ends of every alternate row (every k. row) until 10 more increase rows have been worked and there are 92 sts. on the pins.

Cast on 8 sts. at the beginning of each of the next 2 rows (108 sts.).

Continue straight on these sts. for 18 rows.

Now decrease at both ends of the next row and every following 6th row until 60 sts. remain.

Continue straight on these sts. for length of sleeve desired, less about 3 inches for the cuff.

Change to No. 12 pins and work 36 rows in single rib. Cast off.

The Collar

With No. 10 pins, cast on 38 sts. and k. 5 rows, working into the back of the sts. on the 1st row to give a neat edge.

** *Next row:* K. 2 tog., k. to end.

Next row: K. until 6 remain, turn and k. back.

Next row: All k.

Next row: K. 2 tog., k. to end.

K. 3 rows.

Repeat from ** 8 times more, when 20 sts. will remain.

Continue in plain knitting, working 2 sts. tog. at the beginning of the next row and every following alternate row (shaped end) 5 times. K. 51 rows.

Continue in plain knitting, increasing at the beginning of next row and every following alternate row (shaped end) 5 times. K. 1 row more.

*** *Next row:* K. 1, inc., k. to end.

Next row: K. until 6 remain, turn and k. back.

Next row: All k.

Next row: K. 1, inc., k. to end.

K. 3 rows.

Repeat from *** 8 times more (38 sts.).

K. 5 rows. Cast off.

The Belt

With No. 12 pins, cast on 18 sts. and k. plain for length desired. Cast off. Stitch this to the Petersham ribbon.

The Ties

With No. 10 pins, cast on 26 sts. and k. 2 rows, working into the back of the sts. on the 1st row.

Continue in plain knitting, decreasing at both ends of next row and every following alternate row until 10 remain.

K. 81 rows straight on these sts.

Continue in plain knitting, increasing at both ends of next row and every following alternate row until there are 26 sts. K. 2 rows and cast off.

To Make Up the Jumper

First press all pieces with a hot iron over a damp cloth. Join the shoulder seams, beginning at the armhole end and taking 1 st. from each side at a time. Stitch the shaped edge of collar to neck. Set the sleeves into armholes and press these seams, then join the sleeve and side seams.

Work 1 row of d.c. all round the edge of the jumper.

Fold in the two front edges for about half an inch and press.

THE BUTTONHOLE TABS.—Work 10 ch. and slipstitch to the first st. to form a ring. Work 2 tr. into each chain, and at the end of the round sl.st. to the top of the first tr. to join. Fasten off.

These rings are then stitched over the buttonholes, drawing up the loose threads of wool left across the buttonholes.

The lower part of the jumper is in stocking-stitch knitting.

ENCHANTING—*In* BROWN *and* BLUE!

A Soft Little Jumper with a Most Attractive Lacy Yoke

Materials

Four ounces of W.B. Rosedale 4-ply Fingering in dark shade, and 2 ounces of W.B. A.A. "Shetland Wool" in a light contrast; a pair each of "Acro" knitting pins No. 3 and No. 11; an "Aero" crochet hook No. 13.

Tension and Measurements

Worked at a tension of 4½ sts. to the inch in width on No. 3 pins, and with the thick wool, the following measurements are attained after light pressing: Round the bust, 37 inches; front length from shoulder seam to lower edge, 20 inches; back length, 18 inches; side seam, 13 inches; sleeve seam, 6 inches.

The little puff sleeves are most fascinating.

YOUTHFUL *and* QUITE IRRESISTIBLE!

(Continued from overleaf)

P. 1 row.

With light-coloured wool begin the yoke pattern and armhole shaping as follows :

1st armhole decrease row : (Right side facing) K. 2 tog., k. until 2 remain, sl. 1, k. 1, p.s.s.o.

2nd armhole decrease row : P. 2 tog., p. until 2 remain, p. 2 tog. (79 sts.).

3rd armhole decrease row : K. 2 tog., k. 7, p. 1, * (k. 2 tog.) 5 times, m. 1, (k. 1, m. 1) 9 times, (sl. 1, k. 1, p.s.s.o.) 5 times, p. 1 ; repeat from * until 9 remain, k. 7, sl. 1, k. 1, p.s.s.o. (77 sts.).

4th armhole decrease row : P. 2 tog., p. 12, * (k. into the back of the next st., p. 1) 9 times, k. 1 into the back of the next st., p. 11 ; repeat from * until 3 remain, p. 1, p. 2 tog.

5th armhole decrease row : K. 2 tog., k. 5, p. 1, (k. 29, p. 1) twice, k. 5, sl. 1, k. 1, p.s.s.o. (73 sts.).

6th armhole decrease row : P. 2 tog., k. 4, p. 1, (k. 29, p. 1) twice, k. 4, p. 2 tog. (71 sts.)

7th armhole decrease row : K. 2 tog., k. 3, p. 1, (k. 29, p. 1) twice, k. 3, sl. 1, k. 1, p.s.s.o. (69 sts.).

8th armhole decrease row : P. 2 tog., p. until 2 remain, p. 2 tog. (67 sts.).

9th armhole decrease row : K. 2 tog., k. 1, p. 1, * (k. 2 tog.) 5 times, m. 1, (k. 1, m. 1) 9 times, (sl. 1, k. 1, p.s.s.o.) 5 times, p. 1 ; repeat from * until 3 remain, k. 1, sl. 1, k. 1, p.s.s.o. (65 sts.).

10th armhole decrease row : P. 2 tog., p. 6, (k. into the back of the next st., p. 1) 9 times, k. into the back of the next st., p. 11, (k. into the back of the next st., p. 1) 9 times, k. into the back of the next st., p. 6, p. 2 tog. (63 sts.).

11th armhole decrease row : K. 2 tog., k. 29, p. 1, k. 29, sl. 1, k. 1, p.s.s.o.

There are now 61 sts. on which work straight in yoke pattern as follows :

1st straight pattern row : P. 1, * k. 29, p. 1 ; repeat from * to end.

2nd yoke pattern row : P. 1, * k. 29, p. 1 ; repeat from * to end.

3rd yoke pattern row : All purl.

4th yoke pattern row : P. 1, * (k. 2 tog.) 5 times, m. 1, (k. 1, m. 1) 9 times, (sl. 1, k. 1, p.s.s.o.) 5 times, p. 1 ; repeat from * to end.

5th yoke pattern row : P. 6, * k. into the back of the next st., (p. 1, then k. into the back of the next st.) 9 times, p. 11 ; repeat from *, ending the last repeat with p. 6 instead of p. 11.

Abbreviations

K., knit ; p., purl ; st., stitch ; tog., together ; inc., increase (by working into the back and front of the same stitch) ; m., make (by bringing the wool to the front of the pins) ; p.s.s.o., pass slipped stitch over ; sl., slip. Rib is k. 2 and p. 2 alternately. S.s., stocking-stitch (k. on the right side and p. back). Directions in brackets are worked the number of times stated immediately after the brackets.

To Work the Back

With No. 11 pins and dark wool cast on 108 sts. and work in rib as follows :

1st row : (Right side facing) P. 1, k. 2, * p. 2, k. 2 ; repeat from * until 1 remains, p. 1.

2nd row : K. 1, p. 2, * k. 2, p. 2 ; repeat from * until 1 remains, k. 1.

Repeat these 2 rows 17 times more (36 rows altogether).

Decrease row : (Right side facing) K. 4, * k. 2 tog., k. 2 ; repeat from * ending the last repeat with k. 6 instead of k. 2 (83 sts.).

Change to No. 3 pins and work 47 rows straight in s.s., beginning with a purl row.

Next row : (Right side facing) K. 11, * (k. 2 tog.) 5 times, inc. in each of the next 10 sts., (sl. 1, k. 1, p.s.s.o.) 5 times, k. 1 ; repeat from * once more, then k. 10.

COLOUR-SCHEME No. 1

JUMPER. Chocolate-brown. Shade No. 443. Sky-blue yoke.

SKIRT. Chocolate-brown shantung.

ACCESSORIES. Brown suède court shoes. "Tange" brown stockings. Brown suède Romeo cap.

COLOUR-SCHEME No. 2

JUMPER. Bright navy-blue. Shade No. 846. Baby-pink yoke.

SKIRT. Navy-blue linen, to match.

ACCESSORIES. Navy-blue linen sandals. Pink and blue bracelets. Navy-blue straw hat.

COLOUR-SCHEME No. 3

JUMPER. Ebony-black. White yoke.

SKIRT. White flannel, six-gored style.

ACCESSORIES. Black and white Oxfordettes. White kid belt and gloves. White hat, trimmed with black.

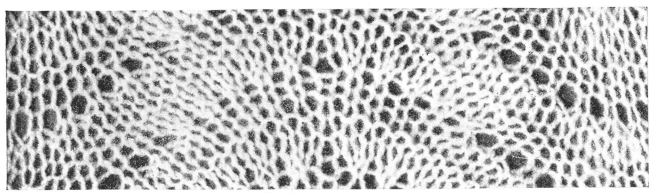

The feathery yoke pattern.

6th yoke pattern row : P. 1, * k. 29, p. 1.

Repeat these 6 rows twice more, then the 1st to the 5th row again.

Next row : Cast off 18 sts. for 1st shoulder (1 st. on pin), k. 11, p. 1, k. 12 (25 sts. for back of neck), cast off 18.

Join the wool to the remaining 25 sts. and work as follows :

1st neck row : (Right side facing) K. 2 tog., k. until 2 remain, sl. 1, k. 1, p.s.s.o.

2nd neck row : Cast off 3 (1 st. on pin), k. 7, p. 1, k. 9, k. 2 tog. (19 sts.).

3rd neck row : Cast off 3 (1 st. on pin), p. 6, k. 1, p. 6, p. 2 tog. (15 sts.).

Cast off the remaining sts.

The Front.—This is worked exactly the same as the back until the armhole shaping is finished and 61 sts. remain.

Work the 6 yoke pattern rows twice, then 5 rows of the next pattern when the neck-line will be reached. On the next row the sts. are divided for the neck opening as follows : (With the right side facing) P. 1, k. 24 and slip these 25 sts. on to a stitch-holder until needed for the Left Front Shoulder, cast off 11, (1 st. on pin), k. 23, p. 1, for Right Front Shoulder (25 sts.).

THE RIGHT FRONT SHOULDER.—*1st row :* (Wrong side facing) P. 1, k. 24.

2nd row : Cast off 4 (1 st. on pin), k. 19, p. 1 (21 sts.).

3rd row : All purl.

4th row : Cast off 3 (1 st. on pin), (k. 1, m. 1) 6 times, (sl. 1, k. 1, p.s.s.o.) 5 times, p. 1 (19 sts.).

5th row : P. 6, k. into the back of the next st., (p. 1, k. into the back of the next st.) 5 times, p. 2.

6th row : K. 2 tog., k. 16, p. 1 (18 sts.).

7th row : P. 1, k. 17.

8th row : K. 17, p. 1.

9th row : All purl.

10th row : K. 2 tog., m. 1, (k. 1, m. 1) 5 times, (sl. 1, k. 1, p.s.s.o.) 5 times, p. 1.

11th row : P. 6, (k. into the back of the next st., p. 1) 6 times.

Cast off the remaining sts.

THE LEFT FRONT SHOULDER.—Join the wool to the neck end of the 25 Left Front Shoulder sts. and work in pattern as follows :

1st row : (Wrong side facing) K. 24, p. 1.

2nd row : P. 1, k. 24.

3rd row : Cast off 4 (1 st. on pin), p. 20 (21 sts.).

4th row : P. 1, (k. 2 tog.) 5 times, (m. 1, k. 1) 6 times, k. 4 (22 sts.).

5th row : Cast off 3 (1 st. on pin), p. 1, (k. into the back of the next stitch, p. 1) 6 times, p. 5.

6th row : P. 1, k. 16, sl. 1, k. 1, p.s.s.o. (18 sts.).

7th row : K. 17, p. 1.

8th row : P. 1, k. 17.

9th row : All purl.

10th row : P. 1, (k. 2 tog.) 5 times, m. 1, (k. 1, m. 1) 5 times, k. 2 tog.

11th row : (P. 1, k. into the back of the next st.) 6 times, p. 6. Cast off.

The Sleeves

With No. 11 pins and dark wool cast on 60 sts. and work 8 rows in rib as on back waist.

Increase row : (Right side facing) K. 1, m. 1, k. 1 all into the first st. (3 on pin). Now inc. 1 st. into each of the remaining sts. by knitting into the front and back of each st. (121 sts. now on).

Change to No. 3 pins and light wool and purl 1 row.

Continue in pattern as follows :

1st, 2nd and 3rd rows : P. 1, * k. 29, p. 1 ; repeat from * to end.

4th row : All purl.

5th row : P. 1, * (k. 2 tog.) 5 times, m. 1, (k. 1, m. 1) 9 times, (sl. 1, k. 1, p.s.s.o.) 5 times, p. 1, repeat from * to end.

6th row : P. 6, * k. into the back of the next st., (p. 1, k. into the back of the next st.) 9 times, p. 11 ; repeat from * ending the last repeat with p. 6 instead of p. 11.

Repeat these 6 rows 3 times more.

To Shape the Sleeve Top : Continue in decrease pattern as follows :

1st decrease row : (Right side facing) Cast off 12 sts. (1 st. on pin), k. 17, p. 1, (k. 29, p. 1) 3 times.

2nd decrease row : Cast off 12 (1 st. on pin), k. 17, p. 1, (k. 29, p. 1) twice, k. 18.

3rd decrease row : Cast off 9, (1 st. on pin), k. 8, p. 1, (k. 29, p. 1) twice, k. 18.

4th decrease row : Cast off 9, (1 st. on pin), p. 78.

5th decrease row : K. 2 tog., k. 7, p. 1, * (k. 2 tog.) 5 times, m. 1, (k. 1, m. 1) 9 times, (sl. 1, k. 1, p.s.s.o.) 5 times, p. 1 ; repeat from * until 9 remain, k. 7, sl. 1, k. 1, p.s.s.o.

6th decrease row : P. 2 tog., p. 12, * (k. into the back of the next st., p. 1) 9 times, k. into the back of the next st., p. 11 ; repeat from * until 3 remain, p. 1, p. 2 tog.

7th decrease row : K. 2 tog., k. 5, p. 1, (k. 29, p. 1) twice, k. 5, sl. 1, k. 1, p.s.s.o.

8th row : P. 2 tog., k. 4, p. 1, (k. 29, p. 1) twice, k. 4, p. 2 tog.

9th row : K. 2 tog., k. 3, p. 1, (k. 29, p. 1) twice, k. 3, sl. 1, k. 1, p.s.s.o.

10th row : P. 2 tog., p. until 2 remain, p. 2 tog.

11th row : K. 2 tog., k. 1, p. 1, * (k. 2 tog.) 5 times, m. 1, (k. 1, m. 1) 9 times, (sl. 1, k. 1, p.s.s.o.) 5 times, p. 1 ; repeat from * until 3 remain, k. 1, sl. 1, k. 1, p.s.s.o.

12th row : P. 2 tog., p. 6, * (k. into the back of the next st., p. 1) 9 times, k. into the back of the next st., p. 11, (k. into the back of the next st., p. 1) 9 times, k. into the back of the next st., p. 6, p. 2 tog. (63 sts.).

13th row : Cast off 12 (1 st. on pin), k. 18, p. 1, k. 29, p. 1, k. 1 (51 sts.).

14th row : Cast off 12 (1 st. on pin), k. 18, p. 1, k. 19 (39 sts.).

15th row : Cast off 9 (1 st. on pin), k. 9, p. 1, k. 19 (30 sts.).

16th row : Cast off 9 (1 st. on pin), p. 20 (21 sts.). Cast off remaining sts.

Work a second sleeve the same.

TO MAKE UP THE JUMPER.—First press all pieces with a hot iron over a damp cloth over the wrong side of the work and join the shoulder seams.

THE CROCHET NECK-BAND —*1st round:* With the No. 13 crochet hook work 1 d.c. into each k. st., but across the centre front where there are open sts. put 1 d.c. between the k. sts. also, 4 ch., turn.

2nd round : * 1 tr. in second d.c. of last round, 1 ch. ; repeat from * to end, sl.st. to the 3rd of the turning ch.

3rd round : * 4 ch., sl.st. to 4th ch. from hook to form a picot, 1 d.c. into next tr., 3 ch., 1 d.c. in next tr. Repeat from * all round ; at the end sl.st. to first st., then fasten off.

Set the sleeves into armholes, gathering the tops of the sleeves to give a puffed effect. Join the sleeve and side seams in one long line and press.

Twist a cord of the two wools, using 4 strands of light Shetland wool and 2 of the dark fingering, and stitch a tassel at each end.

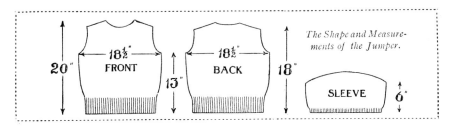

20"   18½" FRONT   18½" BACK   18"
The Shape and Measurements of the Jumper.
13"   SLEEVE   6"

An Embroidered Jumper

decrease ; st.-st. = stocking-stitch ; rib = k. 1, p. 1 ; g.-st. = garter-stitch.

TENSION : 13 sts. and 17 rows = 2 inches.

MEASUREMENTS : Length, 21 inches ; bust, 35 inches ; sleeve seam, 21 inches, sleeve worn pouched.

The Back

Commence at lower edge of back. Using No. 12 needles, cast on 84 sts., and rib for 30 rows.

Change to No. 9 needles and st.-st., and inc. in 1st row by knitting twice into every 7th st. to end. Continue in st.-st., and inc. at each end of 60th, 70th, 80th, and 90th rows (104 sts.). Continue until 96 rows of st.-st. are completed.

Change to g.-st., and to shape armholes dec. at each end of next 10 rows (84 sts.). Continue for 44 more rows.

To shape neck and shoulders, cast off 7 sts., k. 28, cast off 14, k. 35. *Next row.—* Cast off 7, knit to last 2 sts. (neck end), knit them tog. Now dec. at neck edge on each row, and cast off 7 sts. at beg. of each row starting from armhole end, until all sts. are worked. Fasten off.

Work other shoulder likewise.

The Front

Commence with right side in wear. Using No. 12 needles, cast on 49 sts. and rib 43 sts., g.-st. 6 sts. *Next row.*—Right side facing, g.-st. 6 sts., rib 43. Continue as in these 2 rows for 13 rows in all.

14th row.—k. 3, cast off 3, rib 43. *Next row*—In pattern, and cast on 3 sts. over cast-off 3 in previous row. Continue in pattern for 15 rows, 30 in all.

Change to No. 9 needles ; g.-st. 6 sts., st.-st. remainder, knitting twice into 1st, then every 7th, st. to end (56 sts.). Continue on these sts. in pattern for 13 rows.

Make one buttonhole on next row, as for first, then further buttonholes on every 27th row, starting from front edge.

MATERIALS REQUIRED : 10 ounces of Wendy Merino Wool, 4-ply ; 1 pair of Stratnoid knitting needles, size 12, and 1 pair, size 9 ; 6 medium-sized fancy buttons ; 1 crochet hook, size 1 ; wools for embroidery (see " To Make Up " at end).

ABBREVIATIONS : k. = knit ; p. = purl ; sl. = slip ; tog. = together ; rep. = repeat ; inc. = increase ; dec. =

An Embroidered Jumper

Inc. at seam edge on 60th, 70th, 80th, and 90th rows (60 sts.). Continue in pattern until 96 rows of st.-st. are completed.

Now work all in g.-st., and shape for armholes, making buttonholes as before, and dec. at seam end of needle on next 12 rows (48 sts.). Continue in g.-st. until six buttonholes in all are completed. Knit 20 more rows after sixth buttonhole.

To shape neck, cast off 6 sts. at beg. of next row, starting from front edge, and work to end. Knit 14 rows, and dec. at neck edge on each.

To shape shoulder, cast off 7 sts. at beg. of next 4 rows, starting from armhole end, and fasten off.

Work other front to pair, only reversing 6 g.-sts., so that they come at end of needle instead of beg., and with *no buttonholes*.

The Sleeves

Using No. 12 needles, cast on 50 sts. and rib 6 rows. Change to No. 9 needles and st.-st., and knit 1st row, knitting 3 sts. into each st. to end (150 sts.). Continue in st.-st., and dec. at each end of every 5th row until 86 sts. remain. Continue until seam measures 21 inches, then to shape top dec. at each end of every row until 20 sts. remain. Cast off.

Work another sleeve likewise.

To Make Up

Press each part to size and shape, using damp cloth and warm iron. Sew up seams and put in sleeves. Chalk designs as in diagrams on to fronts of jumper exactly as shown in photograph. The rose is worked in pale pink wool and satin stitch, its leaf in green and short stem-stitch. The shamrock is worked in small buttonhole-stitch, with as natural a green as is possible to obtain. The thistle is worked in very dark green wool and stem-stitch, and pale mauve in uneven buttonhole-stitch for the flower. Press all seams and embroidery on the wrong side, using damp cloth and warm iron.

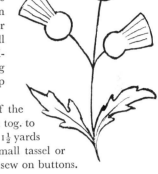

Using three or four shades of the embroidery wools, crochet them tog. to form thick chain for neck, about 1½ yards long. Finish either end with small tassel or fringe. Work buttonholes, and sew on buttons.

D. M. Beckett

Betty's Vases

By G. E. Edwards

FOR the past five years Betty's sitting-room has been a symphony in pale green and rose-pink. Last week, when I went to see her, the room was yellow and cream.

"My fresh flowers this year will be yellow daisies, deep cream and golden-tinted roses, and some white blossoms, too," explained Betty. "And I've been enormously busy, re-enamelling the vases a nice yellow colour to match the room."

"You've been what . . . ?"

My friend waved an airy hand towards a table whereon stood a collection of the queerest vases I have ever seen. Yes, I had seen them the previous year (when they had been either pink or green); but somehow I'd always seen them without paying much attention. Probably because the flowers were in them, more or less concealing the shapes. Now, however, I stared.

"Where did you get them?" I asked. "Are they . . . er . . . Balkan in origin?"

"Not at all. They're absolutely a home article. From the butcher," she added reflectively.

"From the . . . Come now, Betty, you're joking!"

"Upon my honour, I'm doing nothing of the sort. Those vases are nothing more nor less than beef bones—marrow bones—from the local butcher. I sawed them into five-inch lengths, taking care to make a level cut across both ends; and of course I made certain that the bottom of each 'vase' was where the marrow ended and the bone was solid. Then I bought a small pot of enamel and a one and a half-inch paint brush, and set to work to colour the set according to my fancy.

You saw them here all last year—but it never occurred to you they were merely bones, did it?"

"It certainly didn't. I must be singularly unobservant."

Betty laughed. "Not more so than most of my other friends. Some of them have actually admired the 'quaint shapes' of my Balkan vases; and even then not realised the simple truth. The enamel does wonders in hiding a homely origin—especially if one doesn't paint them white. They hold water perfectly: are quite steady on the tables; and are just the very thing for a bunch of short-stemmed flowers. I enamelled a pair for Aunt Margaret this spring. Cherry red, with a fine silver line round the top. They looked quite imposing, I assure you. And now she has asked me to make her a pair of pale blue and gold ones for her bazaar stall. If she has the luck that I had, they'll sell like hot cakes; so I've taken the liberty of asking the butcher to save me a lot of extra soup bones. Poor man! He must think I live on beef broth."

"Marrow-bone vases! What an idea!"

"Isn't it?" agreed my friend, cheerfully. "But I think a nicer name would be 'unbreakable vases'. That's true, you know; they're absolutely proof against disaster. . . . Oh, yes, I was going to tell you that this winter I plan growing bulbs in them: one bulb to each bo— vase. Just as one does in glass hyacinth vases."

"And that will be quite a good idea, too."

Betty considered me with a speculative eye. "Now that I've told you everything, I suppose you'll go home and write it up."

"I think I must let other people know the bare bones of your idea," I murmured, as I took my departure.

The big puff-sleeeves are slightly pleated on to the shoulders.

The Prettiest COLLAR for THIS PARTY JUMPER—

A Bewitching Design Knitted in a Lacy Stitch

READ THIS BEFORE WORK-ING. ABBREVIATIONS.—*K., knit; p., purl; st., stitch; tog., together; inc., increase (by working into the front and back of the same st.); dec., decrease; m., make (by bring-ing the wool to the front of the pin so that it passes over it when knitting*

To parties, wear this lacy jumper with its deep front sailor-collar in stocking-stitch.

MATERIALS.—*7 ounces of "Sirdar" 3-ply Super Shetland Wool; a pair each of No. 10 and No. 13 "Aero" knitting pins; a No. 14 "Aero" crochet hook.*

TENSION AND MEASUREMENTS.—*Worked at a tension that one pattern of 11 sts. measures 1½ inches in width, the measurements on the diagram are attained after light pressing.*

FOR AN OUTSIZE JUMPER.—*To make this jumper suitable for a bust measure of 42 or 43 inches (that is an actual measure on the jumper of 45 inches) use "Sirdar" Majestic wool (4-ply) with No. 8 pins on the main part, and No. 10 for the finer. It will take about 12 ozs. of this wool.*

The Shape and Measurements of the Jumper.

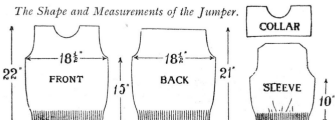

A close-up of the lacy stitch.

If you'd like it in Pink—choose Hydrangea Pink (Shade No. 215). Have a Black Velveteen Skirt. Black Patent-leather Shoes Peachglow Stockings. A Paste or Marcasite Clip.

If you'd like it in Green—choose Blue-Grass Green (Shade No. 284). Have a Matching Green Smooth-Woollen Skirt. Rust-Brown Calf Shoes and Belt. A Novelty Wooden Clip.

If you'd like it in Blue—choose Powder-Blue (Shade No. 214). Have a Plum-Purple Crêpe Woollen Skirt. Matching Suede Shoes. A Posy of Artificial Anemones at the Neck.

THE PRETTIEST COLLAR FOR THIS PARTY JUMPER

(Continued from page 236)

the next st.). *Directions in brackets are worked the number of times stated immediately after the brackets. Single rib is k. 1, p. 1 alternately. S.s., stocking-stitch (k. on the right side and purl back).*

The Back

With No. 13 pins, cast on 110 sts. and work in a k. 1, p. 1 rib for 48 rows.

Next row : Rib 12, * inc., rib 3 ; repeat from * until 6 remain, rib 6. (133 sts.)

Now change to No. 10 pins, and begin the Main Pattern :

1st row : K. 2 tog., * k. 5, m. 1, k. 1, m. 1, k. 2, k. 3 tog. ; repeat from *, ending the last repeat with k. 2 tog. instead of k. 3 tog.

2nd row, and every even numbered row : All purl.

3rd row : K. 2 tog., * k. 4, m. 1, k. 3, m. 1, k. 1, k. 3 tog. ; repeat from *, ending the last repeat with k. 2 tog., instead of k. 3 tog.

5th row : K. 2 tog., * k. 3, m. 1, k. 5, m. 1, k. 3 tog. ; repeat from *, ending the last repeat with k. 2 tog. instead of k. 3 tog.

7th row : K. 2 tog., * k. 2, m. 1, k. 1, m. 1, k. 5, k. 3 tog. ; repeat from *, ending the last repeat with k. 2 tog., instead of k. 3 tog.

9th row : K. 2 tog., * k. 1, m. 1, k. 3, m. 1, k. 4, k. 3 tog. ; repeat from *, ending the last repeat with k. 2 tog., instead of k. 3 tog.

11th row : K. 2 tog., * m. 1, k. 5, m. 1, k. 3, k. 3 tog. ; repeat from *, ending the last repeat with k. 2 tog., instead of k. 3 tog.

12th row : All p.

These 12 rows form one pattern. Work 7 patterns more to the armholes.

To Shape the Armholes.—1st row : Cast off 5 sts., which leaves one st. on the right-hand pin, (k. 1, m. 1) twice, k. 2, k. 3 tog., * k. 5, m. 1, k. 1, m. 1, k. 2, k. 3 tog. ; repeat from * ending the last repeat with k. 2 tog., instead of k. 3 tog.

2nd row : Cast off 5, all p. to end.

3rd row : Cast off 5, k. 3 tog., * k. 4, m. 1, k. 3, m. 1, k. 1, k. 3 together ; repeat from *, ending the row with k. 5.

4th row : As 2nd row.

5th row : Cast off 5, m. 1, k. 5, m. 1, k. 3 tog., * k. 3, m. 1, k. 5, m. 1, k. 3 tog. ; repeat from *, ending the last repeat with k. 2 tog., instead of k. 3 tog.

6th row : As 2nd row.

7th row : K. 2 tog., k. 5, k. 3 tog., * k. 2, m. 1, k. 1, m. 1, k. 5, k. 3 tog. ; repeat from *, ending the row with k. 2, m. 1, k. 1, m. 1, k. 2.

8th row : K. 2 tog., then all p. to end.

9th row : K. 2 tog., k. 3, k. 2 tog., * k. 1, m. 1, k. 3, m. 1, k. 4, k. 3 tog. ; repeat from *, ending the row with k. 1, m. 1, k. 5. (100 sts.) This finishes the armhole shaping.

10th row : All p.

11th row : K. 4, k. 2 tog., * m. 1, k. 5, m. 1, k. 3, k. 3 tog. ; repeat from *, ending the row with m. 1, k. 6.

12th row : All purl.

10th pattern. 1st row : K. 4, k. 2 tog., * k. 5, m. 1, k. 1, m. 1, k. 2, k. 3 tog. ; repeat from *, ending the row with m. 1, k. 6.

2nd, and every even numbered row : All p.

3rd row : K. 4, k. 2 tog., * k. 4, m. 1, k. 3, m. 1, k. 1, k. 3 tog. ; repeat from *, ending the row with m. 1, k. 6.

5th row : K. 4, k. 2 tog., * k. 3, m. 1, k. 5, m. 1, k. 3 tog., repeat from * ending the row with k. 3, m. 1, k. 3.

7th row : K. 4, k. 2 tog., * k. 2, m. 1, k. 1, m. 1, k. 5, k. 3 tog., repeat from * ending the row with k. 2, m. 1, k. 4.

9th row : K. 4, k. 2 tog., * k. 1, m. 1, k. 3, m. 1, k. 4, k. 3 tog. ; repeat from *, ending the row with k. 1, m. 1, k. 5.

11th row : K. 4, k. 2 tog., * m. 1, k. 5, m. 1, k. 3, k. 3 tog. ; repeat from *, ending the row with m. 1, k. 6.

12th row : All purl.

Repeat the 10th pattern 3 times more (13 patterns from the beginning), then repeat from 1st to 5th row inclusive, of 10th pattern. Cast off straight across.

The Front

Work as directed for the Back, until 12 patterns have been worked and 100 sts. remain.

To Shape the Neck.—Now work in s.s. as follows :

Next row : K. 44, and pass these sts. on a stitch-holder for one shoulder. Cast off 12 sts., k. 44 for second shoulder.

** K. 2 tog. at the neck edge of the next 14 rows, when 30 sts. will remain. Work 9 rows more on these 30 sts., then cast off straight across.

Join the wool to the neck end of the first 44 sts., and repeat from ** on first shoulder.

The Sleeves

With No. 13 pins cast on 70 sts. and work 36 rows in single rib.

Increase row : K. 15, inc. 1 st. into every st. until 14 sts. remain, k. 14. (111 sts.)

Purl one row.

Change to No. 10 pins and work 5 complete patterns as on the Back.

To Shape the Top.—6th Pattern. *1st row :* K. 2 tog., k. 6, m. 1, k. 2, k. 3 tog., * k. 5, m. 1, k. 1, m. 1, k. 2, k. 3 tog. ; repeat from *, ending the row with k. 5, m. 1, k. 3, k. 2 tog.

2nd row : K. 2 tog., p. until 2 sts. remain, k. 2 tog.

3rd row : K. 2 tog., k. 5, m. 1, k. 1, k. 3 tog., * k. 4, m. 1, k. 3, m. 1, k. 1, k. 3 tog. ; repeat from *, ending the row with k. 4, m. 1, k. 2, k. 2 tog.

4th row : As 2nd row.

5th row : K. 2 tog., k. 4, m. 1, k. 3 tog., * k. 3, m. 1, k. 5, m. 1, k. 3 tog. ; repeat from *, ending the row with k. 3, m. 1, k. 1, k. 2 tog.

6th row : As 2nd row.

7th row : K. 2 tog., k. 2, m. 1, k. 3 tog., * k. 2, m. 1, k. 1, m. 1, k. 5, k. 3 tog. ; repeat from *, ending the row with k. 2, m. 1, k. 2 tog.

8th row : As 2nd row.

9th row : K. 2, k. 3 tog., * k. 1, m. 1, k. 3, m. 1, k. 4, k. 3 tog. ; repeat from * until 13 remain, then k. 1, m. 1, k. 3, m. 1, k. 4, k. 2 tog., k. 1, m. 1, k. 2 tog.

10th row : As 2nd row.

11th row : K. 3 tog., * m. 1, k. 5, m. 1, k. 3, k. 3 tog. ; repeat from *, ending the row with k. 1.

12th row : K. 2 tog., then p. to end.

Now work the pattern as at the beginning of the back until 10 patterns from the beginning have been completed, then repeat the 6th pattern once more, and cast off.

Work another sleeve in the same manner.

The Collar

With No. 10 pins cast on 100 sts., and work for 10 rows in garter-stitch.

11th row : All k.

12th row : K. 7, all p. until 7 sts. remain, k. 7.

Repeat the last 2 rows 16 times more.

Next row : K. 44 sts. and pass these on a spare pin ; cast off 12, k. the remainder of the row.

Next row : K. 7, all p. until 2 sts. remain, k. 2 tog.

Next row : K. 2 tog., then k. to end.

Repeat the last 2 rows until 30 sts. remain, then work 9 rows straight. Cast off.

Join the wool at the inside edge of the 44 sts. from the spare pin, then k. 2 tog., p. until 7 sts. remain, k. 7.

Next row : K. until 2 sts. remain, k. 2 tog.

Repeat the last 2 rows until 30 sts. remain, then work 10 rows straight. Cast off.

To Make Up the Jumper.—First press all pieces with a hot iron over a damp cloth on the wrong side of the work. Tack the collar piece around the front neck edge, and along the shoulder edges. Sew the shoulders together, beginning at the arm-end and taking 1 st. from each side at a time, and sewing through the collar at the same time. Gather the top of the sleeves, and sew into the armholes, easing the fullness at the top of the sleeve. Press all seams while garment is still open. Sew up the sleeve and side seams in one line and press. With the crochet hook, work a row of double crochet around the neck opening, working through the collar on the front. Gather the collar in front as illustrated, sew neatly in place, and finish with a fancy clip.

SUCH Flattering PUFF SLEEVES!

Knitted all in ribbing, this charming jumper has a simple square neck-line and attractively shaped sleeves.

The puffed sleeves are most cleverly shaped!

MATERIALS.—*6 ounces of Greenock Super Fingering 4-ply (obtainable only from branches of* SCOTCH WOOL & HOSIERY STORES) ; *and a pair each of Stratnoid knitting pins No. 9 and No. 10.*

TENSION AND MEASUREMENTS.— *Worked at a tension of 9 sts. to the inch in width on No. 9 pins, with the ribs closed, the measurements on the diagram are attained after light pressing. It should be remembered, however, that the rib pattern will expand to a bust measurement of 37 inches.*

ABBREVIATIONS : TO BE READ BEFORE WORKING.—*K., knit plain ; p., purl ; st., stitch ; inc., increase (by working into the back and front of the same stitch) ; dec., decrease ; rib is k. 2 and p. 2 alternately. Directions in brackets are worked the number of times stated immediately after the brackets.*

The Back

WITH No. 10 pins cast on 112 sts. and work 24 rows in rib, working into the back of the sts. on the first row to give a neat edge.

Change to No. 9 pins and work 76 rows more in rib to armholes.

To Shape the Armholes.—Continue in rib, casting off 5 sts. at the beginning of each of the next 2 rows, then decrease at both ends of the following row, when 100 sts. will remain.

Work 49 rows straight on these sts. Cast off straight across.

The Front

THIS is worked exactly the same as the Back until the armhole shaping is finished and 100 sts. remain.

Work 25 rows straight on these sts. to neck.

On the next row the sts. are divided for the neck opening as follows : Rib 26 and slip these sts. on a stitch-holder until needed for shoulder, cast off 48 sts. (1 st. on pin), rib to end (26 sts).

Work 24 rows straight on these sts. Cast off.

Join the wool to the neck end of remaining 26 sts. and rib 23 rows. Cast off.

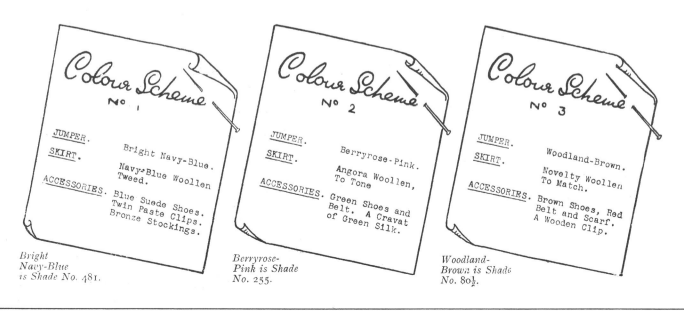

Colour Scheme No. 1

JUMPER. Bright Navy-Blue.
SKIRT. Navy-Blue Woollen Tweed.
ACCESSORIES. Blue Suede Shoes. Twin Paste Clips. Bronze Stockings.

Bright Navy-Blue is Shade No. 481.

Colour Scheme No. 2

JUMPER. Berryrose-Pink.
SKIRT. Angora Woollen, To Tone.
ACCESSORIES. Green Shoes and Belt. A Cravat of Green Silk.

Berryrose-Pink is Shade No. 255.

Colour Scheme No. 3

JUMPER. Woodland-Brown.
SKIRT. Novelty Woollen To Match.
ACCESSORIES. Brown Shoes, Red Belt and Scarf. A Wooden Clip.

Woodland-Brown is Shade No. 80½.

The Sleeves

BEGIN at the arm end, and using No. 10 pins, cast on 64 sts. Work 16 rows in rib. Change to No. 9 pins and work 16 rows in same rib.

Now shape for the puffed top as follows :

** 1st increase row : * (K. 2, p. 2) twice, inc. in each of the next 4 sts. ; repeat from * until 4 remain, k. 2, p. 2 (84 sts.).

A pair of paste clips expertly pinned into the square neck.

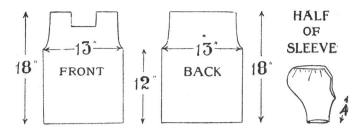

Next row : * K. 2. p. 2 ; repeat from * to end.

Work 4 rows more in rib as set on the last row, decreasing at both ends of each of these rows (76 sts.).

Repeat the last 6 rows from ** once more (92 sts.).

3rd increase row : K. 2, p. 2, * (k. 2, p. 2) twice, inc. in each of the next 4 sts. ; repeat from * until 4 remain, k. 2, p. 2 (120 sts.).

Work 5 rows straight in rib as set on the last row.

*** 4th increase row : K. 2, p. 2, * (k. 2, p. 2) twice, inc. in each of the next 4

sts. ; repeat from * until 8 remain, (k. 2, p. 2) twice (156 sts.).

Work 5 rows in rib as set on the last row.

Repeat the last 6 rows from *** once more (204 sts.).

Work 4 rows in rib, decreasing at both ends of each of these rows (196 sts.).

Next row : * (K. 2, p. 2) twice, (k. 2 tog.) 4 times ; repeat from * until 4 remain, k. 2, p. 2 (148 sts.).

Rib 1 row.

Repeat the last 2 rows once more (112 sts.).

Next row : * (K. 2, p. 2) twice, (k. 2

tog.) 4 times ; repeat from * to end (84 sts.).

Rib 1 row.

Cast off rather tightly.

Work a second sleeve in the same manner.

TO MAKE UP THE JUMPER.—Join the shoulder seams, beginning at the arm-hole end and taking 1 st. from each side at a time.

Gather the cast-off edge of sleeve and set the sleeve top into armhole. Join the sleeve and side seam in one long line.

Press the seams only on the wrong side with a hot iron over a damp cloth.

The *Tunic* DRESS

A Charming Design which Knits Up Quickly

(including the lining portion) : Length, 31 in. Width all around lower edge, 46 in.

Abbreviations : Sts., stitches ; k., knit ; p., purl ; tog., together ; rep., repeat ; rem., remain(s)(ing)(der) ; inc., increase(ing) ; dec., decrease(ing).

Tension :·Approximately 6 sts. to 1 inch.

THE SKIRT Begin at the lower edge. With No. 9 needles cast on 130 sts. and work for 8 rows in garter-st., then continue to work in stocking-st., until the piece measures 13½ ins. from the beginning. Cast off. Work a second piece in exactly the same manner.

THE TUNIC—BACK Cast on 180 sts., and work for 8 rows in garter-st., then continue in stocking-st., working as follows : Work 12 rows more, then : *Row 21* —* K. 18, k. 2 tog., rep. from * to end (171 sts.). Work 13 more rows.

Row 35—* K. 17, k. 2 tog., rep. from * to end (162 sts.). Work 13 more rows. *Row 49*—* K. 16, k. 2 tog., rep. from * to end (153 sts.). Work 13 more rows. *Row 63*—* K. 15, k. 2 tog., rep. from * to end (144 sts.). Work 13 more rows. *Row 77*—* K. 14, k. 2 tog., rep. from * to end (135 sts.). Work 13 more rows. *Row 91*—* K. 13, k. 2 tog., rep. from * to end (126 sts.). Work 13 more rows. *Row 105*—* K. 12, k. 2 tog., rep. from * to end (117 sts.). Work 13 more rows. *Row 119*—* K. 11, k. 2 tog., rep. from * to end (108 sts.). Work 13 more rows. *Row 133*—* K. 10, k. 2 tog., rep. from * to end (99 sts.). Work 13 more rows. *Row 147*—* K. 9, k. 2 tog., rep. from * to end (90 sts.). Continue to work on these 90 sts. without further alteration, until the piece measures 22 ins. from the beginning. *Next row* (with right side of work towards you)—* K. 8, k. 2 tog., rep. from * to end of row (81 sts.). Work for 9 more rows, then inc. 1 st. at both ends of the next row, and likewise every following 10th row, until there are 93 sts. Work for 6 more rows, then— with wrong side towards you—divide the work into two and proceed to work the *Left Side*, thus : *Next row*— P. 45 sts., turn the piece. Transfer the rem. 48 sts. to a

STOCKING-STITCH and garter-stitch are used throughout. The skirt section is attached to a satin top, hidden by the tunic

*M*ATERIALS : 29 ozs. of Templeton's "Mystic" Fancy Yarn ; a pair of No. 9 "Stratnord" knitting pins ; five small buttons ; one press-fastener ; one set of hook-and-eye ; 3 yards of 1-inch wide velvet ribbon (about 60 in. for belt, and 50 in. for neck trimming) ; a short length of elastic for skirt waist ; 1¼ yards of satin lining for top portion of skirt.

Measurements (after pressing) : *Tunic :* Length from lower edge to top of shoulder, 37½ in. ; length of sleeve, along seam, 7 in. To fit from 34 to 36-in. bust. *Skirt*

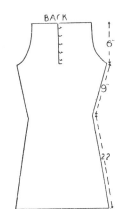

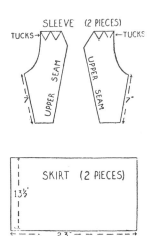

spare needle and leave for the present. Cast on 10 sts. at the beginning of next row (for the under-lap), k. rem. of row (55 sts. on the needle). Now: *Shape armhole as follows:* Row 1—Cast off 3, all p. until 5 sts. rem., k. 5. Row 2—All k. Rep. these 2 rows once more (4 rows in all), then: Row 5—K. 2 tog., all p. until 5 sts. rem. k. 5. Row 6—All k. Rep. the last 2 rows until 46 sts. rem. Work for 39 more rows without further alteration. Cast off.

Now pick up the 48 sts. from spare needle (point of No. 9 needle held towards centre of the work), join in the wool, then: Next row—K. 5, all p. to end. Now: *Shape armhole as follows:* Row 1—Cast off 3, all k. to end. Row 2—K. 5, all p. to end. Rep. the last 2 rows once more. Row 5—K. 2 tog., all k. until 5 sts. rem., cast off 2, k. rem. of row. Row 6—K. 3, cast on 2 sts., all p. to end. N.B. Four more buttonholes are worked in this manner, with 8 rows between each. Row 7—K. 2 tog., all k. to end. Row 8 —K. 5, all p. to end. Rep. the last 2 rows once more (39 sts.). Work without further alteration for 39 rows. Cast off.

THE FRONT Work as for the back until the arm-hole is reached (93 sts. on the needle, but do not divide work). Work one more row, then (with right side of work towards you): *Shape armholes thus:* Cast off 3 sts. at the begin-ning of each of the next 4 rows, then k. 2 tog. at the end of every row, until 75 sts. rem. Work 20 more rows, then: *Shape neck, thus: Next row* (with right side of work towards you): K. 32, cast off 11, k. rem. of row.

Transfer the first set of 32 sts. to a spare needle and leave for the moment, and proceed to work one shoulder, as follows: On the neck edge k. 2 tog. every row, until 25 sts. rem. Work without further dec. until the piece measures one inch longer than the back. Cast off. Pick up the 32 sts. from spare needle, and work the other shoulder in the same way, and to match the first shoulder.

THE SLEEVES (*Two alike—each worked in 2 separate pieces*): (a) *First piece:* Cast on 34 sts. and work for 8 rows in garter-st., then continue in stocking-st., as follows: Row 9— Inc. 1 st. into first st., all k. until 1 st. rem. Row 10—All p. Row 11—All k. until 1 st. rem., inc. Rep. Rows 10 and 11 twice more. Row 16 —All p. until 1 st. rem., inc. ** Rep. Rows 11 and 10 three times more. Row 23—As Row 11. Row 24—As Row 16. ** Now rep. from ** to ** four times more (56 rows from beginning), then: *Shape top of sleeve:* Row 57—K. 2 tog., all k. until 1 st. rem., inc. Row 58—All p. until 2 sts. rem., k. 2 tog. Rep. Rows 57 and 58 eight times more (74 rows from beginning). Row 75 —K. 2 tog., all k. until 2 sts. rem., k. 2 tog. Row 76—All p. until 2 sts. rem., k. 2 tog. Rep. Rows 75 and 76 until 24 sts. rem. on the needle. Cast off.

(b) *Second piece:* Cast on 34 sts. and work for 8 rows in garter-st. Row 9—Inc. 1 st. into first st., all k. until 1 st. rem., inc. Row 10—All p. Row 11—Inc. 1 st. into first st., all k. to end of row. Rep. Rows 10 and 11 twice more. Row 16 —Inc. 1 st. into first st., all p. to end. **Rep. Rows 11 and 10 three times more. Row 23—As Row 11. Row 24—As Row 16.** Rep. from ** to ** four times more (56 rows from beginning), then: *Shape top:* Row 57—Inc. 1 st. into first st., all k. until 2 sts. rem., k. 2 tog. Row 58—K. 2 tog., all p. to end. Rep. Rows 57 and 58 eight times more (74 rows from beginning). Row 75— K. 2 tog., all k. until 2 sts. rem., k. 2 tog. Row 76 —K. 2 tog., all p. to end. Rep. Rows 75 and 76 until 24 sts. rem. Cast off.

TO MAKE UP AND (1) *The Tunic:* Carefully FINISH press all the pieces on the wrong side under a damp cloth with a warm iron. Seam up the shoulders and sew the upper (outer) seam of the sleeve pieces; work 2 tucks on each side of this seam at the top of each sleeve, and neatly sew the tops of sleeves into the armholes. Press all seams while garment is still open. Sew up the under sleeve seam and the side seam in one operation, and press. Sew on the buttons to correspond with the buttonholes. Sew the ribbon to neck, making five loops in front to form the ruff trimming, as shown in the photograph, and fastening at the back by means of the press-fastener. Fit on the tunic, then work a tuck for 2 in. inside the upper edge of each cuff, taking the top seam for its centre.

(2) *The Skirt:* Press as tunic, and sew up the two seams. Sew the lining to the top edge of the knitted portion, and work a hem at the waist. Cut a length of elastic to fit your waist, and thread this through the hem. Press all seams. *Belt:* Work five loops at one end of the ribbon to match collar, fit to the waist, and fasten by means of a hook and eye.

Use More Mint and Parsley!

Says Margaret Welsby

THESE two herbs can be made use of in many more ways than by merely keeping them for flavouring purposes, and for sauces.

Both mint and parsley should be gathered, dried, and bottled when plentiful during the summer, so that a good supply can be assured through-out the winter months.

Mint Tea

This makes an excellent drink as a "night-cap" in very cold weather. It helps to ward off a cold, or to check one already caught. It is much thought of by our neighbours across the Channel, and is frequently served in Egypt and Morocco.

To make it, put a teaspoonful of dried mint into a cup and fill up with boiling water. Leave to infuse for a few minutes, then add the juice of half a lemon. Strain, and sweeten to taste.

Pineapple Mint Tea

Is made as follows. Put the juice from a tin of pineapple into a saucepan and when it is almost boiling, pour it into a tumbler. Add a teaspoonful of dried mint, and the juice of half a lemon and half an orange. Flavour with cinnamon, if liked, and sip while hot.

Mint Julip

Is a very pleasant hot-weather bever-age. To make it, strain the juice from five lemons into a basin and add one and a half teacupfuls of sugar, two teacupfuls of hot water and a handful of bruised mint leaves. Stir well, strain, and set aside to cool. Before serving, add three pints of ginger ale, iced, if possible. Serve in glass jugs with mint leaves floating on top.

Rhubarb Mint Jelly

This makes a delightful accompani-ment to roast lamb instead of the more ordinary mint sauce.

Wipe the rhubarb, and cook until it becomes a pulp, then strain through a sieve. When all the juice is extracted, measure it, and to each pint of liquid allow one pound of sugar.

Put juice and sugar into the preserving-pan, and add a bundle of fresh mint, well washed. Boil until the jelly will set when a little is poured on a cold plate—it should be stirred frequently while cooking. Remove the mint before pouring into jars.

Starring STRIPES

The Jumper of the Month

designed by "*Finella*"

MATERIALS

Three ounces of Femina Botany Fingering, 3-ply, in light blue and 5 oz. in navy ; a pair each of Nos. 8 and 11 Stratnoid knitting pins ; a set of 4 No. 8 needles with points at both ends.

MEASUREMENTS

Round bust, 34 ins. ; length, 19 ins. ; sleeve seam, 20 ins.

TENSION

Six sts. and 8 rows to 1 in.

*W*E *want gay clothes to wear on dullish days, so I know you'll like this smart jumper. The stripes are cleverly arranged to make you look your slimmest, and it is so easy to knit.*

THE *Back.*—Using No. 11 pins and navy wool, cast on 102 sts. and work in k. 1, p. 1 rib for 4 ins., working into the backs of the sts. on the first row. Change to No. 8 pins and st.-st. and continue straight for 18 rows.

Now continue in st.-st. in the following stripes : 2 rows blue, 14 rows navy, 4 rows blue, 12 rows navy, 6 rows blue, 8 rows navy. Change to blue and shape the armholes by casting off 6 sts. at the beginning of the next 2 rows and then dec. at both ends of the following 4 rows. Work 2 more rows in blue, then 6 rows navy, 12 rows blue, 4 rows navy, 14 rows blue, 2 rows navy. Break off the navy wool and continue in blue till work measures 18 ins. from the beginning, then shape the shoulders by casting off 9 sts. at the beginning of the next 6 rows. Place the remaining sts. on a holder.

The Front.—Work as for the back until the work measures 16 ins. from the beginning, then continuing the stripes as for the back, shape the neck as follows : Work across 40 sts., cast off 12, work to end. Put the first set of sts. on a holder and work on the last set only, completing the neck shaping by dec. at the neck edge of the following 13 rows. Continue straight till work measures 18 ins. from the beginning, then shape the shoulders by casting off 9 sts. at the armhole edge of the following 3 alternate rows.

Return to the other side and work to match with all shapings reversed.

The Sleeves.—Using No. 11 pins and navy wool, cast on 48 sts. and work in k. 1, p. 1 rib for 4 ins., working into the backs of the sts. on the first row. Change to No. 8 pins and st.-st. and inc. at both ends of every 6th row, working in the following stripes : 12 rows navy,

2 rows blue, (18 rows navy, 2 rows blue) 4 times, 14 rows navy, 4 rows blue, 8 rows navy.

Shape the top by casting off 6 sts. at the beginning of the next 2 rows and then dec. at both ends of every row until 46 sts. remain. Then dec. at both ends of every alternate row until 18 sts. remain. At the same time work in stripes as follows : 8 rows blue, 6 rows navy, 8 rows blue, 4 rows navy, 12 rows blue, 2 rows navy, break off navy wool and continue in blue to end. Cast off.

Work another sleeve in the same way.

The Neck Ribbing.—Join the shoulder seams, then using the set of four No. 8 needles and navy wool pick up the sts. round the neck and work in k. 1, p. 1 rib for 10 rows. Cast off loosely.

TO MAKE UP

Press all parts but the ribbing carefully on the wrong side with a hot iron over a damp cloth. Sew the sleeves into the armholes, carefully matching the stripes. Join the side and sleeve seams. Press all seams.

IT CANNOT FAIL TO PLEASE!

An Enchanting Design In Leaf Pattern!

MATERIALS

FIVE ozs. of " Greenock " 3-ply Super Fingering (obtainable only from branches of SCOTCH WOOL & HOSIERY STORES) and a pair of Stratnoid knitting pins No. 10 and No. 13 ; 3 press studs.

TENSION AND MEASUREMENTS

WORKED at such a tension that one repeat of the pattern (18 sts.) measures 2¼ inches in width, on the No. 10 pins. the measurements on the diagram are attained after light pressing.

ABBREVIATIONS

K KNIT ; p., purl ; st., stitch ; tog., together ; inc., increase (by working into the back and front of the same st.) ; dec., decrease (by working 2 sts. tog.) ; single rib is k. 1 and p. 1 alternately ; m., make (by bringing the wool to the front of the pin, over it before working a k. st., or by bringing the wool to the front of the pin, over it, and to the front again before working a p. st.). Directions in brackets are worked the number of times stated immediately after the brackets.

TO WORK THE BACK

USING the No. 13 pins, cast on 126 sts. and work 1 row into the back of the sts. to give a neat edge.

Now work 32 rows in single rib, increasing 1 st. at the end of the last row. (127 sts.)

Change to the No. 10 pins and work in pattern as follows :

1st Row (right side facing) : K. 1, * m. 1, p. 2, k. 5, p. 3 tog., k. 5, p. 2, m. 1, k. 1 ; repeat from * to end.

2nd Row : K. 1, p. 1, * k. 2, p. 11, k. 2, p. 3 ; repeat from *, ending the last repeat with p. 2 instead of p. 3.

3rd Row : K. 1, * m. 1, k. 1, p. 2, k. 4, p. 3 tog., k. 4, p. 2, k. 1, m. 1, k. 1 ; repeat from * to end.

4th Row : K. 1, p. 2, * k. 2, p. 9, k. 2, p. 5 ; repeat from *, ending the last repeat with p.3 instead of p. 5.

5th Row : K. 1, * m. 1, k. 2, p. 2, k. 3, p. 3 tog., k. 3, p. 2, k. 2, m. 1, k. 1 ; repeat from * to end of row.

6th Row : K. 1, p. 3, * k. 2, p. 7 ; repeat from *, ending the last repeat with p. 4 instead of p. 7.

7th Row : K. 1, * m. 1, k. 3, p. 2, k. 2, p. 3 tog., k. 2, p. 2, k. 3, m. 1, k. 1 ; repeat from * to end of row.

8th Row : K. 1, p. 4, * k. 2, p. 5, k. 2, p. 9 ; repeat from *, ending the last repeat with p. 5 instead of p. 9.

9th Row : K. 1, * m. 1, k. 4, p. 2, k. 1, p. 3 tog., k. 1, p. 2, k. 4, m. 1, k. 1 ; repeat from * to end of row.

10th Row : K. 1, p. 5, * k. 2, p. 3,

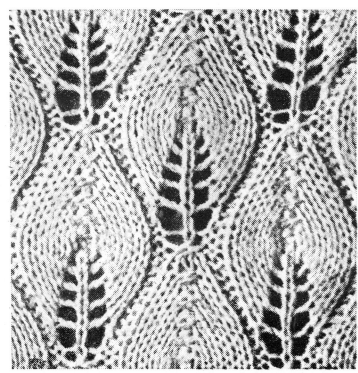

A Close-up Photograph of the Leaf Pattern !

k. 2, p. 11 ; repeat from *, ending the last repeat with p. 6 instead of p. 11.

11th Row : K. 1, * m. 1, k. 5, p. 2, p. 3 tog., p. 2, k. 5, m. 1, k. 1 ; repeat from * to end of row.

12th Row : K. 1, p. 6, * k. 2, p. 1, k. 2, p. 13 ; repeat from *, ending the last repeat with p. 7 instead of p. 13.

13th Row : K. 2 tog., * k. 5, p. 2, m. 1, k. 1, m. 1, p. 2, k. 5, p. 3 tog. ; repeat from *, ending the last repeat with p. 2 tog. instead of p. 3 tog.

14th Row : K. 1, p. 5, * k. 2, p. 3, k. 2, p. 11 ; repeat from *, ending the last repeat with p. 6 instead of p. 11.

15th Row : K. 2 tog., * k. 4, p. 2, k. 1, (m. 1, k. 1) twice, p. 2, k. 4, p. 3 tog. ; repeat from *, ending the last repeat with p. 2 tog. instead of p. 3 tog.

16th Row : K. 1, p. 4, * k. 2, p. 5, k. 2, p. 9 ; repeat from *, ending the last repeat with p. 5 instead of p. 9.

17th Row : K. 2 tog., * k. 3, p. 2, k. 2, m. 1, k. 1, m. 1, k. 2, p. 2, k. 3, p. 3 tog. ; repeat from *, ending the last repeat with p. 2 tog. instead of p. 3 tog.

18th Row : K. 1, p. 3, * k. 2, p. 7 ; repeat from *, ending the last repeat with p. 4 instead of p. 7.

19th Row : K. 2 tog., * k. 2, p. 2, k. 3, m. 1, k. 1, m. 1, k. 3, p. 2, k. 2, p. 3 tog. ; repeat from *, ending the last repeat with p. 2 tog. instead of p. 3 tog.

20th Row : K. 1, p. 2, * k. 2, p. 9, k. 2, p. 5 ; repeat from *, ending the last repeat with p. 3 instead of p. 5.

21st Row : K. 2 tog., * k. 1, p. 2, k. 4, m. 1, k. 1, m. 1, k. 4, p. 2, k. 1, p. 3 tog. ; repeat from *, ending the last repeat with p. 2 tog. instead of p. 3 tog.

22nd Row : K. 1, p. 1, * k. 2, p. 11, k. 2, p. 3 ; repeat from *, ending the last repeat with p. 2 instead of p. 3.

23rd Row : K. 2 tog., * p. 2, k. 5, m. 1, k. 1, m. 1, k. 5, p. 2, p. 3 tog. ; repeat from *, ending the last repeat with p. 2 tog. instead of p. 3 tog.

24th Row : K. 1, * k. 2, p. 13, k. 2, p. 1 ; repeat from * to end of row.

These 24 rows complete 1 pattern.

Work 3 more complete patterns, then 4 rows of the next pattern.

To Shape the Armholes. — Continue in pattern as follows :

5th Row : Cast off 3 (1 st. on pin), p. 1, k. 3, p. 2 tog., k. 4, p. 2, k. 2, m. 1, k. 1, * m. 1, k. 3, p. 2, k. 3, p. 3 tog., k. 3, p. 2, k. 2, m. 1, k. 1 ; repeat from * to end. (124 sts.)

6th Row : Cast off 3 (1 st. on pin) * k. 2, p. 7 ; repeat from * until 12 sts. remain, p. 8, k. 2. (121 sts.)

7th Row : Cast off 3 (1 st. on pin), k. 1, p. 2 tog., k. 3, p. 2, k. 3, m. 1, k. 1, * m. 1, k. 3, p. 2, k. 2, p. 3 tog., k. 2,

The Shape and Measurements of the Jumper.

FRONT 16'

BACK 16'

15' 21'

SLEEVE 6'

So Fresh and Sweet with Puff Sleeves and a Plain Square Neckline.

p. 2, k. 3, m. 1, k.1 ; repeat from * until 15 sts. remain, m. 1, k. 3, p. 2, k. 2, p. 2 tog., k. 3, p. 2. k. 1. (118 sts.)

8TH Row : Cast off 3 (1 st. on pin), p. 5, k. 2, p. 9, * k. 2, p. 5, k. 2, p. 9 ; repeat from * until 8 sts. remain, k. 2, p. 6. (115 sts.)

9TH Row : Cast off 3 (1 st. on pin), k. 2 tog., p. 2, k. 4, m. 1,

It Cannot Fail To Please!

k. 1, * m. 1, k. 4, p. 2, k. 1, p. 3 tog., k. 1 p. 2, k. 4, m. 1, k. 1; repeat from * until 12 sts. remain, m. 1, k. 4, p. 2, k. 1, p. 2 tog., k. 3. (112 sts.)

10TH ROW: Cast off 3, (1 st. on pin) p. 1, k. 2, p. 11, * k. 2, p. 3, k. 2, p. 11; repeat from * until 4 sts. remain, k. 2, p. 2. (109 sts.)

11TH ROW: K. 2 tog., p. 2, k. 6, * m. 1, k. 5, p. 2, p. 3 tog., p. 2, k. 5, m. 1, k. 1; repeat from * until 9 sts. remain, k. 5, p. 2, k. 2 tog. (107 sts.)

12TH ROW: K. 2 tog., k. 1, p. 12, * k. 2, p. 1, k. 2, p. 13; repeat from *, ending the last repeat with p. 12 instead of p. 13, then k. 1, k. 2 tog. (105 sts.)

13TH ROW: K. 2 tog., k. 5, p. 2 tog., * k. 5, p. 2, m. 1, k. 1, m. 1, p. 2, k. 5, p. 3 tog.; repeat from *, ending the last repeat with p. 2 tog. instead of p. 3 tog., then k. 5, k. 2 tog. (103 sts.)

14TH ROW: K. 2 tog., p. 10, * k. 2, p. 3, k. 2, p. 11; repeat from *, ending the last repeat with p. 10, k. 2 tog. instead of p. 11. (101 sts.)

15TH ROW: K. 2 tog., k. 3, p. 2 tog., * k. 4, p. 2, k. 1, (m. 1, k. 1) twice, p. 2, k. 4, p. 3 tog.; repeat from *, ending the last repeat with p. 2 tog. instead of p. 3 tog., then k. 3, k. 2 tog. (99 sts.)

16TH ROW: K. 2 tog., p. 7, * k. 2, p. 5, k. 2, p. 9; repeat from *, ending the last repeat with p. 7, k. 2 tog. instead of p. 9. (97 sts.)

17TH ROW: K. 2 tog., k. 1, p. 2 tog., * k. 3, p. 2, k. 2, m. 1, k. 1, m. 1, k. 2, p. 2, k. 3, p. 3 tog.; repeat from *, ending the last repeat with p. 2 tog. instead of p. 3 tog., then k. 1, k. 2 tog. (95 sts.)

18TH ROW: K. 2 tog., p. 4, * k. 2, p. 7; repeat from *, ending the last repeat with p. 4, k. 2 tog. instead of p. 7. (93 sts.)

19TH ROW: P. 3 tog., * k. 2, p. 2, k. 3, m. 1, k. 1, m. 1, k. 3, p. 2, k. 2, p. 3 tog.; repeat from * to end. (91 sts.)

Now work from the 20th to the 24th row, as on main pattern at the beginning of the Back.

Continue straight in pattern for 1 complete pattern more (omit this pattern on front).

Now begin the neck border as follows:
** NEXT ROW: Work 19 sts. in pattern, k. 53, pattern 19.

Repeat the last row 11 times more.

NEXT ROW: Pattern 19, k. 11, slip these 30 sts. on a stitch-holder until needed, cast off 31, (1 st. on pin) k. 10, pattern 19.

THE FIRST SHOULDER.—NEXT ROW: Pattern 19, k. 11.

NEXT ROW: K. 11, pattern 19.

Repeat the last 2 rows 5 times more. (Repeat 17 times more when working the front shoulder.) K. one row plain and cast off.

Rejoin the wool to the neck end of remaining sts. and work the opposite shoulder to match, remembering to work the k. 11 border at the *neck* end of the rows.

THE FRONT

WORK exactly the same as the Back until the armhole shaping is finished, then continue as from ** on Back, observing the special notes in brackets which refer to the working of the Front.

THE SLEEVES

WITH the No. 10 pins cast on 64 sts. Change to the No. 13 pins and work 22 rows in single rib.

INCREASE ROW: Purl twice into every st. except the last st. (127 sts.)

Change to the No. 10 pins and work 1 complete pattern, then 12 rows of the next pattern as on Back.

TO SHAPE THE SLEEVE TOP.—1ST ROW: (13th pattern row) (k. 2 tog.) twice, k. 3, p. 2, m. 1, k. 1, m. 1, p. 2, k. 5, p. 3 tog., * k. 5, p. 2, m. 1, k. 1, m. 1, p. 2, k. 5, p. 3 tog.; repeat from *, ending the last repeat with k. 3, (k. 2 tog.) twice, instead of k. 5, p. 3 tog.

2ND ROW: P. 2 tog., p. 3, * k. 2, p. 3, k. 2, p. 11; repeat from *, ending the last repeat with p. 3, p. 2 tog. instead of p. 11.

3RD ROW: (K. 2 tog.) twice, p. 2, k. 1, (m. 1, k. 1) twice, p. 2, k. 4, p. 3 tog., * k. 4, p. 2, k. 1, (m. 1, k. 1) twice, p. 2, k. 4, p. 3 tog.; repeat from * until 15 sts. remain, k. 4, p. 2, k. 1, (m. 1, k. 1) twice, p. 2, (k. 2 tog.) twice.

4TH ROW: P. 2 tog., * k. 2, p. 5, k. 2, p. 9; repeat from * ending the last repeat with p. 2 tog. instead of p. 9.

5TH ROW: (K. 2 tog.) twice, (k. 1, m. 1) twice, k. 2, p. 2, k. 3, p. 3 tog., * k. 3, p. 2, k. 2, m. 1, k. 1, m. 1, k. 2, p. 2, k. 3, p. 3 tog.; repeat from * until 13 sts. remain, k. 3, p. 2, k. 2, (m. 1, k. 1) twice, (k. 2 tog.) twice.

6TH ROW: K. 2 tog., p. 6, * k. 2, p. 7; repeat from * until 10 sts. remain, k. 2, p. 6, k. 2 tog.

7TH ROW: K. 2 tog., k. 2, m. 1, k. 3, p. 2, k. 2, p. 3 tog., * k. 2, p. 2, k. 3, m. 1, k. 1, m. 1, k. 3, p. 2, k. 2, p. 3 tog.; repeat from * until 11 sts. remain, k. 2, p. 2, k. 3, m. 1, k. 2, k. 2 tog.

8TH ROW: P. 2 tog., p. 5, k. 2, p. 5, * k. 2, p. 9, k. 2, p. 5; repeat from * until 9 sts. remain, k. 2, p. 5, p. 2 tog.

9TH ROW: K. 2 tog., m. 1, k. 4, p. 2, k. 1, p. 3 tog., * k. 1, p. 2, k. 4, m. 1, k. 1, m. 1, k. 4, p. 2, k. 1, p. 3 tog.; repeat from * until 9 sts. remain, k. 1, p. 2, k. 4, m. 1, k. 2 tog.

10TH ROW: P. 2 tog., p. 4, k. 2, p. 3, * k. 2, p. 11, k. 2, p. 3; repeat from * until 8 sts. remain, k. 2, p. 4, k. 2 tog.

11TH ROW: K. 2 tog., k. 3, p. 2, k. 1, p. 2 tog., * p. 2, k. 5, m. 1, k. 1, m. 1, k. 5, p. 2, p. 3 tog.; repeat from *, ending the last repeat with p. 2 tog. instead of p. 3 tog., then k. 1, p. 2, k. 3, k. 2 tog.

12TH ROW: P. 2 tog., p. 2, k. 2, p. 2, * k. 2, p. 13, k. 2, p. 1; repeat from *, ending the last repeat with p. 2 instead of p. 1, then k. 2, p. 2, p. 2 tog.

13TH ROW: K. 2 tog., k. 1, p. 2, k. 2, * m. 1, p. 2, k. 5, p. 3 tog., k. 5, p. 2, m. 1, k. 1; repeat from *, ending the last repeat with k. 2 instead of k. 1, then p. 2, k. 1, k. 2 tog.

14TH ROW: P. 2 tog., k. 2, p. 3, * k. 2, p. 11, k. 2, p. 3; repeat from * until 4 sts. remain, k. 2, p. 2 tog.

15TH ROW: P. 2 tog., p. 1, k. 2, * m. 1, k. 1, p. 2, k. 4, p. 3 tog., k. 4, p. 2, k. 1, m. 1, k. 1; repeat from * until 4 sts. remain, k. 1, p. 1, k. 2 tog.

16TH ROW: K. 2 tog., p. 4, * k. 2, p. 9, k. 2, p. 5; repeat from *, ending the last repeat with p. 4, k. 2 tog. instead of p. 5.

17TH ROW: K. 2 tog., k. 1, * m. 1, k. 2, p. 2, k. 3, p. 3 tog., k. 3, p. 2, k. 2, m. 1, k. 1; repeat from * until 2 sts. remain, k. 2 tog.

18TH ROW: P. 2 tog., p. 3, * k. 2, p. 7; repeat from *, ending the last repeat with p. 3, p. 2 tog. instead of p. 7.

19TH ROW: K. 2 tog., k. 2, p. 2, k. 2, p. 2 tog., k. 3, p. 2, k. 3, m. 1, k. 1, * m. 1, k. 3, p. 2, k. 2, p. 3 tog., k. 2, p. 2, k. 3, m. 1, k. 1; repeat from * until 18 sts. remain, m. 1, k. 3, p. 2, k. 2, p. 2 tog., k. 3, p. 2, k. 2, k. 2 tog.

20TH ROW: P. 2 tog., p. 1, k. 2, p. 6, k. 2, p. 9, * k. 2, p. 5, k. 2, p. 9; repeat from * until 13 sts. remain, k. 2, p. 6, k. 2, p. 1, p. 2 tog.

21ST ROW: K. 2 tog., p. 2, k. 1, p. 2 tog., k. 3, p. 2, k. 4, m. 1, k. 1, * m. 1, k. 4, p. 2, k. 1, p. 3 tog., k. 1, p. 2, k. 4, m. 1, k. 1; repeat from * until 16 sts. remain, m. 1, k. 4, p. 2, k. 1, p. 2 tog., k. 3, p. 2, k. 2 tog.

22ND ROW: P. 2 tog., k. 1, p. 5, k. 2, p. 11, * k. 2, p. 3, k. 2, p. 11; repeat from * until 10 sts. remain, k. 2, p. 5, k. 1, k. 2 tog.

23RD ROW: K. 2 tog., k. 1, p. 2 tog., k. 2, p. 2, k. 5, m. 1, k. 1, * m. 1, k. 5, p. 2, p. 3 tog., p. 2, k. 5, m. 1, k. 1; repeat from * until 14 sts. remain, m. 1, k. 5, p. 2, k. 1, p. 2 tog., k. 2, k. 2 tog.

24TH ROW: K. 2 tog., p. 3, k. 2, p. 13, * k. 2, p. 1, k. 2, p. 13; repeat from * until 7 sts. remain, k. 2, p. 3, k. 2 tog.

25TH ROW: K. 2 tog., k. 2, p. 2, k. 6, p. 2 tog., * k. 5, p. 2, m. 1, k. 1, m. 1, p. 2, k. 5, p. 3 tog.; repeat from *, ending the last repeat with p. 2 tog. instead of p. 3 tog., then k. 6, p. 2, k. 2, k. 2 tog.

26TH ROW: P. 2 tog., p. 1, k. 2, p. 12, * k. 2, p. 3, k. 2, p. 11; repeat from *, ending the last repeat with p. 12 instead of p. 11, then k. 2, p. 1, p. 2 tog.

27TH ROW: K. 2 tog., p. 2, k. 6, p. 2 tog., * k. 4, p. 2, k. 1, (m. 1, k. 1) twice, p. 2, k. 4, p. 3 tog.; repeat from *, ending the last repeat with p. 2 tog. instead of p. 3 tog., then k. 6, p. 2, k. 2 tog.

28TH ROW: K. 2 tog., k. 1, p. 11, * k. 2, p. 5, k. 2, p. 9; repeat from *, ending the last repeat with p. 11 instead of p. 9, then k. 1, k. 2 tog.

29TH ROW: P. 2 tog., k. 6, p. 2 tog., * k. 3, p. 2, k. 2, m. 1, k. 1, m. 1, k. 2, p. 2, k. 3, p. 3 tog.; repeat from *, ending the last repeat with p. 2 tog. instead of p. 3 tog.; then k. 6, p. 2 tog.

30TH ROW: P. 2 tog., p. 9, * k. 2, p. 7; repeat from *, ending the last repeat with p. 9 instead of p. 7, then p. 2 tog.

31ST ROW: K. 2 tog., k. 4, p. 2 tog., * k. 2, p. 2, k. 3, m. 1, k. 1, m. 1, k. 3, p. 2, k. 2, p. 3 tog.; repeat from *, ending the last repeat with p. 2 tog. instead of p. 3 tog., then k. 4, k. 2 tog.

32ND ROW: P. 2 tog., p. 6, * k. 2, p. 9, k. 2, p. 5; repeat from *, ending the last repeat with p. 6 instead of p. 5, then p. 2 tog.

33RD ROW: K. 2 tog., k. 2, p. 2 tog., * k. 1, p. 2, k. 4, m. 1, k. 1, m. 1, k. 4, p. 2, k. 1, p. 3 tog.; repeat from *, ending the last repeat with p. 2 tog. instead of p. 3 tog., then k. 2, k. 2 tog.

34TH ROW: P. 2 tog., p. 3, * k. 2, p. 11, k. 2, p. 3; repeat from * until 2 sts. remain, p. 2 tog.

There should now be 59 sts. on the pins. Cast off rather tightly.

Work another sleeve in the same manner.

Make up the jumper in the usual way, but fasten the jumper on the left shoulder with press studs.

see overleaf

Could Anything Be Prettier?

The Main Part Of The Jumper Is In A Charming Lacy Stripe, And The Jabot And Sleeves Are Worked In The Daintiest Of Stitches!

MATERIALS

*F*OUR ozs. of " Greenock," 2-ply Super Fingering (obtainable only from any of the branches of the SCOTCH WOOL & HOSIERY STORES). A pair of Stratnoid knitting pins, No. 9 and No. 10, and a pair of wooden pins, No. 4. Six tiny glass buttons.

TENSION AND MEASUREMENTS

*W*ORKED at a tension of 7 sts. to the inch in width, on the plain part, with No. 9 pins, the measurements on the diagram are attained after light pressing.

ABBREVIATIONS

K., KNIT ; p., purl ; st., stitch ; tog., together ; dec., decrease —(by working 2 sts. tog.) ; inc., increase (by working into the back and front of the same st.) ; m., make (by bringing the wool to the front of the pin and over it before working a k. st., or by bringing the wool to the front of the pin, over it, and to the front again, before working a p. st.) ; m.s., moss-st. (k. 1 and p. 1 alternately, and on subsequent rows the sts. are reversed) ; single rib is k. 1 and p. 1 alternately. Directions in brackets are worked the number of times stated immediately after the brackets.

TO WORK THE BACK

*W*ITH No. 10 pins cast on 100 sts., working into the back of the sts. on the first row to give a neat edge.
Now work 34 rows in single rib.
INCREASE ROW : * Rib 4, inc. ; repeat from * to end (120 sts.).
Change to No. 9 pins and work in stripe pattern as follows :
1ST ROW : K. 4, * m. 1, k. 2 tog., k. 1, m. 1, k. 2 tog., k. 7 ; repeat from *, ending the last repeat with k. 3.
2ND ROW : P. 5, * m. 1, k. 2 tog., k. 1, m. 1, k. 2 tog., p. 7 ; repeat from *, ending the last repeat with p. 2 instead of p. 7.
These 2 rows complete one pattern.
Repeat the 2 pattern rows 36 times more to armholes.
TO SHAPE THE ARMHOLES.—1ST ARMHOLE ROW : Cast off 3 (1 st. on pin), m. 1, k. 2 tog., k. 1, m. 1, k. 2 tog., * k. 7, m. 1, k. 2 tog., k. 1, m. 1, k. 2 tog. ; repeat from *, ending the last repeat with k. 3.
2ND ARMHOLE ROW : Cast off 3 (1 st. on pin), p. 1, * m. 1, k. 2 tog., k. 1, m. 1, k. 2 tog., p. 7 ; repeat from * until 4 remain, m. 1, k. 2 tog., k. 2.
3RD ARMHOLE ROW : Cast off 3 (1 st. on pin), m. 1, k. 2 tog., * k. 7, m. 1, k. 2 tog., k. 1, m. 1, k. 2 tog. ; repeat from * to end.
4TH ARMHOLE ROW : Cast off 3 (1 st. on pin), k. 1, m. 1, k. 2 tog., p. 7, * m. 1, k. 2 tog., k. 1, m. 1, k. 2 tog., p. 7 ; repeat from * until 1 st. remains, k. 1.
5TH ARMHOLE ROW : K. 2 tog., k. 1, * k. 7, m. 1, k. 2 tog., k. 1, m. 1, k. 2 tog. ; repeat from * until 9 sts. remain, k. 7, k. 2 tog.
6TH ARMHOLE ROW : K. 2 tog., p. 8, * m. 1, k. 2 tog., k. 1, m. 1, k. 2 tog., p. 7 ; repeat from *, ending the last repeat with p. 6, p. 2 tog.
7TH ARMHOLE ROW : K. 2 tog., k. 6, * m. 1, k. 2 tog., k. 1, m. 1, k. 2 tog., k. 7 ; repeat from *, ending the last repeat with k. 5, k. 2 tog.
8TH ARMHOLE ROW : P. 2 tog., p. 6, * m. 1, k. 2 tog., k. 1, m. 1, k. 2 tog., p. 7 ; repeat from *, ending the last repeat with p. 3, p. 2 tog.
9TH ARMHOLE ROW : K. 2 tog., k. 4, m. 1, k. 2 tog., k. 1, m. 1, k. 2 tog., * k. 7, m. 1, k. 2 tog., k. 1, m. 1, k. 2 tog. ; repeat from * until 5 sts. remain, k. 3, k. 2 tog.

10TH ARMHOLE ROW : P. 2 tog., p. 4, * m. 1, k. 2 tog., k. 1, m. 1, k. 2 tog., p. 7 ; repeat from *, ending the last repeat with p. 1, k. 2 tog.
There will now be 96 sts. on the pins, on which work in straight pattern as at the beginning for 38 rows more.
On the next row the sts. are divided for the neck opening as follows : Pattern 30 and slip these sts. on to a stitch-holder until needed for Right Back Shoulder, cast off 36 (1 st. on pin), pattern to end (30 sts. for Left Back Shoulder).

THE LEFT BACK SHOULDER

**C*ONTINUE in pattern as now set, decreasing at the neck end of the next row and following 6 alternate rows when 23 sts. will remain.
Work 6 rows straight on these sts.
Cast off straight across.

THE RIGHT BACK SHOULDER

*J*OIN the wool to the neck end of the remaining sts., and work 1 row.
Continue as from ** on Left Back Shoulder to end.

THE FRONT

This is worked exactly the same as the Back.

THE SLEEVES

*F*IRST join the shoulder seams, beginning at the armhole end and taking 1 st. from each side at a time.
Holding the work with the right side facing and using No. 9 pins, pick up and k. 111 sts. from all round the armhole edge.
P. 1 row, then change to No. 4 pins and work in pattern as follows :
PATTERN ROW : K. 1, * m. 1, k. 2 tog. ; repeat from * until 1 st. remains, k. 1.
Repeat this row 21 times more.
DECREASE ROW : K. 2 tog. 3 times, * rib 3, rib 2 tog. ; repeat from * until 5 sts. remain, k. 1, then k. 2 tog. twice (86 sts.).
Now change to No. 10 pins, and work 13 rows in single rib. Cast off.
Work a second sleeve in the same manner.

THE JABOT

*U*SING No. 4 pins, cast on 106 sts., and work in pattern as on sleeve for 16 rows.
Change to No. 10 pins, and work 4 rows in m.s.
NEXT ROW : Cast off 35 (1 st. on pin), m.s. to end (71 sts.).
Work 1 row in m.s.
NEXT ROW : Cast on 35 (same end as cast-off sts.), when there will again be 106 sts.
Work 4 rows straight in m.s.
Change to No. 4 pins, and work 16 rows in sleeve pattern.
Cast off.

NECK BAND

*P*RESS all pieces with a hot iron over a damp cloth.
Join the sleeve and side seams in one long line, then stitch jabot in place, so that the cast-off and cast-on pieces go round the front neck.
With No. 10 pins and right side of work facing, pick up and rib 80 sts. from front neck edge, beginning at the shoulders.
Work 4 rows in single rib.
NEXT ROW : * M. 1, p. 2 tog. ; repeat from * until 1 st. remains, k. 1.
Work 6 rows in single rib.
Cast off.

A Photograph of the Lacy Stripe Pattern.

Could Anything be Prettier (cont'd)

The Shape and Measurements of the Jumper.

SLEEVE 5"

18" 17" FRONT 11"

17" BACK 18"

A frilly jabot is most becoming to the figure. It disguises the too-plump, and softens the too-thin.

Work the back neck border to match.

Sew tiny crystal buttons down centre-front of jabot and one on each back shoulder to correspond with the buttonhole loop.

Colour Scheme No 1

JUMPER. — Emerald-Green.
SKIRT. — White Flannel.
ACCESSORIES. — Green Sandals.
Rust Stockings
and White Pin.

Colour Scheme No 2

JUMPER. — Daffodil-Yellow.
Yellow Shantung.
SKIRT. —
ACCESSORIES. — Cherry-Red Belt.
Black Kid Shoes.
A Charm Bracelet.

Colour Scheme No 3

JUMPER. — Cornflower-Blue.
SKIRT. — Linen, To Match.
ACCESSORIES. — Rose-Pink Scarf.
Blue Flower Clip
Navy Blue Shoes.

*Emerald-Green is
Shade No. 259*

*Daffodil-Yellow is
Shade No. 252*

*Cornflower-Blue is
Shade No. 244*

For SUN-SPLASHED DAYS!

*Your Imagination Will Be Captured
By This Charming Design*

Beginners can make this delightful jumper as every row of the shaping is given in full.

MATERIALS.—9 ozs. of Sirdar Majestic wool, 4-ply, or 11 ozs. if long sleeves are made, and a pair each of No. 12, No. 10, and No. 8 Aero knitting pins.

ABBREVIATIONS.—*K., knit ; p., purl ; st., stitch ; sl., slip ; tog., together ; p.s.s.o., pass the slipped st. over ; inc., increase (by working twice into one st., which increases one st. only). To inc. twice k. in the front of a st., then in the back and again in the front, before slipping the st. off the left-hand pin. Directions in brackets are worked the number of times stated after the brackets. Single rib is k. 1 and p. 1 alternately. S.s., stocking-st. (k. on the right side and p. back).*

TENSION AND MEASUREMENTS.—*Worked at such a tension that one repeat measures 2 inches in width, with No. 8 pins, the measurements on the diagram are attained after light pressing. Bear in mind that this wavy rib pattern contracts the knitting, so if desired it will expand or press to a larger size.*

To Work the Back

Cast on 100 sts. with No. 10 pins and work 36 rows in single rib, knitting into the back of the k. sts. on the first row.

Increase row : K. plain, increasing in the third st., then in every alternate st. until 48 sts. are added, k. 3 at end, making a total of 148 sts.
P. the next row.

The Main Pattern

Still retaining the No. 10 pins, work as follows :

1st row (right side facing) : P. 4, * (k. 1, p. 1) twice, k. 1, p. 9, (k. 1, p. 1) 3 times ; repeat from * until 4 sts. remain, p. 4.

2nd row : K. 4, * inc. twice in the next st., (p. 1, k. 1) twice, p. 1, k. 2 tog., k. 5, k. 2 tog., (p. 1, k. 1) twice, p. 1 ; repeat from * until 4 sts. remain, k. 4.

3rd row : P. 4, * (k. 1, p. 1) twice, k. 1, p. 7, (k. 1, p. 1) twice, k. 1, p. 3 ; repeat from * until 4 sts. remain, p. 4.

4th row : K. 4, * inc. in the next st., k. 1, inc. in the next st. (p. 1, k. 1) twice, p. 1, k. 2 tog., k. 3, k. 2 tog., (p. 1, k. 1) twice, p. 1 ; repeat from * until 4 sts. remain, k. 4.

5th row : P. 4, * (k. 1, p. 1) twice, k. 1, p. 5 ; repeat from * until 4 sts. remain, p. 4.

6th row : K. 4, * inc. in the next st., k. 3, inc. in the next st., (p. 1, k. 1) twice, p. 1, k. 2 tog., k. 1, k. 2 tog., (p. 1, k. 1) twice, p. 1 ; repeat from * until 4 sts. remain, k. 4.

The neck and sleeves are edged with knitted rouleaux.

7th row : P. 4, * (k. 1, p. 1) twice, k. 1, p. 3, (k. 1, p. 1) twice, k. 1, p. 7 ; repeat from * until 4 sts. remain, p. 4.

8th row : K. 4. * inc. in the next st., k. 5, inc. in the next st., (p. 1, k. 1) twice, p. 1, sl. 1, k. 2 tog., p.s.s.o., (p. 1, k. 1) twice, p. 1 ; repeat from * until 4 sts. remain, k. 4.

9th row : P. 4, * (k. 1, p. 1) 6 times, p. 8 ; repeat from * until 4 sts. remain, p. 4.

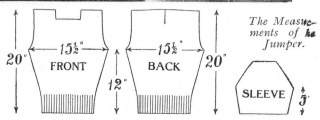

The Measurements of the Jumper.

FOR *Sun-Splashed* DAYS

10th row : K. 4, * k. 2 tog., k. 5, k. 2 tog., (p. 1, k. 1) twice, p. 1, inc. twice in the next st., (p. 1, k. 1) twice, p. 1 ; repeat from * until 4 sts. remain, k. 4.

11th row : P. 4, * (k. 1, p. 1) twice, k. 1, p. 3, (k. 1, p. 1) twice, k. 1, p. 7 ; repeat from * until 4 sts. remain, p. 4.

12th row : K. 4, * k. 2 tog., k. 3, k. 2 tog., (p. 1, k. 1) twice, p. 1, inc., k. 1, inc., (p. 1, k. 1) twice, p. 1 ; repeat from * until 4 sts. remain, k. 4.

13th row : P. 4, * (k. 1, p. 1) twice, k. 1, p. 5, repeat from * until 4 sts. remain, p. 4.

14th row : K. 4, * k. 2 tog., k. 1, k. 2 tog., (p. 1, k. 1) twice, p. 1, inc., k. 3, inc., (p. 1, k. 1) twice, p. 1 ; repeat from * until 4 sts. remain, k. 4.

15th row : P. 4, * (k. 1, p. 1) twice, k. 1, p. 7, (k. 1, p. 1) twice, k. 1, p. 3 ; repeat from * until 4 sts. remain, p. 4.

16th row : K. 4, * sl. 1, k. 2 tog., p.s.s.o., (p. 1, k. 1) twice, p. 1, inc., k. 5, inc., (p. 1, k. 1) twice, p. 1 ; repeat from * until 4 sts. remain, k. 4.

These 16 rows form one pattern, and there should be 148 sts. as at the beginning of the pattern.

Repeat these 16 rows once more, change to No. 8 pins and work 2 patterns more, then work 8 rows of the next pattern.

To Shape the Armholes.—*9th row of pattern :* Cast off 8 sts. (now 1 st. on right-hand pin), p. 1, (k. 1, p. 1) 3 times, p. 8, * (k. 1, p. 1) 6 times, p. 8 ; repeat from * until 4 sts. remain, p.4.

10th row : Cast off 8 sts. (1 st. on right-hand pin), k. 2, k. 2 tog., (p. 1, k. 1) twice, p. 1, inc. twice in the next st. (p. 1, k. 1) twice, p. 1, * k. 2 tog., k. 5, k. 2 tog., (p. 1, k. 1) twice, p. 1, inc. twice in the next st., (p. 1, k. 1) twice, p. 1 ; repeat from * until 16 sts. remain, then k. 2 tog., k. 5, k. 2 tog., (p. 1, k. 1) twice, p. 1, k. 2.

11th row : (K. 1, p. 1) 3 times, k. 1, p. 7, * (k. 1, p. 1) twice, k. 1, p. 3, (k. 1, p. 1) twice, k. 1, p. 7 ; repeat from *, ending the last repeat with p. 4 instead of p. 7.

12th row : Cast off 2 (1 st. on right-hand pin) k. 1, pass previous st. over, (p. 1, k. 1) twice, p. 1, inc., k. 1, inc., (p. 1, k. 1) twice, p. 1, * k. 2 tog., k. 3, k. 2 tog., (p. 1, k. 1) twice, p. 1, inc., k. 1, inc., (p. 1, k. 1) twice, p. 1 ; repeat from * until 14 sts. remain, k. 2 tog., k. 3, k. 2 tog., (p. 1, k. 1) 3 times, p. 1.

13th row : P. 2 tog., (* k. 1, p. 1) twice, k. 1, p. 5 ; repeat from * until 6 sts. remain, (k. 1, p. 1) 3 times.

14th row : P. 2, (k. 1, p. 1) twice, inc., k. 3, inc., (k. 1, p. 1) twice, p. 1, * k. 2 tog., k. 1, k. 2 tog., (p. 1, k. 1) twice, p. 1, inc., k. 3, inc., (p. 1, k. 1) twice, p. 1 ; repeat from * until 11 sts. remain, k. 2 tog., k. 1, k. 2 tog., (p. 1, k. 1) twice, p. 2 (127 sts., and no more decreases for the armhole).

15th row : P. 1, (k. 1, p. 1) twice, k. 1, p. 3, * (k. 1, p. 1) twice, k. 1, p. 7, (k. 1, p. 1) twice, k. 1, p. 3 ; repeat from *, ending the last repeat with p. 1 instead of p. 3.

16th row : P. 2, (k. 1, p. 1) twice, inc., k. 5, inc., (p. 1, k. 1) twice, p. 1, * sl. 1, k. 2 tog., p.s.s.o., (p. 1, k. 1) twice, p. 1, inc., k. 5, inc., (p. 1, k. 1) twice, p. 1 ; repeat from * until 9 sts. remain, sl. 1, k. 2 tog., p.s.s.o., (p. 1, k. 1) twice, p. 2.

This finishes the armhole pattern.

As the pattern is broken at each end, the 16 upper pattern rows (as distinct from the pattern at the beginning of the Back) will now be worked as follows :

1st row : (P. 1, k. 1) 3 times, p. 1, * (k. 1, p. 1) twice, k. 1, p. 9, (k. 1, p. 1) 3 times ; repeat from * to end of row.

2nd row : (K. 1, p. 1) 3 times, k. 2 tog., k. 5, k. 2 tog., (p. 1, k. 1) twice, p. 1, inc. twice in the next st., (p. 1, k. 1) twice, p. 1, k. 2 tog., k. 5, k. 2 tog., (p. 1, k. 1) twice, p. 1 ; repeat from * until 7 sts. remain, inc. twice in the next st., (p. 1, k. 1) twice, p. 2.

3rd row : (P. 1, k. 1) 3 times, p. 3, * (k. 1, p. 1) twice, k. 1, p. 7, (k. 1, p. 1) twice, k. 1, p. 3 ; repeat from *, ending the last repeat with p. 1 instead of p. 3.

4th row : K. 1, (p. 1, k. 1) twice, p. 1, k. 2 tog., k. 3, k. 2 tog., (p. 1, k. 1) twice, p. 1, * inc. in the next st., k. 1, inc. in the next st., (p. 1, k. 1) twice, p. 1, k. 2 tog., k. 3, k. 2 tog., (p. 1, k. 1) twice, p. 1 ; repeat from * until 9 sts remain, inc. in the next st., k. 1, inc. in the next st., (p. 1, k. 1) twice, p. 2.

5th row : K. 1, * (k. 1, p. 1) twice, k. 1, p. 5 ; repeat from * until 6 sts. remain, (k. 1, p. 1) 3 times.

6th row : (K. 1, p. 1) 3 times, k. 2 tog., k. 1, k. 2 tog., (p. 1, k. 1) twice, p. 1, * inc., k. 3, inc., (p. 1, k. 1) twice, p. 1, k. 2 tog., k. 1, k. 2 tog., (p. 1, k. 1) twice, p. 1 ; repeat from * until 11 sts. remain, inc., k. 3, inc., (p. 1, k. 1) twice, p. 2.

7th row : K. 2, (p. 1, k. 1) twice, p. 7, * (k. 1, p. 1) twice, k. 1, p. 3, (k. 1, p. 1) twice, k. 1, p. 7 ; repeat from *, ending the last repeat with k. 1 extra instead of p. 7.

8th row : K. 1, (p. 1, k. 1) twice, p. 1, sl. 1, k. 2 tog., p.s.s.o., (p. 1, k. 1) twice, p. 1, * inc., k. 5, inc., (p. 1, k. 1) twice, p. 1, sl. 1, k. 2 tog., p.s.s.o., (p. 1, k. 1) twice, p. 1 ; repeat from * until 13 sts. remain, inc., k. 5, inc., (p. 1, k. 1) twice, p. 2.

9th row : K. 1, (k. 1, p. 1) 3 times, p. 8, * (k. 1, p. 1) 6 times, p. 8 ; repeat from *, omitting the p. 8 on the last repeat.

10th row : (K. 1, p. 1) 3 times, inc., twice in the next st., (p. 1, k. 1) twice, p. 1, * k. 2 tog., k. 5, k. 2 tog., (p. 1, k. 1) twice, p. 1, inc. twice in the next st. (p. 1, k. 1) twice, p. 1 ; repeat from * until 15 sts. remain, k. 2 tog., k. 5, k. 2 tog., (p. 1, k. 1) twice, p. 2.

11th row : K. 1, (k. 1, p. 1) twice, k. 1, p. 7, * (k. 1, p. 1) twice, k. 1, p. 3, (k. 1, p. 1) twice, k. 1, p. 7 ; repeat from *, ending the last repeat with p. 1 instead of p. 7.

12th row : (K. 1, p. 1) 3 times, inc., k. 1, inc., (p. 1, k. 1) twice, p. 1, * k. 2 tog., k. 3, k. 2 tog., (p. 1, k. 1) twice, p. 1, inc., k. 1, inc., (p. 1, k. 1) twice, p. 1 ; repeat from * until 13 sts. remain, k. 2 tog., k. 3, k. 2 tog., (p. 1, k. 1) twice, p. 2.

13th row : K. 1, * (k. 1, p. 1) twice, k. 1, p. 5, repeat from * until 6 sts. remain, (k. 1, p. 1) 3 times.

14th row : (K. 1, p. 1) 3 times, inc., k. 3, inc., (p. 1, k. 1) twice, p. 1, * k. 2 tog., k. 1, k. 2 tog., (p. 1, k. 1) twice, p. 1, inc., k. 3, inc., (p. 1, k. 1) twice, p. 1 ; repeat from * until 11 sts. remain, k. 2 tog., k. 1, k. 2 tog., (p. 1, k. 1) twice, p. 2.

15th row : K. 1, (k. 1, p. 1) twice, k. 1, p. 3, * (k. 1, p. 1) twice, k. 1, p. 7, (k. 1, p. 1) twice, k. 1, p 3 ; repeat from *, ending the last repeat with p. 1.

16th row : (K. 1, p. 1) 3 times, inc., k. 5 inc., (p. 1, k. 1) twice, p. 1, * sl. 1, k. 2 tog., p.s.s.o., (p. 1, k. 1) twice, p. 1, inc., k. 5, inc. (p. 1, k. 1) twice, p. 1 ; repeat from * until 9 sts. remain, sl. 1, k. 2 tog., p.s.s.o. (p. 1, k. 1) twice, p. 2.

On the next row the sts. are divided for the neck opening and shoulders as follows :

RIGHT BACK SHOULDER.—Repeat the 16 upper pattern rows twice on 67 sts. only, then cast off straight across.

LEFT BACK SHOULDER.—Join the wool to the next st. along the row, and cast on 7 sts., making 67 sts. for this shoulder, then work to match the Right Back Shoulder.

The Front

WORK as for the Back as far as the neck opening row, but here work the 16 upper pattern rows again to the neckline.

LEFT FRONT SHOULDER.—Work the 16 rows of upper pattern once on the first 33 sts., but at the neck edge there will be 6 sts. over the repeat which must be worked in single rib at this end to keep the wave. After the 16th row, cast off straight across.

RIGHT FRONT SHOULDER.—Join the wool to the next st. along the row and cast off 61 sts., which leaves 33 for this shoulder with the one on the right-hand pin after casting off. Work 16 rows on these 33 sts., following the pattern as set by the rows underneath, on this shoulder.

The Short Sleeves

BEGIN at the arm edge and cast on 88 sts with No. 10 pins. Work 16 rows of the pattern as at the beginning of the Back.

Change to No. 8 pins and repeat the same 16 rows. (More patterns may be worked here for a longer sleeve, but this part of the sleeve must finish with the last row of the pattern, so as to begin shaping the top on the 1st row).

To Shape the Top of the Sleeve, Work as Follows : 1st row : P. 2 tog., p. 2, * (k. 1, p. 1) twice, k. 1, p. 9, (k. 1, p. 1) 3 times ; repeat from * until 4 sts. remain, p. 2, p. 2 tog.

2nd row : K. 2 tog., k. 1, * inc. twice in the next st., (p. 1, k. 1) twice, p. 1, k. 2 tog., k. 5, k. 2 tog., (p. 1, k. 1) twice, p. 1 ; repeat from * until 3 sts. remain, k. 1, k. 2 tog.

3rd row : P. 2 tog. * (k. 1, p. 1) twice, k. 1, p. 7, (k. 1, p. 1) twice, k. 1, p. 3 ; repeat from * until 2 remain, p. 2 tog.

4th row : Sl. 1, k. 1, p.s.s.o., then pass the single st. back to the left-hand pin, * inc. in the next st., k. 1, inc. in the next st. (p. 1, k. 1) twice, p. 1, k. 2 tog., k. 3, k. 2 tog., (p. 1, k. 1) twice, p. 1 ; repeat from *, ending the last repeat with p. 2 tog.

5th row : K. 2 tog., k. 1, p. 1, k. 1, p. 5, * (k. 1, p. 1) twice, k. 1, p. 5 ; repeat from *, ending the last repeat with p. 3, p. 2 tog.

6th row : K. 3, inc. in the next st., (p. 1, k. 1) twice, p. 1, k. 2 tog., k. 1, k. 2 tog., (p. 1, k. 1) twice, p. 1, * inc. in the next st., k. 3, inc. in the next st. (p. 1, k. 1) twice, p. 1, k. 2 tog., k. 1, k. 2 tog., (p. 1, k. 1) twice, p. 1 ; repeat from *, ending the last repeat with p. 2 tog.

7th row : P. 2 tog., k. 1, p. 3, (k. 1, p. 1) twice, k. 1, p. 7, * (k. 1, p. 1) twice, k. 1, p. 3, (k. 1, p. 1) twice, k. 1, p. 7 ; repeat from *, ending the last repeat with p. 3, p. 2 tog., instead of p. 7.

8th row : K. 3, inc. in the next st. (p. 1, k. 1) twice, p. 1, sl. 1, k. 2 tog., p.s.s.o., (p. 1, k. 1) twice, p. 1, * inc. in the next st., k. 5, inc. in the next st. (p. 1, k. 1) twice, p. 1, sl. 1, k. 2 tog., p.s.s.o., (p. 1, k. 1) twice, p. 1 ; repeat from *, ending the last repeat with p. 2 tog. after p.s.s.o.

9th row : P. 2 tog., (k. 1, p. 1) 3 times, p. 8, * (k. 1, p. 1) 6 times, p. 8 ; repeat from *, ending the last repeat with p. 2, p. 2 tog., instead of p. 8.

10th row : (K. 2 tog.) twice, (p. 1, k. 1) twice, p. 1, inc. twice in the next st. (p. 1, k. 1) twice, p. 1, * k. 2 tog., k. 5, k. 2 tog., (p. 1, k. 1) twice, p. 1, inc. twice in the next st. (p. 1, k. 1) twice, p. 1 ; repeat from * until 15 sts. remain, k. 2 tog., k. 5, k. 2 tog., (p. 1, k. 1) twice, p. 2 tog.

11th row : P. 2 tog., k. 1, p. 3, k. 1, p. 7, * (k. 1, p. 1) twice, k. 1, p. 3, (k. 1, p. 1) twice, k. 1, p. 7 ; repeat from *, ending the last repeat with p. 2 tog. instead of p. 7.

12th row : P. 2 tog., (k. 1, p. 1) twice, inc., k. 1, inc., (p. 1, k. 1) twice, p. 1, * k. 2 tog., k. 3, k. 2 tog., (p. 1, k. 1) twice, p. 1, inc., k. 1, inc., (p. 1, k. 1) twice, p. 1 ; repeat from *, ending the last repeat with p. 1, k. 1, p. 2 tog., after the last k. 2 tog.

13th row : P. 2 tog., k. 1, p. 5, * (k. 1, p. 1) twice, k. 1, p. 5 ; repeat from *, ending the last repeat with k. 1, p. 1, k. 1, p. 2 tog.

14th row : P. 2 tog., k. 1, p. 1, inc., k. 3, inc., (p. 1, k. 1) twice, p. 1, * k. 2 tog., k. 1, k. 2 tog., (p. 1, k. 1) twice, p. 1, inc., k. 3, inc., (p. 1, k. 1) twice, p. 1 ; repeat from * until 7 remain, k. 2 tog., k. 1, k. 2 tog., p. 1, k. 1.

15th row : K. 2 tog., p. 3, * (k. 1, p. 1) twice, k. 1, p. 7, (k. 1, p. 1) twice, k. 1, p. 3 ; repeat from * until 15 remain, (k. 1, p. 1) twice, k. 1, p. 7, k. 1, p. 2 tog..

16th row : P. 2 tog., inc., k. 5, inc., (p. 1, k. 1) twice, p. 1, * sl. 1, k. 2 tog., p.s.s.o., (p. 1, k. 1) twice, p. 1, inc., k. 5, inc., (p. 1, k. 1) twice, p. 1 ; repeat from * until 4 remain, sl. 1, k. 3 tog., p.s.s.o. (56 sts.).

17th row : K. 2 tog., (p. 1, k. 1) twice, p. 9, (k. 1, p. 1) 3 times, * (k. 1, p. 1) twice, k. 1, p. 9, (k. 1, p. 1) 3 times ; repeat from *, ending the last repeat with p. 8, p. 2 tog.

18th row : K. 2 tog., k. 5, k. 2 tog., (p. 1, k. 1) twice, p. 1, * inc. twice in the next st., (p. 1, k. 1) twice, p. 1, k. 2 tog., k. 5, k. 2 tog., (p. 1, k. 1) twice, p. 1 ; repeat from *, ending the last repeat with p. 1, k. 1, p. 1, k. 2 tog.

19th row : K. 2 tog., p. 1, k. 1, p. 7, (k. 1, p. 1) twice, k. 1, p. 3, * (k. 1, p. 1) twice, k. 1, p. 7, (k. 1, p. 1) twice, k. 1, p. 3 ; repeat from *, ending the last repeat with p. 5, p. 2 tog.

20th row : K. 2 tog., k. 2, k. 2 tog., (p. 1, k. 1) twice, p. 1, * inc., k. 1, inc., (p. 1, k. 1) twice, p. 1, k. 2 tog., k. 3, k. 2 tog., (p. 1, k. 1) twice, p. 1 ; repeat from *, ending the last repeat with p. 1, k. 2 tog.

21st row : K. 2 tog., p. 5, * (k. 1, p. 1) twice, k. 1, p. 5 ; repeat from *, ending the last repeat with p. 2, p. 2 tog.

22nd row : Sl. 1, k. 2 tog., p.s.s.o., (p. 1, k. 1) twice, p. 1, * inc., k. 3, inc., (p. 1, k. 1) twice, p. 1, k. 2 tog., k. 1, k. 2 tog., (p. 1, k. 1) twice, p. 1 ; repeat from * until 15 sts remain, inc., k. 3, inc., (p. 1, k. 1) twice, p. 1, k. 2 tog., k. 1, k. 3 tog.

23rd row : P. 2 tog., p. 1, (k. 1, p. 1) twice, k. 1, p. 7, * (k. 1, p. 1) twice, k. 1, p. 3, (k. 1, p. 1) twice, k. 1, p. 7 ; repeat from * until 6 remain, (k. 1, p. 1) twice, k. 2 tog.

24th row : K. 2 tog., p. 1, k. 1, p. 1, inc., k. 5, inc., (p. 1, k. 1) twice, p. 1, sl. 1, k. 2 tog., p.s.s.o., (p. 1, k. 1) twice, p. 1, inc., k. 5, inc., (p. 1, k. 1) twice, p. 1, k. 2 tog.

25th row : K. 2 tog., (p. 1, k. 1) twice, p. 9, (k. 1, p. 1) 6 times, p. 8, k. 1, p. 1, k. 2 tog.

26th row : K. 2 tog., p. 1, k. 2 tog., k. 5, k. 2 tog., (p. 1, k. 1) twice, p. 1, inc. twice in the next st., (p. 1, k. 1) twice, p. 1, k. 2 tog., k. 5, k. 2 tog., p. 1, k. 1, p. 1, k. 2 tog.

27th row : K. 2 tog., p. 1, k. 1, p. 7, (k. 1, p. 1) twice, k. 1, p. 3, (k. 1, p. 1) twice, k. 1, p. 7, k. 2 tog.

28th row : K. 1, k. 2 tog., k. 3, k. 2 tog., (p. 1, k. 1) twice, p. 1, inc., k. 1, inc., (p. 1, k. 1) twice, p. 1, k. 2 tog., k. 3, k. 2 tog., p. 1, k. 2 tog.

29th row : K. 2 tog., p. 5, (k. 1, p. 1) twice, k. 1, p. 5, (k. 1, p. 1) twice, k. 1, p. 4, p. 2 tog.

30th row : K. 2 tog., k. 1, k. 2 tog., (p. 1, k. 1) twice, p. 1, inc., k. 3, inc., (p. 1, k. 1) twice, p. 1, k. 2 tog., k. 1, k. 3 tog. (23 sts. left). Cast off.

For Long Sleeves

WITH No. 12 pins cast on 68 sts. and work 30 rows in single rib.

Increase row : Knit this row plain as follows : K. 4, inc. in the next st., then inc. in every 3rd st. until 20 sts. have been added, k. to end of row (88 sts.).

Purl back the next row.

Still using No. 12 pins, work 3 patterns of 16 rows each as at the beginning of the Back. Change to No. 10 pins and work 3 patterns on these pins. Change to No. 8 pins and repeat the pattern for length of sleeve seam required, ending with the 16th row of any pattern. Shape the top as given for Short Sleeves.

THE ROLL BANDS.—These are simply worked in s.s. with the No. 12 pins. Cast on 14 sts. and work 2 strips 9 inches long for the sleeves, and 1 strip 18 inches long for the neck.

TO MAKE UP THE JUMPER.—First press all pieces except the Roll Bands, on the wrong side, putting a damp cloth over the work and a thick blanket underneath. Sew the shoulder seams, taking 1 st. from each side at a time. Set the sleeves into armholes and press these seams while the work is open. Sew side and sleeve seams in one line and press. Now sew on the sleeve and collar bands, first tacking them in position with the purl side uppermost, and arrange so that the centre of the strip is on a line with the edge of the sleeve and neck respectively. With the same wool, hem the edge of the sleeve to the Roll Band and the neck edge to the longer roll. Sew the ends of the sleeve rolls on the plain knitted side of the work. These bands will roll into position themselves, without any further adjustment. Sew two press-studs at the back opening, one of them at the centre of the Roll Band.

LLANFAIRPWLLGWYNGYLLGOGERYCHWYRNDROBWLL-LLANTYSILIOGOGOGOCH

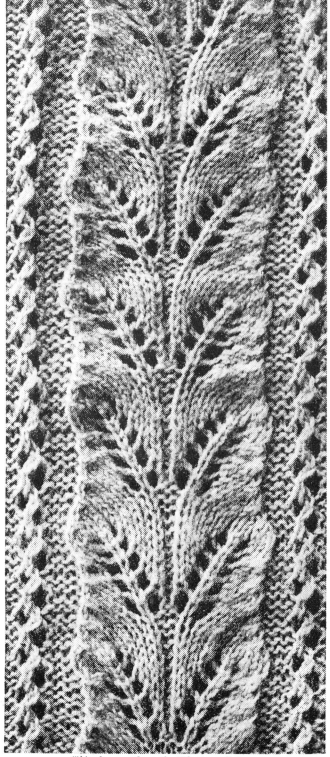

This close-up shows the Wheat-ear Pattern.

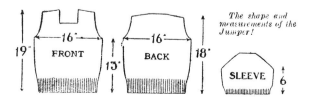

The shape and measurements of the Jumper!

SUCH A DEBONAIR LITTLE JUMPER!

The Ribbed Yoke And Demure, Square Neckline Combine Cleverly With The Lacy Pattern!

MATERIALS

FOUR ounces of " Campanula " Super Fingering, 2-ply ; a pair of " Aero " knitting pins No. 11 and No. 13, also a pair of No. 12 pins if long sleeves are worked ; 1 yard of narrow velvet ribbon. An " Aero " stitch-holder.

TENSION AND MEASUREMENTS

WORKED at a tension of 28 sts. (one pattern) to 3 inches in width, on No. 11 pins, the measurements on the diagram are attained after light pressing.

ABBREVIATIONS

KNIT ; p., purl ; st., stitch ; tog., together ; inc., increase (by working into the back and front of the same st.) ; dec., decrease (by working 2 sts. tog.) ; m., make (by bringing the wool to the front of the pin and over it before working a k. st., or by bringing the wool to the front of the pin, over it and to the front again before working a p. st.) ; sl., slip ; p.s.s.o., pass the slipped st. over. Single rib is k. 1 and p. 1 alternately. Directions in brackets are worked the number of times stated immediately after the brackets.

TO WORK THE BACK

WITH No. 13 pins cast on 128 sts. and work 44 rows in single rib, working into the back of the sts. on the first row to give a neat edge.

INCREASE ROW : K. 8, * inc., k. 5 ; repeat from * to end (148 sts.).

Change to No. 11 pins and p. 1 row.

Now begin the pattern as follows :

1ST ROW : P. 3, m. 1, k. 2 tog., p. 3, * k. 3 tog., k. 5, m. 1, k. 1, m. 1, p. 2, m. 1, k. 1, m. 1, k. 5, sl. 1, k. 2 tog., p.s.s.o., p. 3, m. 1, k. 2 tog., p. 3 ; repeat from * to end.

2ND ROW : (And every even numbered row, wrong side facing). K. 3, p. 2, k. 3, * p. 9, k. 2, p. 9, k. 3, p. 2, k. 3 ; repeat from * to end.

3RD ROW : P. 3, k. 2 tog., m. 1, p. 3, * k. 3 tog., k. 4, m. 1, k. 1, m. 1, k. 1, p. 2, k. 1, m. 1, k. 1, m. 1, k. 4, sl. 1, k. 2 tog., p.s.s.o., p. 3, k. 2 tog., m. 1, p. 3 ; repeat from * to end.

Don't You Love the Decorative Little Bows? Choose them in any colour—but black velvet bows would look very "dressy" on a pale pink jumper.

5TH Row : P. 3, m. 1, k. 2 tog., p. 3, * k. 3, m. 1, k. 1, m. 1, k. 2, p. 2, k. 2, m. 1, k. 1, m. 1, k. 3, sl. 1, k. 2 tog., p.s.s.o., p. 3, m. 1, k. 2 tog., p. 3 ; repeat from * to end.

7TH Row : P. 3, k. 2 tog., m. 1, p. 3, * k. 3 tog., k. 2, m. 1, k. 1, m. 1, k. 3, p. 2, k. 3, m. 1, k. 1, m. 1, k. 2, sl. 1, k. 2 tog., p.s.s.o., p. 3, k. 2 tog., m. 1, p. 3 ; repeat from * to end.

9TH Row : P. 3, m. 1, k. 2 tog., p. 3, * k. 3 tog., (k. 1, m. 1) twice, k. 4, p. 2, k. 4, (m. 1, k. 1) twice, sl. 1, k. 2 tog., p.s.s.o., p. 3, m. 1, k. 2 tog., p. 3 ; repeat from * to end.

11TH Row : P. 3, k. 2 tog., m. 1, p. 3, * k. 9, p 2, k. 9, p. 3, k. 2 tog., m. 1, p. 3 ; repeat from * to end

SUCH A DEBONAIR LITTLE JUMPER

(Continued from previous page.)

12TH ROW : As 2nd Row.

These 12 rows complete one pattern.

Repeat the 12 pattern rows 6 times more to armholes.

TO SHAPE THE ARMHOLES

WORK entirely in single rib for yoke, casting off 10 sts. at the beginning of each of the next 2 rows, then dec. at both ends of the next 8 rows, when 112 sts. will remain.

Continue straight on these sts. for 46 rows more to shoulders.

To SLOPE THE SHOULDERS.—Continue in rib, casting off 9 sts. at the beginning of each of the next 8 rows, then cast off the remaining sts.

THE FRONT

THIS is worked exactly the same as the Back until the armhole shaping is finished and 112 sts. remain.

Work 24 rows straight in rib.

On the next row the sts. are divided for the neck opening as follows :

Rib 36 and slip these sts. on a stitch-holder until needed for Left Front Shoulder, cast off 40, rib to end. (36 sts. for Right Front Shoulder.)

RIGHT FRONT SHOULDER.—Work 32 rows straight in rib on the last 36 sts. to the shoulder line.

To SLOPE THE SHOULDER.—Cast off 9 sts. at the beginning of the next row and the next 3 alternate rows (armhole end) and fasten off.

LEFT FRONT SHOULDER.—Join the wool to the neck end of remaining sts. and work to match the Right Front Shoulder, but work 31 rows only to the shoulder-line.

THE SLEEVES

WITH No. 13 pins cast on 80 sts. and work 20 rows in single rib.

INCREASE ROW : * Inc., p. 1 ; repeat from * to end (120 sts.).

Change to No. 11 pins and work 3 complete patterns as on Back.

Now work entirely in single rib, dec. at both ends of every row until 40 sts. remain.

Cast off.

Work a second sleeve in the same manner.

LONG SLEEVES

WITH No. 13 pins cast on 64 sts. and work 16 rows in single rib. Inc. 1 st. at both ends of the next row, and every third row following, until 16 sts. have been added, making 80 altogether. Work 5 rows more in single rib.

INCREASE ROW : * Inc., p. 1 ; repeat from * to end (120 sts.).

Now work 4 complete patterns as on Back.

Change to No. 12 pins and work 4 patterns more, then change to No. 11 pins and continue the same pattern for length of sleeve seam desired. Shape the sleeve top as for short sleeves to end.

TO MAKE UP THE JUMPER

FIRST press all pieces, except the ribbing, with a hot iron over a damp cloth on the wrong side of the work.

Join the shoulder seams, beginning at the armhole end and taking one st. from each side at a time. Set the sleeves into armholes.

Join the sleeve and side seams in one long line and press.

The lacings are threaded through the rib on each side of the neck-line in a position to suit wearer, or the yoke may be left plain.

To SET OFF Your SUMMER FROCKS

The Big Puff Sleeves of This Delightful Coatee Are Demure And So Smart

THIS coat is just stocking-st. but this special wool makes a fascinating fabric.

MATERIALS : 1 lb. 3 ozs. of Templeton's "Sestal" Bouclè Wool, in white or one of the attractive colours; a pair of No. 8 "Aero" knitting pins. (If you cannot obtain this wool locally write to Messrs. J. Templeton & Son, Ayr, Scotland, for the nearest stockist.)

TENSION . AND MEASUREMENTS : Worked at a tension of 5½ sts. to the inch in width the following measurements are attained after light pressing : Across back at underarms, 20 inches ; across front at same place, 10½ inches ; front length from shoulder seam to lower edge, 22 inches ; back length, 20 inches ; side seam, 14 inches ; sleeve seam, 7 inches.

ABBREVIATIONS : K., knit ; p., purl ; st., stitch ; tog., together ; inc., increase (by knitting into the front and back of the same stitch) ; dec., decrease ; s.s., stocking-stitch (k. on the right side and p. back). Single rib is k. 1 and p. 1 alternately.

To Work the Back

BEGIN at the lower edge by casting on 94 sts. Work 10 rows in garter-stitch.

Now work 42 rows in s.s., after which inc. 1 st. at both ends of the next row and every following 10th row, until there are 104 sts. Work 3 rows more, making 86 rows in s.s. to the armholes.

To Shape the Armholes : Cast off 3 sts. at the beginning of each of the next 4 rows, then k. 2 tog. at the *end* of the next 22 rows, when 70 sts. will remain.

Work 20 rows more in s.s. to the shoulder line and cast off straight across.

The Sleeves

CAST on 46 sts. and work 22 rows in single rib. Now work in s.s. as follows :

1st row : K. 10, inc. into each of the next 26 sts., k. 10 (72 sts.).

2nd row : All p.

3rd row : K. 10, inc. into each of the next 52 sts., k. 10 (124 sts.).

4th row : All p.

Work 22 rows in s.s. without further shaping.

To Shape the Top of the Sleeve : K. 2 tog. at both ends of the next row, and likewise every following 3rd row, until 102 sts. remain.

Next row : K. 2 tog. across the whole row (51 sts.).

Work another row like the last, then cast off the remaining 26 sts.

LONG SLEEVES (with ordinary round top) : Cast on 26 sts. and p. 1 row into the back of the sts.

Now work in s.s., increasing 1 st. at both ends of every row until there are 88 sts.

Continue on these sts., decreasing 1 st. at both ends of every 8th row until the width desired for the forearm is attained. Work in s.s. for length desired, finishing with 22 rows in single rib for the cuff. For a closer fitting cuff use one size finer pins.

The Left Front

CAST on 56 sts. and work 10 rows in garter-st.

Now work 42 rows in s.s., but k. the first 8 sts. on the p. side to produce a border of garter-st. up the front to the shoulder.

To shape the side seam, inc. 1 st. at the beginning of the next row and on every following 10th row until there are 61 sts. Work 3 rows more to the armhole.

To Shape the Armhole and Neck : 1st row : Cast off 3 sts., k. until 10 sts. remain, k. 2 tog., k. 8.

2nd row : K. 8, and p. to end as before.

3rd row : Cast off 3 sts. and k. to end.

4th row : K. 8, p. 2 tog., and p. to end.

5th row : K. 2 tog., k. to end.

6th row : As 2nd row.

Repeat the last 2 rows 10 times more, when there will be 11 single decreases at the armhole edge, and 17 sts. taken away from this end altogether. AT THE SAME TIME, continue to dec. on the neck edge, by knitting 2 tog. on every 3rd row inside the 8 border sts. as before, until 30 sts. remain. Continue without further dec. for 13 rows more, then cast off straight across.

The Right Front

CAST on 56 sts. and work 10 rows in garter-st.

11th row : All k.

12th row : All p. until 8 sts. remain, k. 8.

Keeping these last 8 sts. in garter-st., work to match the Left Front, making the first inc. on the side seam on the wrong side, when the rest of the shaping will follow suit.

When the shoulder line is reached, cast off with wrong side of work facing, until 8 sts. remain. Work 32 rows in garter-st. on these 8 sts. for the back neck-band, then cast off.

*The suit, worn with the skirt is
finished with a white belt at the waist.*

A
DASHING
LITTLE
SWIM-SUIT

With the Halter Neck
That is Ideal for Sun-
bathing

TENSION AND MEASUREMENTS.—*Worked at
a tension of 8 sts. to the inch in width, on No.
12 pins, the measurements on the diagram are
attained after light pressing.*
ABBREVIATIONS.—*K., knit; p., purl; st.,
stitch; tog., together; inc., increase (by working into the back and front of the same st.);
dec., decrease; single rib is k. 1 and p. 1
alternately. Directions in brackets are worked
the number of times stated immediately after the
brackets.*

The Skirt

To work the back, begin at the waist and
with No. 13 pins cast on 112 sts. Work
20 rows in rib, working into the back of
the sts. on the first row to give a neat edge.

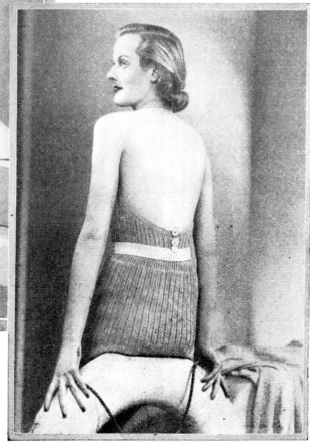

HERE is a really practical swim-suit. The skirt is separate
and can be detached when you go for an energetic swim
MATERIALS.—*12 ozs. of Golden Eagle " Seawul " 4-ply
(or 6 ozs. without the skirt); a pair of Phantom knitting pins
No. 12 and No. 13; 2 large and 3 small buttons; white belt;
large press stud.*

IT IS STYLISH— YET SIMPLE

The Skirt Can Be Discarded for Swimming

Now change to No. 12 pins and work an inc. row as follows :

Increase row : * Inc., k. 1 ; repeat from * until 2 sts. remain, inc. in each of these. (169 sts.)

·Now work in pattern as follows :

1st row (right side facing) : K. 1, * p. 5, k. 1 ; repeat from * to end.

2nd row : P. 1, * k. 5, p. 1 ; repeat from * to end.

3rd row : K. 1, * (p. 2, k. 1) twice, p. 5, k. 1 ; repeat from * to end.

4th row : P. 1, * k. 5, p. 1, (k. 2, p. 1) twice ; repeat from * to end.

Repeat the 3rd and 4th rows once, then 1st and 2nd rows again.

9th row : K. 1, * p. 5, k. 1, (p. 2, k. 1) twice ; repeat from * to end.

10th row : P. 1, * (k. 2, p. 1) twice, k. 5, p. 1 ; repeat from * to end.

Repeat 9th and 10th rows once.

The ribbed stitch gives a wonderfully slim look.

These 12 rows complete one pattern. Repeat the 12 pattern rows 10 times more. Cast off loosely.

The Front

WORK the waist rib as on Back on 112 sts. Now change to No. 12 pins and work an increase row as follows :

Increase row : K. 1, inc., rib until 2 sts. remain, inc., rib 1 (114 sts.)

Now work in pattern as follows :

1st row : P. 1, k. 1, inc in the next st., rib until 3 sts. remain, inc., k. 1, p. 1.

2nd row : P. 1, k. 4, inc., rib until 6 sts. remain, inc., k. 4, p. 1.

3rd row : (K. 1, p. 2) twice, inc., rib until 7 sts. remain, inc., p. 5, k. 1.

The Shape and Measurements of the Swim-Suit.

FRONT — 12" — 27" — 12" — 6"

GUSSET

BACK — 12" — 12" — 6"

SKIRT BACK — 12" — 20"

SKIRT FRONT — 12" — 16" — 16"

A DASHING LITTLE SWIM-SUIT

4th row : P. 1, k. 5, p. 1, k. 2, inc., rib until 10 sts. remain, inc., (k. 2, p. 1) 3 times.

5th row : K. 1, (p. 2, k. 1) twice, p. 3, inc., rib until 11 sts. remain, inc., k. 1, p. 2, k. 1, p. 5, k. 1.

6th row : P. 1, k. 5, (p. 1, k. 2) twice, p. 1, inc., rib until 13 sts. remain, inc., k. 5, (p. 1, k. 2) twice, p. 1.

Continue in this way, working 2 sts. more in pattern at each end of every row, when there will consequently be 4 sts. less in rib at the centre, but on every right side row *only*, increase in the second of the two extra stitches before the centre rib, and in the first of the 2 extra stitches *after* the rib. (If they wish, beginners can follow the easy alternative of the single rib at the centre and stocking-stitch on the " end " stitches instead of pattern, making the purl side the right side to tally with the background of the pattern.)

When 17 increases have been made at each side continue without further increasing until all the sts. are worked in pattern, decreasing 1 st. at the centre of the last row of single rib. (145 sts.)

Work 82 rows straight in pattern and cast off.

To MAKE UP THE SKIRT.—First join the side seams, leaving the ribbed border open at the top on the left-hand side. Fasten opening with the large press stud.

Crochet two loops of 20 ch. sts. and sew these at the top and bottom of the 20 rib rows at waist, and pass the belt through these loops.

The Swim-Suit

To work the front, begin at the edge of the leg and with No. 12 pins cast on 49 sts. (Do not knit into the back of the cast-on sts.)

Now work 14 rows in pattern, then work the hem by folding the work in half so that the cast-on edge is folded to the wrong side of the work, * k. the first st. on the left-hand pin tog. with the first cast-on st. ; repeat from * to end.

Complete this pattern, then work 2 complete patterns more and 5 rows of the next pattern.

Slip these sts. on a stitch-holder until needed.

Work a second leg in the same way.

Do not leave these sts., but work 1 row more, then on to the same pin work the 49 opposite leg sts., decreasing 1 st. at centre to make the pattern correct. (97 sts.)

Work 60 rows straight.

To Shape the Hips.—Continue in pattern, dec. at both ends of the next row and every 3rd row until 10 dec. rows have been worked and 77 sts. remain.

Work 2 rows straight on these sts.

Change to No. 13 pins and work 20 rows in single rib, increasing in the end st. on the last of these rows.

Return to No. 12 pins and begin the front opening as follows :

1st row : K. 1, p. 3, rib until 4 sts. remain, p. 3, k. 1.

2nd row : P. 1, k. 3, rib until 4 sts. remain, k. 3, p. 1.

3rd row : (K. 1, p. 2) twice, rib until 6 sts. remain, (p. 2, k. 1) twice.

4th row : (P. 1, k. 2) twice, rib until 6 sts. remain, (k. 2, p. 1) twice.

5th row : (K. 1, p. 2) twice, k. 1, p. 1, rib until 8 sts. remain, p. 1, k. 1, (p. 2, k. 1) twice.

6th row : (P. 1, k. 2) twice, p. 1, k. 1, rib until 8 sts. remain, k. 1, p. 1, (k. 2, p. 1) twice.

7th row : K. 1, p. 5, k. 1, p. 3, rib until 10 sts. remain, p. 3, k. 1, p. 5, k. 1.

8th row : P. 1, k. 5, p. 1, k. 3, rib until 10 sts. remain, k. 3, p. 1, k. 5, p. 1.

9th row : K. 1, p. 5, (k. 1, p. 2) twice, rib until 12 sts. remain, (p. 2, k. 1) twice, p. 5, k. 1.

10th row : P. 1, k. 5, (p. 1, k. 2) twice, rib until 12 sts. remain, (k. 2, p. 1) twice, k. 5, p. 1.

11th row : K. 1, p. 5, (k. 1, p. 2) twice, k. 1, p. 1, rib until 14 sts. remain, p. 1, k. 1, (p. 2, k. 1) twice, p. 5, k. 1.

12th row : P. 1, k. 5, (p. 1, k. 2) twice, p. 1, k. 1, rib until 14 sts. remain, k. 1, p. 1, (k. 2, p. 1) twice, k. 5, p. 1.

Continue in this way, working 2 sts. more in pattern at each end of the work on every alternate row and consequently 4 sts. less on the centre rib (at the same time increasing at each end of the next row and every following 6th row) until the ribbed point is worked off and all the stitches will be in the main pattern. Inc. in the centre st. on the last of these rows (79 sts.), then continue increasing at each end of every 6th row as before, until there are 95 sts. on the pin.

To Slope the Front.—Continue in pattern, decreasing at both ends of every alternate row until 45 sts. remain.

Next row : * K. 2 tog., k. 3 ; repeat from * to end.

1st buttonhole row : K. 3, cast off 3, (1 st. on pin), k. 24, cast off 3 (1 st. on pin), k. 2.

2nd buttonhole row : K. 3, cast on 3 over those cast off to complete the buttonhole, k. 25, cast on 3 over those cast off to complete the buttonhole, k. 3.

Work 10 rows in plain knitting, increasing 1 st. at each end of every row for half of the mitred point.

Cast off.

The Back

THIS is worked exactly the same as for the Front until the waist rib is completed. (78 sts.)

Return to No. 12 pins and divide the sts. for the back opening as follows :

RIGHT HALF BACK.—Pattern 37, cast on 4 (slip remaining 41 sts. on a stitch-holder until needed).

Work 12 rows more in pattern with the k. 4 border at the inside edge, and increasing 1 st. at the outside edge of every 6th row.

Next row : Cast off 4 sts. at the beginning of this row and work in pattern to end.

Now continue in pattern, decreasing 1 st. at the inside edge of every row, and increasing 1 st. at the seam edge of every 6th row, until 1 st. remains, draw wool through and fasten off.

LEFT HALF BACK.—Join the wool to the remaining 41 sts. and work this half to match the opposite one, but work a buttonhole on the 4th and 5th rows and on the 10th and 11th rows thus : On the wrong side work until 6 sts. remain, cast off 3 sts. and k. to end. On the next row cast on 3 sts.

over those cast off to complete the buttonhole.

Cast off the first 4 sts. at the beginning of the 13th row, bearing in mind the increase at the seam end of every 6th row, and the rest of the shaping will follow suit.

The Borders

FIRST press all pieces with a hot iron over a damp cloth on the wrong side of the work. Join the side seams of bodice, then with right side facing and with No. 12 pins begin at the top of Left Half Back just above the buttonhole border, and pick up 79 sts. from the sloping edge as far as the garter-stitch at the top of the front.

Work 5 rows in plain knitting, increasing at the front end of every alternate row.

Next row : K. 4 (back end), cast off 3 sts., k. to end.

Next row : All k., casting on 3 sts. over those cast off to complete the buttonhole. Work 1 row, then cast off.

Work the opposite side to match, omitting the buttonhole.

THE NECK BAND.—With No. 12 pins cast on 12 sts. and work in plain knitting for 11 ins., or for sufficient length to go round the neck and button through the holes at the top of the front.

Cast off.

The Gusset

WITH No. 12 pins cast on 37 sts. and work 3 complete patterns as on Back, and 6 rows of the next pattern.

Cast off.

To MAKE UP THE SWIM-SUIT.—First press all pieces with a hot iron over a damp cloth on the wrong side of the work, join the side seams of suit, and inset the gusset.

Sew buttons to right half back and one large button at each side of front neck.

Sew press fastener to opening at left side of skirt.

The Love We Know

I DID not know that love could be so
        quiet,
    I thought love made a loud, flamboyant
        show,
When I was young and selfish thoughts ran
    riot ;
But now I know
That love can be true friendship, glorifying
The whole world with its sane and steady
    glow ;
Serene as lamplight, warm as suns,
    undying—
The love we know !

ANNE CAMPBELL.

A close-up of the pattern of openwork and plain squares.

DISTINCTIVE AND SMART IN LACY SQUARES

Wear It As a Jumper— Or As a Cardigan Over a Pretty Blouse

THIS charming cardigan-jumper has a pleasing pattern of alternated plain and openwork squares.

MATERIALS : 6 ozs. of *Sirdar Coronella Knitting Yarn, 3-ply.* A pair each of *Stratnoid knitting pins, No. 8 and No. 11,* 8 buttons.

TENSION AND MEASUREMENTS: *Worked at a tension of 6½ sts. to the inch in width, on No. 8 pins, the measurements on the diagram are attained after light pressing.*

ABBREVIATIONS : *K., knit ; p., purl ; st., stitch ; tog., together ; inc., increase (by working into the back and front of the same st.) ; dec., decrease (by working 2 sts. tog.) ; m., make (by bringing the wool to the front of the pin and over it before working a k. st., or by bringing the wool to the front of the pin, over it, and to the front again, before working a p. st.). Rib is k. 2 and p. 2 alternately. Directions in brackets are worked the number of times stated immediately after the brackets.*

To Work the Back

WITH No. 11 pins cast on 108 sts. for lower edge, and work 1 row into the back of the sts. on the first row to give a neat edge.

Now work in rib as follows :

1st row (right side facing) : P. 1, * k. 2, p. 2 ; repeat from * until 1 st. remains, p. 1.

2nd row : K. 1, * p. 2, k. 2 ; repeat from * until 1 st. remains, k. 1.

Repeat these 2 rows 19 times more.

Increase row (right side facing) : K. 4, inc., * k. 8, inc. ; repeat from * until 4 sts. remain, k. 4. (120 sts.)

P. 1 row.

Change to No. 8 pins and work in pattern as follows :

1st row (right side facing) : K. 6, * m. 1, k. 3 tog., m. 1, k. 3, m. 1, k. 3 tog., m. 1, k. 15 ; repeat from * ending the last repeat with k. 9 instead of k. 15.

2nd row : All p.

3rd row : K. 9, * m. 1, k. 3 tog., m. 1, k. 3, m. 1, k. 3 tog., m. 1, k. 15 ; repeat from *, ending the last repeat with k. 6 instead of k. 15.

4th row : P. 6, * k. 12, p. 12 ; repeat from *, ending the last repeat with p. 6 instead of p. 12.

Repeat these 4 rows twice more, then 1st to 3rd rows again.

16th row : All k.

17th row : K. 1, k. 2 tog., m. 1, k. 15, m. 1, k. 3 tog., m. 1, * k. 3, m. 1, k. 3 tog., m. 1, k. 15, m. 1, k. 3 tog., m. 1 ; repeat from * until 3 sts. remain, k. 3.

18th row : All p.

19th row : K. 3, m. 1, k. 3 tog., m. 1, k. 15, * m. 1, k. 3 tog., m. 1, k. 3, m. 1, k. 3 tog., m. 1, k. 15 ; repeat from * until 3 sts. remain, m. 1, k. 2 tog., k. 1.

20th row : K. 6, * p. 12, k. 12 ; repeat from *, ending the last repeat with k. 6 instead of k. 12.

Repeat 17th to 20th rows twice more, then 17th to 19th rows.

32nd row : All k.

Repeat these 32 rows once more, then 6 rows of the next pattern to armholes.

To Shape the Armholes.—1st row (right side facing) : K. 2 tog., k. 7, m. 1, k. 3 tog., m. 1, k. 3, m. 1, k. 3 tog., m. 1, * k. 15, m. 1, k. 3 tog., m. 1, k. 3, m. 1, k. 3 tog., m. 1 ; repeat from * until 6 sts. remain, k. 4, k. 2 tog.

2nd row : P. 2 tog., p. 3, k. 12, * p. 12, k. 12 ; repeat from * until 5 sts. remain, p. 3, p. 2 tog.

3rd row : K. 2 tog., k. 2, m. 1, k. 3 tog., m. 1, k. 3, m. 1, k. 3 tog., m. 1, * k. 15, m. 1, k. 3 tog., m. 1, k. 3, m. 1

(Continued on page 262)

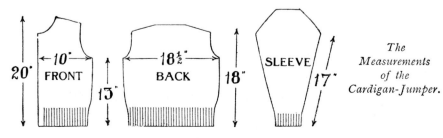

20" FRONT ←10"→ 13" BACK ←18½"→ 18" SLEEVE 17"

The Measurements of the Cardigan-Jumper.

If you'd like it in Pink—Choose Spindleberry-Pink (Shade No. 130), with Novelty Buttons to tone.

Have a Matching Pink Shantung Skirt. Light Blue Sandals, Hat and Gloves.

If you'd like it in Mauve—Choose Deep Dahlia - Mauve (Shade No. 133), with Square Crystal Buttons.

Have a Soft Turquoise Linen Skirt. Turquoise Belt. Turquoise Linen Shoes.

If you'd like it in Yellow—Choose Buttercup-Yellow (Shade No. 122), with Matching Yellow Buttons.

Have a Yellow Woollen Skirt, to tone. White Buckskin Shoes and Belt. A White Flower Brooch.

DISTINCTIVE & SMART in LACY SQUARES

k. 3 tog., m. 1; repeat from * until 7 sts. remain, k. 5, k. 2 tog.

4th row : P. 2 tog., p. until 2 sts. remain, p. 2 tog.

5th row : K. 2 tog. (k. 3, m. 1, k. 3 tog., m. 1) twice, * k. 15, m. 1, k. 3 tog., m. 1, k. 3, m. 1, k. 3 tog., m. 1 ; repeat from * until 2 sts. remain, k. 2 tog.

6th row : K. 2 tog., k. 11, p. 12, * k. 12, p. 12 ; repeat from * until 13 sts. remain, k. 11, k. 2 tog.

7th row : K. 3 tog., m. 1, k. 3, m. 1, k. 3 tog., m. 1, * k. 15, m. 1, k. 3 tog., m. 1, k. 3, m. 1, k. 3 tog., m. 1 ; repeat from * until 3 sts. remain, k. 1, k. 2 tog.

8th row : P. 2 tog., p. until 2 sts. remain, p. 2 tog.

9th row : (K. 2 tog.) twice, m. 1, * k. 3, m. 1, k. 3 tog., m. 1, k. 15, m. 1, k. 3 tog., m. 1 ; repeat from * until 4 sts. remain, k. 2, k. 2 tog.

10th row : K. 2 tog., k. until 2 sts. remain, k. 2 tog.

11th row : K. 2 tog., k. 6, m. 1, k. 3 tog., m. 1, k. 3, m. 1, k. 3 tog., m. 1, * k. 15, m. 1, k. 3 tog., m. 1, k. 3, m. 1, k. 3 tog., m. 1 ; repeat from * until 11 sts. remain, k. 9, k. 2 tog.

12th row : P. 2 tog., p. until 2 sts. remain, p. 2 tog.

Repeat 1st to 6th armhole rows which gives 84 sts.

Now work straight as follows :

1st row (right side facing) : K. 1, k. 2 tog., m. 1, k. 3, m. 1, k. 3 tog., m. 1, * k. 15, m. 1, k. 3 tog., m. 1, k. 3, m. 1, k. 3 tog., m. 1 ; repeat from * until 3 sts. remain, k. 3.

2nd row : All p.

3rd row : K. 3, m. 1, k. 3 tog., m. 1, k. 3, * m. 1, k. 3 tog., m. 1, k. 15, m. 1, k. 3 tog., m. 1, k. 3 ; repeat from * until 3 sts. remain, m. 1, k. 2 tog., k. 1.

4th row : K. 12, * p. 12, k. 12 ; repeat from * to end.

Repeat 1st to 3rd rows again.

8th row : All k.

9th row : K. 12, * m. 1, k. 3 tog., m. 1, k. 3, m. 1, k. 3 tog., m. 1, k. 15 ; repeat from * to end.

10th row : All p.

11th row : * K. 15, m. 1, k. 3 tog., m. 1, k. 3, m. 1, k. 3 tog., m. 1 ; repeat from * until 12 sts. remain, k. 12.

12th row : K. 12, * k. 12, p. 12 ; repeat from * to end.

Repeat from 9th to 12th rows twice more, then from 9th to 11th rows once.

24th row : All k.

Repeat from 1st to 4th rows 3 times more.

To Slope the Shoulders.—Continue in pattern, casting off 7 sts. at the beginning of the next 8 rows (28 sts. on each shoulder).

Cast off the remaining sts.

The Left Front

WITH No. 11 pins cast on 59 sts. and work 1 row into the back of the sts. to give a neat edge.

Now continue in rib pattern as follows :

1st row (right side facing) : P. 1, * k. 2, p. 2 ; repeat from * until 10 sts. remain, k. 10, front end.

2nd row : K. 12, * p. 2, k. 2 ; repeat from * until 3 sts. remain, p. 2, k. 1.

Repeat these 2 rows 19 times more.

Increase row (right side facing) : K. 3, inc., (k. 8, inc.) 5 times, k. 10 front end (65 sts.).

Next row (wrong side facing) : K. 11, front end, p. 54.

Change to No. 8 pins and work in pattern as follows :

1st row (right side facing) : K. 6, (m. 1, k. 3 tog., m. 1, k. 3, m. 1, k. 3 tog., m. 1, k. 15) twice, p. 1, k. 10, front end.

2nd row : K. 11, p. 54.

3rd row : K. 9, m. 1, k. 3 tog., m. 1, k. 3, m. 1, k. 3 tog., m. 1, k. 15, m. 1, k. 3 tog., m. 1, k. 3, m. 1, k. 3 tog., m. 1, k. 12, p. 1, k. 10 front end.

4th row : K. 11, (p. 12, k. 12) twice, p. 6.

Repeat these 4 rows twice more, then 1st to 3rd rows again.

16th row : All k.

17th row : K. 1, k. 2 tog., m. 1, (k. 15, m. 1, k. 3 tog., m. 1, k. 3, m. 1, k. 3 tog., m. 1) twice, k. 3, p. 1, k. 10.

18th row : K. 11, p. 54.

19th row : K. 3, m. 1, k. 3 tog., m. 1, (k. 15, m. 1, k. 3 tog., m. 1, k. 3, m. 1, k. 3 tog., m. 1) twice, p. 1, k. 10, front end.

20th row : K. 23, p. 12, k. 12, p. 12, k. 6.

Repeat from 17th to 20th rows twice, then 17th to 19th rows again.

32nd row : All k.

Repeat these 32 rows once more, then 6 rows of the next pattern to armhole.

To Shape the Armhole.—*1st row* : K. 2 tog., k. 7, m. 1, k. 3 tog., m. 1, k. 3, m. 1, k. 3 tog., m. 1, k. 15, m. 1, k. 3 tog., m. 1, k. 3, m. 1, k. 3 tog., m. 1, k. 12, p. 1, k. 10.

2nd row : K. 11, (p. 12, k. 12) twice, p. 3, p. 2 tog.

3rd row : K. 2 tog., k. 2, m. 1, k. 3 tog., m. 1, k. 3, m. 1, k. 3 tog., m. 1, k. 15, m. 1, k. 3 tog., m. 1, k. 3, m. 1, k. 3 tog., m. 1, k. 15, p. 1, k. 10.

4th row : K. 11, p. until 2 sts. remain, p. 2 tog.

5th row : K. 2 tog., (k. 3, m. 1, k. 3 tog., m. 1) twice, k. 15, m. 1, k. 3 tog., m. 1, k. 3, m. 1, k. 3 tog., m. 1, k. 12, p. 1, k. 10.

6th row : K. 11, p. 12, k. 12, p. 12, k. 11, k. 2 tog.

7th row : K. 3 tog., m. 1, k. 3, m. 1, k. 3 tog., m. 1, k. 15, m. 1, k. 3 tog., m. 1, k. 3, m. 1, k. 3 tog., m. 1, k. 15, p. 1, k. 10.

8th row : K. 11, p. until 2 remain, p. 2 tog.

9th row : (K. 2 tog.) twice, m. 1, k. 3, m. 1, k. 3 tog., m. 1, k. 15, m. 1, k. 3 tog., m. 1, k. 3, m. 1, k. 3 tog., m. 1, k. 12, p. 1, k. 10.

10th row : K. until 2 sts. remain, k. 2 tog.

11th row : K. 2 tog., k. 6, m. 1, k. 3 tog., m. 1, k. 3, m. 1, k. 3 tog., m. 1, k. 15, (m. 1, k. 3 tog., m. 1, k. 3) twice, p. 1, k. 10.

12th row : K. 11, p. until 2 sts. remain, p. 2 tog.

13th row : K. 2 tog., k. 7, m. 1, k. 3 tog., m. 1, k. 3, m. 1, k. 3 tog., m. 1, k. 15, m. 1, k. 3 tog., m. 1, k. 3, m. 1, k. 3 tog., m. 1, p. 1, k. 10.

14th row : K. 23, p. 12, k. 12, p. 3, p. 2 tog.

15th row : K. 2 tog., k. 2, m. 1, k. 3 tog., m. 1, k. 3, m. 1, k. 3 tog., m. 1, k. 15, (m. 1, k. 3 tog., m. 1, k. 3) twice, p. 1, k. 10.

16th row : K. 11, p. until 2 sts. remain, p. 2 tog.

17th row : K. 2 tog., (k. 3, m. 1, k. 3 tog., m. 1 twice, k. 15, m. 1, k. 3 tog., m. 1, k. 3, m. 1, k. 3 tog., m. 1, k. 3 m. 1, k. 3 tog., m. 1, p. 1, k. 10.

18th row : K. 23, p. 12, k. 11, k. 2 tog. (47 sts.).

Now work straight in pattern as follows :

1st row : K. 1, k. 2 tog., m. 1, k. 3, m. 1, k. 3 tog., m. 1, k. 15, m. 1, k. 3 tog., m. 1, k. 3 twice, p. 1, k. 10.

2nd row : K. 11, p. to end.

3rd row : (K. 3, m. 1, k. 3 tog., m. 1) twice, k. 15, m. 1, k. 3 tog., m. 1, k. 3, m. 1, k. 3 tog., m. 1, p. 1, k. 10.

4th row : K. 23, p. 12, k. 12.

Repeat 1st, 2nd and 3rd rows.

8th row : All k.

9th row : K. 12, m. 1, k. 3 tog., m. 1, k. 3, m. 1, k. 3 tog., m. 1, k. 15, p. 1, k. 10.

10th row : K. 11, p. 36.

11th row : K. 15, m. 1, k. 3 tog., m. 1, k. 3, m. 1, k. 3 tog., m. 1, k. 12, p. 1, k. 10.

12th row : K. 11, p. 12, k. 12, p. 12.

Repeat 9th to 12th rows twice, then 9th to 11th rows.

24th row : All k.

Repeat 1st row.

To Shape the Neck.—*26th row* : Cast off 8, neck end (1 on pin), k. 2, p. to end.

27th row : (K. 3, m. 1, k. 3 tog., m. 1) twice, k. 15, m. 1, k. 3 tog., m. 1, k. 3, m. 1, k. 3 tog., m. 1, p. 1, k. 2.

28th row : K. 2 tog., k. 13, p. 12, k. 12.

29th row : K. 1, k. 2 tog., m. 1, k. 3, m. 1, k. 3 tog., m. 1, k. 15, (m. 1, k. 3 tog., m. 1, k. 3) twice, k. 2 tog.

30th row : K. 2 tog., p. to end.

31st row : (K. 3, m. 1, k. 3 tog., m. 1) twice, k. 15, m. 1, k. 3 tog., m. 1, k. 4, k. 2 tog.

32nd row : K. 2 tog., k. 9, p. 12, k. 12.

33rd row : K. 1, k. 2 tog., m. 1, k. 3, m. 1, k. 3 tog., m. 1, k. 15, m. 1, k. 3 tog., m. 1, k. 3, m. 1, (k. 2 tog.) twice.

34th row : P. 2 tog., p. to end.

35th row : (K. 3, m. 1, k. 3 tog., m. 1) twice, k. 15, m. 1, k. 3 tog., m. 1, k. 2 tog.

36th row : K. 2 tog., k. 5, p. 12, k. 12.

37th row : K. 1, k. 2 tog., m. 1, k. 3, m. 1, k. 3 tog., m. 1, k. 15, m. 1, k. 3 tog., m. 1, k. 1, k. 2 tog.

38th row : P. 2 tog., p. to end.

On the remaining 28 sts. work 8 rows in pattern.

To Slope the Shoulder.—Cast off 7 sts. at the beginning of next and following alternate rows (arm end) until all are worked off.

The Right Front

WITH No. 11 pins cast on 59 sts. for lower edge, and work 1 row into the back of the sts. to give a neat edge.

1st row (right side facing) : K. 10, front end, * p. 2, k. 2 ; repeat from * until 1 st. remains, p. 1.

2nd row : K. 1, p. 2, * k. 2, p. 2 ; repeat from * until 12 sts. remain, k. 12, front end.

Repeat these 2 rows 12 times more, then the 1st row again.

1st buttonhole row (wrong side) : Work in pattern until 10 sts. remain, cast off 5, k. to end.

2nd buttonhole row : Work in pattern, casting on 5 sts. over those cast off to complete the buttonhole.

Work 13 rows more to complete 40 rows in rib.

Increase row (right side facing): K. 10, inc. (k. 8, inc.) 5 times, k. 3. (65 sts.)

Next row : P. 54, k. 11.

With No. 8 pins work in pattern as follows :

1st row : K. 10, p. 1, k. 12, m. 1, k. 3 tog., m. 1, k. 3, m. 1, k. 3 tog., m. 1, k. 15, m. 1, k. 3 tog., m. 1, k. 3, m. 1, k. 3 tog., m. 1, k. 9.

2nd row : P. 54, k. 11.

3rd row : K. 10, p. 1, (k. 15, m. 1, k. 3 tog., m. 1, k. 3, m. 1, k. 3 tog., m. 1) twice, k. 6.

4th row : P. 6, (k. 12, p. 12) twice, k. 11.

Repeat 1st, 2nd and 3rd rows again.

8th row : P. 6, (k. 12, p. 12) twice, k. 2, cast off 4 for buttonhole, k. to end.

9th row : K. 5, cast on 4 sts. over those cast off to complete the buttonhole, k. 1. Continue as in 1st pattern row to end.

Repeat 2nd to 4th rows, then 1st to 3rd rows.

16th row : All k.

17th row : K. 10, p. 1, (m. 1, k. 3 tog., m. 1, k. 3, m. 1, k. 3 tog., m. 1, k. 15) twice, m. 1, k. 3 tog., m. 1, k. 3.

18th row : P. 54, k. 11.

19th row : K. 10, p. 1, k. 3, (m. 1, k. 3 tog., m. 1, k. 3, m. 1, k. 3 tog., m. 1, k. 15) twice, m. 1, k. 2 tog., k. 1.

20th row : K. 6, p. 12, k. 12, p. 12, k. 23.

Repeat 17th to 19th rows.

24th row : K. 6, p. 12, k. 12, p. 12, k. 14, cast off 4 (for buttonhole), k. to end.

25th row : K. 5, cast on 4 over those cast off to complete the buttonhole, k. 1 (10 sts. on pin), continue as for 17th row to end.

Work 18th to 20th rows, then 17th to 19th rows.

32nd row: All k. Repeat these 32 rows once more, then 6 rows more to armhole.

To Shape the Armhole.—1st row : K. 10, p. 1, (k. 15, m. 1, k. 3 tog., m. 1, k. 3, m. 1, k. 3 tog., m. 1) twice, k. 4, k. 2 tog.

2nd row : P. 2 tog., p. 3, (k. 12, p. 12) twice, k. 2, cast off 4 (for buttonhole), k. to end.

3rd row : K. 5, cast on 4 over those cast off to complete the buttonhole, k. 1, p. 1, k. 12, m. 1, k. 3 tog., m. 1, k. 3, m. 1, k. 3 tog., m. 1, k. 15, m. 1, k. 3 tog., m. 1, k. 3, m. 1, k. 3 tog., m. 1, k. 5, k. 2 tog.

4th row : P. 2 tog., p. until 11 sts. remain, k. 11.

5th row : K. 10, p. 1, (k. 15, m. 1, k. 3 tog., m. 1, k. 3, m. 1, k. 3 tog., m. 1) twice, k. 2 tog.

6th row : K. 2 tog., k. 11, p. 12, k. 12, p. 12, k. 11.

7th row : K. 10, p. 1, k. 12, m. 1, k. 3 tog., m. 1, k. 3, m. 1, k. 3 tog., m. 1, k. 15, m. 1, k. 3 tog., m. 1, k. 3, m. 1, k. 3 tog., m. 1, k. 1, k. 2 tog.

8th row : P. 2 tog., p. 45, k. 11.

9th row : K. 10, p. 1, k. 15, m. 1, k. 3 tog., m. 1, k. 3, m. 1, k. 3 tog., m. 1, k. 15, m. 1, k. 3 tog., m. 1, k. 2, k. 2 tog.

10th row : K. 2 tog., k. to end.

11th row : K. 10, p. 1, m. 1, k. 3 tog., m. 1, k. 3, m. 1, k. 3 tog., m. 1, k. 15, m. 1, k. 3 tog., m. 1, k. 3, m. 1, k. 3 tog., m. 1, k. 9, k. 2 tog.

12th row : P. 2 tog., p. 41, k. 11.

13th row : K. 10, p. 1, k. 3, m. 1, k. 3 tog., m. 1, k. 3, m. 1, k. 3 tog., m. 1, k. 15, m. 1, k. 3 tog., m. 1, k. 3, m. 1, k. 3 tog., m. 1, k. 4, k. 2 tog.

14th row : P. 2 tog., p. 3, k. 12, p. 12, k. 23.

15th row : K. 10, p. 1, m. 1, k. 3 tog., m. 1, k. 3, m. 1, k. 3 tog., m. 1, k. 3, m. 1, k. 15, m. 1, k. 3 tog., m. 1, k. 3, m. 1, k. 3 tog., m. 1, k. 5, k. 2 tog.

16th row : P. 2 tog., p. until 11 sts. remain, k. 11.

17th row : K. 10, p. 1, k. 3, m. 1, k. 3 tog., m. 1, k. 3, m. 1, k. 3 tog., m. 1, k. 15, m. 1, k. 3 tog., m. 1, k. 3, m. 1, k. 3 tog., m. 1, k. 2 tog.

18th row : K. 2 tog., k. 11, p. 12, k. 14, cast off 4 for buttonhole, k. to end.

Now continue straight in pattern as follows :

1st row : K. 5, cast on 4 over those cast off to complete the buttonhole, k. 1, p. 1, m. 1, k. 3 tog., m. 1, k. 3, m. 1, k. 3, m. 1, k. 3 tog., m. 1, k. 15, (m. 1, k. 3 tog., m. 1, k. 3) twice. (47 sts.)

2nd row : P. 36, k. 11.

3rd row : K. 10, p. 1, (k. 3, m. 1, k. 3 tog., m. 1) twice, m. 1, k. 15, m. 1, k. 3 tog., m. 1, k. 3, m. 1, k. 2 tog., k. 1.

4th row : K. 12, p. 12, k. 23.

Repeat 1st to 3rd rows without buttonholes.

8th row : All k.

9th row : K. 10, p. 1, k. 12, m. 1, k. 3 tog., m. 1, k. 3, m. 1, k. 3 tog., m. 1, k. 15.

10th row : P. 36, k. 11.

11th row : K. 10, p. 1, k. 15, m. 1, k. 3 tog., m. 1, k. 3, m. 1, k. 3 tog., m. 1, k. 12.

12th row : P. 12, k. 12, p. 12, k. 11.

Repeat 9th to 11th rows, then 12th and 9th rows with a buttonhole.

Repeat 10th to 12th rows, then 9th to 11th rows.

24th row : All k.

Repeat 1st and 2nd rows without buttonhole.

To Shape the Neck.—27th row : Cast off 8 (1 st. on pin), k. 1, p. 1, (k. 3, m. 1, k. 3 tog., m. 1) twice, k. 15, m. 1, k. 3 tog., m. 1, k. 3, m. 1, k. 2 tog., k. 1.

28th row : K. 12, p. 12, k. 13, k. 2 tog.

29th row : P. 2 tog., k. 3, m. 1, k. 3 tog., m. 1, k. 3, m. 1, k. 3 tog., m. 1, k. 15, m. 1, k. 3 tog., m. 1, k. 3, m. 1, k. 2 tog., k. 1.

30th row : P. until 2 sts. remain, p. 2 tog.

31st row : K. 3 tog., m. 1, k. 3, m. 1, k. 3 tog., m. 1, k. 15, m. 1, k. 3 tog., m. 1, k. 3, m. 1, k. 3 tog., m. 1, k. 3.

32nd row : K. 12, p. 12, k. 9, k. 2 tog.

33rd row : (K. 2 tog.) twice, m. 1, k. 3, m. 1, k. 3 tog., m. 1, k. 15, m. 1, k. 3 tog., m. 1, k. 3, m. 1, k. 2 tog., k. 1.

34th row : K. 12, p. 12, k. 7, k. 2 tog.

35th row : K. 2 tog., m. 1, k. 3 tog., m. 1, k. 15, (m. 1, k. 3 tog., m. 1, k. 3) twice.

36th row : P. until 2 sts. remain, p. 2 tog.

37th row : K. 2 tog., k. 1, m. 1, k. 3 tog., m. 1, k. 15, m. 1, k. 3 tog., m. 1, k. 3, m. 1, k. 1.

38th row : K. 12, p. 12, k. 3, k. 2 tog. (28 sts.)

Work 9 rows straight in pattern to shoulders, beginning the 1st row with k. 4, then m. 1, k. 3 tog., m. 1, k. 3, m. 1, k. 3 tog., m. 1, k. 15.

To Shape the Shoulder.—Continue in pattern, casting off 7 sts. at the beginning of the next row and every following alternate row (armhole end) until all are worked off.

The Sleeves

WITH No. 8 pins cast on 26 sts. for the top and k. 1 row.

Now shape the top of the sleeve as follows :

1st row : Inc., k. 6, * m. 1, k. 3 tog., m. 1, k. 3, m. 1, k. 3 tog., m. 1; (in following patterns, k. 15 ; repeat from * until 10 sts. remain) k. 9, inc.

2nd row : Inc., p. until 1 st. remains, inc.

3rd row : Inc., k. 11, * m. 1, k. 3 tog., m. 1, k. 3, m. 1, k. 3 tog., m. 1; (in following patterns, k. 15 ; repeat from * until 9 sts. remain) k. 8, inc.

4th row : P. 10, * k. 12; (in following patterns p. 12 ; repeat from * until 10 sts. remain) p. 10.

5th row : Inc., k. 9, * m. 1, k. 3 tog., m. 1, k. 3, m. 1, k. 3 tog., m. 1; (in following patterns k. 15 ; repeat from * until 13 sts. remain) k. 12, inc.

6th row : Inc., p. until 1 st. remains, inc.

7th row : Inc., k. 14, * m. 1, k. 3 tog., m. 1, k. 3, m. 1, k. 3 tog., m. 1; (in following patterns k. 15 ; repeat from * until 12 sts. remain) k. 11, inc.

8th row : K. 1, p. 12, * k. 12, p. 12; (repeat from * in following patterns until 1 st. remains) k. 1.

9th row : Inc., k. 12, * m. 1, k. 3 tog., m. 1, k. 3, m. 1, k. 3 tog., m. 1, k. 15; (in following patterns repeat from * until 1 st. remains) m. 1, k. 1.

10th row : Inc., p. until 1 st. remains, inc.

11th row : K. 1, m. 1, k. 2 tog., m. 1, * k. 15, m. 1, k. 3 tog., m. 1, k. 3, m. 1, k. 3 tog., m. 1; (in following patterns repeat from * until 15 sts. remain) k. 14, inc.

12th row : K. 4, p. 12, * k. 12, p. 12; (repeat from * in following patterns until 4 sts. remain) k. 4.

13th row : K. 1, m. 1, k. 15, * m. 1, k. 3 tog., m. 1, k. 3, m. 1, k. 3 tog., m. 1, k. 15; (in following patterns repeat from * until 4 sts. remain) m. 1, k. 3 tog., m. 1, inc.

14th row : Inc., p. until 1 st. remains, inc.

15th row : Inc., k. 2, m. 1, k. 3 tog., m. 1, k. 15, * m. 1, k. 3 tog., m. 1, k. 3, m. 1, k. 3 tog., m. 1, k. 15; (in following patterns repeat from * until 3 sts. remain) m. 1, k. 2 tog., m. 1, k. 1.

16th row : All k. (50 sts.)

Repeat these 16 rows once more then the first 6 rows again. (84 sts.)

Work 6 rows more in pattern, then continue in pattern dec. at both ends of the next row and every following 8th row until 56 sts. remain.

Work 6 rows straight.

Change to No. 11 pins and work as follows :

Next row (wrong side facing) : P. 12, * p. 2 tog., p. 9 ; repeat from * to end. (52 sts.)

Rib 30 rows. Cast off.

Work a second sleeve the same.

The Collar

WITH No. 11 pins cast on 158 sts. Now work as follows :

1st row : K. 4, p. 2, * k. 2, p. 2 ; repeat from * until 4 remain, k. 4.

2nd row : K. 2, * p. 2, k. 2 ; repeat from * to end.

Repeat these 2 rows 12 times more, then the 1st row again. Cast off.

TO MAKE UP THE JUMPER : First press all pieces with a hot iron over a damp cloth, on the wrong side of the work, with a thick blanket underneath. Join the sleeve and side seams in one long line. Join the shoulder seams. Sew collar to neck edge. Sew the buttons on Left Front Border.

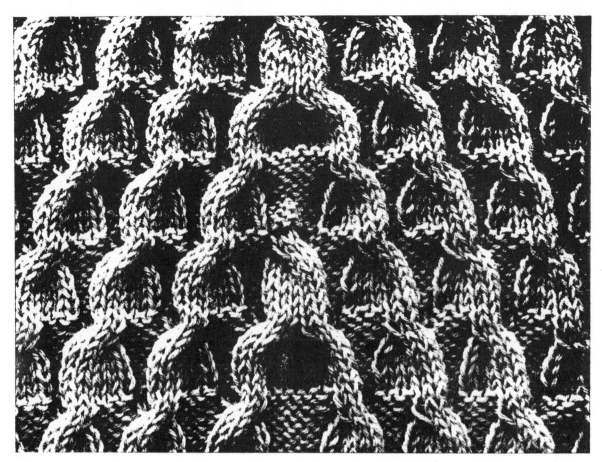

Here is our new variation of Cable-Stitch—diagonal stripes, standing out clearly against the plain background, are cleverly arranged to link up at the centre front and back, forming points. The row at the foot of this illustration is the third row of the pattern above the waist ribbing.

Here's ONE that is "LOTS of FUN"!

This Delightful Jumper Is Knitted In a Clever Variation of Cable-Stitch

A NARROW strip of either crochet or knitting is used for the initial. An alphabet is given on page 50, which will show you how best to make your own initial.

MATERIALS.—*Five ounces of Campanula Super Fingering 2-ply, and an oddment of 4-ply Fingering in white, for the initial ; a pair each of Aero knitting pins No. 9 and No. 10 (also a pair of No. 11 pins if long sleeves are worked) ; a set of four knitting pins No. 9 pointed at each end ; a short spare pin for the cable-stitches, and an Aero crochet hook No. 13.*

TENSION AND MEASUREMENTS.— *Worked at a tension of 9 sts. to the inch in width across the fancy pattern on No. 9 pins, the measurements on the diagram are attained after light pressing.*

ABBREVIATIONS.—*K., knit plain ; p., purl ; st., stitch ; inc., increase (by working into the back and front of the same st.) ; single rib is k. 1 and p. 1 alternately ; directions in brackets are worked the number of times stated immediately after the brackets ; ch., chain ; d.c., double crochet.*

TO CABLE BACK.—*Slip the first 3 sts. on the left-hand pin on to a spare pin and leave these at the back of the work, k. the next 3 sts. on the left-hand pin, then k. the 3 sts. from the cable pin, thus reversing the position of the two sets of sts. ; TO CABLE FRONT, work the same as for the*

If you'd like it in Blue—Choose Dark Navy-Blue (Shade No. 94), with a White Initial.
Have a White Linen-Tweed Skirt. Navy-Blue and White Court Shoes. Peachglow Stockings.

❄ ❄

If you'd like it in Cream— Choose Parchment (Shade No. 660), with a Brown Initial.
Have a Red Skirt in Fine Woollen. Brown Sandals and Belt. Brown, Red and Cream Bracelets.

❄ ❄

If you'd like it in Grey—Choose Smoke-Grey (Shade No. 2,316), with a Jade-Green Initial.
Have a Matching Grey Flannel Skirt. Grey Lizard Shoes and a Jade-Green Belt.

other cable, but leave the cable sts. at the front of the work instead of at the back.

To Work the Back

WITH No. 10 pins cast on 126 sts. and work 32 rows in single rib, working into the back of the sts. on the 1st row to give a neat edge.

Increase row : K. 4, * inc., k. 4 ; repeat from * until 2 sts. remain, k. 2 (150 sts.).

Still using No. 10 pins, begin the main pattern.

1st row : (P. 3, k. 6) 8 times, p. 6, (k. 6, p. 3) 8 times.
2nd row : (K. 3, p. 6) 8 times, k. 6, (p. 6, k. 3) 8 times.

Repeat these 2 rows twice more.
7th row : (P. 3, cable front) 8 times, p. 6, (cable back, p. 3) 8 times.
8th row : As 2nd row.

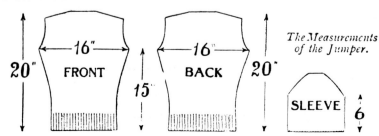

The Measurements of the Jumper.

One of the Year's Little Vanities—Your Initial on Your Jersey! Have It In White on Navy-Blue, Brown on Parchment, or Jade-Green on Grey. Made from a Narrow Strip of Crochet or Knitting the Alphabet on Page 267 Shows You How to Twist It Into Your Own Initial.

"LOTS OF FUN!"

9th row: K. 3, (p. 3, k. 6) 7 times, p. 3, k. 12, (p. 3, k. 6) 7 times, p. 3, k. 3.

10th row: P. 3, k. 3, (p. 6, k. 3) 7 times, p. 12, k. 3, (p. 6, k. 3) 7 times, p. 3.

Repeat the last 2 rows twice more.

15th row: K. 3, (p. 3, cable front) 8 times, (cable back, p. 3) 8 times, k. 3.

16th row: As 10th row.

17th row: * K. 6, p. 3 ; repeat from * until 6 sts. remain, k. 6.

18th row: * P. 6, k. 3 ; repeat from * until 6 sts. remain, p. 6.

Repeat the last 2 rows twice more.

23rd row: (Cable front, p. 3) 9 times, (cable back, p. 3) 7 times, cable back.

24th row: * P. 6, k. 3 ; repeat from * until 6 sts. remain, p. 6.

Change to No. 9 pins, and repeat these 24 patterns rows 3 times more, then the first 8 rows again, to the armholes.

To Shape the Armholes.—*1st row*: Cast off 9 (1 st. on pin), k. 2, (p. 3, k. 6) 6 times, p. 3, k. 12, (p. 3, k. 6) 7 times, p. 3, k. 3.

2nd row: Cast off 9 (1 st. on pin), p. 2, k. 3, (p. 6, k. 3) 6 times, p. 12, k. 3, (p. 6, k. 3) 6 times, p. 3 (132 sts.).

3rd row: K. 2 tog., k. 1, (p. 3, k. 6) 6 times, p. 3, k. 12, (p. 3, k. 6) 6 times, p. 3, k. 1, k. 2 tog.

4th row: P. 2 tog., k. 3, (p. 6, k. 3) 6 times, p. 12, k. 3, (p. 6, k. 3) 6 times, p. 2 tog.

5th row: K. 2 tog., p. 2, (k. 6, p. 3) 6 times, k. 12, (p. 3, k. 6) 6 times, p. 2, p. 2 tog.

6th row: K. 2 tog., k. 1, (p. 6, k. 3) 6 times, p. 12, k. 3, (p. 6, k. 3) 5 times, p. 6, k. 1, k. 2 tog. (124 sts.).

7th row: P. 2 tog., cable front, (p. 3, cable front) 6 times, (cable back, p. 3) 6 times, cable back, p. 2 tog. (122 sts.).

8th row: K. 2 tog., p. 5, k. 3, (p. 6, k. 3) 5 times, p. 12, k. 3, (p. 6, k. 3) 5 times, p. 5, p. 2 tog. (120 sts.).

9th row: P. 1, p. 2 tog., * k. 6, p. 3 ; repeat from * ending the last repeat with p. 1, p. 2 tog., instead of p. 3 (118 sts.).

10th row: K. 2 tog., * p. 6, k. 3 ; repeat from *, ending the last repeat with k. 2 tog. instead of k. 3.

11th row: K. 2 tog., k. 5, * p. 3, k. 6 ; repeat from *, ending the last repeat with k. 5, k. 2 tog. (114 sts.).

12th row: * P. 6, k. 3 ; repeat from * until 6 remain, p. 6 (114 sts.).

Continue in pattern, beginning with the 21st row, but remember that there will be two repeats less of the items in brackets. Finish the present pattern, then work one complete pattern more and 16 rows of the next pattern to the shoulders.

To Slope the Shoulders.—Cast off 9 sts. at the beginning of the next 8 rows, and leave the remaining 42 sts. on a spare pin for the collar.

The Front

THIS is worked the same as the back until the shoulders are reached.

** *Next row*: Cast off 9 (1 st. on pin), pattern 26 more for the Left Front Shoulder. Work 1 row back on these 27 sts., then cast off 9 sts. at the beginning of the next row and following 2 alternate rows, when all will be cast off.

Slip the next 42 sts. on the left-hand pin on to a spare pin and leave them until needed for the collar. Join the wool to the neck end of the remaining 36 sts., and work 1 row back to arm end, then continue from ** on Left Front Shoulder.

The Sleeves

WITH No. 10 pins cast on 96 sts. and work 18 rows in single rib, working into the back of the sts. on the 1st row.

Change to No. 9 pins and work 1 complete pattern as at the beginning of the back and 8 rows of the next pattern. (On the first 8 rows the items in brackets will be worked 5 times instead of 8 times.)

To Shape the Top of the Sleeve : First work the 12 rows of the armhole shaping on the back, remembering to work items in brackets 3 times less, when 60 sts. will remain.

13th row (21st pattern row): K. 2 tog., k. 4, p. 3, * k. 6, p. 3 ; repeat from * until 6 sts. remain, k. 4, k. 2 tog.

14th row: P. 5, * k. 3, p. 6 ; repeat from *, ending the last repeat with p. 5.

15th row: K. 2 tog., k. 3, p. 3, (cable front, p. 3) 3 times, (cable back, p. 3) twice, k. 3, k. 2 tog. (56 sts.)

16th row: P. 4, * k. 3, p. 6 ; repeat from *, ending the last repeat with p. 4.

17th row: P. 2 tog., k. 5, (p. 3, k. 6) twice, p. 6, (k. 6, p. 3) twice, k. 5, k. 2 tog.

18th row: P. 6, (k. 3, p. 6) twice, k. 6, (p. 6, k. 3) twice, p. 6.

19th row: K. 2 tog., k. 4, (p. 3, k. 6) twice, p. 6, (k. 6, p. 3) twice, k. 4, k. 2 tog.

20th row: P. 5, (k. 3, p. 6) twice, k. 6, (p. 6, k. 3) twice, p. 5.

21st row: K. 2 tog., k. 3, (p. 3, k. 6) twice, p. 6, (k. 6, p. 3) twice, k. 3, k. 2 tog.

22nd row: P. 4, (k. 3, p. 6) twice, k. 6, (p. 6, k. 3) twice, p. 4.

23rd row: K. 2 tog., k. 2, (p. 3, cable front) twice, p. 6, (cable back, p. 3) twice, k. 2, k. 2 tog. (48 sts.)

24th row: P. 3, (k. 3, p. 6) twice, k. 6, (p. 6, k. 3) twice, p. 3.

25th row: K. 2 tog., k. 4, p. 3, k. 6, p. 3, k. 12, p. 3, k. 6, p. 3, k. 4, k. 2 tog.

26th row: P. 5, k. 3, p. 6, k. 3, p. 12, k. 3, p. 6, k. 3, p. 5.

27th row: K. 2 tog., k. 3, p. 3, k. 6, p. 3, k. 12, p. 3, k. 6, p. 3, k. 3, k. 2 tog. (44 sts.)

28th row: P. 4, k. 3, p. 6, k. 3, p. 12, k. 3, p. 6, k. 3, p. 4.

29th row: K. 2 tog., k. 2, p. 3, k. 6, p. 3, k. 12, p. 3, k. 6, p. 3, k. 2, k. 2 tog.

30th row: P. 3, k. 3, p. 6, k. 3, p. 12, k. 3, p. 6, k. 3, p. 3.

31st row: K. 2 tog., k. 1, (p. 3, cable front) twice, (cable back, p. 3) twice, k. 1, k. 2 tog.

32nd row: P. 2, k. 3, p. 6, k. 3, p. 12, k. 3, p. 6, k. 3, p. 2.

33rd row: K. 2 tog., k. 3, * p. 3, k. 6 ; repeat from *, ending the last repeat with k. 3, k. 2 tog.

34th row: P. 4, * k. 3, p. 6 ; repeat from *, ending the last repeat with p. 4.

35th row: K. 2 tog., k. 2, * p. 3, k. 6 ; repeat from *, ending the last repeat with k. 2, k. 2 tog.

36th row: P. 3, * k. 3, p. 6 ; repeat from *, ending the last repeat with p. 3.

37th row: K. 2 tog., k. 1, * p. 3, k. 6 ; repeat from * until 6 remain, p. 3, k. 1, k. 2 tog.

38th row: P. 2, * k. 3, p. 6 ; repeat from *, ending the last repeat with p. 2.

39th row: K. 2 tog., p. 3, (cable front, p. 3) twice, cable back, p. 3, k. 2 tog. (32 sts.)

40th row: P. 1, * k. 3, p. 6 ; repeat from * until 4 remain, k. 3, p. 1.

Cast off the remaining sts.

Work another sleeve in the same manner.

Long Sleeves

WITH No. 11 pins cast on 66 sts. and work 32 rows in single rib.

Increase row: K. 4, * inc., k. 1 ; repeat from * until 2 remain, k. 2. (96 sts.)

Still using No. 11 pins work 2 complete patterns as at the beginning of the back, then change to No. 10 pins and work 2 patterns more. Change to No. 9 pins and work 2 patterns (or 3 patterns if a longer sleeve is desired) and 8 rows of the next pattern, then shape the top of the sleeve as for the short sleeve.

The Collar

FIRST join the shoulder seams, beginning at the arm end and taking 1 st. from each side at a time.

Divide the 42 sts. from front neck between 2 double-pointed pins, and on to the end of the first pin with the sts. from the right side of neck pick up 5 sts. at the side, then the first 5 sts. on spare pin at the back of neck ; slip the next 32 sts. on to a second double-pointed pin. With the 3rd pin holding the remaining 21 front neck sts., pick up 5 sts. from the left side of neck, and slip the 5 remaining sts. from the back neck on to this 3rd pin. (94 sts. altogether.)

1st row: Inc., * p. 1, k. 1 ; repeat from * until 1 st. remains, inc.

2nd row: Inc., * k. 1, p. 1 ; repeat from * until 1 st. remains, inc.

Repeat these 2 rows until there are 142 sts. Cast off loosely.

TO MAKE UP THE JUMPER. First press all parts except the ribbing with a hot iron over a damp cloth. Set the sleeves into armholes and press these seams. Join the sleeve and side seams in one line and press. Join the front edges of the collar to form a V.

The Crochet Initial

THE letter on the original jumper is worked in crochet. As the foundation row will vary with each letter, first form the initial with a piece of string and measure the length. From this you should be able to judge how many foundations sts. are required. With the No. 13 crochet hook and 4-ply Fingering you should get 9 d.c. to the inch in width.

For the initial " A " make 85 ch., miss the first ch. by the hook, then one d.c. into each remaining ch., and fasten off. Form this into the required initial, sewing it down with the wrong side of the crochet uppermost.

The Knitted Initial

THOSE who cannot crochet, or who prefer all knitting, can work as follows :

With No. 10 pins and 4-ply Fingering cast on 75 sts. for the letter " A." Now cast off in the following manner :

K. 1, leaving one st. on the right-hand pin, slip this st. back to the left-hand pin and * knit it together with the next st. on the left-hand pin, working through the *back* of the loops ; slip the resulting st. back on the left-hand pin and k. 2 sts. tog. again, but this time knit through the front of the loops in the ordinary way ; slip the single st. back to the left-hand pin and repeat from * to the end of the row.

Fasten off and form the initial as described.

HOW TO MAKE YOUR INITIAL

A B C D
E F G H
I J K L
M N O P
Q R S T
U V W
X Y Z

Each letter should measure about 2½ inches high. First make your initial in string or tape on the jumper to be sure of the length required for the crochet or knitted strip.

The Cap is Tied Round the Neck with Loose Scarf Ends, which is Ideal for Motoring!

The Gayest CAP for a Windy Day!

In Simple Knitting With a Border of Crochet Flowers

MATERIALS

*T*HREE ozs. of Templeton's "Carrick" Knitting Wool, 3-ply, and a pair of Stratnoid knitting pins, No. 8; 1 Stratnoid crochet hook, No. 10; oddments of brightly coloured wool of the same thickness for the crochet flowers.

TENSION AND MEASUREMENTS

*W*ORKED at a tension of 2 ridges to the inch in width on the knitting, the measurements given on the diagram are attained without expanding the knitting, which is very pliable and will accommodate head sizes to 23 inches.

ABBREVIATIONS

*K*NIT; p., purl; st., stitch; inc., increase (by working into the back and front of the same stitch); dec., decrease; ch., chain; d.c., double crochet; tr., treble; sl., slip; st., stitch.

TO WORK THE HOOD

CAST on 69 sts. and work 1 row into the back of the sts. to give a neat edge, then work in pattern as follows:
PATTERN ROW: * K. 2, p. 2; repeat from * until 1 st. remains, k. 1.
Repeat this row 63 times more.
On the next row work 25 sts. in pattern, and put these on a stitch-holder, cast off the next 19 sts., leaving 1 st. on right-hand pin, work in pattern to end, beginning with k. 1 as the first st. is already on the pin. Work 15 rows more in pattern on these sts. and cast off.
Join the wool to the inside edge of remaining sts. and work 15 rows more in pattern, beginning with k. 2. Cast off.

THE SCARF

CAST on 37 sts. and work 1 row into the back of the sts. to give a neat edge, then work in pattern as for hood for 14 inches. Now work 8 rows plain, decreasing at both ends of every row, when 21 sts. will remain. Work 24 rows straight on these sts., then inc. at both ends of each of the next 8 rows, when there will again be 37 sts. on the pins. Work 14 inches in pattern, then cast off.

THE FLOWERS

THESE are made from odd lengths of gaily coloured wool. The original bonnet was worked in navy blue with flowers in purple, mauve, light and dark green, orange, yellow, and red.
Each flower is worked as follows:
Make 6 ch., and sl.-st. to the first st. to form a ring.

TO MAKE UP THE HOOD

FIRST sew the crown in shape as shown on the diagram, sewing from A to A, then B to B. Now sew the two short ends for the top of the hood. Join the strip of flowers to the face edge of the crown, pinning the flowers first so that they are evenly spaced along the edge of the knitting, then catch by 1 tr. only on each flower. To work the face edge, begin on one short end of the flower strip

and sl.-st. into a k. st. on the edge of the crown and into the nearest tr. on the first flower, 4 ch., miss 3 tr., 1 d.c. into next tr., 7 ch., 1 d.c. into the fourth tr. from the side join on next flower, 7 ch., miss 3 tr. on same flower, 1 d.c. into next tr. The front line of the flower strip is now reached, * 7 ch., 1 d.c. into the centre tr. cf next flower; repeat from * along the front edge, then work along the second end like the opposite one, finishing with a sl.st. on the knitting, 1 ch., turn.

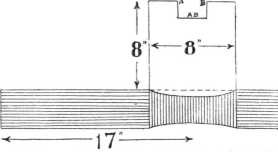

1ST ROUND: 10 d.c. into the ring and sl.-st. to the first d.c. at end of round.
2ND ROUND: 3 ch. which, with the sl.-st., will stand for the first tr., * 1 tr. into next st., 1 ch.; repeat from * all round, then sl.-st. to the 2nd of the 3 ch. at beginning of round, draw wool through and fasten off.
The cup of the flower is made thus: Sl.-st. the wool into the space between 2 d.c. on the first row of the piece already worked, make 3 ch., * 1 tr. into the next space, 1 ch., and repeat from * all round. Sl.-st. to second ch. at end, and fasten off.
Work 31 more flowers in the same way.
Now join the flowers in pairs by oversewing the tops of 2 trs. together, using the main colour, then join the pairs in the same way to form a long strip.

2ND ROW: 1 tr. into each d.c. of previous row, but put 3 trs. into each front corner stitch. Fasten off.
Thread a piece of the main coloured wool into a crewel needle and run through the back neck edge of the knitted crown, and draw up until this edge is the same length as the centre portion of the scarf, which is in garter st. Secure this with a back stitch, then sew the scarf and crown together, over the garter st. only, which finishes the hood.

KNITTED DRESS *in Tweed Effect*

Made on Youthful Lines with a Very Becoming "Swing" Skirt

A BROKEN rib pattern is used for the swing skirt, with the bodice in stocking-stitch

MATERIALS : 1 lb. 4 ozs. Templeton's "Ayrtweed" Knitting Wool. Three press-studs. One pair each Nos. 6 and 10 pins.

Measurements : Length from shoulder, 40ins. Width across underarm, 17½ins. Sleeve length, from shoulder, 22ins.

Tension : Approx. 5 sts. to 1in.

Abbreviations : K., knit ; p., purl ; sts., stitches ; inc., increase ; dec., decrease ; tog., together ; beg., beginning ; pat., pattern ; s., slip.

SKIRT—BACK With No. 6 pins cast on 180 sts. Work in following broken rib : *1st row*—S. 1, k. to end. *2nd row*—S. 1*, p. 7, k. 2. Repeat from * ending k. 1. Work until 10 ins. from cast-on edge (end with 1st row of pat.). *1st decreasing*—S. 1, * p. 3, p. 2 tog., p. 2, k. 2. Repeat from * ending k. 1 (160 sts.). Work until 16ins. from cast-on edge. *2nd decreasing*—S. 1, * p. 2, p. 2 tog., p. 2, k. 2. Repeat from * ending k. 1 (140 sts.). Work until 18ins. from cast-on edge. *3rd decreasing*—S. 1, * p. 2, p. 2 tog., p. 1, k. 2. Repeat from * ending k. 1. (120 sts.). Work until 20ins. from cast-on edge. *4th decreasing*—S. 1, * p. 1, p. 2 tog., p. 1, k. 2. Repeat from * ending k. 1 (100 sts.). Work until 22ins. from cast-on edge. *5th decreasing*—S. 1, * p. 1, p. 2 tog., k. 2, p. 3, k. 2. Repeat from * ending k. 1 (90 sts.). Work until 23ins. from cast-on edge. Cast off.

For skirt front work another piece to correspond.

CENTRE RIBBING With No. 10 pins cast on 32 sts. Rib 27ins., k. 1, p. 1. Cast off in rib.

BACK OF TOP With No. 6 pins cast on 90 sts. Work 5ins. stocking-st., as follows : *1st row*—S. 1, k. to end. *2nd row*—S. 1, p. to last st., k. 1.

To Shape Armholes : Cast off 3 sts. at beg. of next 8 rows. Work 7ins. on remaining 66 sts.

To Shape Shoulders : Cast off 6 sts. at beg. of next 6 rows. Cast off rem. sts.

FRONT OF TOP With No. 6 pins cast on 96 sts. Work as for back until armhole shaping is complete (72 sts.).

To Shape Neck : Work on 1st 36 sts. for 7ins., decreasing 1 st. every 3rd row at neck edge until 22 sts. remain.

To Shape Shoulder : Cast off 6 sts. every armhole end row 3 times. Work back to armhole. Cast off 4.

Return to 36 sts. of right front and work to correspond.

SLEEVES With No. 10 pins cast on 40 sts. Rib 1½ins., k. 1, p. 1. Change to No. 6 pins and work in stocking-st. for 17ins., increasing 1 st. each end of every 6th row until 70 sts. Then cast off 2 sts. at beg. of every row until 10 sts. remain. Cast off.

NECK EDGING With No. 10 pins cast on 4 sts. Rib 20ins., k. 1, p. 1. Cast off.

TO MAKE UP Press lightly with warm iron and damp cloth. Sew side seams of skirt and top and sleeve seams. Sew in sleeves. Sew centre ribbing to skirt and top of dress, overlapping left side for opening. Sew edging to neck. Sew press-studs to side opening.

R

WHAT THEY ASK THE MATRON

We have persuaded the Matron of a big Welfare Centre, whose homely advice brings solace to dozens of mothers every week, to let us publish some of the queries just as they were brought to her, and the advice she gave the anxious mothers. That those who have little ones of their own will find the information invaluable we are confident.

THE EDITRESS.

FOOD BETWEEN MEALS

My children have lately got into an annoying habit of not wanting their food at ordinary meal times. But they get hungry and cry for food between meals. Is it safe to refuse it?

CHILDREN must be taught to have their meals at regular intervals.

All snacks should be forbidden, the only exception being a light lunch at half-past ten in the morning if there are more than four hours between breakfast and dinner.

Find out the reason for their refusal of food at ordinary times. Do they eat between meals? If so, stop this at once.

* * *

WHEN MUMPS ARE ABOUT

Is mumps a serious illness? Should one send for the doctor? What are the symptoms?

MUMPS is a very distressing illness, and it is essential to send for a doctor. You can then be sure of being told all the best ways of alleviating the discomfort for the little patient.

The onset may be simply loss of appetite and slight feverishness —which will put you on the alert in any case.

But, if your child has been in contact with a case of mumps, it is very infectious, and in three weeks the symptoms of swollen glands may begin to appear.

Fortunately it is an illness in which there are no bad after effects; but children need " building up " afterwards.

* * *

A CHILD'S HAIR

How often should I wash my child's hair? My little girl is six, and her hair is very thick, but rather dry.

A CHILD'S head should be washed at least once a week, winter and summer. In winter dry it with hot towels.

Be sure to use a super-fatted soap or shampoo powder if your little girl's hair is inclined to be dry.

You would find it a good plan to rub a little pure olive oil or vaseline into the scalp the night before the bath, and be very sure to rinse out all the soap as this will cause the hair to be too dry. A squeeze of lemon in the last rinsing water will assist this.

* * *

WHEN BABY IS FRETFUL

My baby is inclined to cry before his feeding time. Lately he has been wakeful during the night. As I feed him myself, what can be the reason?

IT would seem as if your health needs more attention. Try to enrich your diet by more milk, or by taking cocoa full cream foods. Have you tried milk tea? Have more fresh air and sleep.

MADE GAY with FLOWERS

The Newest of Embroideries

THE loveliest flower embroidery you can imagine! It is to be worked on your pretties or on a little girl's frock.

The roses are in pink rose-stitch —a small back stitch in the centre with rings of back stitches all round. The forget-me-nots are pale blue satin-stitch, with a yellow French knot in the centre. The leaves are soft green lazy-daisy-loops. The bars are in upright satin-stitch.

To make the little frock (Pattern No. 53,000, 2-6 years) you will require from 1⅜ to 1½ yards of 54-inch material.

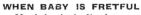

5 The Square look 1940-49

The wartime sweater is warm and comfortable, and worn over a skirt or slacks. It has elbow-length sleeves and a bold all-over pattern of lattice stitch or a raised cable, and the square yoke and shoulders help the Forties woman to look strong and able to cope. After the war the sweater becomes fresh and youthful, with colorful gay plaids and Fair Isle sweater sets. Boleros and pullovers are often worn over a white blouse. For the evening, sequins add sparkle. Romantic, lacy or tuft stitches are worked, or sentimental designs of roses are featured on the yoke.

MARY FLAXMAN'S

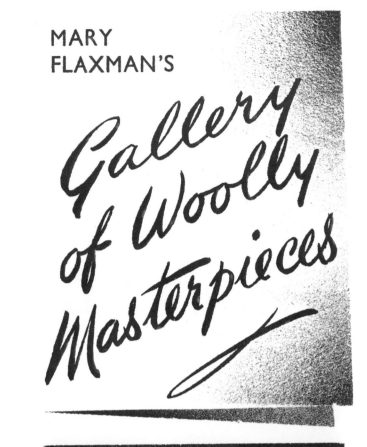

Gallery of Woolly Masterpieces

ASTRAKHAN COAT WITH HOOD OR HAT

MATERIALS.—2 lbs. 4 oz. of Munrospun Astrakhan wool for coat with hat, 3 lbs. 8 oz. for coat with hood, 1 pair of No. 0 knitting needles, 1 yard of crêpe-de-chine lining for coat with hat, 2 button moulds and a braid frog for coat with hat, and 2 buttons the size of a two-shilling piece for coat with hood.

MEASUREMENTS.—Length from shoulder at armhole edge (with hat) 15 inches; with hood, 22 inches; width all round under the arms, 36 inches; length of sleeve seam, 16 inches.

TENSION.—5 stitches to 2 inches in width.

ABBREVIATIONS.—K., knit; p., purl; st.-st., stocking stitch; sts., stitches; dec., decrease or decreasing; tog., together; inc., increase or increasing.

CASTING-ON.—If you cast on with two needles, work into the back of the cast-on sts. to produce firm edges, but if you use the thumb method this is not necessary.

The Back

Begin at the lower edge. Cast on 36 sts. and work 6 rows in garter-st. Change to st.-st. and continue until the work measures 8 inches from beginning (with hat), 15 inches with hood, finishing after a p. row.

The Armhole Shaping

Dec. 1 st. at both ends of the next row, then on every alternate row until 30 sts. remain. Continue without dec. until the armholes measure 7 inches on the straight, finishing after a p. row.

The Shoulder Shaping

Cast off 5 sts. at the beginning of the next 4 rows. Cast off the remaining 10 sts. for the back neck.

The Right Front

Begin at the lower edge. Cast on 28 sts. and work 6 rows in garter-st. Change to st.-st., but keeping 6 sts. at the front edge in garter-st. for the coat with hood, and continue until the work measures 8 inches, 15 inches from the beginning, finishing after a k. row.

The Armhole Shaping

Cast off 6 sts. at the beginning of the next row, then dec. 1 st. at the same edge on every alternate row until 20 sts. remain. Continue without dec. until the armhole measures 5 inches on the straight, finishing after a p. row.

The Neck Shaping

Cast off 6 sts. at the beginning of the next row, then dec. 1 st. at the neck edge on every row until 10 sts. remain. Continue without dec. until the armhole measures 7 inches on the straight, finishing after a k. row.

The Shoulder Shaping

Cast off 5 sts. at the beginning of the next row, then on the next alternate row.

The Left Front

Work this exactly like the right front, but with all shapings at opposite edges.

The Sleeves

Begin at the lower edge. Cast on 44 sts. and work 6 rows in garter-st. Change to st.-st., dec. 1 st. at both ends of the 13th row, then on every 14th row following until 38 sts. remain. Continue without dec. until the work measures 15½ inches from the begin-

through the remaining sts., draw up tightly and fasten off.

The Making-up (Hat)

Join the brim and press the seam. Sew the crown inside the brim. ¾ inch below the top.

The Button Covers

Cast on 6 sts. and work 6 rows in garter-st. Cast off.

The Making-up (with Hat)

Place the coat on to the lining and cut to shape. Join the shoulders, sew in the sleeves and press the seams. Sew up the side and sleeve seams and press them. Cover the button moulds, then sew one button to each front neck. Sew in the lining. Sew the frog to the neck edge of the right front.

The Making-up (with Hood)

Join the shoulders and sew in the sleeves. Sew up the side and sleeve seams. Join the back seam of the hood, then sew the hood round the neck edge of the coat, leaving the border sts. free. Sew a button to each side of the neck edge, then make a button loop on the right neck edge.

JULIET CAP

MATERIALS.—2 oz. of Lister's "Lavenda" 4-ply wool, and 1 pair of No. 10 and No. 12 knitting needles.

MEASUREMENTS.—Width all round the head, when unstretched, 17 inches.

TENSION.—7 stitches to 1 inch in width, and 14 rows to 1 inch in depth measured over the panels.

ABBREVIATIONS.—K., knit; p., purl; sts., stitches; rep., repeat; inc., increase or increasing; dec., decrease or decreasing.

CASTING-ON.—If you cast on with two needles, work into the back of all cast-on sts. to produce firm edges, but if you use the thumb method this is not necessary.

The Panels

Begin at the lower edge of one panel. Cast on 30 sts., using No. 10 needles. 1st row—*K. 2, p. 2. Rep. from * finishing k. 2. This row forms the pattern. Continue in pattern until the work measures 5 inches from the beginning, then shape the top by dec. 1 st. at both ends of every alternate row until 20 sts. remain, and then dec. 1 st. at both ends of every row until 6 sts. remain. Cast off. Make 3 more panels in the same way.

The Brim

Cast on 12 sts. using No. 12 needles. 1st row—K. 2nd row—K. 3, p. 6, k. 3. 3rd row—Like the 1st row. 4th row—Like the 1st row. 5th row—Like the 2nd row. 6th row—Like the 1st row. These 6 rows form the pattern. Continue in pattern, inc. 1 st. at the beginning of the next row, but inside the 3 border sts., then at the same edge on every 6th row until there are 36 sts. on the needle. Work 2 inches on these sts., then dec. 1 st. at the shaped edge on the next row, then on every 6th row following until 12 sts. remain. Cast off.

The Making-up

Press the work on the wrong side with a warm iron and damp cloth. Join the panels and press the seams. Join the brim and press the seam. Sew the brim to the edge of the cap, then roll the brim and stitch lightly round the cap.

ning, measured down the centre. Now shape the top by casting off 4 sts. at the beginning of the next 2 rows, then cast off 2 sts. at the beginning of every row until 8 sts. remain. Cast off.

The Hood

Cast on 48 sts. and work 8 rows in garter-st. Change to st.-st. and continue until the work measures 10 inches from the beginning. Cast off.

The Hat

Begin at the side of the brim. Cast on 9 sts. and work 22 inches in garter-st. Cast off.

The Crown

Begin at the lower edge. Cast on 50 sts. and work 4 rows in st.-st. Now shape the top as follows:— 5th row—*K. 8, k. 2 tog. Rep. from * to end (45 sts.) 6th row—P. 7th row—*K. 7, k. 2 tog. Rep. from * to end (40 sts.) 8th row—P. 9th row—*K. 6, k. 2 tog. Rep. from * to end (35 sts.) 10th row—* P. 5, p. 2 tog. Rep. from * to end (30 sts.) 11th row—*K. 4, k. 2 tog. Rep. from * to end (25 sts.). 12th row—*P. 3, p. 2 tog. Rep. from * to end (20 sts.). 13th row—*K. 2, k. 2 tog. Rep. from * to end (15 sts.). 14th row—P. 1, *p. 2 tog. Rep. from * to end. Cut the wool, thread

MATERIALS : 8 oz. Templeton's " Opal-sheen " knitting wool in green, and 1 oz. in grey. 1 pair No. 9 knitting-needles, 1 spare needle pointed both ends. 12 buttons.

Measurements : To fit 34-36 in. bust. Length from top of shoulder to lower edge, 17½ in., length of sleeve seam 18 in.

Abbreviations : K. = knit ; p. = purl ; sl. = slip ; st. st. = stocking stitch ; dec. = decrease ; inc. = increase ; cont. = continue ; beg. = beginning ; tog. = together ; rem. = remaining.

Back : Using green wool, work in k. 1, p. 1, rib all through. Cast on 110 sts. and work for 2 in. Inc. 1 st. at both ends of next row and every following 6th row until there are 130 sts. on needle. Cont. on these 130 until back measures 11 in.

Shape armholes : Cast off 4 sts. at beg. of next 2 rows, then 3 sts. at beg. of next 2 rows, then 2 at beg. of next 2 rows, and finally dec. 1 st. at beg. of next 2 rows. Cont. on rem. 110 sts. until armhole measures 6 in. in depth.

Shape shoulders : Next 10 rows : Cast off 8, rib to end of row.

11th row : Cast off rem. 30 sts. for back-neck.

Right Front : With green wool cast on 23 sts. ; with grey wool cast on 12 sts. ; with green wool cast on 29 sts.

1st Row : With green wool (k. 1, p. 1) 14 times, k. 1, twisting green wool ; k. 12 twisting grey wool, (k. 1, p. 1) 11 times, k. 1.

2nd Row : (P. 1, k. 1) 11 times, p. 1 twisting green wool ; p. 12, twisting grey wool, (p. 1, k. 1) 14 times, p. 1.

3rd, 4th, 5th and 6th Rows : As 1st and 2nd rows.

7th Row : (K. 1, p. 1) twice, cast off 2 (for buttonhole) rib 23, slip the next 6 grey sts. on to the spare double-pointed needle, putting them to the back of work. K. with grey wool the next 6 sts., bring the 6 slipped sts. forward, k. them (this forms the cable twist), rib 23 green sts.

8th Row : Rib 23, p. 12, rib 23, cast on 2 (for buttonhole) rib 4.

9th-18th Rows : 1st and 2nd rows repeated.

19th and 20th Rows : As 7th and 8th rows.

(The last 12 rows (9th-20th) form the pattern, and are repeated throughout the work.)

Inc. 1 st. at the end of next row (21st) and every following 8th row, until there are 74 sts. on needle. At the same time make 10 more buttonholes in the front border at intervals of 10 rows. Then, casting off for buttonhole, make cable twist in the same row (as indicated in 7th row). When 9th buttonhole has been finished work another row (thus ending at side edge).

Shape armhole : At beg. of next row and every second row cast off first 5 sts., then 4 sts., then 3 sts., then 2 sts. and finally 1 st. Cont. on rem. 59 sts.

When 12th buttonhole has been finished work 3 more rows (thus ending at front edge).

Shape neck : At. beg. of next row and every second row cast off first 5 sts., then 3 sts. twice ; then 2 sts., and finally dec. 1 st. Cont. on remaining 45 sts. for 10 more rows (ending at side edge).

Shape shoulder : Cast off 9 sts. at beg. of next row and every second row till all have been cast off.

Left Front : With green wool cast on 29 sts., with grey wool cast on 12 sts., with green wool cast on 23 sts.

1st Row : (K. 1, p. 1) 11 times, k. 1, twisting green wool, k. 12 with grey wool, twisting grey wool, (k. 1, p. 1) 14 times, k. 1.

Cont. to match right front, reversing shapings and omitting buttonholes.

Sleeve : With grey wool cast on 56 sts. Work in k. 1, p. 1 rib for 10 rows. Change to green wool and rib for 10 more rows. Inc. 1 st. both ends of next row and every following 5th row until there are 80 sts. on needle. Cont. on 80 sts. until sleeve measures 16 in. from cast-on edge.

Evening jumper with novel sleeves

Evening Jumper

Next Row : K. 15, (k. 1, inc. 1) 50 times. K. 15 (130 sts.). P. back. Work in st. st. for 2 ins.

Shape Top : At beg. of next 2 rows cast off 4 sts., at beg. of next 2 rows 3 sts., at beg. of next 2 rows 2 sts., and finally at beg. of next 2 rows 1 st. Cont. on rem. 110 sts. until top measures 6 ins. from beginning of shaping.

Border for Neck : With grey wool cast on 90 sts. Work in k. 1, p. 1-rib for 10 rows. Cast off in rib.

To Make Up :

Press lightly on wrong side under a damp cloth. Sew tog. side, shoulder and sleeve seams. Insert sleeves, gathering fullnes into top. Buttonhole-stitch buttonholes, and attach buttons to match. Sew border to neck-line, within 6 sts. of both the left and right front edge. Give a finishing press.

The frilly neckline is gathered on a ribbon in a pastel colour to contrast with the jacket.

COSY
Yet
Bewitching—

A Sweet Little Affair That Will Suit All Sizes

To Work the Back

BEGIN at the lower edge and cast on 254 sts. K. 2 rows plain, working into the back of the sts. on the first row.

Next row : K. 1, * work 5 in 1 thus : (k. 1, p. 1) twice, k. 1, all into the next st., p. 5 tog. ; repeat from * until 1 st. remains, k. 1.

Now begin the pattern as follows :

1st row (right side) : K. 1, p. until 1 st. remains, k. 1.

2nd row : K. 1, * p. 5 tog., 5 in 1 ; repeat from * until 1 st. remains, k. 1.

3rd row : K. 1, p. until 1 st. remains, k. 1.

THIS little bedjacket will be a special joy to you. It looks so enchantingly fragile, but it is so warm and cosy.

MATERIALS.—*7 ounces of Copley's "Excelsior" Lady Betty Wool, 3-ply ; a pair of Phantom knitting pins No. 7 ; a Phantom crochet hook No. 12.*

TENSION AND MEASUREMENTS.—*Worked at a tension of 3 harebells to 3 inches in width, the measurements on the diagram on page 64 are attained.*

ABBREVIATIONS (TO BE READ BEFORE WORKING).—*K., knit plain ; p., purl ; st., stitch ; tog., together ; inc., increase (by working into the front and back of the same st.) ; dec., decrease (by working 2 sts. tog.) ; m.s., moss stitch (k. 1 and p. 1 alternately and on subsequent rows the sts. are reversed). Directions in brackets are worked the number of times stated after the brackets. Ch., chain ; d.c., double crochet ; tr., treble.*

This shows the harebell stitch.

This Enchanting Bed-Jacket

Warm As Feathers, Luxurious As Swans-Down

The attractive plain yoke makes the shaping easy to do.

4th row : * K. 1, **m.** 2 by winding the wool twice round the pin ; repeat from * until 1 st. remains, k. 1.

5th row : * P. 1, drop the 2 made sts. ; repeat from * until 1 st. remains, k. 1.

6th row : K. 1, * 5 in 1, p. 5 tog. ; repeat from * until 1 st. remains, k. 1.

These 6 rows form the pattern, so repeat them 9 times more.

To Shape the Armholes.—
1st row : Cast off 7 sts., p. until 1 st. remains, k. 1.

2nd row : Cast off 7, return the st. left after casting off to the left-hand pin, * p. 5 tog., 5 in 1 ; repeat from * to the end.

3rd row : K. 2 tog., p. until 2 sts. remain, k. 2 tog.

4th row : K. 2 tog., * k. 1, m. 2 ; repeat from * until 3 remain, k. 1, k. 2 tog.

5th row : K. 2 tog., * drop 2, p. 1 ; repeat from * until 4 remain, drop 2, k. 2 tog.

6th row : K. 2 tog., p. 1, * 5 in 1, p. 5 tog. ; repeat from * until 3 remain, p. 1, k. 2 tog.

7th row : K. 2 tog., p. until 2 remain, k. 2 tog.

8th row : P. 6 tog., * 5 in 1, p. 5 tog. ; repeat from * until 2 remain, (k. 1, p. 1) twice into the next st., k. 1.

Repeat from the 3rd row to the 8th row once more, when 216 sts. will remain.

Dec. row : * K. 2 tog., p. 2 tog. ; repeat from * to the end (108 sts.).

THE YOKE.—Work 5 rows in m.s., decreasing 1 st. at both ends of every row (98 sts.).

Work 26 rows straight in m.s.

To Shape the Shoulders.—Cast off 8 sts. at the

This shows a close-up of the neckline.

COSY Yet BEWITCHING

beginning of the next 6 rows, then cast off the remaining sts.

The Right Front

Cast on 116 sts. and work the same as for the Back until 10 patterns have been worked.

To Shape the Armhole.—1st row : K. 1, p. until 1 st. remains, k. 1.

2nd row : Cast off 7 and return the remaining st. to the left-hand pin, * p. 5 tog., 5 in 1 ; repeat from * until 1 st. remains, k. 1.

3rd row : K. 1, p. until 2 remain, k. 2 tog.

4th row : K. 2 tog., * k. 1, m. 2 ; repeat from * until 1 st. remains, k. 1.

5th row : * K. 1, drop 2 ; repeat from * until 2 remain, k. 2 tog.

6th row : K. 2 tog., p. 1, * 5 in 1, p. 5 tog. ; repeat from * until 1 st. remains, k. 1.

7th row : P. until 2 remain, k. 2 tog.

8th row : P. 6 tog., * 5 in 1, p. 5 tog. ; repeat from * until 2 remain, 5 in 1, k. 1.

Repeat from the 3rd row to the 8th row once more, when 97 sts. will remain.

Dec. row : * K. 2 tog., p. 2 tog. ; repeat from * until 1 st. remains, k. 1 (49 sts.).

Work 8 rows in m.s., decreasing 1 st. at the arm end of every row (41 sts.)

Work 1 row more.

** *To Shape the Neck.*—Cast off 10

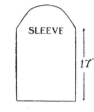

| 20 | ←—13—→ FRONT | 13 | ←——25——→ BACK | 20 |

SLEEVE 17

The shape and measurements of the pretty bed-jacket.

sts. at the beginning of the next row, then dec. 1 st. at the neck edge of the next 7 rows, when 24 sts. will remain.

Work 13 rows more.

To Slope the Shoulder.—Cast off 8 sts. at the beginning of the next row and following 2 alternate rows, then fasten off.

The Left Front

Cast on 116 sts. and work as for the back until there are 10 complete patterns.

To Shape the Armhole.—1st row : Cast off 7, p. until 1 st. remains, k. 1.

2nd row : K. 1, * p. 5 tog., 5 in 1 ; 1epeat from * to the end.

3rd row : K. 2 tog., p. until 1 st. remains, k. 1.

4th row : * K. 1, m. 2 ; repeat from * until 3 remain, k. 1, k. 2 tog.

5th row : K. 2 tog., * drop 2, p. 1 ; repeat from * to the end.

6th row : K. 1, * 5 in 1, p. 5 tog. ; repeat from * until 3 sts. remain, p. 1, k. 2 tog.

7th row : K. 2 tog., p. until 1 st. remains, k. 1.

8th row : K. 1, * p. 5 tog., 5 in 1 ; repeat from * until 7 remain, p. 5 tog., (k. 1, p. 1) twice into the next st., k. 1.

Repeat from the 3rd row to the 8th row once more (97 sts.).

Dec. row : * K. 2 tog., p. 2 tog. ; repeat from * until 1 st. remains, k. 1 (49 sts.).

Work 8 rows in m.s., decreasing 1 st. at the arm end of every row (41 sts.).

Now continue from ** on the right front to the end.

The Sleeves

Begin at the lower edge and cast on 128 sts.

K. 2 rows plain.

Next row : K. 1, * 5 in 1, p. 5 tog. ; 1epeat from * until 1 st. remains, k. 1.

Now work 13 patterns as on the Back, or for length required, finishing with the last row of a pattern.

To Shape the Sleeve Top.—Work the first 7 rows of armhole shaping on the Back (104 sts.).

Work 17 rows straight, beginning with the 2nd pattern row.

Cast off 6 sts. at the beginning of the next 4 rows, working the last row plain, then cast off the remaining sts.

To Make Up the Dressing Jacket. —First join the shoulder seams, beginning at the arm end and taking 1 st. from each side at a time. Set the sleeves into armholes and press these seams with the edge of the iron only, for neatness. Join the sleeve and side seams in one line and press these seams.

The Crochet Edging.—Work a row of 1 d.c. into every st. round the neck edge, 4 ch. ; turn.

2nd row : * Miss the first st. over which the turning ch. stands, 1 tr. into the next d.c., * 1 ch. ; miss 1 d.c., 1 tr. into next st., and repeat from * to the end.

3rd row : 4 ch. and 1 d.c. into the top of each tr. along the row.

4th row : 6 ch., and 1 d.c. into the middle of each loop of the previous row.

5th and *6th rows :* 8 ch. and 1 d.c. into each loop of the last row, then fasten off.

Thread the ribbon through the 2nd row of the crochet edging.

FOR MEN IN THE SERVICES

—socks, helmet with chest and back flaps, and mittens that leave thumbs and forefingers free : they take respectively 4 oz. Viyella 4-ply Unshrinkable Sock Yarn, and 4 oz. and 2 oz. Ramada 4-ply Super Fingering Wool.

The harebell stitch.

KNITTERS' DELIGHT

Here Is One Of Our Loveliest Jumper Designs.   Knit It In A Soft Flower Colour So Appropriate For Springtime

THE harebell stitch of the yoke and the lacy rib of the main part of the jumper make this a specially interesting "knitted."

MATERIALS.—6 ounces of Femina Botany Fingering, 3-ply, a pair each of No. 9 and No. 10 knitting pins ; 1 press stud.

TENSION AND MEASUREMENTS.— Worked at a tension of one repeat of the lace pattern to one inch and a quarter in width with No. 9 pins, the measurements on the diagram are attained without pressing.

ABBREVIATIONS—TO BE READ BEFORE WORKING.—K., knit plain ; p., purl ; st., stitch ; tog., together ; inc., increase (by working into the front and back of the same st.) ; dec., decrease ; m., make (by bringing the wool to the front of the pin and over it before knitting the next st., or by bringing the wool to the front of the pin, over it and to the front again, before a p. st.) ; garter st. is k. plain on every row. Directions in brackets are worked the number of times stated after the brackets.

TO WORK THE FRONT

BEGIN at the lower edge and with No. 10 pins cast on 130 sts. Work in pattern as follows, working into the back of the cast-on sts. to give a neat edge :

1st row : * K. 1, p. 2, k. 1, m. 1, k. 2 tog., k. 1, p. 2, k. 1 ; repeat from * to the end of the row.

2nd row : * P. 1, k. 2, p. 1, m. 1, p. 2 tog., p. 1, k. 2, p. 1 ; repeat from * to the end of the row.

These 2 rows form the pattern, so repeat them 15 times more.

Change to No. 9 pins and inc. 1 st. at both ends of the next row and every following 8th row until the 7th inc. row has been worked, when there will be 144 sts., working the extra sts. in k. 2 and p. 2 rib. Work 29 rows more.

THE YOKE.   *To Shape the Armholes :*
1st row : Cast off 12 (1 st. on pin), k. 1, p. 2, k. 2, p. 2, (k. 1, m. 1, k. 2 tog., k. 1, p. 2, k. 2, p. 2) 5 times, k. 1, m. 1, k. 2 tog., m. 1, k. 1, p. 2, k. 2, p. 2, (k. 1, m. 1, k. 2 tog., k. 1, p. 2, k. 2, p. 2) 6 times, k. 2, p. 2.

2nd row : Cast off 12 (1 st. on pin), p. 1, k. 2, p. 2, k. 2, (p. 1, m. 1, p. 2 tog., p. 1, k. 2, p. 2, k. 2) 5 times, k. 3, p. 1, k. 2, p. 2, k. 2, (p. 1, m. 1, p. 2 tog., p. 1, k. 2, p. 2, k. 2) 5 times, p. 2.

3rd row : K. 2 tog., p. 2, k. 2, p. 2, (k. 1, m. 1, k. 2 tog., k. 1, p. 2, k. 2, p. 2) 5 times, k. 1, m. 1, k. 3, m. 1, k. 1, p. 2, k. 2, p. 2, (k. 1, m. 1, k. 2 tog., k. 1, p. 2, k. 2, p. 2) 5 times, k. 2.

4th row : P. 2 tog., k. 2, p. 2, k. 2, (p. 1, m. 1, p. 2 tog., p. 1, k. 2, p. 2, k. 2) 5 times, p. 1, k. 5, p. 1, k. 2, p. 2, k. 2, (p. 1, m. 1, p. 2 tog., p. 1, k. 2, p. 2, k. 2) 5 times, p. 1.

5th row : P. 2 tog., p. 1, k. 2, p. 2, (k. 1, m. 1, k. 2 tog., k. 1, p. 2, k. 2, p. 2) 5 times, k. 1, m. 1, k. 5, m. 1, k. 1, p. 2, k. 2, p. 2, (k. 1, m. 1, k. 2 tog., k. 1, p. 2, k. 2, p. 2) 5 times, k. 1.

6th row : K. 2 tog., k. 1, p. 2, k. 2, (p. 1, m. 1, p. 2 tog., p. 1, k. 2, p. 2, k. 2) 5 times, p. 1, k. 7, p. 1, k. 2, p. 2, k. 2, (p. 1, m. 1, p. 2 tog., p. 1, k. 2, p. 2, k. 2) 5 times.

7th row : P. 2 tog., (k. 2, p. 2, k. 1, m. 1, k. 2 tog., k. 1, p. 2) 5 times, k. 4 tog., k. 9, k. 4 tog., (p. 2, k. 1, m. 1, k. 2 tog., k. 1, p. 2, k. 2) 5 times, p. 2.

8th row : K. 2 tog., (p. 2, k. 2, p. 1, m. 1, p. 2 tog., p. 1, k. 2) 5 times, k. 13,

p. 1, m. 1, p. 2 tog., p. 1, k. 2, (p. 2, k. 2, p. 1, m. 1, p. 2 tog., p. 1, k. 2) 5 times, p. 2, k. 1.

9th row : P. 1, (k. 2, p. 2, k. 1, m. 1, k. 2 tog., k. 1, p. 2) 4 times, k. 2, p. 2, k. 1, m. 1, k. 2 tog., m. 1, k. 8, m. 1, k. 1, m. 1, k. 8, m. 1, k. 2 tog., m. 1, k. 1, p. 2, (k. 2, p. 2, k. 1, m. 1, k. 2 tog., k. 1, p. 2) 4 times, k. 1, p. 2.

10th row : K. 1, (p. 2, k. 2, p. 1, m. 1, p. 2 tog., p. 1, k. 2) 4 times, p. 2, k. 2, p. 1, (k. 3, p. 8) twice, k. 3, p. 1, k. 2, (p. 2, k. 2, p. 1, m. 1, p. 2 tog., p. 1, k. 2) 4 times, p. 2, k. 1.

11th row : P. 1, (k. 2, p. 2, k. 1, m. 1, k. 2 tog., k. 1, p. 2) 4 times, k. 2, p. 2, k. 1, (m. 1, k. 3, m. 1, k. 8) twice, m. 1, k. 3, m. 1, k. 1, p. 2, (k. 2, p. 2, k. 1, m. 1, k. 2 tog., k. 1, p. 2) 4 times, k. 2, p. 1.

12th row : K. 1, (p. 2, k. 2, p. 1, m. 1, p. 2 tog., p. 1, k. 2) 4 times, p. 2, k. 2, p. 1, (k. 5, p. 8) twice, k. 5, p. 1, k. 2, (p. 2, k. 2, p. 1, m. 1, p. 2 tog., p. 1, k. 2) 4 times, p. 2, k. 1.

13th row : P. 1, (k. 2, p. 2, k. 1, m. 1, k. 2 tog., k. 1, p. 2) 4 times, k. 2, p. 2, k. 1, (m. 1, k. 5, m. 1, k. 8) twice, m. 1, k. 5, m. 1, k. 1, p. 2, (k. 2, p. 2, k. 1, m. 1, k. 2 tog., k. 1, p. 2) 4 times, k. 2, p. 1.

14th row : K. 1, (p. 2, k. 2, p. 1, m. 1, p. 2 tog., p. 1, k. 2) 4 times, p. 2, k. 2, p. 1, (k. 7, p. 8) twice, k. 7, p. 1, k. 2, (p. 2, k. 2, p. 1, m. 1, p. 2 tog., p. 1, k. 2) 4 times, p. 2, k. 1.

15th row : P. 1, (k. 2, p. 2, k. 1, m. 1, k. 2 tog., k. 1, p. 2) 4 times, k. 1, (k. 4 tog., k. 7, k. 4 tog.) 3 times, k. 1, (p. 2, k. 1, m. 1, k. 2 tog., k. 1, p. 2, k. 2) 4 times, p. 1.

16th row : K. 1, (p. 2, k. 2, p. 1, m. 1, p. 2 tog., p. 1, k. 2) 4 times, p. 1, k. 27, (k. 18 sts. more here on each repeat), p. 1, (k. 2, p. 1, m. 1, p. 2 tog., p. 1, k. 2, p. 2) 4 times, k. 1.

17th row : P. 1, (k. 2, p. 2, k. 1, m. 1, k. 2 tog., k. 1, p. 2) 3 times, k. 2, p. 2, k. 1, m. 1, k. 2 tog., m. 1, k. 1, (k. 8, m. 1, k. 1, m. 1) 3 times, k. 8, m. 1, k. 2 tog., m. 1, k. 1, p. 2,. (k. 2,

The main part of the jumper is knitted in this stitch.

The pretty harebell stitches are grouped to make a pointed yoke.

p. 2, k. 1, m. 1, k. 2 tog., k. 1, p. 2) 3 times, k. 2, p. 1 (119 sts.).

Repeat from the 10th row to the 17th row twice more, then from the 10th row to the 15th row again, but on each repeat work the bracketed item at each end once less than on the previous repetition, and the centre bracketed item twice more (105 sts.).

Continued on page 282

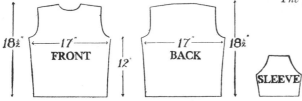

18½" ⟶17"⟵ 12' ⟶17"⟵ 18½"
FRONT   BACK   SLEEVE

The shape and measurements of the jumper.

So suitable for town wear with a printed silk frock and a flowery little hat.

Lacy GLOVES On TWO NEEDLES!

The Prettiest Pair of Gloves to Wear With Your Summer Frocks

MATERIALS.—*One 50-gram ball of Clark's Anchor Stranded Cotton and a pair of No. 13 knitting pins.*

TENSION AND MEASUREMENTS.—*Worked at a tension of 10 stitches to the inch in width on the plain knitting these gloves will fit a hand taking size 6 in skin gloves. This is a small size for a change, but No. 12 pins will make the next size larger, or sts. may be increased after the wristlet and these extra sts. divided equally between the back of hand and the palm. On the back the extra sts. must be knitted plain at each side of the pattern so as to avoid interfering with the centre leaf panel.*

THIS enchanting pair of cotton gloves is ideal for hot weather, and so simple to make. Each lace-panelled glove is knitted in one piece on two needles. The photograph on the page opposite shows one glove before the seams are sewn up.

ABBREVIATIONS. TO BE READ BEFORE WORKING.—*K., knit plain ; p., purl ; st., stitch ; tog., together ; m., make (by bringing the wool to the front of the pin and over it before knitting the next st., or by bringing the wool to the front of the pin, over it and to the front again, before working a p. st.) ; sl., slip ; p.s.s.o., pass the slipped st. over ; inc., increase (by working into the front and back of the same st.) ; dec., decrease (by working 2 sts. tog.) ; s.s., stocking stitch (k. on the right side and p. back) ; single rib is k. 1 and p. 1 alternately. Directions in brackets are worked the number of times stated after the brackets.*

TO WORK THE LEFT-HAND GLOVE

BEGIN at the wrist and cast on 50 sts. Work 36 rows in single rib.

Now begin the pattern as follows :

1st row : K. 26 for the s.s., sl. 1, k. 1, p.s.s.o., m. 1, k. 2, k. 2 tog., k. 2, m. 1, k. 1, m. 1, k. 5, (sl. 1, k. 1, p.s.s.o.) twice, m. 1, k. 6.

2nd row : P. 4, p. 2 tog., m. 1, p. 14, p. 2 tog., m. 1, p. 2, which finishes the pattern, then p. 26.

3rd row : K. 26, sl. 1, k. 1, p.s.s.o., m. 1, k. 2, k. 2 tog., k. 1, m. 1, k. 3, m. 1, k. 4, (sl. 1, k. 1, p.s.s.o.) twice, m. 1, k. 6.

4th row : As 2nd row.

5th row : K. 26, sl. 1, k. 1, p.s.s.o., m. 1, k. 2, k. 2 tog., m. 1, k. 5, m. 1, k. 3, (sl. 1, k. 1, p.s.s.o.) twice, m. 1, k. 6.

6th row : As 2nd row.

7th row : K. 20, inc. in the next st. to begin the thumb gusset, k. 2, inc. for second outline of gusset, k. 2, sl. 1, k. 1, p.s.s.o., m. 1, k. 2, k. 2 tog., k. 5, m. 1, k. 1, m. 1, k. 2 (sl. 1, k. 1, p.s.s.o.) twice, m. 1, k. 6.

8th row : P. 4, p. 2 tog., m. 1, p. 14, p. 2 tog., m. 1, p. 30.

9th row : K. 28, sl. 1, k. 1, p.s.s.o., m. 1, k. 2, k. 2 tog., k. 4, m. 1, k. 3, m. 1, k. 1, (sl. 1, k. 1, p.s.s.o.) twice, m. 1, k. 6.

10th row : As 8th row.

11th row : K. 20, inc., k. 4, inc., k. 2, sl. 1, k. 1, p.s.s.o., m. 1, k. 2, k. 2 tog., k. 3, m. 1, k. 5, m. 1, (sl. 1, k. 1, p.s.s.o.) twice, m. 1, k. 6.

12th row : P. 4, p. 2 tog., m. 1, p. 14, p. 2 tog., m. 1, p. 32.

These 12 rows form the lace pattern, so repeat them twice more, but on every 3rd, 7th and 11th pattern row inc. 2 sts. on the thumb gusset, working 2 sts. more in s.s. between the increases after every inc. row and allowing for these extra sts. on subsequent rows (66 sts.). The first row of the second pattern will begin with k. 30 for the s.s. because 4 gusset increases have been made, and it is a good plan for beginners to add the number of sts. increased after every inc. row and put that number down on paper. It will then be easy to remember to k. the right number at the beginning of right-side rows, and to purl the corresponding number at the end of wrong-side rows. All *increase* rows will begin with k. 20 as on the 7th row of the first pattern

Continued on page 282

Lacy GLOVES On TWO NEEDLES!

Continued

because the extra sts.. are counted between the two increase points.

THE THUMB : K. 40, turn, p. 17, turn and cast on 4 sts.

Work 32 rows in s.s. on these 21 sts., or for length required.

To Shape the Top : K. 2 tog. and k. 1 alternately to the end of the row, turn and p. 1 row. Turn and k. 2 tog. along the row.

Break off the wool, leaving a long end, which thread through the remaining sts.; draw up closely and fasten off, leaving enough wool to sew up the thumb seam.

THE HAND CONTINUED : Holding the work with the right side facing, pick up and k. 5 sts. from the base of the thumb with the pin holding 23 plain sts., then work the remaining 26 sts. from the back of the hand, keeping 20 sts. in lace pattern (54 sts.).

Work 17 rows more, working in pattern as at the beginning, but omit the thumb gusset increases and work 30 sts. in s.s. at the beginning of right-side rows. (More rows may be worked here for a longer hand.)

Now set the sts. in position for the fingers as follows :

THE FIRST FINGER : Holding the work with the right side facing, k. 34, turn, cast on 3 sts., turn and p. 19 for this finger, leaving 18 sts. for the front of the hand and 20 sts. on the back.

Work 32 rows more on these 19 sts., or for length required, then shape the top and finish as for the thumb.

THE SECOND FINGER : With the right side facing pick up and k. 4 sts. from the base of the first finger, k. 7 sts. from the back of the hand, cast on 3 sts., turn and p. 19.

Work 36 rows or for length required, on these 19 sts., then finish the top as for the thumb.

THE THIRD FINGER : Pick up and k. 4 sts. from the base of the second finger, k. 6 from the back of hand, turn, cast on 3 sts., and p. 19.

Work as for the first finger.

THE FOURTH FINGER : Pick up and k. 3 sts. from the base of the third finger, k. the remaining 14 sts., turn and p. 17.

Work 26 rows on these 17 sts., then finish the top as before.

THE RIGHT-HAND GLOVE

WORK the ribbing as for the first glove, then reverse the position of the pattern, by working the rows *backwards* until the thumb gusset is finished, when there will be 66 sts.

To divide the sts. for the thumb : K. 4, pattern 20, k. 19, turn and p. 17, turn and cast on 4 sts. (21 sts.). Now work the thumb as given for the left-hand glove.

To continue the hand, hold the work with the right side facing and on to the working pin with 26 pattern sts., pick up and k. 5 sts. from the cast-on edge at the base of the thumb, then k. the 23 plain sts. across the front of the hand (54 sts.).

Work 17 rows more, keeping 30 sts. in s.s. at the end of right side rows.

THE FIRST FINGER : Work 36 sts., turn and p. 16 turn and cast on 3 sts., leaving 18 sts. for the front of hand and 20 on the back. Work on these 19 sts. as for the first finger of the left hand.

Now work the other fingers as for the left hand, but hold the work with the wrong side facing when beginning each finger, so that the k. and p. rows will be reversed.

TO MAKE UP THE GLOVES : Darn in all ends and press the gloves with a hot iron over a damp cloth and a thick blanket underneath. Join the finger and thumb seams, then join the seam down the side of the hand. Turn inside out and press the seam on the wrong side.

KNITTERS' DELIGHT

Continued from page 279

Now divide the sts. as follows :

Next row (wrong side) : · K. 1, p. 2, k. 2, p. 1, m. 1, p. 2 tog., p. 1, k. 2, p. 1, k. 27, and leave these 39 sts. on a spare pin for the Right Front Shoulder, cast off 27, (1 st. on pin), k. 26, p. 1, k. 2, p. 1, m. 1, p. 2 tog., p. 1, k. 2, p. 2, k. 1 (39 sts. for the Left Front Shoulder).

THE LEFT FRONT SHOULDER.—1st row : P. 1, k. 2, p. 2, k. 1, m. 1, k. 2 tog., m. 1, (k. 8, m. 1, k. 1, m. 1) 3 times, k. 2, k. 2 tog.

2nd row : P. 2 tog., p. 1, (k. 3, p. 8) 3 times, k. 3, p. 1, k. 2, p. 1.

3rd row : P. 1, k. 2, p. 2, k. 1, (m. 1, k. 3, m. 1, k. 8) 3 times, m. 1, k. 3, k. 2 tog.

4th row : K. 2 tog., k. 3, (p. 8, k. 5) 3 times, p. 1, k. 2, p. 2, k. 1.

5th row : P. 1, k. 2, p. 2, k. 1, (m. 1, k. 5, m. 1, k. 8) 3 times, m. 1, k. 2, k. 2 tog.

6th row : K. 4, (p. 8, k. 7) 3 times, p. 1, k. 2, p. 2, k. 1.

7th row : P. 1, k. 1, (k. 4 tog., k. 7, k. 4 tog.) 3 times, k. 4 tog., k. 2, k. 2 tog.

8th row : K. 31, p. 1, k. 1.

To Slope the Shoulder : Work in garter-st. and cast off 11 sts. at the beginning of the next row and following 2 alternate rows, then fasten off.

THE RIGHT FRONT SHOULDER : Begin at the neck end of the remaining 39 sts. and work as follows :

1st row : K. 2 tog., k. 2, (m. 1, k. 1,

m. 1, k. 8) 3 times, m. 1, k. 2 tog., m. 1, k. 1, p. 2, k. 2, p. 1.

2nd row : · K. 1, p. 2, k. 2, p. 1, (k. 3 p. 8) 3 times, k. 3, p. 1, p. 2 tog.

3rd row : K. 2 tog., (k. 3, m. 1, k. 8, m. 1) 3 times, k. 3, m. 1, k. 1, p. 2, k. 2, p. 1.

4th row : K. 1, p. 2, k. 2, p. 1, (k. 5 p. 8) 3 times, k. 3, k. 2 tog.

5th row : K. 2 tog., k. 2, m. 1, (k. 8, m. 1, k. 5, m. 1) 3 times, k. 1, p. 2, k. 2, p. 1.

6th row : K. 1, p. 2, k. 2, p. 1, (k. 7, p. 8) 3 times, k. 4.

7th row : K. 2 tog., k. 2, k. 4 tog., (k. 4 tog., k. 7, k. 4 tog.) 3 times, k. 1, p. 1.

8th row : K. 1, p. 1, k. 31.

K. 1 row plain, then slope the shoulder as for the first shoulder.

THE BACK

WORK this the same as the Front, but instead of dividing the sts. at the neck, repeat from the 10th to the 17th row 3 times more instead of twice, then from the 10th to the 15th row.

To Slope the Shoulders : Cast off 11 sts. at the beginning of the next 6 rows, then cast off the remaining sts.

THE NECK BAND

FIRST join the right shoulder seam, beginning at the arm end and taking 1 st. from each side at a time. Using No. 10 pins pick up and k. 15 sts. from the neck edge of the Left Front Shoulder, 34 sts. across the centre front,

15 sts. from the neck edge of Right Front Shoulder, and 40 sts. across the back neck edge, turn, and cast on 6 sts. (110 sts.).

Work 4 rows in garter-st.

1st dec. row : * K. 20, k. 2 tog. ; repeat from * to the end. K. 1 row (105 sts.).

2nd dec. row : * K. 15, k. 2 tog., repeat from * until 3 remain, k. 3. Cast off.

THE SLEEVES

BEGIN at the arm edge and with No. 10 pins cast on 80 sts. Work 16 rows in pattern as at the beginning of the Back.

Change to No. 9 pins and inc. 1 st. at both ends of the next row and every following 6th row until the 3rd inc. row has been worked (86 sts.). Work 9 rows more.

To Shape the Sleeve Top : Cast off 10 sts. at the beginning of the next 2 rows, then dec. 1 st. at beginning of next 40 rows (26 sts.).

Cast off 4 sts. at the beginning of the next 4 rows, then cast off the remaining sts.

Work another sleeve in the same way.

TO MAKE UP THE JUMPER. Do not press the knitting. Join the left shoulder seam as far as the neck-band, and press the seam with the edge of the iron only, for neatness. Set the sleeves into armholes and press these seams. Join the sleeve and side seams in one line and press. Sew a press-stud to the neck-band on the left shoulder.

CECILE'S
Cake-Making
LESSONS !

OTHELLOS

Little Iced Cakes With a Professional Look

THE CAKE MIXTURE

Two eggs
Three ounces of flour
Three ounces of castor sugar

FILLING

One ounce of plain chocolate
Three-quarters of a gill of cream
Vanilla essence

ICING

One pound of icing sugar
One ounce of plain chocolate
Three dessertspoonfuls of strong coffee
Three dessertspoonfuls of water
Vanilla flavouring
Cochineal

FOR these little cakes you require one or two trays of very shallow cake-tins, with a completely circular base. Grease them sparingly.

Break the eggs into a basin, add the sugar and whisk together until thick and creamy and free from dark streaks. If you draw your whisk slowly across the base, you will see if any dark streaks remain.

Sift the flour on to a sheet of paper, then sift it again by degrees, on top of the whisked eggs and sugar, folding it in lightly with a metal spoon. Drop a small teaspoonful of the mixture into each prepared tin, and bake slowly for about eight to ten minutes. They should be light and spongy. *This quantity should make about twenty-four small cakes.*

THE FILLING

GRATE the chocolate finely, and whisk the cream until it will just hang from the whisk. Mix these together lightly and flavour with vanilla. Spread the flat sides of your cakes (when cold) with filling and clap them together in pairs, moulding them to circular shapes.

THE ICING

RUB the icing sugar through a hair sieve. Divide into two equal portions, and put into separate basins.

Grate the chocolate finely and put into a small pan. Add the strong coffee and stir until dissolved, then cool slightly and add to one portion only of the sugar. Mix the icing to a smooth thick coating consistency, adding a little more coffee as required.

Arrange half the cakes on a cake rack, with a dish below, and taking a spoonful of icing at a time, coat each one carefully.

To the other half a pound of sugar, stir in two or three dessertspoonfuls of moderately hot water and mix as before. Flavour with vanilla, and tint to a very pale pink shade with a few drops of cochineal.

Coat the remaining cakes with pink icing.

When set, decorate the chocolate iced cakes with trails of pink icing, and vice versa.

FOR THE TRAILS.—Pick up the left-over icing and beat until smooth, keeping each colour separate, then put into an icing bag with a piping tube attached, and force on to the cakes, as shown.

WHERE YOU GO WRONG

YOU fill the tins too full and they rise over the top. They should be only half filled.

YOU over-cook the cakes, and they become crisp, instead of being soft and pliable.

YOU over-whip the cream, and it curdles.

YOU do not beat up the left-over icing before putting it into the icing bag, and the "trails" break when forced through the pipe.

Half the cakes are covered with pink icing, the rest with chocolate.

Cross your Heart

—and look your best !

MATERIALS.—7 ozs. of Sirdar Super Shetland Wool, 3-ply ; 1 pair each of No. 9 and No. 12 knitting needles, also 2 spare No. 9 needles with points at both ends.

TENSION.—Approx. 15 sts. to 2 ins. in width.

MEASUREMENTS.—Bust size, 34 ins. ; length from back shoulder to lower edge, 18 ins. ; sleeve down underarm, 5 ins.

ABBREVIATIONS.—K., knit ; p., purl ; st.(s), stitch(es) ; in.(s), inch(es) ; pat., pattern ; rep., repeat ; tog., together ; sl., slip ; p.s.s.o., pass slipped stitch over ; p.u.t., pick up thread lying between the needles and k. it.

The Back

USING No. 12 needles cast on 110 sts. and work in ribs of k. 1, p. 1 for 2½ ins.

Next row : Rib 5, * knit twice into next st., rib 4 ; rep. from * to end. (131 sts.) Change to No. 9 needles and pat. thus :

1st pat. row : P. 1, k. 2, * p. 5, twist 5 thus (sl. next 2 sts. on spare needle and leave at front of work, then sl. next st. on to 2nd spare needle and leave at back of work, k. 2, then p. 1 from 2nd spare needle, now k. 2 from 1st spare needle), rep. from * to 8 sts. of end, p. 5, k. 2, p. 1.

2nd pat. row : K. 1, * p. 2, k. 5, p. 2, k. 1 ; rep. from * to end.

3rd pat. row : P. 1, * k. 2, p. 5, k. 2, p. 1 ; rep. from * to end.

4th pat. row : As 2nd pat. row.

5th pat. row : P. 1, * p.u.t., k. 1, sl. 1, k. 1, p.s.s.o., p. 3, k. 2 tog., k. 1, p.u.t., p. 1 ; rep. from * to end.

6th pat. row : K. 2, * p. 2, k. 3 ; rep. from * finishing last rep. with k. 2 instead of k. 3.

7th pat. row : P. 2, * p.u.t., k. 1, sl. 1, k. 1, p.s.s.o., p. 1, k. 2 tog., k. 1, p.u.t., p. 3 ; rep.

from * finishing last rep. with p. 2 instead of p. 3.

8th pat. row : K. 3, * p. 2, k. 1, p. 2, k. 5 ; rep. from * finishing last rep. with k. 3 instead of k. 5. **9th pat. row :** P. 3, * twist 5 as before, p. 5 ; rep. from * finishing last rep. with p. 3 instead of p. 5.

10th pat. row : As 8th pat. row. **11th pat. row :** K. 3, * k. 2, p. 1, k. 2, p. 5 ; rep. from * finishing last rep. with p. 3 instead of p. 5. **12th pat. row :** As 8th pat. row.

13th pat. row : P. 2, * k. 2 tog., k. 1, p.u.t., p. 1, p.u.t., k. 1, sl. 1, k. 1, p.s.s.o., p. 3 ; rep. from * finishing last rep. with p. 2 instead of p. 3. **14th pat. row :** K. 2, * p. 2, k. 3 ; rep. from * finishing last rep. with k. 2 instead of k. 3.

15th pat. row : P. 1, * k. 2 tog., k. 1, p.u.t., p. 3, p.u.t., k. 1, sl. 1, k. 1, p.s.s.o., p. 1 ; rep. from * to end. **16th pat. row :** K. 1, * p. 2, k. 5, p. 2, k. 1 ; rep. from * to end.

These 16 rows form the pat. Proceed in pat. until work measures 12 ins. from cast-on edge.

Shape the Armholes (taking care to keep the continuity of the pat.) by casting off 5 sts. at start of next 6 rows. (101 sts.) Continue without further shaping until work measures 18 ins. from cast-on edge. Cast off.

The Front

CAST on and work exactly as for back until after armhole shapings have been completed and work measures 15 ins. from cast-on edge, then **Shape the Neck** thus :

Next row : Work in pat. over 45 sts., cast off 11, work in pat. to end.

Now working only over the last group of 45 sts. proceed in pat. but take 2 tog. at neck edge on every row until sts. are reduced to 31. Continue without further shaping until work measures 19 ins. from cast-on edge. Cast off. Join wool to inner (neck) edge of remaining sts. and work this side to match first side.

The Neck Band

USING No. 12 needles cast on 130 sts. and work in ribs of k. 1, p. 1 for 1 in. Cast off.

The Sleeves (two alike)

USING No. 9 needles cast on 91 sts. and work in stocking-st. for 20 rows but do not work into the back of the cast-on sts.

Now make a hem thus :

Next row : Fold work double lengthwise with p. side in, * k. through first st. on needle together with corresponding st. of cast-on row ; rep. from * to end.

Now commencing with a p. row proceed in stocking-st. for a further 4 ins.

Shape the Top by taking 2 tog. at end of every row until sts. are reduced to 45. Work a further 6 rows without shaping, then cast off 15 sts. at start of next 2 rows. Now, using wool double, work a further 16 rows on remaining 15 sts. Cast off.

To Make Up

JOIN all seams. Set sleeves into armholes. Fold neck band double and sew to neck edge.

In My Garden This Week

To grow runner beans without stakes, I know that they should be pinched out when they reach a certain stage of growing. When is that ?

WHEN 18 ins. high, but nip out side shoots when half that length. To prevent the " bushes " from blowing down in windy weather, drive a stake in each end of the row and run a length of string all round. This will keep them in position.

I don't think my brussels sprouts are making the progress they should. What's best to use to hurry them along ?

KEEP the surface of the soil round each plant well hoed. Sprinkle sulphate of ammonia around and water it in. Not too much of this, otherwise your plants will become tall and lanky.

I want to grow the biggest marrow ever. How do I feed it up so that it will ripen off for keeping.

DON'T attempt to grow more than three marrows on a plant, otherwise you won't get them any size. Nip off the end of runners 18 in. long so that they cannot make any further growth. Feed the plants with plenty of water. Regular doses of liquid manure will help, too.

M. E.

Blue Bird

A lovely jumper knitted in a brand-new stitch!

MATERIALS.—7 ozs. of Sirdar Super Shetland Wool, 3-ply; 1 pair each of No. 9 and No. 12 knitting needles; also two spare No. 9 needles with points at both ends.

TENSION.—Approx. 15 sts. to 2 ins. in width measured over pat. section worked on No. 9 needles.

MEASUREMENTS.—Bust size, 34 ins.; length from back shoulder to lower edge, 18½ ins.; sleeve down underarm, 17 ins.

ABBREVIATIONS.—K., knit; p., purl; st(s)., stitch(es); pat., pattern; rep., repeat; sl., slip; tog., together; p.s.s.o., pass slipped stitch over; inc., increase (by knitting twice into same st.); p.u.k., pick up thread lying between the two needles and k. into the back of it.

NOTE.—If difficulty is found in keeping the pat. correct when shaping work, knit any odd sts. at start or end of row in stocking-st. (making the p. side the right side) until the pat. will work in correctly again.

The Back

USING No. 12 needles, cast on 108 sts. and work in ribs of k. 1, p. 1 for 3 ins.

Next row—Rib 8, * inc. in next st., rib 4; rep. from * to 5 sts. of end, rib 5. (127 sts.)

Change to No. 9 needles and work in pat. thus:

1st pat. row—P. **2nd pat. row**—K. Rep. these 2 rows once.

5th pat. row—P. 3, * p.u.k., k. 2, sl. 1, k. 1, p.s.s.o., p. 5, k. 2 tog., k. 2, p.u.k., p. 5; rep. from *, finishing last rep. with p. 3 instead of p. 5.

6th pat. row—K. 4, * p. 3, k. 5, p. 3, k. 7; rep. from *, finishing last rep. with k. 4 instead of k. 7.

7th pat. row—P. 4, * p.u.k., k. 2, sl. 1, k. 1, p.s.s.o., p. 3, k. 2 tog., k. 2, p.u.k., p. 7; rep. from *, finishing last rep. with p. 4 instead of p. 7.

8th pat. row—K. 5, * p. 3, k. 3, p. 3, k. 9; rep. from *, finishing last rep. with k. 5 instead of k. 9.

9th pat. row—P. 5, * p.u.k., k. 2, sl. 1, k. 1, p.s.s.o., p. 1, k. 2 tog., k. 2, p.u.k., p. 9; rep. from *, finishing last rep. with p. 5 instead of p. 9.

10th pat. row—K. 6, * p. 3, k. 1, p. 3, k. 11; rep. from *, finishing last rep. with k. 6 instead of k. 11.

11th pat. row—P. 6, * twist 7 thus: Sl. 3 sts. on a spare needle and leave in *front* of work, sl. 1 st. on to a second spare needle and leave at *back* of work, k. 3, then p. 1 from second spare needle, k. 3 from first spare needle, then p. 11; rep. from *, finishing last rep. with p. 6 instead of p. 11. **12th pat. row**—Same as 10th pat. row.

13th pat. row—P. 5, * k. 2 tog., k. 2, p.u.k., p. 1, p.u.k., k. 2, sl. 1, k. 1, p.s.s.o., p. 9; rep. from *, finishing last rep. with p. 5 instead of p. 9. **14th pat. row**—Same as 8th pat. row.

15th pat. row—P. 4, * k. 2 tog., k. 2, p.u.k., p. 3, p.u.k., k. 2, sl. 1, k. 1, p.s.s.o., p. 7; rep. from *, finishing last rep. with p. 4 instead of p. 7. **16th pat. row**—Same as 6th pat. row. **17th pat. row**—P. 3, * k. 2 tog., k. 2, p.u.k., p. 5, p.u.k., k. 2, sl. 1, k. 1, p.s.s.o., p. 5; rep. from *, finishing last rep. with p. 3 instead of p. 5. **18th pat. row**—K. 3, * p. 3, k. 7, p. 3, k. 5; rep. from *, finishing last rep. with k. 3 instead of k. 5. **19th pat. row**—P. **20th pat. row**—K. Rep. last 2 rows once.

23rd pat. row—P. 3, * k. 2 tog., k. 2, p.u.k., p. 5, p.u.k., k. 2, sl. 1, k. 1, p.s.s.o., p. 5; rep. from *, finishing last rep. with p. 3 instead of p. 5.

24th pat. row—K. 3, * p. 3, k. 7, p. 3, k. 5; rep. from *, finishing last rep. with k. 3 instead of k. 5.

25th pat. row—P. 2, * k. 2 tog., k. 2, p.u.k., p. 7, p.u.k., k. 2, sl. 1, k. 1, p.s.s.o., p. 3; rep. from *, finishing last rep. with p. 2 instead of p. 3. **26th pat. row**—K. 2, * p. 3, k. 9, p. 3, k. 3; rep. from *, finishing last rep. with k. 2 instead of k. 3.

27th pat. row—P. 1, * k. 2 tog., k. 2, p.u.k., p. 9, p.u.k., k. 2, sl. 1, k. 1, p.s.s.o., p. 1; rep. from * to end.

28th pat. row—K. 1, * p. 3, k. 11, p. 3, k. 1; rep. from * to end.

29th pat. row—P. 1, k. 3, * p. 11, twist 7 (as in 11th row); rep. from *, finishing last rep. with k. 3, p. 1 instead of twist 7.

30th pat. row—Same as 28th pat. row. **31st pat. row**—P. 1, * p.u.k., k. 2, sl. 1, k. 1, p.s.s.o., p. 9, k. 2 tog., k. 2, p.u.k., p. 1; rep. from * to end.

32nd pat. row—Same as 26th pat. row. **33rd pat. row**—P. 2, * p.u.k., k. 2, sl. 1, k. 1, p.s.s.o., p. 7, k. 2 tog., k. 2, p.u.k., p. 3; rep. from *, finishing last rep. with p. 2 instead of p. 3.

34th pat. row—Same as 24th pat. row. **35th pat. row**—P. 3, * p.u.k., k. 2, sl. 1, k. 1, p.s.s.o., p. 5, k. 2 tog., k. 2, p.u.k., p. 5; rep. from *, finishing last rep. with p. 3 instead of p. 5. **36th pat. row**—K. 4, * p. 3, k. 5, p. 3, k. 7; rep. from *, finishing last rep. with k. 4 instead of k. 7.

These 36 rows form the pat. When the 22nd row of 3rd pat. from start has been completed **Shape the Armholes** by casting off 5 sts. at start of each of the next 6 rows, then cast off 3 sts. at start of next 2 rows. (91 sts.) Continue without further shaping until the 29th row of 5th pat. from start have been worked. Cast off.

The Front

CAST on and work exactly as for back until armhole shapings have been completed and sts. reduced to 91, then proceed without further shaping until 4 complete pats. from start have been worked. Now **Shape the Neck** thus:

Next row—P. 40, loosely cast off 11, p. to end.

Now, working only over the last set of 40 sts., proceed in pat., but take 2 tog. at neck edge on every row until sts. number 27. Work without shaping until the 32nd row of 5th pat. has been worked. Cast off.

Join wool to inner end of remaining 40 sts. and work this side to match 1st side.

The Sleeves (two alike)

USING No. 12 needles, cast on 60 sts. and work in ribs of k. 1, p. 1 for 3 ins.

Next row—Rib 6, * inc. in next st., rib 3; rep. from * to 2 sts. of end, rib 2. (73 sts.)

Still using No. 12 needles, work 1 complete pat. as set out for back, then change to No. 9 needles and continue in pat., but inc. 1 st. at both ends of needle on the next row and every following 6th row until sts. number 97. Proceed until the 24th row of 4th pat. has been worked. **Shape the Top** by taking 2 tog. at end of every row until sts. are reduced to 51. Work a further 14 rows, then cast off 17 sts. at start of next 2 rows. Work 18 rows in stocking-st. on the remaining 17 sts., using the p. side of work as the right side. Cast off.

The Neck Ribbing

USING No. 12 needles, cast on 130 sts. and work in ribs of k. 1, p. 1 for 16 rows. Cast off.

To Make Up

JOIN shoulder seams. Sew the side edges of extension at top of sleeve to the corresponding cast-off edges, then set sleeve into armhole. Join sleeve and side seams. Join neck ribbing to form a circle, fold double and stitch neck of jumper between. Lightly press work on the wrong side.

The JERSEY With A Soft BOW

It Is Worked In Feather Pattern And Single Rib

MATERIALS

SIX ounces of Patons Beehive Fingering 2-ply Patonised (or 4 ounces if short sleeves are worked); a pair each of No. 13 and No. 10 knitting needles; a No. 10 crochet hook; shoulder pads.

TENSION AND MEAS-UREMENTS

WORKED at a tension of one repeat of the pattern to 2 inches in width with No. 10 needles, the measurements on the diagram are attained without pressing

ABBREVIATIONS — TO BE READ BEFORE WORKING

K., KNIT PLAIN; p., purl; st., stitch; tog., together; inc., increase (by working into the front and back of the same st.); dec., decrease (by working 2 sts. tog.); m., make (by bringing the wool to the front of the needle and over it before knitting the next st.); single rib is k. 1 and p. 1 alternately. Directions in brackets are worked the number of times stated after the last bracket.

TO WORK THE BACK

BEGIN at the lower edge by casting on 120 sts. with No. 13 needles. Work 57 rows in single rib, working into the back of the sts. on the first row to give a neat edge.

INC. ROW: Rib 2, * inc., rib 4; repeat from * until 3 sts. remain, inc., rib 2. (144 sts.)

Change to No 10 needles and work in feather pattern as follows:

1ST ROW (right side): K. 2 tog. 3 times, * (m. 1, k. 1) 6 times, k. 2 tog. 6 times; repeat from *, ending the last repeat with k. 2 tog. 3 times, instead of 6 times.

2ND ROW: All purl.

3RD ROW: All knit.

4TH ROW: All knit.

These 4 rows form the pattern, so repeat them 23 times more to the armholes.

To Shape The Armholes.—Working entirely in single rib cast off 5 sts. at the beginning of the next 2 rows, then dec. 1 st. at both ends of the following 12 rows. (110 sts.)

Work 54 rows straight in single rib to bring the work to the shoulder line.

To Slope The Shoulders.—Cast off 12 sts. at the beginning of the next 6 rows, then cast off the remaining sts.

THE FRONT

WORK this exactly the same as the Back until the arm-hole shaping has been finished and 110 sts. remain, then divide the sts. for the neck opening as follows:

NEXT ROW (Right side): Rib 55, turn; leaving the remaining 55 sts. on a spare needle until needed for the Right Half Front.

** *The Left Half Front.*—Work 28 rows straight in single rib to the neck line.

To Shape The Neck.—Cast off 15 sts. at the beginning of the next row, then dec. 1 st. (neck edge) on every following row, until 36 sts. remain.

Work 24 rows more to the shoulder-line.

To Slope The Shoulder.—Cast off 12 sts. at the beginning of the next row and following 2 alternate rows. Fasten off.

The Right Half Front.—Return to the 55 sts. left on spare needle and with the right side of work facing repeat from ** on the Left Half Front to the end.

THE SLEEVES

BEGIN at the sleeve top by casting on 35 sts. with No. 10 needles. Work in single rib, increasing 1 st. at both ends of every row until there are 119 sts. for the full width of the sleeve.

Work 6 rows straight, then dec. 1 st. at both ends of the next row and every following 8th row, until the 21st dec. row has been worked. (77 sts.)

Work 3 rows straight.

Change to No. 13 needles and work 36 rows in single rib, then cast off loosely in rib with a No. 10 needle.

Work a second sleeve in the same way.

The Shape and Measurements of the Jersey.

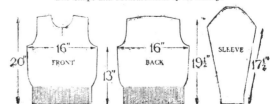

FOR SHORT SLEEVES

WORK the top as for long sleeves until there are 119 sts. for the full width of the sleeve.

Work 6 rows straight, then dec. 1 st. at both ends of the next row and every following 4th row, until the 7th dec. row has been worked. (105 sts.)

Work 3 rows straight.

Change to No. 13 needles and work 12 rows straight, then cast off loosely in rib with a No. 10 needle.

THE NECK BAND

WITH No. 13 needles cast on 16 sts. Work in single rib until strip measures 38 inches, then cast off.

TO MAKE UP THE JERSEY

DO not press. Join the shoulder seams, beginning at the armhole end and taking 1 st. from each side at a time.

Set the sleeves into the armholes and stroke these seams flat with the top of a thimble. Join the sleeve and side seams in one line. Sew the row ends at one side of the neck-band to neck edge, beginning and ending about ¾ of an inch from front opening. Sew in shoulder pads. With crochet hook work a row of double crochet round front neck opening.

The Midas Touch

Golden sequins turn a simple day
jumper into a sparkling one for evening

MATERIALS. — 9 oz. W.B. "Sonata" Crepe; 2 No. 12 and 2 No. 9 knitting needles; about 300 sequins.

MEASUREMENTS. — Bust, 34 ins.; length, 20 ins.

TENSION. — 6½ sts. to 1 in.

ABBREVIATIONS. — K. = knit; p. = purl; st. or sts. = stitch or stitches; rep. = repeat; tog. = together; m.st. = moss stitch (k. 1, p. 1 alternately); st.st. = stocking stitch (1 row k., 1 row p.); inc. = increase or increasing; dec. = decrease or decreasing; patt. = pattern; beg. = beginning; ins. = inches.

BACK. — With No. 12 needles cast on 91 sts. Work ½ in. in moss st.

Next row. — K.

Next row. — P.

Work in patt. thus: —

1st row. — K. 3, * p. 1, p. 3 tog. without slipping sts. off left-hand needle, k. same 3 sts. tog. without slipping sts. off, then p. same 3 sts. tog. and slip off left-hand needle, p. 1, k. 5; rep. from *, ending k. 3 instead of k. 5.

Work 5 rows in st.st., beg. and ending with a p. row.

7th row. — K. 8, * p. 1, p. 3 tog., k. same 3 sts. tog. and p. same 3 sts. tog., p. 1, k. 5; rep. from * to last 3 sts., k. 3.

Work 5 rows in st.st., beg. and ending with a p. row.

Rep. these 12 rows until work measures 5 ins., ending with a k. row. Change to No. 9 needles and continue in patt., inc. 1 st. both ends of next and every following 6th row until there are 111 sts. Work the extra sts. in patt. as sufficient are made.

Continue straight (if necessary) until work measures 11½ ins. Now inc. 1 st. both ends of next and every following 4th row until there are 131 sts., working the extra sts. in patt. as before. Continue straight until work measures 18 ins., ending with a row on wrong side.

Shape Shoulders. — Keeping the continuity of the patt., k. 2 tog. at both ends of next 10 rows (111 sts.), then cast off 3 sts. at beg. of next 8 rows (87 sts.), now cast off 10 sts. at beg. of next 6 rows. Cast off remaining 27 sts.

FRONT. — Proceed as given for back until work measures 11½ ins. Inc. 1 st. both ends of next row, then work 3 rows in patt.

Divide for Neck. 1st row. — Inc. in first st., work across 55 sts., cast off 1 st., work to last st., k. twice in last st. Continue in patt. on last set of 57 sts., keeping neck edge straight, and inc. 1 st. at side edge every 4th row until there are 65 sts. Continue straight in patt. (if necessary) until work measures 17¾ ins., ending at neck edge.

Next row. — Work 10, (work 2 tog.) 13 times, work to end.

Continue on these 52 sts. until work measures 18 ins., ending at sleeve edge.

Shape Shoulder. — Keeping the continuity of the knot patt. (or, if preferred, working from now on in st.st.), k. 2 tog. at beg. of next row, then dec. 1 st. at same edge every row until 42 sts. remain.

Next row. — Cast off 3 sts., work to end.

Next row. — Work to end.

Rep. last 2 rows 3 times more.

Next row. — Cast off 10 sts., work to end.

Next row. — Work to end.

Rep. last 2 rows once.

Cast off remaining 10 sts.

Rejoin yarn at neck edge and work to end. Complete to match first side.

Armhole Borders (make 2). With No. 12 needles cast on 5 sts. Work 11 ins. in m.st. Cast off.

Neck Border. — With No. 12 needles cast on 5 sts. Work 18 ins. in m.st. Cast off.

TO MAKE UP. — Press work lightly on wrong side with hot iron and damp cloth. Join side seams, leaving about 6 ins. open for armholes. Join shoulder seams. Sew borders round armholes and neck. Press seams. Sew on the sequins, using the "knots" of the patt. as a guide, and massing the sequins more closely on the shoulders, and round back and front neck edges.

WOMAN'S WEEKLY

EVERY TUESDAY   № 1829 · VOL. LXX.   NOVEMBER · 23 · 1946

3^{d.}

CARDIGAN TO-DAY * JERSEY NEXT WEEK *

THE CARDIGAN

of a

LOVELY SET

This Week We Give The Instructions For Knitting The Cardigan. The Jersey Instructions Will Appear Next Week

MATERIALS

*E*IGHT ounces of Sirdar Super Shetland Wool, 3-ply, in natural shade, or if you intend knitting the set, get 5 ounces more for the jumper, which will be published in next week's WOMAN'S WEEKLY, ½ ounce of each of the following shades will be enough for the cardigan and jumper, red, yellow, brown, green, and blue; a pair each of No. 9 and No. 12 knitting needles.

TENSION AND MEASUREMENTS

*W*ORKED at a tension of 7 sts. to the inch in width on No. 9 needles, the measurements on the diagram are attained after light pressing.

ABBREVIATIONS—TO BE READ BEFORE WORKING

*K*NIT; p., purl; tog., together; inc., increase (by working into the back and front of the same st.); dec., decrease (by taking 2 sts. tog.); st., stitch; s.s., stocking stitch (k. on the right side and p. back), single rib is k. 1 and p. 1 alternately. Directions in brackets are worked the number of times stated after the last bracket; n., natural; g., green; bl., blue; br., brown; y., yellow.

TO WORK THE BACK

*B*EGIN at the lower edge and with No. 12 needles and n. wool, cast on 115 sts.

1ST ROW (RIGHT SIDE): P. 1, * k. 1, p. 1; repeat from * to end of row.

2ND ROW: K. 1, * p. 1, k. 1; repeat from * to end.

Repeat these 2 rows until 44 rows are worked.

NEXT ROW (RIGHT SIDE): K. 19, (inc. in the next st., k. 23) 1 times. (119 sts.)

Change to No. 9 needles and s.s. 3 rows.

Now work s.s. with an inc. into the 4th st. from each end of the next row and every following 6th row, until 8 inc. rows are worked. (135 sts.)

S.s. 29 rows to the armholes.

To Shape The Armholes.—Cast off 5 sts. at the beginning of each of the next 2 rows. (125 sts.) Then work 2 sts. tog. at each end of the next 13 rows. (99 sts.)

Now dec. 1 st. at each end of the next 2 alternate rows. (95 sts.)

S.s. 37 rows to the shoulder line.

To Slope The Shoulders.—Cast off 7 sts. at the beginning of the next 6 rows, then cast off the remaining sts.

THE LEFT FRONT

*W*ITH n. wool and No. 12 needles, cast on 57 sts.

Work 44 rows in rib as on the Back.

NEXT ROW (RIGHT SIDE): K. 17, (inc., k. 19) twice. (59 sts.)

Change to No. 9 needles and s.s. 3 rows.

Continue in s.s. with an inc. into the 4th st. from the beginning of the next row (seam end) and every following 6th row, until 8 increases have been worked. (67 sts.) P. 1 row.

The front slope is begun on the next row thus: * Dec. 1 st. at the front end. P. 1 row.

Dec. 1 st. at the front end of the next row. S.s. 3 rows. Repeat the last 6 rows from * 4 times more. (57 sts.)

To Shape The Armhole.—Cast off 5 sts. at the beginning of the next row, work until 2 sts. remain, k. 2 tog. for the front slope. (51 sts.) P. 1 row.

Work 2 sts. tog. at the armhole end of the next 13 rows and at the front end of the 1st, 5th, 7th, 11th, and 13th of these rows. (33 sts.) P. 1 row.

Work 2 sts. tog. at the arm end of the next row. P. 1 row.

Work 2 sts. tog. at both ends of the next row. (30 sts.)

** P. 1 row. Work 2 sts. tog. at the front end of next row. S.s. 3 rows.

Work 2 sts. tog. at the front end of the next row. Repeat from ** 6 times more. (16 sts.) S.s. 5 rows.

To Slope The Shoulder.—Cast off 8 sts. at the beginning of the next row and the following alternate row (arm end). Fasten off.

THE RIGHT FRONT

*W*ORK from the Left Front instructions, but reverse the shaping as follows: The first side seam inc. will be made in the 4th st. from the end of the row. When the underarm is reached, work one row more than on opposite front, so as to begin the armhole by casting off 5 sts. at the beginning of a p. row (wrong side) and omit the " p. 1 row " given there. The remainder of the armhole rows will be worked in the same way, but bear in mind that the front slope decrease is at the beginning of rows, when the rest of the shaping will follow suit. Work one row more to the shoulder, so that the sts. will be cast off on the wrong side of the knitting.

THE RIGHT FRONT BORDER

*W*ITH No. 9 needles, pick up and k. 100 sts. with n. wool from the shaped edge at front neck (1 st. from every row).

1ST ROW (WRONG SIDE): P. 1 g., 1 y., * 1 g., 1 y., 3 g., 1 y., repeat from * until 2 sts. remain, 2 tog. g. at front end.

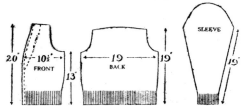

The Shape and Measurements of the Cardigan

2ND ROW : K. 3 tog. front end,
k. to end.

3RD ROW : P. 1 bl., 2 n., * 2 bl.,
2 n.; repeat from * until 2 sts.
remain, p. 2 tog., bl.

4TH ROW : K. 3 tog., bl., front
end, 1 bl., * 2 n., 2 bl.; repeat
from * to end.

5TH ROW : P. * 2 n., 2 red ;
repeat from * until 2 remain,
p. 2 tog. n.

6TH ROW : K. 3 tog. r., k. 1 r.,
* 2 n., 2 r.; repeat from * until
1 st. remains, 1 n.

7TH ROW : P. n. with 2 tog. at
the front end.

8TH ROW : K. 3 tog., y. front
end, 1 g., 1 y., * 3 g., 1 y., 1 g.,
1 y. ; repeat from * until 1 st.
remains, 1 g.

9TH ROW : As 7th row.

10TH ROW : K. 3 tog., * 1 br.,
1 n., 3 br., 1 n., (1 br., 2 n.) twice;
repeat from * to end.

11TH ROW : P. (1 n., 1 br.)
twice, 3 n., 3 br., * 3 n., 1 br., 1 n.,
1 br., 3 n., 3 br. ; repeat from *
until 3 remain, 1 n., 2 tog. n.

12TH ROW : K. 3 tog. y., 1 br.,
1 y., 2 br., 1 y., (1 br., 1 y.) twice,
* 2 br., 1 y., 1 br., 1 y., 2 br.,
1 y., (1 br., 1 y.) twice ; repeat
from * to end.

13TH ROW : P. 2 y., 1 br., 2 y.,
3 br., * 1 y., 3 br., 2 y., 1 br.,
2 y., 3 br.; repeat from * until
2 remain, p. 2 tog. y.

14TH ROW : K. 3 tog. br., 1 br.,
1 y., (1 br., 1 y.) twice, * 2 br.,
1 y., 1 br., 1 y., 2 br., 1 y., (1 br.,
1 y.) twice ; repeat from * to end.

15TH ROW : P. (1 n., 1 br.)
twice, * 3 n., 3 br., 3 n., 1 br.,
1 n., 1 br.; repeat from * until 3
remain, 1 n., 2 tog. n.

16TH ROW : K. 3 tog. n., 1 br.,
2 n., * 1 br., 1 n., 3 br., 1 n.,
(1 br., 2 n.) twice ; repeat from
* to end.

17TH ROW : P. n. with 2 tog.
at the front end.

18TH ROW : K. 3 tog. g.,
k. 2 g., 1 y., 1 g., 1 y., * 3 g.,
1 y., 1 g., 1 y.; repeat from *
until 1 st. remains, 1.g.

Cast off with n. wool.

THE LEFT FRONT BORDER

WORK from the directions for the Right Front Border,
picking up 100 sts. on the right side, from the shoulder
to the lower edge of the front slope, then work the
rows backwards, to reverse the sloped end.

THE SLEEVES

WITH No. 12 needles, cast on 55 sts. with n. wool.   Rib
30 rows.

Change to No. 9 needles and work 2 rows in s.s.

Inc. 1 st. at each end of the next row and every following
6th row, until 17 increases have been worked.   (89 sts.)
S.s. 11 rows.

Inc. at each end of the next row and every following 6th
row, until 6 inc. rows more are worked.   (101 sts.)   S.s. 5 rows.

To Shape The Top.—Work 2 sts. tog. at each end of the
next 3 rows.   P. 1 row.

Repeat the last 4 rows twice more.   (83 sts.)

Work 2 sts. tog. at each end of next row and the following
alternate rows, for 16 dec. rows more.   (51 sts.).   P. 1 row.

Work 2 sts. tog. at each end of the next 16 rows.   (19 sts.)
Cast off.

Work the second sleeve in the same way.

THE FRONT BAND

WITH n. wool and No. 12 needles, cast on 11 sts.

1ST ROW (RIGHT SIDE) : K. 2, p. 1, * k. 1, p.1 ;
repeat from *, ending with k. 2.

2ND ROW : K. 1, * p. 1, k. 1 ; repeat from * to end.

Repeat these 2 rows twice more.

1ST BUTTONHOLE ROW : Rib 6, cast off 4. leaving 1 st. on
needle.

2ND ROW : Rib 1, cast on 4 sts. over those cast off to complete the buttonhole, rib to end.

Work 16 rows.

Repeat the last 18 rows until the 7th buttonhole is completed.

Work straight for length needed for both fronts and back
neck, but do not cast off until the band is sewn on.

TO MAKE UP THE CARDIGAN

FIRST press all parts except the rib,
with a hot iron, over a damp cloth.
Sew the shoulder seams, beginning
at the arm end and taking one stitch
from each side at a time. Now sew on the
front band, after tacking in position,
beginning at the lower end of the right
front, with the buttonhole end of the
band. Stretch the band a little when
tacking round the back of the neck, and
cast off the band sts. when within two
inches of the lower edge of the left front.
Sew on the wrong side alternately taking
1 st. from the edge of the band and one
from the front, so that the seam will be
quite flat when finished and stroked with
the top of a thimble. Set the sleeves into
the armholes and press these seams while
the work is open, then sew side and sleeve
seams in one line and press. Sew on the
buttons opposite the buttonholes.

With FAIR ISLE Across The Yoke

A Lovely Jersey To Match The Cardigan Which Appeared In Last Week's Issue

of each of the next 2 rows. Work 2 sts. tog. at each end of the next 11 rows (103 sts.), then work 2 sts. tog. at each end of the next 3 alternate rows. (97 sts.) S.s. 41 rows.

To Shape Shoulders And Neck.—Cast off 6 sts., then k. until there are 27 on this needle, turn and p. 27.

NEXT ROW : Cast off 6 sts. and k. until there are 17 on needle, turn and p. 17.

NEXT ROW : Cast off 6, k. until there are 7 on needle, turn and p. 7.

Cast off 7 sts. then k. 1 row right across all the sts.

With n. wool begin the second shoulder slope, as given for first shoulder, but p. instead of k. and vice versa. Leave 47 sts. for the neckband.

THE FRONT

WORK as for the Back until the armhole shaping is finished and 97 sts. remain. S.s. 6 rows.

Work in pattern as follows :

1ST ROW (wrong side) : P. 1 g., * 1 y., 3 g., 1 y., 1 g.; repeat from * to end.

2ND ROW : K. n.

3RD ROW : S.s. 1 n., * 2 bl., 2 n.; repeat from * to end.

4TH ROW : As 3rd row.

5TH ROW : S.s. * 2 r., 2 n.; repeat from * until 1 st. remains, 1 r.

6TH ROW : As 5th row.

7TH ROW : P. n.

8TH ROW : K. 1 g., * 1 y., 3 g., 1 y., 1 g.; repeat from * to end.

9TH ROW : P. n.

10TH ROW : K. 1 br., * 2 n., 1 br., 1 n., 3 br., 1 n., 1 br., 2 n., 1 br.; repeat from * to end.

11TH ROW : P. 1 n., * 1 br., 3 n., 3 br., 3 n., 1 br., 1 n.; repeat from * to end.

12TH ROW : K. 1 y., * 1 br., 1 y., 2 br., 1 y., 1 br., 1 y., 2 br., 1 y., 1 br., 1 y.; repeat from * to end.

13TH ROW : P. 1 br., * 2 y., 3 br., 1 y., 3 br., 2 y., 1 br.; repeat from * to end.

Now work from the 12th row back to the 1st row inclusive (25 rows), then from the 9th to the 13th row inclusive (but k. instead of p. and vice versa), then backwards from the 12th to the 8th row inclusive to finish the colour pattern.

Work both shoulders all n. as given on the Back.

BACK NECK BAND

SLIP the 47 back neck sts. on a No. 12 needle.

NEXT ROW : (With No. 12 needle). Pick up and k. 3 at neck edge of shoulder; (k. 4, pick up 1) twice, k. 31 across back of neck, (pick up 1, k. 4) twice, pick up and k. 3. (57 sts.)

Work 5 rows in rib. Cast off with No. 9 needles.

Front Neck Band.—Work exactly the same as back neckband.

MATERIALS

FIVE ounces of *Sirdar Super Shetland Wool, 3-ply,* in natural shade ; ½ an ounce of each of the following shades : red, yellow, brown, green, and blue, but if you have worked the cardigan in last week's WOMAN'S WEEKLY you will have enough left for the colour work ; a pair each of No. 9 and No. 12 knitting needles.

TENSION AND MEASUREMENTS

WORKED at a tension of 7 sts. to the inch in width on No. 9 needles, the measurements on the diagram are attained after light pressing.

ABBREVIATIONS—TO BE READ BEFORE WORKING

K., KNIT ; p., purl ; tog., together ; inc., increase (by working into the back and front of the same stitch) ; st., stitch ; s.s., stocking stitch (k. on the right and p. back) ; single rib is k. 1 and p. 1 alternately ; directions in brackets are worked the number of times stated after the last bracket ; n., natural ; bl., blue ; br., brown ; g., green ; y., yellow.

TO WORK THE BACK

BEGIN at the lower edge and with n. wool and No. 12 needles cast on 111 sts.

1ST ROW (right side) : P. 1, * k. 1, p. 1 ; repeat from * to end.

2ND ROW : K. 1, * p. 1, k. 1 ; repeat from * to end.

Repeat these 2 rows until 40 rows are worked altogether.

NEXT ROW (right side) : K. 6, inc., (k. 13, inc.) 7 times, k. 6. (119 sts.)

Change to No. 9 needles and s.s. 3 rows.

Now begin the slope of the side seam with an inc. into the 4th st., from each end of the next row and every following 6th row until 8 inc. rows have been worked. (135 sts.) S.s. 29 rows.

To Shape The Armholes.—Cast off 5 sts. at the beginning

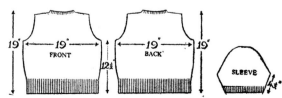

The Shape and Measurements of the Jersey.

THE SLEEVES

WITH No. 12 needles cast on 93 sts. with n. wool.
Work 20 rows in rib as back waist.

With No. 9 needles k. 1 row and p. 1 row. Continue in s.s. with an inc. into the 4th st. from each end of the next row and three following 6th rows. (101 sts.) S.s. 5 rows.

To Shape The Top Of Sleeve.—Dec. 1 st. at each end of next 3 rows. P. 1 row.

Repeat the last 4 rows twice more. (83 sts.)

Work 2 sts. tog. at each end of next row and following 15 alternate rows. (51 sts.) P. 1 row. Work 2 sts. tog. at each end of the next 16 rows. (19 sts.) Cast off.

Work the second sleeve in the same way.

TO MAKE UP THE JERSEY

FIRST press with a hot iron over a damp cloth. Sew the shoulder seams, beginning at the arm end and taking 1 st. from each side at a time. Sew sleeves into armholes and press these seams while the work is open. Sew sleeve and side seams in one line and press.

MATERIALS : 8 oz. (5 oz. Black, 2 oz. Red and 1 oz. White) of " Sirdar " 3-ply Super Shetland Wool ; a pair each of No. 9 and No. 12 knitting needles.

If you prefer a different colour scheme, why not try a green background with stripes of blue and white ; or two shades of blue on a pink background.

MEASUREMENT (after pressing) : Length from lower edge to top of shoulder, 19½ inches. Length of sleeve along seam, 19 inches. To fit a 36-inch bust.

TENSION : 7 sts. and 11 rows to 1 inch.

ABBREVIATIONS : St(s)., stitch(es) ; k., knit ; p., purl ; tog., together ; rep., repeat ; rem., remain(s)(der)(ing) ; inc., increase(ing) ; dec., decrease(ing) ; R, red wool ; W, white wool ; B, black wool.; patt., pattern.

The Back

WITH No. 12 needles cast on 100 sts. in the Black wool and k. 1, p. 1 rib for 35 rows.

36th row : Rib 10, * inc., rib 2 ; rep. from *, ending row by inc., rib 11 (127 sts.).

Now change to No. 9 needles and patt. as follows :

1st row : K 7 R, * 1 W, 8 R, 3 B, 1 R, 3 B, 1 R, 3 B, 8 R ; rep. from *, ending row by 1 W, 7 R.

2nd row : P. 7 R, * 1 W, 8 R, 3 B, 1 R, 3 B, 1 R, 3 B, 8 R ; rep. from *, ending by 1 W, 7 R.

Rep. these 2 rows three times more (8 rows in all).

9th row : K. 7 B, * 1 W, 27 B ; rep. from *, ending row by 1 W, 7 B.

10th row : P. 7 B, * 1 W, 27 B ; rep. from *, ending row by 1 W, 7 B.

11th row : As 9th row. **12th row :** As 2nd row. **13th row :** As 9th row. **14th row :** As 10th row.

15th row : As 9th row ; rep. from 12th row to 15th row inclusive once more (19 rows in all).

20th row : As 2nd row ; rep. 1st and 2nd rows three times more (26 rows in all).

27th row : As 1st row.

28th row : All p. in White.

These 28 rows compose the patt.

Work straight in patt. until the piece measures 11½ inches from the lower edge.

To Shape the Armholes : Cast off 3 sts. at the beginning of each of the next 6 rows, then k. 2 tog. at the end of each row, until 95 sts. rem. Work straight until the piece measures 18 inches from lower edge. Cast off.

The Front

WORK as for the Back, making the same dec. for the armholes (95 sts.) and until the piece measures 16 inches from the lower edge.

To Shape the Neck : Next row : Work patt. for 42 sts., cast off 11, work patt. to end. Leave the first set of 42 sts. for the present and work **One Shoulder thus :** On the Neck edge k. 2 tog. every row until 27 sts. rem. Continue straight until the piece measures 19 inches from the lower edge. Cast off. Now revert to the set of 42 sts. and work the opposite Shoulder in the same way, and to match.

The Sleeves (both alike)

WITH No. 12 needles cast on 60 sts. in Black wool and k. 1, p. 1 rib for 34 rows. Change to No. 9 needles and stocking-st., but inc. one st. at both ends of every 8th row until there are 86 sts. Work straight for the length required.

To Shape the Top of Sleeve : K. 2 tog. at both ends of every row until 10 sts. rem. Cast off.

The Collar

WITH No. 12 needles cast on 130 sts. in Black wool and k. 1, p. 1 rib for 16 rows. Cast off.

Assembly and Finish

SEAM up the shoulders and sew collar (folded in two lengthwise) to neck edge. Neatly sew tops of sleeves into the armholes, then carefully press on the wrong side, while garment is still open, under a damp cloth with a hot iron.

Sew up the rem. seams and press seams.

The Beret

MATERIALS : 4 oz. (3 oz. Red and 1 oz. Black) of " Sirdar," 3-ply Super Shetland Wool ; a pair of No. 12 knitting needles ; a 42-inch long piece of milliners' wire.

MEASUREMENTS : To fit an average-size head.

ABBREVIATIONS : St(s)., stitch(es) ; k., knit ; p., purl ; tog., together ; rep., repeat ; rem., remain(s)(der)(ing) ; inc., increase(ing) ; dec., decrease(ing).

USING the Red wool doubled, cast on 119 sts.

1st row : All k.

2nd row : All p. (and similarly every subsequent **even-numbered** row).

3rd row : K. 16, * inc., (by picking up a double thread from previous row and knitting into the back of it), k. 17 ; rep. from *, end row by inc., k. 1.

5th row : K. 17, * inc., k. 18 ; rep. from *, ending row by inc., k. 1.

7th row : K. 18, * inc., k. 19 ; rep. from *, end row by inc., k. 1.

9th row : K. 19, * inc., k. 20 ; rep. from *, end row by inc., k. 1.

11th row : K. 20, * inc., k. 21 ; rep. from *, end row by inc., k. 1.

13th row : K. 21, * inc., k. 22 ; rep. from *, end row by inc., k. 1.

15th row : K. 22, * inc., k. 23 ; rep. from *, end row by inc., k. 1.

17th row : K. 23, * inc., k. 24 ; rep. from *, end row by inc., k. 1.

Continue to inc. in this manner—except that there will be one st. more to be worked between each inc. in every odd row—until 30 rows have in all been worked (217 sts.).

Now continue as follows : **31st row :** K. 30, * inc., k. 31 ; rep. from * until 32 sts. rem., then inc., k. 22 ; turn the work and leave the rem. 10 sts. unworked on the needle.

32nd row : Purl until 10 sts. rem. ; turn.

33rd row : K. 21, * inc., k. 32 ; rep. from * until 32 sts. rem., inc., k. 12 ; turn.

34th row : P. until 20 rem. ; turn.

35th row : K. 12 * inc., k. 33 ; rep. from * until 33 sts. rem., inc., k. 3 ; turn.

36th row : P. until 30 sts. rem. ; turn.

37th row : K. 37, * inc., k. 34 ; rep. from * until 66 sts. rem., inc., k. 26 ; turn.

38th row : P. until 40 sts. rem. ; turn.

39th row : K. 29, * inc., k. 35 ; rep. from * until 66 sts. rem., inc., k. 16 ; turn.

40th row : P. until 50 sts. rem. ; turn.

41st row : K. 19, * inc., k. 36 ; rep. from * until 66 sts. rem., inc., k. 6 ; turn.

42nd row : P. 187.

43rd row : K. all the sts. across. (247 sts.).

Work straight for 3 rows on these 247 sts., then continue as follows :

1st row : K. 32, * k. 2 tog., k. 35 ; rep. from *, end row by k. 2 tog., k. 32, k. 2 tog., k. 29, k. 2 tog.

2nd row : All p. (Likewise every following even row).

3rd row : K. 31, * k. 2 tog., k. 34 ; rep. from *, end row by k. 2 tog., k. 31, k. 2 tog., k. 28, k. 2 tog.

5th row : K. 30, * k. 2 tog., k. 33 ; rep. from *, end row by k. 2 tog., k. 30, k. 2 tog., k. 27, k. 2 tog.

7th row : K. 29, * k. 2 tog., k. 32 ; rep. from *, end row by k. 2 tog., k. 29, k. 2 tog., k. 26, k. 2 tog.

9th row : K. 28, * k. 2 tog., k. 31 ; rep. from *, end row by k. 2 tog., k. 28, k. 2 tog., k. 25, k. 2 tog.

11th row : K. 27, * k. 2 tog., k. 30 ; rep. from *, end row by k. 2 tog., k. 27, k. 2 tog., k. 24, k. 2 tog.

13th row : K. 26, * k. 2 tog., k. 29 ; rep. from *, end row by k. 2 tog., k. 26, k. 2 tog., k. 23, k. 2 tog.

15th row : K. 25, * k. 2 tog., k. 28 ; rep. from *, end row by k. 2 tog., k. 25, k. 2 tog., k. 22, k. 2 tog. Continue to dec. in this way, working 1 st. fewer between each dec. every row (even-numbered), until 14 sts. rem.

Next row (wrong side) : P. 2 tog. for the entire row (7 sts.). Break off the wool, leaving an end to pass through the seven sts., draw together and secure.

The Band.

WITH the Black wool (used singly), cast on 14 sts. and work in a k. 1, p. 1 rib for 40 inches. Cast off.

Assembly and Finish.

CAREFULLY press on the wrong side under a damp cloth with a hot iron.

Neatly sew up the seams and press, then sew on the band, leaving the two ends loose at the back ; press the seams. Form a circle with the milliners' wire and fit inside. Sew on the feather, as illustrated.

With A Neat Little Collar

**This Pretty Jersey
Is Knitted In A
New Version Of
Tuft Stitch.**

MATERIALS

*E*IGHT ounces of Sirdar Majestic Wool, 3-ply, or six ounces
if short sleeves are worked; a pair each of No. 9 and No.
12 knitting needles.

TENSION AND MEASUREMENTS

*W*ORKED at a tension of 7 sts. to the inch in width on the
stocking stitch with No. 9 needles, the measurements
on the diagram are attained after light pressing.

ABBREVIATIONS—TO BE READ BEFORE WORKING

*K*NIT plain; p., purl; st., stitch; tog., together;
inc., increase (by working into the front and back of the
same st.); dec., decrease (by working 2 sts. tog.); m.,
make (by bringing the wool to the front of the needle and over it
before knitting the next st.); s.s., stocking stitch (k. on the right
side and p. back); single rib is k. 1 and p. 1 alternately. Directions in brackets are worked the number of times stated after the
last bracket.

TO WORK THE BACK

*B*EGIN at the lower edge and with No. 12 needles cast on
100 sts. Work 35 rows in single rib, working into the
back of the sts. on the 1st row to give a neat edge.

INC. Row: P. 6, * inc., p. 2; repeat from *, ending the
row with inc., rib 6. (130 sts.)

Change to No. 9 needles and work in pattern as follows:

1ST Row: P. 2, * k. 1, p. 4; repeat from * until 3 sts.
remain, k. 1, p. 2.

2ND Row: K. 2, * p. 1, k. 4; repeat from * until 3 remain,
p. 1, k. 2.

3RD Row: P. 2, * make a tuft thus: (k. 1, p. 1) twice, k. 1,
all into the next st., turn and k. the 5 tuft sts., turn, cast off
4 sts., which completes one tuft, p. 4, k. 1, p. 4; repeat from
*, ending the last repeat with p. 2 instead of p. 4.

4TH Row: As 2nd row.

Repeat these 4 rows four times more.

21ST Row: As 1st row.

The Shape and Measurements of the Jersey.

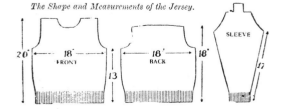

22ND ROW : As 2nd row.
23RD ROW : P. 2, * k. 1, p. 4, tuft, p. 4 ; repeat from *, ending the last repeat with p. 2.
24TH ROW : As 2nd row.
Repeat the last 4 rows four times more.
These 40 rows form the pattern, so repeat them once more and the first 8 rows again, to the armholes.
To Shape The Armholes.—Cast off 3 sts. at the beginning of the next 6 rows, then dec. 1 st. at both ends of the following 11 rows, when 90 sts. will remain. (It is quite easy to keep the pattern correct when shaping if it is noted that on the first 20 rows a line of 5 tufts is worked on every other k. rib, and on the last 20 rows a similar line of 5 tufts is worked on the alternating k. ribs.)
Work 40 rows straight, beginning with the 26th pattern row, when 3 complete patterns and the first 25 rows of the 4th pattern from the beginning will have been worked. Cast off straight across.

THE FRONT

WORK the first 36 rows as on the back. (130 sts.)
Change to No. 9 needles and work in pattern thus :
1ST ROW : P. 2, * k. 1, p. 4 ; repeat from *, ending with p. 2.
2ND ROW : K. 2, * p. 1, k. 4 ; repeat from *, ending with k. 2.
3RD ROW : P. 2, (tuft, p. 4, k. 1, p. 4) 4 times, tuft, p. 4, k. 1, p. 2, (m. 1, k. 2 tog.) 15 times, p. 2, (tuft, p. 4, k. 1, p. 4) 4 times, tuft, p. 4, k. 1, p. 2.
4TH ROW : K. 2, (p. 1, k. 4) 9 times, p. 1, k. 2, p. 30 centre panel sts., k. 2, (p. 1, k. 4) 9 times, p. 1, k. 2.
5TH ROW : P. 2, (k. 1, p. 4) 9 times, k. 1, p. 2, m. 1; k. 2 tog., k. 26, m. 1, k. 2 tog., p. 2, (k. 1, p. 4) 9 times, k. 1, p. 2.
6TH ROW : K. 2, (p. 1, k. 4) 9 times, p. 1, k. 2, p. 30, k. 2, (p. 1, k. 4) 9 times, p. 1, k. 2.
7TH ROW : P. 2, (tuft, p. 4, k. 1, p. 4) 4 times, tuft, p. 4, k. 1, p. 2, m. 1, k. 2 tog., k. 26, m. 1, k. 2 tog., p. 2, (tuft, p. 4, k. 1, p. 4) 4 times, tuft, p. 4, k. 1, p. 2.
8TH ROW : As 6th row.
Repeat from the 5th row to the 8th row 3 times more.
21ST ROW : As 5th row.
22ND ROW : As 6th row.
23RD ROW : P. 2, (k. 1, p. 4, tuft, p. 4) 4 times, k. 1, p. 4, tuft, p. 2, m. 1, k. 2 tog., k. 26, m. 1, k. 2 tog., p. 2, (k. 1 p. 4, tuft, p. 4) 4 times, k. 1, p. 4, tuft, p. 2.
24TH ROW : As 6th row.
Now repeat the last 4 rows four times more.
These 40 rows complete the pattern.
Work one complete pattern more and 8 rows of the next pattern, but instead of the first 4 pattern rows begin at the 5th row and repeat the 5th to 8th pattern rows 4 times instead of 3 times.
To Shape The Armholes.—Cast off 3 sts. at the beginning of the next 6 rows, then dec. 1 st. at both ends of the next 11 rows, when 90 sts. will remain. (Note that the s.s. panel with a row of holes each side, formed by the sts. " m. 1, k. 2 tog.," is continued throughout the 17 armhole rows.)
Work 15 rows more, when there will be 3 complete patterns of 40 rows from the beginning.
The Yoke.—NEXT ROW : K. 2, (m. 1, k. 2 tog.) 15 times, k. 26, (m. 1, k. 2 tog.) 15 times, k. 2.
Purl 1 row, knit 1 row, and purl 1 row.
Now continue in s.s. and shape the neck as follows :
NEXT ROW : K. 40 for the Left Front Shoulder and leave these sts. on a spare needle, cast off 10 sts. for the neck, k. to end. (40 sts.)
The Right Front Shoulder.—Dec. 1 st. at the neck edge of the next 13 rows, when 27 sts. will remain.
Work 16 rows more, than cast off.
The Left Front Shoulder.—Return to the first set of 40 sts. and work this shoulder the same as the first one.

THE SLEEVES

BEGIN at the wrist and with No. 12 needles cast on 58 sts. Work 30 rows in single rib, working into the back of the sts. on the first row to give a neat edge.
INC. ROW : Inc., (p. 4, inc.) 11 times, p. 2. (70 sts.)
Change to No. 9 needles and work one pattern of 40 rows as on the Back, then work the first 10 pattern rows again. Inc. 1 st. at both ends of the next row and every following

6th row until the 10th inc. row has been worked, when there will be 90 sts., working the extra sts. in pattern.
Work 15 rows more, or for length required.
To Shape The Sleeve Top.—Dec. 1 st. at the beginning of the next 40 rows. (50 sts.)
Work 20 rows straight in pattern.
Cast off 17 sts. at the beginning of the next 2 rows. (16 sts.)
Work 18 rows more on the centre 16 sts. then cast off.
Make another sleeve in the same way.

FOR SHORT SLEEVES

BEGIN at the arm edge and with No. 12 needles cast on 80 sts. Work 12 rows in single rib.
INC. ROW : * P. 7, inc.; repeat from * to end. (90 sts.)
Change to No. 9 needles and work 40 rows in pattern as on the Back, then shape the top as for the long sleeves.

THE COLLAR

BEGIN at the neck edge and with No. 12 needles cast on 116 sts. Work 4 rows in single rib, decreasing 1 st. at the end of the last row. (115 sts.)
Change to No. 9 needles and work the first 2 pattern rows as on the Back.
3RD ROW : P. 2, * tuft, p. 4, k. 1, p. 4; repeat from * until 3 sts. remain, tuft, p. 2.
4TH ROW : As 2nd row on Back.
Repeat these 4 rows twice more, then cast off straight across.

TO MAKE UP THE JERSEY

FIRST press all parts except the ribbing very lightly on the wrong side, with a hot iron over a damp cloth. Join the shoulder seams, beginning at the arm end and taking 1 st. from each side at a time. Sew the sides of the last 18 rows at the top of sleeve to the cast-off edges of 17 sts. and set the sleeves into armholes, then press these seams. Join the sleeve and side seams in one line and press. Sew the collar to the neck edge.

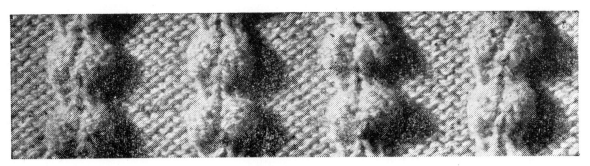

IN BLACKBERRY STITCH

This Good Style Cardigan Looks Smart Over A White Blouse

MATERIALS

TEN ounces of W.B. Melody Knitting, 3-ply, or eight ounces if short sleeves are worked; a pair each of No. 9 and No. 13 knitting needles; 3 buttons.

TENSION AND MEASUREMENTS

WORKED at a tension of 7 sts. to the inch in width on the stocking-stitch with No. 9 needles, the measurements on the diagram are attained after light pressing.

ABBREVIATIONS — TO BE READ BEFORE WORKING

K., KNIT plain; p., purl; st., stitch; tog., together; inc., increase (by working into the front and back of the same st.); dec., decrease (by working 2 sts. tog.); single rib is k. 1 and p. 1 alternately; s.s., stocking-stitch (in this case p. on the right side and k. back). Directions in brackets are worked the number of times stated after the brackets.

TO WORK THE BACK

BEGIN at the lower edge and using No. 13 needles, cast on 124 sts. Work 39 rows in single rib, working into the back of the sts. on the 1st row to give a neat edge.

NEXT ROW (wrong side): (K. 4, k. 2 tog.) 20 times, k. 4. (104 sts.)

Change to No. 9 needles and work in pattern as follows:

1ST ROW: P. 1, * k. 2, p. 8; repeat from * until 3 remain, k. 2, p. 1.

2ND ROW: K. 1, * p. 2, k. 8; repeat from * until 3 remain, p. 2, k. 1.

3RD ROW: P. 1, * work "5 in 1" twice thus: (K. 1, p. 1) twice, k. 1 into each of the next 2 sts., then p. 8; repeat from *, ending the last repeat with p. 1.   (192 sts.)

4TH ROW: All knit.

5TH ROW: All purl.

6TH ROW: K. 1, * p. 5 tog. twice, k. 8; repeat from * until 11 remain, p. 5 tog. twice, k. 1.   (104 sts.)

These 6 rows form the pattern, so repeat them once more, then continue in pattern and inc. 1 st. at both ends of the next row and every following 8th row until 7 inc. rows have been worked, working the extra sts. in s.s., when there will be 118 sts.

Work 23 rows without shaping, finishing with the last row of the 14th pattern from the beginning.

To Shape The Armholes.—1ST ROW: Cast off 10 (1 st. on needle), p. 7, * k. 2, p. 8; repeat from * to the end.

2ND ROW: Cast off 10 (1 st. on needle), k. 7, * p. 2, k. 8; repeat from * to end.

3RD ROW: P. 2 tog., p. 6, * "5 in 1" twice, p. 8; repeat from *, ending the last repeat with p. 6, p. 2 tog.   (168 sts.)

4TH ROW: K. 2 tog., k. until 2 sts. remain, k. 2 tog.

5TH ROW: P. 2 tog., p. until 2 remain, p. 2 tog.

6TH ROW: K. 2 tog., k. 3, * p. 5 tog. twice, k. 8; repeat from *, ending the last repeat with k. 3, k. 2 tog.

7TH ROW: P. 2 tog., p. 2, * k. 2, p. 8; repeat from * until 6 remain, k. 2, p. 2, p. 2 tog.

8TH ROW: K. 2 tog., k. 1, * p. 2, k. 8; repeat from * until 5 remain, p. 2, k. 1, k. 2 tog.

9TH ROW: P. 2 tog., * 5 in 1 twice, p. 8; repeat from *, ending the last repeat with p. 2 tog. instead of p. 8.

Work from the 4th to the 6th pattern row as at the beginning of the Back.   (84 sts.)

Work 7 complete patterns more.

To Slope The Shoulders.—Cast off 7 sts. at the beginning of the next 8 rows, then cast off the remaining sts.

THE RIGHT FRONT

USING No. 13 needles, cast on 64 sts. and work 10 rows in single rib.

1ST BUTTONHOLE ROW: Rib 5, cast off 4 sts., rib to end.

2ND BUTTONHOLE ROW: Rib until 5 sts. remain, cast on 4 sts. in place of those cast off, rib 5.

Work 16 rows more in single rib, then repeat the 2 buttonhole rows.

Rib 9 rows more.

NEXT ROW (wrong side): (K. 6, k. 2 tog.) 6 times, k. 2, turn and slip the remaining 14 sts. on to a spare needle for the front band.

Change to No. 9 needles and work 2 patterns as on the Back on the remaining 44 sts., then inc. 1 st. at the end of the next row and every following 8th row until 7 inc. rows have been worked (51 sts.), keeping the extra sts. in s.s.

Work 24 rows more.

To Shape The Armhole.—2ND PATTERN ROW: Cast off 10 (1 st. on needle), k. 7, * p. 2, k. 8; repeat from * until 3 remain, p. 2, k. 1.

3RD ROW: P. 1, * 5 in 1 twice, p. 8; repeat from *, ending the last repeat with p. 6, p. 2 tog.   (72 sts.)

4TH ROW: K. 2 tog., k. to end.

5TH ROW: P. until 2 remain, p. 2 tog.

6TH ROW: K. 2 tog., k. 3, * p. 5 tog. twice, k. 8; repeat from *, ending the last repeat with k. 1.

7TH ROW: P. 1, * k. 2, p. 8; repeat from * until 5 remain, k. 2, p. 2, p. 2 tog.

8TH ROW: K. 2 tog., k. 1, * p. 2, k. 8; repeat from * until 3 remain, p. 2, k. 1.

9TH ROW: P. 1, * 5 in 1 twice, p. 8; repeat from *, ending the last repeat with p. 2 tog. instead of p. 8.

Work from the 4th to the 6th row of straight pattern. (34 sts.)

Work 7 patterns, as on the Back and the 1st row of the next pattern.

To Slope The Shoulder.—Cast off 7 sts. at the beginning of the next row and following alternate row, then work back to arm end.

5TH SHOULDER ROW: K. 2 sts. tog., cast off 3 sts., K. 3 sts. tog., and pass first st. over, cast off 2, pattern to end.

Work back to arm end, then repeat 5th row, but cast off 3 sts. at end. Draw wool through remaining st. and fasten off.

The Right Front Band.—Rejoin the wool to the 14 sts. left on a spare needle, and using No. 13 needles, rib 7 rows, then on the next 2 rows make a buttonhole as before. Continue in rib until the band measures 21 inches from the cast-on edge when slightly stretched. Do not cast off until the strip has been sewn to the cardigan.

The Shape and Measurements of the Cardigan.

THE LEFT FRONT

WITH No. 13 needles cast on 64 sts. and work 39 rows in single rib.

NEXT ROW: Rib 14, and leave these sts. on a spare needle for the front band, then (k. 6, k. 2 tog.) 6 times, k. 2. (44 sts.)

Change to No. 9 needles and work 2 complete patterns as on the Back, then inc. 1 st. at the beginning of the next row and every following 8th row until the 7th inc. has been worked. (51 sts.)

Work 23 rows more.

To Shape The Armhole.—1ST ROW: Cast off 10 (1 st. on needle), p. 7, * k. 2, p. 8; repeat from * until 3 remain, k. 2, p. 1.

2ND ROW: K. 1, * p. 2, k. 8; repeat from * to end.

3RD ROW: P. 2 tog., p. 6, * 5 in 1 twice, p. 8; repeat from *, ending the last repeat with p. 1.

4TH ROW: K. until 2 remain, k. 2 tog.

5TH ROW: P. 2 tog., p. to end.

6TH ROW: K. 1, * p. 5 tog. twice, k. 8; repeat from *, ending the last repeat with k. 3, k. 2 tog.

7TH ROW: P. 2 tog., p. 2, * k. 2, p. 8; repeat from * until 3 remain, k. 2, p. 1.

8TH ROW: K. 1, * p. 2, k. 8; repeat from * until 5 remain, p. 2, k. 1, k. 2 tog.

9TH ROW: P. 2 tog., * 5 in 1 twice, p. 8; repeat from * ending the last repeat with p. 1 instead of p. 8. (44 sts.)

Work from the 4th to the 6th rows of straight pattern, then 7 complete patterns more. Slope the shoulder as on Right Front but beginning on right side of work.

The Left Front Band.—Return to the 14 sts. left on a spare needle and using No. 13 needles work in rib until the band measures 21 inches when slightly stretched. Do not cast off until it has been sewn in position.

THE SLEEVES

BEGIN at the wrist and using No. 13 needles cast on 64 sts. Work 35 rows in single rib.

NEXT ROW (wrong side): (K. 4, k. 2 tog.) 10 times, k. 4. (54 sts.)

Change to No. 9 needles and work 2 patterns as on the Back, then inc. 1 st. at both ends of the next row and every following 8th row until the 15th inc. row has been worked, working the extra sts. in pattern, or these can be worked in s.s. if there is any difficulty in keeping the pattern correct.

Work 7 rows without shaping, or for length required, finishing with the 6th row of a pattern. (84 sts.)

To Shape The Sleeve Top.—1ST ROW: P. 2 tog., p. 4, * k. 2, p. 8; repeat from * until 8 remain, k. 2, p. 4, p. 2 tog.

2ND ROW: K. 2 tog., k. 3, * p. 2, k. 8; repeat from * until 7 remain, p. 2, k. 3, k. 2 tog.

3RD ROW: P. 2 tog., p. 2, * 5 in 1 twice, p. 8; repeat from *, ending the last repeat with p. 2, p. 2 tog.

4TH ROW: K. 2 tog., k. until 2 remain, k. 2 tog.

5TH ROW: P. 2 tog., p. until 2 remain, p. 2 tog.

6TH ROW: K. 1, * p. 5 tog. twice, k. 8; repeat from *, ending the last repeat with k. 1. (74 sts.)

7TH ROW: K. 2 tog., k. 1, * p. 8, k. 2; repeat from * until 11 remain, p. 8, k. 1, k. 2 tog.

8TH ROW: P. 2 tog., * k. 8, p. 2; repeat from * until 10 remain, k. 8, p. 2 tog.

9TH ROW: P. 2 tog., p. 7, * 5 in 1 twice, p. 8; repeat from *, ending the last repeat with p. 7, p. 2 tog.

10TH ROW: K. 2 tog., k. until 2 remain, k. 2 tog.

11TH ROW: P. 2 tog., p. until 2 remain, p. 2 tog.

12TH ROW: K. 6, * p. 5 tog. twice, k. 8; repeat from *, ending the last repeat with k. 6. (64 sts.)

Repeat these 12 rows once more and the first 6 rows again, when 34 sts. will remain. Cast off.

Work another sleeve in the same way.

For Short Sleeves.—With No. 13 needles cast on 74 sts. and work 12 rows in single rib.

Change to No. 9 needles and work 6 rows in pattern as on the Back, then inc. 1 st. at both ends of the next row and every following 6th row until 5 inc. rows have been worked. (84 sts.)

Work straight for length required, finishing with the 6th pattern row, then shape the top as for the long sleeves.

TO MAKE UP THE CARDIGAN

FIRST press all parts except the ribbing on the wrong side, with a hot iron over a damp cloth. Join the shoulder seams, beginning at the arm end and taking 1 st. from each side at a time. Sew the front bands in position and join them at the back of the neck, stretching the bands slightly when sewing. Set the sleeves into armholes and press these seams. Join the sleeve and side seams in one line and press. Sew the buttons to the left front band, to correspond with the buttonholes.

THE LONDON GIRL'S STAR DRESS ACCESSORY

A charming idea to give a colour-ful finish to a simple dress.

A Flower Belt To Wear With A Plain Dress

The Belt And The Flowers Are In Crochet

MATERIALS

ONE tube (1 oz. each) of Pearsall's Rayon Crochet in each of two colours ; an Archer steel crochet hook, No. 1 ; press studs.

TENSION AND MEASUREMENTS

WORKED at a tension of 8 d.c. to the inch in width, the belt measures 3 inches deep at the centre and 1½ inches on the main part. The belt illustrated is 28 inches long, but any length can be made from these directions.

ABBREVIATIONS — TO BE READ BEFORE WORKING

CH., chain ; d.c., double crochet ; sl.st., slip stitch.

BEGIN at the centre, and using the two colours together, make 24 ch.

1ST ROW : 1 d.c. into the 3rd ch. from the hook, 1 d.c. into each ch. to end, 2 ch., turn. (This turning ch. will stand for the first d.c. of the following row, and has a d.c. worked into it at the end of each row, to keep a straight edge.)

2ND ROW : Miss the 1st d.c., 1 d.c. into each d.c. to end, finishing with 1 d.c. into the 2nd of the 2 ch., then turn with 2 ch.

Repeat the 2nd row six times more.

9TH ROW : Miss the first 2 d.c., 1 d.c. into each d.c. until 1 d.c. remains, miss the last d.c., 1 d.c. into the 2nd of the 2 ch., then 2 ch., turn.

Work 3 rows of 1 d.c. into each st.

Repeat the last 4 rows four times more.

Work 84 rows in d.c. without shaping,

1 d.c. into the next d.c. ; repeat from * 5 times more. (18 d.c.)

3RD ROUND : * 6 ch., miss 2 d.c., 1 d.c. into the next d.c. ; repeat from * 5 times more, sl.st. to first ch. at the beginning of the round.

The petals are now worked as follows :

4TH ROUND : * 2 ch., 9 d.c. into the 1st loop, 2 ch., turn ; miss 2 d.c., 1 d.c. into each of the next 6 d.c., miss 1 d.c., 1 d.c. into the 2nd of 2 ch., 2 ch., turn ; miss 2 d.c., 1 d.c. into each of the next 4 d.c., miss 1 d.c., 1 d.c. into the 2nd of the 2 ch., 2 ch., turn ; miss 2 d.c., 1 d.c. into each of the next 2 d.c., miss 1 d.c., 1 d.c. into the 2nd of 2 ch., 2 ch., turn ; miss 2 d.c., 1 d.c. into the next d.c., 1 ch. ; sl.st. into each st. down the side of the petal and into the first ch. of the next loop on the previous round ; repeat from * 5 times more.

5TH ROUND : Work 1 d.c. into each st. all round each petal.

Cut the thread and fasten off.

6TH ROUND : With the second colour

Sew each flower to the wide part of the belt.

when the strip should measure 14 inches. (More or less rows may be worked here according to the length required.) Fasten off.

Join the thread to the foundation ch. and work the second half exactly the same.

THE FLOWERS

USING a single thread of one colour, make 6 ch. and sl.st. to the 1st ch. to form a ring.

1ST ROUND : Work 12 d.c. into the ring.

2ND ROUND : * 2 d.c. into the 1st d.c.,

* work 1 d.c. into each st. to the top of the petal, 5 ch., sl.st. to the side of the last d.c., work in d.c. to base of petal ; repeat from * 5 times more, sl.st. to first st. and fasten off.

Make 7 flowers more in the same way.

TO MAKE UP THE BELT

PRESS the belt and flowers on the right side, with a warm iron over a dry cloth. With the same colour rayon sew each flower at the centre to the wide part of the belt, as shown in the illustration. Sew press studs to ends of belt to fasten.

This exciting jumper takes only 6 oz. of 3-ply wool

Easter Chic

MATERIALS : 6 oz. Copley's 3-ply "Excelsior" Wool, White ; 1 oz. same wool in Blue, and a small quantity in each Brown, Green and Yellow ; two small black beads for the eyes (optional) ; a pair each of No. 9 and No. 12 knitting needles.

MEASUREMENTS (after pressing): Length from lower edge to top of shoulder, 20½ ins. ; length of sleeve, along seam, 4½ ins. ; to fit a 34 to 36-in. bust.

TENSION : Seven sts. and 11 rows to 1 in.

ABBREVIATIONS : St(s)., stitch(es) ; k., knit ; p., purl ; tog., together ; rep., repeat ; rem., remain(s)(ing)(der) ; inc., increase(ing) ; dec., decrease(ing) ; W., white wool ; Bl., blue wool ; Br., brown wool ; G., green wool ; Y., yellow wool.

THE BACK

WITH No. 9 needles cast on 98 sts. in white wool ; do not work into the backs of the sts. for the 1st row. Work straight for 20 rows.

21st row : Work hem, thus : Fold the piece in two lengthwise, then * k. through the 1st st. on the needle and through the 1st st. of cast-on row ; rep. from * to end. Commencing with a purl row, work straight for 25 more rows. Inc. 1 st. at both ends of the next row, and similarly every following 8th row until there are 122 sts. Work straight for 5 more rows.

To Shape the Armholes : Cast off 3 sts. at the beginning of each of the next 6 rows, then k. 2 tog. at the end of every row until 88 sts. rem. Work straight for 45 more rows. Cast off.

THE FRONT

WORK as directed for the Back until 5 rows have been worked on 122 sts.

To Shape the Armholes : Cast off 3 sts. at the beginning of each of the next 2 rows then commence the " Fair-Isle " pattern, thus :

3rd row : Cast off 3 (1 st. now on right-hand needle—likewise each time there is a dec.), k. 39 W., 1 Bl., 28 W., 1 Bl., 43 W.

4th row : Cast off 3, p. 39 W., 1 Bl., 28 W., 1 Bl., 40 W. (110 sts.).

5th row : Cast off 3, k. 36 W., 1 Bl., 28 W., 1 Bl., 40 W.

6th row : Cast off 3, p. 36 W., 1 Bl., 1 W., 1 Bl., 24 W., 1 Bl., 1 W., 1 Bl., 37 W. (104 sts.)

7th row : K. 37 W., 1 Bl., 1 W., 1 Bl., 24 W., 1 Bl., 1 W., 1 Bl., 35 W., k. 2 tog.

8th row : P. 36 W., 1 Bl., 1 W., 1 Bl., 24 W., 1 Bl., 1 W., 1 Bl., 35 W., k. 2 tog.

9th row : K. 36 W., 1 Bl., 1 W., 1 Bl., 24 W., 1 Bl., 1 W., 1 Bl., 34 W., k. 2 tog.

A LOVELY JUMPER FOR YOU TO KNIT WITH 7 OZ. 3-PLY WOOL

Continued from previous page

10th row : P. 35 W., 1 Bl., 1 W., 1 Bl., 24 W., 1 Bl., 1 W., 1 Bl., 34 W., k. 2 tog.

11th row : K. 30 W., 3 Bl., 2 W., 3 Bl., 24 W., 3 Bl., 2 W., 3 Bl., 28 W., k. 2 tog.

12th row : P. 30 W., 3 Bl., 2 W., 3 Bl., 22 W., 3 Bl., 2 W., 3 Bl., 29 W., k. 2 tog.

13th row : K. 31 W., 4 Bl., 2 W., 3 Bl., 18 W., 3 Bl., 2 W., 4 Bl., 29 W., k. 2 tog.

14th row : P. 31 W., 5 Bl., 2 W., 2 Bl 16 W., 2 Bl., 2 W., 5 Bl., 30 W., k. 2 tog.

15th row : K. 31 W., 7 Bl., 1 W., 2 Bl., 14 W., 2 Bl., 1 W., 7 Bl., 29 W., k. 2 tog.

16th row : P. 31 W., 7 Bl., 1 W., 2 Bl., 12 W., 2 Bl., 1 W., 7 Bl., 30 W., k. 2 tog.

17th row : K. 32 W., 7 Bl., 1 W., 2 Bl., 10 W., 2 Bl., 1 W., 7 Bl., 30 W., k. 2 tog.

18th row : P. 32 W., 10 Bl., 8 W., 10 Bl., 31 W., k. 2 tog.

19th row : K. 33 W., 9 Bl., 8 W., 9 Bl., 31 W., k. 2 tog.

20th row : P. 33 W., 9 Bl., 6 W., 9 Bl., 32 W., k. 2 tog.

21st row : K. 33 W., 9 Bl., 6 W., 9 Bl., 31 W., k. 2 tog.

22nd row : P. 33 W., 8 Bl., 6 W., 8 Bl., 32 W., k. 2 tog.

23rd row : K. 33 W., 9 Bl., 4 W., 9 Bl., 33 W.

24th row : P. 34 W., 8 Bl., 4 W., 8 Bl., 34 W.

25th row : K. 34 W., 8 Bl., 4 W., 8 Bl., 34 W.

26th row : P. 35 W., 7 Bl., 4 W., 7 Bl., 35 W.

27th row : K. 35 W., 7 Bl., 4 W., 7 Bl., 35 W.

28th row : P. 36 W., 7 Bl., 2 W., 7 Bl., 36 W.

29th row : K. 36 W., 7 Bl., 2 W., 7 Bl., 36 W.

30th row : P. 37 W., 3 Bl., 1 W., 2 Bl., 2 W., 2 Bl., 1 W., 3 Bl., 37 W.

31st row : K. 38 W., 5 Bl., 2 W., 5 Bl., 38 W.

32nd row : P. 39 W., 3 Bl., 4 W., 3 Bl., 39 W.

Continue in white only, and work for 13 more rows.

To Shape the Neck.—Next row : P. 39 sts., cast off 10, p. to end. Leave the first set of 39 sts. for the present, and work

One Shoulder, as follows.—On the Neck edge k. 2 tog. every row until 27 sts. rem. Work straight for 19 more rows. Cast off.

Now revert to the set of 39 sts., and work the opposite Shoulder in the same way, and to match.

THE SLEEVES (both alike)

With No. 9 needles cast on 86 sts., and work a hem, as in Back (21 rows). Commencing with a purl row, work straight for 33 more rows.

To Shape the Top : K. 2 tog. at the end of each row, until 51 sts. rem. Work straight for 25 more rows. Cast off 17 sts. at the beginning of each of the next 2 rows (17 sts.)

Using the wool doubled, work straight for 19 more rows on these 17 sts. Cast off.

THE COLLAR

With No. 12 needles cast on 132 sts. and k. 1 p. 1 rib for 17 rows. Cast off loosely.

ASSEMBLY AND FINISH

Seam up the shoulders and sew collar piece (folded in two lengthwise) to neck edge. Carefully press all the pieces on the wrong side with a hot iron over a damp cloth. With yellow wool work a row in chain-st. over the white line in the plumage of the birds, and work also the beaks in yellow. Work the branches in brown wool, and the leaves in green, as illustrated. Sew the outer edges of the last 19 rows at top of sleeve to the cast-off edges of 17 sts. and neatly set the sleeves into the armholes. Press seams while garment is still open ; sew up the rem. seams and press. If desired, sew a bead into each eye

MATERIALS : 7 oz. (5 oz. yellow and 2 oz. white) of Sirdar Majestic Wool, 3-ply, a little green wool ; a pair each of No. 9 and No. 12 knitting needles.

MEASUREMENTS (after pressing) : Length from lower edge to top of shoulder, 19½ inches ; length of sleeve, along seam, 18½ inches ; to fit a 34-inch bust.

TENSION : Eight stitches and eleven rows to one inch.

ABBREVIATIONS : St(s)., stitch(es) ; k., knit ; p., purl ; tog., together ; rep., repeat ; rem., remain(ing)(s)(der) ; inc., increase(ing) ; dec., decrease(ing) ; Y, yellow wool ; W, white wool ; G, green wool ; patt., pattern.

THE BACK

WITH No. 9 needles cast on 94 sts. in the Yellow wool ; do not work into the backs of the sts. for the first row. Work for 20 rows in stocking-stitch, then work a hem, thus :

21st row : Fold the work in two lengthwise, then * k. through the first st. on the needle and through the first st. of the cast-on row ; rep. from * to end.

22nd row : All purl.

Work straight for 20 more rows. Inc. 1 st. at both ends of the next row, and similarly every following 8th row until there are 118 sts. Work straight for 2 more rows. Now commence the Yoke, working with two balls of Yellow, one of White and one ball of Green wool. N.B.—When changing from one colour to the other always twist the wools once, to avoid gaps in the sts.

To Shape the Armholes.—1st row : Cast off 3 sts. (1 st. now already on right-hand needle), k. 45 Y, join in W and k. 9, join in G and k. 1, pass W at the back of G st., and k. 9 W, k. 50 Y.

2nd row : Cast off 3, p. 46 Y, 9 W, 1 G, 9 W, 46 Y.

3rd row : Cast off 3, k. 37 Y, 14 W, 1 G, 14 W, 42 Y.

4th row : Cast off 3, p. 38 Y, 14 W, 2 G, 13 W, 38 Y.

5th row : Cast off 3, k. 29 Y ; continue to work with one ball G and one ball W, but twist the wools at the back of work every 2 sts., taking care not to drag the wool, and keeping it loose ; k. 3 W, 1 G, 12 W, 2 G, 1 W, 1 G, 15 W, 1 G, 3 W, 34 Y.

6th row : Cast off 3, p. 30 Y, 3 W, 1 G, 15 W, 1 G, 1 W, 3 G, 11 W, 1 G, 3 W, 30 Y.

7th row : K. 2 tog., k. 23 Y, 8 W, 1 G, 10 W, 2 G, 1 W, 1 G, 15 W, 1 G, 8 W, 24 Y, k. 2 tog.

8th row : K. 2 tog., p. 23 Y, 8 W, 2 G, 13 W, 2 G, 3 W, 3 G, 9 W, 2 G, 7 W, 22 Y, k. 2 tog.

9th row : K. 2 tog., k. 16 Y, 10 W, 2 G, 1 W, 1 G, 8 W, 3 G, 1 W, 2 G, 9 W, 2 G, 1 W, 1 G, 13 W, 17 Y, k. 2 tog.

10th row : K. 2 tog., p. 16 Y, 13 W, 1 G, 1 W, 3 G, 7 W, 3 G, 1 W, 1 G, 5 W, 2 G, 8 W, 1 G, 1 W, 3 G, 9 W, 15 Y, k. 2 tog.

11th row : K. 2 tog., k. 9 Y, 1 W, 1 G, 11 W, 3 G, 2 W, 1 G, 14 W, 2 G, 2 W, 3 G, 5 W, 3 G, 2 W, 1 G, 15 W, 1 G, 2 W, 10 Y, k. 2 tog.

12th row : K. 2 tog., p. 9 Y, 2 W, 1 G, 14 W, 2 G, 3 W, 3 G, 3 W, 3 G, 3 W, 1 G, 1 W, 2 G, 11 W, 2 G, 3 W, 3 G, 10 W, 1 G, 1 W, 8 Y, k. 2 tog.

13th row : K. 2 tog., k. 2 Y, 6 W, 1 G, 9 W, 3 G, 4 W, 1 G, 1 W, 2 G, 8 W, 3 G, 1 W, 1 G, 4 W, 3 G, 1 W, 1 G, 4 W, 2 G, 12 W, 1 G, 7 W, 3 Y, k. 2 tog.

14th row : K. 2 tog., p. 2 Y, 7 W, 2 G, 10 W, 3 G, 1 W, 3 G, 5 W, 2 G, 1 W, 2 G, 1 W, 3 G, 6 W, 1 G, 1 W, 5 W, 2 G, 9 W, 1 G, 6 W, 1 Y, k. 2 tog. (83 sts.).

Now break off the Yellow wool, leaving a long end to secure at the back and continue thus :

15th row : K. 7 W, 2 G, 15 W, 2 G, 2 W, 3 G, 4 W, 3 G, 3 W, 1 G, 14 W, 2 G, 2 W, 3 G, 7 W, 2 G, 1 W, 1 G, 9 W.

16th row : P. 9 W, 1 G, 1 W, 3 G, 5 W, 3 G, 3 W, 1 G, 1 W, 2 G, 10 W, (1 G, 1 W) twice, 1 G, 2 W, 3 G, 2 W, 3 G, 3 W, 1 G, 1 W, 2 G, 13 W, 1 G, 1 W, 2 G, 5 W.

17th row : K. 4 W, 3 G, 1 W, 1 G, 12 W, 3 G, 1 W, 1 G, 4 W, 3 G, 1 W, 2 G, 4 W, 3 G, 10 W, 3 G, 1 W, 1 G, 4 W, 3 G, 3 W, 3 G, 2 W, 1 G, 9 W.

18th row : P. 8 W, 2 G, 3 W, 3 G, 2 W, 2 G, 5 W, 1 G, 2 W, 3 G, 10 W, 1 G, 8 W, 2 G, 5 W, 1 G, 2 W, 3 G, 10 W, 2 G, 2 W, 3 G, 3 W.

19th row : K. 2 W, 3 G, 3 W, 1 G, 1 W, 2 G, 7 W, 3 G, 3 W, 1 G, 14 W ; join in a ball of Yellow wool again, and k. 3 Y, 8 W, 3 G, 3 W, 1 G, 8 W, 3 G, 4 W, 1 G, 1 W, 2 G, 6 W.

20th row : P. 5 W, 3 G, 1 W, 1 G, 5 W, 2 G, 6 W, (1 G, 1 W) twice, 1 G, 2 W, 3 G, 7 W, 3 Y, 12 W, (1 G, 1 W) twice, 1 G, 2 W, 3 G, 5 W, 3 G, 1 W, 1 G, 4 W, 3 G, 1 W.

21st row : K. 1 W, 2 G, 4 W, 2 G, 2 W, 3 G, 4 W, 2 G, 4 W, 3 G, 12 W, 5 Y, 6 W, 2 G, 4 W, 3 G, 13 W, 2 G, 2 W, 3 G, 4 W.

22nd row : P. 3 W, 3 G, 3 W, 1 G, 1 W, 2 G, 12 W, 1 G, 13 W, 5 Y, 13 W, 1 G, 10 W, 3 G, 3 W, 1 G, 1 W, 2 G, 5 W.

23rd row : K. 4 W, 3 G, 1 W, 1 G, 4 W, 3 G, 8 W, k. 3 Y, 12 W, 5 Y, 12 W, 3 Y, 10 W, 3 G, 1 W, 1 G, 4 W, 3 G, 2 W.

24th row : P. 2 W, 2 G, 5 W, 1 G, 2 W, 3 G, 9 W, 3 G, 12 W, 5 Y, 12 W, 3 Y, 8 W, 2 G, 5 W, 1 G, 2 W, 3 G, 3 W.

25th row : K. 2 W, 3 G, 3 W, 1 G, 14 W, 5 Y, 10 W, 1 Y, 1 W, 2 Y, 1 W, 2 Y, 10 W, 5 Y, 7 W, 3 G, 3 W, 1 G, 9 W.

26th row : P. 7 W, (1 G, 1 W) twice, 1 G, 2 W, 3 G, 6 W, 5 Y, 27 W, 5 Y, 12 W, (1 G, 1 W) twice, 1 G, 2 W, 3 G, 1 W.

27th row : K. 1 W, 2 G, 4 W, 3 G, 13 W, 5 Y, 27 W, 5 Y, 6 W, 2 G, 4 W, 3 G, 8 W.

28th row : P. 9 W, 1 G, 13 W, 5 Y, 27 W, 5 Y, 14 W, 1 G, 8 W.

29th row : K. 7 W, 3 Y, 12 W, 1 Y, 1 W, 2 Y, 1 W, 2 Y, 25 W, 1 Y, 1 W, 2 Y, 1 W, 2 Y, 11 W, 3 Y, 8 W.

30th row : P. 8 W, 3 Y, 62 W, 3 Y, 7 W.

31st row : K. 6 W, 5 Y, 60 W, 5 Y, 7 W.

32nd row : P. 7 W, 5 Y, 60 W, 5 Y, 6 W.

33rd row : As 31st row.

34th row : As 32nd row.

35th row : K. 5 W, 1 Y, 1 W, 2 Y, 1 W, 2 Y, 58 W, 1 Y, 1 W, 2 Y, 1 W, 2 Y, 6 W.

36th row : All p. in White.

Continue in White wool only, and work for 23 more rows. Cast off.

THE FRONT

WORK as directed for the Back until 36th row of yoke patt. has been completed. Work 3 more rows.

To Shape the Neck.—Next row : P. 36 sts., cast off 11, p. to end. Leave the first set of 36 sts. for the present, and work **One Shoulder**, thus : On the neck edge k. 2 tog. every row, until 27 sts. rem. Work straight for 19 more rows. Cast off.

Now revert to the set of 36 sts. and work the opposite Shoulder in the same way, and complete to match.

THE SLEEVES (both alike)

WITH No. 9 needles cast on 40 sts. in Yellow wool and work a hem, as in Back (22 rows). Work straight for 20 more rows, then inc. 1 st. at both ends of the next row, and similarly every following 8th row until there are 50 sts., then inc. every 6th row until there are 70 sts. Continue straight for the length desired, ending on a purl row.

To Shape the Top.—K. 2 tog. at both ends of each of the next 7 rows, then k. 2 tog. at the end of each of the following 9 rows (47 sts.).

Now commence in patt. as follows :

1st row : K. 4 W, 39 Y, 4 W.

2nd row : P. 4 W, 39 Y, 4 W.

3rd row : K. 8 W, 1 G, 29 Y, 1 G, 8 W.

4th row : P. 8 W, 1 G, 29 Y, 1 G, 8 W.

5th row : K. 8 W, 1 G, 5 W, 19 Y, 5 W, 1 G, 8 W.

6th row : P. 8 W, 1 G, 14 W, 1 G, 14 W, 1 G, 8 W.

7th row : K. 7 W, 2 G, 14 W, 1 G, 13 W, 2 G, 8 W.

8th row : P. 8 W, 1 G, 1 W, 2 G, 11 W, 1 G, 14 W, 1 G, 1 W, 2 G, 5 W.

9th row : K. 4 W, 3 G, 1 W, 1 G, 14 W, 1 G, 10 W, 3 G, 1 W, 1 G, 8 W.

10th row : P. 7 W, 2 G, 2 W, 3 G, 9 W, 2 G, 12 W, 2 G, 2 W, 3 G, 3 W.

11th row : K. 2 W, 3 G, 3 W, 1 G, 1 W, 2 G, 8 W, 2 G, 1 W, 1 G, 8 W, 3 G, 3 W, 1 G, 1 W, 2 G, 5 W.

12th row : P. 4 W, 3 G, 1 W, 1 G, 4 W, 3 G, 7 W, 1 G, 1 W, 3 G, 6 W, 3 G, 1 W, 1 G, 4 W, 3 G, 1 W.

13th row : K. 1 W, 2 G, 4 W, 2 G, 2 W, 3 G, 4 W, 3 G, 2 W, 2 G, 6 W, 2 G, 4 W, 2 G, 2 W, 3 G, 3 W.

14th row : P. 2 W, 3 G, 3 W, 1 G, 1 W, 2 G, 8 W, 2 G, 1 W, 1 G, 3 W, 3 G, 2 W, 3 G, 3 W, 1 G, 1 W, 2 G, 5 W.

15th row : K. 4 W, 3 G, 1 W, 1 G, 4 W, 2 G, 1 W, 3 G, 4 W, 1 G, 1 W, 3 G, 6 W, 3 G, 1 W, 1 G, 4 W, 3 G, 1 W.

16th row : P. 1 W, 2 G, 5 W, 1 G, 2 W, 3 G, 4 W, 3 G, 2 W, 2 G, 4 W, 2 G, 7 W, 1 G, 2 W, 3 G, 3 W.

17th row : K. 2 W, 3 G, 3 W, 1 G, 11 W, 2 G, 1 W, 1 G, 3 W, 3 G, 2 W, 3 G, 3 W, 1 G, 8 W.

18th row : P. 6 W, (1 G, 1 W) twice, 1 G, 2 W, 2 G, 2 W, 2 G, 4 W, 1 G, 1 W, 3 G, 8 W, (1 G, 1 W) twice, 1 G, 2 W, 2 G, 2 W.

19th row : K. 7 W, 3 G, 8 W, 3 G, 2 W, 1 G, 13 W, 3 G, 7 W.

20th row : P. 8 W, 1 G, 14 W, 1 G, 3 W, 3 G, 8 W, 1 G, 8 W.

21st row : K. 7 W, 3 Y, 7 W, 2 G, 2 W, (1 G, 1 W) twice, 1 G, 11 W, 3 Y, 7 W.

22nd row : P. 7 W, 3 Y, 12 W, 3 G, 12 W, 3 Y, 7 W.

23rd row : K. 6 W, 5 Y, 12 W, 1 G, 12 W, 5 Y, 6 W.

24th row : P. 6 W, 5 Y, 11 W, 3 Y, 11 W, 5 Y, 6 W.

25th row : K. 6 W, 5 Y, 11 W, 3 Y, 11 W, 5 Y, 6 W.

26th row : P. 6 W, 5 Y, 10 W, 5 Y, 10 W, 5 Y, 6 W.

27th row : K. 5 W, 1 Y, 1 W, 2 Y, 1 W, 2 Y, 9 W, 5 Y, 9 W, 1 Y, 1 W, 2 Y, 1 W, 2 Y, 5 W.

28th row : P. 21 W, 5 Y, 21 W.

29th row : K. 21 W, 5 Y, 21 W.

30th row : P. 20 W, 1 Y, 1 W, 2 Y, 1 W, 1 Y, 20 W.

Continue in White wool only, and work 7 more rows. Cast off 16 sts. at the beginning of each of the next 2 rows (15 sts.).

Using the wool doubled, work straight for 20 more rows on these 15 sts. Cast off.

THE COLLAR

WITH No. 12 needles cast on 132 sts. in White wool, and k. 1, p. 1 rib for 16 rows. Cast off.

ASSEMBLY AND FINISH

SEAM up the shoulders and sew collar, folded in two lengthwise, to neck edge, then carefully press all the pieces, while garment is still open, on the wrong side under a damp cloth with a hot iron. Sew the outer edges of the last 20 rows at top of sleeve to the cast-off edges of 16 sts., and neatly set sleeves into armholes. Press seams while garment is still open. Sew up rem. seams and press.

A JERSEY IN TRELLIS PATTERN

Make It Your Own In Two Shades Of The Same Colour—One Light, One Dark

MATERIALS

*T*HREE *ounces of Copley's 3-ply " Excelsior " Wool in a dark shade and 3 ounces of the same wool in a lighter shade (for a jersey with long sleeves get 4 ounces of each colour) ; a pair each of No. 10 and No. 13 knitting needles ; a short cable needle ; 3 press-studs.*

For a bust measurement of 34 to 36 inches use No. 9 needles for the main part and No. 12 for the finer.

TENSION AND MEASUREMENTS

*W*ORKED *at such a tension that one repeat of the pattern (10 sts.) measures 1¼ inches in width with No. 10 needles, the measurements on the diagram are attained after light pressing.*

ABBREVIATIONS—TO BE READ BEFORE WORKING

K., *KNIT plain ; p., purl ; st., stitch ; tog., together ; inc., increase (by working into the front and back of the same st.) ; dec., decrease (by working 2 sts. tog.) ; sl., slip, single rib is k. 1 and p. 1 alternately. Directions in brackets are worked the number of times stated after the brackets.*

TO WORK THE BACK

*B*EGIN *at the lower edge, and using dark wool and No. 13 needles, cast on 116 sts. Work 39 rows in single rib, working into the back of the sts. on the 1st row to give a neat edge.*

Inc. Row : * P. 8, inc. ; repeat from * until 8 remain, p. 8. (128 sts.)

Change to No. 10 needles and work in pattern as follows :

1st Row : Leave the dark wool hanging and join in the light wool. With light wool k. 1 for an edge st., sl. 1 ; * k. 4, sl. 1 ; repeat from * until 1 st. remains, k. 1 edge st. (Take care not to draw the wool across tightly after each sl. st.)

2nd Row : P. 1, sl. 1, * p. 4, sl. 1 ; repeat from * until 1 st. remains, p. 1.

Repeat these 2 rows once more.

5th Row : Leave the light wool hanging and, using dark wool, k. 1, * cross 2 over 4 thus : slip the first 5 sts. on to a cable needle and pass them to the *back* of the work, k. the next st., taking care not to draw up the wool too tightly, return the 4 light sts. from the cable needle to the left-hand needle and bring the dark st. on the cable needle to the *front* of the work, k. 4, then k. the dark st. from the cable needle ; k. 4 ; repeat from *, ending the last repeat with k. 1 instead of k. 4.

6th Row : Knit in dark wool, making a ridge on the right side.

Repeat the first 2 rows twice more.

11th Row : Using dark wool, k. 6, * cross 2 over 4, as described in the 5th row, k. 4 ; repeat from * until 2 sts. remain, k. 2.

12th Row : All knit, using dark wool.

These 12 rows form the pattern, so repeat them 7 times more.

To Shape The Armholes.—1st Row : With light wool cast off 7 (1 st. on needle), k. 3, * sl. 1, k. 4 ; repeat from * until 2 sts. remain, k. 2.

2nd Row : Cast off 7 (1 st. on needle), p. 3, * sl. 1, p. 4 ; repeat from * to end.

3rd Row : K. 2 tog., k. 2, * sl. 1, k. 4 ; repeat from * until 5 remain, sl. 1, k. 2, k. 2 tog.

4th Row : P. 2 tog., p. 1, * sl. 1, p. 4 ; repeat from * until 4 remain, sl. 1, p. 1, p. 2 tog.

5th Row : Using dark wool k. 2 tog., * cross 2 over 4, k. 4 ; repeat from * until 8 remain, cross 2 over 4, k. 2 tog.

6th Row : Using dark wool k. 2 tog., k. until 2 remain, k. 2 tog.

7th Row : Using light wool k. 2 tog., k. 3, * sl. 1, k. 4 , repeat from * until 6 remain, sl. 1, k. 3, k. 2 tog.

8th Row : P. 2 tog., p. 2, * sl. 1, p. 4 ; repeat from * until 5 remain, sl. 1, p. 2, p. 2 tog.

9th Row : K. 2 tog., k. 1, * sl. 1, k. 4 ; repeat from * until 4 remain, sl. 1, k. 1, k. 2 tog.

10th Row : P. 2 tog., * sl 1, p. 4 ; repeat from * until 3 remain, sl. 1, p. 2 tog. (98 sts.)

Now work from the 5th to the 12th row of straight pattern as at the beginning of the Back, then 4 complete patterns more, and the first 6 rows again.

To Slope The Shoulders.—Cast off 8 sts. at the beginning of the next 8 rows ; fasten off the wool and leave the remaining 34 sts. on a spare needle for the back neck-band.

THE FRONT

*W*ORK *as for the Back until the armhole shaping has been finished and 98 sts. remain. Work from the 5th to the 12th row of straight pattern, then 2 complete patterns more.*

Now divide the sts. for the neck as follows :

The Left Front Shoulder.—1st Row : With light wool k. 1, (sl. 1, k. 4) 7 times, k. 1 (37 sts.), turn, leaving the remaining 61 sts. on a spare needle.

2nd Row : P. 2 tog., p. 3, (sl. 1, p. 4) 6 times, sl. 1, p. 1.

3rd Row : K. 1, (sl. 1, k. 4) 6 times, sl. 1, k. 2, k. 2 tog.

4th Row : P. 2 tog., p. 1, (sl. 1, p. 4) 6 times, sl. 1, p. 1.

5th Row : With dark wool k. 1, (cross 2 over 4, k 4) 3 times, k. 1, k. 2 tog. (33 sts.)

6th Row : With dark wool all knit.

Continue straight in pattern as follows :

1st—4th Rows : As first 4 rows of straight pattern on the Back.

5th Row : Using dark wool k. 6, (cross 2 over 4, k. 4) twice, cross 2 over 4, k. 1.

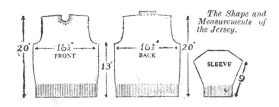

The Shape and Measurements of the Jersey.

20" · 16½" FRONT · 13" · 16½" BACK · 20" · SLEEVE 9"

K. 1 row dark, then work the first 4 rows of straight pattern once more.

11TH Row: With dark wool k. 1, (cross 2 over 4, k. 4) 3 times, k. 2.

12TH Row: Using dark wool all k.

Repeat the last 12 rows once more.

To Slope The Shoulder.—Cast off 8 sts. at the beginning of the next row and following 3 alternate rows. Draw the wool through the remaining sts. and fasten off.

The Right Front Shoulder.—Leave the centre 24 sts. on a spare needle for the neck-band and rejoin the wool to the next st. along the row. (37 sts. for Right Front Shoulder.)

1ST Row: Using light wool k. 1, * k. 4, sl. 1; repeat from * until 1 st. remains, k. 1.

2ND Row: P. 1, (sl. 1, p. 4) 6 times, sl. 1, p. 3, p. 2 tog.

3RD Row: K. 2 tog., k. 2, (sl. 1, k. 4) 6 times, sl. 1, k. 1.

4TH Row: P. 1, (sl. 1, p. 4) 6 times, sl. 1, p. 1, p. 2 tog.

5TH Row: Using dark wool k. 2 tog., sl. 1, (k. 4, cross 2 over 4) 3 times, k. 1. (33 sts.)

6TH Row: All k., using dark wool.

Work the 12 rows of straight pattern twice as at the beginning of the Back then work the 1st row again, making 25 rows more.

Now slope the shoulder, as on the Left Front Shoulder, but begin on the wrong side.

THE NECK-BAND

FIRST join the right shoulder seam, beginning at the arm end and taking 1 st. from each side at a time. Holding the work with the right side facing and using No. 13 needles, pick up 36 sts. from the left side of the neck, 24 sts. on a spare needle at centre front, pick up 36 sts. from the right side of the neck, then 34 sts. from the back neck. (130 sts.)

Work 12 rows in single rib, then cast off in rib thus: K. 1, p. 1, * pass the k. st. over, k. 1, pass the p.st. over, p. 1; repeat from * to end, then fasten off.

THE SLEEVES

BEGIN at the arm edge and using No. 13 needles with dark wool, cast on 76 sts. Work 29 rows in single rib.

Change to No. 10 needles and inc. on the next row thus: K. 5, (inc., k. 2) 22 times, k. 5. (98 sts.)

Now work 5 complete patterns as at the beginning of the Back, or for length required, finishing with the last row of a pattern.

To Shape The Sleeve Top.—1ST Row: With light wool, k. 2 tog., * k. 4, sl. 1; repeat from * until 6 remain, k. 4, k. 2 tog.

2ND Row: P. 2 tog., p. 3, * sl. 1, p. 4; repeat from * until 6 remain, sl. 1, p. 3, p. 2 tog.

3RD Row: K. 2 tog., k. 2, * sl. 1, k. 4; repeat from * until 5 remain, sl. 1, k. 2, k. 2 tog.

4TH Row: P. 2 tog., p. 1, * sl. 1, p. 4; repeat from * until 4 remain, sl. 1, p. 1, p. 2 tog.

5TH Row: With dark wool k. 2 tog., k. 1, * k. 4, cross 2 over 4; repeat from * until 7 remain, k. 5, k. 2 tog. (88 sts.)

6TH Row: All k., without dec., in dark wool.

Repeat these 6 rows 5 times more, then cast off the remaining 38 sts.

Work another sleeve in the same way.

FOR LONG SLEEVES

BEGIN at the wrist edge and with No. 13 needles cast on 58 sts. Work 40 rows in single rib.

Change to No. 10 needles and work 1 pattern of 12 rows as at the beginning of the Back, then inc. 1 st. at both ends of the next row and every following 6th row until the 20th inc. row has been worked, when there will be 98 sts. Work straight for length required, finishing with the last row of a pattern, then shape the top as for the short sleeves.

TO MAKE UP THE JERSEY

FIRST press all parts, except the ribbing, on the wrong side, with a hot iron over a damp cloth, and a thick blanket underneath. Join the right shoulder seam for 1 inch beginning at the arm end and taking 1 st. from each side at a time. Set the sleeves into armholes and press these seams. Join the sleeve and side seams in one line and press. Fasten the left shoulder with 3 press-studs.

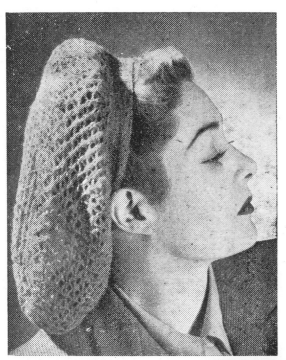

MATERIALS

*O*NE *ounce of Lister's Lavenda Wool, 2-ply ; a pair each of No. 8 and No. 13 knitting needles.*

TENSION AND MEASUREMENTS

*W*ORKED *at such a tension that 2 repeats of the open pattern measure 1¼ inches in width with No. 8 needles, the snood will measure 13 inches along the back seam, 10 inches from centre of head edge to back of snood, and 13 inches round the head edge, expanding to 18 inches.*

ABBREVIATIONS—TO BE READ BEFORE WORKING

*K*KNIT *plain ; p., purl ; st., stitch ; tog., together ; inc., increase (by working into the front and back of the same st.) ; sl., slip ; p.s.s.o., pass the slipped st. over ; m., make (by bringing the wool to the front of the needle and over it before knitting the next st.) ; single rib is k. 1 and p. 1 alternately.*

KNIT IT FOR THE HOLIDAYS

A Little Snood For All Weathers

TO WORK THE SNOOD

*B*EGIN at the head edge and with No. 13 needles cast on 108 sts. Work 28 rows in single rib, working into the back of the sts. on the 1st row to give a neat edge.

Change to No. 8 needles and inc. thus :
INC. ROW : * K. 1, inc. in the next st. ; repeat from * to end. (162 sts.)

Now begin the lacy pattern as follows :
1ST ROW : K. 1, * m. 1, sl. 1, k. 2 tog., p.s.s.o., m. 1, k. 1 ; repeat from * until 1 st. remains, k. 1.

2ND ROW : All purl.

3RD ROW : K. 2 tog., * m. 1, k. 1, m. 1, sl. 1, k. 2 tog., p.s.s.o. ; repeat from * until 4 remain, m. 1, k. 1, m. 1, k. 2 tog., k. 1.

4TH ROW : All purl.

These 4 rows form the pattern, so repeat them 15 times more.

Now divide the sts. equally between two needles and cast off, taking 1 st. from each needle at a time, or an invisible join can be made by grafting the sts. together in the following way :

HOW TO GRAFT

*C*UT the wool, leaving about a yard hanging, thread this into a fine bodkin, and pass it through the first st. of the front row as if about to knit, draw the wool through and pass the st. off the needle ; pass the bodkin through the next st. along the front row as if about to purl, draw the wool through, but leave the st. on the needle. Now pass the bodkin *under* the front needle to the back and reverse the action thus : Pass the bodkin through the first st. purlwise and slip the st. off the needle, pass the bodkin through the next st. knitwise and leave the st. on the needle. Continue along the row until all the sts. are worked off, taking care not to draw up the wool too tightly, or the top will be puckered. Pass the cut end of the wool to the wrong side

and fasten off. You can remember grafting by this little drill :

Front needle, k. and slip off, p. and keep on.

Back needle : P. and slip off, k. and keep on.

The k. and p. refer, of course, to the position of the bodkin when put into the stitch.

Sew the side seam with the same wool.

MAKE THE MOST OF THESE HINTS

Our Beauty Expert Is Ready To Advise You On This All-Important Subject

My boy friend sent me a lovely parcel of beauty aids from America, including a dear little blue velour powder puff. I have never used this type of powder puff, and wondered if they are washable. —DELIGHTED.

*Y*ES, they wash beautifully. They are usually filled with cotton wool, so before washing the puff you will have to unpick the stitching for about an inch and remove it. Give the cover a thorough shake to remove any surplus powder and then soak it in lukewarm soapy water. When it is perfectly clean, press out as much of the moisture as possible and lay it out flat on a towel to dry.

Pack in the new cottonwool filling, stitch up the seam, and your puff will be as good as new.

SMALL DOSES

Do you think it would harm my hair if I added a little peroxide to my rinsing water, after a shampoo ? I am a natural blonde, but my hair is darkening.— HILDA (Devon).

*I*F you add only a little peroxide—a teaspoonful to a bowl of water should be ample—it should not harm your hair.

WOMAN'S WEEKLY

EVERY TUESDAY · N° 1855 · VOL. LXXI · MAY · 24 · 1947

A Special Transfer Offer

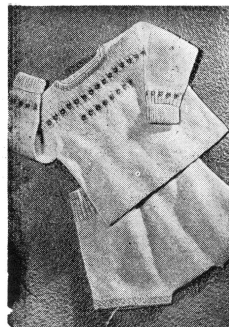

Baby's Little Knitted Suit and a Holiday Snood

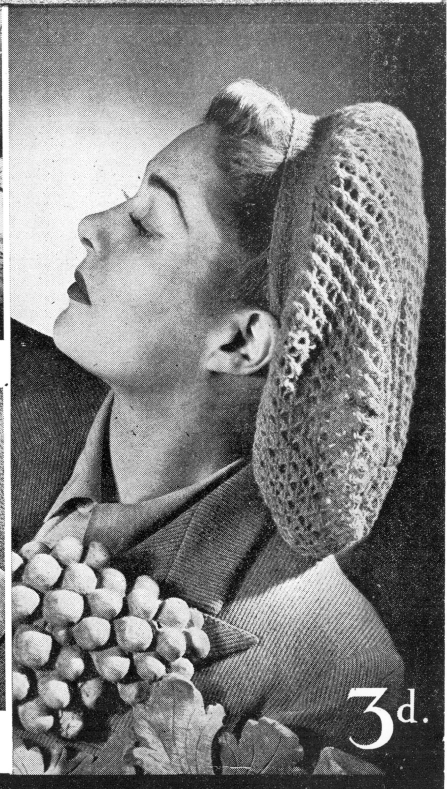

3d.

Instructions for making all these inside !

MATERIALS : 6 ounces in White and a small quantity in Red and in Green of Sirdar Majestic Wool, 3-ply ; a pair each of No. 9 and No. 12 knitting needles ; a medium-sized crochet hook ; a little cottonwool.

MEASUREMENTS (after pressing) : Length from lower edge to top of shoulder, 21½ ins. ; length of sleeve, along seam, 4¼ ins. ; to fit a 32 to 34-inch bust.

TENSION : Seven sts. and 11 rows to 1 in.

ABBREVIATIONS : St(s)., stitch(es) ; k., knit ; p., purl ; tog., together ; rep., repeat ; rem., remain(s) (ing) (der) ; inc., increase(ing) ; dec., decrease(ing) ; W, white wool ; R, red wool ; G, green wool ; d.-c., double-crochet.

June Rose

See picture on page 313

THE BACK

With No. 9 needles cast on 98 sts. in the W wool ; do not work into the backs of the sts. for the first row. Work straight in stocking-st. for 20 rows.

21st row : Work a hem thus : Fold the piece into two lengthwise, then * k. through the first st. on the needle and the first st. of the cast-on row ; rep. from * to end.

22nd row : All p. Work straight for 30 more rows. Inc. 1 st. at both ends of the next row, and similarly every following 10th row until there are 116 sts. Work straight for 5 more rows.

To Shape the Armholes : Cast off 3 sts. at the beginning of each of the next 6 rows, then k. 2 tog. at the end of every row until 88 sts. rem.

Next row : All k. **Following row :** P. 38 sts., turn and leave the rem. 50 sts. for the present. **Next row :** Cast on 6 sts., k. to end of row. (44 sts.) **Following row :** P. 40, k. 4.

Keeping intact in garter-st. the border of 4 sts., work straight for 49 more rows. Cast off.

Now join in the wool on the set of 50 sts.

Next row : Cast on 2, k. 2, p. 50. (52 sts.).

Following row : All k.

Next row : K. 2, p. 3, cast off 2 sts., p. to end.

Following row : K. until 5 sts. rem., cast on 2, k. 5. This completes the first buttonhole—work 6 more (7 in all) in the same way, with 6 rows between each, and complete to match the opposite side. Cast off.

THE FRONT

Work as directed for the Back, until there are 116 sts. on the needle. Work for 5 more rows, then commence the "Fair-Isle" pattern and **Shape Armholes** thus :

1st row : Cast off 3 sts. (1 st. now on right-hand needle), k. 53 more, now join in G and k. 1 G, then k. 58 W.

2nd row : Cast off 3, p. 53 W, 1 G, 53 W.

3rd row : Cast off 3, k. 49 W, 3 G, 54 W.

4th row : Cast off 3, p. 50 W, 3 G, 50 W.

5th row : Cast off 3, k. 39 W, 3 R, 3 W, 5 G, 3 W, 3 R, 44 W.

6th row : Cast off 3, p. 37 W, 2 R, 1 W, 4 R, 2 W, 5 G, 2 W, 4 R, 1 W, 2 R, 37 W.

7th row : K. 36 W, 8 R, 3 W, 3 G, 3 W, 8 R, 35 W, k. 2 tog.

8th row : P. 34 W, 1 R, 1 W, 2 R, 3 W, 1 R, 2 W, 2 R, 2 W, 1 G, 2 W, 2 R, 2 W, 1 R, 3 W, 2 R, 1 W, 1 R, 32 W, k. 2 tog. Break off the Green wool.

9th row : K. 31 W, 4 R, 2 W, 3 R, 1 W, 2 R, 1 W, 2 R, 3 W, 2 R, 1 W, 2 R, 1 W, 3 R, 2 W, 4 R, 30 W, k. 2 tog.

10th row : P. 31 W, 4 R, 1 W, 3 R, 1 W, 4 R, 1 W, 2 R, 1 W, 4 R, 1 W, 3 R, 1 W, 4 R, 29 W, k. 2 tog.

11th row : K. 30 W, 3 R, 1 W, 4 R, 1 W, 5 R, 1 W, 5 R, 1 W, 5 R, 1 W, 4 R, 1 W, 3 R, 29 W, k. 2 tog.

12th row : P. 30 W, 3 R, 1 W, 4 R, 1 W, 5 R, 5 W, 5 R, 1 W, 4 R, 1 W, 3 R, 28 W, k. 2 tog.

13th row : K. 21 W, 2 R, 1 W, 2 R, 3 W, 3 R, 1 W, 5 R, 2 W, (1 R, 1 W) five times, 1 R, 2 W, 5 R, 1 W, 3 R, 3 W, 2 R, 1 W, 2 R, 20 W, k. 2 tog.

14th row : P. 20 W, 8 R, 1 W, 3 R, 1 W, 4 R, 1 W, 2 R, 2 W, (1 R, 1 W) three times, 1 R, 2 W, 2 R, 1 W, 4 R, 1 W, 3 R, 1 W, 8 R, 18 W, k. 2 tog.

15th row : K. 19 W, 8 R, 1 W, 4 R, 1 W, 3 R, 1 W, 2 R, 1 W, 1 R, 1 W, 2 R, 1 W, 2 R, 1 W, 1 R, 1 W, 2 R, 1 W, 3 R, 1 W, 4 R, 1 W, 8 R, 18 W, k. 2 tog.

16th row : P. 17 W, 2 R, 1 W, 1 R, 4 R, 3 R, 1 W, 4 R, 1 W, 3 R, 2 W, 1 R, 1 W, 3 R, 1 W, 3 R, 1 W, 1 R, 2 W, 3 R, 1 W, 4 R, 1 W, 3 R, 4 W, 1 R, 1 W, 2 R, 15 W, k. 2 tog. (88 sts.)

17th row : K. 15 W, 4 R, 1 W, 4 R, 1 W, 1 R, 2 W, 4 R, 2 W, 4 R, 1 W, 3 R, 3 W, 3 R, 1 W, 4 R, 2 W, 4 R, 2 W, 1 R, 1 W, 4 R, 1 W, 4 R, 16 W.

18th row : P. 16 W, 3 R, 1 W, 6 R, 1 W, 2 R, 1 W, 2 R, 4 W, 1 R, 1 W, 1 R, 5 W, 1 R, 1 W, 1 R, 4 W, 2 R, 1 W, 2 R, 1 W, 2 R, 1 W, 6 R, 1 W, 3 R, 15 W.

19th row : K. 15 W, 2 R, 1 W, 1 R, 2 W, 1 R, 1 W, 3 R, 1 W, 2 R, 1 W, 1 R, 1 W, 8 R, 7 W, 8 R, 1 W, 1 R, 1 W, 2 R, 1 W, 5 R, 2 W, 1 R, 1 W, 2 R, 16 W.

20th row : P. 18 W, 4 R, 1 W, 4 R, 1 W, 3 R, 3 W, 2 R, 1 W, 4 R, 7 W, 4 R, 1 W, 2 R, 3 W, 3 R, 1 W, 4 R, 1 W, 4 R, 17 W.

21st row : K. 17 W, 2 R, 3 W, 4 R, 1 W, 3 R, 1 W ; join in Green wool again and 1 G, 1 W, 2 R, 1 W, 3 R, 9 W, 3 R, 1 W, 2 R, 1 W, 1 G, 1 W, 3 R, 1 W, 4 R, 3 W, 2 R, 18 W

22nd row : P. 18 W, 1 R, 1 W, 2 R, 1 W, 4 R, 1 W, 3 R, 2 W, 1 G, 21 W, 1 G, 2 W, 3 R, 1 W, 4 R, 1 W, 2 R, 1 W, 1 R, 17 W.

23rd row : K. 17 W, 1 R, 1 W, 3 R, 1 W, 4 R, 1 W, 2 R, 3 W, 1 G, 21 W, 1 G, 3 W, 2 R, 1 W, 4 R, 1 W, 2 R, 1 W, 1 R, 18 W.

24th row : P. 18 W, 2 R, 2 W, 4 R, 1 W, 3 R, 2 W, 1 G, 4 W, 5 G, 5 W, 5 G, 4 W, 1 G, 2 W, 3 R, 1 W, 4 R, 2 W, 2 R, 17 W.

25th row : K. 18 W, 4 R, 3 W, 1 R, 1 W, 2 R, 2 W, 1 G, 3 W, 5 G, 7 W, 5 G, 3 W, 1 G, 2 W, 2 R, 1 W, 1 R, 3 W, 4 R, 19 W.

26th row : P. 23 W, 5 R, 1 W, 1 R, 3 W, 1 G, 1 W, 5 G, 9 W, 5 G, 1 W, 1 G, 3 W, 1 R, 1 W, 5 R, 22 W.

27th row : K. 19 W, 2 G, 2 W, 3 R, 7 W, 5 G, 11 W, 5 G, 7 W, 3 R, 2 W, 2 G, 20 W. Break off the Red wool.

28th row : P. 19 W, 3 G, 13 W, 1 G, 17 W, 1 G, 13 W, 3 G, 18 W.

29th row : K. 18 W, 4 G, 8 W, 4 G, 19 W, 4 G, 8 W, 4 G, 19 W.

30th row : P. 13 W, 3 G, 4 W, 4 G, 2 W, 3 G, 1 W, 1 G, 3 W, 4 G, 13 W, 4 G, 3 W, 1 G, 1 W, 3 G, 2 W, 4 G, 4 W, 3 G, 12 W.

31st row : K. 10 W, 6 G, 4 W, 5 G, 3 W, 1 G, 4 W, 6 G, 9 W, 6 G, 4 W, 1 G, 3 W, 5 G, 4 W, 6 G, 11 W.

32nd row : P. 10 W, 8 G, 3 W, 3 G, 5 W, 1 G, 5 W, 6 G, 7 W, 6 G, 5 W. 1 G, 5 W, 3 G, 3 W, 8 G, 9 W.

33rd row : K. 10 W, 7 G, 1 W, 2 G, 7 W, 3 G, 5 W, 4 G, 9 W, 4 G, 5 W, 3 G, 7 W, 2 G, 1 W, 7 G, 11 W.

34th row : P. 13 W, 3 G, 2 W, 1 G, 1 W, 1 G, 7 W, 4 G, 25 W, 4 G, 7 W, 1 G, 1 W, 1 G, 2 W, 3 G, 13 W.

35th row : K. 15 W, 2 G, 1 W, 3 G, 6 W, 5 G, 23 W, 5 G, 6 W, 3 G, 1 W, 2 G, 16 W.

Continued on page 313

"My Bonnie"

For pattern see p. 294

"Knitter's delight"

For pattern see p. 279

"With a neat little collar"

For pattern see p. 296

"A gay Fair-Isle pullover"

For pattern see p. 325

June Rose

Continued from page 308

The perfect jumper for you to wear in flower time

36th row : P. 15 W, 1 G, 3 W, 4 G, 5 W, 6 G, 21 W, 6 G, 5 W, 4 G, 3 W, 1 G, 14 W.

37th row : K. 14 W, 1 G, 3 W, 5 G, 5 W, 4 G, 23 W, 4 G, 5 W, 5 G, 3 W, 1 G, 15 W.

38th row : P. 13 W, 2 G, 4 W, 5 G, 6 W, 1 G, 27 W, 1 G, 6 W, 5 G, 4 W, 2 G, 12 W.

39th row : K. 11 W, 1 G, 7 W, 3 G, 43 W, 3 G, 6 W, 1 G, 13 W.

40th row : P. 12 W, 3 G, 6 W, 1 G, 45 W, 1 G, 7 W, 3 G, 10 W.

41st row : K. 8 W, 5 G, 60 W, 5 G. 10 W.

42nd row : P. 10 W, 5 G. 60 W, 5 G, 8 W.

43rd row : K. 7 W, 5 G, 62 W, 5 G, 9 W.

44th row : P. 9 W, 3 G, 66 W, 3 G, 7 W.

45th row : K. 6 W, 3 G, 68 W, 3 G, 8 W.

Break off Green wool and continue in White only.

46th row : All purl.

47th row : All knit.

To Shape the Neck.—48th. row : P. 39, cast off 10, p. to end. Leave the first set of 39 sts. for the present and work **One Shoulder thus :** On the neck edge k. 2 tog. every row until 27 sts. rem. Work straight on these 27 sts. for 17 more rows. Cast off.

Now revert to the set of 39 sts., and work the opposite shoulder in the same way and to match.

THE COLLAR

WITH No. 12 needles cast on 130 sts. in White wool and work for 14 rows in a k. 1, p. 1 rib. Cast off.

THE SLEEVES (both alike)

WITH No. 9 needles cast on 85 sts. and work a hem as for the Back (21 rows). Commencing with a purl row, work for 31 more rows.

To Shape the Top : K. 2 tog. at the end of each of the next 39 rows. (46 sts.)

Work straight for 20 more rows. Cast off 15 sts. at the beginning of each of the next 2 rows. (16 sts.)

Using the wool doubled, work straight on these 16 sts. for 19 more rows. Cast off.

THE BUTTONS (7 alike)

WITH the crochet-hook work 4 chain and fasten so as to form a ring, into which work 8 d.-c. for the first round.

2nd round : Work 2 d.-c. into each d.-c. (16 d.-c.)

Working d.-c. over d.-c., work for 32 more d.-c., then insert a tuft of cottonwool and cover by working d.-c. into every alternate d.-c. until closed. Fasten off.

ASSEMBLY AND FINISH

CAREFULLY press all the pieces on the wrong side under a damp cloth with a hot iron. Seam up the shoulders. Fold collar piece in two lengthwise, and sew to neck edge. Sew the outer edges of the last 19 rows at top of sleeve to the cast-off edges of 15 sts. and neatly set sleeves into the armholes. Sew inside the border of 2 sts. worked in garter-st. along the right edge of vent. Press seams while garment is still open ; sew up rem. seams and press. Sew on the buttons to correspond with the buttonholes. Using Red wool doubled, immediately after the hem at sleeves and neck, work a row of sts. as follows : pick up one knitted st. and pass over two, and so on, as illustrated.

READER'S QUERY

I am very slim (my bust measurement is 30 inches) and can never find a jumper pattern to fit me.—MISS J. M. (Glasgow).

KNIT according to patterns for a 32-inch bust size, using smaller needles to make the jumper smaller in proportion. If you are tall and slim and need the extra length, knit exactly as instructed in the pattern, but when you are sewing up the jumper, take in side seams so that the garment will fit you. Press the seams out flat so that they will not be bulky.

Close-up of flower motif

How charming Miss Joy Frankau, the young film starlet, looks wearing our jersey.

PRETTIEST OF THE SEASON

The Round Lacy Yoke Of This Jersey Is So Very Becoming

2ND ROW: All purl.

3RD ROW: K. 1, k. 2 tog., m. 1, * k. 3, m. 1, sl. 1, k. 2 tog., p.s.s.o., m. 1 ; . repeat from * until 5 sts. remain, k. 3, m. 1, k. 2 tog.

4TH ROW: All purl.

These 4 rows form one pattern, so repeat them 26 times more.

To Shape The Armholes.—1ST ROW: Cast off 3 (1 st. on needle), k. 2 tog., m. 1, * k. 3, m. 1, sl. 1, k. 2 tog., p.s.s.o., m. 1 ; repeat from * until 2 sts. remain, k. 2.

2ND ROW: Cast off 3 sts., p. to end.

3RD ROW: Cast off 3 (1 st. on needle), k. 2 tog., m. 1, * k. 3, m. 1, sl. 1, k. 2 tog., p.s.s.o., m. 1 ; repeat from * until 2 remain, k. 2.

4TH ROW: Cast off 3 sts., p. to end.

Repeat these 4 rows twice more, when 80 sts. will remain.

Work 3 complete patterns as at the beginning of the Back, to the yoke-line, then divide the sts. as follows :

The Right Half Back.—1ST ROW: (K. 3, m. 1, sl. 1, k. 2 tog., p.s.s.o., m. 1) 6 times, k. 4, turn, leaving the remaining 40 sts. for the opposite half.

2ND ROW: Cast off 3, p. to end.

3RD ROW: K. 1, k. 2 tog., m. 1, (k. 3, m. 1, sl. 1, k. 2 tog., p.s.s.o., m. 1) 5 times, k. 4.

4TH ROW: Cast off 3, p. to end. (34 sts.)

Repeat the last 4 rows 4 times more, but work the items in brackets once less on each repeat, when 10 sts. will remain.

Finish the shaping as follows :

1ST PATTERN ROW: K. 3, m. 1, sl. 1, k. 2 tog., p.s.s.o., m. 1, k. 4.

2ND ROW: Cast off 3, p. to end.

3RD ROW: K. 1, k. 2 tog., m. 1, k. 4.

4TH ROW: Cast off 3, p. 3 more.

5TH ROW: K. 4.

6TH ROW: Cast off 3 sts. Draw the wool through the remaining st. and fasten off.

The Left Back Shoulder.—Rejoin the wool to the remaining 40 sts. at the centre of the Back.

1ST ROW: Cast off 3 (1 st. on needle), k. 1, (m. 1, sl. 1, k. 2 tog., p.s.s.o., m. 1, k. 3) 5 times, m. 1, sl. 1, k. 2 tog., p.s.s.o., m. 1, k. 2.

2ND ROW: All purl.

3RD ROW: Cast off 3 (1 st. on needle), k. 1, (m. 1, sl. 1, k. 2 tog., p.s.s.o., m. 1, k. 3) 5 times, m. 1, sl. 1, k. 2 tog., m. 1, k. 2 tog.

4TH ROW: All purl.

Repeat these 4 rows 4 times more, but work the items in brackets once less on each repeat, when 10 sts. will remain.

Finish the shaping thus :

1ST ROW: Cast off 3, k. 1, m. 1, sl. 1, k. 2 tog., p.s.s.o., m. 1, k. 2.

MATERIALS

FOUR ounces of Copley's 2-ply "Excelsior" wool, or 6 ounces if long sleeves are worked ; a pair each of No. 10 and No. 12 knitting needles ; a steel crochet hook No. 3 for the crochet buttons ; a No. 9 crochet hook for the chain on the yoke.

TENSION AND MEASUREMENTS

WORKED at such a tension that one repeat of the main pattern (6 sts.) measures one inch in width with No. 10 needles, the measurements on the diagram will be attained without pressing.

ABBREVIATIONS—TO BE READ BEFORE WORKING

K KNIT plain ; p., purl ; st., stitch ; tog., together ; inc., increase (by working into the front and back of the same st.) ; dec., decrease (by working 2 sts. tog.) ; m., make (by bringing the wool to the front of the needle and over it before slipping or knitting the next st.) ; sl., slip ; p.s.s.o., pass the slipped st. (or sts.) over ; single rib is k. 1 and p. 1 alternately ; s.s., stocking stitch (k. on the right side and p. back) ; ch., chain ; d.c., double crochet ; tr., treble. Directions in brackets are worked the number of times stated after the last bracket.

TO WORK THE BACK

BEGIN at the lower edge and with No. 12 needles cast on 96 sts.

Work 36 rows in single rib, working into the back of the sts. on the 1st row to give a neat edge.

Change to No. 10 needles.

INC. ROW: (Inc., k. 4) 19 times, inc. (116 sts.)

Purl 1 row, then begin the main pattern as follows :

1ST ROW: * K. 3, m. 1, sl. 1, k. 2 tog., p.s.s.o., m. 1 ; repeat from * until 2 sts. remain, k. 2.

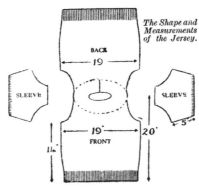

The Shape and Measurements of the Jersey.

BACK
19

SLEEVE

SLEEVE

19
20
5
19
FRONT
11

2ND ROW : All purl.

3RD ROW : Cast off 3, k. 1, m. 1, k. 2 tog.

4TH ROW : P. 4.

5TH ROW : Cast off 3 sts. Draw the wool through the remaining st. and fasten off.

THE FRONT

WORK this the same as the Back, but omit the 3 patterns worked straight immediately after the armhole shaping has been finished, so that the yoke shaping begins on the row following the last armhole row.

THE SLEEVES

BEGIN at the arm edge and with No. 10 needles cast on 80 sts. Work 10 rows in single rib, then work 10 complete patterns as at the beginning of the Back, or according to length required.

To Shape The Sleeve Top.—Work the first 4 rows of armhole shaping once. (68 sts.)

5TH ROW : * K. 3, m. 1, sl. 1, k. 2 tog., p.s.s.o., m. 1 ; repeat from * until 2 remain, k. 2.

6TH ROW : P. 2 tog., p. until 2 remain, p. 2 tog.

7TH ROW : K. 2 tog., m. 1, * k. 3, m. 1, sl. 1, k. 2 tog., p.s.s.o., m. 1 ; repeat from * until 4 remain, k. 4.

8TH ROW : As 6th row.

9TH ROW : K. 1, * m. 1, sl. 1, k. 2 tog., p.s.s.o., m. 1, k. 3 ; repeat from * until 3 remain, m. 1, sl. 1, k. 1, p.s.s.o., k. 1.

10TH ROW : P. 2 tog., p. until 2 remain, p. 2 tog. (62 sts.)

Repeat from the 5th to the 10th row 5 times more, when 32 sts. will remain.

Work 15 rows straight, beginning with the 1st row of pattern at the beginning of the Back.

NEXT ROW : P. 2 tog. all along the row. (16 sts.)

Cast off the remaining sts.

Make another sleeve in the same way.

For Long Sleeves.—Begin at the cuff and with No. 12 needles cast on 56 sts. Work 36 rows in single rib.

Change to No. 10 needles and work 2 patterns as on the Back, then inc. 1 st. at both ends of the next row and every following 8th row until the 12th inc. row has been worked. (80 sts.) If there is any difficulty in working the extra sts. in the lace pattern, keep these in s.s. until there are 6 more at each end, making another repeat of the pattern.

Work straight for length required, finishing with the 4th row of a pattern, then shape the top as for the short sleeves.

THE YOKE

BEGIN at the neck edge and with No. 12 needles cast on 122 sts. Work 3 rows in single rib.

Change to No. 10 needles.

4TH ROW : * Inc., p. 3 ; repeat from * until 2 remain, inc., p. 1. (153 sts.)

5TH ROW : K. 5, * k. 2 tog., m. 1, k. 1, k. 2 tog., m. 1, k. 2 tog. back (by knitting into the back of the sts.), k. 1, m. 1, k. 2 tog. back, k. 9 ; repeat from *, ending the last repeat with k. 9. (145 sts.)

6TH ROW : P. 9, * inc. (inc. purlwise on every wrong side row), p. 17 ; repeat from * 6 times more, inc., p. 9. (153 sts.)

7TH ROW : K. 4, * (k. 2 tog., m. 1) twice, k. 2 tog. back, k. 2 tog., (m. 1, k. 2 tog. back) twice, k. 7 ; repeat from *, ending the last repeat with k. 4. (137 sts.)

8TH ROW : P. 7, * inc., p. 2, inc., p. 13 ; repeat from * ending the last repeat with p. 7. (153 sts.)

9TH ROW : K. 3, * k. 2 tog., m. 1, k. 1, k. 2 tog. back, k. 2 tog., m. 1, k. 2 tog. back, k. 2 tog., k. 1, m. 1, k. 2 tog. back, k. 5 ; repeat from *, ending the last repeat with k. 3 instead of k. 5. (129 sts.)

10TH ROW : P. 8, * inc., p. 15 ; repeat from * 6 times more, inc., p. 8. (137 sts.)

WOMAN'S WEEKLY

EVERY TUESDAY   Nº 1854 · VOL. LXXI.   MAY · 17 · 1947

3ᵈ

A Romantic Design With a Yoke!

OUR MATRON'S CORNER

TALKING ABOUT
LITTLE BOYS

To make this little suit, allow ¾-yard of 36-54 inch material for the knickers, and ⅝ to 1 yard of 36-inch material for the blouse with short sleeves

Although I try to lay my baby down carefully, so as to keep his left ear flat, it will still stick out. What do you advise?—MICHAEL'S MOTHER.

IT is important to get the ears to stay back properly while baby is small, and particularly in the case of a boy, as the ears are more in evidence. The trouble can be remedied by wearing a small net bonnet. You can buy special little net caps at most large chemists, or you could quite well run one up yourself. Make a plain little bonnet of fine net, with tapes to tie beneath the chin. The part over the ears could be reinforced if the net tends to give.

A TINY BOY'S OUTFIT

I am writing to you to see what colours you would suggest for my little boy of three years. He is very fair with blonde hair, and I would like him in a really nice outfit for the Summer.—T. D.

YOU do not tell me what colour your little boy's eyes are, but as he is so fair, I think most shades of blue would suit him.

I would suggest a mid-blue light-weight tweed coat for the Summer, and a navy blue beret for the cooler days. He might have little buster suits of Dayella with checked or striped blouses and plain trousers.

A fine blue and white striped blouse, with plain blue knickers, would be attractive. His second suit could be of soft green and white checked Dayella with plain green knickers, and a third of cherry red with white stitching round the collar and down the front of the blouse. If you do not care for green for a small boy you might like a soft yellow and white or coffee-colour and white check.

Choose white socks and brown or red strap shoes.

11TH ROW: K. 2, * k. 2 tog., m. 1, k. 2, m. 1, k. 1, k. 2 tog. back, k. 2 tog., k. 1, m. 1, k. 2, m. 1, k. 2 tog. back, k. 3; repeat from *, ending the last repeat with k. 2.

12TH ROW AND EVERY FOLLOWING ALTERNATE ROW: All purl.

13TH ROW: (K. 1, k. 2 tog., m. 1, k. 3, m. 1, k. 1, m. 1, sl. 2, k. 2 tog., p.s.s.o., m. 1, k. 1, m. 1, k. 3, m. 1, k. 2 tog. back) 8 times, k. 1. (145 sts.)

15TH ROW: K. 2 tog., * m. 1, k. 4, m. 1, k. 3, m. 1, k. 1, m. 1, k. 3, m. 1, k. 4, m. 1, sl. 1, k. 2 tog., p.s.s.o.: repeat from *, ending the last repeat with k. 2 tog. back instead of sl. 1, k. 2 tog., p.s.s.o. (177 sts.)

17TH ROW: *(k. 2, m. 1, k. 2 tog. back) twice, k. 1, k. 2 tog., m. 1, k. 1, m. 1, k. 2 tog. back, k. 1, k. 2 tog., m. 1, k. 2, k. 2 tog., m. 1, k. 1; repeat from * 7 times more, k. 1.

19TH ROW: * K. 1, (m. 1, k. 2 tog. back) twice, k. 2, m. 1, sl. 1, k. 2 tog., p.s.s.o., m. 1, k. 3, m. 1, sl. 1, k. 2 tog., p.s.s.o., m. 1, k. 2, (k. 2 tog., m. 1) twice; repeat from * 7 times more, k. 1.

21ST ROW: (K. 1, k. 2 tog., m. 1, k. 1, m. 1, k. 2 tog. back, k. 3, m. 1, k. 2 tog. back, k. 1, k. 2 tog., m. 1, k. 3, k. 2 tog., m. 1, k. 1, m. 1, k. 2 tog. back) 8 times, k. 1.

23RD ROW: K. 2 tog., m. 1, k. 3, m. 1, k. 2 tog. back, k. 1, k. 2 tog., m. 1, sl. 1, k. 2 tog., p.s.s.o., m. 1, k. 2 tog. back, k. 1, k. 2 tog., m. 1, k. 3, m. 1, sl. 1, k. 2 tog., p.s.s.o.; repeat from *, ending with k. 2 tog. back instead of sl. 1, k. 2 tog., p.s.s.o. (161 sts.)

25TH ROW: K. 1, * m. 1, k. 2 tog., m. 1, k. 1, (m. 1, k. 2 tog. back) twice, k. 5, (k. 2 tog., m. 1) twice, k. 1, m. 1, k. 2 tog. back, m. 1, k. 1; repeat from * 7 times more. (177 sts.)

27TH ROW: K. 2 tog., m. 1, k. 3, k. 2 tog., m. 1, k. 1, m. 1, k. 2 tog. back, k. 3, k. 2 tog., m. 1, k. 1, m. 1, k. 2 tog. back, k. 1, k. 2 tog., m. 1, k. 3; repeat from * 7 times more, ending the last repeat with k. 2.

29TH ROW: K. 1, (m. 1, k. 2, m. 1, sl. 1, k. 2 tog., p.s.s.o.,

m. 1, k. 2, m. 1, k. 1, m. 1, k. 2 tog. back, k. 1, k. 2 tog., m. 1, k. 1, m. 1, k. 2, m. 1, sl. 1, k. 2 tog., p.s.s.o., m. 1, k. 2, m. 1, k. 1) 8 times. (209 sts.)

31ST ROW: K. 2, * m. 1, k. 2 tog. back, k. 3, k. 2 tog., m. 1, k. 3, m. 1, sl. 1, k. 2 tog., p.s.s.o., m. 1, k. 3, m. 1, k. 2 tog. back, k. 3, k. 2 tog., m. 1, k. 3; repeat from *, ending the last repeat with k. 2.

33RD ROW: K. 1, * (m. 1, k. 2 tog. back) twice, k. 1, (k. 2 tog., m. 1) twice, k. 1, m. 1, k. 2 tog. back, k. 1, k. 2 tog., m. 1, k. 1, (m. 1, k. 2 tog. back) twice, k. 1, (k. 2 tog., m. 1) twice, k. 1; repeat from * 7 times more.

35TH ROW: K. 2, * m. 1, k. 2 tog. back, m. 1, sl. 1, k. 2 tog., p.s.s.o., m. 1, k. 2 tog., m. 1, k. 3, m. 1, sl. 1, k. 2 tog., p.s.s.o., m. 1, k. 3, m. 1, k. 2 tog. back, m. 1, sl. 1, k. 2 tog., p.s.s.o., m. 1, k. 2 tog., m. 1, k. 3; repeat from *, ending the last repeat with k. 2. (209 sts.)

36TH ROW: All purl.
37TH ROW: All knit.
Cast off very loosely.

THE SHOULDER PADS

WITH No. 10 needles cast on 16 sts. Work 10 rows in s.s., then dec. 1 st. at both ends of the next 4 rows. Inc. 1 st. at both ends of the following 4 rows, then work 10 rows straight, and cast off.

Fold the knitting in half, and pad with a little cotton-wool then sew the remaining seam.

Make another pad in the same way.

TO MAKE UP THE JERSEY

THE *Button Band.*—Holding the yoke with the right side facing and using No. 10 needles, pick up and k. 20 sts. from row ends along the left side of the yoke, then work 7 rows in s.s. Cast off, and turn back the cast-off edge on the wrong side, then sew this edge to the 1st row.

The Buttonhole Band.—With No. 10 needles pick up and k. 20 sts. along the right edge of the yoke. P. 1 row, k. 1 row, and p. 1 row.

1ST BUTTONHOLE ROW: K. 2, (cast off 2, k. 3 more) 3 times.

2ND BUTTONHOLE ROW: (K. 4, cast on 2) 3 times, k. 2. K. 2 rows, then cast off.

To mark the position for the sleeves button the yoke and place flat. Now put a pin at each side fold. Measure 1½ inches on each side of the pin and mark with cotton or a small safety-pin. Repeat this at the opposite side. The space of 3 inches between the two safety pins is left free, for the top of the sleeve, when sewing the back and front to the yoke.

Sew the cast-off edge of the yoke to the shaped edges of the back and front of the jersey, beginning at the centre back, and leaving the 3 inches free at each side for the top of the sleeves. Set the sleeves into armholes and press the seams lightly on the wrong side, with a hot iron over a damp cloth. Join the sleeve and side seams in one line and press these seams.

The Crochet Buttons.—With the crochet hook make 3 ch. and sl.st. into the 1st ch. to form a ring. Work 18 tr. into the ring.

NEXT ROUND: Work 1 d.c. into every alternate st. (9 d.c.) Stuff the button cover with cotton-wool and draw the edges together, then fasten off.

Make 2 buttons more in the same way and sew them to the button-band on the yoke.

The Chain.—Take three lengths of wool, each 5 yards long, and using this triple thickness make a chain, using the No. 9 crochet hook. Sew this chain along the lower edge of the yoke.

Sew the shoulder pads in position.

Light and Lovely

MATERIALS : 4 oz. Paton's Beehive Fingering, 2-ply, (" Patonised " shrink-resist finish), pink ; a small quantity of contrasting-colour wool for the crochet edging ; a pair each of No. 9 and No. 12 knitting needles ; a medium-sized crochet hook ; and a little cottonwool.

MEASUREMENTS (AFTER PRESSING) : Length from lower edge to top of shoulder, 21 inches ; length of sleeve, along seam, 8½ inches ; to fit a 34 to 36-inch bust.

TENSION : Two patterns in width to 3½ inches, and one pattern in depth to 2 inches.

ABBREVIATIONS : St(s)., stitch(es) ; k., knit ; p., purl ; tog., together ; rep., repeat ; rem., remain(s)(ing)(der) ; inc., increase(ing) ; dec., decrease(ing) ; m., make ; sl., slip ; p.s.s.o., pass the slipped stitch over ; inst., instead of ; patt., pattern ; ch., chain ; d.c., double-crochet.

THE BACK

With No. 12 needles cast on 100 sts., and k. 1, p. 1 rib for 35 rows.

36th row : * Inc., rib 4 ; rep from *, ending row by inc., rib 3, inc. (121 sts.). Now change to No. 9 needles and patt. thus :

1st row : All k.

2nd row : All p.

3rd row : K. 5, * m. 1, sl. 1, k. 2 tog., and p.s.s.o., m. 1, k. 9 ; rep. from *, end row by k. 5 (inst. k. 9).

4th row : All p. Similarly every following even row.

5th row : K. 3, * k. 2 tog., m. 1, k. 3, m. 1, sl. 1, k. 1 and p.s.s.o., k. 5 ; rep. from *, end row by k. 3 (inst. k. 5).

7th row : As 3rd row.

9th row : All k.

11th row : K. 11, * m. 1, sl. 1, k. 2 tog. and p.s.s.o., m. 1, k. 9 ; rep. from *, end row by k. 11 (inst. k. 9).

13th row : K. 9, * k. 2 tog., m. 1, k. 3, m. 1, sl. 1, k. 1 and p.s.s.o., k. 5 ; rep. from *, end row by k. 9 (inst. k. 5).

15th row : As 11th row.

16th row : All p.

These 16 rows compose the pattern. Work 5 more entire patts. (6 in all).

To Shape the Armholes.—Cast off 4 sts. at the beginning of each of the next 6 rows, then k. 2 tog. at both ends of each of the following 6 rows (85 sts.). Cast off, loosely.

THE LEFT PORTION OF YOKE

With No. 9 needles cast on 45 sts.

1st row : All k.

2nd row : P. 41, k. 4, and similarly following even row. N.B.—These last 4 sts. are worked in garter-st. to the end of piece.

3rd row : K. 11 ; rep. from * in 5th row of patt., ending row by k. 3 (inst. k. 5).

5th row : K. 13 ; rep. from * in 3rd row of patt., ending row by k. 5 (inst. k. 9).

Keeping intact the border of 4 sts. in garter-st. and the next 4 sts. in stocking-st., on the rem. 37 sts. work in patt. as Back, working straight until 52 rows have in all been worked. Cast off.

THE RIGHT PORTION OF YOKE

Cast on 41 sts.

1st row : All k.

2nd row : All p.

3rd row : K. 3 ; rep. from * in 5th row of patt., ending row by k. 7 (inst. k. 5).

Working 37 sts. in patt. as for Back, and the last 4 sts. in stocking-st., work straight to match the Left portion.

THE FRONT

Work as directed for the Back until 6 entire patts. have been completed.

To Shape the Armholes.—Cast off 4 sts. at the beginning of each of the next 6 rows (97 sts.). Work straight for 5 more rows.

Next row (wrong side of work) : P. 21, (p. 2 tog.) 6 times, p. 31, (p. 2 tog.) 6 times, p. 21 (85 sts.). Cast off.

THE YOKE

Cast on 85 sts. and p. 1 row.

Next row : As 13th row of patt.

Work in patt. as usual, until 29 rows in patt. have been worked.

To Shape the Neck.—Next row (wrong side) : P. 37, cast off 11, p. to end.

Leave the first set of 37 sts. for the present, and work **One Shoulder** thus : On the Neck edge k. 2 tog. every row until 27 sts. rem. Work straight for 22 more rows. Cast off.

Now revert to the set of 37 sts. and work the other Shoulder in the same manner, and to match.

THE SLEEVES (both alike)

With No. 12 needles cast on 84 sts., and k. 1, p. 1 rib for 15 rows.

16th row : Rib 6, * inc., rib 2 ; rep. from *, ending row by inc., rib 5 (109 sts.). Now change to No. 9 needles, and work in patt. as for Back, until three entire patts. and the first 8 rows of 4th patt. have been completed.

To Shape the Top.—Cast off 3 sts. at the beginning of each of the next 6 rows, then k. 2 tog. at the end of each row until 51 sts. rem. Work straight for 14 more rows. Cast off 17 sts. at the beginning of each of the next 2 rows (17 sts.). Work straight in stocking-st. for 17 more rows. Cast off.

THE COLLAR

With No. 12 needles cast on 130 sts., and k. 1, p. 1 rib for 10 rows. Cast off.

THE BOWS (2 alike)

With No. 9 needles cast on 16 sts., and work 4 rows in garter-st., then commence in patt., thus :

1st row : K. 2, * m. 1, k. 2 tog. ; rep. from *, end row by k. 2.

2nd row : K. 2, p. until 2 rem., k. 2. These 2 rows compose the patt. Work 5 more patts. (6 in all).

Next row : K. 2 tog. for the entire row (8 sts.).

Next row : Inc. 1 st. in every st. (16 sts.), then rep. 1st and 2nd rows of patt. for 6 patts. more, followed by 4 rows in garter-st. Cast off. Work a second similar piece in the same way.

THE BUTTONS (8 alike)

With the crochet hook work 4 ch., and fasten so as to form a ring, into which work 10 d.c. for the first round. Working d.c. over d.c., work for 20 more d.c., then insert a tuft of cottonwool and cover by working d.c. in every alternate d.c. until closed. Fasten off.

ASSEMBLY AND FINISH

Join together the two pieces of Back Yoke to the Front Yoke by sewing up the shoulder seams. Using pink wool and the crochet hook, work 3 rows d.c. along the inner edge of right portion of Back Yoke, working 8 loops in the last row. Using contrasting wool, work 1 row d.c. all around the outer edges of the yoke ; also round the edges of the bows.

Carefully press all the pieces on the wrong side under a damp cloth with a hot iron.

Neatly sew the lower portions of both Back and Front underneath the d.c. edging of the yoke. Sew the outer edges of the last 17 rows at top of sleeves to the cast-off edges of 17 sts., and neatly sew tops of sleeves underneath the crochet edging of yoke.

Sew collar to neck edge, folded in two lengthwise. Press seams while garment is still open. Sew up rem. seams and press. Sew on buttons at back. Gather each bow in the centre and sew on as illustrated.

A KNITTED WAISTCOAT

So Dashing And Warm!

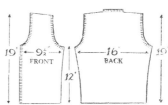

The Shape and Measurements of the Waistcoat.

MATERIALS

SIX ounces of W.B. Melody Knitting Wool, 3-ply; a pair each of No. 10 and No. 12 knitting needles; 5 buttons or button-moulds; a steel crochet hook No. 2 for the crochet buttons.

TENSION AND MEASUREMENTS

WORKED at a tension of 10 sts. to the inch in width with No. 10 needles on the rib pattern, the measurements on the diagram are attained after light pressing.

ABBREVIATIONS—TO BE READ BEFORE WORKING

KNIT plain; p.=purl; st., stitch; tog., together; inc., increase (by working into the front and back of the same st.); dec., decrease (by working 2 sts. tog.); single rib is k. 1 and p. 1 alternately; d.c., double crochet. Directions in brackets are worked the number of times stated after the last bracket.

TO WORK THE BACK

BEGIN at the lower edge and using No. 12 needles cast on 122 sts.

1st Row : K. 2, * p. 1, k. 1 ; repeat from * to end of row.

Repeat the 1st row 6 times more, then k. 1 row.

Now begin the pattern as follows :—

Work 9 rows in rib as set on the 1st row.

10th Row : All knit.

These 10 rows form the pattern, so repeat them twice more.

Change to No. 10 needles and rib 8 rows more.

Continue in pattern and inc. 1 st. at both ends of the next row and every following 4th row, until the 16th inc. row has been worked, when there will be 154 sts.

K. 1 row more.

To Shape The Armholes.—Cast off 16 sts. at the beginning of the next 2 rows, then dec. 1 st. at both ends of the next row and following 9 alternate rows, when 102 sts. will remain.

Work 49 rows in pattern without shaping, finishing with the 10th pattern row.

To Slope The Shoulders.—1st AND 2ND ROWS : Rib until 9 sts. remain ; turn.

3RD AND 4TH ROWS : Rib until 18 sts. remain ; turn.

5TH AND 6TH ROWS : Rib until 27 sts. remain ; turn.

7TH ROW : (Rib 4, k. 2 tog.) 7 times, rib to end of row.

Cast off straight across.

THE LEFT FRONT

WITH No. 12 needles cast on 64 sts. and work exactly the same as the Back until the row before the side increases is completed.

Continue in rib pattern and inc. 1 st. at the beginning only of the next row and every following 4th row until the 16th inc. has been worked, when there will be 80 sts.

K. 1 row.

** To Shape The Armhole And Neck.—1ST ROW : Cast off 16 sts. (arm end), rib to end of row.

2ND ROW : Cast off 12 sts., rib to end of row. (52 sts.)

Work 11 rows more, decreasing 1 st. at the neck edge of every row and at the armhole end of the 1st row and following alternate rows, when 35 sts. will remain.

Work 1 row without shaping.

Dec. 1 st. at both ends of the next row and following 3 alternate rows, when 27 sts. will remain.

Work 50 rows straight in rib pattern, ending at the neck edge.

To Slope The Shoulder.—1st Row : Rib until 9 sts. remain ; turn.

2ND ROW : Rib to end of row.

3RD ROW : Rib until 18 sts. remain ; turn.

4TH ROW : Rib to end of row.

Cast off the 27 sts.

THE RIGHT FRONT

WITH No. 12 needles cast on 64 sts. and work as for the Back until the row before the side increases is completed.

Continue in rib pattern and inc. 1 st. at the end of the next row and every following 4th row, until the 16th inc. has been worked, when there will be 80 sts.

Work 2 rows without shaping, then continue from ** on the Left Front to the end.

THE NECK-BAND

FIRST join the shoulder seams, beginning at the arm end and taking 1 st. from each side at a time. Holding the work with the right side facing and using No. 12 needles, begin at the right front neck edge and pick up 83 sts. evenly along the neck edge, finishing at the right shoulder, then 39 sts. across the back of neck, and 83 sts. down the left front neck edge. (205 sts.)

Work the following rib rows firmly.

1ST ROW : * K. 1, p. 1 ; repeat from * until 1 st. remains, k. 1.

2ND ROW : K. 2, * p. 1, k. 1 ; repeat from * until 1 st. remains, k. 1.

Repeat these 2 rows 4 times more.

Cast off in rib thus : K. 1, * p. 1, slip the k. st. over and off the needle, k. 1, pass the p. st. over ; repeat from * to end. Fasten off.

THE BUTTONHOLE-BAND

USING No. 12 needles and with the right side facing, begin at the lower edge of the Right Front, and pick up and k. 125 sts. along the front edge, including the neck-band edge. Work the 1st and 2nd rows of neck-band once, then the 1st row again.

1ST BUTTONHOLE ROW : K. 2 (p. 1, k. 1) twice, * cast off 2 (1 st. on needle), rib 25 ; repeat from * 3 times more, cast off 2 sts., k. 1, p. 1, k. 2.

2ND BUTTONHOLE ROW : (K. 1, p. 1) twice, k. 1, * cast on 2 sts. over those cast off to complete the buttonhole, rib 26 ; repeat from * 3 times more, cast on 2 sts., rib 6.

Rib 3 rows more, then cast off in rib.

The Button-Band.—Work as for the buttonhole-band, but rib 2 rows more instead of the buttonhole rows.

THE ARMHOLE-BANDS

HOLDING the work with the right side facing and using No. 12 needles, pick up and k. 166 sts. all round one armhole edge.

Work 9 rows in single rib as on the neck-band, then cast off in rib.

Work the other armhole-band in the same way.

TO MAKE UP THE WAISTCOAT

PRESS the knitting very lightly on the wrong side, with a hot iron over a damp cloth and a thick blanket underneath. Join the side seams, and press all seams.

THE CROCHET BUTTONS

USING a No. 2 crochet hook make 6 chain and slip-st. into the 1st chain to form a ring.

Work 1 round of 2 d.c. into every chain. (12 d.c.)

NEXT ROUND: * 1 d.c. into the 1st d.c., 2 d.c. into the next d.c.; repeat from * all round. (18 d.c.)

Work 1 round of 1 d.c. into every st.

Now slip in an old button or button-mould and work rounds of d.c., missing every alternate st. until the back is nearly closed. Cut the wool, leaving about 12 inches hanging, and sew across the button cover at the back to close it.

Make 3 buttons more in the same way.

A LACY JERSEY IN WAVE PATTERN

Instructions For Long And Short Sleeves Are Given

MATERIALS

SIX ounces of " Greenock " Super Fingering, 3-ply, or 8 ounces if long sleeves are worked (obtainable only from branches of Scotch Wool & Hosiery Stores); a pair each of No. 9 and No. 11 knitting needles; a steel crochet hook No. 1 for the double crochet on the shoulder; press-studs.

TENSION AND MEASUREMENTS

WORKED at such a tension that one repeat of the pattern (14 sts.) measures 1¾ inches with No. 9 needles, the measurements on the diagram are attained after light pressing.

For one size smaller (36 inches bust measure) use No. 10 and No. 12 needles.

ABBREVIATIONS—TO BE READ BEFORE WORKING

K., KNIT plain; p., purl; st., stitch; tog., together; inc., increase (by working into the front and back of the same st.); dec., decrease (by working 2 sts. tog.); m., make (by bringing the wool to the front of the needle and over it before knitting the next st.); single rib is k. 1 and p. 1 alternately. Directions in brackets are worked the number of times stated after the last bracket.

TO WORK THE BACK

BEGIN at the lower edge and using No. 11 needles cast on 128 sts. Work 36 rows in single rib, increasing 1 st. at the end of the last row. (129 sts.)

Change to No. 9 needles and begin the pattern as follows:
1st Row: K. 2, * m. 1, k. 5, k. 3 tog., k. 5, m. 1, k. 1; repeat from * until 1 st. remains, k. 1.
2nd Row: All purl.
3rd Row: All knit.
4th Row: As 1st row.
Repeat these 4 rows once more, then the first 3 rows again.
12th Row and 13th Row: All purl.
14th Row: All knit.
15th Row: All purl.
16th Row: All knit.
These 16 rows form the pattern.

Continue in pattern and inc. 1 st. at both ends of the next row and every following 8th row until the 8th inc. row has been worked, when there will be 145 sts. (Work the extra sts. in the stocking-stitch pattern, with the k. or p. sts. on the right side to correspond with the remainder of the row, and remember to count these stitches extra to the lacy pattern.)

Work 7 rows without shaping, finishing on the last row of a pattern.

To Shape The Armholes.—1st Row: Cast off 6 (1 st. on needle), k. 3, * m. 1, k. 5, k. 3 tog., k. 5, m. 1, k. 1; repeat from * until 9 sts. remain, k. 9.
2nd Row: Cast off 6, p. to end.
3rd Row: Cast off 6, k. to end.
4th Row: Cast off 6 (1 st. on needle), k. 3, k. 2 tog., k. 5, m. 1, k. 1, * m. 1, k. 5, k. 3 tog., k. 5, m. 1, k. 1; repeat from * until 11 sts. remain, m. 1, k. 5, k. 2 tog., k. 4.
5th Row: K. 2 tog., k. 2, k. 2 tog., k. 5, m. 1, k. 1, * m. 1, k. 5, k. 3 tog., k. 5, m. 1, k. 1; repeat from * until 11 remain, m. 1, k. 5, k. 2 tog., k. 2, k. 2 tog.
6th Row: P. 2 tog., p. until 2 remain, p. 2 tog.
7th Row: K. 2 tog., k. until 2 remain, k. 2 tog.
8th Row: K. 2 tog., k. 7, * m. 1, k. 5, k. 3 tog., k. 5, m. 1, k. 1; repeat from * until 8 remain, k. 6, k. 2 tog.
9th Row: K. 2 tog., k. 6, * m. 1, k. 5, k. 3 tog., k. 5, m. 1, k. 1; repeat from * until 7 remain, k. 5, k. 2 tog.
10th Row: P. 2 tog., p. until 2 remain, p. 2 tog.
11th Row: K. 2 tog., k. until 2 remain, k. 2 tog.
12th Row: P. 2 tog., p. until 2 remain, p. 2 tog.
13th Row: P. 2 tog., p. until 2 remain, p. 2 tog.
14th Row: K. 2 tog., k. until 2 remain, k. 2 tog. (101 sts.)
Work the 15th and 16th rows of straight pattern as at the beginning, then 3 complete patterns more.

To Slope The Shoulders.—1st Row: Cast off 6 (1 st. on needle, and likewise on every following row), k. 1, k. 2 tog., k. 5, m. 1, k. 1, * m. 1, k. 5, k. 3 tog., k. 5, m. 1, k. 1; repeat from * until 1 st. remains, k. 1.
2nd Row: Cast off 6, p. to end.
3rd Row: Cast off 6, k. to end.
4th Row: Cast off 6, k. 3, * m. 1, k. 5, k. 3 tog., k. 5, m. 1, k. 1; repeat from * until 3 remain, k. 3.
5th Row: Cast off 6, k. 3, k. 2 tog., k. 5, m. 1, k. 1, * m. 1, k. 5, k. 3 tog., k. 5, m. 1, k. 1; repeat from * until 3 remain, k. 3.
6th Row: Cast off 6, p. to end.
7th Row: Cast off 6, k. to end.
8th Row: Cast off 6, k. 5, * m. 1, k. 5, k. 3 tog., k. 5, m. 1, k. 1; repeat from * until 5 remain, k. 5.

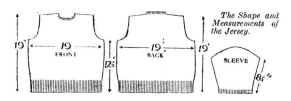

The Shape and Measurements of the Jersey.

Continued overleaf

v

9TH ROW: Cast off 6, k. 5, k. 2 tog., k. 5, m. 1, k. 1, * m. 1, k. 5, k. 3 tog., k. 5, m. 1, k. 1; repeat from * until 5 remain, k. 5.

10TH ROW: Cast off 6, p. to end.

Cast off the remaining 41 sts.

THE FRONT

WORK the same as for the back until the arm-hole shaping has been finished and 101 sts. remain. Work 28 rows more, finishing with the 10th row of a pattern.

The Left Front Shoulder.—1ST ROW: K. 34, turn, leaving the remaining 67 sts. on a spare needle.

2ND ROW: P. 2 tog., p. to end.

3RD ROW: P. until 2 sts. remain, p. 2 tog.

4TH ROW: K. 2 tog., k. to end. (31 sts.)

Work 18 rows more, beginning with the 15th row of straight pattern at the beginning of the Back.

To Slope The Shoulder.—1ST ROW: Cast off 6 (1 st. on needle), k. 1, k. 2 tog., k. 5, m. 1, k. 1, m. 1, k. 5, k. 3 tog., k. 5, m. 1, k. 2.

2ND ROW: All purl.

3RD ROW: Cast off 6, k. to end.

4TH ROW: K. 2, m. 1, k. 5, k. 3 tog., k. 5, m. 1, k. 4.

5TH ROW: Cast off 6 (1 st. on needle), k. 3, k. 2 tog., k. 5, m. 1, k. 2.

6TH ROW: All purl.

7TH ROW: Cast off 6, k. to end.

8TH ROW: All knit.

Cast off the remaining 7 sts.

Slip the centre 33 sts. on to a spare needle for the neck-band, and rejoin the wool at the neck edge of the remaining 34 sts.

The Right Front Shoulder.—1ST ROW: K. 2 tog., k. to end.

2ND ROW: P. until 2 remain, p. 2 tog.

3RD ROW: P. 2 tog., p. to end. (31 sts.)

Work 18 rows more in pattern, beginning with the 14th row of straight pattern on the Back.

To Slope The Shoulder.—1ST ROW: (16TH PATTERN ROW) Cast off 6, k. to end.

2ND ROW: K. 2, m. 1, k. 5, k. 3 tog., k. 5, m. 1, k. 1, m. 1, k. 5, k. 2 tog., k. 2.

3RD ROW: Cast off 6, p. to end.

4TH ROW: All knit.

5TH ROW: Cast off 6 (1 st. on needle), k. 3, k. 2 tog., k. 5, m. 1, k. 2.

6TH ROW: K. 2, m. 1, k. 5, k. 2 tog., k. 4.

7TH ROW: Cast off 6, p. to end.

8TH ROW: Knit.

Cast off the remaining 7 sts.

THE NECK-BAND

FIRST join the right shoulder seam, beginning at the arm end and taking 1 st. from each side at a time. Using No. 11 needles and holding the work with the right side facing, pick up 20 sts. from the neck edge of the left front shoulder, 33 sts. from the spare needle at centre front, 20 sts. from the right side of neck, and 45 sts. from the back of neck. (118 sts.)

Work 9 rows in single rib, then cast off in rib thus: K. 1, * p. 1, slip the k. st. over, k. 1, pass the p. st. over; repeat from * to end. Fasten off.

An unusual aerial view of Ramsgate, one of Thanet's most popular holiday resorts.

IDEAS FOR YOUR HOLIDAY

A Suggestion For The Young Girl Who Is Alone

I want my eighteen-year-old daughter to have a seaside holiday this year, but unfortunately I cannot take her myself, and my husband does not like the idea of her going with friends whom we do not know.

Can you suggest anything that would solve my difficulty ?—Mrs. E. (Luton).

YOU will be pleased to hear that the Y.W.C.A. have organised a series of holiday centres in different parts of England and Wales, and you could safely send your daughter there knowing that she would be in good hands. Perhaps this would interest her friends, too. Each hostel is in charge of a warden as at permanent centres.

Some of these Holiday Centres, such as Shanklin, Bexhill and Eastbourne, are open for the holiday months only ; others, which include Felixstowe, Rhyl and Burnham-on-Sea, are permanent.

If you are interested and would like to have details, write to : The Holidays Bookings Secretary, Y.W.C.A. National Offices, Great Russell Street, London, W.C.1. Ask for Holiday Leaflet and enclose a stamped self-addressed envelope.

IN DEVON

I have spent my holidays chiefly in Scotland and have always enjoyed them very much. This year, however, I shall have to wait until late in September, or even October, for my leave, so I think I should be wiser to have a change and journey south instead of north.

I would prefer a town, on account of the short evenings, but I should like to be near moorland country. Can you suggest a nice district in Devonshire for me ?—Joan (Burslem).

SIDMOUTH, Exmouth, Paignton Torquay, or Teignmouth are good all-the-year-round places with nice shops and amusements.

Then there is Dartmouth, a picturesque little town on the River Dart, but quite near the sea, and in the midst of charming scenery. It has a ferry service which connects it with Kingswear.

All these centres are within easy reach of moorland ; and Summer lingers on a long time in this lovely district.

---

k. 1 ; repeat from * until 7 remain, k. 5, k. 2 tog.

10TH Row : P. 2 tog., p. until 2 remain, p. 2 tog.

11TH Row : K. 2 tog., k. until 2 remain, k. 2 tog.

Repeat the 10th row twice more. Work the 11th, 10th and then 11th rows again.

17TH Row : K. 2 tog., k. 4, k. 2 tog., k. 5, m. 1, k. 1, * m. 1, k. 5, k. 3 tog., k. 5, m. 1, k. 1 ; repeat from * until 13 remain, m. 1, k. 5, k. 2 tog., k. 4, k. 2 tog.

18TH Row : P. 2 tog., p. until 2 remain, p. 2 tog.

19TH Row : K. 2 tog., k. until 2 remain, k. 2 tog.

20TH Row : K. 2 tog., k. 1, k. 2 tog., k. 5, m. 1, k. 1, * m. 1, k. 5, k. 3 tog., k. 5, m. 1, k. 1 ; repeat from * until 10 remain, m. 1, k. 5, k. 2 tog., k. 1, k. 2 tog.

21ST Row : K. 2 tog. twice, k. 5, m. 1, k. 1, * m. 1, k. 5, k. 3 tog., k. 5, m. 1, k. 1 ; repeat from * until 9 remain, m. 1, k. 5, k. 2 tog. twice.

22ND Row : P. 2 tog., p. until 2 remain, p. 2 tog.

23RD Row : K. 2 tog., k. until 2 remain, k. 2 tog.

24TH Row : K. 2 tog., k. 5, * m. 1, k. 5, k. 3 tog., k. 5, m. 1, k. 1 ; repeat from * until 6 remain, k. 4, k. 2 tog.

25TH Row : K. 2 tog., k. 4, * m. 1, k. 5, k. 3 tog., k. 5, m. 1, k. 1 ; repeat from * until 5 remain, k. 3, k. 2 tog. (51 sts.)

P. 1 row, k. 1 row, p. 2 rows, k. 1 row, p. 1 row and k. 1 row, taking 2 sts. tog. at both ends of every row. (37 sts.)

33RD Row : K. 2 tog., k. 2, k. 2 tog., k. 5, m. 1, k. 1, * m. 1, k. 5, k. 3 tog., k. 5, m. 1, k. 1 ; repeat from * until 11 remain, m. 1, k. 5, k. 2 tog., k. 2, k. 2 tog.

34TH Row : P. 2 tog., p. until 2 remain, p. 2 tog.

35TH Row : K. 2 tog., k. until 2 remain, k. 2 tog.

THE SLEEVES

BEGIN at the arm edge and using No. 11 needles cast on 68 sts. Work 15 rows in single rib.

INC. Row : (wrong side) K. 1, (inc., k. 1) 33 times, k. 1 (101 sts.)

Change to No. 9 needles and work 4 complete patterns as on Back.

To Shape The Sleeve Top.—1ST Row : K. 2 tog., * m. 1, k. 5, k. 3 tog., k. 5, m. 1, k. 1 ; repeat from * until 15 remain, m. 1, k. 5, k. 3 tog., k. 5, m. 1, k. 2 tog.

2ND Row : P. 2 tog., p. until 2 remain, p. 2 tog.

3RD Row : K. 2 tog., k. until 2 remain, k. 2 tog.

4TH Row : K. 2 tog., k. 3, k. 2 tog., k. 5, m. 1, k. 1, * m. 1, k. 5, k. 3 tog., k. 5, m. 1, k. 1 ; repeat from * until 12 remain, m. 1, k. 5, k. 2 tog., k. 3, k. 2 tog.

5TH Row : K. 2 tog., k. 2, k. 2 tog., k. 5, m. 1, k. 1, * m. 1, k. 5, k. 3 tog., k. 5, m. 1, k. 1 ; repeat from * until 11 remain, m. 1, k. 5, k. 2 tog., k. 2, k. 2 tog.

6TH Row : P. 2 tog., p. until 2 remain, p. 2 tog.

7TH Row : K. 2 tog., k. until 2 remain, k. 2 tog.

8TH Row : K. 2 tog., k. 7, * m. 1, k. 5, k. 3 tog., k. 5, m. 1, k. 1 ; repeat from * until 8 remain, k. 6, k. 2 tog.

9TH Row : K. 2 tog., k. 6, * m. 1, k. 5, k. 3 tog., k. 5, m. 1,

Cast off the remaining 31 sts.

Work another sleeve in the same way.

FOR LONG SLEEVES

BEGIN at the wrist and with No. 11 needles cast on 60 sts. Work 36 rows in single rib.

INC. Row (wrong side) : K. 8, * inc., k. 3 ; repeat from * to end. (73 sts.)

Change to No. 9 needles and work one complete pattern as on the Back, then inc. 1 st. at both ends of the next row and every following 6th row, until the 14th inc. row has been worked, when there will be one complete pattern more at each end. (101 sts.)

Work straight for length required, finishing with the 16th pattern row, then shape the top as for the short sleeves.

TO MAKE UP THE JERSEY

FIRST press all parts except the ribbing on the wrong side, with a hot iron over a damp cloth. Join the left shoulder seam for one inch, beginning at the arm end. Set the sleeves into armholes and press these seams. Join the sleeve and side seams in one line and press. Work a row of double crochet along the left shoulder and fasten this shoulder with press studs.

The unique, frill-edged yoke is most becoming

KNITTED in ribbing, with a moss-stitch yoke, this jumper is very smooth fitting. Make it in buttercup yellow or sky blue for Summer !

Materials : 7 ozs. of "Jester" Fashion Fingering, 3-ply ; 1 pair of No. 11 knitting needles ; 4 button moulds ; a medium-size crochet hook.

Tension : 17 sts. to 2 inches and 11 rows to 1 inch over the rib, but over the moss-stitch 8 sts. and 12 rows to 1 inch.

Measurements : All round underarms, nearly 30 inches, stretching to 32 inches ; length, just over 19 inches ; sleeve seam, 4¼ inches.

Abbreviations : K., knit ; p., purl ; st., stitch ; sts., stitches ; rep., repeat ; tog., together ; inc., increase (by working twice into the same st.) ; dec., decrease (by taking 2 sts. tog.) ; m.-st., moss-stitch ; d.c., double crochet. Stitches in brackets must be worked all along row, or the number of times stated after 2nd bracket, or until stated number of sts. remain.

THE BACK

Cast on 111 sts.

1st rib row : P. 3, (k. 1, p. 3) to end of row.
2nd rib row : K. 3, (p. 1, k. 3) to end of row.

Rep. these 2 rib rows once, then, keeping the continuity of ribs, dec. 1 st. at each end of next row and every 6th row after until there are 93 sts. Work 13 rows straight. Now inc. 1 st. at each end of next row and every 6th row after until there are 119 sts. Work 5 rows straight.

To shape armholes, cast off 2 sts. at start of next 2 rows, then dec. 1 st. at start of every row until 101 sts. remain.

Work 52 rows without dec. To shape shoulders, cast off 9 sts. at start of the next 8 rows. Cast off remaining 29 sts. for back neck.

THE FRONT

Cast on 123 sts. and work the 2 rib rows of back twice, then dec. 1 st. at each end of next row and every 6th row after until there are 105 sts. Work 13 rows straight. Now inc. 1 st. at each end of next row and every 6th row after until there are 131 sts. Work 5 rows straight.

To shape armholes, cast off 8 sts. at start of next 2 rows, then dec. 1 st. at each end of the following 4 rows, after which dec. 1 st. at each end of next 8 rows. There are now 99 sts. Work 2 rows straight, then divide for front opening and begin m.-st. yoke, as follows :

1st row : (K. 1, p. 1) 23 times, turn. Leaving remaining 53 sts. on a spare needle, continue on the first set of 46 sts. thus :

2nd row : Cast on 7 sts., (k. 1, p. 1) to 1 st. from end, k. 1.
3rd row : (K. 1, p. 1) to 1 st. from end, k. 1.

Rep. 3rd row until you have worked 47 rows m.-st. altogether, ending at centre edge. To start neck shaping, cast off 9 sts. at start of next row. Now continue neck shaping thus : ** Cast off next 2 rows that begin from neck edge, and 2 sts. at the start of the 2 following rows that begin from neck edge. Work 2 rows straight. To shape shoulder cast off 8 sts. at start of next 3 rows that commence from armhole end, then work 1 row, after which cast off remaining 10 sts.**

Return to the 53 sts. on spare needle, join wool to inner end of sts. and cast on 7 sts. for buttonhole facing, so that you have 60 sts. on needle, and proceed thus :

1st row—2nd side : (P. 1, k. 1) to end of row.
2nd row : (K. 1, p. 1) to end of row.

Rep. these 2 rows twice. Make 2 buttonholes on next 2 rows thus :

1st buttonhole row : M.-st. 2, cast off 3, work in m.-st. until you have 4 sts. on needle after the cast-off, then cast off next 3 sts., then m.-st. to end of row.

2nd buttonhole row : M.-st. to last 6 sts., cast on 3, m.-st. 4, cast on 3, m.-st. 2.

Work another 10 rows m.-st.

Rep. last 12 rows twice more, then rep. the 2 buttonhole rows again. Work 2 rows m.-st., then to commence neck shaping, cast off 16 sts. at start of next row. Now work as 1st side from ** to **.

THE SLEEVES (both alike)

Cast on 71 sts. and work the 2 rib rows of back twice. Inc. 1 st. at each end of next row and every 6th row after until there are 85 sts. Work 5 rows straight. To shape top, cast off 4 sts. at start of next 2 rows, then dec. 1 st. at start of every row until 65 sts. remain. Now dec. 1 st. at each end of every 6th row until 51 sts. remain. Cast off 4 sts. at start of the next 10 rows. Cast off remainder.

THE YOKE FRILL

Cast on 136 sts.

1st row : K. **2nd and every alternate row :** P. **3rd row :** K. 2, (inc. 1 st. in each of the next 2 sts., k. 3) to last 4 sts., inc. in each of the next 2 sts., k. 2. **5th row :** K. 3, (inc. in each of the next 2 sts., k. 5) to last 5 sts., inc. in each of the next 2 sts., k. 3. **7th row :** K. 4, (inc. in each of the next 2 sts., k. 7) to last 6 sts., inc. in each of the next 2 sts., k. 4. **9th row :** K. 5, (inc. in each of the next 2 sts., k. 9) to last 7 sts., inc. in each of the next 2 sts., k. 5. **10th and 11th rows :** Work in m.-st. Cast off.

THE BUTTON COVERS (4 alike)

Make 3 chain and join into a ring with a slip-st. **1st round :** Work 6 d.c. into the ring. **2nd round :** 2 d.c. in each d.c. **3rd and 4th rounds :** 1 d.c. in each d.c. **5th and 6th rounds :** 1 d.c. in every alternate d.c. Fasten off. Cover the moulds with the crochet.

TO COMPLETE

Press work very lightly on wrong side with a warm iron over a damp cloth. Join all seams. Sew in sleeves, easing them in over shoulder. Fold the buttonhole facing over to wrong side so that the buttonholes come together, and catch-stitch down. Sew down base of under-flap of left front. Sew frill all round front yoke. Work a row of d.c. all round neck edge. Attach buttons.

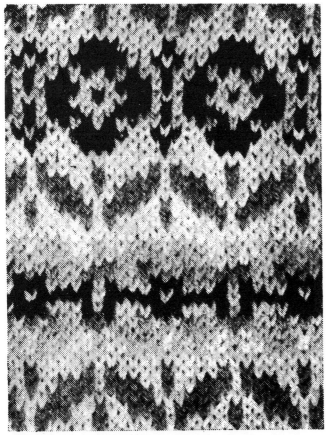

MATERIALS

*T*HREE ounces of Copley's Shetland Floss in natural, and one ounce each of the same wool in pink, brown, and green; a pair each of No. 9 and 12 knitting needles.

TENSION AND MEASUREMENTS

*W*ORKED at a tension of 8 sts. to the inch in width with No. 9 needles on the Fair Isle pattern, the measurements on the diagram are attained after light pressing.

ABBREVIATIONS—TO BE READ BEFORE WORKING

*K*NIT plain; p., purl; st., stitch; tog., together; inc., increase (by working into the back and front of the same st.); dec., decrease (by taking 2 sts. tog.); s.s., stocking-st. (k. on the right side and p. back); single rib is k. 1 and p. 1 alternately; n., natural; g., green; b., brown; pk., pink. Directions in brackets are worked the number of times stated after the last bracket.

You'll Feel HAPPY In It

A Fair Isle Pullover With An Attractive Deep Neckline

MULTI-COLOURED KNITTING

*T*O avoid loose threads at the back of the work, the method known as "weaving in" is adopted by all good knitters.

For this the wool out of action is passed once over the working thread, before working each stitch with the second colour, so that the spare thread is caught at the back of the work with every stitch. If the wool is passed over with a forward movement, then a backward movement, alternately, tangled wool is avoided. Some workers can work more easily by holding the spare wool to the left over the first finger, as in crochet work, then passing the knitting needle alternately under and over it, when working with the second wool. On the purl side see that the spare colour is kept at the front of the work.

TO WORK THE BACK

*B*EGIN at the lower edge by casting on 109 sts. with natural wool and No. 12 needles.

1ST ROW (right side): P. 1, * k. 1, p. 1; repeat from * to end.

2ND ROW: K. 1, * p. 1, k. 1; repeat from * to end.

Repeat these 2 rows 19 times more.

INC. ROW: K. 4, inc., (k. 8, inc.) 11 times, k. 5. (121 sts.) Change to No. 9 needles and p. 1 row in natural.

Now begin the Fair Isle pattern, which is worked entirely in s.s., beginning with a k. row, so only the colour details are given.

1ST ROW (right side): 1 n., * (1 g., 4 n.) twice, 1 g., 1 n.; repeat from * to end.

2ND ROW: 1 n., * 3 g., 2 n., 1 g., 2 n., 3 g., 1 n.; repeat from * to end.

3RD ROW: 2 n., * 3 g., 3 n.; repeat from *, ending the last repeat with 2 n.

4TH ROW: 1 g., * 2 n., 3 g., 1 n., 3 g., 2 n., 1 g.; repeat from * to end.

5TH ROW: 1 g., * 4 n., 1 g., 1 n., 1 g., 4 n., 1 g.; repeat from * to end. Fasten off g.

6TH ROW: All n. Join in b.

7TH ROW: 2 b., * 4 n., 1 b., 4 n., 3 b.; repeat from *, ending the last repeat with 2 b.

8TH ROW: 3 b., * 2 n., 1 b., 1 n., 1 b., 2 n., 5 b.; repeat from *, ending the last repeat with 3 b. Fasten off n. and join in pk.

9TH ROW: 1 pk., * 1 b., 1 pk., (1 b., 2 pk.) twice, (1 b., 1 pk.) twice; repeat from * to end.

10TH ROW: 2 pk., * 3 b., 1 pk., 1 b., 1 pk., 3 b., 3 pk.; repeat from *, ending last repeat with 2 pk.

11TH ROW: 1 b., * 2 pk., 2 b., 3 pk., 2 b., 2 pk., 1 b.; repeat from * to end.

Repeat 10th, 9th, 8th and 7th rows, in that order. Fasten off b.

16TH ROW: Using n. only (p. 3, inc. purlwise) 3 times p. until 12 remain, (inc., p. 3) 3 times. (127 sts.) Join in g.

17TH ROW: 3 n., 1 g., * 4 n., 1 g., 1 n., 1 g., 4 n., 1 g.; repeat from * until 3 remain, 3 n.

18TH ROW: 1 g., 2 n., 1 g., * 2 n., 3 g., 1 n., 3 g., 2 n., 1 g.; repeat from * until 3 remain, 2 n., 1 g.

19TH ROW: 2 g., * 3 n., 3 g.; repeat from *, ending last repeat with 2 g.

20TH ROW: 3 g., 1 n., 3 g., * 2 n., 1 g., 2 n., 3 g., 1 n., 3 g.; repeat from * to end.

21ST ROW: 2 n., * 1 g., 1 n., (1 g., 4 n.) twice; repeat from * until 5 remain, 1 g., 1 n., 1 g., 2 n. Fasten off g.

22ND ROW: All n. Join in pk.

** 23RD ROW: (1 pk., 2 n.) twice, * 3 pk., 1 n., 3 pk., 2 n., 1 pk., 2 n.; repeat from * until 1 remains, 1 pk.

24TH ROW: 2 pk., 1 n., 1 pk., 1 n., * (4 pk., 1 n.) twice, 1 pk., 1 n.; repeat from * until 2 remain, 2 pk. Fasten off n. and join in g.

25TH ROW: 2 pk., 3 g., 2 pk., * 1 g. (1 pk., 1 g.) twice, 2 pk., 3 g., 2 pk.; repeat from * to end. Fasten off g. and join in b.

26TH ROW: 2 pk., 1 b., 1 pk., 1 b., * 3 pk., 3 b., 3 pk., 1 pk., 1 b.; repeat from * until 2 remain, 2 pk.

27TH ROW: 3 b., 1 pk., * 5 b., 1 pk.; repeat from * until 3 remain, 3 b.

Repeat 26th row back to the 23rd row.

32ND ROW: As 16th row. (133 sts.). (145 sts. here on the

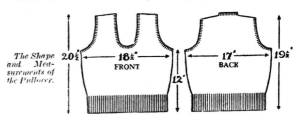

The Shape and Measurements of the Pullover.

20½" 18½" FRONT 17" BACK 19½" 12"

front). These 32 rows complete one pattern.

1ST ROW OF 2ND PATTERN : 1 g., * 4 n., 1 g., 1 n., 1 g., 4 n., 1 g. ; repeat from * to end.

2ND ROW : 1 g., * 2 n., 3 g., 1 n., 3 g., 2 n., 1 g. ; repeat from * to end.

3RD ROW : 2 n., * 3 g., 3 n. ; repeat from *, ending 2 n.

4TH ROW : 1 n., * 3 g., 2 n., 1 g., 2 n., 3 g., 1 n. ; repeat from * to end.

5TH ROW : 1 n., * 1 g., (4 n., 1 g.) twice, 1 n. ; repeat from * to end.

6TH ROW : All n.

7TH ROW : 1 b., * 4 n., 3 b., 4 n., 1 b. ; repeat from * to end.

8TH ROW : 1 n., * 1 b., 2 n., 5 b., 2 n., 1 b., 1 n. ; repeat from * to end.

9TH ROW : 1 b., * 2 pk., (1 b., 1 pk.) 3 times, 1 b., 2 pk., 1 b. ; repeat from * to end.

10TH ROW : 1 b., * 1 pk., 3 b., 3 pk., 3 b., 1 pk., 1 b. ; repeat from * to end.

11TH ROW : 2 pk., * 2 b., 2 pk., 1 b., 2 pk., 2 b., 3 pk. ; repeat from *, ending last repeat with 2 pk.

Repeat from the 10th row back to the 1st row on the 2nd pattern.

22ND ROW : All n.

23RD ROW : 1 n., * 3 pk., 2 n., 1 pk., 2 n., 3 pk., 1 n. ; repeat from * to end.

24TH ROW : 1 n., * 4 pk., 1 n., 1 pk., 1 n., 4 pk., 1 n. ; repeat from * to end.

25TH ROW : 1 g., * 1 pk., 1 g., 2 pk., 3 g., 2 pk., 1 g., 1 pk., 1 g. ; repeat from * to end.

26TH ROW : 2 b., * 3 pk., 1 b., 1 pk., 1 b., 3 pk., 3 b. ; repeat from *, ending last repeat with 2 b.

To Shape The Armholes.—27TH ROW : Cast off 6 (1 st. on needle and likewise on following row), * 5 b., 1 pk. ; repeat from * to end.

28TH ROW : Cast off 6, * 1 b., 3 pk., 3 b., 3 pk., 1 b., 1 pk. ; repeat from * to end.

29TH ROW : 2 tog. g., * 2 pk., 1 g., (1 pk., 1 g.) twice, 2 pk., 3 g. ; repeat from *, ending last repeat with 2 tog. g. instead of 3 g.

30TH ROW : 2 tog. pk., 3 pk., 1 n., * 4 pk., 1 n., 1 pk., 1 n., 4 pk., 1 n. ; repeat from * until 5 remain, 3 pk., 2 tog. pk.

31ST ROW : 2 tog. pk., 2 pk., 1 n., * 3 pk., 2 n., 1 pk., 2 n., 3 pk., 1 n. ; repeat from * until 4 remain, 2 pk., 2 tog. pk.

32ND ROW : All n., decreasing 1 st. at each end of the row.

1ST ROW OF 3RD PATTERN : 2 tog. n., 1 g., * 4 n., 1 g., 1 n., 1 g., 4 n., 1 g. ; repeat from * until 2 remain, 2 tog. n.

2ND ROW : 2 tog. g., * 2 n., 3 g., 1 n., 3 g., 2 n., 1 g. ; repeat from *, ending last repeat with 2 tog. g.

Look ahead towards your Spring hiking and cycle trips and make this colourful pullover in readiness. It is an essential for all kinds of outdoor activity.

3RD ROW : 2 tog. n., * 3 g., 3 n. ; repeat from *, ending last repeat with 2 tog. n.

4TH ROW : 2 tog. g., 1 g., 2 n., 1 g., 2 n., * 3 g., 1 n., 3 g., 2 n., 1 g., 2 n. ; repeat from * until 3 remain, 1 g., 2 tog. g.

5TH ROW : 2 tog. n., 2 n., 1 g., * 4 n., 1 g., 1 n., 1 g., 4 n., 1 g. ; repeat from * until 4 remain, 2 n., 2 tog. n.

6TH ROW : All n., decreasing 1 st. at each end of the row. (101 sts.)

7TH ROW : 1 n., * 3 b,, 4 n., 1 b., 4 n. ; repeat from * until 4 remain, 3 b., 1 n.

8TH ROW : 5 b., * 2 n., 1 b., 1 n., 1 b., 2 n., 5 b. ; repeat from * to end.

9TH ROW : * (1 pk., 1 b.) 3 times, (2 pk., 1 b.) twice ; repeat from * until 5 remain, (1 pk., 1 b.) twice, 1 pk.

10TH ROW : 1 b., * 3 pk., 3 b., 1 pk., 1 b., 1 pk., 3 b. ; repeat from * until 4 remain, 3 pk., 1 b.

11TH ROW : 3 tog. b., * 2 pk., 3 b., 2 pk., 2 b., 3 pk., 2 b., 2 pk. ; repeat from *, ending last repeat with 3 tog. b.

12TH ROW : 2 pk., * 3 b., 1 pk., 1 b., 1 pk., 3 b., 3 pk. ; repeat from *, ending last repeat with 2 pk.

13TH ROW : 1 pk., * 1 b., 1 pk., (1 b., 2 pk.) twice, (1 b., 1 pk.) twice ; repeat from * to end.

14TH ROW : 3 b., * 2 n., 1 b., 1 n., 1 b., 2 n., 5 b. ; repeat from *, ending last repeat with 3 b.

Joan Chandler

THIS WEEK'S
FILM

"ROPE"

Rupert Cadell	..	..	..	..	James Stewart
Brandon	..	..	..	..	John Dall
Philip	..	..	..	..	Farley Granger
Janet	..	..	..	..	Joan Chandler
Mr. Kentley	..	..	..	..	Sir Cedric Hardwicke

THEY achieved the perfect murder; perfect, that is, except that it was without real purpose and that they arranged a meeting with the man's sweetheart, his father and his friends.

Here is grimness indeed! Yet so cleverly worked out—the finding of the clue that leads to the discovery of the murder is so cunning, the whole picture so brilliantly made, and such a screen adventure, with its new and revolutionary technique—that you will surely be thrilled without being too horrified.

Certainly this one is an amazing experience!

15TH Row : 2 b., * 4 n., 1 b., 4 n., 3 b.; repeat from *, ending last repeat with 2 b.

16TH Row : All n., taking 3 sts. tog. at each end of the row.

17TH Row : 3 n., * 1 g., 1 n., (1 g., 4 n.) twice; repeat from * until 6 remain, 1 g., 1 n., 1 g., 3 n.

18TH Row : 1 n., * 3 g., 1 n., 3 g., 2 n., 1 g., 2 n.; repeat from * until 8 remain, (3 g., 1 n.) twice.

19TH Row : 3 g., * 3 n., 3 g.; repeat from * to end.

20TH Row : 2 g., * 2 n., 1 g., 2 n., 3 g., 1 n., 3 g.; repeat from * until 7 remain, 2 n., 1 g., 2 n., 2 g.

21ST Row : * (4 n., 1 g.) twice, 1 n., 1 g.; repeat from * until 9 remain, 4 n., 1 g., 4 n.

22ND Row : All n., taking 3 sts. tog. at each end of the row.

23RD Row : 2 pk., * 1 n., 3 pk., 2 n., 1 pk., 2 n., 3 pk.; repeat from * until 3 remain, 1 n., 2 pk.

24TH Row : 2 pk., * 1 n., 4 pk., 1 n., 1 pk., 1 n., 4 pk.; repeat from * until 3 remain, 1 n., 2 pk.

25TH Row : * (1 g., 1 pk.) twice, 1 g., 2 pk., 3 g., 2 pk.; repeat from * until 5 remain, (1 g., 1 pk.) twice, 1 g.

26TH Row : 1 pk., * 3 b., 3 pk., 1 b., 1 pk., 1 b., 3 pk.; repeat from * until 4 remain, 3 b., 1 pk.

27TH Row : 3 tog. pk., * 5 b., 1 pk.; repeat from *, ending last repeat with 3 tog. pk. (85 sts.)

28TH Row : 2 b., * 3 pk., 1 b., 1 pk., 1 b., 3 pk., 3 b.; repeat from *, ending last repeat with 2 b.

29TH Row : * 1 g., 1 pk., 1 g., 2 pk., 3 g., 2 pk., 1 g., 1 pk.; repeat from * until 1 st. remains, 1 g.

30TH Row : * 1 n., 4 pk., 1 n., 1 pk., 1 n., 4 pk.; repeat from * until 1 st. remains, 1 n.

31ST Row : 1 n., * 3 pk., 2 n., 1 pk., 2 n., 3 pk., 1 n.; repeat from * to end.

32ND Row : All n.

1st to 26th rows of 4th pattern as 1st to 26th rows of 2nd pattern.

27TH Row : 1 pk., * 5 b., 1 pk.; repeat from * to end.

28TH Row : 2 b., * 3 pk., 1 b., 1 pk., 1 b., 3 pk., 3 b.; repeat from *, ending last repeat with 2 b.

To Slope The Shoulders.—29TH Row : Cast off 7, (1 st. on needle and likewise on following rows), * 2 pk., (1 g., 1 pk.) twice, 1 g., 2 pk., 3 g.; repeat from * until 5 remain, 2 pk., 1 g., 1 pk., 1 g.

30TH Row : Cast off 7, * (4 pk., 1 n.) twice, 1 pk., 1 n.; repeat from * until 10 remain, (4 pk., 1 n.) twice.

31ST Row : Cast off 7, (1 pk., 2 n.) twice, * 3 pk., 1 n., 3 pk., 2 n., 1 pk., 2 n.; repeat from * until 9 remain, 3 pk., 1 n., 3 pk., 2 n.

32ND Row : Cast off 7, p. to the end in n.

1ST Row of 5TH Pattern : Cast off 7, 2 n., * 1 g., 4 n., 1 g., 1 n., 1 g., 4 n.; repeat from *, ending last repeat with 3 n.

2ND Row : Cast off 7, * 2 n., 1 g., 2 n., 3 g., 1 n., 3 g.; repeat from * until 6 remain, (2 n., 1 g.) twice.

Cast off the remaining sts.

THE FRONT

WORK as for the Back until the ribbed welt and inc. row have been worked. (121 sts.)

Change to No. 9 needles and p. 1 row, then work the 5th to the 1st row (in that order), as on the 1st pattern on the back, then the 16th row once. (127 sts.)

7TH Row : 3 n., * 1 b., 4 n., 3 b., 4 n.; repeat from * until 4 remain, 1 b., 3 n.

8TH Row : * 2 n., 1 b., 1 n., 1 b., 2 n., 5 b.; repeat from *, omitting 5 b. at the end of the last repeat.

9TH Row : * (1 b., 2 pk.) twice, (1 b., 1 pk.) 3 times; repeat from * until 7 remain, (1 b., 2 pk.) twice, 1 b.

10TH Row : 2 b., * 1 pk., 1 b., 1 pk., 3 b., 3 pk., 3 b.; repeat from * until 5 remain, 1 pk., 1 b., 1 pk., 2 b.

11TH Row : * 2 b., 3 pk., 2 b., 2 pk., 1 b., 2 pk.; repeat from * until 7 remain, 2 b., 3 pk., 2 b.

Repeat the 10th row back to the 7th row, then repeat the 16th row of 1st pattern on back. (133 sts.)

Repeat the 5th row to the 1st row as on the first pattern on the Back, then the 16th row once more. (139 sts.)

Now work from ** on the Back until the 5th row of armhole shaping (31st pattern row) has been worked. (127 sts.)

Divide the sts. for the shoulders on the next row as follows :

32ND Row of 2ND Pattern : Using n. only, p. 2 tog., p. 52, cast off 19 (1 st. on needle), p. 51, p. 2 tog. (53 sts. for each front shoulder).

The Left Front Shoulder.—Repeat from the 1st row of 3rd pattern on the back to the shoulder line, finishing with the 28th row of the 4th pattern. (25 sts.) Then work from the 29th to 32nd row of 3rd pattern, and first 6 rows of the 2nd pattern.

To Slope The Shoulder.—7TH Row of 5TH Pattern : Cast off 7, 4 n., 1 b., 4 n., 3 b., 4 n., 1 b.

8TH Row : 1 n., 1 b., 2 n., 5 b., 2 n., 1 b., 1 n., 1 b., 2 n. 2 b.

9TH Row : Cast off 7, (1 b., 1 pk.) 3 times, 1 b., 2 pk., 1 b.

10TH Row : 1 b., 1 pk., 3 b., 3 pk., 3 b.

11TH Row : Cast off 7, 1 b., 2 pk.

12TH Row : 1 b., 1 pk., 2 b.

Cast off the remaining 4 sts.

The Right Front Shoulder.—Rejoin wool to neck edge of remaining 53 sts. and work from the 1st row of 3rd pattern as on the back to the 28th row of 4th pattern. (25 sts.)

Now work from the 29th to the 32nd row of 3rd pattern on Back and the first 7 rows of the 2nd pattern.

To Slope The Shoulder.—8TH Row of 5TH Pattern : Cast off 7, 1 b., 2 n., 1 b., 1 n., 1 b., 2 n., 5 b., 2 n., 1 b., 1 n.

9TH Row : 1 b., 2 pk., (1 b., 1 pk.) 3 times, (1 b., 2 pk.) twice, 1 b., 1 pk., 1 b.

10TH Row : Cast off 7, 2 b., 3 pk., 3 b., 1 pk., 1 b.

11TH Row : 2 pk., 2 b., 2 pk., 1 b., 2 pk., 2 b.

12TH Row : Cast off 7, 1 b., 1 pk., 1 b.

13TH Row : (1 pk., 1 b.) twice.

Cast off remaining 4 sts.

THE BACK NECK BAND

FIRST join the shoulder seams, beginning at the arm end and taking 1 st. from each side at a time.

With No. 12 needles and n. wool, pick up and k. 37 sts. along back neck edge.

Work 6 rows in single rib.

Cast off in rib thus : K. 1, * p. 1, slip the k. st. over, k. 1, slip the p. st. over; repeat from * to end.

THE FRONT NECK BAND

WITH No. 12 needles and n. wool, pick up and k. 81 sts. from the neck edge of Left Front Shoulder, 19 sts. at centre front, and 81 sts. from neck edge of Right Front Shoulder. (181 sts.)

Rib 6 rows, then cast off in rib.

THE ARM BANDS

WITH No. 12 needles and n. wool, pick up and k. 161 sts all round armhole edge.

Rib 6 rows, then cast off in rib.

TO MAKE UP THE PULLOVER

PRESS all parts except the ribbing with a hot iron over a damp cloth and a thick blanket underneath. Join the side seams and press these seams. Join the small seams of the neck and armhole ribbing.

KNITCRAFT

In this article " FINELLA," our knitting expert, gives you some professional tips which should help you to improve the quality of your work

Knitting is so universally popular nowadays that there must be few who cannot do plain and purl, but alas! the finished garment is often disappointing in its workmanship, simply because the secrets of knitcraft, as distinct from knitting, are not as well known as they ought to be. Let me try to explain the chief of them.

As with all handwork, it is the attention to detail which will produce best results, and it is a mistake to choose too intricate a design to begin with. After all, the simplest patterns are often the most effective, as my experience in designing for WIFE and HOME has shown me.

It is important to obtain the materials stated. Wool of a different kind, and needles of a different gauge, will produce a garment of a different size from that of the model. The " gauge " of the needle is its size, or thickness, which naturally affects the size of the stitches, but even needles of the same gauge may produce a slightly different stitch if one pair has points which are more tapered than the other pair.

One thing which remains unalterable is the required tension of the knitting. If the instructions state that there are 6 stitches to the inch, it is essential that the knitter should produce this number. Before beginning the work itself, cast on about 24 stitches, and knit in the pattern for about 30 rows. Press this specimen, if the finished garment is to be pressed, and place a ruler across the middle of it. Count the number of stitches to the middle inch. Should there be too many, either knit more loosely or use larger needles. If there are too few stitches, knit more tightly or use smaller needles.

CASTING ON

The cast-on edge should have the same elasticity as the rest of the work. There is a great tendency for this edge to be too tight, and to overcome this defect it is a good plan to cast on with needles one or two sizes larger than those which will be employed for the beginning of the work.

There are several methods of casting on, and some knitters use double wool to ensure an edge which will withstand strain. The most common method is probably the " knitting " method. Make a slip loop on the left needle for the first stitch. Insert the right needle in it and draw a loop of wool through the stitch on the left needle. Now there is also a stitch on the right needle. Slip it from the right to the left needle. Proceed in this way for the number required. It is advisable to knit one row into the back of these stitches before proceeding with the work, in order to produce a firm and even edge.

A very good, but less known method is as follows. Make the slip loop on the left needle. Cast on the second stitch as in the previous method. Now insert the right needle, from front to back immediately beneath the left needle, and between the two previous stitches. Draw the wool from back to front on the right needle, thus producing a stitch, and place this stitch on the left needle. Cast on the remaining stitches in this way.

A third method is the old-fashioned way of knitting into loops on the left thumb, using one needle only. This is shown in the diagrams on this page. It has the advantage of producing a firm edge, but cannot be used in the middle of a piece of work.

Good knitting should be even, and the rhythm which is attained by continuous knitting will produce a more even tension than the work which is picked up repeatedly for short periods. Avoid joins where they will be seen. Do not begin a row if the wool is insufficient to finish the row, but commence the new ball, having wound the wool very loosely.

Protect the early stages of the work from soil and rubbing by pinning or tacking the knitting in a large handkerchief or some other piece of fabric, and keep the hands as clean as possible. Try to knit quickly and handle the work lightly.

Not everyone knows the neatest method of decreasing. At the beginning of a plain row, knit 2 stitches together, picking up the backs of the stitches. At the end of a similar row, knit 2 stitches together, picking up the fronts. This ensures that the decreases slope in the right way. Another method of decreasing at the beginning of the row is to slip the first of the 2 stitches from left to right needles, without knitting it, to knit the second of the two stitches, and then to pass the slipped stitch over the knitted stitch.

In purl rows, purl 2 stitches together and work into the fronts of the stitches at the beginning of rows, and purl into the backs of stitches at the end of rows.

To increase, first knit (or purl) a stitch into the front of the stitch on the left needle, and then knit another stitch into the back of the same stitch on the left needle. In lace patterns, where the open design needs a hole, a stitch is made by simply passing the wool over the needle. This is usually called " m. 1 " (make one).

Stitches are sometimes dropped accidentally, and they may run down the work. A skilled knitter can pick up such stitches even in lace patterns, without any mistake. A crochet hook is always useful when a stitch is dropped. Plain stitches can be retrieved by working chain stitches up the rows. Purl stitches are picked up in the same way, but the chain is worked on the wrong side.

Beginners are sometimes puzzled by directions given for repetition of a pattern or group of stitches or rows. Groups of stitches in brackets are repeated for the number of times stated immediately after the bracket. For example, (k. 2 tog., m. 1, p. 3) 4 times. An asterisk (*) serves the same purpose as a bracket. All instructions following the * are repeated for the number of times stated.

(Further hints to help you improve your knitting will appear in next month's WIFE and HOME. If you are entering for our knitting competition, you must be sure to read them.)

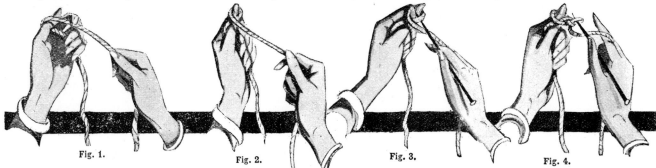

Fig. 1.   Fig. 2.   Fig. 3.   Fig. 4.

HOW TO CAST ON

Measure off a length of wool about four times as long as the row of knitting is to be. Leave this end loose and at this point hold the thread in the left hand and with the right hand bring the main thread round the front of the left thumb (Fig. 1). Wind the wool once round the left thumb, thus crossing the thread already on the left thumb (Fig. 2). Take a knitting needle in the right hand, also holding the thread from the ball in the right hand, and place the needle under the thread at the outside of the left thumb (Fig. 3). Put the thread over the needle, and draw a loop through, still holding the thread tight in the right hand (Fig. 4). Withdraw the left thumb and pull the thread which the left hand is holding, right up to the needle. This is the first stitch. The rest of the stitches are made in the same way. Keep them as even as possible, neither too tight nor too loose.

More About Knitcraft

CASTING OFF

A CAST-OFF edge has a tendency to be too tight, and it is advisable to use a larger needle for the process. Work two stitches in the ordinary way, then, using the left needle, pull the first stitch over the second stitch and drop it. Work the next stitch on the left needle, so that there are again two stitches on the right needle. Pass the first over the second and drop it. Continue thus to the end. Draw the end of the wool through the last stitch and darn it in the back of the fabric, for safety.

It sometimes happens that there are two sets of stitches, equal in number, which will have to be joined to form a seam. They may be grafted together in such a way that the join is invisible. Place the two sets of stitches beside each other, with the wrong sides together and the right sides outside, and cut the wool attached to one set of stitches, so that it is about 5 times the length of the seam. Thread it in a wool needle, and hold the work with this end on the right side of the back needle. Pass the wool needle through the first front stitch purlwise without slipping the stitch off the knitting needle. Pass the wool needle through the first back stitch purlwise, without slipping it off the knitting needle.

* Insert wool needle in next stitch of front needle (through the same stitch as the wool needle has already passed purlwise) knitwise. Slip the stitch off the knitting needle. Pass the wool needle through the next stitch of the front row purlwise, but do not slip it off the knitting needle.

Pass the wool needle through the next stitch on the back needle purlwise (through the same stitch as the wool has previously passed) and slip it off the knitting needle. Pass the wool needle through the next stitch of the back row knitwise, but do not slip this stitch off the knitting needle.

Repeat from * to * to the end, and adjust the tension of the grafting thread so that it is the same as that of the knitting. At the end of the row, fasten off by darning the wool in the back of the knitting.

Knitting in which two or more colours are employed is usually known as Fair Isle knitting, although some of these patterns are not Fair Isle designs. The colour not in use may be carried along the back, at an easy tension, so that it does not hold the fabric tightly. This method certainly has the best effect as regards appearance, but there is a risk that the loops of wool at the back may catch on a button or similar object and will then be tightly dragged, thus spoiling the pattern. The alternative is to weave the colour not in use along the back. Place the wool which is required for use over the first finger of the right hand, and the unused colour over the first finger of the left hand. Lower the left finger, and knit the next stitch so that the unused colour is beneath the knitted stitch. Raise the left finger, and knit the next stitch so that the unused colour is above the knitted stitch. Continue in this way, alternately raising and dropping the left finger, so that the stitches are knitted alternately under and over the unused thread. When the pattern needs a change of colour, reverse the two threads on the right and left first fingers. Press the work heavily for some time on the wrong side under a damp cloth.

MAKING UP

WHEN the knitting is completed there still remains the equally important task of making up the garment. The parts should be the correct size to fit the figure. Pressing may stretch the fabric a little. Some knitting, such as ribbing and raised patterns, is best left unpressed. If there be any doubt as to the way to obtain the best effect, try pressing lightly on the wrong side ; and if it improves the appearance, increase the pressure. For really heavy pressing use a damp cloth and a heavy iron. Sometimes really heavy pressing on the right side under a damp cloth will give the best result. This experimental pressing may be carried out on a small sample piece of the knitting. In the case of competition work it is always advisable to knit a sample of the pattern first, and this may be kept for trial pressing.

If the parts of a garment are rather small it may be possible to stretch them sufficiently while pressing. As an alternative method, strips of knitting may be made and neatly let into the garment at the seams.

Should the parts be too large, a tacking thread can be run in the fabric as a guide to the amount of surplus material. Along this line run two rows of hand or machine stitching, without stretching it out of shape. Cut away the excess, leaving $\frac{1}{4}$ inch edge, and work double crochet over the edge.

Necks and armholes which have a tendency to stretch, or which are too large, may be drawn to size by a row of double crochet

Opinions vary as to the best method of making seams. Shoulder edges which have been shaped are probably best joined like a seam for textiles—with small running stitches and an occasional back-stitch, allowing a narrow single turning on either edge. Straight shoulder edges may be grafted, or the cast-off stitches may be oversewn. Whatever the method, it is essential that this seam be the correct length, which is usually 4 inches for a stock size woman's garment, and from $5\frac{1}{2}$ to 6 inches for a man's. Sleeves may be set in the armholes by either of these two methods. Press each seam as it is finished. Some seams, such as side and sleeve seams, are better if they are free to stretch, otherwise they may break. In such cases, provided the wool be not too thick, it is best to work them in double crochet. This is certainly advisable for underwear.

Any parts which may sag owing to strain, such as front openings, pocket edges, shoulders in heavy garments, should be strengthened by means of strips of tape, ribbon, or similar binding. Should there be any uncertainty as to the position of buttonholes, omit them while knitting, and make them when the garment has been fitted by cutting the wool at the required place, unravelling a few stitches, darning in the ends, and working double crochet into the stitches along the edge.

Ribbing which does not grip the figure as it should, may have a fine elastic threaded along the back, but a better way to overcome this trouble is to join two ends of a waist length of elastic, turn the garment inside out, place the elastic on the ribbing, and work herringbone-stitch over the elastic.

Garments which are in a pattern needing no pressing may have an unfinished appearance when they are completed. In such cases, arrange the garment carefully in shape, place a board on it, and leave it with heavy weights on the top for a day or more.

THE END

notes
on working from the patterns

Yarns have changed a great deal since these patterns first appeared. Some kinds, such as the artificial silk of the 20s, have disappeared altogether. Real wool has also tended to be replaced with wool and nylon mixtures and nylon yarns; they are more practical, though the old garments are nicer and more authentic knitted up in real wool. No modern yarn will be exactly equivalent to the one given in the pattern, so it is *essential* to test your tension before starting on a garment; if you knit with the tension given in the pattern, the garment will come out the right size. An easy method of testing tension is given below.

The *Index of Modern Yarns* suggests a modern yarn and needle size for each pattern. Many of the patterns recommend 2-ply and 3-ply yarns, which are now often very difficult to find. The old 2-ply and 3-ply were thicker than modern 2-ply and 3-ply, and these patterns can be knitted in 4-ply or even Double Knitting if the needle size is adjusted to keep the tension the same. The garment comes out the right size, but with a slightly heavier texture. For these reasons, many 4-ply and Double Knitting yarns are recommended in the Index where the original pattern gave 2-ply and 3-ply.

However, for those particular patterns, 2-ply and 3-ply yarns do reproduce best the soft, silky feel and fine texture of the old garments. If you can find 2-ply and 3-ply yarns, by all means use them, on the needle size given in the patterns; only remember to check your tension first. Since modern 2-ply is finer than the old 2-ply, it may be easier to get the right tension using a 3-ply for a 2-ply.

If the ply is changed up, you will need more wool; slightly more if you use a 3-ply for 2-ply, quite a lot more if you use 4-ply or Double Knitting for 2-ply or 3-ply.

To test tension

Work a sample 3″ square, before starting on the garment. If the tension count in the pattern is, say, 8 stitches to the inch, count 8 stitches and mark them off with pins. If the distance between the pins is exactly 1″, your tension is correct. If the distance is more, the stitches are too loose – try a smaller needle size; if it is less, they are too tight – try a larger needle size. A more attractive garment is produced if the knitting is kept fairly tight and even.

You can often use tension to alter the size of a garment without altering the pattern. For a garment one size larger, use needles one size larger, giving less stitches to the inch. For a garment two sizes larger, use needles two sizes larger.

Knitting Needle Sizes

British	Continental	American
1	9.25	13
2	8.00	11
3	7.00	10½
4	6.00	10
5	5.50	9
6	5.00	8
7	4.75	7
8	4.50	6
9	4.00	5
—	3.50	4
10	3.25	3
11	3.00	2
12	2.50	1
13	—	—
14	2.00	0

Crochet Hook Sizes

International Standard Sizes	Old Wool Sizes	Old Cotton Sizes	American Sizes
0.60	—	7	14 Boye
0.75	—	6½	12 Boye
1.00	—	5½	10 Boye
1.25	—	4½	—
1.50	16	3½	7 Boye
1.75	15	2½	4 Boye
2.00	14	1½	1 Boye or B Bernat
2.50	12	0	0 Boye or D Bernat
3.00	10	3/0	F Bernat
3.50	9	—	G Bernat
4.00	8	—	H Bernat
4.50	7	—	I Bernat
5.00	6	—	J Bernat
5.50	5	—	I Boye
6.00	4	—	J Boye
7.00	2	—	K Boye

index
of Modern Yarns

Glossary of English and American terms

English	American
Knitting and crochet terms	
cast off	bind off
shape cap	shape top
as established	as set
gauge	tension
moss stitch	seed stitch
stocking stitch	stockinette stitch
hanks	skeins
K up	pick up and K
Yarn round hook (yrh)	yarn over hook (yoh)
sewing cotton	sewing thread
g st	garter stitch
wool	yarn
Double Knitting	sportsweight yarn
on the cross	on the bias
double crochet	single crochet
treble crochet	double crochet
half treble crochet	half double crochet
double treble crochet	treble crochet

General terms	
pram	baby carriage
cot	crib
waistcoat	vest
pop-over pinny	smock
plait	braid
polo neck	turtle neck
turtleneck	mock turtleneck
jumper	sweater
siren suit	jump suit
twinset	sweater set
balaclava	cold weather hood
camiknicker (camibocker in the 20s)	all-in-one bodice and pants or "combinations"
costume	suit, outfit

The page number given is that of the page on which the pattern begins. Where no needle size is given, use the size in the original pattern.

Chapter 1 The Tubular Look 1920-32

Index